MW01194733

CRESCENT DAWN

OSPREY
PUBLISHING

DEDICATION
To my children's teachers, coaches,
mentors, and friends

SI SHEPPARD

CRESCENT DAWN

THE RISE OF THE OTTOMAN EMPIRE AND THE MAKING OF THE MODERN AGE

OSPREY PUBLISHING
Bloomsbury Publishing Plc
Kemp House, Chawley Park, Cumnor Hill, Oxford OX2 9PH, UK
29 Earlsfort Terrace, Dublin 2, Ireland
1385 Broadway, 5th Floor, New York, NY 10018, USA
E-mail: info@ospreypublishing.com
www.ospreypublishing.com

OSPREY is a trademark of Osprey Publishing Ltd

First published in Great Britain in 2025

A catalog record for this book is available from the British Library.

ISBN: HB 9781472851468; PB 9781472851475; eBook 9781472851420; ePDF 9781472851444; XML 9781472851437; Audio 9781472851451

25 26 27 28 29   10 9 8 7 6 5 4 3 2 1

Image credits are given in full in the List of Illustrations (pp. 7–8)
Maps by www.bounford.com
Index by Fionbar Lyons

Typeset by Deanta Global Publishing Services, Chennai, India
Printed and bound in Great Britain by CPI (Group) UK Ltd, Croydon CR0 4YY

Editor's note
For ease of comparison please refer to the following conversion table:
1 mile = 1.6 kilometers
1 yard = 0.9 meters
1 pound = 0.45 kilograms

Osprey Publishing supports the Woodland Trust, the UK's leading woodland conservation charity.

To find out more about our authors and books visit **www.ospreypublishing.com**. Here you will find extracts, author interviews, details of forthcoming events and the option to sign up for our newsletter.

CONTENTS

LIST OF ILLUSTRATIONS AND MAPS

ILLUSTRATIONS

Jousting helmet of King Louis II of Hungary. (The Metropolitan Museum of Art, New York)

The Battle of Mohács, 1526. (© Archives Charmet/Bridgeman Images)

The 1529–43 Ethiopian–Adal War. (Science History Images/Alamy Stock Photo)

The Ottoman siege of Vienna, 1529. (mikroman6/Getty Images)

A 360-degree panorama of the siege of Vienna, 1529. (Wien Museum, CC0)

Suleiman the Magnificent with his *divan* during the siege of Vienna, 1529. (The Picture Art Collection/Alamy Stock Photo)

The Habsburg siege of Tunis, 1535. (Sepia Times/Universal Images Group via Getty Images)

The Franco-Ottoman siege of Nice, 1543. (Wikimedia Commons)

Statue of Jean Parisot de Valette. (Author's collection)

The Ottoman siege of Malta, 1565. (Bridgeman Images)

The Hungarian frontier stronghold of Szigetvár. (Wikimedia Commons)

Count Nicholas IV of Zrin's defense of Szigetvár in 1566. (Fine Art Images/Heritage Images via Getty Images)

The Battle of Lepanto, 1571. (Science History Images/Alamy Stock Photo)

The Battle of Lepanto, 1571. (Franco Novacco Map Collection, Newberry Library)

Ottoman *akinji* light cavalry raider and Hungarian *chevalier*. (Wikimedia Commons)

Ottoman saber, helmet, and dagger. (The Metropolitan Museum of Art, New York)

MAPS

Map 1: Ottoman Heartland: Anatolia to Aegean, *c.*1300–1600

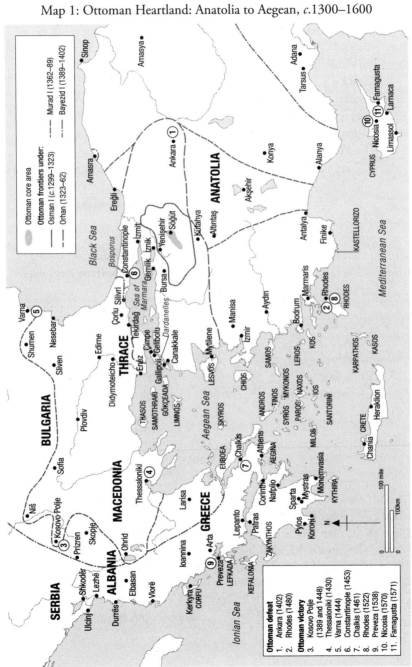

9

Map 2: The Siege of Constantinople, April–May 1453

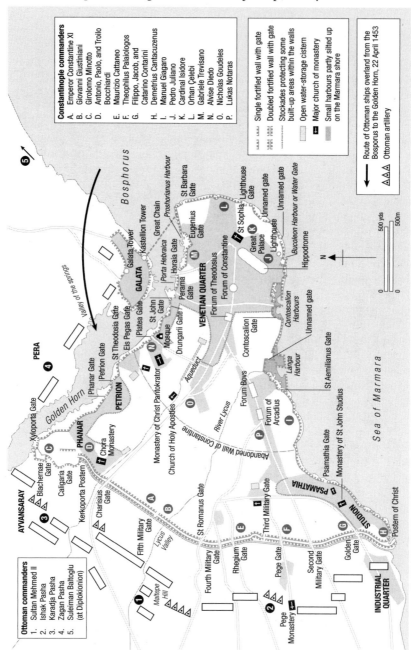

Map 3: Ottoman Frontier: The Balkans, *c*.1300–1600

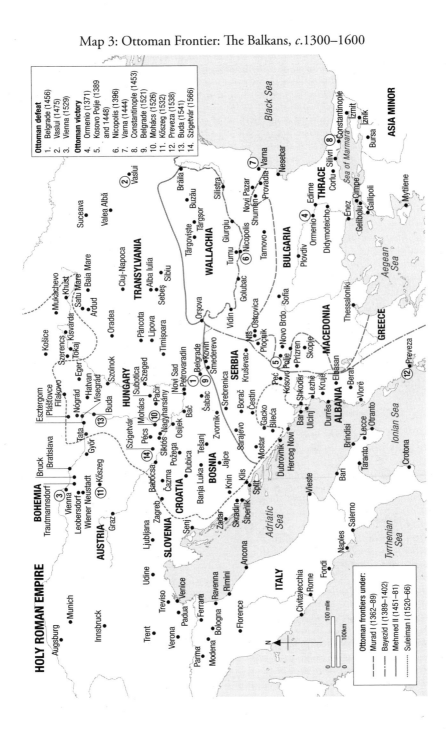

Map 4: The Siege of Rhodes, June–December 1522

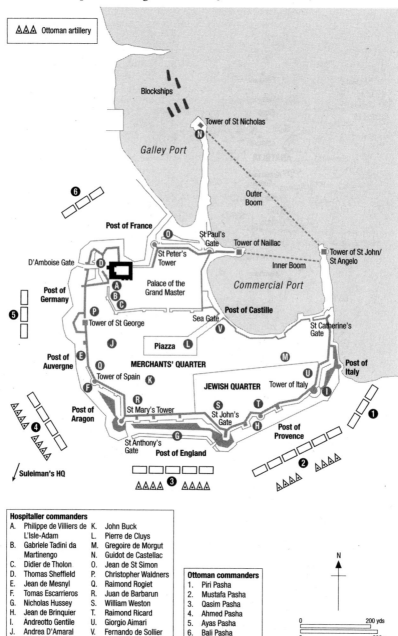

▲▲▲ Ottoman artillery

Blockships

Tower of St Nicholas

Galley Port

Outer Boom

Post of France

St Paul's Gate

Tower of Naillac

Tower of St John/ St Angelo

St Peter's Tower

D'Amboise Gate

Inner Boom

Palace of the Grand Master

Commercial Port

Post of Germany

Post of Castille

Tower of St George

Sea Gate

St Catherine's Gate

Piazza

Post of Auvergne

MERCHANTS' QUARTER

Post of Italy

Tower of Spain

JEWISH QUARTER

Tower of Italy

Post of Aragon

St Mary's Tower

St John's Gate

Post of Provence

St Anthony's Gate

Post of England

Suleiman's HQ

Hospitaller commanders

A. Philippe de Villiers de L'Isle-Adam
B. Gabriele Tadini da Martinengo
C. Didier de Tholon
D. Thomas Sheffield
E. Jean de Mesnyl
F. Tomas Escarrieros
G. Nicholas Hussey
H. Jean de Brinquier
I. Andreotto Gentile
J. Andrea D'Amaral
K. John Buck
L. Pierre de Cluys
M. Gregoire de Morgut
N. Guidot de Castellac
O. Jean de St Simon
P. Christopher Waldners
Q. Raimond Rogiet
R. Juan de Barbarun
S. William Weston
T. Raimond Ricard
U. Giorgio Aimari
V. Fernando de Sollier

Ottoman commanders

1. Piri Pasha
2. Mustafa Pasha
3. Qasim Pasha
4. Ahmed Pasha
5. Ayas Pasha
6. Bali Pasha

N

0   200 yds
0   200m

Map 5: Ottoman Frontier: The Middle East, c.1400–1600

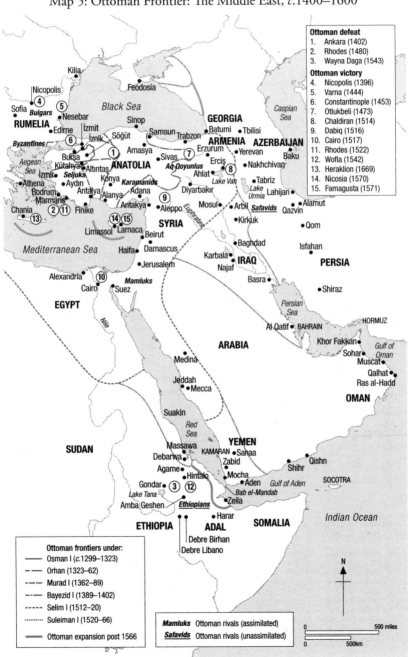

Ottoman defeat
1. Ankara (1402)
2. Rhodes (1480)
3. Wayna Daga (1543)

Ottoman victory
4. Nicopolis (1396)
5. Varna (1444)
6. Constantinople (1453)
7. Otlukbeli (1473)
8. Chaldiran (1514)
9. Dabiq (1516)
10. Cairo (1517)
11. Rhodes (1522)
12. Wofla (1542)
13. Heraklion (1669)
14. Nicosia (1570)
15. Famagusta (1571)

Ottoman frontiers under:
— Osman I (c.1299–1323)
– – Orhan (1323–62)
– ‑ – Murad I (1362–89)
– ‑ ‑ Bayezid I (1389–1402)
- - - - Selim I (1512–20)
·········· Suleiman I (1520–66)
~~~~~~ Ottoman expansion post 1566

Mamluks Ottoman rivals (assimilated)
Safavids Ottoman rivals (unassimilated)

0   500 miles
0   500km

13

Map 6: Ottoman Frontier: The Mediterranean Sea, c.1450–1600

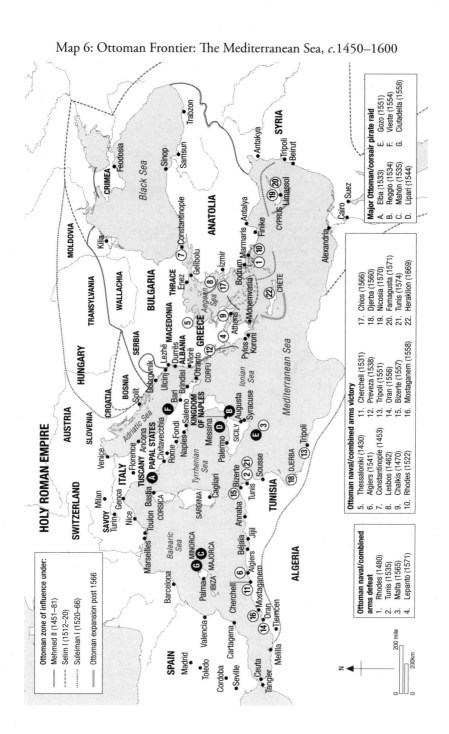

Ottoman zone of influence under:
— Mehmed II (1451–81)
----- Selim I (1512–20)
===== Suleiman I (1520–66)
===== Ottoman expansion post 1566

Major Ottoman/corsair pirate raid
A. Elba (1533)   E. Gozo (1551)
B. Reggio (1534)   F. Vieste (1554)
C. Mahón (1535)   G. Ciutadella (1558)
D. Lipari (1544)

Ottoman naval/combined arms victory
5. Thessaloniki (1430)   11. Cherchell (1531)   17. Chios (1566)
6. Algiers (1541)   12. Preveza (1538)   18. Djerba (1560)
7. Constantinople (1453) 13. Tripoli (1551)   19. Nicosia (1570)
8. Lesbos (1462)   14. Oran (1556)   20. Famagusta (1571)
9. Chalkis (1470)   15. Bizerte (1557)   21. Tunis (1574)
10. Rhodes (1522)   16. Mostaganem (1558)   22. Heraklion (1669)

Ottoman naval/combined arms defeat
1. Rhodes (1480)
2. Tunis (1535)
3. Malta (1565)
4. Lepanto (1571)

Map 7: The Siege of Malta, May–September 1565

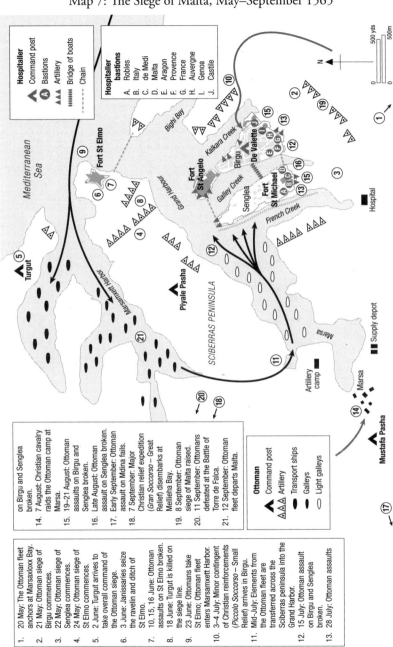

1. 20 May: The Ottoman fleet anchors at Marsaxloxx Bay.
2. 21 May: Ottoman siege of Birgu commences.
3. 22 May: Ottoman siege of Senglea commences.
4. 24 May: Ottoman siege of St Elmo commences.
5. 2 June: Turgut arrives to take overall command of the Ottoman siege.
6. 3 June: Janissaries seize the ravelin and ditch of St Elmo.
7. 10, 15, 16 June: Ottoman assaults on St Elmo broken.
8. 18 June: Turgut is killed on the siege line.
9. 23 June: Ottomans take St Elmo; Ottoman fleet enters Marsamxett Harbor.
10. 3–4 July: Minor contingent of Christian reinforcements (Piccolo Soccorso – Small Relief) arrives in Birgu.
11. Mid-July: Elements from the Ottoman fleet are transferred across the Sciberras peninsula into the Grand Harbor.
12. 15 July: Ottoman assault on Birgu and Senglea broken.
13. 28 July: Ottoman assaults on Birgu and Senglea broken.
14. 7 August: Christian cavalry raids the Ottoman camp at Marsa.
15. 19–21 August: Ottoman assaults on Birgu and Senglea broken.
16. Late August: Ottoman assault on Senglea broken.
17. Early September: Ottoman assault on Mdina fails.
18. 7 September: Major Christian relief expedition (Gran Soccorso – Great Relief) disembarks at Mellieha Bay.
19. 8 September: Ottoman siege of Malta raised.
20. 11 September: Ottomans defeated at the Battle of Torre de Falca.
21. 12 September: Ottoman fleet departs Malta.

Hospitaller
- Command post
- Bastions
- Artillery
- Bridge of boats
- Chain

Hospitaller bastions
A. Robles
B. Italy
C. de Medi
D. Malta
E. Aragon
F. Provence
G. France
H. Auvergne
I. Genoa
J. Castile

Ottoman
- Command post
- Artillery
- Transport ships
- Galleys
- Light galleys

Map 8: Ottoman Frontier: The Indian Ocean, *c.*1500–1600

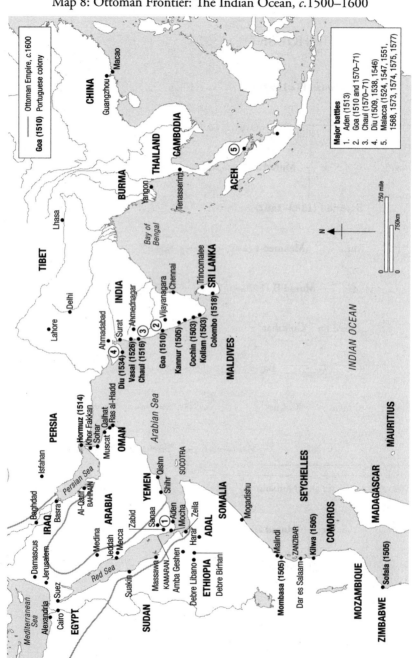

Ottoman Empire, c.1600

Goa (1510) Portuguese colony

Major battles
1. Aden (1513)
2. Goa (1510 and 1570–71)
3. Chaul (1570–71)
4. Diu (1509, 1538, 1546)
5. Malacca (1524, 1547, 1551, 1568, 1573, 1574, 1575, 1577)

750 mile

750km

CHINA
Guangzhou
Macao

CAMBODIA

THAILAND

BURMA
Yangon

Tenasserim

ACEH ⑤

TIBET
Lhasa

Bay of Bengal

Trincomalee
Chennai
SRI LANKA
Vijayanagara
Colombo (1518)
Kollam (1503)
Cochin (1503)
Kannur (1505)
Goa (1510) ②
Chaul (1516) ③
Vasai (1526)
Diu (1534) ④
Surat
Ahmadabad
Ahmednagar
INDIA
Delhi
Lahore

MALDIVES

INDIAN OCEAN

MAURITIUS

Isfahan
PERSIA
Hormuz (1514)
Khor Fakkan
Qalhat
Muscat
Sohar
Ras al-Hadd
OMAN
Arabian Sea
Qishn
Shihr
SOCOTRA

Baghdad
IRAQ
Basra
Persian Sea
Al-Qatif
BAHRAIN
ARABIA
Zabid
Sanaa
Aden ①
Mocha
YEMEN

Damascus
Jerusalem
Medina
Jeddah
Mecca
Harar
Zeila
ADAL
SOMALIA
Mogadishu
SEYCHELLES

Mediterranean Sea
Alexandria
Cairo
Suez
EGYPT
Red Sea
Suakin
SUDAN
Massawa
KAMARAN
Amba Geshen
Debre Libanos
ETHIOPIA
Debre Birhan

Malindi
Mombasa (1505)
ZANZIBAR
Dar es Salaam
Kilwa (1505)
COMOROS
MADAGASCAR
MOZAMBIQUE
Sofala (1505)
ZIMBABWE

16

FAMILY TREES

THE HOUSE OF OSMAN, *C*.1299–1603

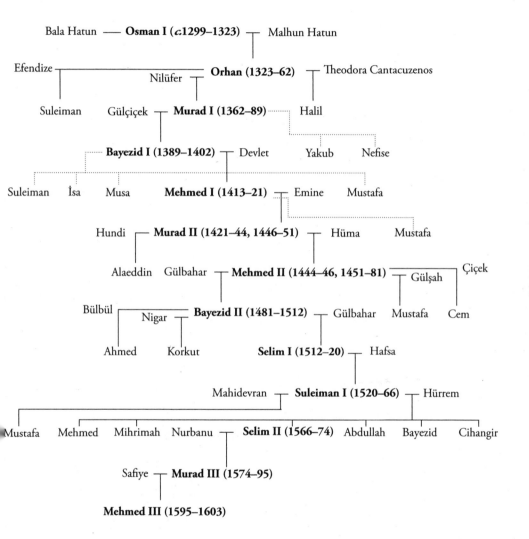

THE ROYAL HOUSES OF EUROPE, 15TH–17TH CENTURIES

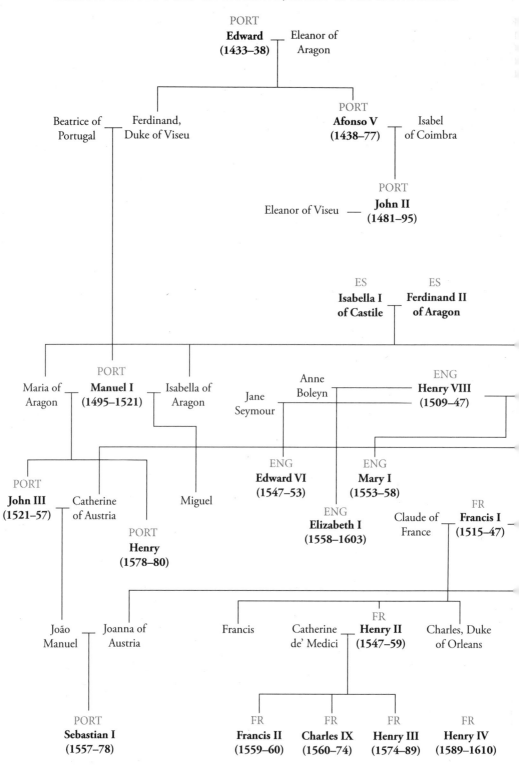

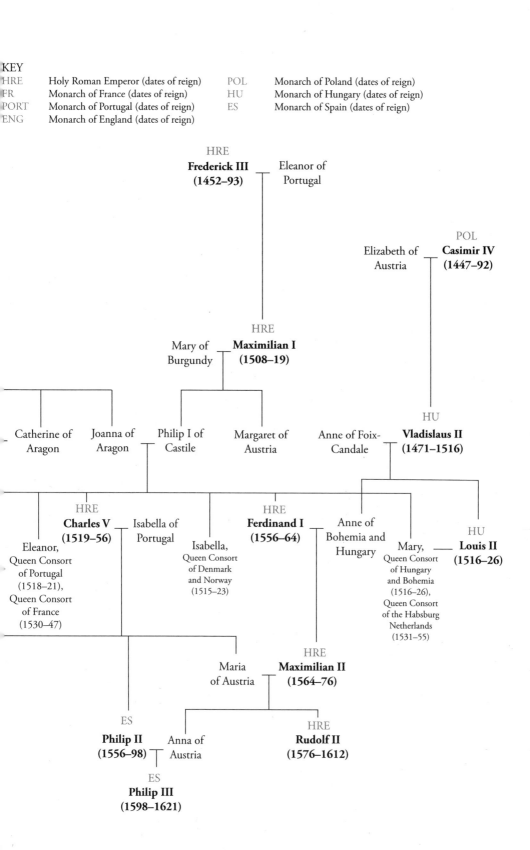

KEY
HRE   Holy Roman Emperor (dates of reign)   POL   Monarch of Poland (dates of reign)
FR   Monarch of France (dates of reign)   HU   Monarch of Hungary (dates of reign)
PORT   Monarch of Portugal (dates of reign)   ES   Monarch of Spain (dates of reign)
ENG   Monarch of England (dates of reign)

HRE
Frederick III — Eleanor of
(1452–93) — Portugal

POL
Elizabeth of — **Casimir IV**
Austria — **(1447–92)**

HRE
Mary of — **Maximilian I**
Burgundy — **(1508–19)**

HU
Anne of Foix- — **Vladislaus II**
Candale — **(1471–1516)**

Catherine of — Joanna of — Philip I of — Margaret of
Aragon — Aragon — Castile — Austria

HRE
Charles V — Isabella of
(1519–56) — Portugal

HRE
Ferdinand I — Anne of
(1556–64) — Bohemia and
Hungary

HU
Mary, — **Louis II**
Queen Consort — **(1516–26)**
of Hungary
and Bohemia
(1516–26),
Queen Consort
of the Habsburg
Netherlands
(1531–55)

Eleanor,
Queen Consort
of Portugal
(1518–21),
Queen Consort
of France
(1530–47)

Isabella,
Queen Consort
of Denmark
and Norway
(1515–23)

Maria — HRE
of Austria — **Maximilian II**
— **(1564–76)**

ES
Philip II — Anna of
(1556–98) — Austria

HRE
Rudolf II
(1576–1612)

ES
Philip III
(1598–1621)

NAMING CONVENTIONS

The geographic range of this study stretches from the Balkans to the Middle East and via the Mediterranean Sea to the Indian Ocean. Given this has been some of the most bitterly contested terrain in human history, with the political and cultural environment repeatedly changing hands between multiple ethnic, linguistic, and religious identities over the course of several millennia, it is unsurprising that the names of key sites have evolved, sometimes on several occasions, over the course of this period. To avoid confusion, contemporary names have been applied wherever possible, with a handful of exceptions. We continue to refer to Constantinople as opposed to Istanbul, because given its centrality and ubiquity using the contemporary term prior to the Ottoman conquest would seem anachronistic; Lepanto instead of the contemporary Nafpaktos, and Nicopolis instead of the contemporary Nikopol, because the battles associated with those names are so iconic; and in India, Calicut instead of the contemporary Kozhikode, and Cambay instead of the contemporary Khambhat, because those names were quoted so often in the sources. Readers are encouraged to consult the following table for reference.

Current Name	Prior Name
Alba Iulia	Gyulafehérvár
Antalya	Attaleia
Bursa	Prusa
Çimpe	Tzympē
Dubrovnik	Ragusa
Edirne	Adrianople
Elbasan	Konyuh
Feodosia	Caffa/Kaffa
Gemlik	Kios
Ilok	Újlak
İzmit	Nicomedia

İznik	Nicaea
Kannur	Cannanore
Krujë	Kruša
Pylos	Navarino
Shkodër	Shkodra
Smederevo	Semendria
Syrmia	Szerém
Thessaloniki	Thessalonica
Trabzon	Trebizond
Urfa	Edessa
Üsküdar	Chrysopolis/Scutari

In addition, for the sake of continuity, where possible, personal names have been Anglicized, e.g., *Albrecht* to Albert von Habsburg, *Erszébet* to Elizabeth of Luxembourg, *Djuradj* to George Branković, *János* to John Hunyadi, etc.

PROLOGUE

On 17 April 1534, a man was incarcerated in the Tower of London on suspicion of committing treason against the reigning monarch, King Henry VIII. This was hardly an unusual occurrence. It was a tumultuous era, and the confluence of England's traumatic transition from a Catholic to a Protestant identity under Henry's tyrannical reign made politics a dangerous game. But the prisoner taken that day, deliberately wearing his gold chain of livery as a solemn token of his service to the king, was none other than former Speaker of the House of Commons and Lord Chancellor of England, Sir Thomas More.

The breach between the two men was now irreparable. Unable to legitimize Henry's divorce from Queen Catherine of Aragon and break with the Catholic Church, More had resigned his office on 16 May 1532. His subsequent decisions to snub as irascible and egotistical a royal will as that of King Henry by refusing to attend the coronation of Anne Boleyn as queen of England, refusing to swear allegiance to the parliamentary Act of Succession, and refusing to sign the 1534 Oath of Succession had inevitably brought him to his current impasse.

Now confined behind bars, More was still free to exercise his powerful intellect via pen and paper. In seeking the consolations of philosophy, More wrote several tracts exploring themes of faith, loyalty, and grace.

One of his texts, *A Dialogue of Comfort against Tribulation*, was with apparent whimsy subtitled *made by a Hungarian in Latin, and translated out of Latin into French, and out of French into English*. It takes the form of a dialogue between a young man, Vincent, who visits his uncle, Anthony, during the latter years of the prior decade in the kingdom of Hungary, then at the farthest extremity of Christian Europe. This was More's characteristically cautious and clever way of putting distance between himself and his literary subjects, making their critiques of heresy and oppression – "for there is no born Turk so cruel to Christian folk as is the false Christian that falleth from the faith" – as abstract and oblique as possible.[1]

But the narrative of his text focused on the very real-world consequences of Christian disunity and the fall from grace, a challenge that More would have been assured his readers, secure as they were in their isolated island redoubt, would have been both aware of and troubled about. The Europe of his *Dialogue* was under the looming threat of imminent invasion, occupation, and assimilation by the great and rising imperial power of the day, the Ottoman Empire. It was a long way from Constantinople to London, but the sultan, Suleiman, dubbed by posterity the Magnificent, was already whispered of in awe and fear even in far-off England.

Vincent speaks plainly to his uncle of the pervasive fear in Vienna that the Ottoman war machine is mobilizing to make that city the focus for its next campaign:

> ... since the tidings have come hither so breme of the great Turk's enterprise into these parts here, we can almost neither talk nor think of any other thing else than of his might and our mischief, there falleth so continually before the eyes of our hearts a fearful imagination of this terrible thing – his mighty strength and power, his high malice and hatred, and his incomparable cruelty, with robbing, despoiling, burning, and laying waste all the way that his army cometh; then killing or carrying away the people far hence, from home.[2]

Anthony grimly confirms his nephew is right to be concerned, for the progress of Ottoman expansion was as irrepressible as it was systematic:

> Greece feared not the Turk when that I was born; and within a while after, that whole empire was his. The great sultan of Syria thought himself more than his match; and long since you were born hath he that empire too. Then hath he taken Belgrade, the fortress of this realm, and since hath he destroyed our noble young goodly king [Louis II]. And now strive there twain [John Zápolya of Transylvania and Archduke Ferdinand of Austria] for us. Our Lord send the grace that the third dog [Suleiman] carry not away the bone from them both. What should I speak of the noble, strong city of Rhodes? The winning thereof he counteth as a victory against the whole corps of Christendom, since all Christendom was not able to defend that strong town against him. Howbeit, if the princes of Christendom everywhere about would, whereas need was, have set to their hands in time, the Turk had never taken any one place of all these places. But, partly dissensions fallen among ourselves, partly that no man careth what harm other folk feel, but each party suffer other to shift for itself, the Turk is in few years wonderfully increased, and Christendom, on the other side, very sore decayed. And all this worketh our wickedness – with which God is not content![3]

Hungary had been left devastated by Suleiman's campaign of 1526. Defeated in the great Battle of Mohács, the king and the flower of the nobility had been slain and half the kingdom subject to Ottoman occupation, the remnant fought over by rival claimants to the the throne. The wreck of the state was wide open to another incursion, and "it is, of very truth, that into this realm of Hungary he will not fail to come. For neither is there any country through Christendom that lieth for him so meet, nor never was there any time till now in which he might so well and surely win it."[4] This had much wider significance, for "if Hungary be lost, and that the Turk have it once fast in his possession... he shall ere it be long after have an open, ready way into almost the remnant of all Christendom. Though he win it not all in a week, the great part will be won after, I fear me, within very few years."[5] Vienna would be the next to fall, and after that, there was no limit to Ottoman ambition. Suleiman's vision stretched beyond Europe to Africa and Asia, and if left unchecked, "he would into Portugal, Italy, Spain, France, Almaine [Germany] and England, and as far on another quarter, too – both Prester John's land and the Great Khan's too."[6]

The only hope lay in collective action against this common enemy. As a statesman, More had been frustrated by the inattention and inaction of his own monarch towards the danger dawning in the East. As Lord Chancellor, speaking on behalf of King Henry on 14 March 1527, he had been obliged to decline the appeal of Johann Faber, the envoy of Archduke Ferdinand, for aid against the Turks. This was much against his own inclination; More had long been a critic of "the blindness of those princes" who refused to come to the aid of their fellow Christian magnates engaged in a life-or-death struggle "against so cruel and implacable an enemy" as the Ottoman foe.[7] Now, he expressed his fervent wish the existential Ottoman threat would serve to unite Christian Europe – Protestant and Catholic – in a common cause. He saw evidence of this in the German states of the Holy Roman Empire, where:

> ... for all their diverse opinions, yet as they agree together in profession of Christ's name, so agree they now together in preparation of a common power in defense of Christendom against our common enemy the Turk. And I trust in God that this shall not only help us here, to strengthen us in this war, but also that as God hath caused them to agree together in the defense of his name, so shall he graciously bring them to agree together in the truth of his faith.[8]

Though he wrote secure in the knowledge that the Ottoman campaigns against Vienna of 1529 and 1532 had, indeed, been repulsed by the collective effort of the Christian West, united under the banner of the Habsburg Holy Roman Emperor, Charles V, More was not destined to live long enough to witness how that struggle would play out. Tried and convicted under the Treasons Act of 1534 on 1 July 1535, he was executed five days later at Tower Hill, still claiming to the last "he died the king's good servant, and God's first." He would have no way of knowing that Henry, the man who consigned him to death, would play no part whatsoever in subsequent campaigns against the Ottomans, a policy maintained by the king's successors, Edward VI and Queen Mary, and that indeed, the last of the Tudors, Queen Elizabeth I, would go so far as to find common cause with the Ottoman sultan against their mutual Catholic Habsburg enemy.

Everything was in a state of flux as the Renaissance evolved into the Reformation. The great chain of being between ruler and ruled that governed the universe broke down, and traditional loyalties could no longer be taken for granted. It was an age of expansion and discovery that transformed the world and laid the foundation for our modern, globalized age. The Ottoman Empire was at the center of this process – geographically, politically, militarily. Contemporaries were well aware of that fact, but its significance has faded with time, lost in the narrative of decline and othering during the 19th and 20th centuries, when the ascendant Western great powers were in a position to marginalize the crumbling Ottoman Empire as the "Sick Man of Europe." This study is intended to introduce a 21st-century audience to Ottoman centrality in shaping the trajectory of our history and structuring the geopolitics that continues to define our reality today.

INTRODUCTION

In December 1512, an envoy from Regent Queen Eleni of Ethiopia arrived at the court of Afonso de Albuquerque, the Portuguese governor of India, in Goa. The envoy, an Armenian named Mateus, had been dispatched in response to a Portuguese mission that had arrived in Ethiopia seeking the land of the legendary Prester John, a Christian monarch reputed to rule a vast empire somewhere beyond the unbroken chain of Islamic realms that kept Europe hemmed in to the south and east. Ethiopia having survived in near-perfect isolation for centuries, Queen Eleni enthusiastically seized this opportunity to establish close relations with the rising power of the West. She passed on intelligence and proposed an alliance: "We have news that the Lord of Cairo is building ships to fight your fleet, and we shall give you so many men... as to wipe the Moors from the face of the earth! We by land, and you, brothers, on the sea!"

Albuquerque forwarded Mateus to Portugal, where King Manuel I wept with joy at his arrival. Albuquerque dispatched a full report of his own with the embassy, outlining the new strategic opportunities partnership with Ethiopia opened up regarding Portugal's empire-building in the Orient. A Portuguese fortress at the coastal town of Massawa, allied to Ethiopian control of the African interior, would dominate the entire Red Sea. "All the riches of the world will be in your hands," Albuquerque informed his king, "and you could moreover prevent any merchandise from Cairo and those ports from entering India except in your ships."

To Albuquerque, these objectives, easily obtainable in the short term, were but a step towards the ultimate victory of Christian Europe, for "I have in mind greater things than these that we could do if once we gain a footing there, and make alliance with the land of Prester John." He was aware the headwaters of the Nile River originated in the Ethiopian highlands. Therein lay the key to certain victory over Egypt: "If the King our Lord would send out some of those engineers who make cuttings through the mountains of Madeira, they could divert the flood of the Nile and turn it aside from watering the lands of Cairo, thus in two years Cairo would be undone, and the whole country ruined."

This plan, almost messianic in its breathtaking geopolitical ambition, spoke to the inner and outer features of the European mindset in this era. The outer mentality was one of limitless optimism. In the space of a single lifetime, Europe had broken the bounds of its marginalization as a peninsula at the western tip of Eurasia. Generations of trial and error in nautical navigation and technology had endowed Europe with unprecedented mastery of the world's oceans. Now, European fleets progressed unhindered via the coast of Africa to the spice islands of the East Indies, and across the Atlantic to the shores of the New World. It was this naval supremacy that had created the context whereby a Portuguese viceroy in India could receive an ambassador from Ethiopia and dispatch him to his own monarch in Lisbon. A network of imperial command and control on such a globe-straddling scale would have been unimaginable in 1453, the year Albuquerque was born.

That year had another significance, one deeply rooted in the inner mentality of the European consciousness. For it had been in 1453 that the Ottoman Turks had at last conquered Constantinople, the city of cities, thereby extinguishing the Byzantine Empire. Those European merchants and monarchs sanctioning ventures into the unknown in search of gold, spices, and glory were as motivated by the primal instinct of fear as they were by pecuniary gain, religious evangelism, and national identity. The European desire to project power outwards therefore was rationalized as a policy of self-defense.

Prior to the Renaissance, with the sole exception of the spasm of imperialist aggression that drove Alexander the Great to the far bank of the Indus River, it was Europe that bore the brunt of invasion and would-be colonization from Asia, not the other way around. The Black Sea serves as a useful dividing line. From north of its shores came wave after wave of steppe nomads – Huns, Magyars, Mongols – battering against the sedentary states of Europe. From south of the Black Sea advanced powerful empires whose stated goal was to conquer and subsume European civilization – the Persians, the Arabs, and, most recently, the Turks.

The early modern period is traditionally understood as being defined by the forced globalization the maritime powers of Western Europe imposed on the world. But in fact, European empire-building was just one manifestation of a global trend towards expansion and consolidation during this era. The tsars of Russia established their hegemony over Eastern Europe while imposing their authority ever eastwards across Siberia until reaching the Pacific Ocean. The Manchu forcibly usurped the Ming with their own Ch'ing dynasty and then expanded the frontiers of China to their greatest ever geographic extent. And the advance of the Mughals into India culminated with their domination of the entire subcontinent.

Above all else in significance, from the perspective of Western Europe, was the rise of the Ottoman Turks, expanding in all directions, in the process inheriting responsibility for leading the orthodox Muslim struggle against the apostates, schismatics, and polytheists both internally and on every frontier. When Suleiman the Magnificent ascended to the Ottoman throne in 1520 he was faced with the strategic challenge of allocating resources and determining the focus of diplomatic and military policy across no fewer than five separate geopolitical theaters. Starting in Constantinople and moving counterclockwise, these were:

1) The Balkan Front, dominated by the struggle with the Habsburgs.
2) The Mediterranean Front, where the struggle for control of the sea lanes and key islands invited confrontation with Spain, the maritime republics of Venice and Genoa, and the Knights Hospitaller.
3) The Indian Ocean Front, where Ottoman commercial and diplomatic interests in India and Africa demanded a response to the empire-building of the Portuguese astride the trade emporiums of the Spice Route.
4) The Persian Front, with its endemic struggle for control of Mesopotamia against the Safavid shahs.
5) The Russian Front, a peripheral theater but one where Ottoman interest in maintaining the Black Sea as a Turkish lake against encroachment by the tsars meant an ongoing commitment to a security perimeter that stretched from the Caucasus to Crimea.

Like the Ottomans, the great empires of antiquity – Persian, Roman, Arab – had all straddled the three continents of Europe, Asia, and Africa. But the wars these superpowers fought around their peripheries were unconnected. The Nubians in Africa, the Byzantines in Asia, and the Franks in Europe had each in their own way fought to defend themselves from the seemingly inexorable expansion of the Arab caliphate in the 7th to 8th centuries, but they had done so on their own terms, without reference to, let alone alliance with, each other. The critical break with the past manifested in the wars of the Ottoman sultanate was their interconnected nature. For the first time in human history, a hegemonic imperial superpower was confronted by a coordinated attempt at its containment that spanned multiple continents across hitherto unimaginable distances.

This process invites parallels with the core strategic parameters of the United States and its allies in their confrontation with the Soviet Union during the Cold

War. As diplomat George Kennan defined it in the wake of World War II, the Western powers must maintain "a policy of firm *containment*, designed to confront the Russians with unalterable counter-force at every point where they show signs of encroaching upon the interests of a peaceful and stable world." Substitute Ottomans for Russians and you have in its broadest outlines the definition of European policy during the transition from the medieval to the Renaissance eras. European imperatives during this period, therefore, were as much reactive and defensive as they were proactive and expansive.

In practical terms, the extent to which those ostensibly dedicated to containing Ottoman expansion were prepared to actually commit men and treasure to its enforcement was patchy at best. This is not the story of a clash of civilizations between East and West. Europe was not united against the Ottoman challenge; the scandal of the age was the alliance between King Francis I of France and Sultan Suleiman the Magnificent. Conversely, the resistance of the Saadi dynasty of Morocco to Ottoman encroachment played a critical role in denying Constantinople direct access to the Atlantic Ocean, with all that implied for the future course of colonization in the Americas. This reflects the reality that, although religious imperatives were critical to the motivations of all the key actors involved, these in no way fell neatly along the Christian–Muslim divide. Holy Roman Emperor Charles V desired nothing more than to eradicate the Protestant heresy metastasizing throughout his domains, but time and again the threat of Ottoman invasion forced him to stay his hand and indulge his Lutheran subjects with the recognition they demanded in order for them to contribute towards the common defense. Meanwhile, the Sunni Ottomans were locked in an endless cycle of war against the Shia Safavid dynasty that governed neighboring Persia. Nevertheless, however fitfully, the collective effort to constrain the expansion of the Ottoman superpower did ultimately succeed in preventing the sultans from prevailing in a struggle for power that might have proved the decisive tipping point in reordering the trajectory of history as we know it.

1

ORIGINS, TO FIRST KOSOVO AND NICOPOLIS

FIRST STEPS

It began, as all things do, with a dream.

The most popular myth the Ottomans themselves told about their origins maintained that a young warrior named Osman fell in love with Bala Hatun, daughter of the saintly Sheikh Edebali. Being poor, Osman's only hope of winning her hand lay in military prowess. This he accomplished, yet it was only when he told the sheikh about a strange dream that the old man allowed Osman to be betrothed to his daughter.

In his dream, Osman saw the moon, representing the fair Bala Hatun, rising from Edebali's chest and setting in the young warrior's own. Thereupon a mighty tree sprouted from Osman's heart and soon spread across the entire sky. From its roots four great rivers flowed – the Tigris, the Euphrates, the Nile, and the Danube. This the sheikh interpreted as a prophecy of imperial destiny; the descendants of Osman and Bala Hatun were fated to rule over the lands watered by those four rivers. Edebali was accordingly happy to allow his daughter to marry the young conqueror to be.[1]

More prosaic, but still perhaps partly legendary, accounts asserted that the Ottomans, or Osmanlis as they called themselves, stemmed from the noble Qayi clan of the Ouz Turks, who originated in the high steppes of Central Asia only to be pushed west by the Mongol invasions of the 12th–13th centuries through Iran and Iraq and into Syria. When this band of refugees, doubtless one among the many peoples dislocated and driven into exile during this era, tried to cross the Euphrates River near the great brick castle of Qala'at Jabar, their leader was drowned. Two of his sons turned back with their followers into Mongol territory, but the third son, Ertuğrul, took his people northward to Erzurum and into Anatolia, where they finally settled around the small town of Söğüt.[2]

It was a period of great instability, but also great opportunity, throughout the Levant. In the wake of the Mongol tide, established authority everywhere had been left fragmented and delegitimized. The line of the Abbasid caliphs had been extinguished in 1258 when Hulagu Khan sacked Baghdad, while in Anatolia (the peninsula of Asia Minor, which had been transitioning to modern Turkey over the past two centuries), the Byzantine Empire was in decline and the Seljuk Sultanate of Rum had collapsed. It was in this fluid environment that the Ottomans enter history, taking their first step on the path to imperial hegemony when Osman, the son of Ertuğrul, defeated the Byzantines in battle, most probably on 27 July 1302 on the plain of Bapheus near İzmit. This first victory would bear the hallmarks of later conquests – intelligence, opportunism, and initiative. The Byzantines had constructed forts along the current course of the Sakarya River in order to demarcate a defensive line. However, in March 1302, floods temporarily diverted the river into its original course, rendering the forts useless and enabling Osman to cross into Byzantine territory.

The Ottomans' first major territorial acquisition was the capture of the Byzantine town of Bursa in 1326 by Orhan, Osman's son and successor, which Orhan promptly made the capital of his emirate. Orhan then defeated a Byzantine advance into northwestern Anatolia at the Battle of Pelekanon on 10–11 June 1329. This was the final attempt by the Byzantines to retain control of their Anatolian provinces. The Ottomans took İznik in 1331, reached the southern coast of the Sea of Marmara at Gemlik around 1333, captured İzmit in 1337, and seized Üsküdar on the shores of the Bosporus opposite Constantinople in 1338.[3]

On the death of the Byzantine Emperor Andronicus III in 1341, civil war erupted between his son and legitimate successor, the eight-year-old John V Palaiologos, and the regent, who assumed the title John VI Cantacuzenos. To support his claim, Cantacuzenos enlisted the aid of Orhan, whose intervention enabled Cantacuzenos to return to Constantinople on 8 February 1347 and assert his right as co-emperor. In return, Cantacuzenos betrothed his daughter, Theodora, to Orhan. Less than a half-century after their first trial of arms with the Byzantines, the Ottomans had elbowed their way into a strong enough position to not only intervene in imperial factional infighting but also claim a Christian bride from one of the claimants in the aftermath. It was soon apparent to Cantacuzenos that his ostensible allies were ultimately answerable only to their own agenda. Powerless, he could only lament how the people of Thrace, their region "ravaged as though by enemies, took refuge in the cities and nothing escaped damage, and very soon inhabited Thrace looked like a Scythian desert as the strength of the Romans was being squandered and destroyed by itself."[4]

Nevertheless, Cantacuzenos continued to request Ottoman aid, having inadequate military resources of his own, and in 1349 Ottoman troops under Orhan's son, Suleiman, were ferried to Thessaloniki by the Byzantine fleet in order to regain that city from the Serbs. When a second civil war between John V and John VI broke out in 1352, Palaiologos enlisted support from King Stephen Dušan of Serbia and Tsar Ivan Alexander of Bulgaria, while Cantacuzenos again called on Orhan for aid, receiving a substantial body of Ottoman troops under Suleiman. At the battle at Demotika in October, Cantacuzenos and Suleiman were victorious. The war dragged on until John V finally emerged as undisputed emperor of what remained of the Byzantine state in 1357. However, by then a fatal threshold had already been passed. To facilitate the transfer of Ottoman troops from Anatolia during the Demotika campaign, Cantacuzenos had granted Suleiman the fortress of Çimpe on the European shore of the Dardanelles. Whether or not this was intended as a temporary expedient, Suleiman refused to return the fortress in the aftermath of the battle. Thus, the Ottomans secured their first bridgehead in Europe, and established a significant precedent; so far as the House of Osman was concerned, wherever their boots once trod belonged to them forever.

The following year, Suleiman rode north as far as Tekirdağ, in a partnership with the Genoese, who presumably hoped that this new alliance would undermine the position of their Venetian rivals in Byzantine trade. Suleiman also captured Çorlu, Lüleburgaz, and Malkara, each of which became a forward base for further raids. In 1354, he took the major prize of Gallipoli and its important Byzantine naval base, taking advantage of its defenses having been destroyed by a devastating earthquake.[5]

Suleiman died in a hunting accident in 1357, so when Orhan died in the spring of 1362, his second son, Murad, acceded to the Ottoman throne in Bursa. This succession was challenged by Murad's younger brothers, Ibrahim and Halil.[*] Murad won the ensuing dynastic civil war, and his brothers paid the ultimate price for their defeat. This fratricide would be a recurring feature of the Ottoman succession in the centuries to come.

In 1366, the Ottomans lost Gallipoli to John V's cousin, Amadeo VI of Savoy, who restored it to the emperor. Hoping to follow up on this

---

[*] Reflecting the tangled dynastic politics of the era, Halil was Orhan's son by his Byzantine bride Theodora. This also made him the son-in-law of the Byzantine Emperor John V Palaiologos, Halil having married John's daughter Irene, whose mother was Theodora's sister, Helena. Please see pages 17–19 for family and dynastic trees.

accomplishment, John took the unprecedented step of going in person to Buda to ask King Louis I for military assistance. This marked the first occasion a Byzantine emperor had ever left his own territories to meet face to face with a foreign monarch.

The emperor's next step in his quest to inspire the Western Christian world to action was his trip to Rome in 1369. Here, he had to tread carefully. The Catholic/Orthodox split, made toxic by the Fourth Crusade and its sack of Constantinople in 1204, rendered Western aid for the Byzantines problematic. The explosive reaction at the street level in Constantinople, not just from the clergy but among the general populace, to any suggestion of subordination to the hated Latin rite in exchange for support from a people they looked down on as barbarous made negotiations extremely delicate for successive emperors even as the Ottoman tide rose ever higher. Conversely, many in the West had little respect and less time for what they regarded as the schismatic apostates of the Balkans.

John pleaded for help against the Ottomans, promising to comply with papal instructions regarding church union, even going so far as to convert to the Catholic faith himself. However, none of these gestures succeeded in budging Western elite or popular opinion, Pope Urban V actively discouraging Louis from intervening against the Ottomans on the grounds John did "not appear to want union by choice alone and through religious zeal," but was "driven to it so as to get your help."[6] Adding humiliation to frustration, on his way back to Constantinople the emperor was detained at Venice for unpaid debts, not being able to return home until late 1371.

While John was absent on his fruitless diplomatic initiatives, after a small but historically significant Ottoman victory over a combined Byzantine and Bulgarian army, Edirne was taken by Murad. At the confluence of the Maritsa and Tundzha rivers, the city secured Ottoman domination of Thrace, Bulgaria, and Macedonia. The fact that Murad made Edirne, the second greatest city in the Balkans behind only Constantinople, his new capital sent a clear signal that the Ottomans were in Europe to stay and that they considered themselves an imperial power with strategic interests both in Europe and Asia. Complementing their holdings in Anatolia, the newly conquered Balkan provinces were organized by the Ottomans as Rumelia, from the Turkish term *Rum Ili* (Roman Lands). That the Ottomans had consolidated their presence in Europe was confirmed when, after a failed attempt to forge an alliance with the Byzantines and Bulgars, the Serbs unilaterally marched on Edirne, which culminated in an overwhelming Ottoman victory at the Battle of Ormenio on the Maritsa River on 26 September 1371. Caught unawares when the Ottoman commander,

Lala Shahin Pasha, launched a night assault, Serbian King Vukašin Mrnjavčević and his brother, Despot Jovan Uglješa, were both killed. Isaiah, the prior of the monastery of St Panteleimon on Mount Athos, resorted to almost apocalyptic language in his description of the aftermath:

> Hunger killed those for whom death came solely; for everywhere there was hunger such as had never been anywhere since the world was created and, with Christ's mercy, such as there will never be again… The land was empty of all that was good; of people, animals, and anything fertile. There was neither prince nor military leader nor any teacher who could liberate and save the people… neither I nor the wisest among the Greeks would be able to portray in words the misfortune that befell the Christians in these regions.[7]

Ottoman raiders overran Macedonia, conquering the lowlands as far as Sofia and forcing the Serbs, like the Byzantines and Bulgars before them, to accept Ottoman suzerainty. The anarchic state of Serb dynastic politics exacerbated the lack of effective resistance, a situation worsened by dynastic civil war in Hungary.[8]

Bowing to the inevitable, John V decided to abandon his policy of proactive resistance and seek peace with the Ottomans. He bound himself to be a tribute-paying vassal of Murad I, following the example of those Serbian and Bulgarian princes who had survived the disaster at Ormenio. In 1373, while the emperor and Murad were campaigning in Asia Minor, their sons, Andronicus and Savcı, plotted against them. The rebellious sons were defeated, and while Murad beheaded Savcı, the emperor spared his son's life. However, obeying Murad's demands, he had Andronicus partially blinded and cut out of the line of succession, which passed to his younger brother, Manuel. In the summer of 1376, Andronicus seized the throne from his father with Genoese and Ottoman help, offering Murad his allegiance and an annual tribute.[9] The once mighty Byzantine Empire was now reduced to the status of an Ottoman client state. As a token of his subservience, the now emperor Andronicus IV also surrendered Gallipoli to Murad.[10] "[T]he old scourge, the Turks, roused to arrogance by the alliance which they concluded with the new Emperor against his father, have become more oppressive for us," the historian Kydones lamented; "Thus they received Gallipoli… and seized many other things belonging to us and exacted such an amount of money that nobody could easily count it… They command everything and we must obey… To such a point have they risen in power and we [have] been reduced to slavery."[11]

With their bridgehead into the Balkans firmly secured, the Ottomans were now in a position to intervene in European great power politics. When Hungary allied with Padua against Venice in 1373, the latter reached out to Murad for support, and by June some 5,000 Ottoman archers were serving in northeast Italy. This intervention alarmed Pope Gregory XI, who was responsible for the security, in addition to the souls, of his flock. In 1375, he wrote to Queen Giovanna of Naples: "Opposing the Turks can not only be considered a work of faith, but it is a better contribution towards the defense of the Principality of Achaea and the Kingdom of Naples; it is easier and more important to help those in danger, lest they perish, than to attempt at present the recovery of the holy land which has been occupied for so long."[12] However, the following year, Gregory left Avignon for Rome, where he died in 1378. The ensuing contested succession led to the Western Schism between rival lines of popes and antipope not resolved until the Council of Constance (1414–18). This division exacerbated factional infighting among the Catholic peoples of the West and seriously compromised the capacity for collective action against the rising Ottoman threat in the East.

Left to their own devices, the Orthodox peoples of the East had to choose between submission or resistance to Ottoman hegemony. When the rumor spread that Vaicu, the *voivode* (ruler) of Wallachia, had sided with the Ottomans, King Louis marched against him in 1375. In Wallachia, the Hungarians clashed with Ottoman troops who supported Vaicu, marking the first clash of arms between the two states. One of the few among the Serb nobility to escape the Ottoman orbit was Prince Lazar Hrebeljanović, whose pocket empire served as a haven for Serbian refugees and grew in strength accordingly. In 1381, the Ottomans were defeated on the Dubravnica River, but the following year they took Sofia.

In 1386, Murad took Niš, but the subsequent year a Serbian–Bulgarian coalition, led by Prince Lazar and Ivan Shishman, the Bulgarian tsar of Tarnovo, routed the Ottoman forces led by Lala Shahin Pasha, the first *beylerbey* (supreme governor) of Rumelia, on the banks of the Toplitsa River at Ploçnik. Shahin Pasha was defeated again in August 1388 at the Battle of Bileća by the Bosnian army of King Tvrtko I, commanded by Vlatko Vuković.

Murad, meanwhile, through force, intimidation, arranged marriages, and purchase, was busy incorporating the neighboring Turkmen principalities of Germiyan, Tekke, and Hamid in western and southwestern Anatolia. He also tried to win over Alaeddin of the Karamanids, the most powerful of the Anatolian Turkmen emirates, by offering a daughter to seal a marriage alliance. Alaeddin, however, challenged his father-in-law repeatedly, and the two clashed in battle at Konya in 1386. Murad's victory opened the passes of the Taurus Mountains, extending the Ottoman frontier to the Mediterranean coast between Antalya and Alanya. On the other side of the Bosporus, in April of 1387, at the climax of a siege that had commenced four years earlier, Ottoman banners were finally raised over Thessaloniki, the second city of the fast-dwindling Byzantine Empire.

The relentless Ottoman onslaught in the Balkans reached a critical turning point in 1389, when Murad led an army on campaign in person against Lazar. The two sides met at Kosovo Polje (the Field of the Blackbirds) on 15 June. This clash has become integral to Serbian national identity. According to the *Slovo o Knezu Lazaru* of Serbian Patriarch Danilo III, in his prayer before battle commenced, Lazar offered up both his body and his soul in martyrdom to the immortal spirit of Serbia, pledging himself and his men to the ultimate expression of collective action: "We bring ourselves before God as a living sacrifice... We die so that we may live forever... And a single grave will be ours."[13]

But the identities involved on each side were in fact quite blurred. Lazar marched to battle at the head of a heterogeneous coalition of Christian factions, with Serbs at its core but incorporating Bosnians, Albanians, Croatians, Hungarians, Wallachians, and Bulgarians. On the other side of the field, Serbian warlords Marko Kraljević and Konstantin Dejanović, as Ottoman vassals, contributed troops and perhaps even fought alongside the sultan against their countrymen.[14]

Murad held the center of the Ottoman line, with his sons Bayezid on his right and Yakub on his left. Lazar took up his station at the center of the Christian line. His son-in-law, Vuk Branković, led the right wing, and Bosnian forces under Vlatko Vuković, sent by Lazar's ally King Tvrtko of Bosnia, were on the left.

The actual course of the battle, and even its outcome, remain uncertain. In a letter to the senate of the Dalmatian city of Trogir, dated 1 August 1389, King Tvrtko claimed a Christian victory: "God's right hand lent us its full help and support and we held the field in triumph. We fought them, defeated them, and stretched them dead on the ground so that only a few of these infidels remained alive. And this, thank God, without a great number of losses on our own side."[15] It was true that Murad did not survive that day – whether he died during the battle or was assassinated in the aftermath remains contested – but neither did Lazar. Both armies were severely mauled, but while the Ottomans could draw upon fresh reserves of manpower, the Serbs were exhausted.[16] Murad's son Bayezid immediately seized the Ottoman throne, liquidating his brother Yakub in order to confirm the succession, while the Serbian state passed to Lazar's son, Stephen Lazarević, who became an Ottoman vassal as despot of Serbia. Lazar's widow, Princess Milica, surrendered her last daughter, Olivera, to Bayezid in 1390. Lazar's son-in-law, Vuk Branković, resisted attacks of the Turks until the autumn of 1392, when he finally submitted to the sultan. The only options open to the Serbian nobility now were flight or vassalage. Of the sons of King Vukašin Mrnjavčević, Dmitar made the first choice, seeking refuge in Hungary and serving King Sigismund, while Marko made the second, being killed in the Battle of Rovine in 1395 as a loyal vassal of Sultan Bayezid.

As the Balkans fragmented, Venice took advantage, swooping in to establish its dominance over coastal Albania by taking possession of such key strongholds as Durrës in 1392, Lezhë in 1393, and Shkodër in 1396. Meanwhile, Ottoman conquests in the Balkans had brought the expanding empire into direct contact with the kingdom of Hungary, the most powerful regional state. In the aftermath of Kosovo Polje, the Hungarians preemptively intervened in Serbia to seize strategic strongholds like Čestin and Borač along the border before the Ottomans could claim them, converting the frontier districts into military zones under the supervision of wardens. These preparations were immediately put to the test as the Ottomans closed up to the border, which roiled with conflict every year for the rest of the decade, with raid and retaliation crossing in both directions. Hungary's southern counties were heavily plundered, and in 1392 the flourishing Syrmia region was depopulated, the ensuing loss of customs tolls and taxes seriously affecting Hungarian state revenue.

Hungary was vulnerable during this period as a crisis in the succession had left the state enervated and divided. At his death in 1382, King Louis I left no sons. He had destined his elder daughter Maria – who at eleven years old was betrothed to Sigismund of Luxemburg, the margrave of Brandenburg and son of Emperor Charles IV – to succeed him on both his thrones, but the Poles terminated their personal union with Hungary, crowning the younger daughter, nine-year-old Hedvig, as their queen after her marriage to Prince Jagiello of Lithuania.

Maria was crowned in Hungary, where the Dowager Queen Elizabeth took over the regency from her base in Bosnia. The Hungarian nobles were divided on the question of female succession, and the guardianship of the widely hated Queen Mother was bitterly resisted. To further complicate the issue, Charles III of Naples, the adopted son of Louis I, maintained that he should have become king of Hungary. He found support among much of the Hungarian nobility and in 1385 he invaded Dalmatia. Maria was forced to abdicate in favor of Charles, only for the Queen Mother to arrange his assassination after a reign of only thirty-nine days. Charles's supporters rose up in rebellion, supported by King Tvrtko I of Bosnia and the Venetians, leading to civil war, the capture of Maria, and the poisoning of Elizabeth. Finally, Sigismund entered the fray, freed Maria and had himself crowned king in 1387. Maria died while pregnant, the result of a riding accident at the age of twenty-four, while Sigismund would go on to reign for fifty years, from 1387 to 1437. However, he had a narrow basis for his authority as king.[17] He was elected by a league as a consort of the queen and was obliged to take a coronation oath that bound him to donate royal properties in exchange for support, which resulted in his granting away over half of the royal estate, considerably weakening his financial position.

Sigismund was forced into an alliance with Mircea the Elder, *voivode* of Wallachia, who in 1389 had seized on the opportunity presented by the Ottomans prioritizing their confrontation with the Serbs to annex the Bulgarian despotate of Dobruja, giving his principality access to the Black Sea and some territory south of the Danube. This provoked an Ottoman response. At the time, Bayezid was on campaign in Anatolia, where the Turkmen emirs had sought to exploit the death of Murad at Kosovo to reclaim their lost autonomy. If Sigismund and Mircea assumed his absence accorded them some advantage, they were swiftly disabused of any such misconception. The institutional professionalism of the fast-evolving Ottoman realm allowed its head of state to delegate critical tasks of administration and military policy to subordinates and expect positive results. A trio of Ottoman generals now made substantive gains in Rumelia. Çandarlızade Ali Pasha seized Nicopolis on the north bank of the Danube, and in 1392 Yiğit Pasha took Skopje, while Firuz Bey occupied Vidin, reducing the Bulgar Tsar Ivan Sratsimir to vassal status.

Bayezid, meanwhile, had swiftly reasserted Ottoman control over his disaffected Turkmen client states, and in 1392 he annexed the Black Sea coastal emirate of Kastamonu. Bayezid returned to Europe in 1393 and, over the course of a lightning campaign that illustrated why he would soon earn the sobriquet *Yildirim* (the Thunderbolt), he reimposed Ottoman hegemony in the Balkans. After a brutal three-month siege, Bayezid took Tarnovo on 17 July 1393, reducing the Bulgar tsar, Ivan Shishman, to vassalage. By 1394, Bayezid was in a strong enough position to assume the title *sultanü'r-Rum* (sultan of [Eastern] Rome/Asia Minor).

The following year, Bayezid intervened in Wallachia, ousting the pro-Hungarian *voivode* Mircea the Elder and replacing him with an Ottoman vassal, Vlad the Usurper. However, Mircea was able to reclaim his throne and defeat the Ottoman army of occupation at the Battle of Rovine, which took place near the Argeş River on 17 May 1395.[18] Ottoman casualties were heavy, including Serb vassals Marko Kraljević and Konstantin Dejanović.[19] Mircea, taking advantage of the sack of Sarai, capital city of the Golden Horde, by Timur the Lame, was also able to seize Kilia, an important port at the mouth of the Danube. On the return south, Bayezid compensated for his setback in Wallachia by seizing Nicopolis, the last stronghold of his erstwhile kinsman by marriage Ivan Shishman, who disappeared from history shortly afterwards.

Meanwhile, key Hungarian strongholds along the Danubian line, Golubac and Orşova, were taken, and the islands of Chios and Negroponte were devastated as Bayezid initiated a new scheme of systematic conquest in the Balkans and the Aegean.[20] The great prize now lay within his grasp. In the spring of 1394, the sultan placed Constantinople under a blockade, which rapidly escalated into an all-out siege. To control navigation along the Bosporus, Bayezid ordered the construction of a castle, the Güzelce Hisar (Beauteous Fortress) on the Asian shore of the strait. Constantinople was effectively cut off from the outside world.

THE CRUSADE OF NICOPOLIS

Under relentless pressure, Hungary was forced onto a permanent war footing, with the burden of conscription and increased taxation falling on the nobility, clergy, and peasant families alike. Sigismund mortgaged the kingdom to the hilt, offering up everything from mines to cities to entire principalities as collateral. Western Europe, meanwhile, was mired in its own bloody conflicts, most significantly, the Hundred Years War, which broke out between England and France in 1337. In 1345, Pope Clement VI wrote separate letters to Kings Philip VI of France and Edward III of England urging them to stop fighting and unite to go on crusade: "Oh, how much better to fight against the Turkish enemies of our faith, than the present fratricidal strife," the pontiff wrote to the English king.[21] This missive fell on deaf ears, as did a similar appeal by Pope Urban V in 1370.

However, the spirit of the crusade was not entirely extinguished, being kept alive by evangelical activists like Philippe de Mézières, an itinerant knight who was one of the first in the West to realize the role of Hungary as *Antemuralis Christianitatis* (Bulwark of Christendom) and who had been evangelizing for a collective European response to the Ottoman threat ever since his own experience serving during the 1343–51 Smyrniote Crusades against the emirate of Aydın in Anatolia.[22] He worked tirelessly for Anglo-French reconciliation in particular, urging the Western monarchs in his *Nova Religio Passionis* to set aside their differences and stand shoulder to shoulder in a new order of knighthood, the *Militia Passionis Jhesu Christi*. Mézières outlined a strategic plan for a joint crusade in his *Le Songe du Vieil Pelerine*, incorporating two great crusader columns, the first that would advance by land via Hungary into Ottoman territory and thereby link up with the second arriving by sea through the cooperation of the Venetian and Genoese naval powers. Other advocates, such as Robert the Hermit and Eustache Deschamps, added their voices to the growing groundswell of support for a crusade. As early as 1392, volunteers from across Europe – English, Silesian, Czech, and Styrian knights – began arriving in Hungary to fight alongside Sigismund against the Ottomans.[23]

In 1394, the rival popes of the Western Schism – Boniface IX in Rome, Benedict XIII in Avignon – each issued bulls authorizing a crusade. In January of the following year, Sigismund reached out to Venice to request her assistance in both transporting a crusader army to the Balkans and preventing Ottoman reinforcements from being ferried across from Anatolia to Rumelia. Venice, the *Serenissima Respublica* (Serene Republic), responded in March that it would provide no more than one-fourth of the fleet for any putative crusade, and even that much only if the rulers of France, Burgundy, and England all responded positively to taking the cross. On 15 May, Charles VI of France wrote a letter to King Richard II of England calling for the raising of a joint Anglo-French crusading army: "Then, fair brother, it will be fair moment… that you and I, for the propitiation of the sins of our ancestors, should undertake a crusade to succor our fellow Christians and to liberate the Holy Land."[24] Both monarchs reached out to Antonio Adorno, doge of Genoa, to secure his cooperation.

This new spirit contributed towards the opening of negotiations to end the war between England and France, which culminated in the signing of a peace treaty between the two antagonists in early 1396 and the marriage of Richard II to Isabel, the six-year-old daughter of Charles VI, later that year.

In February 1396 the alliance between Hungary and the Byzantines was formally signed in Buda. A Burgundian ducal proclamation dated 28 March 1396 fixed Dijon as the place where the Franco-Burgundian crusaders should assemble by 20 April that year. The crusade set out from Dijon on 30 April 1396. The Crusader camp boasted some of the most renowned knights of medieval Europe, including John "the Fearless" of Nevers, son and heir to the Duke of Burgundy, Philip II "the Bold," and Guillaume de la Trémoille, the marshal of Burgundy, to Philip of Eu, the constable of France, Jean II le Maingre (*le Boucicaut*, "the Brave"), the marshal of France, Jean de Vienne, the admiral of

France, and Enguerrand de Coucy, a son-in-law of England's King Edward III. Although he was only twenty-three years old, his dynastic status and the enormous funds his father had committed to the endeavor led to John the Fearless emerging as the at least titular leader of the crusade.[25] Ironically, one of the chief critics of the crusade was Philippe de Mézières. Aged almost seventy and living in the Convent of the Celestines in Paris, he warned the knights were being drawn east by "Vain Madame Ambition, one of the Mightiest Ladies in the World." It would, he proclaimed, end in disaster.[26]

The Western Crusaders arrived without incident at Vienna. From there, a river fleet of seventy ships and barges bore them down the Danube to Buda, followed by the main Crusader army which reached the Hungarian capital late in July. The best option for Sigismund would have been for the main army to march through Transylvania, across the Carpathians, and into Wallachia. This would have confirmed the shaky allegiance of both the Transylvanians and of Mircea of Wallachia. The Crusader commanders, however, feared being held up in the difficult mountain passes and wanted to stay close to their supply route on the Danube. The best path forward from that base would be to separate Serbia from the Ottomans before pushing through Bulgaria to capture Bayezid's capital of Edirne, raising the siege of Constantinople and forcing the Ottomans back into Anatolia.

Nicolas de Gara, the constable of Hungary, led the vanguard down the left bank of the Danube, followed by the French and Burgundians. The host mustered at Orşova. While the bulk of the army crossed to the southern side of the Danube, a Hungarian contingent had taken a different route from Budapest, through Transylvania to Braov and across the Carpathian Mountains into Wallachia. Apart from gathering the perhaps unwilling Transylvanian contingents they also may have had the task of expelling Mircea's pro-Ottoman rival Vlad before driving the small Ottoman garrison from Nicopolis Minor (Turnu Măgurele) on the northern side of the river.

The main Crusader fleet, which left Rhodes in August after picking up the Hospitaller contingent, had sailed via the Sea of Marmara into the Black Sea. It consisted of forty-four vessels under the overall command of the Venetian admiral Thomas Mocenigo. At the end of the month, this armada began sailing up the Danube towards Nicopolis.

The Crusaders meanwhile marched on to take Vidin, where Bulgar Tsar Ivan Sratsimir (half-brother of the late Ivan Shishman) threw open the gates, and Orjahovo, where those of the garrison considered worth ransoming were taken prisoner and the rest were massacred, a gruesome addition to the lengthening catalogue of atrocities visited on the local populations, before linking up with their Black Sea fleet, which had sailed unhindered up the Danube to anchor off Nicopolis on 12 September. However, the Ottoman garrison of Nicopolis stubbornly refused to either surrender, buckle under a siege, or be starved into submission; its defiance was so resolute the commander, Doğan Bey, was subsequently awarded the title of *Şuja al-Din* (Hero of the Faith).[27]

Bayezid ordered the Ottoman regional forces in the Balkans not to attack the Crusaders but instead to assemble in strength between Edirne and Plovdiv, while vassal contingents mustered around Plovdiv itself, with the Serbs under Stephen Lazarević arriving via Sofia. Taking the main Ottoman army, which was already in the field enforcing the siege of Constantinople, and summoning every other detachment immediately available, Bayezid marched northwards via Edirne and the Shipka Pass to Tarnovo, where he linked up with the regional and vassal contingents on 21 or 22 September.

On 24 September, Bayezid advanced to contact, raising his banner on a hill several kilometers south of the Crusader camp. His army could boast officer of singular talent, expertise, and experience, from the *Sadr-ı A'zam* (grand vizier, prime minister, and keeper of the imperial seal) Çandarlızade Ali Pasha, who also served as *Qadi'l-Askar* (judge of the army) and a military commander in his own right, to Evrenos Bey, who had served under no fewer than five Ottoman rulers (and would continue to do so until his death in 1417, rising to become *Uc Bey*, governor of the "Left March" of the frontier, whose task was to extend Ottoman control along the Aegean coast of Greece to Thessaloniki, Macedonia, Albania, and finally down into the heartlands of Greece).[28]

The Crusaders now found themselves with a formidable enemy army to their front with a still vigorous enemy garrison behind them, and with no strong base to fall back upon. A broad river without a bridge also lay between them and the nearest friendly territory in Wallachia. If defeated they would be trapped and this, as well as the traditionally aggressive tactics of the French and Burgundians, impelled the Crusaders to take the offensive.

At a council of war on 24 September, Sigismund recommended that his and the other Central European troops, almost entirely infantry, should be in the vanguard, there to meet the irregular infantry of the Turks who constituted the front line of their own army. They would take a defensive stance and try to provoke the Ottomans into a charge which would either be defeated at the contact of the two infantry forces or could be reinforced by the strong Franco-Burgundian cavalry ordered in the rear. The Franco-Burgundians rejected this strategy outright. That same day, the Crusaders, perhaps fearing a rescue sortie by the garrison in Nicopolis, massacred the prisoners taken at Orjahovo. Such drastic action was common enough on Western European battlefields, but it was new to the Ottomans and, as the Crusaders clearly had no time to bury the dead, it would cost them dear two days later.

The following morning the Franco-Burgundians took up their position at the front of the Crusader army. Behind them, spread along a broader front, were the Hungarians plus the Germans, Hospitallers, and probably Bohemians and Poles. On one flank were the Transylvanians, led by their *voivode*, Stephen II Lackfi, while on the other flank were the Wallachians led by Mircea.

Sigismund made one last attempt to talk his allies out of going on the offensive and thereby sacrificing a strong defensive position. John the Fearless consulted with his advisers. Some, like the Admiral de Vienne, favored a more defensive strategy, only to be overruled by the hotheads like Philip of Eu, who sneered, "Yes, yes, the king of Hungary wishes to gain all the honor of the day. He has given us the vanguard, and now he wishes to take it away, that he may have the first blow. Let those who will believe what he sends to us, but for my part I never will."

Seizing one of the banners of the Virgin, the constable of France shouted, "In the name of God and Saint George, you shall see me this day prove myself a good knight."[29]

Bayezid, meanwhile, used natural features to secure his position, his left flank being close to a wood while his right flank was protected by very broken ground beyond which were steep slopes leading down to broad marshes along the southern shore of the Danube. He was also on slightly higher ground than the plateau south and east of Nicopolis. Most importantly, there was a deep and narrow wooden ravine to his front. Here, he placed infantry archers to screen the main formation of cavalry, which was itself divided into a larger center and smaller wings which could also be thrust forwards, giving the whole array the appearance of a crescent. As was also traditional, the Rumelian provincial cavalry were placed on the right wing because the battle was fought on European soil. The Anatolians would have had this place had the battle been in Asia, but at Nicopolis they were on the left. Infantry were placed in the center protected by a dense thicket of sharpened wooden stakes. The small numbers of the sultan's elite household troops, the janissaries, present were likely to have been stationed with the ordinary *azap* foot soldiers rather than held back with Bayezid's household corps, which almost entirely consisted of cavalry, stationed with the sultan some distance to the rear, out of sight of the enemy behind the brow of a hill. In front of the thicket of stakes were the light cavalry *akinji*, operating as skirmishers or to draw the enemy forward against the main field defenses and thus exposing them to flank attacks by the provincial *sipahi* heavy cavalry, including 5,000 vassal Serbian cavalry led by Stephen Lazarević.

Bayezid clearly planned to draw the Crusaders into an assault and then hit them in the flanks while they were fighting his infantry. Two things, however, did not go as anticipated. The Crusaders attacked so precipitously their army effectively split in half, with the Franco-Burgundians in the vanguard scattering the screening *akinji* and then breaking through the Ottoman infantry more quickly than expected, while leaving their Hungarian, Transylvanian, and Wallachian allies behind them.

In his memoirs, *Deeds of Marshal Boucicault*, le Maingre recalled:

When the Saracens saw that we were near enough, the whole cavalry battalion wheeled away in tight formation like a cloud and moved to the rear, behind the stakes and behind their infantry... The Saracens began to shoot... so thick and fast that never hail or rain fell more heavily from the sky than the arrows now flew, in a few minutes they had killed great numbers of our horses and men.

Speaking of himself in the third person, le Maingre, "who was unable to see the sharp stakes so wickedly set just in front of them," urged his compatriots to renew their frontal assault. "At once they spurred on to charge the Saracens, and rode straight in among the stakes, which were strong, rigid and sharp, so that they drove into the horses' bellies and killed many of them and injured the men who fell from the horses."[30]

The Ottoman tactical position was saved when the Crusaders were struck in the flanks by the provincial *sipahi* heavy cavalry. The Crusaders succeeded in holding their ground, but by now they were almost exhausted, having suffered heavy casualties and being left exposed on a steep slope in the blazing sun. At this critical point, Bayezid committed his household reserve, which struck head on while the *sipahi* again crashed in on the Crusaders' flanks.

If the vanguard had not charged so precipitously the fortunes of the day might still have shifted, for the second wave of the Crusader army was only now coming up, brushing aside the still regrouping Ottoman forces scattered by the first wave. The surviving fragments of a lost account describe how Archbishop Nicholas Kaniszay of Esztergom, witnessing the perilous state of the vanguard, "led his soldiers to the center of the struggle, launched a counterattack against the Turks and slew many. The Christians were shouting, 'Victory! Victory is ours!' and the archbishop was able to put the Turkish troops to flight."[31]

The battle hung in the balance. Now came the decisive moment, as Bayezid ordered his last reserve, Lazarević's Serbian cavalry, into the fray. The sultan's vassals charged towards the banner held by the standard-bearer of Nicolas de Gara, the constable of Hungary, and overthrew it. The second line of the Crusader army now broke and began falling back to the river. Some made it to the Danube, and safety; Bertrandon de la Brocquiére described how 200 Lombard and Genoese crossbowmen held off the pursuit, buying time for Sigismund to board his galley and make good his escape. Others were not so fortunate. Some were cut down as they fled, others as they made last stands on the hilltops. The number who did succeed in reaching the river soon exceeded the capacity of the galleys to evacuate them. Johann Schiltberger, serving as a squire to Lord Lienhart Richartingen, was an eyewitness to what happened next, as the crews of the already overloaded galleys, desperate to pull away, began beating or hacking at the hands of those left on the shore, who were frantically trying to clamber aboard. These unfortunates either drowned or were abandoned to their fate.[32]

Isolated and surrounded, the surviving Crusaders of the vanguard were cut down or forced to yield at sword point to an Ottoman army not in the mood to take prisoners. Unless a captive could command a ransom, his typical fate was either slavery or summary execution. In the aftermath, Bayezid reclaimed Vidin and with it Ivan Sratsimir, whose choice to side with the crusade was rewarded by incarceration in an Edirne prison from which he would never emerge alive.

Those who escaped via the Danube to the Black Sea made for Constantinople, where Sigismund discussed the situation with Emperor Manuel II before embarking once more and returning home via the Adriatic port of Dubrovnik on 21 December. Manuel was despondent at the news; "To prudent men, life is not worth living after that calamity," a disaster greater than the deluge of the Great Flood in Genesis, "as it carried off men better than those of old."[33]

The West responded to word of this catastrophe with equal shock and grief. "A great mourning began throughout the kingdom," a contemporary Parisian recorded; "everybody lamented the noble knights who had fallen there, who represented the flower of France."[34] For some, the outcome was the inevitable price to be paid for the sin of hubris. In his *Épistre lamentable et consolatoire*, Philippe de Mézières accused the Crusaders of following the "three daughters of Lucifer" – pride, cupidity, and luxury – instead of the four virtues of good governance – order, the discipline of chivalry, obedience, and justice.[35] Others, however, searched for a scapegoat, and found it in the conduct and character of the Hungarians generally, and Sigismund particularly. The poet Eustace Deschamps lamented the lost opportunity at Nicopolis, "Abandoned through arrogance and folly; Because of the Hungarians who fled the field."[36] The feeling was mutual. "We lost the battle by the pride and vanity of those French," Sigismund raged to Philibert de Naillac, Grand Master of the Hospitallers.[37]

The outcome of this, the first concerted Christian effort to roll back the Ottoman tide, thus augured ill for the future. Not only had the Ottomans proved they were at least a match for the flower of European chivalry on the battlefield, but also the tangled skein of the alliance between Western and Central European powers, so painstakingly assembled, now completely unraveled in a welter of recriminations and bad blood.

Only too aware his kingdom now stood alone against the Ottoman leviathan, Sigismund immediately initiated reforms upon his return to Hungary, starting in October of 1397 at the *Diet* (legislative assembly) of Timișoara with a new obligation requiring "all landowners among the barons and noblemen of our realm must equip and lead to war… from twenty peasant tenants one archer in soldierly fashion and to make them fight during the present war." This broadening of military service would be dubbed the *militia portalis* (literally, "soldiers of tax plots"). This was complemented by an extensive program of fortress construction along the Danube frontier, and specialists in siege warfare from across Italy and the Holy Roman Empire were encouraged to settle in Hungary by Sigismund, who was eager to solicit their expertise in designing state-of-the-art defensive lines.[38]

Hungary's role as the *scutum atque murus* (shield and rampart) of Christendom was recognized in 1410 by Antipope John XXIII.[39] However, not every Christian state was aligned with Hungary. Venice wrested control of the Dalmatian coast in the wars of 1410–13 and 1418–20, with the exception of the aristocratic republic of Dubrovnik, which had flourished under nominal Hungarian suzerainty since 1358 owing to its extensive trade networks in the Balkans, Adriatic, and Mediterranean. Sigismund acknowledged Venetian rule in Dalmatia only in 1433.

Another persistent Christian antagonist to Hungary during this period was King Ladislaus of Naples, the last of the Angevin dynasty. In October 1392, he sent letters and an embassy to Bayezid offering an alliance against their common enemy, Sigismund, a pact that was intended to be sealed by a marriage between the king and a daughter of the sultan. Ladislaus had inherited a claim to the throne of Hungary through his father, Charles of Durazzo, king of Naples and Hungary, who was assassinated in Buda in February of 1386. Only nine years old at the time, Ladislaus was in no position to contest his claim against Sigismund, who was crowned the following year. Although nothing came of the proposed marriage, Ladislaus continued to scheme against Hungary, encouraging his followers in Bosnia to cooperate with the Ottomans in raiding Hungarian territory, machinations that were only brought to a halt in 1408 when Sigismund's decisive victory at the Battle of Dobor decimated the Bosnian nobility and forced *voivode* Hrvoje Vukčić Kosača to submit to Hungarian authority. Ladislaus subsequently sold his possessions and royal rights over Dalmatia to Venice for 100,000 ducats, essentially abandoning his trans-Adriatic ambitions.[40]

The critical role of Hungary in holding the front line of Christendom was emphasized when, in a major reverse, Sultan Mehmed I launched a punitive campaign against Mircea in 1417, capturing the Danubian fortresses of Giurgiu and Severin, which guarded the river crossings into Wallachia and Transylvania. The sultan reduced Mircea to a tribute-paying vassal, who was also obliged to send his son to the Ottoman capital as a hostage.

In the Hungarian–Serbian treaty concluded in May 1426 at Tata in northwestern Hungary, Sigismund accepted George Branković, the nephew of the aging and childless Despot Stephen Lazarević, as his heir. Branković, whose legitimate sons were to inherit the despotate of Serbia, was to remain the vassal of the Hungarian king and of his descendants, serving his overlord with troops whenever called on. In return for his loyalty and service, Branković would keep his uncle's possessions, save for some strategically important strongholds such as Belgrade and Golubac.

The agreement changed power relations between the Ottomans and the Hungarians, as the Hungarians acquired key fortresses along the Danube River and reasserted their suzerainty over Serbia, which the sultan considered an Ottoman vassal. It is also possible that Sigismund did not trust Branković and wanted to make sure that Belgrade and Golubac reverted to him upon the death of Stephen Lazarević. After the despot passed away on 19 July 1427, Sigismund took possession of Belgrade in late September, but only after Branković ordered its handover to the Catholic Hungarians, which the Orthodox clergy opposed.

Belgrade controlled the Danubian waterways and the most important river crossing, and was the end point of the Niš–Belgrade military corridor. Belgrade's possession was imperative for the Hungarians if they wanted to halt Ottoman incursions into their country and maintain their influence in Serbia and Wallachia. Golubac's castellan, however, ceded the fort to the Ottomans, creating a major gap in the Hungarian defense line. Despite Sigismund's careful preparations, his attempt to recapture the fortress in the summer of 1428 was foiled by the arrival of an Ottoman relief force, with which the king signed a truce. The loss of Golubac was a major blow to the Hungarians, for the castle was a convenient crossing point through which Ottoman *akinji* raiders crossed the Danube River into Hungary.

Notwithstanding these setbacks, considering the extent to which the kingdom had trembled on the precipice of total ruin in the immediate aftermath of the disaster at Nicopolis, Hungary had weathered the last quarter century remarkably well. This was owed less to its own initiatives and more to forces far beyond its control rising in the distant heartland of Eurasia.

With the Ottoman frontier in Europe secure after his great victory at Nicopolis, Bayezid could address unresolved business in Anatolia. In 1398, he defeated and killed both the Karamanid Emir Alaeddin and Kadı Burhaneddin of Sivas, incorporating their lands into the Ottoman realm. The House of Osman was ascendant, and the limitless energy and ambition of its sultan knew no bounds. The crowning achievement of his reign now seemed only a matter of time. Constantinople was still grimly holding on, but for all intents and purposes the city had been abandoned to its own devices. Not only was there now no prospect of relief from the West, but even efforts at resupply – half-hearted and haphazard at best before Nicopolis – completely evaporated in the wake of the battle. By 1402, the specter of famine stalked the city.[41] Its fall was only a matter of time.

However, while the Catholic West had been chastised and the Balkans lay at the sultan's mercy, a new challenge was arising in the East.

Having subdued Central Asia, in 1400 and 1401 the Turco-Mongol warlord Timur sacked Aleppo, Damascus, and Baghdad. Bayezid's refusal to surrender the fugitive sultan of Baghdad and the khan of the Karakoyunlu (Black Sheep) Turks of Azerbaijan to Timur poisoned relations between the two conquerors. An embassy arrived at Bayezid's court with a letter, in which Timur poured scorn on the obscure origins of the Ottoman dynasty, suggesting they were descended from slaves. Bayezid sent the ambassadors back to Timur with their beards shaved off, and a coarse warning that if Timur dared tangle with him, Bayezid would rape his wife. Brushing off that threat, Timur indignantly refuted the Ottoman claim to the status of *ghazi* (holy warriors), arguing that in fact it was his soldiers who "are always grasping the hems of God's grace, while most of yours are poll-tax-paying *kāfirs*" (non-Muslims).[42] He warned that any confrontation between the two of them "would be the aiding of the religion of the *kāfirs*," for "while

Muslims fall upon each other, the abject *kāfirs* might stretch out their hands" and reclaim territories taken by the *ghazi* faithful.[43]

The ensuing clash between the two conquerors took place northeast of Ankara on 28 July 1402, and ended with Timur's total victory. Two of Bayezid's sons – Mustafa and Musa – were taken prisoner alongside their father, while another three – Suleiman, İsa, and Mehmed – managed to escape. Bayezid would die in captivity, and the struggle to inherit his crown over the course of the ensuing decade would be remembered in Ottoman history as the Interregnum (1402–13). This reflected the inherent vulnerability of the Ottoman model of government, which centralized all power in the individual sultan. There was no respect for primogeniture. Following an old Turkish tradition, the Ottoman system endowed all male heirs with an equal right to the throne. The first prince (*şehzade*) to successfully assert that right was the only legitimate ruler, as his victory was evidence that he benefited from divine favor (*kut*). Consequently, every succession would be defined by fratricide at best, civil war at worst.

This was the great crisis of the Osmanli dynasty. Defeated, demoralized, and divided, it would never again be so vulnerable as it was when left in the dust of Timur the Lame. A concerted effort by the Western powers at this moment might well have driven the Ottomans entirely out of Europe. Such a shock to the system coming so soon after the humiliation at Ankara might even have permanently fragmented the Ottoman holdings in Anatolia, leaving squabbling dynasts scavenging over the remnants of Osman's dream. But it was not to be. Just when it was gifted with the most perfect opportunity it would ever receive, the crusading impulse faltered, and none of the Latin states elected to intervene. The shriven nub that remained of the Byzantine Empire along with the other regional Christian principalities did seek to take advantage of the very fluid environment during the Interregnum by aligning with the rival contenders to the Ottoman throne, but they lacked the weight to decisively tip the scales in any direction.[44]

İsa's powerbase was western Anatolia, while Mehmed dominated in the east and Suleiman controlled Rumelia. İsa, defeated by Mehmed in the Battle of Ulubad in 1403, was run to ground and executed later that year. Having being released by the Timurids following the death of Bayezid, Musa forged an alliance with Mehmed and in 1411 succeeded in taking Edirne, Suleiman being killed while attempting to flee into Byzantine territory. The last two brothers then turned on each other. Mehmed defeated and killed Musa at the Battle of Çamurlu on 5 July 1413, thereby ending the Interregnum by taking the throne as Sultan Mehmed I. In 1417, the sultan defeated Mircea the Elder of Wallachia and subdued him into vassalage. Mircea agreed to pay a tribute and to send his sons as hostages to the sultan's court. To strengthen his hold over the Danube, Mehmed placed Ottoman garrisons at Turnu and Giurgiu on the north bank of the river and Silistra on its south bank in 1419, effectively ending Bulgar independence. Meanwhile, the Ottoman advance recommenced in Bosnia. In May 1415, the Ottomans had pushed all the way to Ljubljana in Slovenia. In July of that year, King Sigismund, who was then busy at the Council of Constance, sent an army into Bosnia, but this was defeated in a decisive battle at Lašva. In August, the Ottomans penetrated all the way to Friuli in northeast Italy.

The return of stability under the reign of one sovereign was welcome, but the scars of civil war ran deep. Mehmed I's son and successor, Murad II, faced many of the same challenges as his father. Using every tool at his disposal – military force, diplomacy, appeasement, vassalage, and marriage alliances – Murad not only asserted his right to reign, but expanded and consolidated the Ottoman realm, bequeathing to his successor the most dynamic state in Eurasia. At his accession, his uncle (baselessly dubbed the "False" Mustafa in official Ottoman chronicles) and his thirteen-year-old brother (called "Little" Mustafa), contested his right to the throne, while the former lord of Aydın rebelled against him.

At this point, the Byzantines badly overplayed their hand. Timur had done no greater favor to any man than the Byzantine Emperor Manuel II Palaiologos. Constantinople had been reduced to the brink of starvation when the Ottoman war machine finally met its match at Ankara in 1402. In the fractious aftermath, the following year Bayezid's son Suleiman, now referring to the emperor as his "father," not only ended the siege of Constantinople but restored to Manuel by treaty significant territories, including Thessaloniki, the Thracian coast north to Mesembria, and the islands of Skiathos, Skopelos, and Skyros. In addition to these concessions, Suleiman freed Constantinople from its tribute obligation, guaranteed the release of all the emperor's subjects held captive, and promised his ships would not sail through the straits without the permission of either the emperor or the other Christian co-signatories of the treaty. Relations between the Byzantines and Ottomans remained relatively peaceful during much of the reign of Mehmed I, who immediately upon his accession acknowledged the terms of the treaty of 1403 as well as his position as the "obedient son" of the emperor.[45]

However, Byzantine policy fractured over its best course of action after Mehmed I's death in 1421. Manuel II favored recognition of Mehmed's eldest son and designated successor, Murad, as sultan. But he was overruled by his own son and co-emperor, John VIII, who urged support for a rival claimant to the Ottoman throne, the "False" Mustafa, whom the Byzantines had held in their custody on Limnos since 1416. This use of a proxy to incite civil war in the Ottoman domains backfired. In reprisal, Murad laid siege to both the Byzantine capital Constantinople and the empire's second city Thessaloniki in 1422, keeping them marginalized while he focused on his uncle (who he defeated and then executed that year) and his brother, "Little" Mustafa, who was subjected to the same fate in February 1423.

Effectively abandoned to their own devices – the contemporary chronicler Doukas relates that Constantinople "was suffering her own calamities and was unable to send help" – the civic leaders and population of Thessaloniki conceded control of the city to Venice in 1423 (it would remain under their authority until 1430, when Murad II finally subjugated it).[46]

Constantinople itself was hardly in fit condition to confront the revitalized Ottoman war machine. The city had never recovered from the siege imposed on it by Bayezid from 1394 to 1402. The Castilian ambassador Clavijo, who arrived in Constantinople in 1403, was shocked by the city's ruined houses, churches, and monasteries, its conspicuously sparse population, and the almost village-like appearance of what had once been a great urban metropolis. Other foreign eyewitnesses who visited the city over the ensuing decades, such as Cristoforo Buondelmonti and Bertrandon de la Broquiére, also commented on its dilapidated state. Efforts at urban renewal had not been helped by outbreaks of plague in 1410, 1417, and 1420.

As far as relief from the West was concerned during the siege of 1422, on 26 August the Senate of Venice rejected a proposal for a naval operation against the Ottoman fleet blockading Constantinople, and informed the emperor it could not send any military or financial assistance to the besieged city before the following spring. The senate suggested the emperor should instead seek assistance from the Genoese and the Hospitallers of Rhodes, unless, they added, he should be amenable to making peace with Murad II, in which case Venice would gladly offer its services to facilitate a mediation between the two parties.[47]

The war – such as it was – wound down in February 1424. Taking advantage of the fact John VIII was absent undertaking a sojourn to the courts of Venice, Milan, and Hungary in a bid to rally support, Manuel II concluded new terms of peace with the Ottomans, by which the Byzantines conceded most of the gains from the treaty of 1403 and were again reduced to the status of a tribute-paying Ottoman vassal. Murad rounded out the consolidation of the Ottoman realm when he re-annexed the Anatolian principalities of Aydın, Menteşe, Germiyan, and Teke, and reclaimed territory from the Karamanid emirate, which had shrugged off the Ottoman yoke after Timur's triumph at Ankara in 1402.

Having ended the generation of strife during the Interregnum and its aftermath and restored unity and purpose to the Ottoman state, Murad would now set in motion the next chapter in the fulfillment of Osman's dream.

MEASURES OF SUCCESS

What explains the relentless Ottoman expansion from refugee outcasts to world power? Perhaps the simplest answer is, they were in the right place at the right time.[48] Settling on the frontier between Anatolia and the Balkans when both regions were splintered into a kaleidoscope of minor powers enabled the Ottomans to start small and build slowly, beneath the notice of any surrounding great power until it was too late for direct intervention because the Ottomans had already expanded to the point where they had parity. The only existential threat to the Ottoman ascendancy was Timur, who dealt the Ottomans a potentially fatal blow at Ankara in 1402. However, this was mitigated by three factors. First, Timur died only three years later, and his empire lacked the institutional staying power necessary to keep the Ottomans in check. Second, by the beginning of the 15th century, the Ottoman state was already as European as it was Asian. Even had the Anatolian provinces been entirely subsumed by Timur, Bayezid's successors would have rebuilt from the far side of the Bosporus in Rumelia.[49] And third, any attempt to take advantage of the Ottoman crisis during the Interregnum would have required a capacity for collaborative effort among the surrounding states that simply did not exist. The complete eradication of the Ottoman presence in Europe would have required the manpower reserves of Western Europe, the active participation of the navies from both Venice and Genoa, the total commitment of Hungary and what was left of Serbia, Bulgaria, and the Byzantine Empire, and at least the passive consent of the Muslim emirates in Anatolia. This grand coalition never arose and so, and rather than work together, its potential partners allowed themselves to be picked off one by one until the Ottomans were at the gates of Vienna in the north and the mouth of the Red Sea to the south.

If timing and geography were key to the rise of Ottoman power, so was governance. Few, if any, dynasties can have produced a line of succession comprising such consistently top tier leaders of men. From Osman to Suleiman, the Ottoman realm was nursed from infancy to hegemony by individuals of singular vision, ambition, and energy. As statesmen, they presided over their responsibilities to stimulate agriculture and trade, to balance the secular and religious needs of their diverse subjects, to leave their mark in the arts and architecture, and to conduct diplomacy, with an ideal blend of personal intervention and delegation to qualified subordinates in a highly responsive bureaucracy. As warriors, they forged a war machine of unsurpassed discipline and professionalism that they led from the front to victory after victory.

The Ottomans were a warrior state. In the dog-eat-dog environment that shaped them, victory in war was a precondition of life, first as a requisite for survival, then as a means by which to achieve glory. This precondition ensured there was no division between the military and the administration of the state, for each was inextricably bound up with the other.

The term *sanjak* (flag, standard) originally designated an army unit, without territorial association, under a standard that the unit commander received from the ruler as a symbol of transferred authority. The *sanjak* soon became the basic Ottoman territorial administrative unit. It was headed by a governor (*sanjak-bey*), who commanded the *timariot* cavalry troops within his *sanjak*.[50]

It was the second sultan, Orhan (1323–62), and his vizier Ala' al-Din who regularized the Ottoman military. The *müsellem* (tax-free) cavalry were organized under the overall command of *sanjak-bey*s and theoretically divided into units of 100 (led by a *subais*) and 1,000 (led by a *binbashi*). The foot soldiers, known as *yaya*, were similarly divided into tens, hundreds, and thousands. They fought as infantry archers and were occasionally recorded in Byzantine service, where they were called *mourtatoi*. Both *müsellems* and *yayas* were at first paid regular wages, but by the time of Murad I they were more normally allocated fiefs in return for military service, the *yaya* also having responsibility for the protection of local roads and bridges.[51] By the late 14th century the *müsellems* and *yayas* had been relegated to second-line duties, and by the end of the 16th century they would either be abolished altogether or be reduced to a non-military status.

As the empire expanded, rationalization of the territorial units became necessary. Murad I reorganized the army so that each *sanjak* would derive income from land grants (*timar*) responsible for maintaining the heavy cavalrymen (*sipahis*) who formed the strike force of his army. For a specific campaign, the *sanjak* could raise conscript infantry (*azaps*) and light cavalry suitable for raiding (*akinjis*). Murad also appointed the first governor-general to command the *timariot* forces of all the *sanjaks* in Rumeli. The Ottoman term for the governor-general of a province was *beylerbey* (the *bey* of [*sanjak*] *bey*s, or lord of lords). The provinces in time would come to be known as *vilayet*, and from the late 16th century on, *eyalet*.

For a long period in the formative phase of Ottoman history the motors of its expansion into Europe were the marcher lords (*uçbeyis*) and their extended households along the frontier, who commanded the *akinji* and dominated the border districts (*uç kenar yer*).[52] Until the reign of Murad II (1421–51), when centralized authority began to be systematically applied in order to curtail their authority, these hereditary clans – the Evrenos, Mihal, Turahan, and Malkoçoğlu – were laws unto themselves within their own spheres of influence, a reality the sultans were prepared to indulge provided the arrangement kept the empire's restless military energy facing outwards and extending the Ottoman aegis ever onwards.[53]

From the earliest times, the Ottoman rulers could count on their military entourage, members of which were known as *kul* (slave) and *nöker* (companion, client, retainer). These were the forerunners of the sultan's salaried household troops, the *kapıkulu* (slaves of the sultan's gate). This included the legendary *yeni çeri* (new corps, renowned and feared in the West as the janissary) infantry and the elite cavalry units, the *süvarileri* or *bölük halki* (regiment men).

The *devshirme* system was introduced in order to ensure the janissary corps remained at strength. Under this system non-Muslim children were levied and then Ottomanized. Subsequently, they were trained for government service or became members of the salaried central corps of the sultan. The institution of military slavery was brutally pragmatic in its induction process. At the capture of Novo Brdo in 1455, the population was lined up in the ditch outside the walls and 340 youths were taken from their families to be forcibly enrolled in the janissary corps or as auxiliaries. Nineteen of this number escaped only to be recaptured, beaten, and dragged behind horses until comrades stood surety for their future good conduct.[54] Nonetheless, the relentless training and indoctrination of the young men taken created the highest and most loyal pillar of support for the House of Osman, an elite unit that, in periods of greatest crisis, prevented the break-up of the state. Indeed, it was they who, acting out of their own interests, pressed continuously for renewed conquests. This placed a double-edged sword in the hands of the sultans, for if the *kapıkulu* were not kept satisfied with the constant prospect of war, glory, and plunder, the slaves could turn on their masters.[55]

The Ottomans were early and enthusiastic converts to the potential of gunpowder weapons, adopting firearms in the latter part of the 14th century, and established a separate artillery corps as part of the sultan's standing army in the early 15th century, well before any European rival. The standard infantry firearm was the matchlock arquebus (*fitilli tüfek*). Ottoman artillery included field pieces (*darbzens*) and siege guns (*bacaloşkas* and *şaykas*). This not only gave the Ottomans parity in terms of firepower with their Western enemies, but consistently gave them a cutting edge in confrontations with their fellow Muslims.[56] The failure to link up with his Venetian allies beforehand cost the Aq Qoyunlu khan Uzun Hasan dearly when he confronted the Ottomans at the Battle of Otlukbeli on 11 August 1473, for the Venetians had brought firearms and specialists to teach the Aq Qoyunlu how to use them. In effect, Uzun Hasan, who, as Ottoman historian Neşri noted, had "not seen battle with guns and cannon" before, was predestined to defeat.[57] According to Ibn Zunbal, when the last sultan of Egypt's Mamluk dynasty, Tuman Bey II, was brought before Selim the Grim, he hissed defiance, insisting, "amongst us are the horsemen of destiny and red death. A single one of us can defeat your whole army. If you do not believe it, you may try, *only please order your army to stop shooting with firearms*."[58] And the Safavid Shah of Iran, Tahmasp, chided Suleiman the Magnificent for acting like a "veiled woman" by hiding behind a curtain of artillery, and challenged him to come out and fight like a man.[59]

The imperial budget for 1528 accounted for some 120,000–150,000 members of the regular units, including 38,000 provincial *timar*-holders, 20,000–60,000 men-at-arms brought to the campaigns by the *timar*-holders, and 47,000 mercenaries. This force included the 24,000 members of the *kapıkulu* – everyone from the janissaries, gunners (*topçu*), gun carriage drivers (*top arabacısı*), and bombardiers (*humbaracı*) of the artillery corps to the military police (*martalos*), armorers (*cebeci*), and sappers (*lağımcı*) – plus the 23,000 garrison troops on station manning strongholds throughout the empire, and the marines of the navy. These figures do not include the various auxiliary troops – the *müsellems*, who repaired the roads and bridges in front of the marching armies; the *yayas*, who helped to transport the cannons; the *yörüks*, who collected the draft animals and cast the cannon balls in the mines; the *cerehors*, who performed engineering work; the *beldar*, who were specialist trench diggers; the *akinji* raiders; and the auxiliaries.[60]

The Ottoman navy was very much the junior partner to the army. Ottoman naval personnel in 1609 accounted for only 3 percent of manpower and 4 percent of salary payments for the armed services borne by the central treasury.[61] The Ottomans remained competitive in the struggle for control of the Mediterranean Sea by outsourcing the responsibility for naval power projection to the opportunistic corsair raiders operating out of bases on its southern shore, such as Tunis and Algiers, with whom they maintained a mutually productive and profitable relationship. The Ottomans would describe their Tatar auxiliaries on the Ukrainian steppe and the corsairs of North Africa as the two wings of the sultan.[62]

The beginning of the campaigning season coincided with the growing season for crops (especially grass), and the onset of winter – when food became impossible to forage and expensive to procure – marked its conclusion. The military calendar was thus defined by the period of mobilization for the campaign season (*Hizir Ilyas Günü*, late April to early May) and demobilization of the army as it dispersed to enter winter quarters (*Ruz-I Kasım*, late October to early November).

Up to the end of the 16th century, Ottoman armies (even without their Tatar and other auxiliaries, who typically went on campaign with several spare mounts in tow) was characterized by a three- or even a four-to-one ratio of cavalry to infantry. The capacity to project power therefore depended enormously on the capacity to meet the need for fodder. This is reflected in an anonymous Ottoman account of the Battle of Varna in 1444, in which a speech attributed to the military leaders of the Christian coalition worried about the advance of the Ottoman host warns, "The Turk keeps constant watch for the appearance of the first grass shoots in Spring. As soon as the grass springs from the earth he will close the gap and be upon us."[63]

Religion was significant to Ottoman recruitment, morale, and motivation. From the beginning, the Ottomans emphasized their commitment as *ghazi* (holy warriors) to spreading the faith of Islam through *jihad* (holy war) as a core rationale for their expansion. An inscription in Bursa dated 1337 labeled Osman "the exalted great emir, *mujāhid* [the one striving in jihad] in the way of God, sultan of the *ghazis*, *ghazi*, son of the *ghazi*." As late as 1484, Sultan Bayezid II mobilized for war with the following words: "All those wishing to enjoy the pleasure of *ghaza* and *jihad*, and those who desire booty, those brave comrades who gain their bread by their sword, and those wishing to receive *timar* by comradeship, are requested to join me with their weapons and military equipment in this blessed *ghaza*."[64]

Ottoman frontier epics such as the *Kutbname*, *Düsturname*, and *Saltukname* celebrated in the *gazavatname* style such legendary *ghazi* as Umur Bey, Sarı Saltuk, and Kasım Voyvoda.[65] And Ottoman texts drew a distinction between the true Muslim God, *Allah*, and the false Christian God, the *Nar-ı Nur* (Fire of Light), while the Ottomans affected disdain for the *ayin-i batıl* (superstitious rituals) and flagrant idolatry of the *küffar-ı güraz-siret* (pig-like infidels), for example, the veneration of the *put-ı Marko* (idol of Marco) in Venice, a reference to St Mark, patron saint of the city.

To the Ottomans, morality was lax in the West, and men effeminate; they allowed their women to be sexually promiscuous and accorded them freedom of action, even equality. In his travelogues, Evliya Çelebi recounted in amazement that in Vienna, the Habsburg emperor himself politely stood aside to let a woman pass, and even respectfully doffed his hat when a woman addressed him. For the benefit of his baffled readers, he attributed such unusual comportment to the infidels' over-reverence for the Virgin Mary.[66]

However, the Ottomans were also pragmatic in their relationship with both the Christian states they encountered and the Christian subjects they accrued over the course of their campaigns.[67]

The Ottomans considered the lands of their Christian neighbors the *memleket-i küffar* (land of the infidel), where dwelt the *düşman-i din* (enemy of the faith). By contrast, Ottoman chroniclers and official documents referred to their polity as the *memalik-i mahrusa-yi İslamiyye* (well-guarded lands of Islam) whose *serhadd-i mansure* (victorious frontier) was secured by the *serhad gazileri* (holy warriors of the frontier). Strategically important border strongholds such as Buda, Eger, and Zvornik were known as the *sedd-i sedid-i İslam* or *sedd-i sedid-i İslamiyye* (strong rampart, or bulwark of Islam). The Ottomans also designated the key crossroads of Belgrade as the *darü'l-cihad* (house of the holy war).[68]

The Ottomans referred to the *Ifranja* or *Frenks* (pl. *Efrenç*) who inhabited the realm of *Frengistan* (land of the *Frenks*). Much like the generic term "Turk" was used in early modern Europe to identify "Muslims" more than ethnic "Turks", "Frenk" became the common denominator referring to Western European Christians in Ottoman parlance. Other appellations included *Beni Asfar*, the *Asfari* ("Blond Race") originally used to refer to Byzantines and later to Eastern European (mostly Slavic) Christians, or more conventional expressions such as *kâfir*, ("infidel") *nasara*, or *tersa* ("Christian"). The Ottomans were able to distinguish between distinct groups or "nationalities" within the *Frengistan*, noting the existence of different *Frenks* such as the Genoese (*Ceneviz*), Venetians, (*Venedik*), Hungarians (*Üngürüs*), Germans (*Alaman*), *Nemçe* (Austrians), Poles (*Şah-ı Leh*), and Czechs (*Şah-ı Çih*), and understood that these represented a form of commonwealth that in religious matters was presided over by the *Rim-Pap* (Roman Pope) in opposition to the noble *ehl* (people) and *asakir* (soldiers) of Islam. References to Latin countries such as *Frençe* (France) and *Espan* (Spain) appear clearly, even in the earliest sources. However, besides the rather value-free terms of *Frengistan* or *Latin Diyarı* (Latin Lands), the broader universe which these ethnicities were thought to inhabit had been disapprovingly labeled *Kâfiristan* ("the land of infidels"), *dar-ül harb* ("the abode of war", in opposition to the "abode of Islam"), or *dar-ül käfirf* ("the abode of unbelief").[69] To this end, Ottoman folklore spoke of ultimate victory through acquiring the Red Apple of myth; originally associated with Constantinople, after that city fell in 1453, it was increasingly identified with the pope's city of Rome, and when a new sultan came to power, the janissaries would shout, "Let us meet at the Red Apple!"[70]

Within that framework, the only appropriate relationship of any foreign realm to the sultan, the inner circle of his government – the Sublime Porte, as it was known – and the Ottoman realm was that of the tributary state.[71] In practice, Ottoman diplomacy appreciated that among those polities powerful enough to remain – for now – outside of the sultan's direct or indirect control, there were specific individuals who had to be considered potential rivals or could be bargained with as potential allies. In the former category were Charles V, the king of Spain (*İspanya vilayetinin kıralı*) – the Ottomans refused to recognize him by his title as Holy Roman Emperor, as that implied parity with the sultan – and his brother, Ferdinand, the archduke of Austria, who was referred to as the king of Vienna (*Beç kıralı*). The Ottomans were on better terms with Francis I, the king of France (*Rida Frans*), and Elizabeth I of England, who was addressed as queen (*kraliçe*). To such favored individuals, the sultan might be inclined to offer *ahdnames* (capitulations) endowing them with certain trade and other privileges. In the long-term interests of the state, truces could be arranged with the unbelievers, and in extreme circumstances, even an alliance; this was particularly the case with France, where converging anti-Habsburg interests led to a partnership between Paris and the Porte. Thus, softening the harsh edges of the traditional division of the world into the *dar-ül islâm* (the realm of Islam) and *dar-ül harb* (the realm of war), the Porte recognized the possibility there could be a *dar-ül ahd* (the realm of treaty).[72]

This flexibility allowed for diplomatic initiatives to take advantage of the evolving spectrum of factional politics in Europe. The Ottomans, who had long experience in exploiting divisions between Christian sects, using preexisting anti-Catholic sentiment among the Orthodox communities of the Balkans to their advantage, were able to apply this strategy in a wider context during the Reformation, seeking to undermine the Porte's Catholic enemies by encouraging domestic Protestant resistance within the Habsburg realms over the course of the 16th century. "The Turks are very threatening," Maurice of Nassau, the leader of the Protestant revolt in the Netherlands against the Catholic King Philip II, wrote to his brother in 1566, "which will mean, we believe, that the king will not come [to the Netherlands on campaign] this year." Indeed, the Protestant rebels were in receipt of correspondence from Ottoman Grand Vizier

Sokollu Mehmed Pasha, promising "friendship, compassion and favor" to the "Lutherans" and vowing assistance in their struggle against their common enemy, "the Papists."[73] After Spain lost its outpost at La Goulette just offshore Tunis in 1574, the French ambassador to the Netherlands made a similar point. He thought this setback "may make Philip II more anxious to seek [peace here] so that he will be able to turn all his forces and resources against the Turks in order to put up a better resistance to them, the war in the Mediterranean being of greater importance to him."[74]

While prepared to cut deals with Christian states and statesmen abroad, from the beginning a central pillar of Ottoman domestic policy was the propitiation and, ideally, cooption of its own Christian subjects, a logical alternative given that until the conquest of the Mamluk sultanate in 1517, Muslims were a minority within the Ottoman Empire.[75] Non-Muslims were obliged to accept subordinate status as *dhimmi* (in the Turkish form, *zimmi*). The main fiscal obligation of non-Muslim subjects in the Ottoman Empire was the *haraj*, a tax per capita paid to the sultan. Subjects paying *haraj* were freed from the obligation to serve the Ottoman army and had the right to practice their faith.

Not every Christian exempted from military service elected to do so, as participation in the sultan's wars was a viable path to social advancement for all of his subjects. Thus a contradictory reality emerged whereby a *ghazi* sultan would march into battle at the head of *kāfir* troops. To cite just one example, when Mehmed II set out on campaign against Belgrade in the spring of 1456, "to open the padlock of the abode of infidelity with the key of *jihad*," at least half of his army was made up of Balkan Orthodox Christians, converts, and renegades (including his grand vizier and most of his commanders).[76]

At the local level, the Ottomans practiced a policy of accommodation (*istimalet*), absorbing local administrative practices and institutions in order to cushion the process of assimilation. At the elite level, the Ottoman sultans strengthened their claim to territorial aggrandizement through marriage and inheritance. When Murad I married Kera Tamara, the sister of the Bulgarian tsar Ivan Shishman of Tarnovo, the latter became an Ottoman vassal. Bayezid I's marriage in 1392 to Olivera Lazarević, the sister of Despot Stephen Lazarević, and Murad II's marriage in 1436 to Mara Branković, the daughter of Despot George Branković, reinforced the two Serbian rulers' vassal status. However, in these instances, the sultans were careful not to produce children by these marriages, denying the wives' families an opportunity to claim Ottoman patrimony, the basis of the power of the House of Osman. Except for Murad I's and Selim I's mothers, the Ottomans produced heirs through slave concubines.[77]

Even these could wield enormous influence; the role played by Roxelana (Hürrem), a Christian slave girl abducted from her Ukrainian homeland to be inducted into the harem of Suleiman the Magnificent, was pivotal in the trajectory of Ottoman history.[78]

Nonetheless, while Christians could never hope to rule the Ottoman state, it was astonishingly open to their progression up the ladder of promotion to the highest ranks possible. Conversion was the path to promotion, and there was no stigma whatsoever attached to an aspirant's background in family or faith.[79] Three of the four most famous marcher lord dynasties in Rumelia on the Ottoman frontier – the Evrenos, Mihal, and Malkoçoğlu – were of Christian origin.[80]

Talent was the only determinant of promotion in Ottoman government, up to the inner circle of the sultan's advisers, the viziers who constituted his *divan* (council). Mehmed II's longest-serving grand vizier was Mahmud Pasha Angelović, who held the empire's highest office from 1456 to 1468 and again from 1472 to 1474 and was grand admiral of the Ottoman fleet from 1469 to 1472. A descendant of the great Byzantine families of Angeloi and Palaiologi, Mahmud Pasha came from a noble Byzantine–Serbian family. Ottoman frontier raiders had captured him and his mother in Serbia, probably in 1427, when he was about seven years old.[81]

Three times *beylerbey* of Anatolia (1486, 1489, 1493–96), three times grand admiral of the Ottoman navy (1488, 1500–01, 1506–11), and five times grand vizier between 1497 and 1516, Hersekzade Ahmed Pasha was the youngest son of Stephen Vukčić Kosača. The childhood friend of Suleiman the Great, Pargalı Ibrahim Pasha, who served his master as grand vizier from 1523 to 1536, was a Christian taken as a slave in his youth, and known, long after his conversion to Islam, as Frenk (the Westerner) Ibrahim Pasha.

An even more remarkable story is that of Stephen Hercegović. Born in 1456 in Herceg Novi, the youngest son of powerful Bosnian magnate Stephen Vukčić Kosača (whose title, *herceg*, is the source of the name Herzegovina), in 1472 he departed for Constantinople, converted to Islam, took the name Hersekzade Ahmed, and entered palace service, rising to the very inner circle of the Ottoman governing elite. Marrying the daughter of Sultan Bayezid II, he was appointed as *sanjak* of Hüdavendigar (Bursa), then governor-general of Anadolu province in western Asia Minor, and subsequently served as grand vizier three times under Bayezid II (1497–98, 1502–06, 1511) and two more times as grand vizier under Selim I (1512–14, 1515–16).

Hersekzade Ahmed Pasha, who married Hûndi-Hâtûn, the daughter of Sultan Bayezid II, and served as grand vizier on no fewer than five separate occasions, was originally baptized as Stephen Hercegović, uncle to Sigismund Tomašević, half-brother of the last king of Bosnia, Stephen Tomašević, who was executed by Sultan Mehmed II in 1463. Sigismund too converted to Islam, taking the name Ishak Bey Kraloğlu and fighting for the Ottoman cause at the Battle of Otlukbeli in 1473, during the Mamluk war of 1485–91, and at the Battle of Krbava in 1493, in addition to serving as *sanjak-bey* of Karasi in Anatolia.

Another Christian, allegedly the son of a shoemaker from Tolna in Hungary, who was captured at the Battle of Mohács in 1526, would convert to Islam, adopt the name Piyale, and take to a life at sea as a corsair in the service of the sultan, capturing the islands of Elba and Corsica in 1554 and being appointed *kapudan pasha* (grand admiral) of the Ottoman navy the following year. In 1560, Piyale Pasha took Djerba; in 1565 he was at the center of the Ottoman attempt to seize Malta, and in 1570, the conquest of Cyprus.

Another great corsair captain who rose to the pinnacle of Ottoman naval authority started life as Giovanni Dionigi Galeni, a fisherman from the village of Le Castella on the Calabrian coast of Italy. Captured by the Algerian corsair Ali Ahmed and forced to serve as a slave at the oars of a galley, he earned his freedom by converting and taking the name Uluç Ali. He subsequently served under the legendary corsair Turgut Reis, on his recommendation being promoted to captain of his own galley in 1551. After his service during the 1560 Djerba campaign, in 1562 the sultan appointed Uluç commander of the squadron escorting the convoy sailing from Alexandria to Constantinople.[82] Upon the death of Turgut Reis during the siege of Malta in 1565, Uluç was appointed to succeed him as *bey* of Tripoli. In 1568, he was appointed *bey* of Algiers. The only Ottoman naval commander to survive the disaster at Lepanto in 1571, as Kılıç Ali Pasha he was appointed *kapudan pasha* in the aftermath, serving in that role until his death in 1587.

Finally, although there are many other such personal histories to relate, there is the story of Hasan Veneziano, who, as his name implies, was born in 1544 in Venice and baptized as Andrea Celeste. At the age of sixteen, he was enrolled as a scrivener in a ship out of Dubrovnik, the *Fabiana*, which was captured in 1563 by Turgut Reis. In captivity, he converted to Islam, taking the name Uluç Hasan. When Turgut died during the siege of Malta in 1565, another corsair, the Calabrian renegade Uluç Ali, became his new master. Hasan quickly gained Ali's favor, becoming his majordomo (*kahya*) and, under his master's patronage, rising to serve the sultan in multiple prestigious administrative roles; two terms (1577–80, 1582–87) as pasha of Algiers (Miguel de Cervantes, who was a captive there from 1575 to 1580, would owe his life to Hasan's clemency after repeated failed attempts to escape); as pasha of Tripolitania (1585–87); and pasha of Tunis (1587–88). From 1572 to 1587, Hasan was stationed at the Porte, where he served as grand admiral of the Ottoman navy.[83]

And, of course, the Ottoman capacity for recognizing and utilizing talent wherever they found it was not restricted to Christians. Throughout the Renaissance, those Jewish communities that, having survived generations of ghettoization, bigotry, and violence were now subjected to forced conversion or expulsion throughout the Christian West – from Spain in 1492, from Portugal in 1496, from Naples in 1510 – found new homes, vocations, and freedoms in the Ottoman East.[84]

Cumulatively, these assets – effective leadership, military power, financial security, social mobility, administrative professionalism, adroit diplomacy – impelled the upward trajectory of the Ottoman state to the point where, by the mid-16th century, it was second only to Ming China as the single wealthiest and most secure polity on Earth. Certainly, nothing in Europe came close, an irrefutable fact that was reflected in the – grudging – respect accorded the Porte throughout Western Europe. In his *Methodus* (*Methods*, 1566), the prominent French political philosopher and theorist of sovereignty Jean Bodin argued:

> This fact is obvious to everyone – if there is anywhere in the world any majesty of empire and of true monarchy, it must radiate from the sultan. He owns the richest parts of Asia, Africa, and Europe, and he rules far and wide over the entire Mediterranean and all but a few of its islands. Moreover, in armed forces and strength he is such that he alone is the equal of almost all the princes.[85]

This analysis is borne out by an analysis of the financial reserves available to the sultan as opposed to those of his chief rival in Western Europe. The balance sheet of the Ottoman imperial treasury for 1527–28 recorded a total revenue of about 10 million gold ducats: 5 million in cash revenue, 3.6 million from the *timar* military fiefs, and an additional 1 million via contributions from pious foundations. By contrast, the Holy Roman Emperor Charles V's combined revenue from Spain, the Kingdom of Naples, and the Low Countries' core provinces – the Habsburg realms that yielded the most income – amounted to about 2.8 million gold ducats, his brother Ferdinand, the archduke of Austria, being able to contribute an additional 1.7 to 1.9 million Venetian ducats.[86]

The Spain that Charles inherited was a still new and fragile political construct where the Crown was forced to share political authority with a powerful nobility and was dependent on a very modest stream of tax revenues from the *alcabala* (sales tax) and two irregular imposts, the *servicio* and papal *cruzado*, supplemented by the sale of noble titles and offices, monopolies, state lands, and annuities and government certificates (*juros*); extortion of forced loans; extracting tribute from client states; and looting defeated enemies.[87] The reign of Charles V was in many ways defined by his constant struggle to find the funds necessary to fulfill his imperial ambitions, a task delegated to his secretary of state from 1529 to 1547, Francisco de los Cobos.

The lesson, bitterly brought home time and again on the battlefield, was that unity trumped division. In his 1588 exegesis on the causal factors in the rise and fall of states, *De la Naissance: Durée et Cheute des Estats*, French historian Rene de Lucinge openly conceded: "Among all the things that we admire today, there is nothing so marvelous as the fortune of the Ottomans, with the progress of their greatness."[88] He pointed out that unity and singularity of purpose was the key advantage the centralized Ottoman state enjoyed over its dispersed Habsburg rival. Philip II's empire was so scattered over Europe, Africa, Asia, and America that "there is, in the fact that it is held together, more of a miracle than a sign of human planning and prudence." Conversely, the Ottomans had shown themselves to be "more judicious," allowing no motives of short-term advantage to tempt them into "leaping forwards unwisely, or throwing themselves into any distant undertaking." So, unlike the Habsburgs, "they have marched step by step from country to country," and for that reason they had enjoyed "the good fortune of so many victories, the benefit of such great and rich conquests, and also the consequence that it is easy for them to maintain and preserve what they had acquired."[89]

In the second volume of his *Historia sui Temporis* (*History of the Times*), published in Paris in 1560, Paolo Giovo maintained that the Christian powers, by their feuds and rivalries, had failed to crush the Turks while it was still in their power to do so, and that the Turks were now so strong that they were likely to conquer the whole world. This had been a common refrain throughout Europe for more than a century, never more so than for those coming to terms with the fall of Constantinople. "Here is a second death for Homer and for Plato too," Aeneas Sylvius Piccolomini mused in the aftermath; "Now Muhammad reigns amongst us. Now the Turk hangs over our very heads."[90] Years later, having ascended to become Pope Pius II, he continued to ascribe the relentless Ottoman advance and Christian retreat to the failure of Europe to find common ground and come together; for, "when I consider the failure to act of our rulers and the mutual enmities of our peoples, it seems to me that

I am looking at our destruction; we are all agents of the sultan, all paving the way for Mehmed II."[91]

To a degree, the Ottomans served as the definitive "other" by which Europe could collectively define itself.[92] In fact, it could be argued the Ottomans created the concept of Europe in the first place. In his *Ad defendenda pro Europa Hellesponti claustra (On the necessity of defending the straits of the Hellespont for the sake of Europe)* the scholar George of Trabzon made an impassioned plea in 1452 to Pope Nicholas V that he safeguard Constantinople because it served as a bulwark protecting the West, which he chose to call Europe, where in the past Christendom would have been the preferred term.[93]

But any sense of unity created by the need for collective resistance against a common existential threat was always only partial and transient. In fact, as the Middle Ages evolved into the Renaissance, the complexity of European society increased and the potential for all nations, all peoples, to rally under a single banner correspondingly decreased. By the mid-16th century the Western milieu was split not just *vertically* – on a *national* basis, between rival dynasties and republics (e.g., the Valois vs. the Habsburgs, Venice vs. Genoa) – but also *horizontally*, on a *transnational* basis. There had always been an endemic class divide between the haves and have-nots, and the frustration of the poor always threatened to boil over into murderous insurrectionary bloodshed, most infamously during the Great Peasants' War of 1524–25, which shook the established social order in Germany to its foundations before the elites reimposed their monopoly on political power through the application of almost genocidal violence. Exacerbating this perennial simmering class tension was the new contest for souls between the rival doctrines of the established Catholic Church and the upstart Protestant insurgency that cut across territorial borders (which was immediately significant within the loose federal structure of the Holy Roman Empire, and would become increasingly relevant inside the unitary states of France and England).[94] Thus did the contrast between the Ottoman East and Christian West only become more vivid as the 16th century progressed. Whereas the sultans consolidated their centralized authority over the realm they governed as it ever expanded, Christendom continued to fracture and devolve into essential anarchy even as the territory under its control continued to shrink before the Ottoman advance. "For the Turk with his sword is not so cruel, but the bishop of Rome on the other side is more fierce and bitter against us," the firebrand Protestant preacher John Foxe lamented; "stirring up his bishops to burn us, his confederates to conspire our destruction, setting kings against their subjects, and subjects disloyally to rebel against their princes, and all for Thy name. Such dissension and hostility Satan hath sent among us, that Turks be not more enemies to Christians, than Christians to Christians, papists to protestants; yea, protestants with protestants do not agree, but fall out for trifles."[95]

Theoretically, it was impossible for any Christian to advance the cause of Islam in any way. As early as the 9th century, Pope John VIII invoked the words of St Paul: *nolite iugum ducere cum infidelibus* ("Do not be yoked together with unbelievers") to formulate the doctrine of the "impious alliance," which strongly condemned any form of collaboration with the Muslims. By making such an alliance a Christian ruler was understood to have excluded himself from the Christian commonwealth (*respublica christiana*), becoming *exterus inimicus* (a foreign enemy) and *Christo adversus* (against Christ), to be treated in the same way as the infidels themselves.

In reality, Christians from the beginning had been prepared to break bread with their Muslim counterparts if it served their needs, whether conducting business – for profits will always outweigh prophets – or in the interests of national security, even at the expense of fellow Christians. Venice had been a past master of playing this double game for centuries before the Ottomans first set foot in Europe.[96] But nowhere was the failure of Christian collective action against the Ottoman threat throughout the Renaissance more explicit than during the Italian wars between the Habsburgs and the French House of Valois, which would drag out for generations and render the peninsula an ever-shifting kaleidoscope of alliances between rival factions, good Catholics all. The papacy would be continuously frustrated by the fact it was always much, much easier to mobilize the rival powers of the peninsula to keep the French out of Italy than it was to lead them on a crusade to stop the Ottomans getting in. Charles VIII of France justified his intervention by announcing in a decree to all Christian nations on 22 November 1494 that his invasion of Italy represented a first step towards driving Ottomans first out of Europe and then the Holy places. After his entry into Naples, Charles had himself crowned emperor of Constantinople and king of Jerusalem. The monarchs of Spain, Ferdinand and Isabella, who not two years earlier had consummated the *Reconquista* of the Iberian Peninsula by conquering Granada, its last Muslim emirate, contested this claim, and its assumption that Christendom looked to the king of France, and not them, to lead its war against the oncoming tide of Islam.[97]

Thus, the struggle for the Mediterranean was never a simple matter of Christianity against Islam; it was more of a struggle between the two great empires of Madrid and Constantinople counterpointed by the feud between

Spain and France and the extraordinary alternating hostility and mutual dependence of Venice and the Porte. When the two conflicts coincided and France joined with the Ottomans against Spain, or Spain joined with Venice against the Ottomans, the alliances were never satisfactory because each partner was ultimately working towards a different end game. Charles V would not benefit were he to smash Ottoman naval power so decisively that Venice would become undisputed master of the eastern Mediterranean. Nor would Venice gain from aiding the emperor against his French rivals or the Barbary corsairs who interfered with his lines of communication if Charles subsequently consolidated his control over all of Italy, especially after Charles secured the allegiance of Genoa, the ancestral enemy of the *Serenissima Respublica*.[98] In short, the two halves of the sea each supported its own system of trade rivalry and conquest, and the powers of the other half, together with small independent squadrons from the Knights of St John, the Papal States of central Italy, and the princes of Savoy, Tuscany, and Monaco, were called in by subsidy and diplomacy to tilt or redress the balance when it was threatened.

Throughout the 16th century, France would decline to be associated with any diplomatic initiative, trade embargo, or military alliance against the Porte that offered any advantage to Spain. Quite the contrary; France saw the Ottoman Empire as a welcome counterweight to Spanish imperial ambition, vital to her own national self-interest. "I cannot deny," King Francis I confessed to a Venetian envoy in March 1531, "that I keenly desire the Turk powerful and ready for war, not for himself, because he is an infidel and we are Christians, but to undermine the emperor's power, to force heavy expenses upon him and to reassure all other governments against so powerful an enemy."[99]

Savary de Brèves, French ambassador to Constantinople from 1591 to 1605, would argue that, so far as the king of Spain was concerned, "when we have been at war with him, and when he has used his forces and means to stir up our internal quarrels, it is certain that he would have fared altogether differently were it not for the trouble and expense that he was obliged to go to in order to defend his sea-coasts, both the Italian ones and the Spanish," from the Ottoman threat. In particular, de Brèves noted, the territories of Algiers and Tunis "are so necessary and important to him, because if he had them he could pass from Spain to Italy with full security and total freedom, and as a result he would be much better enabled to make himself master of the whole of Italy" – another long-standing concern of the French.[100]

All of this rebounded to the benefit of the Porte. In a *relazione* sent to the *Serenissima Respublica* from Constantinople around 1560, the Venetian ambassador Marino Cavalli, commenting on Ottoman assistance to French campaigns against the Habsburgs, noted that:

> Every time the French plead for help to wage war, they will get it. Surely, even if it will be like the food that doctors give to the sick, which does not restore them to vigor, nor let them die either, but barely keeps them alive. The Turks will thus help the French so that they continue the war, because they neither want them fat nor thin, neither winners nor losers.[101]

Finally, the human factor – the impact of interpersonal dynamics – should never be discounted in the narrative of history. The prospect of any meaningful working relationship between Charles V and Henry VIII, for example, whether directed against Francis I or the Ottomans, foundered when the king of England divorced his wife, Catherine of Aragon – who happened to be the emperor's aunt – and broke with the Catholic Church in order to do so.

Thus, the West remained inherently, inevitably, willfully divided even as the Ottoman wolf crept inside the door, until the entire southeast quarter of Europe and more than half the coastline of the Mediterranean were under the control of the Sublime Porte. At the signing of the Declaration of Independence in 1776, Benjamin Franklin reminded his peers, representatives of the American states, "we must all hang together, or most assuredly we shall all hang separately." During the critical years of the 14th to 16th centuries, the statesmen of Europe did elect to hang separately, and many did so.

2

VARNA, SECOND KOSOVO, AND CONSTANTINOPLE

VARNA, 1444

The steady hand of Murad II had stabilized the Ottoman state and left the Interregnum in its past. By 1440, with their strength restored and unity reestablished, the Ottomans would roll back onto the offensive. Their primary antagonist would be the kingdom of Hungary, which still held the line of the Danube, effectively unaided. Among those sensing the impending storm and proselytizing for collective action was the bishop of Kraków, Zbigniew Oleśnicki, who made great efforts at the Council of Basel (1431–37) to rally both financial and military support for Hungary, and called upon the other European states to declare a common crusade against the Ottomans.[1] This would not materialize, and Hungary would be left to shoulder the burden of meeting the oncoming Ottoman tide divided and alone.

Sigismund, king of Hungary since 1387, had a mania for collecting titles, crowns, and kingdoms, becoming king of Germany in 1410, king of Bohemia in 1419, and Holy Roman Emperor in 1433. But the more authority he wielded on paper, the less well he performed in the field, most obviously in his futile and failed crusades against the Hussites of Bavaria (1420–22). When he died on 9 December 1437, he was succeeded as king of Hungary by his son-in-law, Albert von Habsburg, the first of that house to take the Hungarian throne, having married King Sigismund's daughter Elizabeth.

Albert's brief reign was consumed by war, as the Ottomans staged major raids into Transylvania in 1437 and 1438. "Three great mountains of heads have been made there from the dead," lamented Bartolomeo di Giano, a Franciscan theologian then resident in Constantinople: "Priests and monks, young and old, were led away in iron fetters tied to the backs of horses, at least as long as they were able to walk. But the rest of the crowd, including women and children, were herded by dogs without any mercy or piety."[2]

Ottoman pressure was equally relentless in Bosnia. Borač was taken in 1438, followed by Zvornik and Srebrenica in 1439. Serbia was targeted next. After a siege of three months, Smederevo fell to Murad on 18 August 1439. The despot, George Branković, fled, ultimately finding asylum in Dubrovnik. Two of his sons, Stephen and Gregory, were taken as hostages; two years later, accused of plotting against the sultan, both were blinded on his orders. Meanwhile, the despot's remaining possessions on the Dalmatian coast were seized by Stephen Vukčić Kosača, an Ottoman protégé and pretender to the Bosnian throne, only to then be snatched away by the Venetians in order to keep them out of the hands of the Ottoman enemy.

By this point the Ottomans were raiding at will across the Danube. As Murad would boast to Sayf ad-Din Jaqmaq, the Mamluk sultan of Egypt, between June 1439 and May 1440, "the mujahedeen crossed the river into the kingdom of Hungary five times in boats. They raided, sated themselves with ample plunder, smashed [the Christian's] idols and their crosses, ravaged their homes and palaces, scorched their countryside and villas, suppressed their images and engravings, and reduced their castles stone by stone as they fell upon their heads."[3] This depiction is echoed in the *Chronica Hungarorum* of historian Johannes Thuróczy:

> The southern regions of the Kingdom of Hungary as far as the Tisza river, and the whole of Slavonia and all the territory situated between the rivers Sava and Drava were being savagely plundered by the Turks; cities and villages and towns were being consumed by fierce fires, and possessions were being looted; people without distinction of sex and age were either being killed or led away to be sold forever into slavery.[4]

At this critical juncture, Albert's death on 27 October 1439 created a power vacuum that would consume the Hungarian state in bloody internecine conflict. Elizabeth, the late king's pregnant widow, gave birth to a son, Ladislaus, on 22 February 1440. Two days previously, her entourage, acting on the queen's orders, had removed the holy crown of Hungary from the castle of Visegrád and smuggled it to Austria. Having gained the acquiescence of Denes Szecsi, cardinal archbishop of Esztergom, on 15 May, Elizabeth succeeded in having her now three-month-old child crowned King Ladislaus V at Székesfehérvár with the stolen crown, thus confirming the consecration, a crucial condition of legitimacy since the extinction of the Árpád dynasty.

However, her claim was rejected by a majority of the nobility, who feared that as regent Elizabeth would embody the centralizing and authoritarian tendencies of her father, Sigismund, and in any event, the necessity to rally around a functional leadership in order to hold the line against the looming Ottoman threat proved more valid than primogeniture in the line of succession. Accordingly, the *diet* instead elected the sixteen-year-old Polish King Władysław III Jagiello as King Vladislaus I of Hungary in return for a promise that through his person the union of the two kingdoms would more effectively fulfill their role as the "wall and shield of the faithful" throughout Christendom as a whole.[5] The same Cardinal Szecsi who had administered the coronation rites to the infant Ladislaus in May was willing to crown Władysław king of Hungary in the same church at Székesfehérvár on 17 July. The *diet* then ceremonially declared the coronation of Ladislaus null and void.

Civil war erupted, and Elizabeth initially had the upper hand, advancing to Esztergom, just thirty miles west of Buda. But a column of her supporters marching up was annihilated by a joint force under Miklós Újlaki, *ban* (governor) of Macsó, and John Hunyadi, *ban* of Szörény, who had experience fighting on the frontier and as a *condottiere* in Italy, at the Battle of Szegszárd on 10 September. Elizabeth fled to Austria and the protection of Frederick IV, Habsburg King of the Romans (an archaic term for what amounted to being king of Germany), while Újlaki and Hunyadi proceeded to pacify Hungary, being rewarded by Vladislaus with appointment as joint *voivodes* of Transylvania, counts of the Székelys, and castellans of Timişoara, Szeged, Belgrade, and the other border castles along the Danube, in addition to the right of collecting the tax revenue from the royal salt monopoly. In real terms, they divided the state between them, Újlaki taking the west, Hunyadi the east.

However, the Habsburg party remained defiant and effectively controlled most of northern Hungary through Elizabeth's Bohemian mercenary warlord, John Jiskra of Brandýsa, while loyalists to Elizabeth continued to hold out in western Hungary, including the counts of Cilli (the family of Elizabeth's mother), the influential Garai family, and the despot of Serbia, George Branković, whose daughter Catherine was the wife of Ulrich II of Cilli.

The Ottomans were poised to take advantage of the civil strife now consuming Hungary. In April 1440, Murad invaded Serbia and laid siege to Belgrade, which since 1427 had been the linchpin of Hungary's southern frontier network of fortified strongholds. Located at the confluence of the Danube and the Sava rivers, Belgrade was of enormous strategic importance to both sides. As the Ottoman historian Aşıkpaşazâde put it, "Sultan Murad, having visited Hungary, afterwards knew that this Belgrade was the doorway to the country. He wanted to undertake an expedition to open this door."[6] The defense of the city was led by John Tallóci, a Hospitaller who commanded the priory of the Knights of St John in Vrana, and the younger brother of Matthew Tallóci, the *ban* of Croatia. According to Johannes Thuróczy, Ottoman artillery "shattered the high fortifications of the towers together with the walls, razing them down to the ground."[7] Having softened up the defenses, the Ottomans geared up for a two-pronged final assault, loading their galleys on the Danube with troops in preparation for an attack via the river, while filling in the moat protecting the landward side of the city with branches and wood. Tallóci responded by quietly scattering gunpowder through this combustible fill. When the assault jumped off the following morning and the first Ottomans began scaling the walls with ladders, the garrison hurled torches, firebrands, and hot coals onto the flammable wood and gunpowder mix below. Any of the enemy who survived being consumed by the flames were suffocated by the smoke. Meanwhile, the naval assault also came to grief, the ships either being driven back by cannon fire or driven forward by the wind against the walls, where they wallowed, helpless, until being captured. Frustrated, Murad broke off the siege and withdrew to Edirne, his army despoiling the countryside on its line of retreat, taking such a booty in slaves that, as the chronicles relate, "a beautiful girl sold for the same price as a pair of boots."[8]

In October 1441, Hunyadi raided into Ottoman territory, defeating the *bey* of Smederevo, Ishak Pasha. There would be much higher stakes the following year. The prize was Wallachia, where Vlad II had become *voivode* in 1436. His affiliation with Hungary was a source of concern to Murad. Accordingly, sometime between late October 1441 and early 1442 the Ottomans cajoled Vlad into traveling to Edirne. Soon after arriving he was imprisoned, being replaced on the throne by his fourteen-year-old son, Mircea II, whose compliance with Ottoman interests was guaranteed not only by his father being held hostage in Gallipoli, but also by the confinement of his two brothers, Vlad and Radu, in Egrigöz.

An Ottoman force of *akinji* led by Mezid Bey of Nicopolis then broke into Transylvania either through the Vaskapu (Iron Gate) pass or through the upper valley of the Lotru River. Mezid established his headquarters east of Alba Iulia and set about the systematic plundering of the region. Bishop György Lépes rallied the local resistance and met Mezid's raiders somewhere near the village of Sântimbru. The resulting battle, fought on 18 March 1442, ended with the rout of the Transylvanians, the bishop himself being among the slain.

Hunyadi turned the tables a week later. Aware Mezid Bey had unleashed many of his *akinjis* on forays, Hunyadi ordered the main body of his army to Borbánd, north of Alba Iulia, led by Simon of Kamonya who wore the armor and colors of his commander to deceive the enemy, while Hunyadi made a turning maneuver with the smaller part of the army to the west, concealed by the high ground of Bilag. Kamonya's light cavalry attacked the Ottoman vanguard on 25 March, drawing Mezid Bey into committing his army in force. Simon was killed in the ensuing melee, but when Hunyadi sprung his trap, the Ottomans panicked, broke, and fled. Many thousands were cut down in the ensuing rout, including Mezid Bey and his son. Having occupied the Ottoman camp, Hunyadi then stationed most of his army in the surrounding countryside while dressing some of his men in the uniforms of their slain enemies to hold the site itself. The outlying *akinjis*, returning from their raids burdened with plunder and driving slaves before them, saw nothing amiss as they returned to their camp. When Hunyadi sprung his ambush, their annihilation was total.

Hunyadi then countermarched into Wallachia, inducing Murad to reinforce Hadım Şehabeddin, the *beylerbey* of Rumelia, with Anatolian troops and order him to reimpose Ottoman prestige by leading this combined army against Hungary. Şehabeddin crossed the Danube at Nicopolis in June. Though heavily outnumbered, Hunyadi advanced to meet the Ottomans at Vaskapu; in the ensuing battle on 6 September, he won a triumphant victory.[9]

Victory at the Battle of Alba Iulia had brought Wallachia back into the Hungarian orbit as Hunyadi deposed Mircea as *voivode*, elevating Basarab II in his place. In order to reassert Ottoman hegemony, Murad ordered Şehabeddin Pasha to take command of another army, this one incorporating units from Anatolia, including both *sipahis* and janissaries to support the *akinjis*, and march into the disputed border region. Şehabeddin duly crossed the Danube and entered Wallachia in the summer of 1442, taking and burning the capital, Târgovişte.

Using the terrain to his advantage, Hunyadi elected to make his stand at the Iron Gate Pass, where the Ottomans could not exploit the advantage of their numerical superiority and had limited space for turning maneuvers. Hunyadi also introduced a new element to the battlefield, the war wagon. Bristling with firepower, these mobile bastions had been a critical factor in the successful Hussite resistance against imperial authority, and Hunyadi recognized their potential to perform the same role against the Ottoman foe.

Hunyadi attacked the Ottoman center with his heavy cavalry, but the janissaries held the line while the *sipahis* pushed back Hunyadi's light cavalry on the flanks. When Şehabeddin ordered the janissaries to wheel around the heavy cavalry's flanks in order to encircle them and cut them off from the rest of the Hungarian army, Hunyadi ordered them to disengage and retreat, thereby funneling the Ottomans as they followed up into a chokepoint. Exploiting the terrain, Hunyadi fell back to his line of war wagons, shouldering his flanks in the valley by deploying his light infantry on the heights to either side. The Ottoman pursuit was halted by the war wagons and when it formed into a new line of battle, this was harassed by the light infantry holding the high ground. Sensing weakness, Hunyadi ordered his infantry and reorganized heavy cavalry to charge into the Ottoman center. This swiftly collapsed, and the Ottoman retreat devolved into chaos as fleeing men bottlenecked in the constrained space.

Hunyadi then tracked the Ottoman withdrawal towards the Danube, waiting until an advantageous moment to strike. This opportunity presented itself when Şehabeddin arrived at the banks of the Ialomiţa River. There was neither a bridge nor ford, so the army had to be ferried across in whatever boats it could find, having its horses swim alongside. Hunyadi waited until half the enemy force had transited to the south bank, then, on the morning of 2 September, launched his attack.

Şehabeddin rallied the force trapped on the north bank, which held out all day. But that evening, the *beylerbey* ordered a general retreat under cover of darkness, and the fighting continued, becoming more desperate as the night wore on and the prospects of escape diminished. Their own panic was at least as great an enemy to the Ottomans as the bullets, bolts, and blades of the foe; according to the account of a Hungarian royal letter published in 1453, "retreating in headlong flight, in the waves not a smaller number of them died than those who died by the sword." The casualty list from the campaign was enormous, and not limited to the rank and file. Ottoman sources state all sixteen *sanjak-beys* present were killed, the loss of roughly half of their number in the empire.[10] At Vladislaus's behest and with royal reinforcements, Hunyadi followed up by crossing over into Bulgaria, where he laid waste to the border town of Vidin before pushing west on a raid into Serbia.

By the end of 1442, the momentum seemed to have shifted against the Ottomans. Hungary had stood its ground on the battlefield and even its domestic political crisis appeared to have finally been resolved when Elizabeth recognized Vladislaus as king on 13 December.

Seeking to seize the moment, in his bull of 1 January 1443 Pope Eugene IV announced his intention to launch a crusade by both land and sea against the infidel, to be financed from a tenth of church revenues all over Europe and the fifth of the income of the Apostolic Chamber. Byzantine Emperor John VIII Palaiologos, desperately struggling for the survival of the tiny fraction of the empire that remained, engulfed by the Ottoman flood but still of enormous strategic importance in controlling the Bosporus, renewed his political efforts to raise help in the West, and Duke Philip of Burgundy, whose father had fought with Sigismund at Nicopolis, was willing to contribute to a fleet to close both the Bosporus and the Dardanelles.

Word then spread in the West concerning the revolt in Anatolia unleashed by the sultan's brother-in-law, the Karamanid Emir Ibrahim, who seized the cities of Akşehir and Yenişehir that Murad had taken from him in 1437. Nor was Ibrahim alone in taking advantage of the sultan's absence. The increasingly singular Ottoman focus on Europe had created the context for simmering local dynastic resentments to erupt in outright defiance of central authority in the empire's neglected eastern territories. Upon the death of the emir of Menteşe in 1424, Murad annexed this province to the empire. One of the members of the Menteşeoğulu dynasty, likely İlyas Bey son of Ahmed Bey, had sought refuge with the Karamanids. While Ibrahim was conducting operations against the Ottomans in the north, İlyas Bey moved to retake the province of Menteşe with Karaman assistance. He succeeded in seizing the major cities of Balat, Beçin, and Milas, and then remained camped near Selçuk. Ibrahim's soldiers seized the stretch of the southern coast from Antalya up to Balat with assistance from another ally, one of the sons of Kara Yülük, a former leader of the Aq Qoyunlu federation.

Canceling his planned offensive against Hungary, the sultan set out to punish Ibrahim. His eldest son, Alaeddin, mustered the army of Anatolia. Murad joined him soon after with a strong detachment from the army of Rumelia. While the Ottomans ravaged Karaman, Ibrahim fled to Taş-ili in Syria. He was forgiven and reinstated, only because Murad, only too aware of the preparations for a crusade in the West, did not want to fight a war on two fronts. He also released Vlad II from captivity, allowing him to return to Wallachia and depose Basarab II as *voivode*. However, Vlad's two sons, Radu and the future Vlad III, remained in the Porte's possession as hostages, surety to their father recognizing his place as a vassal.

The momentum of the crusade, meanwhile, had ground to a halt through the failure of Pope Eugene IV and the Republic of Venice to arrive at an agreement about the fitting out and financing of the fleet needed to block Ottoman transit from Asia to Europe. Bargaining came to definitive halt in August and this, alongside the structural problem constituted by the impossibility of raising sufficient supplies before late summer, was the main reason for Hunyadi's departure from Buda at the beginning of September, very late in the campaign season. After mustering at Belgrade, the Crusader army set out again around the middle of October, catching the Ottomans, who were not properly mobilized for action at this time of year, off guard. Hunyadi easily took Niš and then destroyed an Ottoman army under Kasım Pasha, the *beylerbey* of Rumelia, while marching to Kruševac on 3 November.

Murad received word of the Hungarian invasion just after the news of the death of his eldest and favored son, Alaeddin. He ordered a general mobilization, urging "everyone in Rumelia who is capable of wielding a mace set out, whether on foot or horseback."[11] But the urgency of this summons only highlighted the lack of available manpower. Though the *kapıkulu* elite were on call, the vast majority of the Ottoman army was composed of the provincial cavalry serving underneath the various *sanjak-beys* of Anatolia and Rumelia, and it took time to bring these contingents together. The mobilization for Mezid Bey's invasion of Wallachia in 1442 had been announced six months in advance. After his defeat, it had taken Şehabeddin several months to raise another army. The sultan was now hoping to mobilize all of Rumelia and Anatolia in a matter of weeks. This effort was further hindered by the series of defeats the Ottomans had suffered in Rumelia over the past eighteen months, including the capture or death of a number of *sanjak-beys* and other key leaders. This had a depressive effect on the provincial cavalry, who were hesitant to fulfill their obligation of military service with the memory of their fallen comrades still fresh. Many of the men had experienced these defeats personally. Another inhibiting factor was the lateness of the year. Winter was approaching and the regular campaigning season had ended. Finally, since it was a defensive campaign on Ottoman soil, it was clear there would be scant opportunity for securing plunder or spoils or captives by way of compensation for service to the sultan, which had a commensurately depressive effect on motivation. In short, the risks were great and the potential gains minimal. Conversely, Christian communities were rallying to the crusader banner. The Ottoman account of the campaign sourly admits of the sultan's Christian subjects, "that year they paid their *jizya* to the infidels who are as low as the dust, and many of the subject infidels mounted their horses and joined [Hunyadi's] army."[12]

With the *kapıkulu* and whatever other detachments he had been able to muster, Murad advanced from Edirne via Plovdiv to Sofia. Given the mood of the army, at a council of war Turahan Bey urged the sultan not to seek open battle with the Crusaders. In that event, first the Anatolian and then the Rumelian cavalry would flee and only the janissaries would remain. "A bird without either wing is useless," he offered by analogy.[13] Accepting this advice, Murad opted to burn Sofia and leave scorched earth in his wake as he fell back to Edirne, ordering the mountain passes be blocked with rubble and felled trees to form a new defensive line.[14]

Having brushed aside Ottoman screening forces, on 12 December Hunyadi attempted to storm the Zlatitsa Pass but was repulsed, his own horse being shot out from under him. The Christians were on the offensive, taking the fight to the enemy further south than any campaign in generations, but, frustratingly, it was now winter and the Crusaders could no longer maintain their army in the field so far from home. With no alternative, they broke camp and set out on the long return march north. Hunyadi covered the retreat, deploying his war wagons to anchor the rearguard. As the Ottomans began to swarm down from the heights, seeking to overtake and destroy the Crusader army while it was in transit, Turahan Bey sought out the sultan and urged him to rein in the counteroffensive: "Give the command to the troops of Islam to retreat, because if we attack the infidels, they will dig in between the carts and kill our soldiers with cannon and arquebus fire."[15] Murad accepted this advice and the two sides disengaged, maintaining a standoff for the rest of the day. That evening, the Crusaders departed under cover of darkness.

As they pulled back towards the Danube, Hunyadi continued to command the rearguard against the pursuing Ottomans, led by the sultan in person, facing down the enemy at Melshtitsa on 24 December by concentrating his force into a defensive circle (*wagenburg*) behind the war wagons. In the aftermath, Murad returned to Sofia, leaving the pursuit to his subordinates. On 2 January 1444, they charged into an ambush in the hill country of Kunovitsa and were routed, Mahmud Chelebi, Murad's brother-in-law and the brother of Grand Vizier Çandarlı Halil Pasha, being among those captured.

At this point, winter settled in with a vengeance, and "dame fortune who until then had been so kind to the Christians turned her back on them," as Jean de Wavrin described it. "A great cold with wind and frost set in among the mountains, and for three days so much snow fell." The march home was brutal for the Crusaders, their host finally returning to Belgrade on 22 January and Buda on 2 February, "in mourning for their friends who had perished as martyrs amidst the snow and ice."[16] So ended the *Longum Belli*, the Long Campaign of 1443 – so named not because of its duration, but rather its geographic range.

Unsettled by the demonstrated ability of the Western powers to hold their own in battle at the tactical level and coordinate a long-range offensive at the strategic level, Murad was also under pressure to stamp out the Karamanid dynasty in Anatolia before it could metastasize into a wider threat to the empire's authority in the east. Intercepted correspondence proved Byzantine agents had contacted the Karamanid Emir Ibrahim, assuring him Murad had been exhausted by the Long Campaign, so "if you need territory and act in time, you can seize his land while there is an opportunity... If you are afraid that you cannot withstand the son of Osman if he attacks you, have no fear, because the King of Hungary, the Despot [Branković] and the Zupan Yanko [Hunyadi] will be marching from the west."[17] Cleverly, Halil Pasha acted to isolate Ibrahim diplomatically by securing a legal justification for war against a fellow Muslim state from the chief justices of the heads of the four schools of Islamic Law in Cairo. This kept the Mamluks at arm's length, preventing them from being added to the Ottoman Empire's lengthening list of adversaries.

In order to concentrate on the Karamanid challenge, Murad needed a secure frontier in the Balkans, for he could not fight in both East and West at the same time. The sultan also had a personal imperative that induced him towards seeking peace with the Christian powers. He hoped to abdicate in favor of his son, Mehmed, but to do so at an advantageous moment, bequeathing to his successor an empire that was stable and secure. His choice of war in the East would obligate him to offer peace in the West, even at a steep price both materially and in terms of prestige. To facilitate negotiations, he appealed to his father-in-law, the despot of Serbia, George Branković, to mediate peace with Hungary, promising him the restoration of territories and the release of his two sons if he could forestall a new Christian campaign. Branković worked to obtain Hunyadi's support, offering in return his own estates in Hungary.

Terms were arrived at in early June that incorporated significant Ottoman concessions. In exchange for a ten-year truce, Murad offered to pay the enormous sum of 100,000 florins to Vladislaus by way of indemnity and supply 25,000 troops to Vladislaus when needed to fight his enemies, and undertook to restore to Branković his sons and a broad swath of Serbian lands, including Smederevo, Golubac, Srebrenica, and Novo Brdo, with its rich silver mines. Having ratified the treaty, Murad departed for Anatolia to settle his score with Ibrahim Bey, who in the absence of the sultan had taken more cities, including Akşehir, Sivrihisar, and Ankara.

However, Christian mobilization for a crusade was too far advanced for a negotiated settlement to avert an inevitable war. On 24 April Vladislaus had sworn an oath to the papal legate, Cardinal Julian Cesarini, that he would undertake an expedition against the Ottomans that year.

The Venetian Senate formally notified Vladislaus of its resolution to join the crusade and commit a naval force to the Sea of Marmara to cut off Ottoman communications between Asia and Europe. This fleet, consisting of nineteen galleys – eight Papal, five Venetian, four Burgundian, and two from Dubrovnik – mustered under the authority of another cardinal, Francis Condulmer, and left Venice on 22 July.[18] In May and June, Vladislaus concluded truces with the Habsburg Frederick IV and John Jiskra of Brandýsa, thus securing his rear and enabling him to concentrate his forces in the Balkans. On 2 July, Vladislaus wrote to the Republic of Florence expressing his intention to continue the war against the Ottomans. On 24 July he made the same declaration to King Tvrtko II of Bosnia. Vladislaus also received a letter dated 30 July from the Byzantine Emperor John VIII Palaiologos informing him now was an opportune moment to destroy the Ottomans, since Murad had crossed over to Anatolia, and the peace treaty, from Hungary's point of view, had thus served its real purpose. In the Morea, the emperor's brother, the Despot Constantine, invaded Attica, capturing Athens and Thebes.[19] Finally, Vladislaus received word from Condulmer assuring him the fleet was in position off Constantinople and could guarantee Murad would not be able to return from Anatolia; the cardinal therefore urged the king "to back up his promises with deeds and swiftly lead an army into the land of Rumelia," for in the absence of the sultan, "he could recoup all of Europe with little effort."[20]

At Szeged on 4 August Vladislaus swore an oath to Cesarini "to do whatever possible by our might and power that the Turks might be expelled this year from Christendom to beyond the sea, notwithstanding any manner of treaties or negotiations whether they be terms or stipulations of truces concluded or to be concluded with the Emperor of the Turks… whether under any wording or oath affirmed or to be affirmed."[21] The treaty with the sultan was therefore ratified at Várad on 15 August not by Vladislaus but by Hunyadi, who took the oath "for the king, for himself, and for the whole people of Hungary."[22]

The Christian front was not a united one. Branković, who had mediated the peace and gained most by it, understandably refused to participate in the campaign after the Ottomans had fulfilled their part of the bargain. The absence of Serbia from the coalition would make joint action with the rebel Albanian warlord, George Kastriota or "Skanderbeg," impossible. Meanwhile, the Polish

Diet wrote to Vladislaus on 26 August, urging him to keep the peace with the Porte and return to Poland to prepare the fight against the Tatars, who were ravaging Russia and Podolia. The *diet* also wrote to the *voivode* of Moldavia, informing him that he owed allegiance to Vladislaus only in his role as king of Poland, but not of Hungary, thereby giving Moldavia a reason for boycotting the crusade.

While Murad crossed to Asia to take command of the Anatolian army in person, he did not bring the *kapıkulu* or any detachments of the Rumelian army with him, leaving them in place to contain any opportunistic ventures at Ottoman expense in his absence. In the event, the Karamanid insurgency collapsed at the first show of force, Ibrahim begging for terms and accepting the Ottoman demand that he become "a friend to their friend and an enemy to their enemy," and pledging "I will send neither agent, nor word, nor letter, in secret or in public, to the enemies of Murad."[23]

This accomplished, Murad abdicated and retired to Manisa, bequeathing the throne to his twelve-year-old son, Mehmed II. The Byzantines sought to take advantage of the situation by releasing from his sanctuary in Constantinople Orhan Çelebi, the grandson of Suleiman Çelebi, the eldest son of Sultan Bayezid, and the elder brother of Sultan Mehmed I. As Mehmed II's uncle, Orhan was his rival and the only legitimate alternative to the throne. However, his bid to rally support for his claim failed. He sought to establish an alternative court at Dobrudja but was cut off from Edirne, and upon the approach of troops under Şehabeddin Pasha, the *beylerbey* of Rumelia, fled back to Constantinople. Nonetheless, the mood in Edirne was dark, the city being roiled by religious infighting and a major fire at a time when apprehension over the prospect of imminent invasion and war was at its height. The capital was fortified and an urgent order to mobilize was issued, but young Mehmed was wise enough to accept the fact that he was outmatched. He sent his father an urgent letter demanding that he return to Europe and take command of the war effort. "If you are the sultan, come and lead your army," Mehmed wrote. "If I am the sultan, I order you to come and lead my army."

Having reached the designated assembly point at Orşova in such numbers, the plain where it mustered "resembled the sea of pitch in Hell," as the Ottoman account describes it, the Crusader army began to cross the Danube on 18 September.[24] The Ottoman fortress of Tekii opposite Orşova resisted the crossing as best it could, but with naval support the Crusaders succeeded in reducing the fortress and its garrison. The crossing at Orşova was completed by 22 September, and the Crusaders headed east downriver along the south bank of the Danube. The army seized the town of Vidin on 29 September, but could not take its citadel. Interestingly, in the Ottoman account of the campaign, Vladislaus emerges as the more mature commander at this juncture. When Hunyadi approached him seeking authority to storm the citadel, promising "I will reduce the castle to rubble and tip it into the Danube," Vladislaus pulled rank and replied:

> I know that you are capable of this, but the garrison will not surrender the castle so easily. It would mean that we would have to stay here for a few days, while our aim is to reach Edirne as soon as possible and seize the city while the son of Osman is off his guard. After that, the castle will be ours for the taking. I admit it is wrong to spare these castles, but if we delay here, the son of Osman might somehow or other cross the sea to meet us. Then we shall be in trouble. But if we occupy Edirne, the son of Osman will not dare to attack us.[25]

The Crusaders broke off the siege and continued their march. However, it still took more than two weeks to reach Nicopolis on 19 October, where again they were able to storm the town but proved unable to take the citadel. The *voivode* of Wallachia, Vlad Dracul, then arrived in the Crusader camp. He bluntly warned Vladislaus his army was smaller than the sultan's hunting entourage, and urged the king to abandon "this foolishness" and turn back before it was too late.[26] When this advice was rejected, the *voivode* nonetheless generously offered 4,000 Wallachian cavalry under the command of his son, Mircea, to the Crusader cause.

Moving on, the Crusaders skirmished with an Ottoman screening force at Tarnovo, but elected to continue their march eastwards instead of turning south after ascertaining Şehabeddin Pasha had moved faster and succeeded in blocking the Shipka Pass. Unwilling to repeat the experience of Zlatitsa the previous year, the Crusaders were obliged to abandon their original intention of entering Thrace via the diagonal road network linking Belgrade–Niš–Sofia–Edirne. That route was now abandoned in favor of the alternative, marching south along the shore of the Black Sea, which at least allowed for the left flank of the line of march to be screened by the coast and the prospect of being resupplied and reinforced by vessels at sea, arriving either downstream via the Danube or up from the Aegean by way of Constantinople.[27] In the event, the Crusaders did succeed in storming the strongholds of Shumen, Novi Pazar, Provadia, Petricha, and Mihalitsh en route, offering no quarter to their garrisons, but these small victories afforded no strategic advantage, and the long-sought general uprising of the Christian population failed to materialize.[28]

The entire outcome of the campaign thus hinged on the ability of the Crusader fleet to prevent Murad returning from Anatolia. However, the fleet was significantly under strength for its assigned task of blockading the entire strait of water between Europe and Asia, a situation worsened by its being split to cover the narrow channels at both ends of the Sea of Marmara. Condulmer commanded the fifteen vessels assigned to patrol the Dardanelles, leaving only four, under the command of the Burgundian Waleran de Wavrin, warding the Bosporus. Murad resolved to cross via the latter channel north of Constantinople, at the site of the Güzelce Hisar, a fortress Bayezid had constructed in 1394 in preparation for his siege of the city. The sultan dispatched orders to Edirne for Halil Pasha to send a force to the Bosporus in order to "guard both the near and far shore with cannon, so that the cannon on either side should be able to kiss each other."[29]

Wavrin urged the emperor to intervene. Unless he prevented Halil Pasha from setting up his guns on the European shore, the Crusader fleet could not effectively patrol the strait. John VIII responded that the forces at his disposal were too meager to contest with those of the grand vizier. He could only muster an expeditionary force by stripping the garrison from the walls, leaving the city wide open to assault. If Constantinople fell, the blockade would fail, and with it the crusade. The emperor did, however, agree to add two galleys to the Crusader fleet, raising the total under Wavrin's command to six.

On the evening of 18 October, a violent storm broke out and scattered the Western ships. By the time they regrouped, the bulk of the Ottoman force was already embarking on transports provided by the Genoese, and a powerful cannon fire from guns stationed on both sides of the straits stopped the galleys from intervening, sinking one of the Byzantine vessels.[30] Over the course of the next two days and nights, the Ottoman reinforcements crossed over to the European shore and then immediately marched to Edirne.[31] Mehmed pleaded with his father to accompany him on campaign, but the sultan was unmoved. "No, my son, do not say this. You do as I tell you. The enemy is strong, and when I march against him, you defend this city from the infidels of Constantinople, for who knows how things will turn out. You just offer prayers." Delegating real authority to Halil Pasha ("you stay here and busy yourself with my son's affairs… protect the city of Edirne from the infidels of Constantinople, and let me know whatever it is that happens"), Murad marched out to link up with Şehabeddin and the troops of Rumelia at Hisarlık.[32] The following day, the combined Ottoman army set out to intercept the Crusaders. Having arrived at Varna on the Black Sea, at dawn on 9 November Vladislaus suddenly found himself pinned against the coastline when the sultan and his army formed up along the high ground dominating the western horizon. At a council of war that day, the king and his advisers arrived at an inescapable conclusion; though outnumbered by as much as three to one, they could neither advance, withdraw, nor hold their ground. There was no alternative but to fight. The Crusaders slept that night in their armor and arrayed for battle the following morning.

The Ottomans had the advantage of the high ground, but as Wavrin notes, this was mitigated by the limited approaches it allowed, for "Varna is in a valley, and the Turk could not come down from the mountains to fight except through narrow passes."[33] Hunyadi set up a defensive perimeter in an arch formation west of Varna, shouldering his flanks on Lake Devna to his left and with the high ground of the Frangen plateau to his right. The left flank, where the lake and its swampy shores limited Ottoman freedom of maneuver, was commanded by Hunyadi's brother-in-law, Michael Szilágyi. This wing was arranged in five divisions (*banderia*) extending out from the household troops of George Orosz, Szilágyi, and Hunyadi, to the Szeklers under Thomas Székely and, at the far end of the line, the Transylvanians. These men were veterans of mobile warfare and were intended to serve as Hunyadi's hammer.

The right flank was likewise comprised of five *banderia* under the overall command of the bishop of Oradea, John de Dominis. From left to right, this flank consisted of the Wallachians led by Mircea II; the bishop of Bosnia Raphael of Zegev; the bishop of Eger Simon Rozgoni; the troops of the *ban* of Slavonia, Franko Tallóci; and the crusade volunteers under the command of Cardinal Cesarini. A larger percentage of the soldiers on this flank were heavily armored knights. Due to the difficulty of advancing uphill they were designated primarily for defense against the Ottoman left wing, in particular against any attempt to outflank the Crusader line.

In the center were the two *banderia* of the king, one under Stephen Bathory, the palatine of Hungary, flying the crusade banner of St George, the other under Vladislaus Banffi of Losoncz, who bore the royal flag. The king's own retinue and royal knights served in these ranks, as well as the mercenaries and the several hundred Polish troops led by Leshko Bobzhitski comprising the king's bodyguard. The war wagons were arranged in a parallel line behind the army, close to the sea shore. Bristling with guns, these were manned by Bohemian and Ruthenian troops, commanded by Hetman Ceyka.

The Ottoman army lined up in a standard tripartite formation. The Anatolian troops on the right were commanded by Murad's son-in-law, Güyeğü Karaca bin Abdullah Pasha, who took his station at the inner edge of the line. The divisions extending out from this position were led in turn by Suleiman Bey, Fenarioğlu

Hasan Pasha, and Isa Bey Evrenos, who served on the far right of the formation and was assigned the task of leading his men to outflank the enemy line opposite.

The Rumelian troops took position to the left of the sultan under their *beylerbey*, Şehabeddin Pasha. From innermost to outermost on the line, his subordinates were Mehmet Bey Ferizbeyoğlu, with the men he had led in screening the march of the Crusaders throughout the campaign, Isa Bey Hasanbeyoğlu, and two *sanjak-beys*, Malkoçoğlu Murad Bey of Chirmen, and, on the far left, Davud Bey of Priştina, who also was tasked with finding a route around the flank of the Crusader army.

Murad himself observed from the high ground in the center. He stationed the *azaps* and the elite janissaries with the Anatolian *sipahis* in reserve at his camp to the rear of the battlefield. Murad also ordered the Anatolian *akinji* light cavalry and *azap* light infantry to take the high ground northwest of Varna, using the terrain to conceal their movement as they took up this position. In addition to his banner, the sultan had been sure to display the Treaty of Szeged, impaled on a spear, to symbolize the violation of the oath taken by Vladislaus.

The battle opened when Davud Bey on the far left of the Rumelian line succeeded in outflanking the Crusader right wing, which broke ranks and fled, the bishops of Bosnia and Eger being killed in the rout. The Ottoman light cavalry broke through to the war wagons warding the Crusader camp. The only Christian commanders to hold their ground were Tallóci and Cesarini, who rallied 200 men under the banner of St Vladislaus and held the line until relieved by Hunyadi, who led a detachment from the royal cavalry reserve in the center.

Fortunes were reversed on the opposite side of the battle, where the Crusader left wing bent and then broke the Anatolians on the Ottoman right, their *beylerbey*, Karaca Pasha, being killed in the melee. With the Wallachians pursuing the routed Anatolians off the battlefield, Hunyadi was now free to deploy his left against its Ottoman counterpart. "If we can move their left wing even a little bit out of position, you can be sure that all of the son of Osman's army will be defeated," the Ottoman account records him having advised Vladislaus.[34]

Şehabeddin and the Rumelians began to break under the pressure of Hunyadi's troops from the Crusader left flank now working in combination with the remaining troops of their right. An Ottoman account describes how the sultan's left wing "fought furiously, but the cowards in their midst began to flee towards the mountains in groups. When [Şehabeddin] Pasha saw this, he placed the soldiers from the general levy and his own *azaps* in front. The worthy among the

Rumelians stood by them and continued to fight more fiercely than can be described."[35] Hunyadi was knocked from his horse, stunned, when he was shot in the head by an arrow, his life only being saved by his helmet. After coming to his senses, he remounted and withdrew from the battlefield to have his head bandaged so that he could return to the fray. The Crusaders now had the momentum, however, as the king, accompanied by the knights of his entourage, now tore into the enemy ranks like "a new Caesar," in the words of one Crusader, Andreas de Pallatio, driving the Ottomans back up the slope of the valley, "and whomever we came upon we put to death, so that around three thousand Turks fell in this place and were wiped out."[36]

Murad was aware his right wing "had been routed and scattered, while the left, after fighting for a while, had begun to flee in groups to the mountains." However, his *azaps* and janissaries were still fresh and he committed them now, advancing down the slope to close with the Crusaders, who regrouped and charged to meet them. The two armies clashed all along the line, "and that day there was a battle such as words cannot describe. As the fight increased in fury, both the troops of Islam and the infidels displayed such zeal that, in the marketplace of death, father could not recognize son nor son father, and the angels in heaven and the fish in the sea wondered at the fury of the fight." In a grueling contest of attrition, the Crusaders slowly began to roll the enemy center step by step back up the incline. It was a question of who could stand the pressure and who would break first. Ottoman resolve was wavering, as the veterans holding the line were ground down while "the novices among the janissaries and *azaps* began to scatter, group by group."[37] On the other side of the line, men and horses of the Crusader host began to drop out of the fight, exhausted.

Late in the day, Murad, concerned at the grinding Crusader progress and with most of his army now dead, incapacitated, or having fled, withdrew to his fortified camp. This was the critical moment. According to Ottoman historian Neşri, Murad was on the verge of withdrawing from the battlefield altogether when Dayı Karaca Bey dismounted from his horse, grabbed the sultan's horse's reins, and declaimed, "Hey, my sultan! What is this? If you go, the infidel will follow behind our backs to Edirne." Ignoring the demand of Kazancı Doğan, the commander (*agha*) of the janissary corps, to depart, Karaca Bey refused to surrender the reins. "The infidel has crushed us," Murad insisted, to which Karaca Bey replied, "We will crush them, God willing."[38] Either shamed or emboldened, the sultan overruled the objections of his janissaries and resolved to hold his ground.

Taking the sultan would be checkmate, and Vladislaus, urged on by Cesarini, was determined to end the battle, and the war, with one decisive stroke. Hunyadi implored his monarch against committing himself. "The day is yours," he insisted, according to Wavrin; "Do not put yourself at risk... The strongest part of all the enemy army has been routed," and tomorrow the sultan "must either flee or surrender to you... For the sake of God, do not put yourself in a position to lose everything that has been gained."[39] But Vladislaus was won over by the advice of Cesarini that if Murad "escapes from our clutches again, he will return to battle... Let us strike when the iron is hot."[40] The cardinal also contributed by threatening with excommunication anyone who refused to follow the king into the fray.

Announcing, "Since God is granting us so many victories, I do not want to give up unless I see the [sultan] himself," at the head of the flower of chivalry from his two kingdoms, Vladislaus charged with 500 fully armored Hungarian and Polish knights directly at the sultan's banner.[41] Ottoman accounts recalled the spectacle with mingled awe, fear, and loathing: "Then those accursed men with no religion, those lawless reprobates, abandoned their lust for life and love for home and family and attacked so fiercely that the earth could not withstand the heat of battle, the air could not endure their harshness and, out of fear, the sun took flight to the safety of the dust."[42]

The initial impact of this charge was devastating. But Murad was far from easy prey. The Ottoman camp was fortified by a surrounding trench and bulwark, with thousands of iron stakes lining the parapet, behind which the garrison lay in wait with cannon and arquebus. Should the Crusaders punch through these defenses they would have to fight their way through the *kapıkulu*, then a row of camels chained together so as to further impede any assault, and, finally, the *solaklar*, the sultan's personal bodyguards handpicked from the janissary corps, drawn up around Murad himself.

Many of the Crusader knights became entangled in one obstacle or another and were shot or hacked down, their numbers dwindling the deeper they penetrated into the Ottoman stronghold. Vladislaus finally broke free of the trench and spurred directly for the sultan only to be intercepted by one of the *solaklar*, Koca Hızır. Wielding his *balta*, or short battle-axe, he hamstrung the king's mount with a single blow, and when Vladislaus fell to the earth, Koca Hızır lopped off the king's head and presented it to Murad, who ordered it impaled on a pike and raised aloft for both armies to witness.

What happened in the aftermath is contested. According to the Ottoman account, the scattered survivors from the two wings of their army now rallied, and those "who had fled in defeat recovered their zeal and began to come in from all directions and rejoin the ranks," whereas when the Crusaders "saw the disaster that had befallen the evil-doing King, they at once turned to flight."[43] Contrarily, the account of Wavrin records the death of Vlaldislaus brought no immediate end to the struggle. To the contrary, the battle continued to rage until dusk, and then into the darkness. "The Hungarians and Poles continued, until the night became pitch black, to fight so hard it was unclear which side could claim victory," Wavrin recorded. "First one side fled and then the other, believing each other to be defeated. Here a hundred reassembled and there two hundred, here thirty and there forty."[44]

When the two sides finally disengaged, the survivors of the Crusader host had to choose between two alternatives – take their chances by trying to escape under cover of darkness, or hunker down behind a hastily assembled *wagenburg* perimeter. Some of those who opted for the first choice were able to slip through the Ottoman net and return to Hungary. The Wallachians were long gone; having harried the Ottoman right wing off the battlefield, they paused only long enough to snipe at the Ottoman camp before riding for home. Another to escape was Hunyadi. Traveling via Wallachia, he was incarcerated by Vlad Dracul, who was anxious to placate his nominal Ottoman overlords. It was only the Hungarian *Diet*'s threat of war that induced Vlad to release Hunyadi, who he personally escorted to the border. There was no hope for any of those who opted to remain at Varna. The day after the battle the Ottomans stormed the *wagenburg* and, "after enslaving the fresh-faced lads from the infidels who are as low as the earth, they put all their grown men to the sword."[45]

The price paid by the Hungarian elite for this defeat was severe. The Ottomans sent the decapitated head of Vladislaus on a tour of their empire. Preserved in a jar of honey, it would be removed and cleansed before being placed on a spear and paraded from city to city. In addition to the king, Cesarini and Bathory fell in the battle, as did Hunyadi's brother-in-law, his vice-*voivode* of Transylvania, Pongrác Dengelegi. In the aftermath, the Hungarian ruling class had to find a successor to Vladislaus. To avoid the civil war that occurred after the death of King Albert in 1439, both parties agreed to bring the child Ladislaus the Posthumous back to Hungary from the court of Frederick IV. However, Frederick refused to release the boy king. In the absence of the monarch, on 5 June 1446, the *diet* elected Hunyadi as regent of Hungary. Now at the peak of his career, he could call himself master of 2.3 million hectares of land, twenty-eight castles, fifty-seven towns, and about 1,000 villages.

KOSOVO POLJE, 1448

Meanwhile, the war continued. Waleran de Wavrin had remained with Cardinal Condulmer in Constantinople over the winter of 1444–45. In the following spring, the Burgundian ships set out for the Black Sea, raiding the coast of Anatolia before sailing up the Danube, linking with the Wallachians to seize and burn Tutrakan, Giurgiu, and Ruse. They continued towards Nicopolis, where they laid siege to the fort of Turnu Măgurele opposite the town on the north bank of the river. On 15 September, Hunyadi arrived, and on 29 September he crossed at Orjahovo, to engage in a few indecisive skirmishes with the Ottoman force that had been tracking the fleet. All parties involved broke off to go into quarters before winter arrived; the Burgundian fleet returned to Constantinople on 2 November.

Murad had again abdicated in favor of Mehmed and retired to Manisa after the Battle of Varna, only to be recalled to office once more two years later. The first rebellion of the janissaries – known to history as Buçuk Tepe (the Half Akça Hill) – broke out in May 1446, as a reaction against the attempt by the young sultan to pay their wages using a new coin of lower quality and value. The janissaries also refused to go on campaign under the command of Şehabeddin Pasha, *beylerbey* of Rumelia, whom they blamed for the deaths of so many of their comrades in the 1442 campaign against Hunyadi. The rebels threatened to support a pretender claiming to be the son of Bayezid I. While Mehmed II sought to pacify the rebels by authorizing an increase in their wages, the faction at court led by the grand vizier, Halil Pasha, convinced Murad to return to the throne, and he arrived in the capital at the end of August.

This incident reflected a deeper power struggle playing out at the Ottoman court, where a rivalry had emerged between Anatolia and Rumelia, between the ancient Ottoman regime centered on Bursa (the *dar al-ulema*, the scholars' house) and the new one, centered on Edirne (the *dar al-guzat*, the *ghazi*'s house), which was openly manifested in the enmity between the old Anatolian aristocracy, represented by Halil Pasha, and the new *ghazi* aristocracy in Mehmed's aggressive inner circle of *lalas* (advisers), such as Zaganos Pasha.[46] This would have significant implications in 1453 when Mehmed moved against Constantinople. In the short term, his ascension to sultan having been rescinded – for the second time – the outcome was humiliating for Mehmed, who was relegated to governing the minor Anatolian province of Manisa. He would be taken on campaign against the Hungarians in 1448 and the Albanians in 1450 in a bid by his father to instill the confidence, experience, and authority he would need some day as sultan.

Having regained control of the army, Murad stormed the Hexamilion, the defensive wall across the Isthmus of Corinth, and ravaged Byzantine Morea, forcing the Despot Constantine to seek terms. The Venetians had pulled their fleet out of the Aegean in February, a peace treaty with the Ottomans coming into effect in September. These steps were preparatory for a fresh campaign against Hungary.

While the flat plain north of the Danube was their primary objective in Europe, the Ottomans chafed at their inability to stamp out the protracted resistance they encountered in the mountains of Albania to the west. The independence of Albania, which persisted long after kings and emperors had fallen in battle with the sultans, was owed to a single man, one of the great guerilla fighters of the military canon, George Kastriota, known to history as Skanderbeg.[47]

A member of the Albanian Kastrioti noble family, Skanderbeg had been sent to the court of Murad II in Edirne as a hostage in 1423 after his father was forced to accept Ottoman suzerainty. Having been educated and converted to Islam in the sultan's court, he served the Ottomans for some twenty years, including as *sanjak* governor of Debar in northern Albania. When the sultan ordered his *sanjak* governor at Kroja to take control of the Kastrioti family's forts, Skanderbeg deserted the Ottoman army that was marching against the Crusaders in 1443. He sent his cousin in advance to seize Dibra, and he himself swiftly marched to take Krujë. On 28 November, he proclaimed himself a Catholic and Albania an independent republic. Skanderbeg was quick to ally with other rebels, most prominently George Arianiti, who had raised his banner eight years earlier, defeating Ottoman armies of occupation during the 1432–36 Albanian revolt. Skanderbeg would eventually marry Donika, Arianiti's daughter.

Under Venetian patronage, a confederation of Albanian principalities dubbed the League of Lezhë was formed on 2 March 1444. Headed by Skanderbeg, this military alliance rapidly won two major battles, at Elbasan and Berat, and seized a number of Ottoman strongholds, including Krujë and Kodžadžik. After routing an Ottoman counteroffensive at the Battle of Torvioll on 29 June, Skanderbeg drove into Rumelia as far east as Skopje.

These achievements are all the more remarkable in that the basis of Skanderbeg's authority in Albania was extremely narrow. The development of a sense of national identity was hindered by the fact that some Albanians were Catholic Christians, known as Arbanites, while others were Orthodox Christians, generally known as Epirots. Skanderbeg's clan, the Kastriotas, was small and the other leading clans, such as the Thopias, Balshas, and Dukaghinis, resented his leadership. The anarchic nature of clan society in Albania, where generational blood feuds proliferated like creeper vines around every branch of each dynastic family tree, made collaborative decision making and collective action highly problematic. Skanderbeg was obliged to be as much a diplomat as he was a warrior, and domestic social occasions sometimes exceeded the threat level of the battlefield, a representative exemplar being the death toll among the guests in a clan brawl at the wedding of Skanderbeg's youngest sister Mamica to Karl Muzaka Thopia at Krujë in 1445. And while the primary antagonist was the Ottoman foe to his front, Skanderbeg always had to keep a wary eye on the Venetians behind his back. The republic aspired to dominate the entire Adriatic seaboard and a united Albania represented a threat to this ambition. At one point, Skanderbeg had a considerable bounty on his head. But his victories kept coming. In 1445, Skanderbeg isolated and annihilated an Ottoman army in the Mokra Valley, killing its commanding officer, Firuz Pasha. The following year, Skanderbeg scored two more victories, including a decisive defeat of Mustafa Pasha at the Battle of Otonetë on 27 September 1446. In August 1448, Skanderbeg triumphed again at the Battle of Oranik, this time taking Mustafa Pasha captive.

Hunyadi had been kept busy consolidating Hungary's frontier by tightening Hungarian control over the border principalities. In 1447, Vlad II and his son Mircea II, suspected of having colluded with the Ottomans, were executed on his orders, being replaced by a pro-Hungarian candidate, Vladislav Dan, as *voivode* of Wallachia. Hunyadi also enthroned Petru II as *voivode* of Moldavia, and in January 1448 the stronghold of Kilia came under Hunyadi's direct control, the garrison he stationed there fighting off the sultan's fleet in June.

On 8 April, the papal bull *Admonet nos ille* proclaimed a crusade. With financial support from King Alfonso V of Aragon, Hunyadi mustered an army at Kovin on the banks of the Danube. The force was constituted of Hungarian, Bohemian, Wallachian, and Moldovan detachments, and was state of the art, incorporating heavy and light cavalry, war wagons, and artillery. "I can scarcely think of another army better in its array," enthused Pasquale de Sorgo, seconded to the campaign by the Republic of Dubrovnik, "and, in our time, more heavily armed to have existed."[48] The flower of Hungarian nobility participated in the campaign; Imre Pelsőczi Bebek, *voivode* of Transylvania; Hunyadi's two brothers-in-law, Michael Szilágyi and John Székely, *ban* of Slovenia; and the papal nuncio, Cristoforo Garatoni.

Hunyadi had hoped to receive material or at least financial support from the pope. Instead, when he arrived in camp at Kovin where the Hungarian army was mustering at the beginning of September, he received a message from Nicolas V advising him to postpone the "hastily" organized campaign and wait another year before proceeding. The timing for a crusade was unpropitious; no help could be expected from the Holy Roman Empire or Poland; Venice was at war with Portugal over Milan. Noting with disappointment that he had expected the pope to follow in the footsteps of his predecessor "and double the zeal of his achievements in humiliating the enemies of Christendom," Hunyadi replied that he would gladly comply with the pope's suggestion; however, "the enormous preparation of the Turks do not let me do so," for "when our old enemy has gained new powers as a result of its latest victories over Christianity and is gathering great forces at our borders, it is useful for us to take up arms, so that an attack does not find us unprepared." In any event, Hungarian mobilization was too far advanced; "The war has been decided, the army has been gathered, the orders have been given. Power is always greater when used in attack rather than in defense, and the outcome of the war smiles more favorably upon the one who pursues the enemy in its own land."[49] If he postponed the campaign, "is the army going to gather next year, and if it does, will it have the same enthusiasm that it has now?"

In the final analysis, conflict was inevitable, and, as he chided the Holy Father, the support of the entire Christian *oikomene* was critical, for it was the Hungarian obligation "to endeavor to humiliate the enemy by force and continue the war until we bring it to its heels. But [the Ottoman Empire] is enormous and one nation is too weak to defeat it on its own, and to pay the costs of the adequate army for that. This is the cause of the Christianity and not that of the Hungarian nation's only."[50]

When Hunyadi summoned Branković to take part in the campaign, the Serbian despot responded by pleading military incapacity. In fact, his troops were committed to fighting the Bosnians of Stephen Tomaš for possession of Zeta and Srebrenica. Branković, de Sorgo noted, "is openly still undecided as to whether to follow the army; I think as long as it is within his power, as long as he is able to remain neutral, he will take care to stay in the middle."[51] Ultimately, Branković elected to side with Murad, who was awaiting Hunyadi's challenge at Plovdiv, having mustered his Anatolian and Rumelian cohorts, under the command of *beylerbey* Skuras Pasha and the Grand Vizier Çandarlı Halil Pasha respectively.

Hunyadi crossed the Danube late in the campaign season, on 10 September. The Crusader force advanced from Subotica on 21 September to take Niš on 28 September, then crossed the Morava, changing direction to the southwest and taking Prokuplje. On 15 October, Hunyadi arrived at Pristina, on the edge of Kosovo Polje, the field of blackbirds, where the great clash between Serbs and Ottomans had played out in 1389. Murad, taking advantage of intelligence provided by Branković regarding Hunyadi's disposition and intentions, arrived two days later, his *akinji* vanguard immediately skirmishing with Hunyadi's hussars. The following day, Hunyadi drew out his army in three lines. In the middle of the first line was the heavy cavalry from Croatia, Slovenia, and Transylvania, under the command of John Székely and Franko Tallóci. Hunyadi commanded from the center of the second line, comprising the royal troops, the mercenaries, and the contingent from Transylvania. On the right flank, the troops of the magnates were commanded by Benedict Losonczi, with the light cavalry in the first line and the heavy cavalry in the second line. The left flank was arranged in the same way, the Wallachian prince Dan Vladislav in the front line, Stephen Bathory in the second. The third line of the army consisted of the infantry and the artillery inside the fortification of war wagons.[52]

Facing the Hungarian army, along the entire 10–11 kilometer width of the valley, from the Sitnica River to its eastern extremity, was the Ottoman army, also drawn up in two lines, the *akinji* and *azaps* in the front line, the *sipahis* in the second. The Anatolian troops held the right flank, towards the Sitnica River, commanded by their new *beylerbey*, Skuras Pasha, with the Rumelian troops on the left, under the command of Bey Karadja.

The Ottoman left flank initiated the battle. At the first clash, the first line of the Hungarian right flank, formed of light cavalry, retreated without dispersing and made room for the heavy cavalry. The latter entered the fray and a fierce fight began that raged across the entire eastern side of the field. The battle was also joined on the other flank, developing in the same manner. Hunyadi weakened his center by committing troops to aid the flanks. Observing these maneuvers, Murad sent his first line against the center of the Hungarian army. The *azaps* made progress, but the intense fire of the artillery and from the gunners stationed in the war wagons halted them, and the Hungarian infantry, counterattacking, drove them back.

Finally, nightfall intervened, and the two sides drew apart. The Crusaders had held their ground, but the Ottoman army was still intact, and the janissaries had not yet been committed. According to the account of the Byzantine chronicler Laonikos Chalkokondyles, at a council of war that evening, Saudji (Daud Çelebi), a grandson of Murad I who had defected to the Christians, advised Hunyadi:

> ... not to delay in attacking the center of the enemy's line, the sector held by the
> *kapikulu*. We have attacked the armies of Asia and Europe enough. If we continue
> to turn our attention to them and do not bring the battle to Murad himself, we

are laboring in vain… I believe that we should move our entire camp, along with the wagons on which we have placed our cannons and firearms, and engage in close combat with the Porte this very night.[53]

Given it meant sacrificing the capacity to retain command and control over their army once committed, fighting after sunset was a gamble few commanders were willing to risk in the preindustrial era. It was a roll of the dice Hunyadi was now prepared to make. Under cover of darkness, he unleashed a general assault. The Crusaders "immediately attacked the sultan's camp with their wagons, in the first watch of the night," Chalkokondyles chronicled. Breaching the outer defenses, the Crusaders fought their way up to the sultan's tent, where "they terrified the janissaries with their cannons and firearms." Units became intermingled and isolated, some on both sides breaking in the confusion, but the battle continued to rage "until the crack of dawn," when the Crusaders finally pulled back.[54]

Hunyadi still faced a strategic dilemma. He couldn't break off, not with a larger and more mobile enemy at his heels. He had to bleed the Ottoman host on the battlefield, holding his ground long enough for Skanderbeg to arrive in support. On 19 October, Hunyadi again drew up his army, this time with the left flank reinforced by several squadrons of heavy cavalry under the command of John Székely. On the Ottoman side, Murad detached the corps of *sipahis* and *akinji* from Thessaly, commanded by Turakhan Bey, stationing them on his far right wing. This initiative proved decisive, as the intervention of the detached corps at the critical moment tipped the balance in an otherwise even fight. The Crusader line collapsed, those who could escape being encircled streaming back to seek sanctuary in their camp. John Székely, Franko Tallóci, and Stephen Bathory were killed, and Hunyadi himself was unhorsed, only being saved by a soldier from Hunedoara, Teodor Cnezul, who gave him his mount. The strategic position of the depleted Hungarians was now entirely untenable. Around 3am or 4am the following day, a detachment led by Hunyadi's brother-in-law Michael Szilágyi feigned an escape, drawing the attention of the Ottomans away from the real breakout led by Hunyadi himself, who exited the camp from a different direction. The end came at dawn the following day, as Murad ordered a general assault on the wagon laager Hunyadi had established. In desperate, bloody combat the janissaries finally broke through and the Crusader last stand degenerated into a massacre as four days and nights of exhausting combat drew to a bloody conclusion.

Hunyadi succeeded in fighting his way clear, only to be captured by the Serbs and brought before Branković. His release was ultimately negotiated against a ransom of 100,000 florins and the return of the estates he had secured during the peace negotiations four years earlier, Hunyadi's eldest son, the seventeen-year-old Laszlo, being detained at Smederevo as a hostage for surety.[55] It was the lowest point of Hunyadi's career, but, the cost to his pride and reputation notwithstanding, while the Hungarians were beaten, they were not broken. Hunyadi's chancellor, John Vitéz, wrote to Pope Nicholas V on September 17, 1448, assuring him "For over sixty years, we have firmly withstood the scorching wrath of war, relying on our own resources and with the arms of a single nation. Though exhausted by the numerous defeats, the warfare and the mourning, we are persevering."[56]

Once again, Christian disunity played a vital, perhaps even decisive role, in the outcome. Critically, it was the Serbs who blocked the Albanian mountain passes, preventing Skanderbeg from linking up with Hunyadi before the Ottoman sultan brought him to battle. This failure was of critical significance; "Skanderbeg will join us very soon with substantial help," Hunyadi assured his troops just the day before he was surprised by Murad's vanguard, and advance units of Skanderbeg's guerillas were indeed only twenty miles to the west of Hunyadi's position when he engaged the Ottomans, but none of them were able to intervene.[57] This may have been due to the Venetians, who had committed an army led by Andrea Venier against Skanderbeg that summer. He had smashed the Venetian army in a decisive battle on 23 July, but negotiations to arrive at a peace settlement, although including a pledge by Venice to fund Skanderbeg to the tune of 1,400 ducats per year, had dragged out until 4 October. Though Skanderbeg had expressed his impatience to set off with his army in order "to join the lord János," when the treaty was finally signed it was too late for him to arrive at Kosovo Polje in time.[58]

In the final analysis, the outcome of the clash at Kosovo Polje had profound geopolitical implications. The last field army in the Balkans capable of taking offensive action against the Ottomans no longer existed. If – when – the Ottomans next moved against Constantinople, the garrison could harbor no illusions about a relief force marching to the rescue. The city would stand – or fall – alone.

CONSTANTINOPLE, 1453

The religious devotion of the Byzantines, with its infinite capacity to both unite and divide the populace, would dominate their identity and relations with outsiders to the very end. After years of wrangling over points of doctrine, in the cathedral of Florence on 6 July 1439 the union between the Catholic and Orthodox Churches, the stiff price the papacy had demanded for military support against the Ottomans, had finally been agreed upon. However, it was almost unanimously rejected in Constantinople. In 1451, the unionist Patriarch Gregory II Mammas was forced to flee the city and take refuge in Rome, leaving the patriarchal see vacant.

Pope Nicholas V dispatched Cardinal Isidore, a Greek by birth and the metropolitan of Kiev, to take control of the situation.[59] He arrived in Constantinople with a force of 200 armed retainers on 26 October 1452. After enforcing the suppression of the anti-unionist faction, which centered on the monk George Scholarios from the Monastery of the Pantokrator, Isidore proceeded with the long-delayed proclamation of the Union of Churches on 12 December 1452 with a common liturgy in Latin and Greek in St Sophia. Though consummated at the official level, the Union was repudiated by the clergy and common people, and there was rioting in the city's streets. Lukas Notaras, the grand admiral of the Byzantine fleet, spoke for many when he snapped: "It would be better to see the turban of the Turks reigning in the center of the City than the Latin miter."[60]

That exact scenario was now on the very near horizon. On 3 February 1451, Murad II died, and his son, still not quite twenty years old, succeeded – at last in his own right – as Mehmed II. The new sultan did not appear to be in any hurry to stamp his authority with martial prowess. On 10 September 1451, peace was renewed with the Venetians; on 20 September a three-year truce was signed with Hungary that placed Wallachia under the joint suzerainty of Buda and the Porte. On 20 November, Mehmed not only renewed the treaty his father had made with the Byzantines two years previously, but also offered Emperor Constantine XI an annual sum of 300,000 akçes towards the expenses of maintaining the incarceration of the Ottoman pretender Orhan Çelebi.

Early in his reign, Mehmed was confronted by yet another opportunistic uprising on the part of that perennial irritant to his father, Ibrahim Bey of Karaman, who no doubt intended to test the mettle of this young successor to the throne. Constantine took this opportunity to send emissaries to Edirne with a veiled threat that he would release Orhan if the sultan did not immediately double the stipend for the pretender's upkeep. Enraged, Mehmed canceled the existing grant of revenues and commenced building a fortress, the Boğaz Kesen (Strait-Cutter), later renamed the Rumeli Hisar (European Castle), on the European shore of the Bosporus opposite the Güzelce Hisar (Beautiful Castle), later renamed the Anadolu Hisar (Asian Castle).

The construction of the fortress – on what was nominally Byzantine territory – was completed between April and August 1452, giving Mehmed control over the entry and exit of shipping to and from the Black Sea. On 25 November, a Venetian ship attempting to run the straits was sunk by the Rumeli Hisar's guns. Its captain and crew were captured and executed. These were the first shots fired in the final death agonies of Constantinople.

Once again, appeals were made for aid to the wider Christian world, and once again, the response was platitudes, excuses, or silence. Duke Philip III of Burgundy and the Holy Roman Emperor Frederick III were focused on their own domestic concerns. England and France were fighting out the last act of their Hundred Years War.

In Greece, Constantine's brothers and co-despots, Demetrius and Thomas, were subjected to a raid in force by Ottoman troops under Turahan Bey of Thessaly and his sons Ahmed and Ömer, who attacked the Morea on 1 October 1452. They stormed the Isthmus of Corinth, ravaged Arcadia and the plateau of Tripolista as far as the Ionian Sea, and captured Pylos. However, they failed to take Siderokastron and a unit which had been sent towards Leondarion was defeated by Byzantine troops under Matthew Asanes, brother-in-law of Demetrius. Ahmed was captured and taken to Mistra, the capital of the despotate. It was a small and perhaps surprising success for Byzantine arms, but the Ottoman raiders had fulfilled their task. No help for Constantinople would come from the Morea.[61]

In Hungary, the young King Ladislaus the Posthumous came of age in 1453. Hunyadi was relegated from regent to captain general, while Ladislaus was obliged to take the field against a major revolt led by Peter Aksamit of Liderovic. Hunyadi reportedly proposed a seaborne campaign to outflank the Ottomans, but this would come at a price. According to the Byzantine statesman and chronicler George Sphrantzes, Hunyadi had demanded Nesebar (on the Black Sea) or Silivri (a suburb of Constantinople on the Sea of Marmara) in return for aiding the beleaguered Byzantines. "When the war began," Sphrantzes asserted, "Nesebar was conceded to [Hunyadi]. I personally drafted the gold-sealed document." Sphrantzes also claimed one of the empire's few remaining possessions, the northern Aegean island of Limnos, which was offered to King Alfonso V of Aragon for use as a naval base from which to help Constantinople. Nothing came from either of these proposals.[62]

It was a similar story throughout the rest of the Balkans. George Branković, the despot of Serbia, remained loyal to his son-in-law, the sultan, providing sappers and engineers who would prove vital to the Ottoman cause during the siege. The rival claimants Peter III and Alexander II of Moldavia were squabbling with each other and were in any case more concerned about their relationship with Hungary and Poland. The *voivode* Vladislav II of Wallachia refused to turn against the Ottomans without direct support from Hungary. Skanderbeg continued to hold out in Albania but was in no position to advance from the Adriatic to the Bosporus.

A report from Venice – the one state best positioned to intervene with decisive impact – on the response of the senate to the emperor's desperate appeal for aid was a masterclass in the indifference of realist geopolitics:

> The representative of the most serene lord emperor of Constantinople appeared before us and reported to our leadership on the preparations that are being made by the lord of the Turks to take the city of Constantinople. No doubt, unless something is done with regard to provisions and the garrison, the city is under great danger... The same envoy is to present a similar report to Florence, to the Pope in Rome, and to other states in Italy... When he asked for our help, we answered that he should understand that our situation in Lombardy presents us with great difficulties and that for the most part our hands are tied. Consequently, we cannot accommodate his lord.[63]

When Venice did finally mobilize the commitment was half-hearted, the strategy was overly complicated and cumbersome, and the pace was glacial. Gabriele Trevisano, the Venetian Vice Captain of the Gulf, was sent to Constantinople, where he was supposed to remain if the city came under Ottoman attack. In such a case he, all his ships, and their crews were to help in whatever manner they could. The senate also resolved to arm two large transports, each to carry 400 soldiers, accompanied by fifteen galleys to sail for Constantinople on 8 April. Meanwhile, Venetian authorities in Crete sent two warships to Evvoia, where they would be placed under the command of Zaccaria Grioni, who had recently arrived from Constantinople. Then the naval command structure was changed, and the fleet for Constantinople was placed under the command of Giacomo Loredan, the Captain General of the Sea. He was already on his way east when he was then ordered to wait at Modon to be reinforced by another squadron of galleys commanded by Alvise Longo. Further delays followed and in the end Longo was told to take his fleet through the straits to Constantinople but only if they could avoid a direct clash with the Ottoman navy. There he should put himself and his men under Girolomo Minotto, the Venetian *bailo* (magistrate), until Loredan arrived to replace Trevisano and take overall command.

Meanwhile, the Venetians already in Constantinople had to decide what to do. Minotto persuaded Trevisano to disobey his standing orders and remain in the Byzantine capital under the *bailo*'s authority. In December, Minotto summoned a meeting of his council, with the emperor present. Here most of the leading Venetian citizens voted to remain and it was therefore agreed that no ship should leave without the *bailo*'s permission on pain of a massive fine of 3,000 ducats. Nevertheless, on 26 February 1453 six ships from Venetian Crete and one from Venice itself defied the *bailo*'s orders and fled from the Golden Horn carrying 700 people.

If the emperor couldn't win over statesmen via diplomacy, he could still buy fighting men on the open market. He couldn't afford to pay the asking price for the most qualified gunsmiths, who sold their services to the sultan, but on 26 January 1453, Giovanni Guglielmo Longo Giustiniani, a Genoese *condottiere*, arrived in Constantinople with a contingent of 700 Latin mercenaries. The emperor promptly appointed him commander (*dux militiae*) of the entire garrison with the rank of *protostrator*, and promised him the island of Limnos as a reward for his service, "if Mehmed were repelled and returned empty-handed, without realizing his hope of seizing the city."[64]

The emperor desperately needed men-at-arms, for the city was woefully under-garrisoned. Constantinople was far past its prime; the population had dwindled, and its infrastructure was in severe decline. The great Land Walls now largely enclosed empty space, but those ramparts still stood, defying any foreign invader along their triple length on the landward side as they had for the past thousand years – Hun, Avar, Persian, Bulgar, Arab, Rus, and now Turk. The problem lay in manning those battlements. Having conducted a census, Sphrantzes recorded that, "in spite of the great size of our City, our defenders amounted to 4,773, without counting the foreigners," a total he presented to the emperor "in the greatest possible sadness and depression."[65] Constantine ordered the figures suppressed so as to not further damage morale, but the reality was plain to see; Niccolo Tignosi noted with disgust that Constantinople "was not able to muster defenders, with the exception of some pirates and Italian merchants."[66]

The most vulnerable stretch of the Land Walls was at the middle of the line, the Mesoteichion, between the Gate of Charisius and the Gate of St Romanus, where the fortifications dipped down into the valley of the Lycus River, exposing them to the fire of artillery placed on the higher ground outside the city. The emperor and Giustiniani were well aware that Mehmed was likely to focus on reducing this section with his cannon and therefore stationed themselves there with their best men. Also at risk was the emperor's palace of Blachernae at the northern end of the line where the Land Walls met the Golden Horn, for it extended out from the line of the Land Walls like a salient and so would be a natural target for undermining. This stretch was defended by the Venetian *bailo* Minotto, and the crews of five of the Venetian merchant ships in the Golden Horn. Numbering about 1,000 men, they disembarked and marched proudly to the Land Walls, flying their banners of St Mark. Included among their number were the three Bocchiardi brothers from Venice – Antonio, Paolo, and Troilo – leading a company of men they paid for out of their own pockets.

The southern section of the Land Walls stretching to the Sea of Marmara was defended by Maurizio Cattaneo at the Gate of Rhegium, Theophilus Palaiologos at the Pege Gate, and the Contarini brothers – Filippo, Jacob, and Catarino – at the Golden Gate, with Demetrius Cantacuzenos holding the section where the defenses met the Sea of Marmara.

Responsibility for the walls along the Sea of Marmara, the least-threatened sector of the defenses, was assigned to a contingent of monks under the command of Manuel Giagaro. The harbors and the most built-up urban district at the tip of the peninsula were defended by Orhan Çelebi, while the Catalan consul Pedro Juliano guarded the old palace district from a look-out tower near the Hippodrome, and Cardinal Isidore was stationed near St Sophia. The walls along the Golden Horn, where the ships were docked, were defended by their crews under the command of the Venetians, Gabriele Trevisano and Alvise Diedo. Two companies of mobile units, one under Notaras, the admiral, the other under Nicholas Goudeles, the *eparch* (urban prefect) of Constantinople, were stationed in reserve.[67]

Although on 13 April the Genoese government had authorized its citizens to assist Constantinople, the Genoese colony of Pera on the opposite shore of the Golden Horn under its governor (*podestà*), Angelo Lomellino, was officially neutral, although many residents, including Lomellino's own nephew, Imperiali, would serve with the emperor.

The garrison would conduct an active defense, though with its limited numbers had to be careful not to take undue risks. "It was easy to reckon that one Roman had to face twenty Turks," the chronicler Doukas asserted; "What would be achieved then with hand-to-hand combat and sorties?"[68]

The Ottoman army, comprising at least 80,000 men-at-arms and auxiliaries, arrived under the walls of the city on 6 April. The sultan reminded them what was at stake in this campaign: "The *ghaza* is our basic duty as it was in the case of our fathers. Constantinople, situated in the middle of our domains, protects our enemies and incites them against us. The conquest of this city is, therefore, essential to the future and the safety of the Ottoman state."[69]

Mehmed raised his banner on the high ground of Maltepe Hill, overlooking the Lycus Valley. To his right were the Anatolian troops under Ishak Pasha. To his left were the Rumelian troops under Karadja Pasha. A detachment under Zagan Pasha was stationed north of the Golden Horn to both screen Constantinople and keep a wary eye on Galata. According to Nicolo Barbaro, a Venetian eyewitness and diarist of the siege, the Ottoman fleet, which weighed anchor at Diplokionion, two miles north of the city, consisted of 145 sails, including seventy to eighty light galleys (*fustae*) and up to twenty-five heavier vessels (*parandarie*); the rest were all brigantines.

The Ottoman artillery, the best in the world at that moment, had been hauled to the city by teams of thirty wagons yoked to sixty oxen. The largest gun, a great bombard that could fire balls weighing over 650 kilograms (1,433 pounds), was escorted by a corps of 200 men to ensure that it did not slip off its carriage and by fifty skilled carpenters with 200 laborers to construct bridges for its passage over rough terrain.

The sultan lost no time in setting up his guns against the Land Walls. Three he placed outside the Pege Gate, three at Blachernae, and two at the Gate of Charisius. Four, including the largest, were reserved for the Gate of St Romanus, to maximize the advantage in relative height afforded by the Mesoteichion.[70] In the event, the great bombard was put out of action early, but the other siege guns subjected the defense to a relentless barrage. In his account of the siege, contemporary Italian author Antonio Ivani da Sarzana described how the Ottomans "heavily bombarded the wall, without a respite, for ten days and turned it to ruins; in many places they razed it."[71] The garrison was limited in its capacity to retaliate by the smaller caliber of its guns, which were outranged; by the scarcity of gunpowder; and by the nature of walls themselves, which were state of the art for an earlier, pre-gunpowder era, but now suffered structural damage to the battlements and towers from the recoil of whatever cannon had been emplaced there. Ironically, the best option for the defenders to deploy their firepower was in the breaches blasted open in the walls by the Ottoman artillery. Every time a tower or section of the wall subsided, the garrison would immediately reinforce the debris with timber and barrels filled with earth, and could defend it with guns without fear of collateral damage now that the battlements had already collapsed. Ottoman storming parties seeking to exploit the compromised sectors of the defense by scrambling through the rubble into these gaps in the fortifications found they were by no means soft targets.

All the while, Ottoman sappers were pushing forward mines under the walls. When these had advanced far enough to be detected by the garrison, from 16 to 25 May the defenders retaliated by countermining and flooding out, smoking out, or burning out the enemy tunnels before they could bring down any of the fortifications. The Ottomans also deployed a siege tower against the Pege Gate in the sector defended by Maurizio Cattaneo and his 200 Genoese crossbowmen. A sortie led by the Venetian Stornado and the Genoese Molisrus brought the tower down in flames.

On 12 April the Ottoman navy failed to force entry into the Golden Horn, which had been closed by means of a great chain stretched across the harbor mouth from the city to Galata ten days earlier. On 18 April, the defenders beat back an assault on the Land Walls with comparative ease.

On 20 April, five Genoese ships were sighted sailing north across the Sea of Marmara towards Constantinople in an attempt to run the Ottoman naval blockade with supplies of food from the island of Chios. It was too good an opportunity to miss, and almost the entire Ottoman fleet, under the personal command of its admiral, Baltoglu, set out from the harbor at Diplokionion to intercept them. The two fleets met just as the Genoese vessels were about to round the tip of Constantinople's peninsula and enter the Golden Horn. At that moment, the wind died and the five ships found themselves surrounded by a forest of enemy vessels. Their crews fought back desperately, taking advantage of the fact their ships were much higher above the waterline than the light and swift Ottoman galleys. They hurled missiles down on their attackers and held them at bay long enough for the wind to change and guide the Christian ships into the safety of the Golden Horn. Mehmed had watched the entire episode on horseback from the shore, so intent on the action he rode into the surf up to the hem of his robe. Enraged by the failure of his admiral, he had Baltoglu replaced by Hamza, the former *beylerbey* of Anatolia, who had established a good reputation for seamanship during amphibious operations supporting the siege of Thessaloniki in 1430.

On 21 April, after a day-long bombardment near the Gate of St Romanus, an entire tower and large sections of the wall on either side were brought crashing down, but the garrison plugged the gap by erecting a stockade from the rubble and with barrels packed full of rocks and earth.

Mehmed now summoned the *divan*. Halil Pasha was already advising him to abandon the siege, but the more militant faction led by Zaganos Pasha, supported by Şeyh Aq-Şemseddin, a Sufi who had become a *mürşid*, a spiritual guide to the sultan himself, was adamant Constantinople would fall if Ottoman resolve did not falter.

Mehmed, determined to follow the siege through to its end, had an ace to play. On 22 April, seventy-two ships from the Ottoman fleet were dragged overland from the Bosporus and launched into the Golden Horn, thus bypassing the chain that was blocking the harbor's entrance. Byzantine scholar aristocrat Michael Kritoboulos was one of many eyewitnesses marveling at this spectacle; "what a strange sight to behold! No one would ever believe a description, one simply had to have seen it: ships moving over land as if sailing over the sea, crews on board, with sails and all equipment!"[72]

These light vessels were not meant to assume absolute control of the harbor, as they were no match for the Venetian war galleys. They were intended to harass the defenders and to provide diversions, forcing the besieged to transfer troops that were desperately needed at the land walls, and to screen construction of a bridge across the Golden Horn from Galata to Ayvansaray. Now, the walls along the Golden Horn "were open to attack and had to be guarded," Kritoboulos noted, which was problematic because the garrison "did not have sufficient soldiers, either residents of the city or foreigners, to man the other walls; and so each soldier defended two or three battlements." Aware that it was by overwhelming precisely these defenses along the Golden Horn that the Fourth Crusade had broken into the city in 1204, the emperor was obliged "to strip the other battlements of their defenders and to transfer these men to this sector. The danger was manifest: the outer walls were emptied of the defenders and the few that remained were not sufficient to guard the abandoned walls."[73]

Determined to eliminate the threat by burning out the enemy ships, the defenders launched an amphibious operation on 28 April, two hours before daybreak. The task force comprised two fire ships escorted by two war galleys and three *fustae*. However, according to Barbaro, the galley from Trabzon commanded by Jacomo Coco, who was overly eager to attack, moved ahead of the other vessels, and broke from the planned formation. This vessel was struck by the first bombard missile that was fired and sank, taking her captain with her to the bottom of the harbor. The operation was broken off, and Ottoman artillery was now redirected towards the Christian ships sheltering in the Golden Horn, sinking one. The survivors clustered under the walls of Galata to avoid destruction. The garrison retaliated by setting up their own guns at the harbor gates to target the enemy flotilla, with some success, sinking a few Ottoman ships and forcing the rest to pull back to the north shore of the Golden Horn.

A blockade runner, disguised as an Ottoman vessel, slipped out of the harbor on 3 May to seek out the long-hoped-for relief fleet from the West. It returned twenty days later with dire news. There was no relief fleet. No help was coming. Barbaro recounted that the emperor despaired, for no one in the West was "willing to give me help against this treacherous Turk, the enemy of Christendom."[74]

Having finally been returned to the line, the great bombard went back into action on 6 May, when it started battering the walls once more. The following day, Mehmed unleashed an assault on the Land Walls, but this was beaten back by the garrison. The sultan launched another assault on 12 May. "Five thousand Turks attacked the wall around the palace to the accompaniment of the usual cries and the discordant sound of drums and trumpets," according to Barbaro, but again the assault was repulsed.

Thus far, the garrison had successfully repelled everything the enemy had thrown at them, for remarkably little cost. Anconitanus Benvenuto, the consul of Ancona, who was an eyewitness of events, reckoned by this point the defenders had only lost forty men against the 7,000 killed on the Ottoman side.[75] Even assuming these figures are exaggerated, by the end of May, the sultan had little to show for more than seven weeks of determined effort. He resolved to stake the entire campaign on one coordinated grand assault, throwing everything he had against the Land Walls while launching simultaneous amphibious assaults against the walls along the Golden Horn and the Sea of Marmara.

The city's defenders knew the supreme crisis of the siege was approaching. On 28 May, the emperor rallied his exhausted commanders with one final speech: "Well, then, my brothers and fellow soldiers, be prepared for the morning. With the grace and strength granted to you by God and with help from the Holy Trinity, in which we have placed all our hope, let us force our enemy to depart from here in shame."[76]

The garrison then took up their posts along the ramparts and stockades of the outer wall, locking off the gates to the inner wall behind them. Two hours before daylight on 29 May, the sultan ordered his ships to close in on Constantinople while he unleashed his army in three waves against the Land Walls.

The first wave of the assault consisted of the sultan's expendable irregulars, the *bashi-bazouks*, poorly trained and inadequately armed Christian renegades and adventurers from Serbia, Hungary, Germany, Transylvania, and Greece, attracted by the prospect of booty. This first wave was easily beaten back and nearly annihilated by Giustiniani's professionals. The second assault consisted of the sultan's regular *azap* Anatolian regiments, which were also repelled with heavy losses. Before the defenders could recover, the third wave, the elite janissaries, were upon them. The garrison was stretched to the limit, yet, after hours of desperate fighting, the Ottomans still had not breached the Land Walls, while the amphibious operations had also failed to penetrate into the city anywhere along the Golden Horn or the Sea of Marmara. Could the city hold?

Ultimately, the outcome of the siege would hinge on two critical moments.

Constantine had ordered one small postern gate in the inner wall, known as the Kerkoporta, remain unlocked so his men could reach their positions along the outer wall more quickly. A group of about fifty Ottoman soldiers who had broken through the outer wall discovered this gateway, rushed through it and clambered up into a tower on the inner wall along its stretch just south of the Blachernae Palace. Some janissaries forced their way to the Gate of Charisius, the highest point on the Land Walls, and raised their standard, where it was visible to the Byzantine and Latin defenders along the Mesoteichion, and to the Ottoman forces still outside the walls.

At this critical juncture, Giustiniani, who had led from the front throughout the siege, was wounded – mortally, it transpired – and withdrew from the action, the Gate of St Romanus being opened for the sake of his evacuation, only for his mercenaries to depart with him. The remaining defenders, losing heart and now aware there were Ottoman banners on the walls, began to waver. Mehmed, sensing weakness, now renewed the offensive. One janissary, a giant of a man named Hasan of Ulubat, led thirty companions in a furious assault, storming the rampart and planting the Ottoman banner. The defenders desperately rallied, killing seventeen members of this detachment and finally battering Hasan to his knees before hacking him to pieces. But more and more janissaries, rallying to this sector, began to swarm the rampart and penetrate the stockades.

It was now that the defense really began to crack as more and more men started to slip away from their posts. The trickle became a flood and finally the defense broke completely, men fighting each other to escape through the inner wall and into the city. Most of them crowded into the Gate of St Romanus, but it was so narrow and so great were the numbers frantic to escape that many were trampled to death in the crush, "so that they made a great mound of living men by the gate which prevented anyone from having passage."[77] Others, trapped against the inner wall and with nowhere to run, were massacred by the now rampant janissaries. It is likely the emperor met his end this way, although exactly how, and where, will forever remain a mystery.[78]

As more and more gates were forced, districts of the city – Petrion, Stoudios, and Psamathia – began surrendering. Terrible scenes played out as the defenseless civilian population of Constantinople was hunted down for its worth in ransoms or its value at the auction block. St Sophia, jammed with penitent noncombatants, offered the motherlode of human bounty.

Any resident of the city who still could now fled to the Golden Horn seeking passage out via the galleys on station at the harbor. Many of these vessels had lost their captains and the fighting men of their crews, who had been committed to the walls. Massively outnumbered, undermanned, and commanded by inexperienced or second-rate captains, they should have been easy prey for the Ottoman navy, and the sultan's victory consummated by the enemy being completely overwhelmed at sea as well as by land. Indeed, as Doukas notes, "if the ships of the tyrant had not been busy pillaging and looting the city, not a single [Christian] ship would have escaped."[79] But the Ottoman vessels in the Golden Horn made no attempt to engage or pursue them. When it became clear the defenses at the Land Walls had collapsed, the crews of the Ottoman ships beached their vessels on the foreshore in front of the Sea Walls and hurried into the city so as not to be left out in the scramble for loot. The main fleet under Hamza moved south from Diplokionion, but it too was more intent on plunder. That gave the Christian ships a clear run out of the harbor and into the Bosporus. This was a short-sighted policy on the part of the Ottoman crews and commanders. Reeling in the fleeing enemy would have provided them with a bonanza in slaves who would have commanded highly remunerative ransoms from their compeers in the Latin West. But the risk of taking the fleeing but formidable galleys was apparently outweighed by the lure of easy pickings within the fallen city. The sultan was enraged at the lost opportunity, but could not impose his will as the men of his navy abandoned their ships and "rushed furiously, like dogs, into the territory to search for gold, jewels, and other riches, as well as to capture merchants," Barbaro recounted; "above all, they searched the convents."[80] After standing out to sea for as long as possible in order to give any last refugees the opportunity to come aboard, the galleys set sail for the Aegean. It is a reflection on the limitations of Ottoman naval power during this period that the over-burdened flotilla passed right by Gallipoli and through the Dardanelles without incident. Among those who made it out was Giustiniani, but he died of his wound on Chios a few days after the fall of the city. Paolo Bocchiardi was slain during the final assault, but Antonio and Troilo were able to escape.

Where was the relief fleet? Alvise Longo had set sail from Venice on 19 April with only one warship, another fifteen vessels remaining in port because of a shortage of funds. A handful of them set out after 7 May, but in the event the Venetian fleet which eventually assembled in the Aegean was too late to save Constantinople; when the city fell it had proceeded no further than the Venetian naval base of Chalkis on the island of Euboea. On 11 April, Pope Nicholas V had appointed the archbishop of Dubrovnik commander of the papal fleet to go to the rescue of Constantinople, but it was still at Chios when survivors brought news of the city's fall.

Some accounts maintain the fall of Constantinople was inevitable, even fated. That perspective is incorrect. The plain fact is, Constantinople did not have to fall; it was allowed to fall. Impressive as it was, the Ottoman siege would have been rendered utterly impotent if the naval powers of the West – Venice, Genoa, Aragon, the papacy – had cooperated and acted with energy to mobilize and dispatch their fleets to the aid of the city. The Ottoman navy in 1453 was completely outclassed; had it tried to intercept the massed galleys of the Christian West, it would have been annihilated. The Sea of Marmara was an open highway, and with or without Ottoman opposition, the West could have reinforced and resupplied Constantinople at will at any time during the siege. To the bitter end, the walls still stood, and the garrison remained unbroken. As Cardinal Isidore proudly recorded, "we were few and yet we managed to fight, as long as we possessed strength."[81] But, to their eternal shame, the minimal effort required on the part of key statesmen in the West to sustain that strength never materialized.

For that reason, Constantinople now belonged to Mehmed II. As he entered St Sophia, the sultan was heard to recite a couplet of Persian poetry:

The spider serves as doorkeeper in the palace of Khosroes;
The owl sounds the changing of the guard in the fortress of Afrasijab.

This refrain, which reflected on the fall of Sasanian Ctesiphon to the *ghazi* of a previous generation, now bracketed the fall of Christian Constantinople to the House of Osman, which at this moment embodied a consummation of both the heritage of *jihad* and the inheritance of the Caesars. Truly, Mehmed had earned the sobriquet *Fātiḥ* (the Conqueror).

In the aftermath, the last vestiges of Byzantine authority were ruthlessly snuffed out. Isidore himself, wounded during the fighting on 29 May, eventually made good his escape. But the grand admiral Notaras, the Venetian *bailo* Minotto, and the Catalan consul Pedro Juliano were all executed, alongside their sons. Preferring death at his own hand, Orhan Çelebi threw himself from the Sea Walls to perish on the rocks below. George Sphrantzes bought his own way out of captivity and was able to ransom his wife, but not his two children. His son, John, was executed; his daughter, Thamar, was inducted into the sultan's harem, where she died in 1455, aged only fourteen.

George Scholarios was redeemed from slavery in Edirne and returned to Constantinople where on 6 January 1454 he was elevated as Orthodox patriarch with the name Gennadios II. Having assumed the title *Kayser-I Rum* – Caesar of Rome – the sultan, keen to emphasize continuity in his own person, fulfilled the traditional ceremonial role of the emperors, personally presenting the new patriarch with his staff of office. The ceremony took place in the Church of the Holy Apostles, the largest in the city now that St Sophia had been consecrated as a mosque; it was assigned to Gennadios as the new seat of the patriarchate. But Mehmed then expropriated the church, ordered it torn down and built in its place his own mosque, the Fatih Camii. This was symbolic of the intellectual, cultural, and spiritual death spiral that Byzantine civilization now entered in what had been its imperial core. As Gennadios lamented, "Oh, best of native cities, how can we, your dearest children, survive your loss and how can you bear to be without us? Worse, how can we endure still to be alive, when you are beyond the reach of men? For though apparently still here, you are gone forever."[82]

This agony and despair in the East was echoed by the guilt and shame of the West, where the fall of Constantinople resonated throughout Christendom for generations. As the author of the early 16th-century poem *Capystranus* lamented:

Thus is Constantyne the noble cyte wonne,
Beten donne with many a gonne,
And Crysten people slayne.[83]

3

FIRST BELGRADE, FIRST RHODES, AND OTRANTO

BELGRADE, 1456

Having definitively and at last emerged from the shadow of his father, after the fall of Constantinople, Mehmed II undertook to stamp his authority over the Ottoman state. Significantly, he ordered the execution of Grand Vizier Halil Pasha, thus ending the primacy of the old school Anatolian elite at the highest levels of administration. From that point on, most of the grand viziers were of Christian slave origin. The sultan also restructured the bureaucracy, expanded the janissary corps, created a professional artillery corps, and, with his decree in 1470 commissioning the construction of ninety-two galleys, laid the foundations of a vastly expanded Ottoman navy.

Meanwhile, the expansion of the empire continued. Opening new horizons, the sultan allied himself with the new lord of the northern Black Sea region, Haci Giray of the Crimean Tatar khanate, a successor state of the Golden Horde. However, a joint Ottoman–Tatar campaign in 1454 against Feodosia, the Genoese colony and the center of their trade in the Crimea, failed. In June, Mehmed invaded the rump Serbian state. The despot George Branković tried to oppose the Ottoman army but was defeated and his lands were devastated; he fled Smederevo to seek shelter in his Hungarian castle of Bečej.[1] The only Serbian resistance was offered by Nikola Skobaljić, who clashed with an Ottoman detachment marching in from Macedonia, winning a first encounter on 24 September near Vranja, but being bested in a second on 16 November at Trepanja, after which he was taken prisoner and impaled. After taking Ostrovica and the Serbian crown treasure deposited there, Mehmed returned to Edirne.

In response, Hunyadi led an army from Szeged to Belgrade and then across the Danube, defeating the Ottoman forces stationed at Kruševac under the command of Firuz Bey, who was taken captive, before invading Bulgaria, advancing as far as the walls of Vidin. This was a major fillip for Hunyadi, whose star had lost much of its luster after the defeats at Varna and Kosovo Polje, and who had struggled to impose internal order during his regency, failing to subdue the Bohemian mercenary warlord John Jiskra of Brandýsa, who had consolidated his control of several counties in northern Hungary, over the course of four unsuccessful expeditions against him in 1447, 1449, 1451, and 1452.

Mehmed invaded Serbia again in 1455, taking Prizren, Peć, and the key city of Novo Brdo, which fell on 1 June after a forty-day siege. In a classic manifestation of a zero-sum equation, these conquests would have significant economic as well as strategic implications, for with the fall of Novo Brdo the Ottoman state both acquired the output of the region's silver mines, the most productive in the Balkans, and correspondingly denied that output to the West. This exacerbated a system-wide economic malaise that had been afflicting Western Europe since the Black Death of the previous century. The loss of so many people to the bubonic plague had created a scarcity of labor, which naturally pushed up prices. This led to a curtailment of silver production in Europe in a bid to impose deflation, but this coincided with an increase in European demand for Eastern trade goods, which were largely paid for with silver.[2] The net impact was a decline in the available stock of silver currency in Europe, a phenomenon John Day described as the great bullion famine of the 15th century.[3] The inexorable advance of the Ottoman war machine now deprived its Western antagonists of access to the sources of mineral wealth just when they were needed most. By the 1460s, as Peter Spufford concludes, "The economy of Europe ground to a halt at every level, from the humblest... up to the great merchants."[4] The only mint in northwestern Europe that stayed open was the royal mint in the Tower of London, and the £65,000 minted in England in 1474 was only half of that issued in 1350.[5]

With the Ottomans at his gates, King Stephen Tomaševiç warned Pope Pius II that Bosnia was now the front line of Christendom:

After me he will attack the Hungarians and the Dalmatians who are subjected to Venice, and then through Carniola and Istria he will seek Italy which he aspires to rule. He often speaks of Rome, and his heart pulls him there. If the Christians permit him to obtain my kingdom, he will have the most suitable province and appropriate places to achieve his desire. I expect the first storm, and after me the

Hungarians and the Venetians will taste their fate, and not even Italy will be able to rest; this is the enemy's design. I am submitting this information to you so that you cannot say that it was not foretold, and accuse me of negligence. My father predicted the calamity which befell Constantinople to your predecessor Nicholas and to the Venetians – but he was not believed.[6]

This missive fell on receptive ears, for the West, retrospectively appalled at its lethargy during the siege of Constantinople, had been jolted into at least taking the Ottoman challenge more seriously. On 30 September 1453, Pope Nicholas V had issued a papal bull, *Etsi Ecclesia Christi*, describing Mehmed as "a rabid beast" and "a herald of the Antichrist," and commanding "all Christian princes, whatever imperial, kingly, queenly, ducal or other worldly dignity they might hold… to come to the defense of the Christian religion and of the faith with their goods and persons, as genuinely and insistently as is possible," under pain of excommunication.[7] Papal diplomats sought to persuade the powers of Western Europe to coordinate a military response. In the Holy Roman Empire, a series of imperial *diets* were convened at Regensburg (April 1454), Frankfurt (October 1454), and Wiener Neustadt (February 1455) to discuss this issue. One of the most important figures at these conclaves was papal envoy and former imperial secretary to Frederick III, Aeneas Silvius Piccolomini, bishop of Trieste and Siena. In his address to the *Diet* of Frankfurt, *Constantinopolitana Clades*, he stated simply, and accurately: "The Fall of Constantinople was a great victory for the Turks, a total disaster for the Greeks, and a complete disgrace for the Latins."[8]

In April 1454 the major Italian powers, including the Papal States, concluded the peace of Lodi, which ended more than half a century of intermittent warfare between Venice, Milan, Florence, and Naples. The guarantor of continued peace in Italy was the Holy League, formed under the aegis of the papacy to hold Ottoman aggression in check. While the West slowly drew together, the prospects for immediate direct intervention in the Balkans were limited. However, the crusading spirit in its most essential form, not directed by the magnates to serve their own ends but as an expression of the popular will, would be extraordinarily influential during the campaign season of 1456 and culminate in a dramatic and unlikely victory.

Already ill-omened, the year 1456 erupted with millenarian, even apocalyptic speculation when Halley's Comet returned on the latest cycle of its seventy-six-year sojourn around the sun, innocently impinged upon the escalating struggle for control of the Balkans. In 1470, the humanist scholar Bartolomeo Platina wrote in his *Lives of the Popes* that fourteen years earlier:

A hairy and fiery star having then made its appearance for several days, the mathematicians declared that there would follow grievous pestilence, dearth and some great calamity. [Pope Calixtus III], to avert the wrath of God, ordered supplications that if evils were impending for the human race He would turn all upon the Turks, the enemies of the Christian name. He likewise ordered, to move God by continual entreaty, that notice should be given by the bells to call the faithful at midday to aid by their prayers those engaged in battle with the Turk.[9]

While the pope sought to spin the appearance of the comet as an adjunct to ultimate Christian victory over the Ottomans, others speculated that it presaged the exact opposite. In a letter of that year addressed to Henry of Eckenfelt, the author related that:

… sometimes in the shadow of the night I would go out with the crowd; sometimes they were even armed. It was such a novelty that there was no one who did not get up to go and see the portent. In every alleyway of the city, through the streets, on the walls, and in the piazzas alike, everyone stood around in bunches. Each crowd said that the comet was a portent of something different. But all were united in sharing this one common opinion: that the comet signaled the fall of Hungary and the Slavic lands, and that future evils would soon come to ours.[10]

The Ottomans were indeed again on the move, and on this occasion, the intent of the sultan was to take the critical stronghold of Belgrade, the cornerstone of Hungary's defensive line on the Danube.

Belgrade was built on a triangular promontory at the confluence of the Danube and Sava rivers. Its defenses, already formidable when the Ottoman siege of 1440 was repulsed, had subsequently been further strengthened. The castle stood on the highest point at the tip of the promontory and was subdivided into sections that could be defended even if the rest had been taken by the besiegers. Below it lay the town, separated from the castle by strong walls, with only one fortified gate and a drawbridge leading into the citadel. On the river side, the high land on the bank offered sufficient protection against assault, and on the landward side, which was flat, the town was defended by a double wall and a moat. Due to its location, Belgrade could only be besieged from the south, but a blockade of the two rivers above the fort with sufficient naval forces could choke off the transport of additional supplies into the castle. These could only be landed at the fortified port, which was protected by a chain stretched between two towers.

When they arrived below the city on 3 July, the Ottomans immediately established a blockade, consisting of anchored vessels chained together, across the Danube. King Ladislaus had already fled Buda, but in February a *diet* had appointed Hunyadi supreme commander of the Hungarian armies. A general levy was ordered, but most of the elite, jealous of Hunyadi, remained aloof. He was able to station 5,000 troops in Belgrade, mostly mercenaries, under the command of his brother-in-law, Michael Szilágyi.

Hunyadi mustered a relief force at Szeged, the bulk of which was composed of his own personal *banderium* (division), and assembled a river fleet at Szalánkemén, where the Tisa meets the Danube. But while Hunyadi rallied the official rejoinder to the Ottoman invasion, another response was rising up from the grassroots all around him. The key individual involved was the singular figure of Giovanni da Capistrano. Born on 24 June 1386 in the Kingdom of Naples, he studied law at the University of Perugia and served as governor of that city from 1412 to 1416. He was well on track for a meritorious if conventional career when suddenly he was inspired to put all that behind him in exchange for the ascetic life of an itinerant monk. From 1420 onwards he wandered as one who, in the words of an English contemporary, "prechest Goddes words wyde In the countree, on every syde, In diverse lande," attracting huge crowds throughout the Holy Roman Empire, Bohemia, Italy, Hungary, and Poland.[11] As inquisitor in Ferrara, Sicily, Poland, Venice, Hungary, and Bohemia, he prosecuted and sentenced heretics, Jews, and especially Hussites. His unique combination of legal credentials and evangelical populism made him a useful asset to the Curia, and he would lead diplomatic missions for popes Eugene IV and Nicholas V to Milan, Burgundy, France, and Austria. In 1454, Pope Calixtus III charged the septuagenarian Capistrano with preaching the crusade and mobilizing the general public against the Ottoman threat menacing Christian Europe. And the people came when he called. A scholar cleric, John Goldener, reported on the mobilization of the faithful in Vienna: "There was not a vassal, magnate, or nobleman among them – shame on so many effeminate knights who, clinging to their pride and chasing after vanities, have neglected the hard and manly work of the soldier!" He described how "cobblers and tailors and other poor folk came along, without a head or a captain. What a pity for the king and the higher-ups... The artisans have become the soldiers!"[12]

Capistrano arrived in Belgrade with five ships full of crusaders on 2 July. Setting off again along the Danube later that same day with three ships to link up with Hunyadi, he encountered a storm that obliged him to return to the city. Had this little fleet proceeded just half a mile further downriver it would have blundered into the Ottoman galleys *en route* to Belgrade, and the entire party would have been captured or killed.

The following day, even as the Ottoman army appeared beneath the walls of Belgrade, Capistrano dispatched a desperate missive from the city to Francis Oddi, bishop of Assisi, notifying him that "today we await their siege of this fortress, because the Turks have never before been present in such power and strength," and urging him to appeal for support throughout Latin Christendom. Hungary, "if it offers no resistance, will come under the hand of the Turks, under their subjection and command," and the limitless ambition of the sultan would only continue to drive the banners of the Ottomans relentlessly onwards. The message to the potentates and people of the West was simple; "they should not wait for the day when they will have to drive the Turks from their own homes, since here is a proper and fitting place to resist them."[13]

The fields surrounding Belgrade now appeared "covered in snow, so many were the pavilions," John of Tagliacozzo, one of a small group of companions who had accompanied Capistrano on his mission, recalled in his *Relatio de Victoria Belgradensi* (*Relation of the Belgrade Victory*), published four years after the siege.[14] He described how the Ottoman siege artillery, which commenced its bombardment of the wall on 4 July, comprised "nineteen cannons so large and destructive that truly nothing in human history had ever been made like them... The stones are so large that they are some two or three palms larger than a man's embrace."[15] The multinational nature of the Ottoman military is reflected in the admission that the world's four foremost practitioners of the art of siege warfare were present at Belgrade in the service of the sultan – one a Venetian, one a German, another a Hungarian, and the fourth a Bosnian. So intense was the barrage one Ottoman galley was sunk by friendly fire from a poorly judged shot that passed over the city and landed in the Danube.

Capistrano slipped out of the city to inspire more volunteers for the Crusader host. And they came. "The poor rose up," Tagliacozzo reported; "the rich and the noble sat at home."[16] Those responding to Capistrano's appeal were indeed not the nobility but:

> ... commoners, rustics, paupers, priests, secular clerics, students, monks, brothers of various orders, mendicants, those from the Third Order of Saint Francis, hermits... We saw no horses there except those used to carry supplies, and no lances. Those who appeared covered in armor looked like David armed by Saul against Goliath. They were fully armed with swords, clubs, slings, and

staves like those that shepherds usually carry, and they all had shields. They had among them crossbows, bows, arquebuses, lead-ball springalds, iron hooks for grappling.

An Augustinian prior arrived with seven brothers of his convent, "burning with the zeal of the faith and love of the martyrs, wearing armor under their habits, girded with swords, protected with helmets, and shields across their shoulders, running to martyrdom."[17] Capistrano was extraordinarily holistic in his appeals: "All who wish to come to our aid against the Turks are our friends. Serbians, schismatics, Wallachians, Jews, heretics, and whatsoever infidels who wish to fight with us in this storm, let us embrace them as friends. The fight now is against the Turks."

"And so," Tagliacozzo concluded, "the father, inquisitor general of heretical depravity, although one who had always persecuted, uprooted, and confounded these kinds of people most severely, now refused to make any trouble for them as long as they took up arms" against the Ottoman enemy.[18]

Hunyadi and Capistrano now advanced with this vast host to Belgrade. Having established his headquarters at Zemun northwest of the city, Hunyadi drew up his regular troops on the left bank of the Danube, stationing Capistrano's volunteers on the left bank of the Sava.

On 14 July, the Hungarian river fleet arrived and broke the Ottoman naval blockade. The Ottoman fleet on the Danube upriver of Belgrade was trapped between the garrison and these newly arriving reinforcements, which sank three Ottoman galleys and captured another four. Hunyadi was able to transfer a large force from his *banderium* to reinforce the garrison inside the city; he "now not only placed on the towers of the fortress a sufficient number of infidel troops who were large, strong, and fully armed, but he also deployed a well-supplied regiment in front of every damaged breach" in walls, according to Ottoman chronicler Tursun Bey in his *Târîh-i Ebü'l-Feth* (*History of the Conqueror*).[19]

But the Ottoman siege guns continued to pound the walls, blasting additional breaches in several places. According to Capistrano, in a post-battle report to Pope Callixtus III, the Ottomans "breached the outer walls, lest I exaggerate, through perhaps thirty holes, after which they then worked to fill in the rampart and the moat surrounding the fortress of Belgrade. Having done this, they were more easily able to climb the destroyed towers and walls."[20] The garrison scrambled to dig a ditch and erect a palisade behind the collapsed sections of the wall in order to shore up the defenses prior to the imminent Ottoman assault.

This commenced in full force after sundown on 21 July. Tagliacozzo's account captures the intensity of the struggle:

> Oh, it was something unheard of! Three times the Turks fought their way in and were repelled. The Turks had made tunnels under the ground, so that they could enter secretly inside the moat. They had gathered together innumerable small objects and things to fill the moats, which were quite wide, and on one side there were already pine planks on the fallen walls. It is impossible to write about the multitude of dead Turks.[21]

Tagliacozzo was particularly impressed by the women who had joined the Crusader ranks:

> … who seemed to be not human but like lionesses, for they were armed, and carried themselves in a certain distinguished, manly way. They aided those in the fight by providing arrows, stones, and other instruments of war. They inspired the men, whether attacking or defending. They also carried the wounded down from the walls and into the castle, using their hands and their teeth to pull out the metal of the arrows. These women appeared often, engaged for long hours in this warlike work. They did not move about in the way typical of women; rather, they pressed on about their business in the fortress with manly strength.[22]

Having penetrated the walls, the Ottomans fell to looting, as "the avarice of the world began to impose itself on their hearts," Tursun Bey recorded. "And so they poured out and scattered to ransack the city, and failed to remain near to one another. Since the desire of worldly riches caused disunity to fall down upon them, they were unable to confront the enemy, who was ready and waiting in ambush."[23] Hunyadi, who had pulled the garrison back to the citadel, was able to counterattack. The savage street fighting continued to rage past dawn; Hunyadi reported to Ladislaus Garai, the palatine of Hungary, that the brawl "lasted all through the night and into the next day up to midday, such that we engaged them twice in the middle of the fortress, as if in an open field."[24]

The contest was no safer outside the walls, where the *beylerbey* of Rumelia, Karaca Bey, and the *agha* of the janissaries, Hasan Bey, were both cut down by cannon fire. The turning point was reached when Hunyadi, having ordered the production of flammable material from planks of wood soaked in tar to sulfur-saturated blankets, had this debris tossed into the moat, which was swarming with Ottoman reserves now making their way into the city, and then ignited. As Tagliacozzo recalled that moment:

Oh, God! None could flee from the face of the fire; all who were in the moat, a number that could hardly be counted, were consumed by flame, and not one of them remained alive. Those who were about to descend into the moat all retreated in fear. But those who were already in the fortress and who were struggling so mightily to take the drawbridge [to the citadel], seeing that they were now surrounded on all sides by such walls of flame, abandoned the fight. Terrified, and with great cries, they rushed to escape the fortress. Some, struck by a certain fear and blindness and confusion, believed that they could escape by leaping off the walls; they jumped into the fire, and were consumed there.[25]

With those survivors of the Ottoman assault who had penetrated into Belgrade having been hunted down and wiped out, the siege now approached its climax when Capistrano's Crusaders, caught up in an ecstasy of fervor, spontaneously burst out of the city and launched their own assault against the Ottoman camp. Ignoring Hunyadi's orders to remain within the walls, Capistrano reported to Callixtus:

> ... the crusaders cared nothing for his command and instead rushed upon the enemy, placing themselves in great danger. And when I, the least of the servants of Your Holiness, was unable to call them back from beyond the walls, I went forth into the field of battle and ran here and there, now calling them back, now encouraging them, and setting them in order so that they would not be surrounded by their enemies.[26]

Caught off guard, the Ottomans were driven out of their siege lines and back to their tents. Rallied by the sultan, and bolstered by the return of the *akinji* raiding and foraging parties, the Ottomans then counterattacked, and the Crusaders were pushed back to the trenches. The advantage had shifted yet again, and now it was the Ottomans who "had in hand defenseless infidels, now at the end of their rope," Tursun Bey related; "knaves wrapped in armor, caught between their rivers of wine, their exhaustion, and the heat of the sun."[27] The battle, hanging in the balance, was finally decided when Hunyadi led his cavalry in a sortie from the city. In the ensuing fighting the *beylerbey* of Anatolia and the khan of the Tatar auxiliaries were both killed, and the sultan himself was wounded. His army survived until nightfall but, aware it was in no condition to resume the fight the next day, under cover of darkness that evening Mehmed ordered a retreat.

News of this resounding Ottoman defeat, all the more astonishing in that it represented the triumph of enthusiastic amateurs over hardened professionals, swept like wildfire throughout Christendom.[28] It seemed the ambition of the sultan could be checked after all by those who had true faith. In his *Inter Divinae Dispensationis* of 6 August, Pope Callixtus III formally acknowledged how "the siege was lifted by crusaders and Hungarians, all of them commoners, though few in number and almost completely unarmed."[29] In his *Chronicle of Austria*, written a decade after the siege, Thomas Ebendorfer, Dean of the University of Vienna, observed:

> Where is the Roman empire, that once so thoroughly tamed the barbarian nations?
> Where are its electors, those fearsome princes?
> Where is the king of France, who wanted to be called "most Christian"?
> Where are the kings of England, Denmark, Norway, Sweden, Poland, and Bohemia?
> Where are all the powers of Germany and the East?
> Behold the unarmed farmers, the blacksmiths, fullers, tailors, and shoemakers, artisans and scholars, inspired by God, so it is believed, to their distinguished and strong acts in defense of the faith, and who in this way prove their worth as soldiers![30]

"We captured all of their catapults and their diabolical machines, through which they thought they would subjugate all of Christendom,"[31] Capistrano proudly reported to Callixtus. He conceded the outcome was a near-run thing. Belgrade was no longer a fortress, "but an open field, because it is so broken apart and totally destroyed."[32]

So far as both the victorious commanders were concerned, the time to strike was now, while the iron was hot. Hunyadi, ever optimistic the liberation of the entire Balkans was just one final victory away, wrote to Palatine Garai that, with the cream of the Ottoman army having been destroyed at Belgrade, "if anyone now only wanted to proceed with an army against the [sultan], it would be easier to occupy his realm than ever before."[33] Citing figures of more than 24,000 Ottoman dead, Capistrano urged the pope to seize the moment and take full advantage of this great victory: "Now is the time to fulfill the desire of Your Serenity, that we proceed not only to recover Greece and Europe, but to recover the Holy Land of Jerusalem, which almighty God will grant us easily, if Your Serenity will not let go of the holy desire that you have embraced."[34]

Callixtus needed little urging. He wrote with frantic energy to the magnates of Europe exhorting them to contribute towards a general crusade. One such subject was Francesco Sforza, Duke of Milan, who received a letter from the pope dated 23 August urging him to join in the crusade, "as we strive breathlessly for the total eradication of the people of Muhammad."

Now is precisely the time to pursue the victory promised to us from heaven, as the Christian faithful gather their strength and strike out against the kingdom of the Turks, which (since their leader is defeated and confused and uncertain as to what he should do and turns himself shamefully in flight) should be most easily captured... because this moment of great victory must be followed through to the final extermination of not only the Turks but of all the damned sect of the treacherous Muhammad, lest all the grace that has been granted to us from heaven somehow be dragged down by neglect... for its completion we are in need of no small amount of money. Therefore we urge Your Nobility and, in God, with all the urgency we can, we require you, that you come together with us for this most glorious labor, and that you add your forces to the effort... We do so in order that we may fight for the recovery of Constantinople, the total extermination of the infidel, and the liberation of all of Europe, and indeed that we may aspire for the recovery of the Holy Land and all of Asia, and either the restoration or conversion of the lands of the infidel to the Catholic faith, or the thorough expulsion of the infidel from them.[35]

"Shame, shame on those who think otherwise, and let them beware of the wrath of God!" the Holy Father concluded. "For the one who frustrates our plans in this matter, whoever he might be, will suffer judgment."[36]

But the strange lassitude that seemed to grip Christendom continued to apply its own tortured logic. On the one hand, if the Ottomans were in the ascendant, as after their successful siege of Constantinople, then it was too risky to go on crusade. Conversely, if the Ottomans were turned back, as after their unsuccessful siege of Belgrade, then what need was there to go on crusade? One anonymous observer conceded in the aftermath "how astonished I was that so many simple, unarmed, and poor men, untrained in war, unskilled with the bow, flew so quickly into battle." And yet, "now I am struck with even greater wonder," they noted, "that such a great sloth should begin to creep in along the frontiers (where the defense of the faith ought to be most useful!)," and that now, "everyone should turn back to their own business."[37]

In any event, the opportunity to follow up on breaking the siege of Belgrade had already passed. Disease was rampant in the Crusader camp – the negative corollary of assembling a host of amateurs with no experience of maintaining even minimal standards of hygiene while on campaign. Hunyadi was among those afflicted, and he died on 11 August. Capistrano died ten weeks later on 23 October, and was interred in the convent of the Observant Friars Minor in the town of Ujlak.

The death of Hunyadi unleashed a new phase in the smoldering power-struggle at the Hungarian court, where his enemies sought to dispose of his family, especially his sons Laszlo and Matthias, and divide up the Hunyadi estates among themselves. The anti-Hunyadi faction received critical support from King Ladislaus, who, after being crowned king of Bohemia in Prague on 28 October, appointed his uncle, Ulrich II of Cilli, as the new captain general. On 9 November, Laszlo Hunyadi trapped Ladislaus and Cilli when they arrived at Belgrade, murdering the captain general and holding the king hostage until Ladislaus confirmed Laszlo as captain general and swore he would not be punished for Cilli's death. Naturally, the moment he regained the upper hand, the king had the two Hunyadi brothers and their entourage, including the influential Bishop John Vitéz, arrested on 14 March 1457. Two days later, Laszlo was beheaded in the main square of Buda before the entire court.

Civil war now raged between the king and the party of Hunyadi, led by his widow, Elizabeth, and her brother, Michael Szilágyi. Matthias was taken as the king's hostage, first to Vienna and then to Prague, where the king died of a sudden illness on 23 November 1457. Matthias's mother and uncle arrived at a peace agreement with the hostile Palatine Garai, who had enforced the death penalty against Laszlo only a few months earlier. The Garai clan were now willing to accept the accession of Matthias, provided he married the daughter of the palatine and did not wreak vengeance on his brother's murderers. The magnates and prelates agreed to his election, and on 24 January 1458 the nobility proclaimed the fifteen-year-old Matthias king. The *diet* appointed his uncle Szilágyi as regent for five years.

Barely five months after his election the oligarchs, supported by the regent Szilágyi, conspired against the king, but Matthias reacted swiftly, dismissing the principal plotters, the palatine and Nicholas Újlaki, *voivode* of Transylvania and *ban* of Slavonia, from their offices; his uncle Szilágyi was forced to resign as regent in the summer of 1458 and was arrested a few weeks later for his subversive activities. In response, twenty-five magnates, led by the dismissed Garai, rebelled against Matthias and elected Emperor Frederick III – who had maintained the holy crown of St Stephen in his possession since 1440 – as king of Hungary at Nemetujvar on 27 February 1459.

Szilágyi fell into Turkish captivity at the end of 1460 and was beheaded on the orders of the sultan. The conflict between Matthias and Frederick III lasted another five years until the peace of Wiener Neustadt on 19 July 1463, in which the emperor was obliged to hand over the crown of St Stephen, although at an exorbitant price; Matthias had to pay 80,000 gold florins (two-fifths of the royal revenues in 1454) for the crown and for the town of Sopron, mortgaged twenty-two years earlier by his mother, Queen Elizabeth. Furthermore, the emperor kept the title of king of Hungary, and he or his son Maximilian retained the right to inherit the throne should Matthias die without issue.[38]

SKANDERBEG

In the aftermath of the failed siege of Belgrade, Ottoman accounts were careful to downplay the extent of the disaster. Tursun Bey described the campaign as "a holiday for the Muslims" (*ehl-i Đslama bayram*). Emphasizing that the stronghold was "almost" conquered, he explained that the "merciful *pâdishah* was satisfied with this clear victory" and fully intended to return at the opportune moment in order to complete the reduction of Belgrade, which he regarded as his legitimate prey (*av kılınmış sikârumdur*). In any event, through the death of Hunyadi, the sultan's primary intention, namely "the death of the rival" (*katl-i rakîb*), had been realized.[39]

Whether it was his legitimate prey or not, Mehmed never did return to Belgrade. His focus shifted to resolving the ongoing insurrection in Albania, which meant settling an old score. Mehmed had accompanied his father on Murad's last campaign, against the elusive Skanderbeg. On 14 May 1450, the Ottomans had commenced the siege of Krujë. Delegating command of the garrison to Vrana Konti, Skanderbeg had remained at large, constantly harassing the besiegers until on 26 October the sultan was forced to break off and withdraw to Edirne before winter set in and he was trapped in the mountain passes. It was a disappointing end to Murad's storied career, as he died a few months later. Mehmed succeeded to the throne, but the experience can only have rankled.

Skanderbeg, meanwhile, signed the Treaty of Gaeta with King Alfonso V on 26 March 1451, by which he was formally recognized as a vassal of Aragon in exchange for military aid. The following year, Skanderbeg scored two more successes against a twin-pronged Ottoman invasion. At Modrič on 21 July, he routed one wing of the Ottoman advance under Hamza Pasha, who was captured. At Meçad he outflanked and crushed the other wing under Tahip

Pasha, who was killed. In 1453, Mehmed ordered yet another army to bring Albania to heel. On the dark and stormy night of 22 April, Skanderbeg assaulted the Ottoman camp at Polog, scattering the enemy and killing their commander, Ibrahim Pasha.

In 1455, Skanderbeg attempted to reduce the stronghold of Berat, which had been claimed by the Ottomans in 1449. However, his brother-in-law, Karl Muzaka Thopia, who had been delegated responsibility for the siege, was outmaneuvered and killed by an Ottoman relief force from Edirne whose commander, Isa Bey Evrenos, was an old hand at warfare in Albania, having crossed swords with Arianiti as far back as 1434. Much of Skanderbeg's army was destroyed, and in the aftermath one of his key subordinates, Moisi Golemi, defected to the sultan. In 1456, Mehmed sent Golemi back into Albania at the head of an Ottoman army, but Skanderbeg defeated him at the Battle of Oranik on 18 May. Subsequently spurned by the Ottomans for his failure, on top of his faithlessness, Golemi threw himself on Skanderbeg's mercy. The two were reconciled and Golemi served loyally until his death.

The same could not be said for Hamza Kastrioti, Skanderbeg's nephew and right-hand man since the inception of the struggle in 1443, who defected to the Ottomans in 1456 after his hopes of inheriting the Kastrioti title evaporated with the birth of a son to Skanderbeg, George Kastrioti II. He returned to Albania in the summer of 1457 in co-command of an Ottoman army with Isa Bey Evrenos. Once again, Skanderbeg refused to meet an invasion by offering battle until the circumstances were in his favor. Having dispersed his fighters and gone to ground for months, he concentrated his forces to confront the enemy at Albulena on 2 September. Though massively outnumbered, he split his army into three divisions in order to hit the Ottoman camp from multiple directions simultaneously. Isa Bey Evrenos was forced to flee in the chaos, while Hamza Kastrioti was captured.

In the wake of this, perhaps his greatest victory, on 23 December 1457 Pope Calixtus III declared Skanderbeg a captain general of the Curia with the title *Athleta Christi* (Champion of Christ), affirming, "We see Skanderbeg standing, almost alone, as a stout bastion against the fury of the unbridled Turks, who has barred their entry, that they may not burst into Christendom."[40] Skanderbeg's Italian connections led to his playing an important role in the succession war following the death of Alfonso V, his campaign in the Kingdom of Naples during 1461 being decisive in confirming the succession of Ferdinand I.

Upon his return to Albania, Skanderbeg swiftly demonstrated he had lost none of his edge against the Ottomans, smashing no fewer than three separate invasions in the space of one year. The first, under the command of Sinan Pasha, was defeated on the Macedonian border at Mokra. The second was defeated in Ohrid, its commander, Hasan Bey, being captured. The third, under Karaza Bey, was defeated at Skopje. Exasperated, Mehmed agreed to a ten-year truce, effective from April 1463.

This ceasefire was not destined to survive to the end of the year for, finally, it had dawned on key decision makers in the West that Albania represented a critical beachhead that would allow for concerted anti-Ottoman action in the Balkans. On 20 August 1463, Venice not only renewed the 1448 peace treaty but did so on terms more favorable to Skanderbeg. This was an opening gambit in a grand enterprise that had been slowly gathering momentum for years. The prime mover was Pope Pius II. At the Council of Mantua on 26 September 1459 he called for collective Christian action against the Ottomans. On 14 January 1460 he proclaimed the official inception of a crusade that was to last for three years.

Nothing was accomplished during that period, for as always, the monarchs and republics of Europe prioritized the immediate physical security of their own sovereign states over the abstract collective defense of Christendom as a whole. Participation in a crusade carried with it a triple risk. First, for a state to antagonize the Ottomans might result in the loss of trade and other privileges in a best case scenario, and in the worst case, bring the wrath of the sultan down upon its head next. Second, the nature of war guaranteed a large proportion of any expeditionary force dedicated to a crusade would never return home, and there was a distinct possibility the entire army would be wiped out. Third, any state contributing men and materiel to a venture against the distant Porte would be leaving its own borders invitingly open, and there were no guarantees other states within the cockpit of Europe would not take advantage of the opportunity. Thus it was, Pius lamented, that "no king could be found who did not stand in terror of his neighbor and fear to leave his own house empty."[41]

But the dogged determination of the pope did eventually lead to a bilateral alliance being forged between Hungary and Venice on 12 September 1463 at Petrovaradin, and a trilateral agreement being arrived at between the Papal Sates, Venice, and Duke Philip III (the Fair) of Burgundy on 19 October in Rome. This was followed three days later by the papal bull *Ezechielis prophetae*, calling on all Christians for service in a crusade. The able-bodied (*validus*) were invited to come in person and serve for six months, while others could send surrogates, with up to ten sponsors permitted for each combatant. The crusader host would muster at Ancona for a scheduled departure to the far side of the Adriatic on 5 June 1464. Such was the enthusiasm of Pius to the venture he pledged to "lay down our life for our flock since in no other way can we save the Christian religion from being trampled by the forces of the Turk. We will equip a fleet as large as the resources of the Church will permit. We will embark, old as we are, and racked with sickness. We will set our sails and voyage to Greece and Asia."

The pope undertook to ensure that those who answered the call to arms would be able to find shipping at a fair price at Venice. "If the Hungarians receive aid they will attack the Turks energetically with all their forces," the pope insisted. He anticipated France, the Holy Roman Empire, Castile, Portugal, and Genoa would all contribute; even the Venetians, "although they have promised nothing publicly, when they see the Crusade actually ready will surely not fail us nor endure to seem inferior to their ancestors." Poland, threatened by the Ottoman encroachment on Moldavia, "will not dare to desert their own cause." Even the apostate Hussites "we shall be able to hire." Though radiating optimism, the Holy Father was still realistic; "England, now racked with civil war, holds out no hope, nor does Scotland, remote as it is at Ocean's farthest bounds. Denmark, Sweden and Norway also are too far away to be able to send soldiers and they have no money to contribute, as they are content with fish alone."[42] With the prospect of receiving active support for the first time in his confrontation with the intractable enmity of the Porte, on 27 November Skanderbeg answered the papal summons to a crusade by declaring war on the Ottomans. In the grand strategic plan envisaged by Pius, he was to attack the Ottomans from the west while the Hungarians drove against them from the north and the Venetians harried them in the Aegean.

But the date set for departure from Ancona passed before the pope had even left Rome on 18 June 1464. Throughout June and July Matthias clamored for news of action so that he could launch his land campaign. Those crusaders arriving at Ancona had to contend with stifling midsummer heat; a shortfall in accommodation, food, and water; the outbreak of plague; and a lack of clear direction. Doge Cristoforo Moros didn't arrive with the Venetian galleys until 12 August. The troops Philip sent under his bastard son, Anthony, engaged in a diversion to Portuguese Ceuta en route to Italy.

Pius died on 14 August 1464, and the crusade immediately began to fall apart. When the Burgundian force under Anthony called in at Marseilles for extra galleys and the news reached them of the pope's untimely demise, the entire expedition was promptly canceled. As Cardinal Jacopo Ammannati Piccolomini lamented, "such was the fruitlessness of the congress at Mantua, such the empty and pointless hope of setting out against the Turks."[43]

Venetian support for Skanderbeg, including a mixed force of mercenary light cavalry (*stradioti*) and hand gunners under the *condottiere* Antonio da Cosenza, had helped him maul the Ottoman garrison of Ohrid in September 1464. After that, he was essentially left, once again, to his own devices, as the Venetians reoriented their military assets in an increasingly frantic bid to hold on to their existing colonial assets, while the Hungarians dropped out of the war entirely. When the new Pope Paul II wrote to Corvinus sharply criticizing him for arriving unilaterally at a truce with Porte in 1465, the king wrote back to point out, "if your holiness really wants to stop me making peace with the enemies of the faith, he has to give me the means to keep the war going."[44]

Undaunted, in April 1465 Skanderbeg defeated yet another Ottoman army, this one under the *sanjak-bey* of the *sanjak* of Ohrid, Ballaban Bader Pasha, at the Battle of Vaikal.[45] Skanderbeg defeated Bader Pasha again in a rematch at Vaikal later that year, and then another Ottoman army, under the command of Jakup Bey, at Kashari. The following year, Mehmed took personal command of operations in Albania, marching at the head of his army to invest Krujë. Appointing Bader Pasha with responsibility for siege operations, the sultan departed in June to oversee construction of a powerful fortress at Elbasan intended to establish a permanent Ottoman presence in the heart of Albania. Repeating his tactics from the first siege, Skanderbeg delegated command of the garrison to a trusted subordinate, in this instance Tanush Thopia, while he remained at large with his mobile detachments. Skanderbeg spent the winter abroad in Italy in fruitless attempts to secure desperately needed funding for his war effort. Upon his return he was able to reactivate the League of Lezhë with the support of key warlords like Lekë Dukagjini. Advancing to the relief of Krujë, on 19 April 1467 he employed his established tactic of multiple coordinated assaults to defeat a detached Ottoman column, capturing its commander, Ballaban's brother Yonuz, and his son, Haydar. Four days later, he attacked and broke the Ottoman forces besieging Krujë. Ballaban was killed in the process and his army fragmented; most of those who survived the initial battle and fled into the surrounding mountains were tracked down and annihilated. In the aftermath, Skanderbeg moved on Elbasan but, lacking a siege train, couldn't reduce it.

Mehmed had to again personally intervene in Albania the following year. Rebuffed once more at Krujë, he unleashed his fury on the surrounding villages. The core territories loyal to Skanderbeg were made to pay for their fealty; in Mati and Dibër, between two-thirds and three-quarters of the entire population was either killed or abducted into slavery.[46] Skanderbeg escaped, however, and early the following year convened the surviving leaders of the resistance to strategize for the next phase of the struggle. However, he passed away on 17 January 1468. He was buried in the cathedral of St Nicholas, where he had founded the League of Lezhë twenty-four years earlier. When the Ottoman troops took the site several years later, they opened Skanderbeg's tomb and pilfered his bones with superstitious reverence, wearing them as amulets.

Lekë Dukagjini took command of the League of Lezhë and the war continued. Skanderbeg's son, George Kastrioti, held out in Krujë until 1474 when he ceded the castle to the Venetians. On 16 June 1478, Krujë was finally starved into submission by Mehmed, who had participated in the siege led by his father twenty-eight years earlier. The survivors of the garrison were put to the sword. The Ottoman vise was closing. When Venice ratified the Treaty of Constantinople on 25 April 1479, conceding the city of Shkodër, the war for Albania was effectively over.[47]

DRACULA

The Ottoman setback at Belgrade in 1456 could not save Serbia, which was subsumed in 1459. This was followed by the subjugation of the despotate of the Morea in 1460 (with the exception of Monemvasia, which held out until it was acquired by Venice in 1464) in Greece, and the Empire of Trabzon on the north coast of Anatolia in 1461.

While these last, scattered remnants of the Byzantine Empire each collapsed in the course of a single campaign, the death of Serbia was a protracted one. The despot, George Branković, died on Christmas Eve 1456, being succeeded by his son Lazar, the other two sons, Stephen and Gregory, being considered ineligible; accused of plotting against Sultan Murad II in 1441, both had been blinded on his orders. Lazar may have retained his eyesight, but he apparently lacked vision; after he poisoned their mother, Despina Irina in May 1457, his siblings fled Serbia, Stephen escaping to Hungary and then to Albania, while Gregory and his sister Mara, the former sultana, sought refuge with the Ottomans,

Stephen seized the throne after the sudden (and presumably violent) death of Lazar on 20 January 1458. However, his sister-in-law, Lazar's widow Helena Palaiologina, arranged the marriage of one of her daughters to Stephen Tomašević, a prince of Bosnia. She thus managed to secure the throne for her new son-in-law when Tomašević's father Stephan Tomaš Kotromanić, the king of Bosnia, in alliance with King Matthias Corvinus of Hungary, dethroned Stephen Branković on 8 April 1459. After seeking sanctuary in Albania, the following year Stephen married Angelina Arianit Komneni, sister of Skanderbeg's wife Donika Kastrioti. Stephen finally moved to Venice before retiring to Friuli, where he died in 1476.

Meanwhile, Gregory, who naively believed he could ascend to the Serbian throne with Ottoman support, participated in the pacification campaign of Grand Vizier Mahmud Pasha Angelović in Serbia in the spring and summer of 1458, which had annexed Resava and Golubac, reducing Serbia to little more than Smederevo and its environs, while his illegitimate son, Vuk Grgurević, contributed to the Ottoman incursions on Hungarian territory in Srem and southern Banat. In the event, Gregory was sidelined to a monastery in 1459 after Mehmed ordered an army under the command of Grand Vizier Angelović to impose direct Ottoman control. Smederevo was taken in June 1459; after a reign of just two months, Stephen Tomašević fled back to Bosnia, and Serbia ceased to exist as an independent state. Belated Hungarian intervention in 1460 came to grief when Michael Szilágyi, uncle to King Matthias and one of the heroes of the Belgrade campaign in 1456, was defeated in battle by Mihaloğlu Ali Bey, captured, and dragged to his execution in Constantinople.

Many Serbians found refuge in Hungary, which welcomed the additional manpower they offered along the frontier. Vuk Grgurević became a retainer of Matthias Corvinus, who he served loyally in battle alongside other Serb exiles, the Jakšić brothers Dmitar and Jovan, against the king's enemies during campaigns in Bohemia (1468–71) and Poland (1473–74) and against Emperor Frederick III (1477–79). In 1476, he played a prominent role in the siege and capture of the key Ottoman fortress at Šabac. He then rode with *voivode* Vlad Ţepeş (Dracula) of Wallachia in a raid that seized, looted, and torched the fortresses and towns of Srebrenica, Kučlat, and Zvornik. In the summer of that year, Vuk and several other Hungarian commanders, including Dmitar Jakšić, defeated the Smederevo *sanjak-bey* Mihaloğlu Ali Bey at Požežena on the Danube while returning from a raid into Banat. Vuk and one of the Jakšić brothers led the Serbian light cavalry squadrons in the Battle of Breadfield (Kenyérmező) in Transylvania on 13 October 1479. At the end of the same year, alongside the *ban* of Croatia and Slavonia and the *ban* of Jajce, Vuk penetrated to and devastated the city of Sarajevo.

Vuk and Jovan Jakšić also participated in the November 1481 campaign of Paul Kinizsi, the Hungarian Count of Temes County in Serbia, Vuk supporting the naval forces under Ladislaus Rozgonyi that defeated the Ottoman flotilla on the Danube, enabling the majority of the Hungarian forces to cross the river.

After Kinizsi and Jakšić beat and killed the *voivode* of Golubac, the Hungarian army took the city of Kruševac, subsequently returning north of the Danube with tens of thousands of Serbian Christians, who were settled on Hungarian territory (mainly in Banat). In September 1482, Vuk was among the Hungarian commanders who near Bečej successfully beat back another *akınji* raid from the Smederevo *sanjak* into the territory of Banat. The last known Battle of Vuk with the Ottomans occurred at the Una River in October 1483, when he, the Croatian *ban* Matthias Geréb, and Count Bernardin Frankopan defeated *akınji* raiders returning from an incursion into Croatia, Carinthia, and Carniola. Liberally rewarded with castles and estates by a grateful Matthias Corvinus, Vuk died in 1485. Serb exiles would continue to serve the Hungarian state with distinction throughout the constant low-intensity war of raid and counter-raid that characterized life along the Ottoman frontier into the 16th century.[48]

As Eastern Europe convulsed in violence after the death of Hunyadi, there was one man whose blood-soaked legend would ultimately eclipse that of any other warlord to emerge from a violent age: Vlad III, *voivode* of Wallachia, better known to history as Dracula.

His story starts with that of his father, also named Vlad, an illegitimate son of *voivode* Mircea I of Wallachia, who is first referenced in the texts during the Ottoman siege of Constantinople in 1422. He subsequently sought to claim the throne of Wallachia, but, finding little support, by 1431 he had relocated to Nuremberg, where he became a member of the Order of St Ladislaus and of the Order of the Dragon, a chivalric order instituted by King Sigismund, hence his moniker, Vlad *Dracul* (the Dragon). In the same year, an Ottoman invasion killed the *voivode* of Wallachia, Dan II. Vlad was again passed over when the nobility (*boyars*) elected Alexander Aldea to succeed. The new *voivode* refused to pay tribute to the Porte, and so another Ottoman invasion resulted in the conquest of the fortresses at Giurgiu and Turnu.

Aldea died in 1436. With military help from King Sigismund and supported by some of the *boyars*, Vlad crossed the Carpathian Mountains in September 1436 and at last took the throne as *voivode* Vlad II. His real power was limited; having accepted Ottoman suzerainty, Vlad was summoned to Brusa in 1442, where he was locked up. While his elder son, Mircea, remained in Wallachia and was acknowledged as *voivode*, his younger sons, Vlad and Radu, were taken as hostages by the Ottomans and maintained under close supervision, first at isolated Egrigöz in Anatolia, ultimately at court in Edirne. In 1444, Vlad took back his throne with Ottoman support in exchange for pledging an annual tribute of 10,000 gold ducats and 500 boys for the *devshirme* to the Porte. At great personal risk – Vlad and Radu were still under the sultan's knife – he contributed a Wallachian detachment under Mircea to the crusade of 1444. But Hunyadi never forgave him for the brief incarceration in the wake of the defeat at Varna, and in 1447, the Hungarians crossed again into Wallachia in support of another claimant to the title of *voivode*, Vladislav II, whose Danesti line rivaled Vlad's in terms of legitimacy. In late November 1447, Vlad and his son Mircea were defeated in battle somewhere south of the capital of Târgoviște. Mircea was captured by the *boyars* and leading citizens of Târgoviște, who ripped his eyes out before burying him alive. Vlad, who fled after the battle, was pursued and assassinated in the marshes of Bălteni.[49]

Ironically, because Vladislav was the Hungarian candidate, the Ottomans then released their hostage, the eldest surviving son of Vlad *Dracul*, Vlad *Dracula* (Son of the Dragon), in order for him to advance their cause in Wallachia as a legitimate alternative *voivode*. When Vladislav accompanied Hunyadi on campaign in September 1448, Dracula, taking advantage of his rival's absence, entered Wallachia with Ottoman support in early October and seized the throne as Vlad III. However, his reign was terminated within two months. After Hunyadi was defeated at the Battle of Kosovo, Vladislav returned with the remnant of his army, enough to force Vlad back into Ottoman territory.

Vlad spent the next several years wandering in exile before reconciling with Hunyadi, who had fallen out with Vladislav. When Mehmed moved on Belgrade in 1456, Hunyadi ordered Vlad to remain at Sibiu where he could threaten the Ottoman right flank. Vlad, who was plotting to invade Wallachia, moved ahead with his own plans when Mehmed was defeated. On 22 July 1456, Vlad led a small army of mercenaries into Wallachia, where they were intercepted by Vladislav and his men near Târgșor. According to folklore, the rivals agreed to settle their dispute in single combat. One way or another, Vladislav was dead by the end of that summer and Vlad had returned to the throne as *voivode*.

The legend of Vlad Dracula has been embellished by propaganda, both his own and that of his enemies, to the point where it becomes difficult to parse fact from fiction. However, Vlad's propensity for sadistic cruelty must have been grounded in some truth in order for his reputation to stand out in an environment so saturated with violence as the medieval Balkans. The titles with which he was endowed – *Kaziklu Bey* (Impaler Prince) by the Ottomans, *Tepes* (Impaler) by his own subjects – were well earned.

Wallachia was nominally an Ottoman client state. However, opportunistic and arbitrary as he was otherwise, Vlad was consistently anti-Ottoman, and by 1461 his tribute to the Porte, both in ducats and young boys for service in the

129

janissary corps, was years in arrears. Outmaneuvering an Ottoman attempt to apprehend and depose him, he launched a preemptive winter raid into Ottoman territory along the south bank of the frozen Danube. His intention was to degrade the Ottoman capacity to retaliate by inflicting severe damage on the harbor facilities of the Danube, disrupting Ottoman recruiting grounds, and undermining his domestic rivals who had been endowed with fiefs by the sultan in order to cultivate a pro-Ottoman faction at court.

In pursuit of these objectives, Vlad rampaged through the Ottoman frontier. In a message to Corvinus from Giurgiu on 11 February 1462 he boasted of having killed 23,884 people in these actions. His own very precise figures listed 6,414 left dead at Giurgiu; 343 at Orşova; 6,840 at Dârstor, Cartal, and Dridopotrom; 1,350 at Obluciţa and Novoselo; 840 at Vectrem; 630 at Turtucaia; 210 at Marotin; "384 were killed at Turnu, Batin, and Novigrad; at Sistov and in two other villages near it, 410 were killed; likewise, the crossing point at Nicopolis was burned and completely destroyed, the same at Samnovit; and at Ghighen 1,138 were killed; at Rahova 1,460 were killed, and, likewise, the crossing point was completely burned." In the course of these actions, "at the above places where there were crossing points, they were burned and destroyed, the people, men, women, children, and babies were all killed, and in all these places nothing remained." The listed figures included only those whose heads "were brought to our officials who were everywhere; but those who were not presented to them, or who were burned in their houses, could not be counted, because there were so many."[50]

Vlad was only too aware Wallachia could not stand alone against the wrath of the sultan. He urged Corvinus to offer support against the Ottoman response to his provocations that would inevitably come during the summer campaign season: "Your Majesty should know that we have broken our peace with them [the Ottomans], not for our own benefit, but for the honor of Your Majesty and the Holy Crown of Your Majesty, and for the preservation of Christianity and the strengthening of the Catholic faith… And if, God forbid, this war goes badly for us, and this country of ours perishes, no more will Your Highness benefit from it, because it will be detrimental to Christianity as a whole."[51]

While Vlad mobilized by hiring mercenaries, raising the banners (*steaguri*) of the loyal *boyars*, and drawing on the militias maintained by local magistrates (*knezi*), Mehmed ordered Grand Vizier Mahmud Pasha to take the Wallachian port of Brăila. This was accomplished, but Mahmud overreached by undertaking raids against the surrounding villages and farms. Vlad descended on the Ottoman rearguard during one such *razzia* and badly mauled it.

By now, Vlad's reputation was beginning to spread throughout the Christian world. An English pilgrim to the Holy Land, William of Wey, who had happened to sojourn on the island of Rhodes on his way home, remarked on how the Knights Hospitaller "had *Te Deums* sung to the praise and honor of God who had granted such victories."[52] Pope Callixtus III was inspired enough to conceive of Vlad as the cutting edge of a new crusade. The Venetian representative at Buda, Pietro Tommasi, expressed his hope to the republic's senate that once the promised subsidies were sent from Rome and Venice on 4 March 1462, "the Hungarian king will do all he can to help Dracula… He promised that he would descend at the head of his army and cross into Transylvania."[53] This was wishful thinking. Not only did Hungary fail to stir on Wallachia's behalf, Poland and Moldavia joined in a de facto alliance against Vlad. On 22 June, with Ottoman naval support, Stephen III (the Great), *voivode* of Moldavia, attacked Kilia, but failed to seize it.

Mehmed, meanwhile, had led his army out of Constantinople in person on 17 May, marching north from Edirne along the Via Militaris to Sofia and from there to Nicopolis, where the Ottomans had to build new harbor facilities and a pontoon bridge with construction materials brought by their fleet.[54] The Ottoman vanguard, led by Mahmud Pasha, crossed at Vidin under the cover of darkness on the night of 3–4 June. The Wallachian troops holding the northern bank of the Danube put up significant resistance, desperately trying to delay the crossing attempts, seeking to buy time for their *voivode's* preparations as well as allow civilians to be evacuated to the northern, less accessible regions of the land. However, they were ultimately driven off by Ottoman artillery, and the *akinji* raiders under the command of Mihaloğlu Ali Bey were unleashed in Wallachian territory. These inflicted some sharp reverses on any Wallachian contingents unable to counter or escape their relentlessly aggressive incursions. According to Tursun Bey, upon returning to camp after one successful encounter, after "loading the heads of the infidels on the files of the camels and mules, a head was set up on the lance of each warrior, each lance seemed like a snake with a human head."[55]

Vlad pulled back, ordering a scorched-earth policy along the line of march of the sultan's army, and carrying out repeated hit-and-run attacks into its flanks, harassing the lengthening Ottoman logistics chain and targeting isolated foraging parties, which had an unnerving tendency to disappear. Unwilling to risk a set-piece battle, he staged an assault on the Ottoman camp south of Târgoviște on the night of 16–17 June with the specific intention of decapitating the enemy command structure by eliminating the sultan himself. According to the Byzantine historian Chalkokondyles, the attack went in at 11pm on a dark, moonless night:

"At first there was great terror in the camp, as the sultan's men believed that some large foreign army had attacked them, coming from abroad, and they believed that they were utterly doomed, and were reduced to great fear and trembling. For Vlad marched with torches and horns, to signal the attack," and "the Turks became terrified and were paralyzed, each staying where his tent was pitched."[56] Konstantin Mihailović, a janissary who was present in the sultan's camp, never forgot the near anarchy of that affray, how "the Wallachians striking us in the night they beat and killed men, horses, and camels and cut down tents, so that they killed several thousand Turks and did the [sultan] great harm. And other Turks fleeing before them towards the janissaries, the janissaries also beat back and killed so as not to be trampled by them."[57]

The Wallachian objective was the sultan's tent, but in the darkness and confusion they fell upon the tents of his viziers. Initially thrown into confusion by the impetus of this sudden attack, the janissaries soon regrouped, and the deeper Vlad penetrated into the camp, the more he risked becoming entangled in the snarl of tents, pack animals and enemy troops. Breaking off the assault, he rode out to the east at dawn.

After more than two weeks of slow advance towards Târgovişte, the Ottomans finally arrived at the outskirts of the capital. It was here they finally uncovered the mystery of what had happened to so many of their missing comrades. As Chalkokondyles described it:

There were large stakes there on which, as it was said, about twenty thousand men, women, and children had been spitted, quite a sight for the Turks and the sultan himself. The sultan was seized with amazement and said that it was not possible to deprive of his country a man who had done such great deeds, who had such a diabolical understanding of how to govern his realm and its people. And he said that a man who had done such things was worth much. The rest of the Turks were dumbfounded when they saw the multitude of men on the stakes. There were infants too affixed to their mothers on the stakes, and birds had made their nests in their entrails.[58]

Mehmed and his army now headed eastwards towards Brăila. Vlad launched a second major night assault against the Ottoman camp near Buzău on the evening of 22–23 June. "On a dark night, his heart full of wickedness and accompanied by his Infidel army, he flew like a black cloud toward the army of the wise sultan, attacking him," Sa'adeddin Mehmed Hodja Efendi recorded in his *Tadj ut-Tewarikh* (*Crown of Histories*). The battle was a sanguinary one, indeed; by dawn "an ocean of blood had covered the earth in those places" where the fighting was fiercest, "so that no matter what direction his horse took he had to walk in blood and on wounded bodies."[59] But again, Vlad was frustrated in his attempt to eliminate the sultan. After linking up with the fleet at Brăila, where he celebrated the feast of Bayram marking the end of Ramadan on 28 June, Mehmed set out on the return march to Edirne, where he arrived on 11 July.

Vlad had successfully faced down the mighty Ottoman sultan, but from this pinnacle of success his descent would be sudden, anticlimactic, and complete. Wallachia had been left exhausted and depleted by the campaign, and Mehmed had a trump card left to play – his candidate for the throne as *voivode*, Vlad's brother Radu the Handsome, who was able to win over many of the disaffected *boyars*. With the tide running against him, Vlad retreated southeast along the Argeș River to Poienari. When placed under siege he slipped out and crossed the border into Hungary to seek support. But, as Tursun Bey gloated, "Trying to escape from the lion's claws, he had chosen the claws of a bird of prey."[60] Instead of offering aid, Corvinus ordered Jan Giskra, the commander of his Black Army, to arrest Vlad on trumped-up charges of collusion with the Ottomans. The erstwhile *voivode* would be kept imprisoned in Hungary, mostly at the city of Visegrád, for the next dozen years. But this was not the end of his saga.

THE WIDER WAR

The fall of Constantinople and the subsequent ominously persistent two steps forward, one step back progress of Ottoman expansion in Europe was responsible for a spate of alarmist, even apocalyptic literature throughout the Latin-speaking West. Authors such as Antoine Marini of Grenoble, *Tractatus pacis toti christianitati fiendae* (*A tract for making peace throughout Christendom*), 1463; Cardinal Bessarion, *Orationes contra Turcas* (*Orations against the Turks*), 1471; Philippus Buonacorsi Callimachus, *Ad Innocentium VIII de bello Turcis inferendo oratio* (To Innocent VIII: An address concerning bringing war to the Turks), 1490; Feliks Petančić, *Libellus de modo belli Turcis ingerendi* (*A little book concerning the manner of waging war against the Turks*), 1502; and Jacob Wimpfeling, *Epitome rerum Germanicarum* (*Epitome of German things*), 1505, all made the same point; Christian disunity was opening the door to the collective enemy.

In the Aegean, Mehmed attacked various islands, including Kos, clashed with the Genoese on Chios, and took Limnos in 1456, the inhabitants suing for peace "before the explosion of cannon had even had time to deafen the ears of the effete infidels," according to the account of Tursun Bey.[61] Mehmed's aggressive policy resulted in the dispatch of a papal fleet, which claimed Limnos, Samothraki, and Thasos in 1457. The Ottomans countered by taking Athens in 1460 and Lesvos in 1462, its ruler, Nicolò Gattilusio, "drawn into the chain of subjection" while "the clanging and echoing of bells [was] rendered silent by the call to prayer."[62] Venice, whose commercial interests in the region were threatened by this expansion, declared war in 1463, initiating a conflict which was to play out over the next sixteen years.

In 1462, "relying on [who] knows what hope," as Pope Pius II noted in his diary, Stephen Tomašević, the erstwhile despot of Serbia, who had succeeded his father as king of Bosnia the previous year, refused to meet his obligations for tribute to the Porte. An Ottoman army marched into Bosnia in May 1463, meeting little effective resistance. Stephen was run to ground at Gacko by Mahmud Pasha Angelović and brought before the sultan on 25 May. Mehmed promptly had Stephen beheaded, giving him the unenviable distinction of being the last ruler of two states wiped off the map by the Ottomans. Pausing only long enough to establish two new *banats* in Jajce and Srebrenica, the sultan returned to Constantinople.[63]

King Matthias Corvinus of Hungary implored the West to aid Bosnia on the basis that its recovery was a matter of concern for "not just Europe's corners or peripheries but its heartlands."[64] The Venetians, too, warned that the sultan was not satisfied with the capture of Bosnia, but that he was "striving for further conquests and more spacious lands, promising his army even more," not fearing "to arrogantly bring his arms to the seashore at Senj, to the very gate and entrance of Italy."[65] Predictably, no response from the West was forthcoming, but with financial help from Venice, Hungarian forces moved into northern Bosnia in the fall of 1463. The *ban* of Slavonia, Jan Vitovec, pledged allegiance to Corvinus and assisted the attack on Ottoman Bosnia. On 26 December, the Hungarians recaptured Jajce. The following year, Mehmed personally led a campaign to retake this stronghold. Corvinus informed Pope Pius II of the renewed Ottoman offensive and its implications, warning him the sultan had "again invaded Bosnia, which is certainly, so to speak, the key and gate of the whole of Christendom, from where paths in all directions towards the west and north can easily be accessed." Jajce was placed under siege from 10 July to 24 August 1464. But the garrison, commanded by Emeric Zápolya, *ban* of Croatia, Dalmatia, and Slavonia, held firm, and the sultan had to pull back when word arrived that Corvinus had crossed the Sava with a relief army. The king of Hungary was even able to claim Srebrenica in the wake of the Ottoman retreat. Writing to Pius to inform him of this success, Corvinus mixed biological and geopolitical metaphors when he noted that his victory would allow the wound which had been inflicted on the Christian body through the ruin of Bosnia to heal more easily and completely than before, and that this was important, "since the said wound affected not only the corners and sides of Europe, but its very heart, from where it could easily have spread and infected all of its parts."[66]

Venice had scored some early successes against the Ottomans, taking Limnos and Gökçeada in 1464, but in 1470 Mehmed launched an assault against Chalkis, the main Venetian naval base in the Aegean on the isle of Euboea, which fell on 5 August. In the aftermath, the Venetians lamented that the Ottomans – "the eternal and implacable enemies" of Christendom – had not seized just any island, but "had overcome the shield and bulwark of all Christians, opening the path and removing all obstacles to invade, assault and spoil Italy itself." Venice and the Holy See responded by establishing the Holy League, but this came to nothing, largely because the struggle between Poland and Hungary for the Bohemian succession frustrated all efforts to pursue a general anti-Ottoman policy, and forced the two great Christian rivals to separately undertake a policy of rapprochement with the Porte. Meanwhile, the Ottomans continued the grinding advance of their frontier in Bosnia, with the conquest of Počitelj in 1471 and Ljubuški the following year, exposing the hinterlands of the Dalmatian towns of Zadar, Šibenik, and Split to intensifying raids, and in Albania, through the capture of the strongholds of Krujë and Lezhë in 1478 and Shkodër the following year.

The only new ally to enter the anti-Ottoman coalition was the Aq Qoyunlu Empire of Uzun Hasan (Hasan the Tall). The Aq Qoyunlu ("White Sheep" Turks) had forged a powerful state that extended over Azerbaijan, northern Iraq, and eastern Anatolia after the defeat of their rivals, the Karakoyunlu ("Black Sheep" Turks). In 1458, Uzun Hasan had married Princess Theodora Comnena, the daughter of Emperor John IV of Trabzon, in order to seal an anti-Ottoman alliance. This failed to save the Empire of Trabzon from being conquered by Mehmed II in 1461, but Despina Khatun, as she was known, remained an influential adviser to her husband, encouraging him to reach out to the Western powers in search of partners with which to contain the ongoing expansion of the Ottoman Empire at his expense.

Pope Pius II apparently had high hopes of Uzun Hasan, whom he described in a letter he sent in January 1460 to Duke Philip the Good of Burgundy as one of the "friends of the Christians," and whom he counted among those powers "expressing support for the destruction of the most arrogant Turk."[67]

On 2 December 1463, the Venetian Senate approved the dispatch of Lazzaro Quirini to the court of Uzun Hasan, where he would reside until 1471. Meanwhile, two Aq Qoyunlu envoys reached Venice in 1464 and 1465 respectively. In 1471, upon the return of Lazzaro Quirini accompanied by an envoy from Uzun Hasan, the Venetian Senate voted by a margin of 148 to 2 in favor of the alliance and sent Caterino Zeno, a nephew of Despina Khatun resident in Venice, to act as its representative. Venice mobilized a fleet in order to provide the Aq Qoyunlu with artillery, with the expectation Uzun Hasan would open a corridor to the coast through Karaman or preferably through Syria, which would enable delivery of the guns and coordination of joint action by land and sea.[68] Venetian diplomatic activity during this period was intense. In October 1471 a Venetian embassy arrived at the court of King Alexander of Georgia. Venice even dispatched a representative to distant Sarai on the lower Volga River to discuss the possibility of an alliance with the Golden Horde.[69] Hasan also reached out to Poland, his emissaries arriving in Krakow along with Venice's ambassador, Caterino Zeno, offering the hand of one of the Aq Qoyunlu sultan's daughters and with her as a dowry the entire former realm of Byzantium, once those territories were freed from Ottoman rule. Hasan also pledged to support the claims of King Casimir IV of Poland to Hungary and Bohemia.

In 1472, a naval force committed by King Ferdinand I of Naples fought its way through the Dardanelles and sacked the Ottoman naval base at Gallipoli, while another fleet under the Venetian captain general Pietro Mocenigo raided İzmir, Bodrum, and Antalya along the western and southern coasts of Anatolia, and landed troops in support of the Karamanids, who had risen up in a last bid to assert their independence.

These actions were highly lucrative in terms of booty acquired but failed in terms of their strategic imperative of linking up with Uzun Hasan, who had invaded Ottoman territory in 1471, pillaging and destroying Tokat and advancing as far as Akşehir. However, another Aq Qoyunlu invasion of Anatolia the following year was smashed by the Ottomans at Kıreli on 19 August 1472. Uzun Hasan dispatched another embassy, this time to King Matthias Corvinus of Hungary, suggesting terms for an anti-Ottoman alliance, but his ambassadors fell into the hands of the Porte. After a rough start to the campaign of 1473 – the impetuous young *beylerbey* of Rumelia, Hass Murad Pasha, being drawn into an ambush and killed – Mehmed won a decisive victory over the Aq Qoyunlu at Otlukbeli on 11 August 1473, which settled – once and for all – Ottoman hegemony over Asia Minor.[70] A final Venetian embassy headed by Giosafat Barbaro failed to convince Uzun Hasan to continue the war. The Ottoman victory both eliminated a dangerous rival that controlled eastern Anatolia, Azerbaijan, Iraq, and western Iran from its capital Tabriz, and opened those territories up to future Ottoman expansion.

Meanwhile, the primary axis of resistance to the Ottomans in the Balkans shifted to Moldavia, where *voivode* Stephen III had annexed Kilia in 1465.[71] He defeated an Ottoman army under the *beylerbey* of Rumelia, Hadım Suleiman Pasha, at Vaslui on 10 January 1475, many of the Ottoman rank and file drowning in their retreat when the ice of the Siret River collapsed under their weight. On 25 January, Stephen reached out to the European great powers, warning that the sultan would return for his revenge on Moldavia, "which is the gate of Christendom and which God has protected until now. But if this gate which is our country will be lost – God forbid! – then the entire Christendom will be in great danger."[72] And so it came to pass. Stephen was awarded the title *Athleta Christi* (Champion of Christ) by Pope Sixtus IV, but was unable to win any practical European support against the Ottomans, while Mehmed sent an Ottoman fleet to detach Feodosia and other key ports in the Crimea from the Genoese, transforming the Black Sea into an Ottoman lake. Mengli Giray, the khan of northern Crimea and the adjacent steppes, a Genoese ally since 1468 when its mercenaries contributed to his emerging victorious from a disputed succession, was taken captive, dispatched to Constantinople, and condemned to death. On the eve of his execution, the sultan ordered his life spared. He was returned to the Crimea and restored as khan, now a puppet ruler, supervised by an Ottoman garrison stationed in Feodosia.

Reflecting the interconnected nature of medieval trade networks, the consolidation of Ottoman power in the Black Sea also had a profound impact in the Middle East, by cutting the largely Genoese maritime link between the Mamluk sultanate of Egypt and Syria, and the Mongol Khanate of the Golden Horde north of the Caspian and Black seas. This strategic partnership had existed for centuries, not only bringing wealth to the three partners but also serving as the channel through which slaves were recruited for the Mamluk army. Without it, the entire Mamluk system gradually withered.[73]

In 1474, Ottoman *akinjis* raided deep into Hungarian territory, sacking the city of Oradea. Matthias Corvinus was under pressure to mobilize every available fighting man for a renewed bloody struggle, especially those with command ability and experience fighting the Ottomans, who had also invaded Moldavia.

One figure to benefit from this shift in the geopolitical environment was none other than the erstwhile *voivode* of Wallachia, Vlad Dracula, who had spent the last dozen years languishing in a succession of Hungarian prisons. Stephen III urged Corvinus to make use of Vlad in order to depose the current, Ottoman-aligned, *voivode* of Wallachia, Basarab the Elder, who had usurped the throne from Vlad's brother, Radu.[74] Basarab had expelled numerous anti-Ottoman *boyars*, who found asylum in Hungary. These refugees were the natural constituency to form a court in exile centered on Vlad, with the hope of returning home once he regained his throne.

Corvinus released Vlad on the condition that he convert from the Orthodox faith to Catholicism, and dispatched him with his newfound entourage to Belgrade, the plan being for him to support a Hungarian offensive commanded by the king's judge royal, Stephen V Báthory, into Ottoman territory outside the campaign season during the winter of 1475–76. The target was the stronghold of Šabac on the far side of the Sava River. The garrison held out for four weeks, from 16 January to 15 February 1476. Vlad then led a raid on Srebrenica, a mining town renowned for its huge silver deposits, alongside Vuk Branković, who had inherited the (albeit by this point entirely nominal) title of Serbian despot. In a forced march, the two armies covered the distance to the Drina River by the end of February, crossing it at night and unnoticed by the Ottomans. Srebrenica was taken by complete surprise. After being thoroughly plundered, the town was put to the torch, its population massacred. Sending wagons full of booty, including five fully loaded with silver, back to the crossing point on the Drina, Vlad, and Vuk pressed on towards Kušlat and Zvornik, which were both thoroughly sacked, finally retiring before Ottoman reinforcements could intercept them.[75] In addition to exhibiting his characteristic ruthless aggression on campaign, Vlad did not hesitate to employ his by now signature use of terror as a psychological weapon. "He tore the limbs off the Turkish prisoners," and impaled them on stakes, papal legate Gabriele Rangoni reported, "and displayed the private parts of his victims so that when the Turks see these, they will run away in fear!"[76]

Meanwhile, Stephen appealed to Poland for support, but Casimir IV chose not to act, fearing that his involvement in the war against the sultan might strengthen the position of Corvinus, who could thus settle the thorny problem of the Bohemian succession in his favor. Casimir saw Mehmed as his natural ally in his rivalry with Hungary and had no interest in making a foe of the Ottomans. Consequently, Stephen had no choice but to tighten his relationship with Hungary instead. On 12 July 1476, Stephen signed a treaty of alliance with Corvinus. But by that time, an Ottoman army was already in Moldavia, which was squeezed in a grand pincer movement, Mehmed marching up from the south while his Crimean Tatar clients advanced out of the east. This forced Stephen to split his forces, and though the Tatars were routed, Stephen himself suffered a serious defeat on 26 July when the sultan personally led the Ottoman army into the Battle of Valea Albă. However, the Ottomans subsequently proved unable to reduce the key strongholds of Neamț and Suceava, or reclaim Bilhorod-Dnistrovskyi and Kilia. Upon receiving news of the outcome at Valea Albă, Pope Sixtus IV urged Charles of Burgundy to help the common Christian cause, because "if Hungary is conquered Germany will be next, and if Dalmatia and Illyria are overrun Italy will be invaded."[77] Nothing came of this, but in the summer of 1476, Vlad and Báthory moved into Moldavia in support of Stephen III, contributing to his defeat of an Ottoman army at the Siret River in mid-August. They then defeated Basarab the Elder in a battle in the valley of the Prahova, and on 8 November, Vlad reported he had taken Târgoviște. He and Báthory were joined by Stephen in laying siege to Bucharest, which fell on 16 November. Basarab succeeded in fleeing to the Ottomans, taking the treasury with him. However, having secured control of Wallachia's twin capitals, after an interregnum of thirteen years, Vlad finally returned to the throne as *voivode* on 26 November.

He was not indulged with much time in which to savor this triumph. The Ottomans brought the Crimean Tatars into the war in support of Basarab, and this tripartite army marched on Wallachia. Vlad probably took a position at the ford of the Neajlov River, south of Bucharest and west of the Comana Monastery, in anticipation of a coming invasion. He was killed sometime in late December 1476 or early January 1477, either in battle or at the hands of an assassin.[78] Though his severed head would be presented as a trophy to Mehmed, through a quirk of literary fate the legacy of this otherwise obscure warlord would eclipse that of his contemporaries to transcend history and ultimately evolve into supernatural myth.

Meanwhile, the war ground on. In November 1477, Stephen III again invaded Wallachia, defeating an Ottoman army and installing a new *voivode*, Basarab the Younger, only for him to immediately seek patronage from the Porte. An Ottoman army commanded by Koca Isa Bey then entered Transylvania on 9 October 1479, advancing as far as Orăștie. Matthias ordered an army under Stephen Báthory to intercept them, and the two forces clashed on 13 October at the Breadfield (Kenyérmező), near the Saxon village of Șibot. Báthory commanded from the center of his army. The right flank was led by Paul Kinizsi, while on the left was the Serbian light cavalry under Vuk Branković and Dmitar Jakšić with the Saxons. On the Ottoman side, Isa Bey held the center, with Mihaloğlu Ali Bey on the right and his brother Mihaloğlu Iskender Paşha on the left. Isa Bey had the advantage early, Báthory being unhorsed and nearly captured, but Kinizsi succeeded in overwhelming the Ottoman left wing and then falling upon its center. The Ottoman army broke and was routed, Isa Bey being among the many thousands slain. This setback for the Ottomans, coming on the heels of their defeat at Vaslui four years earlier, was a huge boost to the morale of those beleaguered Balkan states desperately trying to hold the line against them. After the clash at the Breadfield, Kinizsi, who had fought with a sword in both hands that day, was said to have danced holding an enemy corpse under each of his arms and another with his teeth.

RHODES, 1480

If there was one thorn in the Ottoman side that Mehmed would relish eliminating more than any other, it was the presence of the Order of Knights of the Hospital of St John of Jerusalem, the Hospitallers, on the island of Rhodes. Founded by papal bull in 1113 and charged with the defense of the holy places in the newly won crusader kingdoms of Outremer, from its inception, as Edward Gibbon described it, this Order embodied "the strange association of a monastic and military life, which fanaticism might suggest, but which policy must approve." In the struggle against the infidel, "they neglected to live, but they were prepared to die, in the service of Christ." The Order had fought to the bitter end throughout the decline and fall of Outremer, making its last stand in the defense of Acre in 1291.[79] Evicted from the Levant, the Hospitallers regrouped in the Kingdom of Cyprus before resolving to establish an empire of their own. The island of Rhodes – wealthy, defensible, and close to the action in Anatolia – was the perfect fit, and under Grand Master Foulques de Villaret the Hospitallers set out to wrest control of it – ostensibly from the Byzantines, in practice from the Genoese. On 5 September 1307, Pope Clement V confirmed the Hospitallers in their possession, but it was to be another three years before they were to secure the island, when the city of Rhodes surrendered on 15 August 1310.[80] Efforts to carve out a presence on the Anatolian mainland failed, but other islands were seized, stretching from Leros in the north via Kos to Kastellorizo in the south.

From this new stronghold, the Order proceeded to exercise its mission statement, which, as Grand Master Juan de Homedes explained to one of his knights in 1536, seemed clear enough: "Our profession is primarily to fight infidels, and to drive the corsairs away from the coasts and seas of the Christians."[81] The Hospitallers commenced a naval war against Muslim shipping and coastal settlements in the Aegean and the Levant in 1312, when its galleys destroyed a Turkish force of twenty-three ships off Amorgos and, allied with the Cypriots, defeated another Turkish fleet at Ephesus. In 1314 the Order, in alliance with France and Venice, routed a Turkish fleet off İzmir, and ten years later led the fleet of the Holy League in capturing that city, which was to be occupied and held by the knights until its fall to Timur in 1402.

In 1347, the Hospitallers smashed a Turkish fleet off Imbros, and in 1361 contributed to the victory of King Peter I of Cyprus at Antalya. In 1365 Alexandria was stormed and sacked. In 1367 the whole Syrian littoral was attacked and looted from Tripoli to Alexandretta. The Mamluks initiated a campaign to eliminate the Knights in 1440, but their landing force never got off the beach, and the Mamluk navy was destroyed in a naval battle, twelve out of seventeen vessels falling into the hands of the Hospitallers. Undeterred, the Mamluks tried again in 1444, but were forced to retreat at the conclusion of a fruitless forty-day siege.

The defenses of the city of Rhodes were state of the art, and constantly expanded and updated. Its critical commercial and military harbors were protected by the towers of Naillac on the extremity of the short mole jutting into the commercial port and of St John (or St Angelo) on its longer mole. After the fall of Constantinople, Grand Master de Lastic called in Florentine experts to strengthen and modernize the defenses. They doubled the enceinte by adding a second series of curtains and ramparts, and deepening and widening the ditch. In 1461, Grand Master Zacosta completed the Tower of St Nicholas on the extremity of the mole in the military port.

In 1476 the Ottomans began probing the island's defenses by attacking the outlying forts on Symi and Kos. The following year they landed a raiding party at Archangelos on the east coast of Rhodes, and in 1479 the city of Rhodes was subjected to a three-month siege, from May to August, while the island suffered considerable damage as *sipahi* cavalry were unleashed to burn villages and despoil the countryside. When the Hospitallers mobilized to drive off these raiders their commander, *kapudan pasha* Misac Palaiologos Pasha, pulled back to winter at Marmaris on the coast of Asia Minor opposite Rhodes. The intelligence he accrued on this venture led to his being appointed by the sultan vizier and commander-in-chief of a full-scale invasion force intended to take the island and eradicate the Hospitallers once and for all.[82]

By 1462, the Order had been divided into eight tongues (langues) based on the nationality of its constituent members. These were, ranked by seniority: Provence, Auvergne, France, Italy, England, Germany, Spain, and Portugal. Each langue was subdivided into priories; on 24 July 1479, Pierre d'Aubusson, Grand Master of the Order of St John since 1476, commanded each of these to mobilize and arrive at Rhodes before the following summer. Nevertheless, by the time the siege commenced the garrison of the city amounted to no more than 2,500 men, with at most 600 of the elite knights and sergeants at arms of the Hospitaller Order itself, the rest comprising mercenaries and local militia. Some reinforcements did reach the garrison during the siege, and a notable addition to its power arrived shortly before the Ottoman landing in the person of d'Aubusson's elder brother Antoine, Count of Monteil, who was returning, with a considerable retinue, from a particularly opportune pilgrimage to the Holy Places. With him were six other Auvergnats with their train of professional soldiers. Grand Master d'Aubusson had been granted plenary powers by the Order's council, and although Antoine, being married, was not a Hospitaller, he was appointed captain general of the city.

Soon after dawn on 23 May 1480, look-outs sighted the Ottoman armada bearing on a southeasterly course towards Akra Milos. That evening, the Ottoman vessels anchored in the sheltered and well-watered Bay of Trianda and began disembarking. Misac Pasha established his headquarters on the slopes of Mount St Stephen. All of the inhabitants of the island were evacuated to the city or its outlying castles, burning whatever they could not bring with them. The next day the city was surrounded by Ottoman troops on land and ships imposing a blockade offshore. A heavy siege battery was set up in the garden of the Church of St Anthony directly opposite the Tower of St Nicholas. According to d'Aubusson, this included "three great bronze basilisks of an incredible size and power, capable of firing balls of nine palms [about seven feet] in circumference."[83]

The Ottoman guns immediately compromised the defense. Guillaume Caoursin, the Hospitaller vice-chancellor, wrote an account of the siege that was widely published throughout Europe. John Kay's English translation of his *Descriptio* recounts how the Ottomans threw "alle theire ordonnance and theire myghte agaynest the pryncypal strenghte and moste neweste walles of the cyte of Rhodes: howe be hyt that they were large, newe, and fortefyed wyth myghty toures and bollewerkes: neverthles wyth castyng of thre thousand and fyfe hondred grete bombardes stones: they were horrybly brused and thrawen downe." A grim d'Aubusson reported to Emperor Frederick III that within a few days of the barrage commencing nine towers had been destroyed and the Grand Master's palace razed to the ground.

The Tower of St Nicholas was the key to the city. If the Ottomans could bring it down and occupy the mole, they could bring their ships into the port, prevent outside aid from reaching the city, and, perhaps, effect an entry by one of the two northern gates of St Peter or St Paul, thus outflanking the Post of France. But the twenty-four-foot thick walls of the tower made reducing it no easy task. And the rate of fire from the siege guns was not very rapid – perhaps fourteen shots a day for each basilisk, whose breech mechanism had to cool between rounds – and communication by way of the mole was never entirely interrupted by Ottoman arquebus or crossbow fire from the opposite shore, enabling the garrison to maintain a continuous resupply and reinforcement of the tower. The besiegers, too, were under constant crossfire from the batteries in the city, and from the marksmen posted along the mole and in entrenchments constructed along the foreshore at the shallow, southern bight of the galley port, under the guns of France.

Finally, after taking 300 rounds of shot, the westward-facing wall of St Nicholas collapsed. Grand Master d'Aubusson immediately improvised a new defense line, assigning a hand-picked company of knights under Fabrizio del Carretto, with supporting arquebusiers and archers, to hold off the Ottomans while setting hundreds of noncombatants to work night and day excavating a trench, erecting timber palisades, and shoring up the great heaps of rubble scattered around the base of the tower.

A carrack from Sicily slipped into the port bearing grain and reinforcements, while a blockade runner slipped out, bearing an appeal from d'Aubusson, dated 28 May, to every brother of the Order, reminding them "entry to our port is open and that it cannot be denied to anyone while the westerlies blow in the summer and autumn." Therefore, "we command and charge each and every one of you... to move with all haste to the succor of our City of Rhodes," to either "earn fame and glory," or "fall in the fight, which is a soldier's lot, and win the crown of martyrs."[84]

All the while, the besiegers kept the garrison under a constant bombardment. After ten days under fire, the first attempt to storm the ruins of St Nicholas came early in June. The Ottomans embarked in specially modified galleys from which the masts, sails, and all unnecessary rigging had been removed. Platforms were built out over the bows, and the sides were buttressed with extra high bulwarks. Some mounted light cannon, and all were packed with *sipahis* armed to the teeth. Characteristically, there was no attempt at surprise. Even before dawn the besiegers set up a raucous din of pipes and cymbals and drums and eldritch screams.

The gunners in the ruins of St Nicholas could not load fast enough to do much damage as the galleys approached, and the Ottoman vessels then deliberately steered so close to the tower they could sail safely under its guns and pass by unhindered; but those which made for the inner end of the mole came under fire from the bombards on the walls of the Post of France. One of the galleys was set alight and exploded. The others succeeded in disgorging their cargoes, but the *sipahis* were immediately swept by a murderous crossfire of arquebus balls, crossbow bolts, and arrows and then broke against the halberds and two-handed swords of the knights. Routed, they fled back for the relative safety of their ships.

Two more attempts were made on the tower, with similar results. The last assault went in on 9 June and ostensibly cost the Ottomans 600 men killed and as many wounded while the defenders did not lose a single man.

Misac Pasha had already redirected the focus of his attack. On 7 June, he shifted the main target of his heavy ordnance to the southern perimeter of the city in the sectors opposite the posts of England, Provence, and Italy, which enclosed the Jewish Quarter. His plan was to attack simultaneously from north and south and thus divide the defense. Eight great basilisks concentrated on the tower and curtain of Italy, and one more was trained on the Tower of St Angelo on the eastern mole of the commercial port. It soon became apparent the obsolete fortifications in this sector were far more vulnerable than the state-of-the-art Tower of St Nicholas and would soon fall. Grand Master d'Aubusson set about ensuring that when the Ottomans poured through the breaches made by their artillery they would be met by a new line of retrenchments. He cleared the Jewish Quarter, demolishing every building and pressing every soul under his command, from knights and men-at-arms to priests and nuns, into working around the clock erecting palisades, constructing gabions, digging trenches, and setting pit traps. As Caoursin described it in Kay's translation of the *Descriptio*, "they of Rhodes alleway besy and provident stopped wyth trees the grete ruyne of theyre walles and made also many dyches wythinne the cytee."[85]

The Ottomans had been busy, too, digging a complex of trenches snaking and zigzagging towards the counterscarp of the moat. At night, they brought up cart-loads of rubble which they emptied into the moat to fill it up to ground level. To buy himself more precious time, d'Aubusson ordered miners to excavate a passage under the walls and retrieve the stone by bearing it with them back into the city. At dawn, the baffled besiegers were at a loss to explain how their night's work had been undone.

Meanwhile, Misac kept up the pressure on St Nicholas. A great wooden tower was set up on the shore opposite the mole, and filled with archers and arquebusiers, protected by hides, who fired from their commanding platform at any movement. On 13 June a new and furious bombardment of the mole and ruined tower commenced and was kept up without relief for four days and nights. Under cover of this barrage, materials were brought overland from Trianda and a great pontoon bridge was constructed, long enough to reach from the foreshore to the mole, and wide enough for six men to advance across it abreast.

Using rafts, on the night of 18 June the Ottomans began to maneuver the pontoon bridge into position. The janissaries were assembled on the beach, while a fleet of more than a dozen heavy store ships (*parandarie*) carrying cannon, powder, and shot, escorted by thirty modified galleys and a flotilla of smaller craft, crept silently around Akta Milos, half taking up station close in to the seaward side of the tower, the remainder approaching the inner side of the mole. The janissaries had boarded the pontoon bridge and it had almost docked before the alarm was raised. Suddenly, the janissaries were ashore, scrambling up the damaged glacis of St Nicholas with ladders and hook-ropes, while the *sipahis* flung themselves at the defenders of the mole from both sides. But Fabrizio del Carretto and his men, who had slept in their armor, held the line, joined by d'Aubusson who, leading from the front, had his helmet smacked from his head by ricocheting shrapnel. The city's guns soon found their mark in the harbor, smashing the pontoon bridge into matchwood and sending its occupants tumbling into the water.

The Grand Master had prepared fireships, and these were now unleashed on the Ottoman flotilla. Four galleys and several *parandarie* laden with munitions went up in flames, the ghastly light of their demise illuminating the fighting that raged on throughout the night, as wave after wave of attackers were flung back into the harbor or slaughtered in the ruins of the tower and on the palisade of the mole. Still the besiegers came on, as the *Descriptio* chronicled: "Neverthelesse the turkes from thother banke manly and stoutely faughted and defended their people aforsayd wyth castyng to the cyte & the toure grete stones of bombardes and of gonnes & wyld fyre and arowes of bowes and balestres."[86]

Finally, by mid-morning, the assault forces were spent. For the next three days, the corpses of fallen Ottoman combatants continued to wash up along the shore, and not just of the rank and file; among the slain were Ibrahim Bey, a favored son-in-law of the sultan, and Merlah Bey, admiral of the Ottoman fleet.

While this outcome ended the direct threat to the Tower of St Nicholas, day by day Misac Pasha's siege lines, shrugging off sorties by the garrison, snaked inexorably closer to the Jewish Quarter. The *Descriptio* relates how "the turkes fylled a certayne place of the dyche of the citee wyth trees and stones and suche other thynges: so that the dyche was made equall and playnnyssed unto the heyght of the broken walle: soo that lyghtely they myghte come for to feyghte hande for hande with the Rhodyans."[87] At dawn on 27 July, the assault began, *bashi-bazouk* irregulars in the first wave, followed by the disciplined ranks of the janissaries. As the Ottomans swarmed into the breaches, the defenders fell back from the ruined wall to the retrenchment, which completely enclosed a crescent-shaped area that had been cleared of buildings to create an open field of fire. The Ottomans entering this space charged directly into the guns of the retrenchment while being caught in the crossfire from the ruined towers of Italy and Provence on either flank. Most were cut down, and while a detachment of 300 janissaries did penetrate into the city they were isolated from the main force and slaughtered.

The defense was weakest at the ends of its line, where the jagged ruins of the ramparts overtopped the retrenchment. Should the assault force seize the Tower of Italy it would gain access to a short length of wall that connected directly to the commercial port. In that eventuality, Ottoman troops on the wall's walkway could advance into the heart of the city under the covering fire of the tower itself.

Accordingly, d'Aubusson immediately appreciated the stakes when he saw the Ottoman banner flying from the Tower of Italy after it was taken by the *bashi-bazouks*. Ignoring the pain from an arrow wound in his thigh, the fifty-seven-year-old Grand Master immediately clambered up the nearest ladder onto the walkway, followed by a handful of knights and three standard bearers carrying the sigils of the Cross of the Holy Religion, the banner of St John the Baptist, and the banner of Our Lady.

Fighting in the front line, d'Aubusson was wounded four more times before a janissary finally put him out of action by thrusting a spear clean through his breastplate and into the right side of his chest, puncturing a lung. But his desperate gambit had turned the tide. The Ottomans were driven out of the Tower of Italy and their banner was cast from its shattered battlements. The *bashi-bazouks* now broke and began streaming back through the breaches, panic mounting as they turned on each other in the jammed bottlenecks. The janissaries initially sought to restore discipline by cutting their erstwhile comrades-in-arms down as they fled, but the Ottoman elite, too, were ultimately caught up in the rout as the garrison, sensing its advantage, pressed onto the offensive, pursuing the demoralized foe into their camp on the slopes of Mount St Stephen, which was thoroughly looted, even the gold and silver standard of the sultan being seized as plunder.

Ten days after this debacle, Misac Pasha broke the siege, falling back to Trianda and setting sail for Constantinople on 17 August. Thus, as Kay brought Caoursin's *Descriptio* to a triumphant conclusion, "Rhodes was and ys preserved and kepte fro the turkes captyvyte."[88]

146

OTRANTO, 1480–81

Even as the struggle for Rhodes approached its climax, Mehmed unleashed another amphibious operation, this one directed against Italy. Having contacted the Venetians at Modon to request safe passage and supplies, both of which were granted by the resident authorities, on 26 July 1480 an Ottoman fleet of twenty-eight galleys, 104 light galleys, and enough transport ships to convey not just an army but 4,000 horses set out from Avlonya. This naval expedition, which to the chronicler Kemalpaşazade resembled "a 1,000-handed giant," crossed the Adriatic unopposed.[89] It was bound for Brindisi, but, owing to contrary winds, on 28 July it arrived offshore the Neapolitan city of Otranto in Apulia on the heel of the peninsula. In command was Gedik Ahmed Pasha, who had rendered meritorious service to the House of Osman in Anatolia against the Karamanids and in the Crimea against the Genoese. He had participated in the 1478–79 siege of Shkodër, and had considerable experience in combined arms operations, having taken the islands of Lefkada, Kefalonia, and Zakynthos from Venice.

The city fathers of Otranto refused a summons to surrender, making the theatrical gesture of throwing the key to the city gate into the Adriatic as a symbol of their defiance. On 11 August, after a fifteen-day siege, the city was taken and its population sold into slavery or put to the sword. This was the first territory on the mainland of Italy to be occupied by a Muslim power since the Emirate of Taranto had been eradicated by the Byzantines exactly 600 years earlier in 880. From this base, the port town of Vieste was assaulted later in August, while on 12 September, the monastery of San Nicholas di Casole, which could boast one of the finest libraries in Europe, was put to the torch. By October, the coastal cities of Lecce, Taranto, and Brindisi had all come under attack. The expeditionary force imposed a one ducat tax on every family under its authority, melted down church bells to make cannon, and deported 8,000 slaves to Albania, measures that did little to win the hearts and minds of the local populace. As residents of the occupation zone increasingly opted to flee, Ottoman policy became more conciliatory, offering a ten-year tax break and religious freedom in an attempt to defuse the tension. Leaving a garrison behind to hold Otranto, Gedik Pasha returned to Albania with the bulk of his force to overwinter.

Pope Sixtus IV was appalled. "We have the enemy before our very eyes," he wrote to the princes of Italy on 27 July, while the Ottomans were still at sea: "He has already been sighted, poised to strike at the province of Apulia with a large fleet."[90] After this force made landfall the pontiff continued to rail against a world in which "this enemy of the Christian name, seeking to subvert religion and all things sacred, had set foot in Italy, and unless he was rapidly dealt with, he would entirely destroy the papacy and the Roman name."[91]

Having summoned a meeting of the great powers at Rome for 1 November, on 8 April 1481 Sixtus issued the papal bull *Cogimur iubente altissimo*, pleading with the magnates of Christendom to rally to the defense of Italy even as he drew up contingency plans to evacuate the Holy City:

> How perilous it has become for all Christians, and especially the Italian powers, to hesitate in the assumption of arms against the Turks and how destructive to delay any longer, everyone can see... And so if the faithful, and especially the Italians, want to keep their lands, homes, wives, children, liberty, and the very faith in which we are baptized and reborn, let them believe us that they must now take up arms and go to war.[92]

A joint program of action was decided upon by which a fleet would be mustered from commitments made by the Italian states, with the pope contributing twenty-five galleys, Naples forty, Genoa five, Ferrara and Siena four each, Bologna two, and Lucca, Mantua, and Montferrat one apiece. Venice, which had only recently concluded peace with Mehmed after its long war, adamantly refused to play any role, and reacted to the pope's summons with cold-blooded cynicism: "Many noble and impressive things will be said and proposed, but they will resemble the fantasies of the past rather than anything substantial and appropriate."[93]

Having mobilized in the spring, King Ferdinand I of Naples appointed his son Alfonso, Duke of Calabria, to lead his army against the Ottoman threat. With support from a contingent of Hungarian troops under the command of Blaise Magyar forwarded by King Matthias Corvinus, Alfonso laid siege to Otranto on 1 May 1481.[94]

Mehmed had set out in person on campaign just days earlier. He had progressed no further than İzmit, only fifty miles from Constantinople, when he died suddenly on 3 May, probably of dysentery, aged just forty-nine. With the Ottoman Empire now ascendant in both the Balkans and Asia Minor, Mehmed had earned his claim to be "Lord of two Continents [Europe and Asia] and of the Two Seas [Aegean and Black]." Christendom issued a collective sigh of relief at news of his passing. God had not conceded any blessing, Caoursin rejoiced in Kay's translation of the *Descriptio*, more important, better or more appreciated than the death of the sultan, who had "proposed & ordeyned grete myght & strenghte to undo & subverte the holy cytee of Rome, & putte Italye to his subiectyon & after lightly to overcome & oppresse the resydue of crystendome."[95] Had he lived to take personal command of his beachhead on the far shore of the Adriatic and led the main Ottoman army in a march on Rome, the course of history might well have taken a very different trajectory. In his *Storia d'Italia*, Renaissance historian Francesco Guicciardini reminded his Christian audience how Mehmed "had by an improvised attack conquered the city of Otranto, and opened a door and fixed a position from which he [would] continuously vex the Italians (if death had not intervened)."[96] In his *Esposizione del Pater Noster*, humanist scholar Antonio de Ferrariis Galateo shuddered to think how, had Otranto not been recovered, "we would not be in Bari today, nor the Pope in Rome, nor would this kingdom [Calabria] be in the Christian faith, nor Sicily, nor Lombardy."[97]

Instead, the Ottoman state devolved into civil war. When Grand Vizier Karamani Mehmet Pasha ordered the army Mehmed had mobilized to stay in camp while the succession was negotiated, the soldiers rose up and killed him. While the troops rebelled, the populace of Constantinople rioted, and the Porte was paralyzed. Mehmed's eldest son, Bayezid, rode day and night for the Topkapi Palace in order to halt the meltdown of authority. He was best placed to succeed, for not only had he healthy adult sons of his own – Ahmed, Selim, and Korkud – but he had made politically astute alliances, marrying off one daughter to the *beylerbey* of Anatolia and another to the *beylerbey* of Rumelia. Arriving in Constantinople on 21 May, he took the throne as Sultan Bayezid II.

Repudiating this claim, Mehmed's younger son, Cem, declared himself sultan on 28 May, establishing his capital at Bursa. He proposed to divide the empire, taking the Anatolian provinces while Bayezid retained Europe. Bayezid furiously rejected this compromise and marched to war against his brother. Critically, Bayezid had the support of Gedik Pasha, the general whose garrison still held out at Otranto. The army he commanded in Albania was redirected away from returning to Italy in order to cross swords with fellow Muslims. The tribal levies that Cem had been able to rally from the central plains of Anatolia were no match for Gedik Pasha's disciplined regulars. Defeated in battle at Yenişehir on 19 June, Cem fled to seek refuge at the Mamluk court in Cairo, where he brooded over his next move.

The states of Christian Europe, spectators to the internecine succession struggle playing out before their eyes, were the primary beneficiaries as the Ottoman world turned in upon itself. The besieged garrison of Otranto, now with no hope of relief or reinforcement, finally surrendered on 10 September. While Italy was relieved from having to confront a serious challenge, Rhodes was delivered from impending annihilation. The ranks of the Order had been bled white and the defenses of the Hospitaller stronghold, already shattered during the siege, were reduced to rubble by an earthquake. Had Mehmed II survived just one more campaign season, Rhodes would have tumbled into his lap.

Instead, with the Ottoman state unsettled, a truce was arrived at between d'Aubusson – who had survived his wounds – and the Porte.[98] Both sides would enjoy navigation rights on the open sea while retaining sovereignty over their own coastal waters. Letters of marque subsequently issued by the knights often referred to customary limits (*limites et confinia*) within which Ottoman ships had to be respected.[99] This arrangement endowed the increasingly isolated Hospitallers with another four decades of service as the *propugnacula fidee* (bulwarks of the faith) on Rhodes.

In a final stroke of good fortune for the Hospitallers, after rallying supporters, Cem invaded Anatolia in 1482, and on 27 May laid siege to Konya only to be defeated and again forced to flee, this time to Rhodes. The Order now had a trump card it could hold over Bayezid, for Cem had a legitimate claim to be sultan and with Western support could make another bid for the throne at any time. Bayezid was forced to settle. By the terms of a treaty dated 8 December 1482, the Order was to receive indefinitely an annual compensation of 10,000 ducats for the damage inflicted during the siege of 1480, and a further 35,000 ducats annually in a per diem for meeting the expenses of an Ottoman prince – diplomatic cover for what was essentially a bribe to keep Cem contained in a gilded cage. He was fated to spend the rest of his life in exile, politely evading the solicitations of both Pope Innocent VIII and King Matthias Corvinus of Hungary to serve as the figurehead for their planned anti-Ottoman crusade. This transient existence only ended with Cem's death in 1495.[100]

4

PERSIA, AND THE FALL OF THE MAMLUKS

BAYEZID II

The pace of Ottoman expansion slowed under Mehmed II's successor, Bayezid II. The new sultan did succeed in advancing the Ottoman frontier in the Balkans; he annexed Herzegovina in 1482, while raiding parties regularly wreaked havoc in Carniola and Styria, spreading devastation all the way to Friuli by the end of the century. Croatia was wide open to Ottoman incursions, which continued over the ensuing decades, year after year. Everywhere, the outcome was the same. Those who could, fled. Those who remained, worn down and desperate for a way out of the cycle of violence, leaned ever closer to capitulation as the only path to security.[1] The situation reached its climax in 1493, when Hadım Yakup Pasha, *sanjak-bey* of Bosnia, led an *akinji* raid into Carniola and Styria. At the same time, a rebellion broke out against Vladislaus II Jagiello, king of Hungary, Bohemia, and Croatia. After receiving news that the rebels had besieged the royal city of Senj, the king committed a force under *ban* Emerik Derenčin of Bajna to restore order. The *ban* won over the rebels by appealing to them for joint action against the marauding Ottoman invaders. The Croatian force mustered at Krbava, cutting off the Ottoman line of retreat. Yakup Pasha initiated negotiations for free passage home to his strongholds in Bosnia, but Derenčin rejected any such settlement. Although the Croatian army had the advantage in numbers, the Ottomans were veterans with more cavalry. Knowing this, and having experience in conflicts with the Ottomans, Ivan Frankopan Cetinski, the count (*knez*) of Cetin Castle, encouraged Derenčin to trap the Ottomans in one of the numerous passes crisscrossing the area. This advice was ignored, and the *ban* arranged his army on the open field below the castle at Udbina. The ensuing battle did not last long. Taking advantage of his greater mobility, Yakup Pasha had stationed a detachment of his force under cover of the adjacent forest. A feigned withdrawal pulled the Croatian line into the trap. The left wing of the Croatian army was hit on its open flank and collapsed, the rest of the line being rolled up and destroyed. The Ottomans took only the most important noblemen as prisoners to be ransomed (including Derenčin, who died in captivity, having already lost his son and brother, who were killed in the battle, as was Ivan Frankopan) while the rest were slaughtered.[2]

Just fifteen days after the battle, on 27 September 1493, Juraj Divnić, the bishop of Nin in Croatia, lamented to Pope Alexander VI that the oncoming tide of the Ottoman foe, possessed of an "insatiable spirit which craves the slaughter of the faithful and greedily wants to appropriate the whole world," could not be halted, for "no one opposes him, Holy Father, and there is nobody whose strength could equal and be compared with his."[3]

On the opposite shore of the Balkan peninsula, in the summer of 1484 the Ottomans conquered the last major free Christian port cities in the Black Sea. Moldavia had traditionally been a bone of contention between Poland and Hungary, so Bayezid was careful to secure a five-year truce with King Matthias Corvinus of Hungary in 1483. While the Hungarians turned on the Habsburgs, it took the sultan less than a month to relieve Moldavia of its entire maritime frontage by annexing Kilia and Bilhorod-Dnistrovskyi (at the mouths of the Danube and Dniester rivers, respectively), thus completing the transition of the Black Sea into an "Ottoman Lake" for the next three centuries.[4] The sultan represented this campaign as a great victory that opened "new gates" for the empire. In a letter addressed to the city fathers of Dubrovnik, the sultan exulted that he had conquered Kilia, "gate of Moldavia and Hungary" and Bilhorod-Dnistrovskyi, "gate of Poland, Russia and Tartaria."[5] Stephen III turned to Poland for support, and 3,000 Polish cavalry, led by Jan Karnowski, contributed to the Moldavian victory at the Battle of Cătlăbuga on 16 November 1485. Stephen was able to arrive at peace terms with Bayezid in April of the following year.

King Casimir IV of Poland, meanwhile, despite having been twice excommunicated because of his hostile attitude towards Hungary, asked for and received approval for a crusade from Pope Innocent VIII, who on 12 July 1486 published the bull *Catholice fidei defensionem*, through which he granted plenary indulgence to all those who would fight with Casimir against the Ottomans. However, the following year the Polish army drove not south towards Moldavia but rather into the east, winning a victory over the Tatars at the Battle of Kopystrzyn in Podolia (September 1487). This only increased the pressure on Poland's steppe frontier; only after concluding a two-year truce with the Ottomans in 1489 were the Polish–Lithuanian forces able to obtain a decisive victory over the Tatars on the other side of the Volga in the Battle of Zaslow (January 1491).

The situation turned farcical when Casimir's successor as king of Poland, John I, convened with King Ladislaus II of Hungary and Elector Johann Cicero of Brandenburg in April 1494 at the conference of Levoča, where plans were hatched for a crusade against the Porte. However, John was also scheming to place his own brother, Sigismund, on the throne of Moldavia. Stephen struck first, preemptively invading Ruthenia, before John's army pushed into Moldavia, laying siege to Suceava on 26 September. With Wallachian and Tatar allies, plus the support of 600 janissaries committed from Constantinople, Stephen routed John in a three-day (26–29 October 1497) battle at Codrii Cosminului (Cosmin's Forest), driving him back into Poland.

Bayezid had played the role of suzerain adroitly. Now he moved to follow up on the opportunity presented by Christian infighting. In 1498, he unleashed 4,000 *akinjis* under the command of the *sanjak-beys* of Kilia and Bilhorod-Dnistrovskyi, together with Malkoçoğlu Bâli Bey, the *sanjak-bey* of Silistra, who carried out devastating successive incursions into Poland, sacking Braclaw, Sambor, and Jaroslaw. These coincided with Tatar raids in Podolia, and Moldavian counterattacks in Pokucie.[6] Poland sued for a truce in 1499, an arrangement that would be renewed, regardless of various provocations, over the course of more than a century until 1617, a policy enhanced by the fact the Ottoman vassals, the Crimean Tatars, often cooperated with the Jagiellonian dynasty of Poland in its wars against the rising power of Muscovy. This powerful piece would thus be marginalized to the edge of the geopolitical chessboard during the critical years of Ottoman expansion.

On 11 July 1499, Stephen III ratified the treaty which his envoys had signed at Krakow and declared a solemn peace between Moldovia and Poland. On 14 September 1499, Stephen ratified a separate anti-Ottoman treaty with Grand Duke Alexander of Lithuania, who warned his father-in-law, Ivan III of Muscovy (whose son had married Stephen's daughter), that the Ottoman threat might soon target him too: "Stephen's realm is the gateway to all the Christian lands of our continent, and God forbid that he should be defeated and his land entirely occupied, for if that happened neither our realms nor yours would ever again have peace from that powerful enemy."[7] Instead of cooperation, war soon broke out between Lithuania and Muscovy; on 14 July 1500 a Lithuanian army was defeated by the Muscovites at the Battle of the Vedrosha River.

Bayezid was able to take full advantage of this squabbling among the great powers to his north, which effectively nullified any threat to his Balkan frontier, by advancing Ottoman interests in the Aegean and Adriatic through an extensive campaign against the Venetian outposts in the Morea and Dalmatia. After the fall of Lepanto on 29 August 1499, the call for a collective response began to echo throughout Christendom. On 5 October 1500, three papal legates were elected in consistory to evangelize for a crusade: Cardinal Raymond Peraudi for the Holy Roman Empire and the Nordic kingdoms; Juan Vera for France, England, and Spain; and Pietro Isvalies for Hungary, Bohemia, and Poland. Additional active propagandists included Stefano Taleazzi, bishop of Torcello, and the bishop of Patras, Alessio Celidonio. Serving as a key intermediary was Felix Petančić, who had served in the chancellery of his native city, Dubrovnik, and then in Buda under King Matthias Corvinus and his successor Vladislaus II, becoming the latter's envoy to Rhodes, Venice, France, and Constantinople.[8]

Isvalies, the cardinal archbishop of Reggio, was tasked with reaching an understanding between the Jagiellonian kings and Venice, if it should prove impossible to build an alliance between all Christian princes. He was a soldier by profession and governor of Rome before being created cardinal, and was a close confidant of the pope's son, Cesare Borgia. In November 1500, the pope appointed Isvalies apostolic legate for Hungary, Poland, and the "adjacent provinces." The pope's plan envisaged three years of war against the Turks, waged by three main armies. A powerful fleet was to be assembled by the Holy See, France, Spain, and Venice to attack the Turks by sea. The first land army would set out from Germany, led by the emperor, while King Vladislaus II and the papal legate together would lead the second army, made up of Hungarian, Polish, and Moldavian forces. Two papal bulls announcing a crusade were issued in 1500, *Quamvis ad amplianda* on 1 June and *Domini et salvatoris* on 26 October.

Meanwhile, the Ottomans were on the march in the Peloponnese, the campaign of 1500 being commanded by the sultan himself. On 9 August Modon fell to Bayezid, and Pylos and Koron subsequently surrendered. In conjunction with French, Spanish, and papal forces, the Venetians retook Pylos (only to lose it again to Kemal Reis in May 1501), then went on to plunder Thessaloniki and establish control over the Ionian islands, including Corfu, Lefkada, Kefalonia, and Zakynthos.

On 13 May 1501, Vladislaus II of Hungary officially announced his adherence to the anti-Ottoman alliance, alongside the papacy, Venice, and the Hospitallers of Rhodes. The pope promised the Hungarians annual assistance of 40,000 ducats; Venice was prepared to pay another 100,000 and would fight at sea. On 30 August, thirteen galleys prepared by the pope (five of them armed in Venice, six in Apulia, and two in Ancona) took Santa Maura on the island of Lefkada. The following year, Pierre d'Aubusson, Grand Master of the Hospitallers, was elected captain general of the allied fleet, which was headed by two brothers from Venice, Benedetto Pesaro (commanding the Venetian ships) and Giacomo Pesaro (commander of all the papal ships and the three committed by the Hospitallers). The allies assembled at Cerigo in the summer of 1502 and resolved to continue the campaign in the Ionian islands.

Efforts were ongoing to induce the recalcitrant magnates of the Holy Roman Empire into joining the war. In an address to the Imperial *Diet* in July 1501, Cardinal Peraudi pointedly asked the assembled representatives where they planned to seek refuge once the Ottomans invaded Germany; did they plan to gather at Lübeck to sail off to England, Ireland, or the Orkneys? In November 1501, Maximilian warned that Regensburg might become a front-line city, in the event that the Ottomans overran both Hungary and Poland, and the following month, he reasoned it was far preferable to take up arms "for the faith and for the protection of other Christians and for glory" on distant battlefields than to fight "not just for the faith but also for country, hearth, children, wives, freedom, and life itself" at home, thereby incurring "warfare, massacre, arson, destruction, and captivity" in the Empire's heartland.[9] In January 1502 Maximilian, without any reference to convening the *diet*, issued a call to arms against the Ottomans. The army was to assemble for 1 June, but, once again, the momentum for collective action broke down.

Unable to sustain the pressure in this war of attrition, it was Venice that finally broke. Pushed to the brink financially – the war had "eaten its soul," Ottoman chronicler Kemalpaşazade gloated: "The knife had bitten to the bone and its strength was gone" – the republic sued for peace on 14 December 1502. Under the treaty concluded in May 1503, Venice lost Modon, Koroni, Lepanto, Durrës, and Lefkada. Bereft of Venetian naval power and subsidies, the crusade could not continue, and Vladislaus II of Hungary also negotiated a truce with the sultan.

A seven-year general peace between Christendom and the Ottoman Empire was ratified on 20 August 1503 in Buda and on 5 November 1503 in Constantinople. As well as the kingdom of Hungary and the other lands of St Stephen's crown, including Wallachia and Moldavia (which were to be ruled as an Ottoman–Hungarian condominium), the treaty mentioned the beneficiaries of the peace as the pope, the Holy Roman Emperor, the kings of France, Spain and England, Venice and the whole of Italy, and the Grand Master of the Knights of Rhodes. The treaty recognized Ottoman rule over fortresses which they had conquered, among them Kilia and Bilhorod-Dnistrovskyi with their adjacent hinterlands.

In the East, however, progress in consolidating Ottoman hegemony over Asia Minor stalled as the Porte encountered its first real great power rival since the era of Timur. Over the course of the inconclusive Ottoman–Mamluk War (1485–91) for control of the Cilician plain and the Turkmen emirate of Dulkadir in southeastern Anatolia, Bayezid proved incapable of pushing south of the Taurus Mountains into the Fertile Crescent.

After the Ottomans suffered a major defeat outside Adana in February 1486, Bayezid sent a larger force under the command of his son-in-law Hersekzade Ahmed Pasha, the *beylerbey* of Anatolia, only for him to be captured by the Mamluk commander Amir Azbak on 15 March. Andrea Gritti, who was sent by the consul of Venice as an ambassador to Bayezid, called the debacle "the greatest defeat ever inflicted upon the Ottoman House."[10] The Ottomans suffered another humiliating defeat at the Battle of Ağaçayırı on 16 August 1488. The situation reached its nadir in 1490, when Mamluk raiders under the command of Amir Azbak penetrated into the heart of the Karaman territory, pillaging their way through Asia Minor from January through October 1490, even reducing some strongholds such as Kevere. Clearly, Ottoman expansion beyond its Anatolian heartland was losing momentum. But Cairo was not destined to be the counterweight to Constantinople in the Levant. That role would pass to a new power rising in the east. Exploring the geopolitical roots and consequences of this phenomenon requires some background in history and geopolitical theory.

SAFAVID PERSIA

Nature abhors a vacuum. This truism of the natural sciences applies equally to interactions between social organisms like human beings. In a power vacuum, something will inevitably evolve to fill that space with its own authority and then continue to expand until it is checked by an alternative authority of equivalent potency.

This understanding of the human condition informed the geopolitical theory of German academic Friedrich Ratzel (1844–1904). His works *Anthropo-Geographie* (1882) and *Politische Geographie* (1897) argued that the most successful peoples historically were those constantly driven to occupy physical and cultural space within available new regions. The physical barriers inhibiting this process in the past – ocean, steppe, desert, etc. – were ultimately overcome through advances in technology. Accordingly, the state was an essentially biological organism and this was the motive force driving international relations. The key lesson of human history, therefore, was that naturally, inevitably, the more dynamic states constituted of more motivated peoples would continue to absorb the less dynamic with a tendency towards the emergence of great empires of equivalent potency to balance against each other.

A classic exemplar of this process in action was the trajectory of Rome. Having absorbed her neighbors in Italy – Latin, Etruscan, Samnite – she continued to expand, defeating, subjugating, and forcibly incorporating more and more rivals – Punic, Celt, Greek – into her empire, the accumulation of territory, population, and wealth empowering the next stage of the process until, in the 1st century BC, this expansion crashed to a halt when Rome finally encountered a people equally motivated and a state equally dynamic expanding in the opposite direction. This was Parthia of the Arsacid dynasty, which had emerged as the dominant force on the Iranian plateau, inheriting and harnessing an ethno-cultural identity that had proved under the previous Achaemenid dynasty it possessed the vision and ambition necessary for empire building. The division of the fertile crescent between Rome and Parthia (and its successor, the Sasanid dynasty) that endured for the next 700 years reflected the inherent rivalry between two great empires whose vision and ambition balanced against each other.

The trajectory of the Ottomans clearly paralleled that of Rome. From humble beginnings, the vision and ambition of its leaders facilitated it continuing to absorb less dynamic neighbors until it attained great power status, each conquest facilitating the next stage of the process until by the second decade of the 16th century it was capable of absorbing and assimilating the Mamluks, a state of equivalent size and population. But this expansion was also paralleled by its conclusion, as the Ottomans, too, ultimately encountered a people equally motivated and a state equally dynamic expanding in the opposite direction. Rome and Parthia had taken advantage of the power vacuum created by the infighting between the successors to Alexander the Great to incorporate its territory into their own, Rome from the west, Parthia from the east. Centuries later, the Ottomans and a new political entity centered on the Iranian plateau, the Safavid dynasty, would repeat this process, contesting over a region still destabilized by the empire building of the Mongol khans, leading to a fresh division of the Fertile Crescent between West and East, with each aspiring hegemon balanced against the other.

The Safavids entered history in the shadow of their Ottoman rivals. The marriage of Uzun Hasan and Despina Khatun had ultimately failed to check

Ottoman expansion in Anatolia, but it did have one important legacy, for their daughter Halima married Haydar, the head of the Safaviyya order of Sufi mystics and the father of Ismail, the founder of the Safavid Empire.

Ismail inherited leadership of the Safaviyya at the age of seven after the death of his brother in 1494. For the rest of the decade, he lived in the city of Lahijan near the Caspian Sea in northwest Iran under the protection of its Zaydi Kiya'id ruler, Mirza Ali of Gilan. In his first campaign, still just thirteen years old, Ismail took the city of Derbent in 1500, and then defeated Shah Farrokhyashar of Shirvan in the Caucasus, avenging both his father Haydar and grandfather Junaid, who had lost their lives in battle against this rival. The following year, despite being outnumbered four to one, Ismail smashed the Aq Qoyunlus at the Battle of Sharur and then occupied Tabriz, where he acclaimed himself as shah. Ismail then defeated the Aq Qoyunlus in three separate battles during 1503, ending forever the dominance of the White Sheep Turks over Iran, where the Safavid dynasty would rule until 1736.[11]

While Iranian cultural identity extends in an unbroken chain through history from at least the Achaemenid era two and a half millennia ago, for generations after the fall of the last pre-Islamic Persian dynasty, the Sasanians, in the 7th century, as a political entity Iran had been dominated by outsiders – Arabs, Turks, Mongols. The triumph of Ismail culminated in the restoration of an Iranian nation state, one that in its contemporary republican form remains critically relevant today. The explosive expansion of the Safavids from marginalized cult to founders of a dynastic empire profoundly altered the balance of power in the Middle East, for the new regime was dedicated not merely to territoriality but to social revolution. The Safavids were militant adherents to the Shia branch of Islam, and focused on the forging of a collective cultural identity centered on Shia principles.[12] Thus, Iranian nationalism would be forged in the explicit association of a defined physical space with a dogmatic interpretation of faith – a potent combination, especially as it put the new regime at odds with all of its neighbors. Horrified at the persecution and forced conversion of fellow Sunnis, so far as the Ottomans were concerned, the Safavids were apostates (*mürted*) who had unleashed a new dark age (*cahiliyye*) upon the lands they had conquered. They were not simply unbelievers (*kâfir*) but heretical unbelievers (*kâfir wa-mulhid*) who misgoverned a realm where the *hutbe* summoning the faithful to Friday prayer was recited in the name of Ismail, instead of the names of the *hulefâ-i raşidîn*, the four righteously guided caliphs who succeeded the Prophet.[13]

The Safavids aggressively proselytized Shiism not just within their own realm but across the Levant. Ismail's followers in Asia Minor were known as the Qizilbash

(Redheads) after their twelve-tasseled red hats that symbolized Twelver Shiism. Their increasingly strident agitation on behalf of the shah inevitably led to friction with the Sunni Ottomans and ultimately triggered the downfall of a sultan.[14]

Bayezid sought to staunch the flow of converts to Shiism, first by closing the border with Iran and then by the forced resettlement of Shia communities away from the zone of Safavid influence. From eastern Anatolia, they were deported to the southwest of the peninsula, even to the Balkans, to get them as far away from Ismail as possible. This plan, however, completely backfired. Instead of dissipating and hence neutralizing the cancer of Shia proselytization, Ottoman policy only succeeded in spreading the infection to every corner of the empire.[15]

In 1505, Shah Ismail's brother Ebrahim crossed the frontier at the head of an army intent on pillage and plunder in Ottoman territory. It was in response to this provocation that a major player made his debut on the stage of world history. Ebrahim's incursion provoked a response from the *bey* of Trabzon on the mountainous Black Sea coast, sultan Bayezid's son, prince (*şehzade*) Selim. He raised a motley army of janissaries, mercenaries, and tribal warriors, and then not only drove the intruders out of Ottoman territory but pursued them as far as Safavid-held Erzincan, just north of the Euphrates, massacring many and seizing their arms and munitions. He then sent a separate retaliatory force to raid the western territories of the Safavids in the Caucasus.[16]

In 1507, Ismail raided the neighboring emirate of Dulkadir. This was a violation of Ottoman sovereignty, as the shah marched through Ottoman lands and recruited into his army Turkmen fighters, who were Ottoman subjects. It was also a humiliation, as the emir Alaüddevle's daughter, Ayşe Gülbahar Hatun, was a consort of Bayezid and the mother of his son, Selim. Ismail also seized Harput and executed its governor, Bekar Bey, the son of 'Alā ad-Dawla, who was ruler of the Zū al-Kadr principality and nominally a Mamluk vassal but also Selim's grandfather.

Bayezid opted not to retaliate, but Selim did, winning another battle against a Safavid army at Erzincan. Selim's successes were commemorated by Ottoman court historian and theologian Hoca Sâdeddin: "He had raised the Ottoman standard many times in these cities, devastating and baffling the Qizilbash, who are bloodthirsty people with stained swords."[17] These actions were undertaken independently and not in pursuit of official policy as determined by the Porte; in fact, Bayezid wrote to Selim many times warning him not to act on his own recognizance. "We were told that you wage untimely wars in that region," the sultan admonished his son. "You should be on the safe side, confining yourself solely to self-defense of your city. We do not give you consent to increase our enemies."[18] Selim chafed against what he perceived as a defeatist stance of appeasement towards the "faithless Qizilbash," as he warned his father:

> From day to day, their properties are significantly increasing. It is known that they are the enemies of the Ottoman dynasty in terms of religion and nation. Great disorder and sedition is expected from that faction. If they continue to be approached with negligence and inattention as it was case in the past, the disorder it causes may reach a level beyond control. And these disorders and tumults may spread everywhere in the country.

So far as Selim was concerned, "it is now obligatory that someone should assume this religious and civil duty" to put the Qizilbash in their place.[19]

Making a significant statement of his ultimate intent, Ismail took Baghdad, the former seat of the caliphs, in 1508. Recrossing the Euphrates, Ismail left a screening force in Mesopotamia under Khan Muhammad Ustājlū, who he appointed governor of Diyarbakır. The vengeful 'Alā ad-Dawla launched multiple campaigns in order to evict the Safavids from Diyarbakır, only to lose three more sons in the process – Kasım, Ahmed, and Shah Ruh – whose heads were sent as trophies to Ismail.

The shah was preoccupied with affairs at the other end of his domain, where the Iranian plateau opened out onto the steppe of Central Asia. Here, the squabbling successors of Timur were finally being swept away by the Uzbek khan Muhammad Shaybani, who conquered the great entrepôts of the Silk Route – Bukhara (1499), Samarkand (1500, 1501, 1505), Balkh (1505), and Herat (1507).[20] This run of successes ended on 2 December 1510 when Shaybani lost his army, and his life, in a confrontation with Ismail at the Battle of Merv. The shah informed the Porte of this victory by sending Bayezid the straw-filled skin of Shaybani's decapitated head.[21]

Meanwhile, Selim continued to make a name for himself on the Ottoman frontier. In 1508, he marched a fighting force northeast into the Caucasus. It took him less than a week to cover the 150 miles into southern Georgia, where his force decimated a disorganized, stunned foe, "the people of unbelief and hatred," as the *Selimname* described them. According to this account of the expedition, Selim "caused a vast area, throughout its length and breadth, to be trodden underfoot by horses swift as the wind… he made its inhabited places waste and desolate, and its prosperous regions the home and nest of the owl whose power is death." By the conclusion of the campaign, Ottoman troops were "spoil-laden and satiated through looting and plundering all its riches, goods, chattels and farms." An estimated 10,000 Georgian noncombatants were dragged into slavery: "Into the possession of the *ġāzīs*, the guides of the *ġazā*, the army of mail-clad warriors... Many jasmine-complexioned girls were taken, girls who imparted gladness and whose beauty was a delight."[22] Such exploits won Selim a favorable impression within the Ottoman military establishment, a reputation only further enhanced when he repelled another Safavid incursion in 1510.

That same year, a major Qizilbash revolt broke out in Teke in southwestern Anatolia, led by a holy man known as Şahkulu (Shah Kulu, the Slave of the Shah, or as the Ottomans labeled him, Şeytan Kulu, the Slave of the Devil), whom his supporters hailed as Messiah. Şahkulu declared himself sultan in Antalya, capital of Teke *sanjak* and a Qizilbash stronghold.

Bayezid ordered Karagöz Pasha, the *beylerbey* of Anatolia, to smash the Shia upstarts. Karagöz Pasha pursued Şahkulu out of Teke and through western Anatolia. In town after town, he witnessed the carnage the rebels left in their wake. Some 20,000 strong, Şahkulu's marauding Shia forces even burned Sunni mosques and Qur'ans. Townspeople recounted tales of murder and rape, pillage and destruction. Karagöz Pasha finally caught up with Şahkulu in Kütahya. But the outnumbered Ottoman army was routed, and Karagöz Pasha fell into the rebels' hands. On 22 April 1511, in front of the citadel of Kütahya, they impaled him for all to see, then beheaded him and burned the body.

Although not directly involved in the Şahkulu rebellion, Ismail had nevertheless exploited the ensuing chaos, sending his general Nur-Ali Khalifa into Anatolia, where he gathered many followers, including, Murad the son of *şehzade* Ahmed, who "girded the Qizilbash crown" and joined this revolt. Murad ultimately took refuge with Ismail, thus providing him with a useful royal Ottoman pawn he could deploy against whoever ultimately emerged as sultan.[23]

Another Ottoman force, under Ahmed and Grand Vizier Hadım Ali Pasha, successfully ran Şahkulu to ground near Altıntaş, but instead of fighting, Ahmed tried to win over the janissaries to endorse his claim to the throne. Failing to achieve this, he departed for Constantinople, allowing Şahkulu to escape. Ali Pasha tracked him down at Çubukova in July. At the ensuing battle on 2 July, both he and Şahkulu were killed.

The immediate threat was over as the Qizilbash dispersed upon the death of Şahkulu – the Ottoman historian Celalzâde records how "this group of hyenas were scattered in four directions as if by wind."[24] But the political implications were enormous. Though he was the preferred candidate of the Porte for the succession, Ahmed's failure to resolve the Qizilbash threat delegitimized him in the eyes of the janissaries, who blocked his attempt to cross over to Constantinople. Another uprising in Anatolia – this time among the Turkmen, stirred up by Nur-Ali Khalifa – was the final straw. Ahmed sent his vizier and *lala* (tutor), Yular Kısdı Sinan Pasha, to suppress the revolt, only for him to be defeated and killed by the rebels in a battle at Sivas.

The Ottoman state was devolving into anarchy as Bayezid had lost control of the janissaries and his three sons were all in open revolt against him. Ahmed was raising an army in Amasya to advance his claim to the throne, as was his brother and fellow *şehzade* Korkud, with limited success, in Manisa. With the support of his father-in-law, Mengli Ghiray I, khan of Crimea, Selim resolved to make his own bid. According to the chronicle of İdris-i Bitlîsî, Selim justified his insurrection against his father on the grounds:

> *Gazâ*, the tradition of my ancestors, calls for the extension of the circle of Islam through *jihad*, as allowed by the Quranic verse "O Prophet! Rouse the Believers to the fight!" To this end, our ancestors unceasingly motivated the warriors, but this tradition – obligation, even – has been disregarded for years. Old warriors have almost forgotten this heroism; adolescents have no experience of war. This good tradition of the Ottoman dynasty has been abandoned.[25]

On 3 August 1511, Selim's forces were defeated near Çorlu by troops loyal to his father. Selim had to withdraw by sea to Feodosia in the Crimea, where his son, Suleiman, was serving as *bey*, his prospects of succeeding as sultan apparently dead. Bayezid openly declared his intention to concede the throne to his favorite son, Ahmed, who in March of 1512 sought to consolidate his control over Anatolia by concluding a marriage alliance with the Safavids, pledging his son to Ismail's daughter. But ultimately, it was the support of the janissaries that proved decisive. Bayezid finally yielded to their demands and invited Selim to the capital, appointing him commander-in-chief of the army. After Selim arrived in Constantinople he deposed his father and was proclaimed sultan on 24 April. It was the first time the janissaries had orchestrated the abdication of a sultan. Bayezid died on 10 June, on his way to exile in Didymoteicho, his birthplace in Thrace.

SELIM THE GRIM

To eliminate the risk of any further contestation over his legitimacy, Selim murdered one brother, Korkud, on 13 March 1513, and bested the other, Ahmed, in battle near Bursa on 24 April 1513, ordering his defeated rival's immediate execution. He then systematically hunted down and liquidated his nephews, purging all seven unfortunate enough to be ensnared in his dragnet.[26] This brutality was a prerequisite for restoring order to the Ottoman state, which could only function on the basis of the absolute centralization of power in the Porte. "A carpet is big enough for two Sufis," Selim was quoted as saying; "The world is not big enough for two sultans." Selim's capacity for sociopathic violence – encapsulated in his sobriquet, *Yavuz* (the Grim) – was proverbial, and not in any way restricted to his own family. Rival members of the Ottoman military ruling elite would curse each other by wishing for their opponents to be granted high offices under Selim, and of the six men who served him as grand vizier, only one, Piri Mehmed Pasha, survived to tell the tale.[27]

Selim's priority upon consummating his ascendancy to the throne was pacifying the eastern frontier through imposing his authority over Shah Ismail. In order to focus on chastising the *kızılbāş-ı evbāş* (Qizilbash rabble), Selim first needed to secure his western frontier. The new sultan was only too aware that the rise of the Safavids had caught the attention of the Christian West, and he could not risk allowing this to culminate in an alliance between Europe and Persia that would confront him with the prospect of fighting a war on two fronts.

It was true that from the first years of the Safavid ascendancy, Europeans had expressed a genuine fascination with this hitherto unknown dynasty rising in the East. As early as 1502, Constantino Laschari, a Venetian spy, reported to the senate that, "The Sophi [Sufi] religion has always fought against the Ottoman royal house because the Ottomans are heretics and usurpers of the territories of many Muslims. Ismail is considered a prophet, rich, just, generous, and divinely inspired. He is much beloved of his sect which is a certain religion – Catholic in their way."[28]

That last clause was the utmost in wishful thinking, but it reflected the all-pervasive desperation throughout an isolated and friendless Europe to find like-minded souls somewhere out there in the wider world, a perspective suffusing the argument of a Portuguese observer ten years later that "those who wear the red cap are more like Portuguese than like people from anywhere else."[29] It was this mentality that led the Portuguese into searching for Prester John in Africa and convincing themselves Hindu temples in India were Catholic churches. The Venetians would indulge in the same illusions. Reporting to the senate in 1507, Giovanni Morosini also extolled the martial qualities of Shah Ismail; while admitting he could not exactly confirm the nature of the Sophi's faith, he conjectured it was "more Christian than otherwise."[30]

In 1507, Giles of Viterbo pleaded a case before Pope Julius II assuring him the wars between the Ottomans and the Safavids created the perfect opportunity for a crusade. That same year, Morosini made the same point to the *Signoria*: "This is the opportune moment to form an alliance among the Christian princes and Persia to engage in the most holy endeavor to throw the Turk out of Europe."[31] Bestselling books by Giovanni Francesco Rota (*La vita de Sophi, Re di Persia et de Media*, 1508) and Martín Fernández de Figueroa (*Tratado de la conquista de las Islas de Persia y Arabia*, 1512) kept Western interest alive in the intriguing possibility of a powerful potential ally on the far side of the Ottoman colossus. From out of nowhere, Ismail was now second only to Prester John as a messianic figure in whom Christendom saw its salvation.

In 1513, Pope Leo X received a memorial, the *Libellus ad Leonem Decimum*, from two Camaldulensian monks, Pietro Querini (who had served his native Venice as a diplomat) and Paolo Giustinian. Their geopolitical analysis offered a glimmer of hope for a beleaguered Europe; the good news was that "now, when the infidels are at odds among themselves, and not only peoples against people, ruler against ruler, but even brother against brother, they wage savage wars with overwhelming hatred of one another, victory is more easily assured you!"[32] The primary source of this division within the ranks of the infidel was the rise of a new power in Persia, a messianic leader they dubbed the Sophy. Although this figure was an infidel, the Holy Father was urged to enlist his aid against the Ottomans, "for when the Christians attack the Turks from one direction, and this most powerful sovereign has begun an attack upon them from the other, you will certainly be delivered, most blessed Father, of your enemies."[33]

However, while Europe was clearly open to the possibility of a partnership with the Safavid state, arriving at specific covenants would prove more problematic. After seizing Baghdad in 1508, Ismail had dispatched an embassy to the doge via Pietro Zeno, the Venetian consul in Damascus, requesting that Venice send artillery masters by way of Syria and that the Venetian navy keep the Ottomans occupied in the Aegean while Ismail attacked them in Asia Minor. Venice responded sympathetically but without committing itself, preoccupied as it was with the war against the pope and his allies in the League of Cambrai, and unwilling to upset the status quo of its existing trade privileges in the Levant.[34]

In the event, Selim found the European powers receptive to his overtures. The prevailing attitude among the risk-averse Western governing elite towards a war between the great Muslim powers was not to pick sides in order to keep both weak and one grateful but rather to let them fight and enjoy the peace while it lasted.

This perspective was neatly encapsulated later that century in the account of Giovanni-Tommaso Minadoi, a renowned Italian physician who spent many years in Aleppo and Constantinople in the diplomatic service of Venice. His commentary on the 1578–90 Ottoman–Safavid War was published in many translations, rendered in English as *The Historie of Warres between the Turkes and the Persians* (1595). He acknowledged the prowess in battle of the Ottomans and Safavids, "both of them among the Barbarians beeing most mightie & most warlike Princes." The conflict between them was therefore heaven-sent, for it constituted "A warre not onely long & bloudie, but also very commodious and of great oportunitie to the Christian Commonwealth: for that it hath granted leisure to the Champions of Christ to refresh and encrease their forces, being now much weakened by warres both Forreine and Ciuill."[35]

On this basis, King Matthias Corvinus and Sultan Bayezid II had concluded a five-year truce in 1483, followed by a two-year truce in 1488, which would be renewed in 1495, 1498, 1503, 1509, and 1510. In 1514, Selim arrived at another three-year truce with King Vladislaus II of Hungary, and a separate three-year truce with Vladislaus's brother, King Sigismund I of Poland.[36]

CHALDIRAN, 1514

With diplomacy having enabled him to concentrate all his forces against the Safavids, in order to legitimize his war against Ismail, the sultan secured *fatwas* from two influential theologians, Hamza Saru Görez (who authorized Selim to have the Qizilbash "men killed and their possessions, women and children divided among the army") and Kemal Paşazade (who ruled "their status is that of the apostates, and once conquered… their possessions, women and children would be considered spoils; as for their men, they should be killed unless they become Muslims").[37]

With that mandate, Selim set out from Edirne on 20 March 1514, having dispatched additional diplomatic missions to Sultan Qansuh al-Ghawri in Cairo to prevent any Mamluk rapprochement with the Safavids and to 'Ubayd Allāh Khan, the dominant figure within the Uzbek confederation, proposing he attack Ismail from the east as the Ottomans approached from the west. He also ordered the Qizilbash of Anatolia exterminated to prevent any disruption within his own domains. Early in his reign he had created a register of all Shia "age seven to seventy" living in the towns of Tokat, Samsun, Sivas, Amasya, and Yozgat. Now, as his army passed through these communities, it rounded up and executed everyone on the register who could be found, just one phase of a wider massacre that took the lives of an estimated 40,000 Shia.[38]

A most undiplomatic war of words presaged the actual fighting between sultan and shah. Any correspondence from the Porte was addressed from Selim, "the Caliph of God Most High in this world… the Solomon of Splendor, the Alexander of eminence; haloed in victory… slayer of the wicked and the infidel, guardian of the noble and the pious; the warrior in the Path, the defender of the Faith; the champion, the conqueror; the lion, son and grandson of the lion; standard-bearer of justice and righteousness," to Ismail, "the possessor of the land of tyranny and perversion, the captain of the vicious, the chief of the malicious, the usurping Darius of the time, the malevolent Zahhak of the age, the peer of Cain."[39]

Selim accused Ismail of having "incited your abominable Shia faction to unsanctified sexual union and the shedding of innocent blood."[40] Therefore, "the ancient obligation of extirpation, extermination, and expulsion of evil innovation must be the aim of our exalted aspiration," Selim declaimed. "[T]he lightning of our conquering sword shall uproot the untamed bramble grown to great heights in the path of the refulgent Divine Law and shall cast them down upon the dust of abjectness to be trampled under the hooves of our legions."[41] Accordingly, the sultan vowed to "crown the head of every gallows tree with the head of a crown-wearing Sûfî [Shia] and clear that faction from the face of the earth."[42]

For his part, taunting Selim – indeed, daring him to invade – Ismail replied with a threat couched in verse:

Bitter experience has taught that in this world of trial
He who falls upon the house of 'Alî always falls.[43]

In the event, for all his aggression on paper, Selim found asserting his authority in the field when he invaded Safavid territory frustratingly difficult. The city of Diyarbakır was taken without resistance, but the Safavids refused to stand their ground, pulling back into the Armenian highlands and leaving scorched earth in their wake. As the army marched ever deeper into an apparently trackless wilderness in pursuit of an elusive enemy whose *köpek savaşı* (dogfight) hit and run tactics took a constant toll, Ottoman supply lines were soon stretched, and the rank and file grew mutinous. The janissaries demanded the campaign be abandoned. Selim had the bearer of this ultimatum, the *beylerbey* of Karaman, Hemden Pasha, executed. In response, disaffected janissaries actually loosed shots at the sultan's tent in protest. Selim dismissed his viziers Hersekzade Ahmed Pasha and Dukaginzade Ahmed Pasha during the Chaldiran campaign and humiliated them by pulling their tents down on their heads before personally stabbing the latter and ordering his decapitation.

Ismail was winning this campaign by simply refusing to give Selim the decisive battle he wanted and letting attrition take its course. Selim knew this, and accordingly escalated the war of insults. After he sent the shah a gift of several barrels of wine – for "it more becomes the son of the Sufi to sit in the *tekke* [gathering place of a Sufi order]" than go to war – Ismail responded by delivering to the Ottoman camp opium paste and a golden opium pot, with a note blithely maintaining that the sultan's letters could only have been written by scribes lost in the oblivion of narcotics. The subtext may have been the implication that Selim, like his father, was himself an opium addict. In any event, the enraged Selim had Ismail's envoy executed and sent the shah in return a set of female garments, including a veil, advising Ismail to dress in women's clothing, as "masculinity is *haram* [forbidden] for you."[44]

Had the Safavids kept their distance until winter, the Ottomans would have had to withdraw. But Selim had succeeded in infiltrating a double agent, Şeyh Ahmed, into the shah's inner circle. This turncoat informed Ismail that the Turkmen and Kurdish *beys* ostensibly loyal to the sultan were only waiting for the opportunity to switch sides, and the advent of battle would provide them with the decisive moment to do so. And indeed, by this point, Ismail, never defeated in battle, had fully internalized the Qizilbash perception of him as the *mürşid-i kâmil* (perfect guide). Written in his own hand, his poetry reflected his messianic sense of destiny:

I am the living *Khidr* [angel] and Jesus, son of Mary.
I am the Alexander of my contemporaries.[45]

Trusting to his divine calling, and perhaps smarting under the ceaseless string of insults he was being subjected to by Selim (who accused him of continually running away "like a woman," in which case, "You had better wear a *chador* instead of your armor"), Ismail was finally prepared to meet the sultan in a clash of arms, and in fact play with a weaker hand in doing so. It is a reflection of the key difference between the more corporate, centralized Ottoman state and that of the more feudal Safavids, where loyalty was still owed to a cult of personality and not the state, which in turn lacked the administration necessary to effectively mobilize the empire's military assets, that Ismail went into the battle badly outnumbered, with some pledged units not yet arrived in his camp – Deev Sultan of Balkh only reached Azerbaijan after the battle was decided. In addition, Ismail took the field entirely outgunned. In his epic poem the *Lusiads*, Luís Vaz de Camões asks his reader to:

> See mighty Persia, that noble empire,
> Its warriors forever in the saddle,
> Scorning the use of smelted bronze,
> Or to have hands uncalloused by weapons.[46]

While the Ottomans had integrated the smelted bronze of gunpowder technology into their military machine generations earlier, the Safavids still went to war in a style familiar to their ancestors – heavily reliant on cavalry, both light, armed with the compound bow for killing at a distance, and heavy, for its shock value in close quarters.

The two sides came together at Chaldiran, northeast of Lake Van, on 22 August 1514. Two leading Safavid commanders, Mohammad Bey Ustājlū and Nur-Ali Khalifa, who had experience fighting the Ottomans, urged Ismail to attack immediately before the enemy had time to complete setting up their cannon and deploying troops, and avoid frontal attacks due to the threat of Ottoman firepower; "We must give battle to them when they are on the move," Ustājlū insisted.[47]

But Ismail was swayed by the arguments of another highly influential Qizilbash leader, Durmish Khan Shamlu, who counseled that a pre-emptive attack before the Ottomans were prepared would be "unmanly" and the actions of a coward. Ismail bought into this chivalric, almost romantic perspective on warfare; "I am not a caravanserai thief," he is alleged to have said.[48] So Selim was given ample time to complete the positioning of his artillery to best effect. The guns were chained together, which would block the Iranian cavalry from charging through the spaces between them. The Ottomans then stationed their arquebus-armed janissaries behind their own artillery.

Selim arranged his army into three divisions. At the center were the janissary troops under the command of Selim himself, with the Rumelian troops on the left under the command of Hasan Pasha (the *beylerbey* of Rumelia) and the Anatolian troops on the right under the command of Sinan Pasha (the *beylerbey* of Anatolia). Conversely, Ismail organized his army into two wings: on the right were the 20,000 *qizilbashes* under the command of Ismail, while the left was composed of 15,000 fighters who were commanded by Mohammad Bey Ustājlū and his brother Karahan. Ismail also detached some 10,000 men under the command of his grand vizier Seyyid Abdülbāki and his chief judge (*kadıasker*) Seyyid Serif to serve as his tactical reserve and protect his standard.

At the appointed hour on 23 August, Ismail initiated the battle, leading the Safavid right flank in a charge that killed the commander of the Ottoman flank opposite, Hasan Pasha. It is a testament to Ottoman discipline that their line buckled but did not break. Meanwhile, Ustājlū, leading from the front, was killed by artillery fire, whereupon his wing scattered.

Ismail responded by leading charge after charge against the Ottoman center. One account of the battle records how the shah "entered that frightful field in person, supervising the course of the battle and performing deeds of valor surpassing those of [ancient heroes]." Ottoman histories acknowledge that Ismail "several times forced his horse right up to the gun carriages and the barricade, and with blows of his sword severed the chains linking the gun carriages."[49] One Ottoman historian derived an account of the battle from his grandfather, Hafız Mehmed, a veteran of Chaldiran, who witnessed the shah personally lead seven assaults into the Ottoman ranks, changing his horse each time.

The secondhand account of the Venetian ambassador to the Porte, Caterino Zeno, maintains the battle turned when Sinan Pasha, on his own initiative, led the Ottoman right wing in a charge against Ismail's open flank. This perspective emphasizes the decisive impact of Ottoman firepower, and the ultimate price the Safavids paid for their affected disdain towards gunpowder technology:

> The monarch [Selim], seeing the slaughter, began to retreat, and to turn about, and was about to fly, when Sinan, coming to the rescue at the time of need, caused the artillery to be brought up and fired on both the janissaries and the Persians. The Persian horses hearing the thunder of those infernal machines, scattered and divided themselves over the plain, not obeying their riders' bit or spur any more, from the terror they were in. Sinan, seeing this, made up one squadron of cavalry from all that which had made been routed by the Persians, and began to cut them into pieces everywhere, so that, by his activity, Selim, even when he thought all lost, came off the victor. It is certainly said, that if it had not been for the artillery, which terrified in the manner related the Persian horses which had never before heard such a din, all his forces would have been routed and put to the edge of the sword; and if the Turk had been beaten, the power of Ismail would have become greater than that of Tamerlane, as by the fame alone of such a victory he would have made himself absolute lord of the East.[50]

The Safavids finally broke. For the first time, the shah was forced off the battlefield. He was thrown from his horse and only escaped through the sacrifice of one of his disciples, who impersonated the shah in order to draw off the Ottoman pursuit. In the aftermath, Ismail's camp was stormed and one of his wives – Tajlu Khanum according to the Ottomans, Behruzeh Khanum according to the Safavids – was taken captive, borne back to Constantinople, and forced into an arranged marriage. Any prisoners-of-war who fell into Ottoman hands were executed on Selim's orders.

It was a decisive set-piece victory, but in the event, Selim was unable to fully exploit his triumph. The Ottoman army entered the undefended Safavid capital of Tabriz on 5 September, only to abandon the city just eight days later. The onset of winter was imminent, and the Ottomans were too deep in unfamiliar and unfriendly territory, with their communication and supply lines dangerously exposed to interdiction. Ismail reoccupied Tabriz without incident, but as he withdrew, Selim took Kars to the northwest of Azerbaijan, as well as Nakhchivan, and Yerevan in the Caucasus. The geopolitical alignment of the Middle East would now take on a character remarkably similar to that which had prevailed between the Battle of Carrhae in 53 BC and the rise of Islam more than six centuries later. Just as the Fertile Crescent had once been divided between East and West, between a Roman empire centered on Constantinople and a Persian dynasty whose heartland was the Iranian plateau, the Battle of Chaldiran marked the inception of a new rivalry between superpowers along the same axis, with the same stakes. In time, the Ottomans would drive the Safavids out of Mesopotamia altogether, pushing down the Tigris and Euphrates to claim Baghdad and then Basra on the Persian Gulf, thus establishing the frontier between contemporary Iran and Iraq. But the Shia revolution inspired by Ismail and his successors lives on today in terms of demographics and identities that do not conform so neatly to territorial borders.

CONQUEST OF THE MAMLUKS

With Ismail chastened and his eastern flank secure, Selim was now free to pursue his annexation of the Dulkadir emirate in 1515, setting up the confrontation he wanted with the Dulkadirs' nominal sovereigns, the Mamluks, who were now clearly a spent force.[51] Portuguese intervention in the Indian Ocean had crippled Mamluk finances, the Mamluk military had not kept pace with the gunpowder revolution, and Bedouin raids on the caravan traffic to and from Mecca had culminated in the 1505–06 suspension of the *hajj*, a grave embarrassment for the

Mamluk sultan, whose legitimacy in the Muslim world depended upon his ability to protect pilgrimages to the holy places.

In 1516, Selim annexed the Zū al-Kadr principality and sent the head of ʿAlā ad-Dawla to the sultan of Cairo with an attached formal declaration of war. Selim was totally victorious at the Battle of Marj Dabiq on 24 August 1516. The seventy-eight-year-old Mamluk Sultan Qansuh was killed, his army disintegrated, and in the aftermath the Ottomans occupied Aleppo, Damascus, and Jerusalem without a struggle. Selim's name was incorporated into the sermon (*hutbe*) during the next Friday prayer, performed in the great mosque of the Umayyad caliphs in Damascus.

Selim was relentless. The Ottoman army covered the 200-mile gap across the Sinai desert from Gaza into the Mamluk heartland of Egypt in just five days in mid-January 1517. The Mamluks suffered a second crushing defeat on 23 January 1517 at the Battle of Raydaniyya on the outskirts of Cairo. The last Mamluk sultan, Tuman Bey II, was hunted down and held in the Ottoman camp for two weeks before being paraded in his misery through Cairo on 13 April and handed over to Şehsuvaroğlu Ali Bey, who hanged him at the Zuwayla Gate, from which the Mamluks had hanged his father, Şehsuvar, the *bey* of Dulgadiroğlu, forty-seven years earlier.

So ended the Mamluk dynasty, which had ruled for more than 250 years in Egypt and Syria. Selim had triumphed in one of the most complete, and decisive, victories in military history. The Middle East now passed to an Ottoman hegemony that would persist for the next four centuries until the Porte was finally dispossessed during the First World War. The extent of Ottoman territory – 341,100 square miles when Selim took the throne – had five years later expanded to 576,900 square miles. In addition to its territorial aggrandizement, because of these conquests, the Ottoman Empire was fundamentally transformed.

Fiscally, the additional revenues derived from the annexation of Syria and Egypt would massively expand the Ottoman state's economic base. Previously, the Porte had derived the vast bulk of the financing necessary to fund its war machine from taxes on agriculture, supplemented by tolls and tariffs and as much as fifty tons of silver extracted annually from the mines of Rumelia.[52] Income to the treasury now rose from 72.9 million akçe (1.4 million Venetian gold ducats) in 1509 to 116.9 million akçe (2.2 million gold ducats) in 1523, and to 141 million akçe (2.6 million gold ducats) in 1524, primarily due to the acquisition of the advanced markets of Syria and Egypt. By 1527, income to the treasury had reached 277 million akçe (5 million gold ducats), excluding revenues from *timar* lands. Of this revenue, 42 percent came from the province of Egypt, and 9 percent from Syria. In other words, a decade after they were forcibly incorporated into the Ottoman state, Egypt and Syria accounted for about half of Ottoman state revenue.[53]

Socially, for the first time, the polyglot Ottoman milieu would have a majority Muslim population. Indeed, in the aftermath of the 1517 campaign, the sharif of Mecca, Abu al-Barakat II bin Muhammad, sent his son and co-ruler, Abu Numayy II ibn Barakat, to Cairo to pledge loyalty to Selim and beg the Ottoman sultan to confirm him as emir of the Hijaz. Abu Numayy handed Selim the keys to the Kaaba on 6 July, signifying he had earned the Islamic honorific *kahdim al-haramayn ash-Sharififayn* (servant of the two Holy Cities). Selim thus emerged with recognized authority over the Islamic world's religious heartland in addition to his enormously enhanced secular power. At that moment, his regime was in its ascendancy, having wrenched the global geopolitical center decisively away from Europe and its peripheral expansion by sea. As Andrew Hess concludes, "the doubling of the Ottoman empire in 1517 not only began the sixteenth-century world war but it also tilted the balance of power in the Afro-Eurasian area toward [Constantinople] and not the Atlantic Ocean."[54] Giancarlo Casale also argues it is "no exaggeration to declare the Ottomans victors in the opening round of history's first truly global struggle for dominance."[55]

That Selim would next hurl his peerless war machine against Christendom was received wisdom in the West, where the folly of buying a temporary reprieve from Ottoman aggression by allowing the sultan to first discipline the Safavids and then eradicate the Mamluks was beginning to be appreciated. As Pope Leo X wrote to Cardinal Thomas Wolsey (Sir Thomas More's predecessor as Lord High Chancellor of England and right-hand man to King Henry VIII) on 20 August 1518, where there had formerly been two "most ample empires" in the East, and hence a balance of power, after Selim's destruction of the Mamluks only one now remained. With this accomplished, the sultan, "inflated by this victory, as we have heard, is preparing a great fleet in the East for an attack, as many people suspect, upon Christian territories since he has no other enemies left whom he can assail by sea."[56] Now, the storm was up, for Selim, if not confronted by a united front, "would in a short time doubtless lead to the ruin of the whole of Christendom. Since the most ferocious Turk has brought Alexandria, Egypt, and almost the entire Eastern Roman Empire under his control and has fitted an imposing fleet... he no longer craves only Sicily or Italy but the empire of the entire Earth."[57]

The West was only spared the wrath of Selim by the ongoing defiance of Shah Ismail in the East. On 30 December 1517, Cardinal de' Medici wrote to a French correspondent that Selim "is returning to Constantinople victorious and secure without hindrance or fear of the sophi, with the certain intention of launching an attack upon Christians."[58] But in fact, Ismail remained professedly unintimidated by the outcome of the 1514 campaign, and Safavid pressure began to build in Mesopotamia in 1518. In response, the Ottoman war machine had to remain focused on campaigning in the Levant. The terms of their confrontation had evolved, however. Using guns recently acquired from the Portuguese, the Safavids inflicted a stinging defeat on an Ottoman force in Anatolia in March 1519. They then went on to seize Mosul later that spring, slaughtering its Ottoman garrison, then did the same in Baghdad that summer, killing some 12,000 Ottoman soldiers and civilians. Refugees reported that Ismail had somewhere between 60,000 and 80,000 cavalry in Iraq, many guns from the Portuguese, and many mercenaries on his payroll, including Georgians, Tatars, and about 1,500 Ottoman defectors.[59] Selim also had to put down Safavid-inspired uprisings throughout his own domain. In just one example, in March 1520, a rebellion some 10,000 strong erupted in the north-central Anatolian towns of Amasya and Tokat.

Ismail continued his outreach to the West in search of prospective partners with which to contain the Ottoman threat. In 1515, Pope Leo X wrote to King Sigismund of Poland with the intriguing news that Fabrizio del Carretto, Grand Master of the Knights Hospitaller headquartered on the island of Rhodes, had received a Safavid envoy bearing an offer of alliance against their common Ottoman enemy:

We have been lately advised by letters of the Grand Master of Rhodes that the Sophy, king of Persia, who now for long past had conceived a hatred against the Tyrant of the Turks, had delegated an envoy to him [the Grand Master] to say that the latter should use every endeavor to report to all Christians and to stir up them, both kings and princes, to take arms against this same Turk, manfully and courageously, from our side. Because, if he shall perceive us likewise ready and armed for this crisis, he [i.e., the Persian king] promised of his own free will that he on his side likewise would rise and attack that enemy in hostile array, and all the cities formerly belonging to the Christians he would cede to the Christians themselves to hold and possess.[60]

Ismail was also active in initiating negotiations with the Portuguese, who had unexpectedly arrived in the Indian Ocean and then Persian Gulf just as he was consolidating his control over Iran. In 1510, the shah's envoy to the court of

Bijapur had offered the Portuguese governor of India, Afonso de Albuquerque, a vaguely worded offer of military cooperation against the Mamluks. Further diplomatic initiatives are recorded in 1515, when Ismail sought to enlist Portuguese assistance for his plans to take Bahrain and Qatif.

In response, Albuquerque dispatched Fernão Gomes de Lemos to Ismail with instructions to conclude an offensive alliance with the shah against both Sunni superpowers in the Middle East. In a campaign against the Mamluks, Albuquerque insisted, "you can reckon upon great assistance from the Armada of the King my Lord by sea, and I believe that with small trouble you must gain the lordship of the city of Cairo and all his kingdom and dependencies." In a campaign against the Ottomans, "my Lord can give you great help by sea against the Turk, and thus his fleets by sea and you with your great forces and cavalry by land can combine to inflict troublous injuries upon them."[61] Although Albuquerque even went so far as to claim Ismail was "a thunderbolt launched by the Almighty for the destruction of Islam," nothing came of this initiative, nor from the subsequent embassy of Baltasar Pessoa to Tabriz in 1523.[62] The Safavids were content to utilize the Portuguese as a conduit to trade with the wider world, especially in order to import the gunpowder technology they needed to face off against the Ottomans, but did not perceive them as peers or partners.[63]

5

SULEIMAN, PART I – SECOND BELGRADE, SECOND RHODES, AND MOHÁCS

BELGRADE, 1521

The Western powers lost a potentially golden opportunity to take advantage of the inner turmoil roiling the Ottoman regime during the twilight years of Sultan Bayezid II. On 18 July 1511, Pope Julius II issued a bull announcing the meeting of a church council at the Lateran Palace to be held beginning in April of the following year. Among the items on the agenda was the unification of Europe so as to "prosecute a holy war against the Turks." The first session of the council assessed the danger the Ottomans posed to Christendom, with the archbishop of Split defining the threat in the most apocalyptic terms:

> Within the confines of Europe they have usurped no mean dominion with the effusion of much Christian blood. They could easily transport themselves to the gates of Rome in the space of one night from their domain in Dalmatia... Not one among them has learned respect for the female sex, for the piety of youth, or compassion for the aged... They snatch children from the arms of their parents and infants from the breast of their mothers; they violate wives in front of their husbands, they snatch virgins from the embrace of their mothers in wild lust, they cut down aged parents as though useless, in full view of their children; they yoke youths to the plough as if they were oxen and they destroy the cultivated land.[1]

On 3 December 1512, Emperor Maximilian established an alliance with the papacy for the purpose of a general campaign against the Ottomans but, as was the case in previous attempts, any genuine fervor for a crusade expired with its chief instigator when Pope Julius died two months later.

Selim's victories in the East jolted the papacy into making preparations for renewed conflict with the *Turcarum tyrannus* (Tyrant of the Turks). Pope Leo X charged a select commission of cardinals to examine Selim's military potential and report on the feasibility of a crusade. In November 1517 this body reported that Selim already had a navy of 300 galleys, with more being built. For the planned crusade, the report suggested recruiting 60,000 Swiss, Spanish, Czech, and *Landsknecht* infantry; 4,000 French and Italian heavy cavalry; and 12,000 Spanish, Italian, Albanian, and Greek light cavalry. An armada of 110 galleys – twenty each from France, Spain, and Genoa, forty from Venice, and ten from the papacy – plus carracks and galleons from France, England, Spain, and Portugal would be necessary to secure control of the sea lanes. The commission outlined three main directions of attack: through Germany and Hungary, through Dalmatia and Illyria, and through Italy.[2]

But there was little popular enthusiasm for a crusade at that time. Most European states were recovering from their exertions in the War of the League of Cambrai (1509–17), fought between Venice and its allied foes France, the Holy Roman Empire, Spain, the papacy, Ferrara, and Mantua. Suffering defeat after defeat on its mainland, Venice had renewed its treaty with the Ottomans in September 1517, agreeing to pay the sultan an annual tribute of 8,000 ducats.

And papal authority to speak for, let alone mobilize, Christendom was itself beginning to unravel. A prominent critic of the concept of the crusade was the humanist scholar Desiderius Erasmus. In his *Dulce bellum inexpertis* (*War seems sweet to those who have not experienced it*, 1515), he asked: "What do you suppose the Turks think, when they hear of Christian kings raging against each other, with all the madness of so many evils let loose? And raging for what? Merely on account of a claim set up for power, for empire, and dominion."[3] Those who declaimed for holy war were in effect saying: "I am really hankering after the riches of the Ottomans, and I cover it up with the defense of religion."[4]

The sale of indulgences, an established mechanism by which the papacy had encouraged its flock to contribute towards raising the necessary financial reserves for a crusade, on this occasion touched off an explosive backlash in the Holy Roman Empire, where the intersection between an emerging German nationalism and a wider demand for ecclesiastic reform found expression in the writing of a previously obscure Augustinian cleric named Martin Luther. His *Ninety-Five Theses* of October

1517 was a direct challenge to papal dominion in matters of faith, and it immediately found a receptive audience, both at the grassroots and at the elite level.

Writing in defense of his theses the following year, Luther complained of the pope's foolish arrogance in thinking that he could drive away "the Turks and Tatars and other infidels whom every single Christian knows to be the whips and rod of God." Indeed, it was a sin for the pope to "dream of fighting a war against the sultan," for that represented a "war against the punishment for iniquity and not against the iniquities, and to struggle against God, who says that He uses that rod to punish our sins, as we do not punish them ourselves."

When asked by George Spalatin, secretary to the imperial elector Frederick the Wise, on his opinion regarding the intention of the papacy for a crusade against the Ottomans, Luther responded:

> If I rightly understand you, you ask whether an expedition against the Turks can be defended by me on biblical grounds. Even supposing the war should be undertaken for pious reasons rather than for gain, I confess that I cannot promise what you ask, but rather the opposite...
>
> It seems to me, if we must have any Turkish war, we ought to begin with ourselves. In vain we wage carnal wars without, while at home we are conquered by spiritual battles...
>
> Now that the Roman Curia is more tyrannical than any Turk, fighting with such portentous deeds against Christ and against his Church, and now that the clergy is sunk in the depths of avarice, ambition and luxury, and now that the face of the Church is everywhere most wretched, there is no hope of a successful war or of victory. As far as I can see, God fights against us; first, we must conquer him with tears, pure prayers, holy life and pure faith.[5]

Rather than going to war, especially if it was conceived of as a crusade, Germany should, for the present, "Let the Turks be Turks." In *Von den guten Werckenn*, Luther suggested that "Christendom is being destroyed not by the Turks, but by those who are supposed to defend it." In *An den Christlichen Adel deutscher Nation*, he argued that, "If we want to fight against the Turks, let us begin here where they are worst of all."[6] Proof that this message resonated was established in July 1518, when the Imperial *Diet* at Augsburg refused to contribute military funding against the Ottomans, declaring that Christianity had "more to fear from the pope than from the Turks. Much as we may dread the ravages of the infidel, they can hardly drain Christendom more effectually than it is now drained by the exactions of the Church."[7]

Even as the pillars of papal hegemony crumbled beneath him, in a final effort to impose the moral authority of any pope claiming to at least theoretically preside over Christendom, Leo X issued a bull dated 6 March 1518 announcing a five-years' truce (*quinquennales treugae et induciae*) among all Christian princes on penalty of excommunication. A flurry of diplomatic negotiations to resolve differences and unite Christendom culminated in the Treaty of London on 4 October 1518, confirming a five-year peace among the great powers. However, the death of Emperor Maximilian just three months later and the resultant jostling for advantage between the Habsburgs and the French, which erupted into outright war in 1521, consumed European military resources and again destroyed any possibility of collective action. Those states along the eastern frontier of Europe were thus abandoned and left to their own devices at the precise moment Ottoman power waxed greater than ever before.

Perhaps the key persona in this process emerged on the scene at that moment. Charles Habsburg was born on 24 February 1500, the son of Philip the Handsome, the Duke of Burgundy, and Joanna, Queen of Castile. When his father died on 25 September 1506, he inherited Burgundy, and upon the death of his maternal grandfather, King Ferdinand, on 23 January 1516 he inherited Spain. When his paternal grandfather, Emperor Maximilian, died on 12 January 1519, he was proclaimed in absentia King of the Romans in Frankfurt am Main on 23 October 1520. Three days later, he was elected Holy Roman Emperor Charles V in Aachen.

Aged just twenty, and without conflict, Charles had emerged with sovereign power over the Holy Roman Empire, the Duchy of Burgundy (including the Netherlands), and Spain (including its Italian dependencies, such as Sicily, Naples, Sardinia, and Corsica, and its evolving colonial empire in the Americas). Theoretically, no one individual in the history of Christendom, not even Charlemagne, had ruled over so much territory or presided over so many souls since the time of the Caesars. In reality, Habsburg power was circumscribed by the very breadth and diversity that made it look so impressive on a map. Charles ruled through outsourcing responsibility for local governance to key family members. The Netherlands and Burgundy were administered in his stead by his aunt, Margaret, and, after her death, by his sister, Mary of Hungary. Spain was also governed by regents, first his wife, Isabel of Portugal, and then his son, the future King Philip II. His brother Ferdinand first ruled as viceroy (*kaiserlicher Statthalter*) in the Habsburg heartland of Austria, then from 1531 as King of the Romans before finally succeeding Charles as emperor from 1556 until his death in 1564.

And Habsburg authority was by no means absolute. The process of governance was one of constant negotiation between Charles and his subjects, a point brought home immediately upon his assumption of power in Spain, where he had to make concessions in order to secure the support of each *cortes* (legislature) in Castile, Aragon, Catalonia, and Valencia to legitimize his regime, and where a bloody uprising, the Revolt of the Comuneros, raged from April 1520 to October 1521. It was a similar story in the Holy Roman Empire, where winning over the fractious Imperial *Diet* was a necessary precursor towards accomplishment of any initiative in domestic or foreign policy. Even in his native Netherlands, Charles complained, "everyone demands privileges that are contrary to my sovereignty, as if I were their companion and not their lord."[8] And those were just the formal institutions of governance. Always hard pressed to find the means by which to pay for the wars that were an endemic feature of his reign, Charles was permanently engaged in haggling over financial terms with the major movers and shakers of Renaissance capitalism, in particular the great German banking families, such as the Fugger, the Welser, the Höchstetter, and the Imhof. It was a key harbinger of the new age that a self-made man like Jakob Fugger could make himself so indispensable to the great dynastic crowned heads of Europe. The collateral he demanded from Maximilian in exchange for the loans the emperor so desperately needed had enabled him to corner the Habsburg silver and copper mining interests in the Balkans by 1508. It was the Fugger loan of 543,000 florins that enabled Charles to accumulate the 850,000 florins necessary to bribe the seven German electors critical to his succeeding Maximilian as emperor in 1519.[9] Habsburg and Fugger interests would continue to be almost symbiotically intertwined for the rest of the century.

Finally, on top of all of these obligations, Charles was also burdened with his responsibility for the religious welfare of his subjects, leading to constant friction between the secular authority of the emperor and the parallel spiritual authority of the pope.

Those were the internal constraints on Habsburg freedom of action. Externally, Charles was circumscribed by the ingrained resistance to the centralization of power inherent to the balance of power that defined the European state system. From the beginning, Charles had sought to use the looming shadow of Ottoman expansion as a rationale for his aggrandizement of imperial authority. In his speech to the *cortes* of Castile on 31 March 1520 justifying his bid to become Holy Roman Emperor, Charles insisted, "I have not sought this responsibility of such extent for myself." Indeed, it was only an unfortunate "fatal necessity" that compelled him to accept the task of leading the defense of Europe, "whose [Ottoman] enemy has expanded so much that neither the repose of Christendom, nor the dignity of Spain, nor finally the welfare of my kingdoms are able to withstand such a threat. All these are hardly able to exist or be maintained unless I link Spain with Germany and add the title of emperor to king of Spain."[10]

Though his personal motto, *Plus Ultra* (Further Beyond), implied universal ambition, the essential personal quality of Charles V was his fundamental conservatism. With the notable exceptions of Italy and the Maghreb, where he led campaigns in person, and the New World – where colonial aggrandizement was undertaken by freebooting conquistadors at a far remove from imperial oversight, let alone direction – the path of Habsburg policy as regards territoriality was fundamentally defensive as opposed to expansionist. While his grandfather, Ferdinand, had aspired to lead a crusade to the east and liberate the Holy Land, Charles inherited no such messianic ambition.[11]

This fact did nothing to allay the suspicions of the other monarchs of Europe. They saw the unprecedented accretion of power by Charles not as a potential rallying point for collective action against the Ottomans, but rather as an existential threat to their own sovereignty. If Charles was allowed to become strong enough to wrest control of Constantinople from the sultan, he would be more than strong enough to subdue any state in Christendom. Nowhere was this fear more all-pervasive than in France, where it was the primary determinant of foreign policy from the moment Charles was crowned Holy Roman Emperor through the Thirty Years War in the 17th century to the War of the Spanish Succession in the 18th. For this reason, it was Francis I, the Valois king of France from 1515 until his death in 1547, who would emerge as the primary antagonist to Charles, not the Ottoman sultan.

On 22 September 1520, at the height of his power, Selim the Grim died, no doubt raging to the bitter end against this premature abridgment of his insatiable ambition. Having restored the Ottoman state and elevated it to unparalleled triumphs, his last accomplishment was ensuring a smooth succession. There would be no repeat of the anarchic circumstances by which Selim himself had secured the throne, for, though the sultan had six acknowledged daughters from his many wives, no other boy had been permitted to survive infancy and hence emerge as a rival to his chosen heir, Suleiman.

The relief as word of Selim's death spread throughout Europe was palpable. Pope Leo X commanded that the litany and common prayers should be sung throughout Rome in celebration. The common assumption was that a fearsome tyrant had been cut down before he could turn his attention westwards, and that his successor was of an altogether different – and more passive – nature. Suleiman "has neither the talent nor the will to continue down the road of the conquerors as his father," Italian historian Paolo Giovio confidently asserted; "he is a child without experience and high ability, a soft, peace-loving personality that thinks little about war and the glory of arms, a lamb that follows the lion."[12] Guicciardini was relieved Selim had left his "great empire to Suleiman, his son, a young man but reputed to be more mild-spirited and not disposed to make war." Contarini, too, described the new sultan as a "peaceful man who wanted to attend to his pleasure."[13] These impressions were understandable. Born on 6 November 1494, and thus in his mid-twenties when he ascended to the throne, Suleiman had lived very much in his father's shadow. He had administrative experience, but no military record to his name. And Suleiman would indeed cultivate a reputation for scholarly and intellectual achievement – he was dubbed with the sobriquet *Kānūnī* (the Lawgiver) by his own people. But it was his achievements on the battlefield that would ultimately command the respect of his Western rivals, who would remember him by a more martial title: Suleiman the Magnificent.

Although Suleiman was young, he inherited the institutional bureaucracy and superlative war machine bequeathed to him by his father, which allowed for continuity in policy making and both administrative and military enterprise on a scale and with a professionalism unimaginable in Europe, indeed, unparalleled anywhere outside of Ming China. As a new and largely untried sultan, Suleiman would need to commence his reign by imposing his authority and proving he had the mettle to lead the army to war. After long campaigns in the East against coreligionist Muslims (albeit deeply flawed ones) it was natural there would be a desire to unleash *jihad* against the infidels of the West, and Hungary was the logical target.

At a practical level, Hungary was effectively already under siege. Selim's preoccupation with the Safavids and Mamluks had enabled Buda to renew the truce with Constantinople in 1513, 1516, 1517, and 1519. But these formal diplomatic arrangements did not alter the harsh reality of life on the frontier, where even in the absence of the sultan his largely autonomous regional governors continually raided in force across the border. The Ottomans besieged Knin, the residence of the *ban* in the center of Croatia, in 1511 and 1514. In 1513 both Skradin and Klis fell under siege. In the autumn of 1512, Ottoman border troops overran Srebrenica, Tešanj, and Sokol, thus reaching the Sava. In the late summer of 1513, Peter Berislavić, bishop of Veszprém and *ban* of Dalmatia, Croatia, and

Slavonia, defeated the *sanjak-bey* of Bosnia at Dubica. However, in July 1515, the Hungarian attempt to take Smederevo just south of Belgrade ended in disaster when by means of a ruse Yahyapaşaoğlu Bali Bey, *sanjak-bey* of Smederevo, crushed the army of the *voivode* of Transylvania, John Zápolya, as the latter lay siege to the Ottoman fortress. After enduring an Ottoman siege for most of 1517, Jajce was finally relieved by Berislavić, only for him to be killed in battle in May 1520.

Hungary was compromised in its capacity to resist. When King Matthias Corvinus died on 6 April 1490 the Habsburgs laid claim to the Hungarian crown, asserting it was their due through the 1463 Treaty of Wiener Neustadt. However, the magnates elected Vladislaus II, the king of Bohemia, who, as the eldest son of Casimir IV, had expected to inherit the throne of Poland and Lithuania. The price for his accession was his concession of the ancient rights and privileges of the nobility, which in effect meant the decentralization of power to an oligarchy and its concomitant weakening of the monarchy, particularly in its capacity to raise taxation. This negatively impacted the military, most obviously realized on 3 January 1493 with the abolition of the Black Army, the elite unit of mercenaries maintained by Corvinus, for lack of funds to maintain it.

In addition to these machinations in the elite circles of the kingdom, Hungary was roiled by socio-religious revolutionary violence among the masses. Cardinal Tamás Bakócz, chancellor to King Vladislaus, aspired to the papacy but was narrowly defeated in the election of 1513 by Giovanni de' Medici, who took the papal throne as Leo X. By way of consolation, Bakócz was subsequently entrusted with a papal bull by the new pope, empowering him to evangelize for a crusade against the growing Ottoman menace, in the same spirit as Capistrano during the siege of Belgrade in 1456. However, the popular fervor whipped up among the lower classes swiftly spiraled out of control, with the massed peasants, suddenly aware of their collective power, electing to turn against their own aristocracy rather than embark on campaign against the sultan. It took months of savage fighting before the uprising of 1514 was finally put down by loyalist forces led by John Zápolya and Stephen VII Báthory, the Count of Timişoara.[14] To set an example, the rebel leader György Dózsa was subjected to a mock coronation, a smoldering iron crown being affixed to his head while his body was torn open by red hot pincers. The other rebel ringleaders, having been starved over the preceding two weeks, were then impelled to devour their erstwhile commander while he was still alive or be summarily executed before his eyes.[15]

The nobility now punished the entire class of peasants for their "faithlessness" with "perpetual servitude" in the Tripartite Code that was made law that winter by the *diet*. This declared that the Hungarian peasants had "forfeited their liberty and become subject to their landlords in unconditional and perpetual servitude." The peasant had no right over his master's land save bare compensation for his labor. Every species of property was judged to belong to the landlord and the peasant was to be denied the right to ever invoke justice or law against a noble.[16]

It was hardly auspicious for the future of Hungary that, when Vladislaus died on 13 March 1516, his dysfunctional kingdom was inherited by his ten-year-old son, Louis II.

Suleiman's intentions and Ottoman preparations for a major campaign in Hungary were no secret, but Europe was already fixated on the Habsburg–Valois rivalry. The Hungarians had done everything in their power to intertwine their cause with that of the emperor. Habsburg ties to Hungary were intimate and personal. In 1521, Charles V's sister, Mary, married King Louis II, while his brother, Ferdinand, married Louis's sister, Anne, that same year. However, these familial bonds proved worthless to Louis. When he pleaded for aid against the Ottomans from his brother-in-law, the emperor made his priorities clear. "We have a bad neighbor," Charles explained, referring to Francis. "First we have to defend ourselves against him, and only after that shall we go against the Turks."[17] He had nothing to offer beyond forwarding the problem to the king of England, writing to Henry VIII that:

> ... the ambassador of my brother-in-law, the king of Hungary, has told me of the distress in which his country is, from the invasion of the Turk. Many towns have been taken, and the rest will be soon subdued, if aid is not given by other Christian princes. I have done what I can, considering the war which Francis has so unjustly commenced against me, and am determined to do more when my affairs will allow of it. The said ambassador has a commission to the King and yourself and has asked me to write to you in his favor. His petition is reasonable and necessary for the preservation of Christendom.[18]

The distant English were in no position to contribute anything, and the Germans, just across the border, were not inclined to. Hungarian envoy Stephen Werbőczy submitted a request for help against the Turks to the Imperial *Diet* at Worms, emphasizing the dire condition of the borderlands, which "have been destroyed due to the constant attacks by the Ottomans... in many places, especially in Bosnia and Croatia, only desolate fortresses have remained, only desolate walls."[19] Unmoved, the *diet* voted the emperor 20,000 infantry and 4,000 cavalry for his use against the king of France, and nothing to the Hungarians for their struggle against the Ottoman sultan. Hungary stood on its own against an Ottoman Empire which by 1520 possessed five times as much territory, four times as much population, and a treasury in Constantinople that dwarfed its meagre counterpart in Buda.

The sultan set out for the campaign rather late, on 18 May 1521, but the path forward had been well prepared. Before marching into Hungary in 1521, Suleiman ordered Mihaloğlu Mehmed Bey to meet with the Wallachian army and pass on to Transylvania to block any potential external aid arriving for the Hungarian cause.

One interesting feature observed in the campaign diary was the rallying of religious students (*suhte*) to the march from each major stop. On 2 June, the *suhte* of Edirne are reported to have raised their banner and joined the *ghaza*. Those of Plovdiv and Sofia did the same on 12 June. During the march, the sultan also accepted various envoys, Moldavian on 22 May and Tatar on 5 June, who took this opportunity to present gifts and kiss his hand.

Perhaps each expecting the other to take the initiative, neither the inexperienced young sultan nor the veteran councilors he had inherited from his father had defined the strategic objective of the campaign either before, or even after, setting out from Constantinople. This was finally raised at a council meeting in Sofia on 19 June. Grand Vizier Piri Mehmed Pasha recommended the conservative option of taking Belgrade, thus securing the Danube and the route into the Carpathian basin. The strategic value of the city was considerable. Writing from Buda on 6 July 1521, the Venetian ambassador, Lorenzo Orio, described Belgrade as "the gate of this Kingdom" and asserted that should the Ottomans seize it, they could advance over the plains to "wherever they pleased."[20] The Ottomans had long been aware of Belgrade's significance, having twice already subjected the city to protracted sieges, in 1440 and 1456. The Ottoman chronicler, Sa'di, identified the city as a "throne on the way of *ghaza*" and the "strong key to the infidel lands."[21] Suleiman's brother-in-law, Ferhad Pasha, the husband of the sultan's sister, Beyhan, also emphasized the importance of Belgrade as the "key to the lands of the infidels and [the] source of evil."[22]

However, Third Vizier Ahmed Pasha proposed the much bolder plan of capturing Šabac and using it to cross the Sava into Srem and strike against the Hungarian capital, Buda. Piri Pasha retorted that if the Ottomans marched against Buda without taking Belgrade, the Hungarians could cut off their line of retreat. Ultimately, and perhaps uncertainly, Suleiman opted to split the difference. Adopting Ahmed Pasha's plan, he would march with the main army against Šabac. However, Piri Pasha would simultaneously march against Belgrade with the regional army of the *bey* of Smederevo.

Ahmed Pasha led the Rumelian vanguard ahead to deliver the main blow against Šabac, storming it in a single bloody assault on 8 July, and then pushing south along the Sava to secure his rear by taking the stronghold of Zemun on the north bank of the Sava opposite Belgrade on 11 July. Suleiman himself had reached Šabac by this time, Ahmed Pasha having thoughtfully lined the severed heads of the garrison along the road by way of welcome.

On 19 July, a flood on the Sava swept away the pontoon bridge that had taken ten days to build, spoiling the army's chance of a quick and easy crossing. The sultan had to ferry his forces across the river in boats, and this loss of momentum ended any prospect of following through on the original plan by undertaking a forced march north to seize Buda. Accordingly, Suleiman marched in the opposite direction, downstream along the left bank of the river via Zemun towards Belgrade. His arrival north of the city was greeted by loud cheers from the detachments under Piri Pasha, which had commenced their siege of Belgrade from the south on 4 July.

The riverside fortifications were the main focus of the siege, which was divided between a left wing under Çoban Mustafa Pasha, another brother-in-law of Suleiman, the husband of the sultan's sister, Hatice, concentrated against the Lower Fortress, and a right wing under Piri Pasha focused on the Western Outer Town. To facilitate communication between the two camps, the sultan ordered the construction of a pontoon bridge over the Sava above Belgrade, which was completed on 17 July. The Ottoman artillery, now deployed in its full strength, meanwhile continued to batter the walls.

On 2 August, siege troops from both wings mounted an assault at the town walls. This was unsuccessful, and the following day, the garrison again managed to fend off an Ottoman assault. In response to these initial failures, Suleiman commanded the siege guns be deployed on War Isle in the river itself in order to bring them closer to the walls.

By 8 August, the artillery bombardment had blasted so many breaches in the wall along the Sava it was impossible for the garrison to cover all possible entrances to the town. Equally unhappily for the defenders, the water level of both the Danube and the Sava had by then decreased enough to make it possible for Ottoman infantry, crossing the rivers by boat, to take up position along the bank.[23] Thus, the assault could be made simultaneously from three directions – from the far side of the Sava, by Piri Pasha; from the far side of the Danube, by Mustafa Pasha; and from War Isle by Ahmed Pasha. Under this pressure, the defenders were forced to abandon the town, burning it behind them as they pulled back into the citadel.

The Ottomans now redeployed their artillery within the town itself and started to batter the already damaged walls of the citadel from close range. Some guns were even installed in the tower of the Franciscan church, which was almost as high as the citadel itself.

Despite his complete isolation, on 12 August the commander of the garrison, *viceban* Balázs Oláh, refused an Ottoman summons to surrender which offered him the alternatives of a substantial monetary reward if he complied or being tortured to death if he declined. Allegedly, he replied that the holdouts in the citadel had so many enemy dead to eat that they had plenty of time to wait for the king's army.

Owing to poor coordination between the dispersed assault forces, a general assault launched against the citadel on 16 August was a costly failure. Another attempt to storm the walls failed on 26 August, but at dawn the following day, the mines Ottoman sappers had emplaced below the Nebojsa tower of the citadel were detonated, destroying the key fortification protecting the citadel on its Sava River side. Janissaries immediately swarmed into the breach, overwhelming the defenders. The last remnant of the garrison – only seventy-two men, including a badly wounded Oláh – dug in for a last stand in the palace of Count Ulrich II of Cilli, but their situation was hopeless, and on 29 August, Oláh finally surrendered on terms.[24] The following day, the Orthodox cathedral temple of the Dormition of the Theotokos was converted into a mosque, and the sultan entered Belgrade to lead the Friday prayer in person.

The fall of Belgrade unhinged the entire Hungarian network of fortified strongholds screening the southern border. From the linchpin of the defensive line holding the Ottomans at bay, the city was now a critical staging ground for further Ottoman advances into the exposed Hungarian heartland. "Our country is now open to the Turk both on land and water," the fifteen-year-old King Louis wrote to his uncle, King Sigismund I of Poland. "It cannot be happy and safe so long as Šabac and Belgrade remain in the hands of the enemy."[25] Of the key fortresses of the southern defense line, only Orşova and Severin in the eastern edge, and Jajce and Klis in the western edge remained under Hungarian control. The Ottomans conquered Orşova in 1522 and Severin in 1524, thus assuming control over the lower Danube valley. In 1522, they also captured Skradin and

Knin. Jajce fell in 1528, while Klis held out until 1537 before finally succumbing to overwhelming Ottoman power.

The fall of Belgrade sent alarm bells ringing throughout Europe. On 30 August, Georgius de Eggi, captain of Gorizia, wrote to Vicenzo Capello, deputy of Udine, of the "mournful" news by way of Graz that "the malignant Turk captured Belgrade, which is the shield of the realm of Hungary and these upper parts, through his unending force and power." On 10 October, a letter arrived for Cardinal Wolsey from Rome lamenting that "the Turk has destroyed Belgrade; – much fear for Hungary, as the King is young and his council divided. If there be war in Hungary, in Italy and in France, the earth will be satiated with Christian blood."[26]

Suleiman could be well pleased by the outcome of his first year at the helm of the Ottoman state. "He seems to have in his hand the key to Christendom for having conquered Belgrade," the Venetian ambassador to Constantinople, Marco Minio, informed the senate, concluding with a significant warning: "The expedition he made to Belgrade has given him the expectation that he can win every great campaign."[27]

RHODES, 1522

In the aftermath of the siege of 1480, Rhodes lay in ruins, so devastated the local peoples were exempted from paying taxes for the next five years. The critical task of rebuilding and renewal was undertaken by Pierre d'Aubusson, who continued to serve as Grand Master until his death on 30 June 1503, aged eighty. A gifted military engineer, over the ensuing decades of reconstruction he substantively improved the defenses to compensate for vulnerabilities exposed during the Ottoman siege. Two of the five gates were blocked up, and formidable outworks were emplaced in front of the remaining three. The thickness of the main wall was significantly increased, up to twelve meters' depth in some sections, allowing for the stationing of powerful cannon on its wall-walk as well as the speedy transfer of troops. He also considerably widened the ditch fronting the wall and incorporated *tenailles*, massive advanced bulwarks featuring formidable polygonal bastions that could subject any assault on the walls to a withering flanking crossfire. The linchpin of this network of defenses was the St George Bastion, one of the earliest pentagonal bastions in history, which was redesigned to feature two-tier mural galleries with gun ports added on each of its sides, enabling the garrison to sweep the ditch with an enfilading barrage.

On the seaward-facing side of the city, the Tower of the Windmills and the St Nicholas Tower were reconstructed and expanded into forts, and the Sea Gate was either built or rebuilt.

This work was carried on by d'Aubusson's successors, including Fabrizio del Carretto, the Italian knight who had held the Tower of St Nicholas during the siege of 1480. He served as Grand Master from 1513 to 1521, benefiting from the professional direction of Basilio dalla Scuola di Vicenza, Emperor Maximilian's personal military engineer, who was stationed at Rhodes from 1519 to 1521. He built a semicircular bulwark in front of the Tower of Italy, and *caponiers*, low structures to enable flanking fire into the moat. He also upgraded the older parapet on the walls with a new one of a rounded shape designed for mounting artillery, and considerably increased the thickness of the main wall on the mainland side. The Knights' outlying strongholds on the island, the ancient towns of Lindos and Pheraklos, which look east towards the Turkish mainland, were also reinforced, as was Monolithos, perched alone on the mountainous west coast.[28]

These defenses were constantly being probed. In August 1503, sixteen Ottoman galleys descended on the coast of Rhodes, sacking villages along the shore and sending raiding parties inland. As the fleet retired northwards it was intercepted by Hospitaller galleys commanded by Don Diego Almeida, Grand Prior of Portugal. In the ensuing action, eight Ottoman galleys were sunk and two captured. Another Ottoman squadron which approached Leros was repulsed by the expedient of lining the battlements of the undermanned fort with peasants and their wives dressed in the red surcoats of the Order.

The Hospitallers continued to win numerous naval encounters at the expense of the Mamluks. In the autumn of 1506, two galleys of the Order captured all seven *fustae* of a Mamluk squadron bent on the plunder of Kos. The following year, the Hospitaller flagship encountered its Mamluk counterpart, the *Mogarbina*, off Heraklion, and took her intact. In 1510, the Order achieved the greatest naval victory of its history off Alexandretta, taking eleven great ships and four galleys of the Mamluk timber fleet, then landing shore parties to set alight the stocks of timber awaiting shipment.

Ironically, these victories at the expense of the Mamluks ultimately only contributed to their downfall, thereby undermining the Hospitallers' strategic position as "defenders of the borders of the Christian Empire in the East," according to Jacob Fontanus, a member of the Order. With the entire Levant now under Ottoman occupation, Rhodes was even more exposed in its role as what Guicciardini called "a bulwark of [the] Christian religion."[29]

To meet this challenge, Philippe de Villiers de L'Isle-Adam, having previously served as seneschal of Rhodes, captain general of the galleys, and grand prior of France, was elected 44th Grand Master of the Order in January 1521, succeeding Del Carretto. Resident in Paris at the time of his election, L'Isle-Adam didn't arrive in Rhodes until 19 September, whereupon he was immediately presented with a letter dated 10 September that had just arrived from Constantinople. Ostensibly offering felicitations at the Grand Master's ascension to his new office, Suleiman was in reality sending a warning shot across his bow:

> I also mean to cultivate your favor; rejoice then with me, as a very dear friend, that following in the footsteps of my father, who conquered Persia, Jerusalem, Arabia, and Egypt, I have captured that most powerful of fortresses, Belgrade, during the late autumn; after which, having offered battle to the *kāfir*, which they had not the courage to accept, I took many other beautiful and well-fortified cities, and destroyed most of their inhabitants either by sword or fire, the remainder being reduced to slavery.[30]

L'Isle-Adam certainly got the hint, writing to Francis I that, regarding Suleiman's correspondence, "we do not accept it as a token of friendship; but rather as a veiled threat."[31]

The sultan had indeed determined that the extirpation of the Order's presence in the Aegean across the vital arteries of Ottoman trade and pilgrimage would be his priority for the campaign season of 1522. The Hospitaller presence had been an insult to the faith for long enough. "Only the city of Rhodes, located at the heart of my empire, at the doors of my best provinces, stands in the way of my grandeur," Suleiman declared. The knights:

> … intercept my messages, they steal my tributes, they rob our merchants, they intimidate my galleys, they receive Christian corsairs, criminals, the disowned, fugitives, and rebels against our faith and my justice… they haggle and negotiate with me as if we were equals, are these things not unbearable? Is it not a shame and a reproach to us Ottomans to further defer punishment and vengeance? To this end, I sent as many ships, cannons, soldiers, and good captains, as if it were a question of conquering an entire kingdom.[32]

On 10 June 1522 – by which time Suleiman's armada had already assembled at Constantinople and an advance squadron was attacking Kos – L'Isle-Adam received the sultan's ultimatum: "Your monstrous injuries against my most afflicted people have aroused my pity and indignation. I command you, therefore, instantly to surrender the island and fortress of Rhodes," and either depart under a guarantee of safe conduct, or submit and serve the sultan as his vassal. If it came to war, the Hospitallers could not be saved, not by their own strength of arms, "nor by external aid, nor by the strength of your fortifications which I will overthrow to their foundations."[33]

Second Vizier Mustafa Pasha was appointed *serdar-ı ekrem* (the rank given to viziers in battle) with overall command of the operation. The admiral of the fleet was Pilaq Mustafa Pasha, the *kapudan* of Gallipoli, but his chief-of-staff, Kurtoğlu Muslihiddin Reis, a former corsair who had entered the sultan's service in 1516, commanded the fighting vessels. For him, the campaign was personal; the Hospitallers had killed two of his brothers and taken a third prisoner.

By the end of April, all crops and farm animals on Rhodes had been brought into the city. The gardens and villas in the approaches to the city were left devastated as part of a scorched-earth policy intended to leave nothing of value to the enemy. L'Isle-Adam had, meanwhile, assigned responsibility for the defense. Four Grand Crosses commanded a mobile reserve, by sectors: the prior of Castile and chancellor, Andrea D'Amaral, for Auvergne and Germany; the English *turcopilier*, John Buck, for Aragon and England; the French grand prior, Pierre de Cluys, for France and Castile; and the prior of Navarre, Gregoire de Morgut, for Provence and Italy. Didier de Tholon, bailiff of Manosque, was in overall command of artillery.

The key Tower of St Nicholas was commanded by the Provençal Guidot de Castellac. Each national post was under a separate command: Raimond Ricard at Provence, Jean de St Simon at France, Raimond Rogiet at Auvergne, Giorgio Aimari at Italy, William Weston at England, Juan de Barbarun at Aragon, Christopher Waldners at Germany, and Fernando de Sollier at Castile and Portugal.

The Palace of the Grand Master (whose northern wall was an integral part of the Post of France) was entrusted to the Englishman Thomas Sheffield, commander of Beverley and seneschal of the Grand Master. Each of the five major bastions had its commander: Jean de Mesnyl for Auvergne, Tomas Escarrieros for Aragon, Nicholas Hussey for England, Jean de Brinquier de Lioncel for Provence, and Andreotto Gentile for Italy. The Grand Master's standard was entrusted to Henry Mansell of England.

Capable outsiders were also recruited to take responsibility for key aspects of the defense. Gabriele Tadini da Martinengo, an engineer then in the service of Venice, arrived from Heraklion in response to an appeal from L'Isle-Adam, who was only too aware of the Ottoman propensity for mining and sapping during siege operations and needed a professional to direct the Order's countermeasures. The commercial port was closed with two great chains backed up by booms, and the galley port was blocked, except for a single narrow channel, by sunken hulks full of stones.

The garrison had covered every contingency possible on its own behalf in order to hold out for as long as it could.[34] But only external support could break the siege. The Hospitallers were prepared to be the anvil. But would the hammer come?

Pope Leo X died on 1 December 1521, and his successor, Adrian VI, did not arrive in Rome until 29 August 1522. Although he was urged to intervene by members of the Curia, including Cardinal Giulio de' Medici (later Pope Clement VII), himself a member of the Order of St John, the new pope had neither time nor opportunity to organize Christian forces.

Hospitaller legates were dispatched to the Emperor Charles V, to Francis I and Henry VIII; but there was little to be expected beyond the usual promises. In a letter dated 24 July 1522, Charles de Lannoy warned the emperor that Rhodes was the "bulwark between the *Turco* and Christendom." If the emperor failed to relieve the island, it would be lost, exposing Habsburg Sicily to worse danger. But the dynastic ambition of their imperial rivals was of far greater significance to the great powers of Europe than the fate of distant Rhodes. In his eyewitness account *De Bello Rhodia*, Jacob Fontanus highlighted the divisions that defined the European milieu and the ensuing improbability of Christian help for the Hospitallers in the terms with which Kurtoğlu Muslihiddin Reis advised his sultan: "And if you consider well, you will see that the Prophet Muhammad looking out for you, has given you a divine occasion; that is Christians are occupied among themselves in civil war, they have the mood for everything else other than you."[35]

This cut to the heart of the matter, for instead of uniting in a common cause, Europe's great magnates found it easier to blame each other for their own inactivity and hold each other responsible for the incoming tide of Ottoman expansionism. As late as 18 December 1522, the emperor's chancellor, Mercurino di Gattinara, wrote to the pope complaining about the king of France keeping Charles from fighting the Ottomans: "As Francis bestirs himself to collect an army, he compels the Emperor to do the same… When the Turk sees these things, he will turn his arms against the Two Sicilies, will find them unprepared, conquer them, strike a blow at Rome, and subvert the Holy See, unless God in His mercy interfere to save it."[36]

On 26 June, the Feast of Corpus Christi, the Ottoman advance squadron anchored some six miles to the south of Rhodes in Kalitheas Bay, behind Cape Voudhi. Over the ensuing fortnight, convoys of transports and auxiliary craft continued arriving, depositing a constant stream of men, munitions, and materiel.

To confront this enormous host, which incorporated vast numbers of engineers, pioneers, miners, and logistical personnel in addition to the tens of thousands of front-line troops, the Hospitallers could muster an estimated 500 knights and servants-at-arms, 1,000 mercenary soldiers, and perhaps 500 Rhodian militia.

The first Ottoman battery was emplaced on the hillside known from a church of that name as Saints Cosmas and Damian, facing the Post of England. The second battery faced the Post of Provence and the third the Tower of Spain, in the Post of Aragon. The initial exchanges were discouraging for the besiegers. A furious return fire from the city wrecked the batteries and drove the pioneers beyond cannon shot. The Ottomans had been harassed by sorties throughout their disembarkation, and these continued to cut off small bodies and working parties throughout the siege.

The siege nonetheless proceeded in characteristic Ottoman fashion with the slow, methodical process of sapping a zigzag trench (*siçan yolu*) to the edge of the moat. In the next phase, high earthen ramparts (*tabiya*) would be constructed level with the city wall on the far side of its moat. Cannon would then be hauled up to the top of these ramparts, from which they could dominate the so-called "covered way" between the edge of the moat and the walls. To protect the gunners on top of the ramparts, shields resembling the bristly hairs on the back of a wild boar (*doñuz dami*) would be erected.[37]

Suleiman was delayed in taking personal command of the operation by a minor Shia uprising led by Shah Suwar Oghli Ali Bey, dispatching his brother-in-law, Ferhad Pasha, to deal with the problem. Suleiman himself marched for Kütahya, where he was joined on 1 July by the *beylerbey* of Anatolia, Qasim Pasha, the *agha* of the janissaries, Bali Pasha, and the *agha* of the *azaps*, Ali Bey. Ten days later, Ferhad Pasha met the sultan on the march with the severed heads of the rebel Shah Suwar and his three sons. On 26 July Suleiman reached the Aegean coast at Marmaris, crossing over to Rhodes two days later.

While Suleiman assumed personal command of the siege his subordinates took their assigned places along its line. Grand Vizier Piri Mehmed Pasha held the eastern end with his right flank anchored on the Bay of Acandia, facing the

Post of Italy. Second Vizier and *serdar-ı ekrem* Mustafa Pasha was next in line on Piri Mehmed's left, facing Provence, with Qasim Pasha on his left, facing England. Third Vizier Ahmed Pasha, who had been promoted to *beylerbey* of Rumelia after the siege of Belgrade, faced the Tower of Spain, with Ayas Pasha, a former *agha* of the janissaries and *beylerbey* of Anatolia who would later succeed as *beylerbey* of Rumelia and rise to become grand vizier in 1536, on his left, before Auvergne. Bali Pasha faced Germany and France, with his left flank extending towards the galley port, but not too close to the sea, in order to keep out of range of the powerful batteries of St Nicholas. This roster of personalities reporting directly to him – the elite of the Ottoman establishment, veteran administrators and military tacticians, many of them personally related to the sultan by marriage – clearly indicates how seriously Suleiman approached the campaign.

The Ottoman artillery park was substantial, ranging from large-caliber bombards and basilisks to much smaller pieces. Four of the heaviest guns were stationed opposite England and Aragon, and two opposite Italy. Eight mortars were concentrated against England, two against Auvergne, and two against St John's Gate.

On 29 July the siege opened in earnest. Under cover of a furious bombardment, the Turks commenced digging trenches and carting stones and earth to construct earthworks parallel to the walls. Furious counter fire killed vast numbers of the crews working this hazardous task, but day by day the earthworks rose higher and higher until, as Jacques de Bourbon, a Hospitaller knight who survived the siege ruefully recalled, "this earth was higher than the walls of the town by ten or twelve feet, and at the end they made a mountain of this earth between the post of Spain and Auvergne."[38]

On 1 August, the Ottomans focused their guns on the Post of Germany, keeping it under fire for ten days, then shifted their attention to the Tower of St Nicholas. All guns were then concentrated in Ahmed's sector, where the earthwork now overtopped the battlements. From behind this screen, Ottoman gunners "battered our people who were on the posts of the wall and boulevards, so that no person could get up there," de Bourbon lamented.[39] In the artillery duel, the Spanish master gunner was killed while his Ottoman counterpart lost both legs. There were now fourteen batteries – virtually the whole of the heavy artillery – concentrated here, and by 14 August Juan de Barbarun, commanding in the Post of Aragon, was killed, and the Ottomans had succeeded in battering open breaches in the walls of England and Provence, the fallen masonry filling the moat.

By 19 August there was a breach in the Post of Italy and the Ottoman trenches had reached the counterscarp, their sappers burrowing into the fallen masonry to construct a covered way under the ravelin and right up to the ramparts. L'Isle-Adam ordered sorties by the garrison to break up the impending assault in Piri Pasha's sector on 19 and 20 August, and in Ahmed and Ayas Pasha's sectors on 22 and 24 August. Despite these proactive gambits, by the end of the month there were so many breaches in the walls it was clear a general assault could not long be delayed. Increasingly desperate messages were dispatched to the great Christian powers – blockade runners had so little apparent difficulty in penetrating the cordon established by Kurtoğlu that a frustrated Suleiman finally resorted to having the former corsair bastinadoed on the quarter deck of his own flagship. But the sultan need not have been overly concerned. Those vessels that returned to the beleaguered city brought little with them beyond hopes and prayers.

Tadini was now constructing traverses on the walls on either side of all the breaches, and mounting mixed batteries of heavy cannon covering the approach trenches and the breaches themselves. If his contributions to the defense above ground were exemplary, his role in the subterranean war was critical. By early September it was estimated the besiegers had undermined five-sixths of the enceinte with a warren of at least fifty tunnels running in different directions. However, Tadini had rendered most of them abortive. He had cut his own tunnels at right angles to those of the Ottomans, setting off countermines or unleashing raiding parties to grapple with their adversaries in the dark, claustrophobic confines of the underground passageways.

Nonetheless, the defenders could not intercept every Ottoman approach, and on 4 September two mines were detonated, one between the towers of Spain and St George and the second at St Mary's Tower. The first seems to have done little damage, but the second, wrote de Bourbon, "was so furious, that a large part of the town shook," and multiple breaches were blasted in the wall.[40]

Ottoman infantry rushed to take advantage and secured a foothold on the bastion itself, planting their banners on the wall. After two hours of fighting they were finally evicted, but the cost was high; the captain of the galleys, Michel D'Argillemont, Grand Commander Gabriel de Pommerols, and the Grand Master's standard-bearer, Henry Mansell, were all fatally wounded in the melee.

On 9 September Tadini intercepted two mines under Provence, but a third beneath England was partly effective, and again the Ottomans had to be repelled from the breach. Hospitaller counterattacks were becoming riskier because the besiegers, too, were adapting to the demands of this type of warfare. Mustafa had learned to cut foxholes along the length of the counterscarp of the moat and man them with sharpshooters. More assaults went in on 11, 13, and 14 September. A major offensive surged against the Post of Italy on 20 September, supported by simultaneous assaults on Provence, England, and Aragon. The Ottomans occupied the remains of the tower and the bastion of Aragon and it took hours of desperate fighting to evict them. On 23 September, the detonation of mines under Aragon and Auvergne shook the entire city and would have collapsed the wall had the impact not been mitigated by Tadini, who had bored a series of spiral vents into the mine shafts through which much of the blast was dispersed.

Under cover of a smokescreen, at dawn on 24 September the janissaries surged against the walls from Aragon to Italy. Nicholas Roberts, an English knight, described how breaches had been blasted in the defense line so wide that in some places five "men on horseback myght come in at once; and after that the wall of the towne was downe, they gave us battall often tymes upon even ground, that we had no manner of advantage apone them."[41] After six hours of bloody combat, in which the *beys* of Tekke and Valona were among the slain, the assault was finally driven off. Suleiman, dismayed at the lack of progress in the siege and its tremendous cost, now turned on his commanders. He condemned Mustafa to death, and when Piri Pasha tried to intervene, the sultan ordered his death also, clapping Ayas Pasha in chains for good measure. He ultimately relented, but Mustafa was relieved of his command and succeeded by his rival, Ahmed Pasha.[42]

The subterranean war continued. On the night of 4 October an Ottoman tunnel under the Post of Italy was demolished by Tadini. That same evening, a blockade runner arrived from Naples with news of a relief force mustering at Messina. But it was too late in the sailing season; the winds were contrary, and no fleet would come. With attrition steadily depleting the ranks available to him, the Grand Master authorized the evacuation of the Order's outlying garrisons, including Kos and Bodrum, so as to concentrate all available fighting men in the struggle for Rhodes itself. And on their own recognizance, some small parties did arrive from further abroad to offer what help they could. On 14 October a brigantine arrived from Naples by way of Heraklion, bringing four Italian knights and a young aspirant to the Order, the nephew of the bailiff of San Stefano, Giovanni di Gesualdo. He was admitted on 15 October, and killed in a sortie the following day.

Ahmed continued the work of widening the breaches by bombardment and undermining while keeping the garrison under constant pressure with wave after wave of assaults against the key bastions of Aragon and England. During one of these Bali Pasha, leading his janissaries from the front, was badly wounded and had to be relieved of his command.

There were only two serviceable cannons remaining in the ruins of the Tower of Spain, at the lowest level, where they were screened from the fire of the Ottoman batteries. Tadini recommended the tower be demolished to provide masonry for the retrenchments which he was continually building in the city. Subsequently, the guns of Auvergne and at the Gate of Koskino were the only ones operating in this sector.

On 11 October, Tadini was shot in the right eye, the ball passing clean through his head and putting him out of action for six weeks. By this point, the ravelins, ramparts, and curtain walls at the posts of Aragon, England, Provence, and Italy had been breached or compromised by undermining, and the city was open to the enemy. But each post was screened by Tadini's retrenchments, and with the exception of Spain, the towers and bastions at each post, though in varying states of ruin, still stood and were still capable of murderous flanking fire. The Ottomans did not yet dare advance into the breaches they had created.

As the siege lengthened and hope of relief from the outside faded, the strain within the garrison began to show. The prior of Castile, the chancellor, Andrea D'Amaral, was arrested on suspicion of negotiating with the sultan to surrender the city. Tortured, tried, and convicted, he was executed by hanging on 6 November, his head and the quartered remains of his body being displayed on different sectors of the battlements, spitted upon pikes.

On 28 October Mustafa Pasha handed over the command of his sector to Qasim Pasha on receipt of the news of the death of Khair Bey, the *beylerbey* of Egypt, whom he succeeded. During a council of war in the Ottoman camp on 1 November the decision was made – contrary to established military practice – that while the fleet would withdraw to the sheltered harbor of Marmaris, the army, and the sultan, would spend the winter on the island.

On 9 November, Hospitaller reinforcements arrived in two brigantines carrying twelve knights and 100 men-at-arms, along with welcome supplies of victuals, powder, and shot. On 21 November a fresh Ottoman assault gained a foothold on the bastions of England and Italy, but after fierce fighting the Hospitallers again drove the enemy back to their lines. By now, the approach of winter was imminent and the garrison enjoyed a respite of several days while rain and hail driven by bitter easterly gales swept over the island. The besiegers huddled in their flooded trenches, unable to sustain their artillery barrage with sodden gunpowder. The conflict had ground into a war of attrition in which the weather was as much a factor as leadership, courage, and logistics.

When the skies cleared, Suleiman drove his men forward in another furious assault that raged through the day and night of 28–29 November. The Ottomans were slaughtered in such numbers that Nicholas Roberts described how, in the aftermath, "the turkes purposed to give us no more batall, but to come into the towne by trenches in so much, yt they mad [many] gret trenches, and by the space of a month did come allmost into the mydst of our towne, in so much that ther lay nightly wtin our towne [many] thousand turkes."[43]

On 1 December Tadini, now fit again for action, led a sortie against the Ottoman sappers boring yet more tunnels beneath the Post of Aragon, only to be almost immediately badly wounded in one knee. Two days later, Suleiman sent Mathieu de Via, a Genoese Christian merchant, to petition the Hospitallers to surrender. L'Isle-Adam refused, acknowledging, in Bourbon's words, the Ottomans "did have great advantage, but they were still outside the town by the grace of God, [and the Hospitallers] could still receive them and feast them well, if they made other assaults."[44]

L'Isle-Adam was determined to resist to the death. But when he convened a council of war, one by one his subordinates informed him the fight was already lost. The citizens of the city were exhausted; there was no workforce left to continue shoring up the defenses. The garrison's powder and shot were almost expended. Tadini pointed out the walls were already compromised both above and below ground, and the city was beyond saving. Lopes de Pas of the Langue of Aragon urged the Grand Master not to "make the enemy's victory the more splendid by our deaths." If L'Isle-Adam still clung to the forlorn hope of relief from the West, "either it will not come at all, or it will be too little and, by failing at the first encounter with Suleiman, will merely worsen our condition." As he concluded, "Where all human hope is gone, it is our duty to try to come to terms, so that we may vindicate our loss at another time and place. Wise men surrender to necessity. No matter how praiseworthy our death, let us consider whether it may not be more damaging to the Holy Religion than our surrender."[45]

Bowing to reason, on 10 December L'Isle-Adam accepted an Ottoman delegation bearing a message from the sultan in which Suleiman again offered his terms; free passage for the knights and their dependents to depart the island, or the massacre of every Christian soul on Rhodes. L'Isle-Adam now concluded that, rather than continue a hopeless fight against an implacable enemy, and thus condemn "so much small people, as women and children, that they would torment and cut some in pieces, others take, and perforce cause them to forsake their faith, with innumerable violences, and shamefull sinnes that should be committed and done, if the town were put to the sword... it were better, and more agrreable to God, for to take the treaty, if it were proferred, then for to die as people desperate and without hope."[46] A ceasefire was arranged, but negotiations broke down and when the truce expired on 15 December the Ottoman guns opened up again all along the line. Assaults were beaten back on 17 and 18 December, but by this point, the Rhodians were almost in open revolt. They demanded to be allowed to send a delegation of their own to Suleiman.

On 24 December, the Ottoman guns again fell silent. Suleiman was now willing not only to let the Order depart with honor, but to furnish them with ships if their own did not suffice. He repeated his promises to protect the lives and property of the citizens, vowed that no church would be desecrated or turned into a mosque, and now added that the citizens would be free to leave his domain at any time up to three years subsequent to his taking the island.

After one final Christmas Day – the last under Christian auspices on Rhodes until 1912 – on 26 December 1522, L'Isle-Adam entered the Ottoman camp to make his formal submission. As he left, Suleiman turned to Ibrahim Pasha and remarked, "It saddens me to be compelled to cast this brave old man out of his home." The following day, the sultan entered Rhodes through the Gate of St John. He insisted on dismissing his guard, saying, "My safety is guaranteed by the word of a Grand Master of the Hospitallers, which is more sure than all the armies in the world."[47] On 2 January 1523, Suleiman led the faithful in public prayer in the mosque which days earlier had been the Church of St John. The outlying Hospitaller islands also passed under Ottoman dominion; the largest, Kos, was occupied on 6 January.

Ottoman panegyrists were understandably ecstatic. Kemalpaşazade exulted that before the ascendancy of Suleiman, "the hand of no groom of *jihad* has ever touched the skirt of the bride of conquest."[48] The mood in the West was correspondingly downcast. Pope Adrian VI sent a letter to Cardinal Wolsey in February 1523 referencing the fall of first Belgrade and now Rhodes. With these two "outworks of Christendom" both in Ottoman hands, the sultan could easily conquer Hungary, Sicily, and Italy. The pope urged Wolsey to make it clear to Henry VIII "what a disgrace it would be if the see of the vicar of God were taken by them, owing to the dissension of the Christian princes."[49] In March, Adrian issued a three-year ceasefire demand to all Christians in order to make preparations for a crusade. In June, he wrote to Francis ordering him to settle his private quarrels and commit himself to collective action against the sultan, who "has committed much wrong, and stands ready at the door to do much worse."[50]

None of this made the slightest impression. "Thus ended the year 1522, ignominiously for Christendom," Guicciardini observed; "such fruit reaped the discord of our princes, which would have been tolerable if at least the example of the harms suffered had served them as a lesson for the future. But the disagreement among our princes continued, and therefore the troubles of the year 1523 proved no less than before."[51]

When Charles V was informed that Rhodes had fallen to Suleiman, he is said to have responded, "Nothing in the world was ever so well lost." The Hospitallers would have had good cause to reflect with justified bitterness on why a man so powerful and so capable of expressing such fine sentiments had been so utterly removed from offering any practical assistance whatsoever when it was so desperately needed and might so easily have tipped the balance. With keen insight, an Ottoman chronicler, Lüfti Pasha, described how the Hospitallers reproached the leaders of the Latin West for having betrayed them, saying "what shameless people you are that you did not send us troops and did not help us that the Turk came and despised and insulted St John and the religion of Jesus and us." This censure was something the "great men of Frengistan" had to live with.[52]

MOHÁCS, 1526

Upon his triumphant return from Rhodes, Suleiman had outsourced much of the day-to-day business of managing the affairs of state to his boyhood friend Pargalı Ibrahim Pasha, also known as Frenk Ibrahim Pasha in reference to his Western, Christian, origins. Ibrahim, "the darling of *Signor Turco*," as the Venetian *bailo* in Constantinople Prioli described him, succeeded Piri Mehmed Pasha as grand vizier in 1523.[53] Suleiman was careful to remain distant from the more menial responsibilities of government in order to cultivate his image as the ideal sovereign, particularly among the powerful and influential religious elite. According to the *Selimname* of Sa'dî bin 'Abd el-Mute'al, his stated rationale behind the campaign of 1521 was to achieve "victory in the conquest of the gate of *jihad*" by conquering Belgrade.[54] In his proclamation of victory following the taking of that city, Suleiman asserted that from the moment he ascended the throne he knew he had to direct his efforts to *jihad* and *ghaza*. Therefore, he investigated those who were in error and judged that the "desperate Hungarians" were such. In his proclamation of victory following the conquest of Rhodes the following year, Suleiman again insisted it was his God-given duty to "conquer and remove the signs of unbelief (*küfr*)" and "to remove and restrain the oppression of oppressors." It was for this reason that he continuously put "his sword to *ghaza* and *jihad* against the infidels."[55] This was one aspect of a broad-based policy intended to retain the favor and fervor of the devout. By organizing the annual pilgrimage to Mecca, protecting the pilgrimage routes, sending the annual charity for the populations of the two Holy Cities, building and restoring mosques and other public buildings in Mecca and Medina, and restoring the Kaaba, Suleiman strengthened his legitimacy in the Muslim world. From the 1540s, the sultan also adopted the title of caliph. His propagandists sought to define his image as *sahib-kıran*, the ruler of a new universal empire.

Meanwhile, the war continued. Although the sultan had concentrated the elite troops of his regime against the Hospitallers, the pressure applied against Hungary by his provincial subordinates was relentless both during the Rhodes campaign of 1522 and every year thereafter. In May 1522, King Louis II named archbishop Pál Tomori of Kalosca commander-in-chief of lower Hungary and moved his headquarters from the east of his realm, in Timişoara, to its center, in Petrovaradin. Nonetheless, the initiative remained entirely with the Ottomans. Two *sanjak-beys*, Yahyapaşaoğlu Bali Bey of Smederevo and Gazi Hüsrev Bey of Bosnia, coordinated their advances into the Lower Danube region, in Bosnia, Croatia, and Dalmatia. In 1522, they seized and destroyed the fortresses of Orşova, Pét, and Miháld, and occupied Knin and Scardona. A counter raid by John Zápolya kept Wallachia out of Ottoman hands that year, but Ottoman raiders crossed the Sava in 1523. They were driven back by a force under István Bárdi at the culmination of a running battle at Szávaszentdemeter in August, but they did succeed in capturing Ostrovica, the most important coastal fortress after Klis, in 1523, and Szörény, the other bulwark on the Lower Danube, fell in 1524. It was demolished and replaced by the newly built Feth-i İslam at Kladovo on the far side of the Danube.[56] One of the few Hungarian victories during this period was the relief of the Ottoman siege of Jajce in 1525 by Count Krsto Frankopan. Otherwise, by the summer of 1526, of the Hungarian defensive line only two minor castles, Petrovaradin and Ilok, remained to check the Ottoman invasion.[57]

Christendom remained apathetic to the fate of Hungary, transfixed as it was by the confrontation between Charles and Francis in the secular realm, and an escalating spiritual crisis within the Church.

On 24 October 1518, an enraged Pope Leo X wrote to Elector Frederick blaming Martin Luther, Satan's "son of perdition," for obstructing the papacy's plans for a coordinated European "crusade against the Turk's unholy wrath."[58] On 15 June 1520, Leo issued the papal bull *Exsurge Domine*, threatening Luther with excommunication if he failed to recant within sixty days of receiving it. Listed at thirty-four among Luther's forty-one alleged heretical and scandalous teachings denounced by the papacy was a summary of an early statement he had made with regard to the Ottomans: "To fight against the Turks is to fight against God's visitation upon our iniquities."

In one of the four rebuttals that he wrote to the papal bull, the 1521 *Grund unnd ursach aller Artikel* (*Ground and cause of all Articles*), Luther retorted:

> This article does not mean that we are not to fight against the Turk, as that holy manufacturer of heresies, the pope, charges. It means, rather, that we should first mend our ways and cause God to be gracious to us. We should not plunge into war, relying on the pope's indulgence, with which he has deceived Christians in the past and is deceiving them still…
>
> All the pope accomplishes with his crusading indulgences and his promises of heaven is to lead Christians with their lives into death and with their souls into hell. This is, of course, the proper work of the Antichrist. God does not demand crusades, indulgences, and wars. He wants us to live good lives. But the pope and his followers run from goodness faster than from anything else, yet he wants to devour the Turk.[59]

It was for this reason that the advance of the sultan had been so inexorable, "so that where he formerly held one mile of land he now holds a hundred. But we still do not see it, so completely have we been taken in by this Roman leader of the blind."[60] For the corruption of the church was nowhere more obvious than the role the papacy's minions played in "selling indulgences and licenses, most shamelessly, for an anti-Ottoman war." Luther denounced the pope's "lackeys and whores" as "fiercer, more cruel, and more insatiable Turks" than the Ottomans, who were, by comparison, "the better Turks."[61]

Called to account for his increasingly obdurate and strident opposition to papal authority by the emperor himself, Luther concluded his defense at the *diet* of Worms on 18 April 1521 by insisting he "neither can nor will retract anything, for it is both sinful and dangerous to act against conscience. I have no choice. Here I stand. I can do no other." He appealed directly to Charles, "begging and exhorting the emperor not to try and impede the spread of his ideas, because that might prove detrimental not only to the most famous German nation but also to his other kingdoms and dominions."[62] As his allies formed a protective escort around him and bore him from the hall on their shoulders as if he had just won a tournament, Luther raised his arms and flashed the sign with his hands and fingers that German knights threw as a sign of victory when they had just won a joust. The emperor was not impressed. The following day, he ruled, "A single monk, led astray by private judgment, has set himself against the faith held by all Christians for a thousand years and more, and impudently concludes that all Christians up till now have erred. I have therefore resolved to stake upon this cause all my dominions, my friends, my body and my blood, my life and soul."[63]

Charles forbade Luther "to preach or teach his evil doctrine," and reaffirmed his determination by issuing the Edict of Worms on 6 May 1521, officially outlawing Luther and his doctrine throughout the entire Holy Roman Empire. The Lutherans were offensive to Charles for reasons both spiritual – he was a devout Catholic – and secular – he opposed the rise of an identity-driven state within a state as a threat to imperial unity. In a letter to his brother Ferdinand on 25 June 1525, Charles referred to "the movement of the Lutherans, and the evil they have done, and to all appearance mean to do; it has annoyed, and does continue to annoy me bitterly. If it were in my power to remedy it speedily, I would spare neither my person nor my estates" in order to enforce the Edict of Worms. For the immediate future, imposing his authority in Italy and securing universal recognition of his title as Holy Roman Emperor had to be his priority. "When that is done, I mean to exert all my power in the extermination of this sect."[64]

Absent support from the emperor, Ferdinand seemed resigned to the Ottoman threat. "We are both lost," he wrote to his brother-in-law, King Louis, in May of 1523. "It is impossible to resist so powerful an enemy as the Turks. As for assistance from the [Holy Roman] Empire, it is not worth a wooden penny."[65]

In a letter to Pope Clement VII in July 1524, Louis stressed that the fate of Hungary hinged on peace between the Christian states. He desperately reached out to the great powers of Western Europe – the emperor, and the kings of France, Portugal, and England – making it clear the situation on the frontier was dire and Hungary would not be able to stand out against the Ottoman pressure any longer without immediate aid. In his letter to Charles, Louis pleaded, "this kingdom, together with our own crown and person could be wiped off and brought to an end" if the sultan led his army against Buda, and if so, the gate to Western Europe would be broken wide open.[66]

The king took a similar tone in his appeal to Andrea Gritti, the doge of Venice, reminding him:

> … the Turkish Caesar is himself a three or four day journey away from Belgrade, and he doesn't delay, he will come against us and our kingdom with all his power, and your illustrious Lordship has understood how unequal we are to him on account of our much diminished forces… For this reason we ask and appeal to your most illustrious Lordship by immortal God and by the safety of Christendom to come to our aid as we struggle in this present danger with whatever help and support is possible, and indeed without any delay. For it will be pointless if help is brought later, when the enemy has penetrated into the guts of our kingdom.[67]

Once again, all Louis received was vague assurances of goodwill. A passage in an Ottoman poem by Lüfti Pasha beautifully encapsulates the sanguine indifference of contemporary Europe. When Louis writes to his brother heads of state in Christendom that the sultan is on the march his counterparts offer nothing more than empty praise: "you are the hope of Christendom / you are the lock of the realm of unbelief."[68]

That hope was dying. The Hungarian treasury, already months in arrears in paying the wages of its garrison troops, ran completely dry in November 1525. Absent deliveries of food and fodder, the castle guards began drifting away from their posts in greater and greater numbers. Some key strongholds were simply abandoned.

Two events in 1525 confirmed in the sultan's mind the campaign season of the following year would be an active one. The first was the unrest of the janissaries. A military elite who lived for battle and plunder, they chafed against the inactivity that had settled in since the fall of Rhodes. On 25 March a revolt broke out, the rebels ransacking the palace of Grand Vizier Ibrahim Pasha and looting the Jewish Quarter. The boldest of the mutineers broke into the quarters of the sultan himself and threatened his life. Suleiman had to reassert control by having the *agha* of the janissaries executed, alongside the ringleaders. But the point had been made; the army must march to war and disperse its restless energy outwards as opposed to allowing it to erupt within the walls of the Porte itself.

The second game-changing event of 1525 was the emperor's decisive victory in the Battle of Pavia on 24 February, where he not only smashed the army of his rival, Francis, but took the king himself captive. Alfonso de Valdés propagandized this triumph for public consumption as an expression of the divine will that Charles rally all Christendom under his banner for the final reckoning with the Ottomans:

> ... so that after the end of these civil wars (for that is what they should be called, since they are among Christians), he could seek out the Turks and Muslims in their own lands and, exalting our Holy Catholic faith as his ancestors had done, win the empire of Constantinople and the Holy City of Jerusalem, which are occupied because of our sins, so that (as many have prophesied) under this most Christian prince everyone may accept our Holy Catholic faith, and the words of our Redeemer may come true: let there be one flock and one shepherd.[69]

Francis arrived at the exact opposite conclusion. Only too willing to set aside any scruples over collaborating with the archenemy of the one true apostolic church against a fellow Catholic, he dispatched emissaries to Constantinople warning Suleiman that unless Charles was checked he threatened to become "ruler of the world." This outreach had two profound implications. First, it laid the foundation for a Franco-Ottoman alliance that would persist, in a patchy but persistent manner, for more than 300 years, until the Crimean War of the mid-19th century.[70] Second, it opened the door to Ottoman intervention in European great power politics. It was an invitation for the Porte to challenge the new world order the Habsburgs sought to create, an invitation Suleiman was only too happy to accept. "Now it is not befitting for rulers to cower and to be imprisoned," the sultan wrote to Francis. "Keep your spirits high, do not be heartbroken. Our glorious ancestors have never refrained from expelling the enemy and conquering lands. I also follow in their footsteps, conquering nations and mighty fortresses with my horse saddled and my sword girthed night and day."[71] It would be the fate of Hungary to tremble beneath the hoofs of that horse, and feel the weight of that sword.

Ottoman diplomats worked assiduously to keep the Hungarians isolated. In the autumn of 1525, Suleiman signed a three-year truce with King Sigismund of Poland, who considered safeguarding his eastern and southeastern borders from the Ottoman–Tatar menace more important than offering a helping hand to his nephew, Louis. That same year, the Porte abandoned its attempts to subsume Wallachia, recognizing the rule of the tenacious *voivode* Radul in return for his submission and an increased annual tribute.[72]

In order to secure his release from captivity, on 14 January 1526, Francis was forced to sign the Treaty of Madrid, by which he renounced all his claims in Italy, Artois, and Flanders and surrendered Burgundy to the emperor. Once safely back in Paris, the king repudiated the terms of the treaty on 10 May, and forged an anti-Habsburg front consisting of France, the papacy, Venice, Florence, and Milan – the League of Cognac – twelve days later.[73] This immediately demanded the complete attention of Charles V, reducing to nothing any possibility of his being able to intervene on behalf of Louis against Suleiman. "If we could have peace, you can be sure that I would deploy everything I have to Hungary," he wrote to Ferdinand. "But if the wars concerning my own possessions are going to continue – and I see for sure that they will – I leave you to judge whether I should not look to my own defence and deploy all my resources for that." Even when a final plea from Louis arrived, Charles still would not budge. "I already have a tiresome Turk to deal with," he replied: "the king of France."[74]

While the emperor set off on campaign, his empire was turning in upon itself. On 23 June, as the sultan's army approached Belgrade, an Imperial *Diet* convened at the town of Speyer on the Rhine River in the Lower Palatinate in southwestern Germany. Rather than focusing on the Ottoman question, this assembly immediately devolved into internecine sniping between Catholics and Lutherans over points of doctrine. Twice, on 30 June and 7 July, Ferdinand had tried to center the debate on the invasion of Hungary, imploring the delegates to "Save our neighbor's house, in order to save your own house from the oncoming fire!"[75] By a supreme irony, on this occasion, the Lutherans found themselves the beneficiaries of Habsburg grand strategy. On 27 July, in a spiteful corollary of his antagonism towards Pope Clement VII, who had enlisted in the League of Cognac against him, the emperor authorized Ferdinand to advise the *diet* the penal provisions of the Edict of Worms were abolished, and of his decision to negotiate with the papacy in order to summon a church council to seek terms of reconciliation, if the Lutherans agreed to obey the determinations of that conclave. It was only on 31 July that the Ottoman threat was addressed, and the only conclusion reached by this assembly was a tepid and toothless motion of support issued on 23 August, just six days before the decisive clash at Mohács: "As a Christian nation, the Crown and the Hungarian Kingdom are not to be left without help."[76]

Four days later, on 27 August, the *Diet* of Speyer issued its unanimous proclamation. Ignoring papal opposition, Ferdinand promised that, subject to his brother's approval, a church council would be called within eighteen months, and, to satisfy the Lutheran desire for guarantees during this interval, he agreed to have inserted in the Recess a statement that "until the meeting of the council, [everyone] would live, act and rule their subjects in such wise as each one thought right before God and his Imperial Majesty."[77] With this official imprimatur, Saxony, Hesse, Prussia, Anhalt, Lüneburg, East Friesland, Schleswig-Holstein, Silesia, and the imperial cities of Nuremberg, Augsburg, Frankfurt, Ulm, Strassburg, Bremen, Hamburg, and Lübeck all became officially Lutheran. Only Bavaria in the south remained loyal to the papacy.[78] While momentous in its implications for the course of the Reformation, this proclamation contributed nothing to the defense of Hungary, which was fast approaching its crisis.

In a further irony, the only state expressing any interest in siding with Hungary was Safavid Persia.[79] Louis had sent Petrus of Monte Libano, a Maronite friar from Lebanon, as his emissary to Ismail in 1516 in order to establish a dialogue. He received no response until 1523, when Petrus returned bearing letters from the shah for both Louis and Charles proposing an alliance and unified military action against the Ottomans, copies of which seem to have circulated around the major courts of Europe; the Venetian ambassador in Rome, Foscari, forwarded copies of both letters to the *Signoria*, and a report to Cardinal Wolsey from his agent at the Imperial court, dated 28 May 1524, confirmed "The Sophy has sent an ambassador to seek the Emperor's alliance with him."[80] However, Shah Ismail died in May 1524. His son and heir, Tahmasp, was only twelve years old, and needed to undertake a long apprenticeship in securing his domestic authority before he could begin to contemplate any action, concerted or otherwise, against his Ottoman neighbor. Vividly illustrating the limitations inherent to maintaining diplomatic relations over such distances, word of Ismail's death and the accession of Tahmasp had still not reached Charles by February 1529.

Isolated and seething with internal tension, Hungary was ill-prepared for the looming Ottoman onslaught.[81] Antonio da Burgio, the papal nuncio in Buda, lamented that "Everything needed for war is lacking. Among the Estates reign hate and need. And the subjects would, if the sultan promises them freedom, raise an even more gruesome revolt against the nobles than in the time of the crusade [1514]. But if the King gives them freedom, then he will alienate the nobility."[82]

On 20 March, Pál Tomori arrived in Buda and presented a detailed report on the imminent Ottoman invasion. Louis summoned the *diet*, which voted on 23 April to assemble the noble levies at Tolna on 2 July. At the same time, messengers were dispatched to Moravia and Bohemia ordering their contingents to march to the aid of their king. Using church monies, Louis recruited 4,000 German and 1,500 Polish mercenaries. John Zápolya, *voivode* of Transylvania, was ordered to harass and distract the Ottomans by crossing the Carpathians to invade Wallachia, thereby falling on the enemy's right flank and rear.

Suleiman had departed Constantinople on 23 April in full pomp and majesty; Ottoman chronicler Kemalpaşazade describes elephants walking like the graceful clouds before the sultan as he led his army out of the city. Marching via Edirne and Plovdiv, he entered Sofia on 28 May, where he held court for five days while the contingents led by the Rumeli *beys* arrived in his camp. The combined Ottoman army progressed via Niš and Kruševac to arrive at Belgrade on 29 June. A vanguard under Ibrahim Pasha then marched ahead to secure passage over the Sava and construct a bridge enabling the rest of the army to cross once it arrived.

The Hungarians had accomplished little in the meantime. "His Majesty has decided together with his council to take to the field, and to mobilize the whole realm," Burgio remarked on 30 May: "But until this very day nothing has been done by way of preparation."[83] Over a month later, on the appointed day for the muster, 2 July, not a soul had arrived at Tolna. Louis ordered the palatine, Stephen VIII Báthory, to advance with his troops to the Sava and prevent the Turks from crossing. The nobles, however, refused to go, arguing that if the king was not with them, they would not fight. The Turks thus crossed the Sava unopposed and immediately commenced the siege of Petrovaradin on the south bank of the Danube about midway between the Sava and the Drava on 12 July. After two mines opened up a breach in the walls the citadel surrendered on 28 July with a loss to the besiegers of only twenty-five men. The castle of Ilok, once the seat of King Miklós Újlaki and his son Lőrinc, who had died in 1524 without an heir, was besieged on 1 August and only held out for a week before capitulating. The defenders of both Erdőd and Osijek then fled, leaving the crossing of the Drava undefended.

There was despair in Buda. Burgio, who had been dispatching increasingly pessimistic reports to the Curia, concluded as early as 10 July that "the affairs in Hungary are most desperate; and Your Sanctity may be assured that this year there will be left in Hungary only what the enemy wishes to leave."[84] Louis finally set out from Buda on 20 July with his household retainers, a mere 3,000 men. Only after he arrived at Tolna on 2 August – a full month after the specified date for the muster – did contingents begin to trickle in.

Tomori, who was shadowing the Ottoman advance, sent urgent messages warning Suleiman was approaching the Drava. Louis ordered Báthory to hold the river at Osijek, but again, the nobility refused to recognize their obligation to serve under any banner save that of the king. Suleiman was thus able commence construction of a pontoon bridge over the Drava on 15 August, crossing unopposed once this was completed four days later. The Hungarian defense line had been shattered almost without resistance. "I have written letters to Your Majesty week after week," Tomori bitterly reproached the king, "but Your Majesty and the lords have failed even to shoe the horses."[85] Significantly, once the Ottoman army had mustered on the north side of the Drava, the bridge was destroyed, along with Osijek, its houses, churches, and gardens. Suleiman had deliberately closed off his own line of retreat. The only alternative was to march forwards to victory.[86]

As they continued their advance, the Ottomans now found themselves wading into an unforeseen physical obstacle – a swampy floodplain of the Danube that stretched five miles north to the Karasso River. Here, the Hungarians missed yet another opportunity to compensate for their numerical inferiority. "The terrain is so swampy that it can carry neither man nor horse," an Ottoman chronicler wrote. "Wherever one steps, you are bound to sink. If the miserable king [Louis] with his dogs comes to the edge of the swamp, sets up his batteries, and fires against us, he can prevent the soldiers of the true faith from entering the game pack of jihad."[87] But no such resistance materialized, and on 28 August Suleiman set up camp ten miles south of Mohács on the Danube, where Louis had established his headquarters.

In stark contrast to the well-oiled Ottoman military machine, synergy within the Hungarian military was distinctly lacking, a flaw that started at the very top. The twenty-year-old King Louis had no military experience and lacked a steady hand to guide him. The Hungarian government had tried to convince the veteran imperial officer, Nicholas von Salm, to assume supreme command of the army, but he declined the offer. Krsto Frankopan, the hero of the 1525 Jajce campaign, volunteered, but he arrived too late, and John Zápolya was still in Transylvania. Finally, Tomori and György Zápolya, the *voivode's* younger brothers, were appointed as co-commanders-in-chief, both against their will.

The Hungarian military elite was also divided over its best course of action. Aware they were outnumbered two to one, some argued the royal host should hold its ground and await the arrival of reinforcements. Units were continuing to trickle into camp; the king's artillery train was landed by boat from Buda, then 3,000 Croatians marched in, the *ban* of Slavonia, Ferenc Batthyány, finally arrived with his men, and large numbers of fortified wagons also trundled into the lines. A Polish officer, Lenart Gnoiński, even suggested the war wagons, which were now available in great numbers, should be arranged in a *wagenburg* formation around the camp in order to buy the army more time. However, John Zápolya and his Transylvanians were no closer than Szeged, 100 miles to the east, and the Bohemian vanguard had not even passed Bratislava. Others recommended a scorched-earth policy, pulling back to Buda and leaving Suleiman to risk setting off in pursuit across the wastes of the Carpathian Plain. But the counsel of Tomori, who insisted on giving battle immediately, ultimately prevailed. This decision did not register with every participant. Ferenc Perényi, the bishop of Varad, cynically remarked that Hungary would have 20,000 martyrs the day after the battle, so the pope had better be ready to canonize them all.[88]

The Ottoman camp, too, was considering its options. At a council of war, Ibrahim suggested constructing a fake camp to lure the enemy into a trap. Bali Bey suggested the age-old steppe strategy of the simulated retreat in order to draw the Hungarians into an ambush. Ultimately, the consensus was to remain in position and let the enemy show his hand first.

Accordingly, early in the morning on 29 August, Louis crossed to the south bank of the Borza, a stream that wended its ways across the field separating the two armies, and formed up his army in two parallel lines on its southern bank. The first line comprised one-third of the Hungarian cavalry, two-thirds of the infantry, and fifty-three guns. The right wing was led by Ferenc Batthyány, the left by Peter Perényi (the bishop of Varad's brother), two young aristocrats with no military experience who owed their commands to their social status. In the second, or main, battle line, the remaining infantry held the flanks while the cavalry massed in the center. Rallying to the king and his royal banner, kept aloft by Judge Royal János Drágfi, was the flower of the Magyar elite, 1,000 mounted and fully armored knights. A single squadron of horsemen under Gábor Ráskay was detached and stationed on the extreme right as insurance against any attempt to outflank the Hungarian line by Ottoman troops believed to be concealed beyond the village of Majs at the foot of the southwestern ridge. No equivalent precautions were taken on the left wing, which was anchored by the Borza as it wended its way through a virtually impassable mixture of swamp and flooded forest towards the Danube.[89]

The Ottoman army did not arrive in force until the afternoon, filing onto the field in separate detachments behind a screen of *akinji* light cavalry. Knowing he needed to distribute his force in a manner calculated to absorb the shock of a

Hungarian mounted charge, Suleiman distributed his forces in depth across three lines. The Anatolian and Rumelian cavalry, supported by the light artillery, comprised the first and second lines, commanded by Ibrahim Pasha and Behrem Pasha respectively. The third line, which incorporated the heavy artillery and the 15,000 janissaries, with the *sipahis* on the flanks, was under the personal command of the sultan himself. Additional units of cavalry were held in reserve on the right, while Bali Bey and Korsev Bey were stationed far to the left with a squadron of *akinji* to contest any threat that might materialize on that flank.

Ironically, it was the Ottoman decision to withdraw their forces to camp and postpone the clash until the following day that precipitated the battle. Observing the retrograde movement in the enemy line, Tomori, confident the Ottomans could be broken before they completed their redeployment, urged Louis to attack; "it is less dangerous to engage part of the enemy forces now than the whole army tomorrow," he advised the king.[90] The first two Turkish lines did indeed buckle, being steadily driven back onto the third. "Since the Rumelian army was dispersed," Suleiman wrote in his diary, "it was unable to resist, and part of it fled in the direction of the ruler."[91] Ráskay, meanwhile, fought a private duel with Bali and Korsev, scattering their *akinji* but failing to drive them from the field.

The tide turned completely when the advancing Hungarians stumbled upon the Ottoman artillery anchoring their third line. Sheltered in revetments and chained together, these guns were positioned in a depression that Tomori's reconnaissance had failed to discover, a lapse that would prove critical. The Ottoman first and second lines now retreated to reform on the flanks of the third, giving the guns a clear field of fire. Tomori immediately recognized continuing to press ahead with a cavalry charge against entrenched artillery supported by the janissaries would be suicidal. He therefore ordered Batthyány and Perényi to attack the *sipahis* on the Ottoman flanks, hoping at least one of them could break through and roll up the Ottoman third line from its rear while he pinned Suleiman in place by launching a frontal assault with the Hungarian infantry. Tomori also sent word to Louis; now was the time for him to advance and deliver the decisive stroke.

Batthyány made good progress and succeeded in swinging around the Ottoman left, some isolated horsemen penetrating as far as the sultan's tent. But the janissaries repulsed the Hungarian infantry assault against the center of the Ottoman line in what may have been the first example of volley fire in European history; the Ottoman chronicler Celalzâde Mustafa described 4,000 janissaries deployed in nine consecutive rows ranked behind two chained field pieces, firing their matchlocks row by row. Meanwhile, Perényi could not break through the superior Ottoman numbers on the right, reinforced by their reserves.

As the Hungarians faltered, Suleiman ordered a general counterattack on both flanks, which swiftly enveloped the enemy in a double encirclement. The detached Ottoman units of *akinji* under Bali Bey and Korsev Bey, whom Gábor Ráskay had so regrettably allowed to regroup, advanced from Majs in two sections, one against the flanks of the melee, and the other on towards the king's position at the rear. "Three or four times the Janissary division rake the infidel with gunfire, and at length, with the help of majestic God and the Prophet, the people of Islam hurl back the wicked ones," Suleiman noted with satisfaction in his journal; "and when they no longer have the strength to throw themselves into a fresh attack, they are put to the sword like dogs."[92] The Hungarian army disintegrated as men desperately turned in flight. "Shields cracked like the heart of a rose, helmets filled with blood like the lips of a rose-bud. Mists of blood rising like a purple cloud to the horizon were like a rosy sky above the head of victory's betrothed," poeticized the Ottoman historian Kemalpaşazade, who was present at the battle.[93]

Few escaped, and the field was left scattered with corpses, most significantly, that of King Louis II, who drowned, thrown from his horse and weighed down by his own armor. His body was only found and identified two months later when the floods of the Danube had subsided.[94] Hungary's political elite was indeed subject to the decimation of its most senior figures from Crown and Church in this battle. In addition to the king, Tomori was killed, along with the chancellor, Laszlo Szalkai, archbishop of Esztergom. Many who survived the battle only to be taken prisoner found their status as captives offered them scant relief. "The Sultan, seated on a golden throne, receives the homage of the *viziers* and *beys*," Suleiman noted in his diary entry for 31 August, dispassionately written in the third person; "massacre of two hundred prisoners, the rain falls in torrents." This was the opening phase of a systematic slaughter, for Suleiman did not want the army encumbered while it pressed forward to the next phase of the campaign. On 2 September the sultan commanded great trenches to be dug where "twenty thousand Hungarian infantry and four thousand of their cavalry are buried," for he had ordered all the remaining prisoners-of-war to be executed.[95]

News of the disaster arrived in Buda on the evening of 30 August. Queen Mary, escorted by fifty horsemen, fled the city with the most precious royal treasures, first to Bratislava and then to her brother in Vienna. Whoever could among the general populace followed her example, leaving behind, as one report concluded, only "the poor, the lame, the blind, and the Jews" to await the sultan when he arrived. On 11 September, Suleiman entered Buda, encountering no resistance. The city was methodically plundered, from the Cathedral of the Virgin to the great library of Matthias Corvinus, and then, with the exception of the royal palace, put to the torch. On 13 September the Ottoman army crossed the Danube into Pest. It too was gutted before being burned to the ground. The only resistance the Ottomans encountered was north of the capital near Esztergom on the Austrian border, where many refugees had gone to ground in the fortress of Pilismarot. Ottoman artillery soon reduced this last refuge to rubble. Only the women were spared.

On 25 September, Suleiman divided his forces in two, the sultan himself advancing along the Danube to the south, while Ibrahim Pasha, who took the bulk of the cavalry, marched directly for Szeged, where Ottoman intelligence reported Zápolya and his army were mustering.

Ibrahim seized and plundered Kecskemet on 27 September and pushed on towards Szeged but found the city abandoned and no sign of Zápolya. An outrunning detachment of his force independently laid siege to Subotica, but its citizens and those inhabitants of the surrounding villages who sought refuge behind its walls resisted fiercely. Constrained by bad weather and aware the fact Zápolya maintained an army in being obliged him to keep the bulk of his forces together, Ibrahim elected not to detach reinforcements for the siege of Subotica, which held out. Following his instructions to reunite with the sultan at Petrovaradin, Ibrahim moved on to take Senta, Perlek, Pačir, and Kanjiža en route before arriving at the fortress of Titel on 2 October. Strategically positioned at the confluence of the Tisza and Danube rivers, the fortress was stoutly constructed and well provisioned, and Ibrahim anticipated a tough siege. But the defenders had fled upon his approach, and Titel was occupied without any resistance. Stationing his own garrison in the fortress, Ibrahim set out the next day for Petrovaradin via Novi Sad. The only resistance he encountered on the march was from the leader of the Hungarian Danube River fleet, Radić Božić, who fell on the Ottoman rearguard, killing 500 men and taking 400 more captive.

Suleiman, meanwhile, had seized Baja and then Bački Monoštor, which he left ablaze in his wake as he moved on to Bač. The Ottoman chronicler Kemalpaşazade recounted how Suleiman's army advanced "across the mountains and valleys, in the gardens and granges, like bloodthirsty dogs and wolves, catching the spawns of hell like lions, leaving nothing for the evil of the natural enemy, no plains, no houses on the mountains, no fields, their own property and the grain necessary for their existence mercilessly destroyed."[96]

Once the besiegers had penetrated the outer walls of Bač, the last Christian holdouts fled to its Franciscan church, which Ottoman chronicler Mustafa bin Dzelal described as being "as big as a fortress." In his account:

> Near the bank of the Danube there was a town called Bač, which was a great city of the beaten king; it had one big church devoted to the devil, which was full of idols of these spawns of hell. A happy army robbed this place, which became part of hell, of all the population the army killed the men, while many women were captured and the loot was endless.[97]

Suleiman continued south for Petrovaradin, encountering unexpected resistance between Bač and Futog, near Plavna, where many refugees had set up a wagon laager deep in the surrounding marshes and bogs. Scouring these wetlands proved a frustratingly protracted endeavor. According to the account of Brodarics Istvan, the royal chancellor of Hungary and bishop of Syrmia, who had survived the catastrophe at Mohács:

> ... thousands of Hungars retired themselues, with their wiues and children, trusting vpon the straight and narrow passages which were strongly shut vp. With those the enemie often came to handy strokes, and always they receiued the worst, and were put to the foile. In the end the Turks seeing by no means they could force the barracado, which the Hungars had made with their wagons, they were constrained to bring thither their artillerie, by means wherof al those wagons & other such defences were broken & ouerthrowne to the ground, and almost all the people put to the sword.[98]

It was 6 October before the sultan succeed in finally subduing the last holdouts, after losing many officers and men in the process. Irritated, Suleiman ordered all prisoners executed before pressing on to Vašaroš Varad, where he arrived on 8 October. With the approach of autumn, the campaigning season was over. After linking up with Ibrahim, Suleiman ordered detachments be left behind to garrison Petrovaradin and Ilok while he led the bulk of the combined army back into Ottoman territory via Belgrade, returning to Constantinople in triumph on 13 November. In his official report on the progress of the campaign, he described how at Mohács, "we combated for two hours, and with the help of God almighty, we broke him [Louis] and we sliced his army into pieces." In the aftermath, "praiseworthy conquests which were not granted to famous rulers and powerful monarchs, or even to the companions of the Prophet, fell to my lot with the help of God."[99]

The Western response was guilt-ridden angst tinged with self-serving recriminations.[100] Seeking to maximize the propaganda value of the disaster, on 6 October, Francis I took the opportunity to blame his archrival for the Ottoman triumph, on the grounds Charles had refused the king's offers to settle their differences and unite against the common enemy, no matter how many times he:

> ... exhorted the Emperor to lay aside private quarrels, and form a league of Christian princes, offering to resign his just rights in Italy that there may be no impediment to peace. The Emperor says that he will refuse no fair terms of peace; but while he is wasting the time by various delays Christian fields and cities are being devastated and burnt. Does not know what other proposals to make to the Emperor, for it is impossible to rouse him, if the danger of Austria and Germany, and the miserable condition of his own sister, do not excite him.[101]

Charles was having none of it. As he instructed his ambassador at the English court:

> You are to request the King and Wolsey, for the love of us, to hear the whole matter that they may understand who is to blame for these wars now in Christendom. It is strange that every time the Turk searches the entry and the destruction of Hungary, and when we and our brother the infant Archduke have made preparations to resist the Infidel and suppress the Lutherans, we are forced to abandon so good business for our own defense.[102]

In a letter dated 23 October to Pope Clement VII, Henry VIII piously related how he "greatly regrets the evils of the times," and that he "could not help shed tears" over the fate of Hungary, which he attributed to the "dissensions of Christendom." He solemnly reaffirmed his pledge that "when other princes have agreed, he will not be behindhand in joining the crusade."[103]

Guicciardini mentions that in the aftermath of Mohács, Clement may have thought that God had chosen to teach Christendom a lesson through the Hungarian defeat, "since perhaps for some good end, it had pleased God that the body of Christendom should be wounded, and at a time when all other members of this body were distracted by other thoughts than those relating to the security of all, he was forced to believe that it was the will of God that the curing of so great a malady be sought by other means."[104] If so, the Holy Father quickly pulled himself together, calling for Charles, Francis, and Wolsey to devise a plan for concerted action against the Ottoman presence in Hungary. Otherwise, according to Gregory di Casale, Henry VIII's representative in the Holy City, Clement was in no doubt "we shall forthwith see the Turks in Rome spoiling his palace."[105] Casale was of like mind, convinced that if the Ottomans consolidated their gains in Hungary, Germany would be the next domino to fall: "I never feared the Turk till now; but I shall fear him more if measures be not taken this spring which would make us secure."[106]

On 14 March 1527, Habsburg envoys arrived in England with an appeal from Ferdinand to Henry VIII, outlining the extent of Ottoman power and referencing the Christian defeats at Belgrade, Rhodes, and Mohács, "to the great rebuke (as he sayd) of the kings christened." The ambassadors "most humbly besought the king" to assist in the struggle against the Ottoman enemy, "in that godly warre and vertuous purpose." Henry responded that while "much hee lamented" the fall of Hungary, he couldn't help but point out, "if it were not for the warres which were betweene the two great princes, he thought that the Turke would not have enterprised that acte." Accordingly, "he with all his studie would take paine, first, to set an unitie and peace throughout all Christendome, and fater that, both with money and men he would be readie to helpe toward that glorious warre, as much as any other prince in Christendome."[107]

None of this finger pointing did anything to alter the fact that the balance of power in Europe had fundamentally shifted over the course of that one fateful day at Mohács. In 1589, Louis de Gonzague, duc de Nevers, neatly encapsulated its significance when he lamented: "Louis was killed there with twenty thousand Christians, and so Hungary – which had served as a bulwark for Christianity against the Muslims for more than 150 years – was reduced nearly completely to obedience to the Turk."[108]

Indeed, although the bulk of Hungary remained unoccupied, Suleiman could be well pleased with his accomplishments, for the kingdom had been effectively neutralized. Mohács had functionally emasculated the Magyar aristocracy, its surviving claimants to the throne rudderless and riven by factions, while the sultan's subsequent *chevauchée* had demonstrated the southern defensive line of Hungary for all intents and purposes no longer existed, leaving the country wide open to future Ottoman incursions. The frontier between East and West that had run along the Danube for generations was now in complete flux. The implications would be profound, for the Ottoman star now approached its zenith, impelled by its absolute unity of purpose. By contrast, even as Europe subsumed entire new worlds in the Americas, it was turning in upon itself, riven by incompatible egos and agendas into irreconcilable identities. In an era where ambition fed upon opportunity, such discord could only whet the appetite of the Sublime Porte.[109]

And yet, as James Reston notes, while the victory over Hungary was complete, perhaps all Suleiman had accomplished was to destroy a weak buffer state on his border, thereby creating endless friction with the far more powerful Ferdinand, who rushed to fill the power vacuum created by the extinction of the ruling Jagiellon dynasty. Thus, in the struggle for dominance in Eastern Europe, "instead of pushing the Habsburgs back, the Turkish victory had sucked them farther in."[110] The wreckage of the Hungarian state would thus become the battleground between rival Habsburg and Ottoman interests for nearly four centuries, not emerging in its own right as a – much reduced – independent state until 1919 in the wake of the First World War. The wounds inflicted at Mohács still scar the Magyar psyche to this day, as reflected in the fifth stanza of the Hungarian national anthem, which, far from celebrating the glorious past, laments:

O, how often has the voice
Sounded of wild Osman's hordes,
When in songs they did rejoice
O'er our heroes' captured swords![111]

6

SULEIMAN, PART II - VIENNA

The shockwaves from the clash at Mohács resonated throughout Europe, nowhere more so than in the Holy Roman Empire, confronted with the reality that its eastern marches now represented the frontier with Islam. Within just two days of the battle the first reports reached the free imperial city of Frankfurt, where a priest named Wolfgang Königstein noted "fair many letters and messages concerning the Turks arrived, how they have engulfed Hungary with war, and how the king of Hungary together with other princes and lords died in a battle. They are gradually advancing on Austria and have taken Buda and other castles." With the emperor entangled in his struggle with Francis I for the political hegemony of Christendom, and with Martin Luther over the unity of the faith, "There is much unpleasantness, war, and complaint in German lands." This vulnerability made Vienna the logical next target for Ottoman expansionism.[1] The Ottomans had long spoken of the major cities lined up in their path to universal dominion as golden apples, which since ancient times had been considered symbols of sovereignty. Constantinople was the first golden apple to fall into the Ottoman lap. Belgrade, and now Buda, had followed. Vienna would be next. Rome was the final objective.

Complicating matters, the death of the childless king Louis II at Mohács had created a power vacuum in Bohemia and Hungary. Archduke Ferdinand had learned of Louis's death before Suleiman did. Wasting no time, on 8 September, only ten days after the Battle of Mohács, he began to circulate a petition among the surviving nobles and towns of Hungary asserting his right to the Hungarian throne. His claim was centered on the treaty of 1463 between Emperor Frederick III and King Matthias Corvinus which stipulated that if Matthias died heirless either Frederick or his son Maximilian would inherit the

Hungarian throne. When Maximilian asserted that right upon the death of Matthias he was repudiated by the Hungarian nobility. Thus a new treaty was signed with Vladislaus III in 1491 upholding the previous one, this treaty being renewed again in 1506, with the additional stipulation that the two houses be further bound together by the double marriages of Ferdinand to Anne, and Mary to Louis. Adding weight to his claim, Louis's widow, Mary, Ferdinand's sister, had fled to Bratislava when Buda surrendered to the Ottomans. She convoked a *diet* which on 17 December 1526 recognized her brother as the new king of Hungary. A few weeks later the great houses of Croatia, Dalmatia, and Slavonia endorsed Ferdinand as king on the grounds he offered the only plausible alternative to Ottoman rule. Ferdinand was crowned as king of Bohemia in Prague on 24 February 1527.

This ascension was contested by the *voivode* of Transylvania, John Zápolya, who appealed to an ancient law by which no one but a born Hungarian could occupy the throne of Bohemia. With the assent of many of the magnates, including Valentin Terek of Subotica, Radić Božić, commander (*vajd*) of the river fleet (*šajkaši*), and the Serbian resistance leader Stevan Berislavić (popularly known as "emperor" Jovan Nenad), he proclaimed himself king, being crowned on 10 November at Székesfehérvár.

Ferdinand received no support from the electors of the Holy Roman Empire for his agenda in Hungary. The Catholic majority was convinced that any army a *diet* voted into existence would only be appropriated by Charles in support of his rivalry with Francis. The Lutheran minority, headed by Philip, Landgrave of Hessen, and John Frederick, elector of Saxony, eager to preserve the gains achieved in the Recess of Speyer, feared to strengthen the Habsburgs lest an empowered Ferdinand retract the concessions he had been obliged to make. As a corollary, they did not wish to support any action that could lead to the elimination of Zápolya, seeing him as useful leverage against any Habsburg backsliding on religious tolerance.

The dual claims of Ferdinand and Zápolya split the already desperately destabilized kingdom of Hungary into rival factions. "The Hungarians have reached the point where if a family has two growing sons, they encourage one to join the cause of Ferdinand, the other the party of King Janos," György Szeremi recorded.[2] Their confrontation had wider implications. Because Zápolya was the alternative to Ferdinand, the anti-Habsburg League of Cognac naturally acknowledged him as Hungary's legitimate ruler. His joining the League was announced in July 1527 in Buda, in the presence of the French envoy, Antonio Rincón.

Zápolya was graced with little time to celebrate this diplomatic recognition, for it brought with it no practical support. That summer, Ferdinand dispatched an army against Zápolya under the command of Nicholas, Graf von Salm, who drove him out of Buda on 20 August and defeated him in battle near Tokaj on 27 September, then captured Győr, Komoron, and Esztergom along the line of the Danube. Zápolya fled to his base of Transylvania only to find the Saxon towns of the region had risen up against him and his *voivode*, Peter Perényi, had defected and handed the Holy Crown of St Stephen to Ferdinand. Having taken the solemn oath pledging to uphold Hungary's ancient laws and the nobles' privileges, Ferdinand was crowned on 3 November at the *Diet* at Székesfehérvár. Attended by the majority of barons and nobles, the ceremony was performed by Stephen Podmaniczky, the same bishop of Nyitra who just a year earlier had crowned Zápolya. Defeated again, this time by Habsburg general Hans Katzianer near Szina on 8 March 1528, Zápolya was forced to take refuge in Poland. Though on all sides deserted, and destitute of troops and money, he persevered in his designs, and made every exertion to gain over to his cause the nobility of Poland and their king, Sigismund, his brother-in-law by marriage to his sister, Barbara. Zápolya succeeded in gaining the support of Hieronymus Łaski, *voivode* of Sieradia, who advised him an alliance with the Ottomans would be a prerequisite of any bid to assume power in Hungary.

Łaski thus undertook a journey to Constantinople in October 1527, accompanied by a renegade Venetian, Alvise Gritti (son of the doge Andrea Gritti), who served him as interpreter, to plead the case for Zápolya. Their embassy would find its path smoothed by the injudicious arrogance of Ferdinand's ambassadors, John Habardanecz, a Hungarian–Slavonian aristocrat, and Siegmund Weichselberger, a courtier from Carniola. The negotiations got off to a bad start when the Habsburg representatives proposed that Suleiman return the border castles of Belgrade, Šabac, Slankamen, Severin, Orşova, Jajce, Banja Luka, Knin, and Skradin in exchange for Ferdinand offering a substantial indemnity. This was a provocative opening gambit to play against the ascendant Ottomans; "I am surprised that he did not ask for Constantinople," Ibrahim mockingly retorted, and then reminded his interlocutors of the Ottoman proverb, "Wherever the hoof of the sultan's horse has trod, that land belongs to him."

"I can only say no more than that my king holds Buda," Habardanecz replied.

"Why has he sent you to ask for peace and friendship if he holds Buda, which the sultan has conquered?" Ibrahim responded.[3] The grand vizier made it clear that if Ferdinand wanted peace, he had to first surrender Hungary: "After that, we can talk about Germany."[4]

Having repudiated the obdurate Habsburgs, Ibrahim next took the opportunity to instruct Łaski in the nature of power. "We killed King Louis," he reminded Zápolya's ambassador. "His kingdom is ours."[5] Nonetheless, on 27 January 1528, in exchange for an annual tribute and free passage through the kingdom for Ottoman forces, the Porte announced that Zápolya was now under the protection of the sultan and was recognized as the king of Hungary.[6] "I accept with pleasure the devotion of your master," the sultan assured Łaski; "Not only do I cede him Hungary, but also I will protect him so effectively against Ferdinand of Austria that he will be able to sleep on both ears."[7] This was a patron–client relationship, not a partnership between peers. "His country, conquered by war and sword, has hitherto belonged to me, not to him," Suleiman said of Zápolya. "Still, having heard about his intentions, I hereby not only return the country to him but shall also assist him against the Austrian Ferdinand."[8] The unfortunate Habsburg ambassadors then spent the next nine months under arrest on trumped-up charges of espionage before finally securing an audience with the sultan, who dismissed them with the menacing promise "that he would soon come to drive [Ferdinand] out of a kingdom which he had unjustly acquired; that he would look for him on the field of Mohács, or even in Pest; and should Ferdinand shrink from meeting him at either, he would offer him battle under the walls of Vienna itself."[9]

Now with the considerable weight of Ottoman acknowledgment buttressing his claim to the legitimate title of king, Zápolya continued to press his case for diplomatic recognition in the West. He reached out to nearly all the powers of Europe, even Pope Clement VII, whom he knew to be on bad terms with the emperor, urging them to support what he termed his just cause. These embassies were unavailing; the pope replied by excommunicating him, by exhorting the magnates of Hungary to support Ferdinand, and by urging the latter to draw the sword without delay in defense of Christendom.

With his pretext of advancing to the support of an embattled vassal now established, Suleiman could proceed with his predetermined agenda of subjugating Habsburg Austria, boasting that he would not lay down his arms until he had erected a monument to his victory and to the faith on the banks of the Rhine River. The Ottomans had laid the groundwork for their campaign through substantive diplomacy. In September 1528 they sweetened their relationship with Francis I by confirming the trade privileges originally obtained from the Mamluks in 1513 for French and Catalan merchants in the Mediterranean. In October, the Porte signed a three-year truce with King Sigismund of Poland, which ruled out any possibility of the Habsburgs receiving assistance from that quarter in the now imminent conflict. That same month, Francis and Zápolya signed an agreement asserting there would be "everlasting brotherhood, union, confederation and friendship" between the two monarchs. However, this treaty was entirely one-sided. Although Francis offered no military aid to his Hungarian ally, he was obliged to wage war against Ferdinand until "the most Christian king [Francis] recovers his sons, who are being held as hostage by Charles," and denied the right to arrive at a truce or peace with Ferdinand "without the expressed consent and agreement of the most Christian king." It was also stipulated that, in the event Zápolya died childless, his kingdom would pass to Henry, Duc d'Orleans, the second son of Francis.[10]

The incorporation of Zápolya did little to reverse the declining fortunes of the League of Cognac, for Charles had steadily won the upper hand over Francis. On 6 May 1527, an imperial army had taken, and then systematically sacked, Rome, placing the pope under the emperor's authority. The French siege of Naples was broken in August of the following year when Andrea Doria of Genoa defected to the imperial cause, and the imperial victory at the Battle of Landriano on 21 June 1529 effectively destroyed any remaining French pretensions to authority in Italy. A flurry of diplomatic initiatives then proceeded to end the war, all of them on terms favorable to Charles.

On 29 June 1529, the Treaty of Barcelona was signed between the emperor and the pope, in which the two signatories jointly expressed their earnest intent to bring peace to Europe in order to contain *"lupus ille, rapax inimicissimus Turcha"* ("that wolf, the ravenous enemy the Turk"). Charles recognized the papal right to reclaim Ravenna and Cervia from Venice, and Modena, Reggio, and Rubiera from Alfonse d'Este, Duke of Ferrara, and pledged to restore Medici control over Florence, which had proclaimed itself a republic in the aftermath of the sack of Rome. In return, Clement renounced the League of Cognac and conferred upon Charles a "new investiture" over the Kingdom of Naples.[11]

Francis came to terms with Charles in the Peace of Cambrai on 3 August 1529, dubbed the *Paix des Dames* (Peace of the Ladies) because it was negotiated by Louise of Savoy, Francis's mother, and her sister-in-law Margaret, who was regent of the Netherlands for her nephew the emperor. Francis recognized Charles's rights to Flanders and Artois and renounced his own claim to Milan, Genoa, and Naples, while agreeing to pay 2 million French crowns (valued in Spain at 1.2 million ducats) as a ransom for his two sons, still held in Spain in consequence of their father's renunciation of the 1526

Treaty of Madrid. A marriage was also negotiated between Francis and Charles's sister, Eleanor.[12]

This at least ensured Suleiman would not receive any direct assistance from the West. Only in Florence, the last holdout of the League of Cognac and besieged by imperial forces, was there support for the sultan's cause. And even there, as evidenced in correspondence dated 20 October 1529, emotions were intensely mixed regarding the Ottoman intentions: "As for the ultimate remedy to the affairs of Italy we have come to the point of wishing for the prosperity and felicity of the Turkish affairs. Poor Christendom! Here and elsewhere we remain with our mouths open to see which great campaign of theirs will hopefully change the current evils."

The Ottoman army that left Constantinople on 10 May 1529 was considerably larger than the invasion force that had triumphed at Mohács three years earlier. It consisted of at least 75,000 men, with thousands of camels and mules and hundreds of elephants to haul the supplies and the artillery train.[13] The target was Vienna, predicated upon the Ottoman assumption that Charles could not risk the immense loss of prestige he would incur if the Habsburg capital were to fall. Even setting aside its political significance, occupying Vienna would endow the Ottomans with a profound strategic advantage. The Marchfeld plain that surrounds the city forms a corridor that connects the German lands to the west with the Hungarian and Slavic lands to the east.[14] Beyond it lay the great central plain of Hungary, the ample pasturage of which had made it the staging ground for centuries of invasions of Western Europe by Huns, Magyars, and Mongols. Taking Vienna would therefore afford the Ottomans a critical bridgehead for further campaigns to the west, just as it then represented a bulwark for the Habsburg forces facing east. For all these reasons, Suleiman believed Charles had no option other than to make a stand either in or before the city, and the sultan had every confidence his professional and battle-hardened army would prevail over its makeshift Habsburg equivalent in the ensuing battle. It was to be a truly apocalyptic clash of civilizations, and the crowning achievement of the sultan's reign.

Alas, this grand design was not to be. As with so many strategic masterplans when drawn up on paper, the reality on the ground refused to comply with Ottoman timetables, hopelessly compromising the mobility of the army and its assumed capacity to project force.

Almost immediately upon departing Constantinople, the Ottoman expedition was dogged by terrible weather. This is not just an anecdotal impression. Statistical analysis confirms the summer of 1529 was among the coldest and wettest of the last 500 years.[15] Central European records from that year indicate it rained on twenty-four days during May, followed by rain falling almost without interruption from 18 June to 5 July, from 22 July to 6 August, from 9 to 23 August, from 31 August to 8 September, and again from 25 September to 6 October.[16] Rivers were swollen; plains were flooded; roads were washed out; temperatures fell to record lows; and the winds were high. At the first way station of Edirne, the bridges had been destroyed. Several weeks later, near Plovdiv, the Maritsa River raged over its banks, drowning a number of men and horses, and forcing many more soldiers to climb trees to escape the flooding. Inevitably and perhaps critically, the weather slowed down the march north through Sofia and Niš. Suleiman had only advanced as far as Osijek by 6 August, while the arrival at Belgrade was a month later than had been planned. Crossing the Drava River was dragged out over six agonizing days by a raging storm, and lightning killed nine men. Not until 18 August did the army finally reach the fields of Mohács in southern Hungary. There Suleiman greeted Zápolya, who arrived with 6,000 reinforcements.[17]

In exchange for his homage, Zápolya was rewarded with four ceremonial robes, one on top of another, in the Ottoman tradition, and officially proclaimed to be the king of Hungary. He was accorded the singular honor of having a bodyguard of janissaries, while a simple iron crown was placed on his head, for the sacred crown of St Stephen was still in Habsburg hands.

A few days later the massive force stood before Buda. The garrison consisted of only about 1,000 German and Hungarian soldiers under Baron Tamás Nádasdy. After four days of sustained fire from Ottoman artillery emplaced on the neighboring heights, the garrison, with the few remaining inhabitants, retired into the citadel, and the Ottomans occupied the town. Nádasdy was resolved to hold out to the last, but the rank and file spontaneously reached out to the Ottomans for terms, answering Nádasdy's pleas for loyalty by throwing him into confinement. The citadel capitulated on 7 September. Suleiman, only too happy to neutralize this obstacle to his advance as quickly as possible, had offered generous terms. However, he was not master of his own camp. When his janissaries received word they would be denied their anticipated plunder of the citadel they responded by hurling imprecations and stones at their own officers. It was through the ranks of these men the garrison had to defile, amid expressions of contempt for their cowardice. A German soldier, provoked by this conduct, insisted that if he had been in command no surrender would have exposed them to it. This information being received, as might be expected, with redoubled insult, the German lost patience, and with his sword he struck a janissary to the ground. The general massacre which naturally ensued was certainly not by the order, and probably against the will, of the sultan. Nevertheless, not more than sixty men escaped this slaughter. Ironically, one of them was Nádasdy, who was dismissed on his parole not to serve against the Ottomans during the war. The generosity of the sultan in this instance is all the more remarkable in that it was exercised in defiance not only of the embittered janissaries but of the Hungarian vassals aligned with Zápolya.

On 14 September, another installation ceremony was held for Zápolya. Interestingly, by this time, under the direction of Ibrahim Pasha, Ottoman soldiers had recovered the stolen crown of St Stephen from Ferdinand's soldiers, who were trying to squirrel it out of Hungary. Though the relic was now in hand, Zápolya again received only a stolid iron crown. Importantly, neither Suleiman nor Ibrahim Pasha attended this perfunctory ceremony, being represented only by the *segbanbaschi*, or second-in-command of the janissaries, and by the sultan's commissioner in Hungary, Alvise Gritti. Zápolya could have no doubts about his place.[18]

Meanwhile, the pasha of Smederevo, Mohammed Bey, was sent on in advance towards Vienna to obtain intelligence and clear the roads. On 15 September, Suleiman prepared to move north. Before he left Buda, he issued a proclamation to the effect that, "Whosoever in Hungary should withhold obedience and subjection from [Zápolya], whom the sultan had named king, had replaced in the sovereignty, and had engaged himself to uphold, should be punished and extirpated with fire and sword; but that those who should submit themselves should be stoutly protected, and maintained in the possession of their property and privileges."[19]

On 18 September, *akinji* raiders swept across the Austrian border, fanning out before the main body and spreading desolation in every direction.[20] At their head was Mihal Oglou, a descendant of Kose Mihal, or Michael of the Pointed Beard, who traced his roots on his father's side to the Palaiologoi, the last ruling dynasty of Byzantium, and on his mother's side to the royal houses of France and Savoy.[21]

From the foot of the Kahlenberg, from Heiligenstadt and Döbling to the shore of the Leitha, the presence of the *akinjis* was proclaimed by the smoke of burning villages, and their march was tracked by wasted fields and vineyards. At Döbling the pastor, Peter Heindl, was flung on a burning pile of the registers and archives of the district. Hütteldorf, St Veit, Brunn, and Enzersdorf were burnt. In

Perchtoldsdorf the inhabitants held out in the castle, but everything beyond its walls was destroyed. In Closter-Neuburg the upper town and the ecclesiastical buildings held out, but the lower was destroyed. Baden shared its fate. The raiders penetrated into Upper Austria as far as Styria, where, however, they on several occasions met their match, for the people rose upon their scattered bands, and burned alive those whom they overpowered. One detachment, having crossed the Danube in thirty vessels and set fire to the village and castle of Schmida, was surprised and in great part destroyed by a body of 200 cavalry under Count Hardegg. Another detachment was surrounded and cut to pieces by the bailiff George von Leuchtenberg and the Bavarian colonel of cavalry Wolfgang von Weichs. In spite of these isolated acts of resistance, upwards of 30,000 villagers and townsfolk were slaughtered or dragged into slavery.

The irresistible advance of the main Ottoman army, the threats of the sultan, and the relentless fury of the *akinjis* combined to force the surrender of most of the strongholds the Austrians had recently captured from Zápolya. Fünfkirchen, Stahlweissenburg, and Pest fell without a blow into the hands of the enemy. In Esztergom, the inhabitants were so intimidated they refused to admit the garrison sent by Ferdinand; the Archbishop Pal Tomori sojourned to the sultan's camp to surrender both the town and the citadel to Suleiman in person. Komoron was abandoned by its garrison. Győr also fell, but not until after it had been set on fire by the fugitives. Conversely, Wiener Neustadt defended itself with spirit, over the course of one day repelling five attempts to storm its defenses. Several other places, among them Closter-Neuburg and Perchtoldsdorf and some castles, also held out, and the guns of Bratislava bombarded the accompanying Ottoman fleet as it sailed up the Danube.[22]

On 21 September, Suleiman with the main body of his army crossed the Raab at Mosonmagyaróvár in Hungary, taking its 300-strong garrison prisoner. On the same day a detachment of his *akinjis*, after spreading terror far and wide around them, reached the outskirts of Vienna, where they destroyed the vineyards of Heiligenstadt. Unfortunately for them, they were subsequently intercepted by a detachment of hussars under Pavle Bakić, a Serbian émigré who had opted to serve with the Habsburgs. The few prisoners taken were racked or otherwise tortured to extract intelligence before being bound together with ropes and flung into the Danube.

With increasing urgency Ferdinand had been petitioning Charles for reinforcements to bolster the empire's threatened eastern frontier. When Ferdinand's scouts reported the arrival of the Ottomans in Belgrade in June, he wrote a last desperate appeal to his brother, then quartered at Piacenza:

The Great Turk, with a force larger than has ever been seen before, has arrived in Belgrade with full intentions to march straight for Vienna. May God come to rescue us! I will do as much as I can with the little force that I have to fight him off. I hope, sire, that you will not abandon me, for otherwise Christianity will be in grave danger. I can not say what the outcome will be. I have every intention to act in your honor and glory.[23]

Charles was conflicted. "I am wholly decided and resolved to go in person to help my brother, because his need is so great and the peril so extreme that it does not merely threaten him but places all Christendom at risk," he wrote to his aunt Margaret. "I cannot and must not abandon him, because of the office I hold and the obligations of fraternal friendship; and also because he is such a good brother to me." However, that same day Charles adopted a very different tone in a letter written to his "good brother." While recognizing the risks involved in the fall of Vienna for Christendom in general and for the Habsburg patrimony in particular, he feared that "without the prior pacification of Italy, it could happen that as soon as I leave to succor you, Venice, Florence, Ferrara and Francesco Sforza will ally together, pool all their resources, and invite the French to support them." Now focused on receiving a formal coronation as Holy Roman Emperor at the hands of Pope Clement VII in Bologna, Charles rated the loss of Austria as "the lesser evil" compared to the loss of all his gains in Italy. Ferdinand would receive no support from this quarter.[24]

Left to his own devices, Ferdinand undertook frantic efforts at recruitment through the Austrian provinces of Styria, Carinthia, and Tirol. Within the confines of his own domain – the Archduchy of Austria, the Kingdom of Bohemia, and the Margravate of Moravia – Ferdinand had more success. He laid down the requirement that every tenth man in his archduchy step forward to defend Vienna. The estates of Bohemia, Moravia, Silesia, and Lusatia promised 9,000 foot soldiers and 800 cavalry in their gathering in České Budějovice in July. To meet the financial demands of mobilization, an extraordinary levy was applied throughout Austria. At a time when a considerable country house might be purchased for fifty florins, bishops were taxed five florins, prelates and counts four, the rest of the noblesse, including the secular clergy and all citizens who were accounted to possess 100 florins, one florin each, all the way down the social hierarchy to the ten pennies extracted from day laborers.

An endemic drag on imperial mobilization was the obduracy of the Lutherans, who continued to maintain the Ottomans represented a lesser danger than the existential threat embodied by the papacy.[25] Luther had dismissed the pope's bull *Coena Domini*, in which Leo X had reiterated the standing interdiction against supplying weapons of war to the infidels: "What evil does the Turk do? He occupies his provinces and governs them reasonably." In Luther's opinion, between the Porte and the pope, the former was the lesser of two evils, for "the Roman Curia is more tyrannical than any Turk."[26] Even in the wake of Mohács, Luther only repeated what he had said before: "Because Germany is so full of evil and blasphemy, nothing else can be expected. We must suffer punishment if we do not repent and stop the persecution of the Gospel."[27] Luther repudiated the concept of a crusade, which would be "opposed to Christ's teaching and name," both in principle and in practice, for "in such an army there are hardly five real Christians and perhaps many people worse in the sight of God than the Turks. Yet they all want to go by the name of Christians. This is the worst of all sins, a sin that no Turk commits. For here Christ's name is used for sin and unrighteousness." He also emphatically denied that Charles V was entitled to any universal authority, secular or divine: "The Emperor is not the head of Christendom or the defender of the Gospel," for he was nothing more than "a poor mortal, a future victim of worms."[28] Only faith could save Christendom, for ultimately, "our hope rests not in weapons but in God. If anyone is able to defeat the Turk, it will be the little children praying the Lord's Prayer."[29] In the final analysis, "The person of the Antichrist is at the same time the Pope and the Turk. Every person consists of a body and a soul. So the spirit of the Antichrist is the Pope, his flesh is the Turk. The one has infested the Church spiritually, the other bodily. However, both come from the same Lord, even the devil."[30]

This attitude enraged Catholics, who became convinced Luther was mobilizing a fifth column actively working to betray Europe into Ottoman hands. Sir Thomas More condemned the Lutherans, who by "sowing schisms and seditions among Christian people, lay the loss thereof to the withstanding of the Turk's invasion."[31] Through their repudiation not just of the one true apostolic church but the common cause of Christendom itself, Luther's disciples were "beasts were more hot and more busy than would the great Turk – and that because their sect is yet, in manner, worse than his."[32] In his *Sperandam esse victoriam* (*Victory is to be hoped for*, 1532), Luther's old antagonist, Johann Eck, went so far as to argue that, since the Lutherans were blaspheming, robbing monasteries, and committing other crimes, "it would be better to live among the Turks than among those apostate and faithless Christians."[33]

An Imperial *Diet* had been convened at Speyer in March 1529, attended by most of the electoral and other princes of the Holy Roman Empire, ostensibly to arrive at a collective response to the Ottoman challenge. The Catholic majority was instead preoccupied with actively containing not the expansion of the Ottomans but rather that of the Lutherans. Ferdinand made his intentions clear in his opening address, in which he delivered the verdict of the emperor – revocation of the terms expressed in the Recess of Speyer, imperial condemnation of "seduction by false beliefs," and the prohibition of any additional deviation from orthodoxy in ecclesiastical affairs until decisions could be arrived at via a church council. In the meantime, Ferdinand emphasized, "Those that until now have followed the Edict of Worms should continue to do so," while "the sects which contradict the sacrament of the true body and blood shall absolutely not be tolerated."

On 19 April, a majority of the *diet* voted to accept these terms. In response, six princes and representatives of fourteen free imperial cities walked out. The following day, the Lutheran faction petitioned the *diet* against its decision in their Letter of Protestation, which Ferdinand, who insisted they "accept and obey the decision" of the majority, refused to receive. In their defense of freedom of conscience as the only true path to God, Luther's loyalists had thus definitively broken not just with the papacy but with the highest secular authority in Christendom, the emperor himself. From their Protestation came the definitive title by which they would henceforth be recognized: Protestants.

The emperor's confessor, García de Loaysa y Mendoza, urged Charles to take a moderate course:

> Your Majesty should come to terms with all of Germany: just pretend that its heresies do not exist, and allow the Germans to live however they wish. You should work with them to abandon some past errors, and everyone should accept those that are easy. In this they should serve you as their lord, obey you as is only right, and join together to defend Germany and Hungary from the Turk. To that end they should provide you with paid troops for a time.[34]

Instead, on 19 November 1530, Charles issued a decree condemning "the doctrine previously outlawed" at Worms, "which has kindled many errors among the common people." All who failed to accept Catholic doctrine within five months would be declared outlaws.

The Lutheran magnates within the Holy Roman Empire concluded they had no choice but to come together in a pact that offered mutual guarantees of collective security. Sworn into being on 27 February 1531 in the Hessian town of Schmalkalden by Landgrave Philip of Hessen and Elector John Frederick of

Saxony, the two most powerful Protestants in the Holy Roman Empire, this Schmalkaldic League declared that its members, "solely for the sake of our own defense and deliverance... have agreed that whenever any one of us is attacked on account of the Word of God... all the others shall immediately come to his assistance."[35] In time, the League would expand and evolve into a temporal power block balanced against the political authority of the emperor as much as it was a counterweight to the spiritual authority of the pope.[36]

However, the inescapable fact that Suleiman and his army were now at the gates proved pressing enough to allay, for the moment, the widening and deepening divisions engendered by the Reformation. A popular contemporary doggerel verse summed up the dawning awareness that the sultan presented a threat to all of Western Europe even as it splintered on the rocks of doctrinal difference:

> From Hungary he's soon away
> In Austria by break of day
> Bavaria is just at hand,
> From there he'll reach another land,
> Soon to the Rhine perhaps he'll come.[37]

The publication of such anti-Ottoman propaganda, which began in the spring of 1522, a few months after the fall of Belgrade, reached a crescendo after the Hungarian debacle at Mohács.[38] Increasingly, Lutherans as well as Catholics were caught up in the apocalyptic atmosphere suffusing the Holy Roman Empire. In a series of texts published over the course of the decade, Martin Luther himself had clarified his position in relation to the Ottoman threat. His 1523 tract *Von welltlicher Uberkeyt* addressed the question of legitimate war. If a foreign realm was disrupting the general peace the first measures to be taken by the ruler of a state should be negotiations to reestablish "justice and peace." If such appeals fell on deaf ears, the ruler was obliged to defend his people "against force by force." In fact, "Since your entire land is in peril you must make the venture, so that with God's help all may not be lost. If you cannot prevent some from becoming widows and orphans as a consequence, you must at least see that not everything goes to ruin until there is nothing left except widows and orphans."

"In this matter subjects are in duty bound to follow, and to devote their life and property, for in such a case one must risk his goods and himself for the sake of others," Luther concluded. "In a war of this sort it is both Christian and an act of love to kill the enemy without hesitation," and to employ "every method of warfare until he is conquered."[39]

Three years later, in *Ob Kriegsleute auch ynn seligem stande* (*Whether soldiers, too, can be saved*), Luther offered a simple, clear rationale for a doctrine of "just war." God has established two kinds of government among men, he explained. The first "is spiritual; it has no sword, but it has the word, by means of which men are to become good and righteous, so that with this righteousness they may attain eternal life." The second "is worldly government, which works through the sword so that those who do not want to be good and righteous to eternal life may be forced to become good and righteous in the eyes of the world." This authority is administered "through the sword."[40] In this restatement of Christ's admonition to render unto Caesar, "If I were a soldier and saw a priest's banner in the field, or a banner of the cross," Luther averred, "I should run as though the Devil were chasing me." However, "if the banner of Emperor Charles or of a prince is in the field, then let everyone run boldly and gladly to the banner to which his allegiance is sworn."[41]

In his *Unterricht der Visitatorn* (*Lessons for the Visitors*) of 1528, Luther reiterated it was the duty of the civic authorities "to make defense against those who would destroy the worship of God, the peaceful order of the country, law, and justice. On this account we are to defend ourselves against the Turks, who not only seek to destroy countries, violate and murder women and children, but also to obliterate justice and divine worship and all forms of good order." This was the essential nature of the separation between the secular and divine, for "Even if there were no Christian faith we would yet need to war against the Turks for the sake of our wives and children. For we would rather choose death than to see and tolerate such shame and vice among our own. For the Turks drive the people to market, buy and sell and use them as animals, be they man or woman, young or old, married or unmarried – so evil is the Turkish nature."[42] Accordingly, while the essential task must always be the inner-directed struggle to achieve purity of faith, it was important for the Lutheran flock to also uphold their worldly obligations, among which was, under the proper circumstances, to recognize what "a rightful service it is before God to fight against the Turks when the authorities so command."[43]

Thus, by 1529 Luther could be entirely practical in his call for those who waged spiritual war against the Catholic Church to rally to the banner of a Catholic emperor. Luther explained he had previously remained silent on the Ottoman question because the papacy insisted on confronting Ottoman imperial aggression with a crusade; the pope "undertook to fight against the Turk in the name of Christ, and taught and incited men to do this, as though our people were an army of Christians against the Turks, who were enemies of Christ." Luther considered this to be "absolutely contrary to Christ's doctrine and name" and "the greatest of all sins." Luther insisted that traditional incitements to war against the Ottoman enemy based on their infidel religion should be abandoned. To "wipe out the Turk's religion" was not the duty of the military; rather, one should fight "unbelief with word and with prayer."[44]

To confront the Ottoman juggernaut required secular unity on the part of the Christian potentates, "and not, as before, let individual kings and princes set upon him – yesterday the king of Hungary, today the king of Poland, and tomorrow the king of Bohemia – until the Turk devours them one after another and nothing is accomplished except that our people are betrayed and slaughtered and blood is shed needlessly."[45] This was because "Fighting against the Turk is not like fighting against the king of France, or the Venetians, or the pope; he is a different kind of warrior," Luther argued, for "his people are always under arms so that he can quickly muster three or four hundred thousand men. If we were to cut down a hundred thousand, he would soon be back again with as many men as before."[46]

In *Vom Kriege wider die Türcken* (*On War against the Turks*, published 1529), and *Türkenbüchlein, Eine Heerpredigt wider den Türcken* (*Military Sermon against the Turks*, published 1530), Luther argued the emperor was empowered to wage war, but not for the "winning of great honor, glory, and wealth, the extension of territory, or wrath and revenge... By waging war for these reasons men seek only their own self-interest."[47] Rather, it was the emperor's obligation to wage a war of self-defense – in this instance, where "the Turk is attacking his subjects and his empire, and it is his duty as a regular ruler appointed by God, to defend his own."[48] Accordingly, a war against the Ottoman threat "should be fought at the emperor's command, under his banner, and in his name. Then everyone can be sure in his conscience that he is obeying the ordinance of God, since we know that the emperor is our true overlord and head and that whoever obeys him in such a case obeys God also... If he dies in this obedience, he dies in a good state, and if he has previously repented and believes in Christ, he will be saved."[49] To Luther, only the faith expressed in the second article of the Apostles' Creed was a valid standard for the truth of religion, for "this article makes us children of God and brothers of Christ, so that we may become eternally like him and be his co-heirs." As Luther now saw it, the renewed vigor of the Muslim armies at the time of the Reformation reflected the anxiety of Satan, who worried that the rediscovery of the Gospel might endanger his empire on Earth, and therefore, through the agency of the Ottomans, was making these powerful attempts to conquer all Europe to snuff out this threat before it could fully evolve. Thus, in the final analysis, "the army of the Turks is actually the army of the devil."[50]

These themes were picked up on and rebroadcast by fellow Lutherans. In 1531, Johannes Brenz, the leading pioneer of the Reformation in the town of Schwabisch-Hall and the duchy of Württemberg, issued a tract entitled *Türcken Büchlein: Wie sich Prediger und Leien halten sollen, so der Türck das Deudsche Land vberfallen würde* (*Booklet on the Turk: How Preachers and Laymen Should Conduct Themselves if the Turk Were to Invade Germany*). He patiently explained that "the authority of the [Holy] Roman Empire stems from God; it is a divinely appointed order which will endure until the end of the world. Consequently, even if the emperor were personally a complete pagan, all his subjects would still owe him obedience in those things in which an emperor, by virtue of being an emperor, has authority, and which are not contrary to the will of God."[51] As he concluded:

> Every civil authority owes it to God to maintain law and order, to protect the land and the people from wrongful violence and murder, as St Paul teaches in Romans 13 [3–4]. Now, the Turk is attacking Germany even though he has no right or provocation to do so; his assault is like that of a murderer. Just as the government is obligated to punish thieves and murderers, or to take preventive action as soon as the aggressive intentions of such persons become known, so the government is obligated to resist the Turk, an undisguised brigand and murderer... That they are nothing but undisguised criminals the Turk themselves prove, not only by their deeds but by their law, for their Mahomet commanded them to commit perpetual aggression, to conquer lands and peoples. They are under the illusion that God promised to Mahomet sovereignty and power over the earth; they allege that only through the Mahometan empire will God fulfill His promise to Abraham, namely to make him lord of all the world. Since the Turks boast that this is their law, it is fitting for all civil authorities to combat them as avowed criminals.[52]

There was give on the imperial side also. García de Loaysa y Mendoza again recommended the emperor allow the Lutherans to "live as heretics provided they do not spread their errors to other Christians," and "make the best deal possible with them so that they will help you against the Turks."[53] Charles, finally, followed Loaysa's advice. In July 1532, by the Peace of Nuremberg, he promised the German Lutherans that he would suspend the Edict of Worms until the pope convened a general council, and in return they agreed to provide and pay 40,000 foot and 8,000 horse to serve against the Ottomans. In the long term, this represented a decisive victory for the Lutherans, for, despite the intended temporary nature of the religious peace, neither Charles nor Ferdinand was able to revoke it for nearly fifteen years.[54] In the immediate term, the Habsburgs could be satisfied with the bargain. Marco Antonio Contarini, ambassador of the Venetian Republic at the imperial court, witnessed the gathering strength of the imperial army. "The Turks had counted on the Lutherans," he observed, "but they will be disappointed because they will soon bring to the imperial camp twice the number of men that they agreed to provide."[55]

Thanks to the blessing of Martin Luther, Catholics and Protestants united to vote a *Reichshilfe*, or quota for the defense of the Holy Roman Empire.[56] While by no means did Ferdinand get the 16,000 soldiers the *Diet* of Speyer had authorized, he did get perhaps a third of that number, and they were not the usual feudal levies palmed off to satisfy the obligation, composed of men left over from Charles's recruiting. Most significantly, the battle-hardened Nicholas von Salm arrived with 1,000 pikemen and 700 Spanish musketeers.[57] Ferdinand ultimately succeeded in assembling a force of 17,000 infantry, 1,400 heavy cavalry, and 1,200 light horse to defend Vienna.[58] Mobilization took time, however. Had Suleiman not been delayed due to the heavy rains, the imperial troops would not have been able to reach Vienna before the siege commenced.

The news of the fall of Buda, which reached Vienna on 17 September, created panic. In defiance of an urgent summons on the part of the authorities, addressed to all capable of bearing arms, many burghers fled the city on the pretense of bearing their women and children to places of safety, and few of these returned.

The imperial troops encamped at Mosonmagyaróvár barely amounted to 5,000 men, and on the first appearance of the enemy these effected a rapid retreat in order not to be cut off from Vienna. The reinforcements promised by Ferdinand were not forthcoming, though messenger after messenger was sent to hurry their advance. Even the Bohemian troops under their leader, John of Bernstein, approached by slow marches. Duke Frederick of the Palatinate, the prince elected as leader of the imperial army, arrived at Linz on 24 September with the scant levies, amounting to just a few thousand men, he had been able to raise. After consulting with Ferdinand, he then hastened forward to reach Vienna before the Ottomans did. But having advanced to Grein on 26 September he received news the enemy had already appeared in force on the outskirts of the city. His first instinct was to cut his way through at all costs, but when he learned that both the bridges over the Danube had been seized by Suleiman, he decided to halt at Crems for reinforcements. However, his cousin, *Pfalzgraf* (count palatine) Philip, succeeded in forcing his way through to the city with a small number of Spanish and German troops three days before it was surrounded by the Ottomans. Others arrived even later; two young nobles left cooling their heels in Frederick's camp at Crems – Rupert, Count of Manderscheid, and Wolf, Count of Oettingen – were so zealous in the cause that after Vienna had been invested they swam across the Danube and were drawn up over the wall near the Werder gate.

Vienna in 1529 remained a small medieval town of narrow streets, cramped houses with shingle roofs, a few Gothic towers, and a magnificent cathedral, St Stephen's, at its center. Its circular, three-mile-long wall, called the *Ringmauer*, had been built in the 13th century on the ruins of the old Roman fortifications.[59] Barely six feet thick, the wall incorporated none of the features now standard for the conditions of 16th-century siege warfare. The name *Stadtzaun*, or city hedge, which it bears in the municipal records of the time, was literally as well as figuratively appropriate. The citadel of Vienna scarcely deserved the term; it was merely an old building, with no particular defensive attributes, built into the southwestern wall. The surrounding trench was choked with years of accumulated garbage.[60]

Clearly, the garrison had work to do. Given the constricted timeframe available to them, they worked wonders. Where the wall was especially weak or out of repair, a new entrenched line of earthen defense was constructed and palisaded. Within the city itself, from the Stuben to the Carinthian gate, an entirely new wall twenty feet high was constructed with a ditch interior to the old.

The berm along the bank of the Danube was also entrenched and palisaded, and from the drawbridge to the Salz gate protected with a rampart capable of resisting artillery. As a precaution against fire, the houses were stripped of their shingles throughout the city. To minimize shrapnel from the "splash" effect of incoming artillery rounds, the pavement was removed from the streets to expose the bare earth beneath, thereby muffling the impact of the enemy's shot. Most of the extracted paving stones were used to construct a new loose wall inside the old on its east side along the Wiener Bach creek where the old defenses were weakest.[61]

The city had nine gates, the most important being the Scottish, the Stuben, the Hofburg, the Carinthian, and the Salz, which funneled into a bridge over the Danube. Only the latter was left open, the others being bricked up save for narrow sally ports which would allow the defenders to launch raids against the besiegers.

To provide a clear field of fire from the ramparts, and deny cover to the enemy, all the buildings in Vienna's burgeoning suburbs which lay too near the wall had to be destroyed. Any property that could be saved was first conveyed into the city before 800 structures, great and small, were burnt to the ground over four days, including the city hospital, the Franciscan convent at St Theobald's, the churches of St Anthony and St Coloman, the nunneries of St Nicholas and St Magdalen, and the castle on the Leopoldsberg, formerly the residence of Margrave Leopold.

Parties were detached to scour the neighboring country in search of provisions, and to bring in cattle and forage. Finally, to provide against the possibility of a protracted siege, noncombatants – women, children, the elderly, and the ecclesiastics – were, as far as possible, forced to evacuate the city. Though this latter measure was successful in terms of taking pressure off the provisions reserved for the garrison during the siege of the city, it had the unhappy consequence that many of the fugitives were massacred or fell into captivity at the hands of the *akinjis*.[62]

Nominally, Pfalzgraf Philip had assumed command in the city. However, effective control was vested in Nicholas von Salm.[63] His leadership qualities tempered through fifty-six years of service in the field, the seventy-year-old veteran had seen action during the siege of Rhodes in 1522 and the Battle of Pavia in 1525, where he had crossed swords and exchanged wounds with the French king, Francis I. He had served most recently in Hungary on behalf of Ferdinand against John Zápolya.

The other commanders were William, Baron of Roggendorf, general of the cavalry, a Dane who had distinguished himself in the Italian wars and was now the marshal of Austria; Marcus Beck, of Leopoldsdorf, commissary general; Ulrich Leyser, master of the ordnance; John Katzianer; Leonhard, Baron of Vels; Hector Eck, of Reischach; and Maximilian Leyser. The imperial contingent consisted of two regiments, under Kuntz Gotzman and James von Bernan. Luis de Avallos, Melchior de Villanel, Juan de Salinas, and Juan de Aquilera commanded the Spaniards. The Styrian troops were commanded by Abel von Holleneck; the Bohemian, by Ernst von Brandenstein.[64]

The garrison altogether amounted to 20,000 infantry and 2,000 horse; the armed burghers to about 1,000. Pfalzgraf Philip occupied, with 100 cuirassiers and fourteen companies of imperial troops, the Stuben quarter from the Rothenthurm to the middle of the curtain towards the Carinthian gate. At that point the line of defense was taken up to the Augustine convent by Eck von Reischach, with 3,000 infantry. From there to the Burggarten were posted the Styrian troops under Abel von Holleneck. The citadel was held by Leonard von Vels, with 3,000 chosen troops; from there to the Scottish gate Maximilian Leyser was in command, and from the Scottish gate to the Werder gate were posted 2,000 Austrians and 700 Spaniards under Rupert von Ebersdorf. In this sector, the Elend tower was strengthened with a rampart and mounted with heavy guns to harass the Ottoman flotilla, which covered the Danube as far as Nussdorf. Finally, from the Werder gate to the Rothenthurm, including the Salz gate, were posted 2,000 Bohemians under Ernst von Brandenstein and William von Wartenberg, with a detachment of cavalry under John, Count of Hardegg. A cavalry reserve was posted in the four principal squares of the city under William von Roggendorf, ready to advance in any direction. The total number of heavy guns appears to have consisted of between sixty and seventy pieces of the various calibers in use at this period. Directly responsible for working the artillery were seventy-four gunners under the master of the ordnance, Ulrich Leyser.[65] These would prove at least a match for their Ottoman counterparts. However, the desperate eleventh-hour effort to augment its defensive framework notwithstanding, Vienna was by no contemporary measure effectively fortified to withstand a professionally conducted siege when the Ottomans arrived. Not only did the walls lack depth, there were no bastions on which the guns could be properly sited, and no magazines for the storage of powder and shot. Several of the pieces which had been stationed at embrasures or loopholes opened in the wall were found useless in those positions, and had to be re-sited to the roofs of neighboring buildings. Over the course of the past seventy-five years the Ottomans had forced the submission of such mighty strongholds as Constantinople, Rhodes, and Belgrade. The defenses of Vienna were child's play by comparison.

The hour of trial was fast approaching. Bruck on the Leitha and Trautmannsdorf capitulated without a struggle, and having reduced these last minor obstacles, there was now no organized resistance between Suleiman and Vienna. Among those determined to remain in the city was Habsburg Secretary of War Peter Stern von Labach. His primary contribution was to posterity as an eyewitness; "if there is a battle, I shall not be able to fight. My eyes are too weak, my bones too fragile. So day after day I shall do my duty and record the fate of Vienna in the greatest of detail."[66] As he wrote those words, every road which led north and west away from the city was crowded with refugees endeavoring to save themselves and their movable goods. Few of these fugitives escaped. Von

Labach's account of the Ottoman advance spares no details in its description of the attendant atrocities:

> After the taking of Bruck on the Leitha and the castle of Trautmannsdorf, the Sackman and those who went before him, people who have no regular pay, but live by plunder and spoil, to the number of 40,000, spread themselves far and wide over the country, as far as the Ens and into Styria, burning and slaying. Many thousands of people were murdered, or maltreated and dragged into slavery. Children were cut out of their mothers' wombs and stuck on pikes; young women abused to death, and their corpses left on the highway. God rest their souls, and grant vengeance on the bloodhounds who committed this evil.[67]

From the opposite camp, one of the secretaries in attendance upon Suleiman also contributed an account of the siege. He confirms that upon the Ottoman army's arrival in the vicinity of Vienna, "Our warriors forced their way into a farmstead, sounding their Muslim battle cry they drew their sabers and cut down all the infidels, they seized the girls and boys and secured rich booty, this too is further proof of the grace of Allah."[68]

On 23 September, with the suburbs of Vienna in full conflagration, a strong body of Ottomans pressed forward as far as St Mark's, cut to pieces a number of invalids who had scandalously been left there to their fate, and ventured still further on the high road. This provoked the first sally from the city, 500 cuirassiers under Count Hardegg. These having pressed too far forward, the Ottomans took advantage of the ruins of some of the burnt houses to attack them in their flank while their front was also engaged against superior numbers. The cuirassiers fell back in disorder without waiting for the support which was detached to their assistance, losing three killed and six taken prisoner. Suleiman subsequently released four of these captives, presented each with three ducats, and sent them back to Vienna with the following message:

> If the city would surrender on terms, the conditions should be arranged with its commanders without the walls, none of his people should be allowed to enter the city, and the property and persons of the inhabitants should be secured. It was Suleiman's sole desire to follow [Charles V] till he should find him, and then to retire to his own dominions.
>
> Should the city, however, venture to resist, he would not retreat till he had reduced it, and then he would spare neither old nor young, not the child in the mother's womb, and would so utterly destroy the city that men should not know

where it stood. He would not rest his head till Vienna and the whole of Christendom were under his subjection, and it was his settled purpose within three days, namely on the feast of St Michael, to break his fast in St Stephen's Cathedral.[69]

In his account, von Labach commented that "Suleiman is thus trying to strike an agreement with the leaders of our city, he vows not to let any of his men enter it and do harm to its people, but if we do not surrender he will not stop until he has conquered Vienna and slaughtered young and old." Apparently, neither terms nor threats moved the garrison; "noble and common companions at arms swore to remain in the city as long as there was still life in their bodies and swore to die for the Christian faith."[70] In reply to the sultan's ultimatum, Pfalzgraf Philip merely dispatched in return a like number of Ottoman prisoners, as richly provided with presents and apparel, but without an answer either to his threats or promises.

The full force of the Ottoman army was still drawing up on the approach roads, and access to the city was not yet entirely cut off. On the 25th, two companies of imperial troops, raised from Nuremberg, effected their entrance through the Salz gate with drums beating and colors flying. They related that between Tuln and Traismauer they had fallen in with a body of 5,000 fugitives on foot and 3,000 in boats, mostly women, children, and regular clergy, who on the following day had been overtaken and destroyed by the *akinjis*.

The diplomatic games continued. On the 26th, Suleiman sent into the city a Bohemian, one of the garrison which had surrendered in Mosonmagyaróvár, with the contemptuous offer that he would send the other Bohemians there taken to strengthen the garrison of Vienna. The man was sent back accompanied by two Ottoman prisoners, each of whom was presented with two ducats, with the reply that they had more garrison than enough in Vienna, and that Suleiman might keep his Bohemian prisoners.

When the main Ottoman army drew up in front of Vienna a mobile city rose up from the ground overnight. The country within sight of the walls as far as Schwechat and Trautmannsdorf was covered with tents, the number of which was calculated at 30,000. Suleiman's royal tent rose above all others at Simmering. Hangings of the richest fabrics separated its numerous compartments from each other. Costly carpets, and cushions and divans studded with jewels, formed the furniture. Its numerous pinnacles were terminated in bulbs of gold. The color of the chief compartment was green striped with gold. The sultan's security throughout the siege was entrusted to the pasha of Anatolia, who ordered defensive trenches dug and assigned 500 archers of the royal guard to keep watch night and day.

Surrounding the sultan's abode, in great though inferior splendor, were the tents of his subordinates, each of whom was assigned responsibility for a sector of the siege line. Güzelce Kasım Pasha, the *beylerbey* of Rumelia, was posted opposite the Stuben gate, and thence down to the Danube, securing the baggage and its attendant train of horses, mules, and camels; the latter, some 20,000 in number, were at pasture in the meadows. Grand Vizier Ibrahim was in command from Simmering over the Wienerberg as far as Spinnerin, and thence down the declivities as far as Wieden and the high road opposite the Stuben and Kärnthner gates. The *bey* of Bosnia occupied the line of the Wien River, from St Ulrich and St Theobald to Penzing. From St Veit to near Döbling the line was occupied by the *beys* of Shkodër and Smederevo. The corps of the *bey* of Belgrade, which extended itself from Schönbrunn to beyond Laxenburg, secured the rear of the besieging force. The meadows and islands of the Lobau floodplain as far as Nussdorf were occupied by the crews of an Ottoman flotilla of 400 vessels which had arrived on 25 September and were stationed to watch the banks and interdict any imperial attempts at relief or resupply.[71] Ferdinand had lost control of the Danube in June when the unpaid Serbian crews of the Habsburg river flotilla defected to their Ottoman counterparts near Erdut.[72]

The investment of the city was completed, and the passage of the Danube effectually closed on the 27th. From that point, on a daily basis, Ottoman sappers drove trenches towards the walls above ground, while Ottoman miners sought to undermine them from below. The primary focus for the Ottoman siegeworks was the stretch of wall that extended from the rampart near the Augustine convent to the tower situated between the Stuben and Rothenthurm gates, where Eck von Reischach commanded, the Carinthian tower being their principal point of assault. The flower of the Ottoman force, the janissaries, took possession of the ruins of the suburbs, which afforded them an excellent cover from the fire of the besieged. They also cut loopholes in the walls still standing, from which they subjected the city to a steady drumbeat of archery and musketry shot.[73]

While the Ottoman war machine was operating with its characteristic professionalism and efficiency, it soon became apparent that in order to be driven to a successful conclusion the siege would have to overcome three serious challenges.

The first was the lack of siege artillery. Because the appalling weather on the march up to Vienna had rendered the roads impassable to heavy ordnance, the larger bore guns had been left behind in Belgrade. Suleiman had about

300 pieces at his disposal, of which not more than thirty were able to throw a respectable weight of shot. The lighter field guns could make little impression on the walls.

The second problem was the garrison, which was determined to be proactive rather than simply hunker down behind its defensive works. On the very day the Ottomans completed their isolation of Vienna, von Salm sent a clear message that the besiegers would not be left unmolested in their work, ordering three companies of German and Spanish horse to sally from the Burg gate. These sorties became an endemic threat to those Ottoman personnel engaged in the backbreaking labor of driving forward the sultan's trenches and tunnels. One raiding party returned to the city with thirty Ottoman heads and ten prisoners. Another sally resulted in the capture of eighty prisoners and five camels. On one occasion, some 200 Ottomans and several of their officers were killed. The Spaniards at the Werder gate also opposed with success the landing of a cargo of arms, which had arrived by the Danube from Kahlenberg. While the material results from these forays were pitifully inadequate from a strictly military point of view, the value in terms of keeping up the spirits of the besieged was incalculable.

The third issue, this one beyond human intervention, was the ongoing, and now accelerating, deterioration of the weather. The rains continued to pelt down, flooding tents, trenches, and tunnels alike, and there was now an ominously, and unseasonably early, distinct chill to the air. On 29 September – that very St Michael's day on which Suleiman had boasted he would be eating his breakfast in St Stephen's cathedral – the sultan instead received a memorandum from inside the city which contained one of the most singularly insulting messages in history:

Your breakfast is getting cold.

The Viennese regretted their being unable to indulge the sultan in person, suggesting he content himself with such poor entertainment as they could send him from the guns on the wall. To emphasize the point, about midday, Eck von Reischach and Luis de Avallos led a vigorous sortie from the Carinthian gate which killed many of the Ottomans, who had been attracted by the grapes of the neighboring vineyards.

From St Michael's Day onwards the continuous rain and now early frosts at night spread much suffering among the besiegers. "It is bitter cold day and night, and impossible to describe how much rain fell," Suleiman's secretary recorded.[74]

Doubtless speaking on behalf of the entire garrison, an unsympathetic Peter Stern confirmed, "It rained and rained the whole day, and we hoped the baboons outside our walls would freeze to death."[75] The cold continued after the rain abated, and was aggravated by severe storms.

In the teeth of the deteriorating weather, Suleiman continued to press forward with the siege. There was little action on 30 September other than an Ottoman assault on the guard at the drawbridge at the Carinthian gate, which was driven into the city with some loss. On 1 October, 300 *Landsknechte* sallied from the Scottish gate. This sortie soon petered out, but the garrison did receive an unlooked-for intelligence windfall when a defector sought refuge within the walls. This man was subjected to both interrogation and torture – "put to the question," as Peter Stern put it. This distasteful process yielded invaluable perspective on Ottoman strength and dispositions and, most crucially, "the man finally admitted that charges had been placed to the right and left of the Carinthian Gate," Stern noted. "No one had any previous knowledge of this."[76]

To meet the subterranean threat, guards were placed in all the cellars near the walls, trenches were dug near the foot of the ramparts, and drums with peas strewed over the skin, or tubs filled with water, were placed at strategic locations to indicate by their vibration the precise whereabouts of Ottoman mining operations.

Having confirmed that one mine was directed against the Carinthian tower, and the other against the convent of St Clara, the garrison commenced driving countermines at those two points, at the same time propping up the walls with posts and beams so that if the mines were detonated the shattered ramparts might fall outwards and impede access to the breach. That evening a heavy fire was kept up on both sides, which led to the expectation of an assault, but none ensued.

On 2 October, the Ottoman mine under the Carinthian tower was detected and destroyed. Some of the most vicious hand-to-hand combat of the entire campaign would play out in such encounters, with men fighting and dying in the claustrophobic confines of these dank, dark, fetid chambers deep underground. On the surface, a large body of Ottomans pressed forward nearly to the Scottish gate, and retired, after a lively skirmish, with ten prisoners and thirty heads of the slain.

On 3 October, Ottoman fire was intensified and protracted far into the evening. An assault was again anticipated and the garrison remained under arms night and day. Nothing, however, ensued except considerable damage to the Carinthian tower and the adjacent bastion. On 4 October, orders were issued in the Ottoman camp to accelerate construction of the mines. The *akinjis* were ordered to convey ladders and bundles of straw to the trenches, and every preparation was made for a general assault.

On the evening of 5 October a council of war was held in the city, which ordered a sortie in force the following day, with the primary objectives of discovering and destroying the Ottoman mines and driving the janissaries out of the ruins of the suburbs, from where their incessant fire was goading the garrison beyond endurance. A total of 8,000 men of all arms and nations were assigned to these tasks. The operation commenced at 6am. Its initial impact was irresistible. The Ottoman batteries were first overwhelmed and then left behind as the garrison swarmed into and over the enemy's siege lines. But as dawn broke, ever greater numbers of Ottoman reinforcements began converging at the point of contact and wading into the fray.

Even more than the gathering strength of the foe, it was fear, a sudden collective spasm of dread that making a stand out in the open would be to risk being cut off from the city, that led to the sortie's collapse. This apprehension quickly degenerated into panic, the imperial troops losing cohesion and then breaking in flight. At least three officers – Wolf Hagen, George Steinpeiss, and Garcia Gusman – were slain in the rout, and Eck von Reischach was severely wounded.

So desperate was the crush to return via the Carinthian gate that many were forced off the side of the drawbridge into the ditch, and, crippled by the fall, were left at the mercy of the enemy, who pursued so closely up to the walls they were only driven back from them at push of pike. The Ottomans had suffered considerable injury, but their losses could be made good, the progress of their siege had been barely set back, and they had the satisfaction of returning to their camp with several prisoners in tow and 500 heads to pile up at the feet of their sultan.

At noon, there was a fresh alarm that camels were conveying fascines of wood, straw, and vine-sticks to fill up the ditch. The expected assault, however, did not take place. The Ottoman batteries recommenced their fire at 5pm, and this was maintained without cessation, which forced the garrison to remain at their posts through the night. At 9am on 7 October, the Ottomans assaulted two bastions and detonated a mine at the Carinthian gate, which collapsed a section of the wall opposite the nunnery of St Clara.[77]

On 8 October, the city was subjected to its most intense bombardment yet. The timber bulwark in front of the Carinthian gate was set on fire, and the walls, deprived of their breastwork, threatened to fall inwards. To avoid this, possibly fatal, catastrophe, trunks of trees and huge beams were brought to their support, and a new breastwork was erected. A similar work was constructed before the Scottish gate, and mounted with two guns, which did much mischief in the Ottoman camp towards Sporkenbühel.

At 3pm on 9 October, mines were detonated to the right and left of the Carinthian gate. The explosions would have been more effective if the besieged had not succeeded in locating some of the mine chambers and by countermining removed a considerable portion of the charge. The impact of the detonations was considerable enough, however; several members of the garrison were buried in the rubble or blown into the air, and the detonation on the left opened a breach in the wall wide enough for twenty-four men to advance in order. Three successive waves of assaults were nevertheless repulsed by the garrison under the personal command of von Salm.

In the city, when quiet was restored, the old wall was rapidly repaired, a new one constructed, the houses which interfered with it leveled, and their building materials employed to fill up the wooden breastwork.

On 10 October, all was quiet, and the work of repair proceeded. Two mines were discovered and destroyed, and in a small sally of some eighty men, five camels were captured. The following day, towards 9am, a mine was detonated between the Carinthian and Stuben gates, which made an enormous breach, equivalent to an open gateway in the wall. As the janissaries rushed to the assault a second mine was detonated at the Stuben gate, and, according to some accounts, the city was finally entered at this point by some of the enemy; it is certain that an Ottoman standard-bearer had mounted the wall when he was shot down into the ditch. The assault was pressed forward with fanatical determination for the next three hours, but to no avail. By midday, the breach had been choked with the heaped-up corpses of 1,200 Ottoman dead. Though rank after rank of assailants were committed to the assault, they could make no progress against the massed pikes of the *Landsknechte* and were decimated in the crossfire from the garrison's small arms and artillery. Losses were heavy on both sides. At a general muster of the garrison that evening, 625 men were missing from the total assembled at the beginning of the siege. Ottoman casualties, however, now numbered many thousands.[78]

On the following day the assault was renewed. Two mines were detonated in the same quarter, and again a large section of the wall collapsed into ruin. Again the Ottomans poured into the breach, but again the defense stood firm. Wave after wave of attacks were launched into the evening, but with diminishing returns. For the first time since the siege had commenced, the garrison sensed hesitation in the enemy's ranks. This crisis of confidence in fact now extended from the rank and file all the way up into the Ottoman high command. That evening, the sultan summoned the *divan* to a council of war (*harp meclisi*) to decide whether or not to continue the siege. Ibrahim, voicing the views of the majority, favored withdrawal. Morale was low, winter was approaching, supplies were running short, the janissaries were grumbling, and the defenders expected reinforcements from the emperor at any moment. Delicately, it was pointed out that three significant assaults had now been repulsed from the walls, fulfilling the mandate of Islam, by which no more than three attempts against a foe are required of the faithful. Suleiman, however, decided on a fourth and final major assault, conceding, should this fail, he would raise the siege. To maximize the possibility of success, he offered exceptional pecuniary rewards. The troops were each given a cash payment of 1,000 asper (an asper being 1/52 of a piastre), an amount roughly equivalent to twenty European gold ducats or forty silver thalers, and the sultan promised to the first man who should mount the wall promotion to the next respective military rank and a bonus of 600 ducats.

The following day passed without incident as the Ottoman camp made preparations for the final effort. Those within the city were no less idle. While the soldiers stood to their arms, the citizens of both sexes, and of all classes, ages, and professions worked ceaselessly removing rubble, digging new entrenchments, throwing up works, strengthening the ramparts, and filling up the breaches. The subterranean war continued without respite, the defenders intercepting one tunnel and seizing the mine intended for the destruction of the Carinthian tower.

At daybreak on 14 October, the Ottoman army was arrayed in three powerful bodies for the assault, which commenced towards 9am. But that desperate courage and cheerful contempt of death which had for so long been the defining quality of the Ottoman war machine was now ebbing. Though urged forward with stick and whip, more and more units refused to advance, crying out that they preferred to die at the hands of their own officers rather than to face the harquebuses of the Spaniards and the German spits, as they called the long halberds of the *Landsknechte*.

Towards noon two mines were detonated to the right and left of the Carinthian gate, but a third, which had been carried under the Burg, was detected, and its entire charge of twenty barrels of powder fell into the hands of the counter-miners. A substantial breach, nevertheless, was created, and through this, supported by the fire of all their batteries, the Ottomans made repeated attempts to storm the city. But once again, these were repulsed. "Some of the Infidels fought in the breaches we had created," Suleiman's secretary recorded; "a fierce battle developed but because the breach was not wide enough we could not take the city."[79] Peter Stern, too, was an eyewitness to the final moments of the siege: "The enemy mounted a fierce [final assault] but the storm soon abated. Enemy losses amounted to about 350 dead. On our side just one [Spaniard] was shot and numerous wounded – Praise the Lord!"[80]

The garrison did suffer one last, cruel blow when in this final clash von Salm, unscathed to this moment throughout the siege, was wounded around 2pm by shrapnel and carried from the breach, which till then he had never quitted. He never fully recovered, and died in May of 1530 at his Salm Hoff residence.

The Ottomans had shot their bolt. It was clear now Vienna could not be taken and, given the increasingly mutinous mood of his men, Suleiman could not risk extending his campaign, already deep inside enemy territory, into an ever more desolate winter. The janissaries broke up the Ottoman encampment an hour before midnight, setting on fire the huts, forage, and every combustible article which they could or would not carry with them. This included most of the vast congregation of prisoners they had accumulated over the course of the campaign. Of these only the youngest, boys and girls, were deemed worthy to be included in the army's retreat, tied together by ropes, and destined for slavery. The rest were for the most part flung alive into the flames of the burning camp, or cut to pieces, or impaled. The glare of the conflagration and the wailing of those consigned to it led to a sleepless night for the exhausted garrison and citizens of Vienna.

Only with the first light of morning came assurance of the city's deliverance, which was hailed by a general discharge of artillery from the walls, and by the pealing of bells. A solemn *Te Deum* and high mass were celebrated in St Stephen's.[81]

Early the following day the Ottoman flotilla began to fall back down the Danube, not, however, unmolested by artillery fire from the city, which sank several vessels. Ibrahim Pasha remained for some time in the neighborhood of the Wienerberg, partly to cover the retreat, partly to rally the light troops dispersed on plundering expeditions.

Determined above all to maintain his dignity, Suleiman refused to make any concession to the fact his bid to take Vienna had ended in failure. He summoned a *divan* in which he received the staged felicitations of his subordinates on the fortunate termination of the campaign, each being endowed in return with rich rewards for their service. Ibrahim Pasha alone received a jeweled saber, four costly pelisses, and five purses stuffed with a total of 6,000 ducats. Ottoman propaganda kept to this official line, describing the conclusion of the siege in the following terms:

> An unbeliever came out from the fortress and brought intelligence of the submission of the princes and of the people, on whose behalf he prayed for grace and pardon. The padishah received his prayer with favor, and granted them pardon. Inasmuch as the German lands were unconnected with the Ottoman realm, that hence it was hard to occupy the frontier places and conduct their affairs, the faithful would not trouble themselves to clear out the fortress, or purify, improve, and put it into repair; but a reward of 1,000 aspers was dealt out to each of the Janissaries; and security being established, the horses' heads were turned towards the throne of Solomon.

On 17 October, the grand vizier commenced his retreat under a heavy snowstorm which lasted from early morning till late into the night. The day's march, which extended as far as Brück on the Leitha, was difficult and further slowed by the loss of much baggage. The garrison actively sought to take advantage of these circumstances. A sally took place on the same day, under command of John Katzianer, Pavle Bakić, and Sigismund von Weichselburg, with eight squadrons of cavalry and four companies of foot, which took many prisoners, rescued Christian captives, and seized a rich booty in tents and baggage, together with some camels.

Another sally the following day was attended with still happier results. Near the village of Laa on the Wienerberg upwards of 200 Ottomans were slain, a pasha captured, and many children rescued from captivity. The Ottoman rearguard was continuously harassed until, on 20 October, it crossed the Hungarian frontier. The invaders, however, left fearful traces of their incursion over a vast extent of country, and on their line of retreat wreaked to the last their vengeance for the failure of their main purpose on both the inhabitants and their livelihoods. In the villages caught up in the wake of the Ottoman retreat, Alvise Gritti informed the *Signoria*, "neither a cock nor hen sings there, nor is a single house intact, nor even a tree."[82]

To their usual practices of massacre, plunder, and arson, the Ottomans added the destruction of fruit-trees, vineyards, and gardens; and the wretched inhabitants who had saved their lives by flight or concealment returned to scenes of desolation which required years to repair. Having toured the war zone less than two months after the siege, Habsburg diplomat Sigismund von Herberstein recorded his vivid impressions:

> Arrived in Vienna on the first of December. It bore little resemblance to the place I once knew. All of the outlying districts, which were not that much smaller than the city proper, were razed and burned out... The enemy had done the same thing throughout the entire region for the same reason; everywhere, from Vienna down to Wiener Neustadt, one could not look as far as a crossbow's range without spotting a human corpse, a dead horse, pig, or cow lying about. The sight was pathetic.[83]

In the meantime, Vienna faced one final challenge, this time internal. The imperial troops who had played such a key role in saving the city now threatened to run amok if they didn't receive their promised bonuses. The authorities were in real danger of losing control of the situation, and Vienna was threatened with the same fate that had befallen Rome two years earlier. Only the arrival of Pfalzgraf Frederick stabilized the situation. His offer of triple pay satisfied most of the rank and file, but it was not until the ringleaders of the incipient mutiny had been executed that order was ultimately restored. The troops were finally divided and marched off, some to Bratislava, others to Mosonmagyaróvár in Hungary.

On 25 October, ten days after raising the siege, Suleiman entered Pest, where he was received with all honors by Zápolya. Three days later, Zápolya renewed his homage, and was presented with ten caftans and three horses, with bits and chains of gold. Alvise Gritti, now his chief minister while also, by virtue of his close relationship with Ibrahim Pasha, effectively serving as the Ottoman plenipotentiary in Hungary, received 20,000 ducats. On 31 October, the iron crown Zápolya had received in August was ceremoniously removed and replaced with the sacred golden crown of St Stephen, a definitive statement that, so far as the Ottomans were concerned, Zápolya was the legitimate – and only – king of Hungary. Significantly, however, this act was performed on the sultan's behalf by Pál Várdai, the archbishop of Esztergom. Again, neither Suleiman nor Ibrahim Pasha attended the ceremony, the sultan having recommenced his march the previous day, continuing via Peterwardein to Belgrade, which he reached only on 20 November, having been much delayed by the weather. Once again, the swollen rivers, including the Danube at Győr, were crossed with great difficulty and with considerable loss of artillery and provisions. Heavy snow began to fall, and in one of the last entries in his diary, Suleiman's secretary wrote: "It rained incessantly from dawn to dusk, some of the soldiers lost their entire equipment in the endless deluge and many men along with their horses sank and drowned in the mire. The suffering was indescribable."[84]

These incidents notwithstanding, for public consumption, the official Ottoman line was that the campaign had been a success.[85] While in Belgrade, Suleiman wrote in a triumphant tone to Andreas Gritti, describing how he had:

> ... taken from Ferdinand the kingdom of Hungary and invested with the same the *voivode* of Transylvania... and had looked for King Ferdinand in Vienna... As it came to the ear of His Majesty that a portion of the Christian Army had shut itself up in the city, and from this it was to be conjectured that the accursed Ferdinand was among them; the victorious army besieged the said fortress for fifteen days, and overthrew the walls in five places by mines, so that the unbelievers prayed for mercy from the faithful. As some of the garrison were taken prisoners, and from these it was ascertained that the accursed was not in the fortress, the Imperial mercy forgave their offence, and listened to their entreaties; but His Majesty, who governs the world, to gain the merits of this holy war, and to ruin the aforesaid accursed, had sent out the *akinjis*, the runners and burners, in all directions into Germany, so that the whole country was trodden down by the hoofs of the horses, and even the lands north of the Danube wasted with fire by the crews of the vessels. Cities and hamlets, market-towns and villages, blazed up in the fire of vengeance and destruction. The beautiful land, the treasury of spring and abode of joy, was trodden down by the horsemen and filled with smoke. Houses and palaces were left in ashes. The victorious army dragged away captive the inhabitants, great and small, high and low, men and women, strong and weak. In the bazaars were sold many fair ones... the booty was incalculable. Property, moveable and immoveable, men and cattle, the speaking and the dumb, the rational and the senseless, were destroyed and slaughtered at the edge of the sabre. Thus, on the page of time was written the fulfilment of the prophecy of the Koran, "Thus deal we with the wicked."[86]

Suleiman arrived at Constantinople on 16 December and made his triumphal entry with that portion of his army which had least suffered on the march. The festivities celebrating the magnificence of his victory over the infidels lasted five days. Significantly, the greater part of his exhausted surviving troops remained at Belgrade, Niš, and Edirne. However enthusiastic the revels in the Topkapi Palace, however much the Sublime Porte might bluster in its diplomatic correspondence, there was no disguising the fact the Ottoman war machine had suffered its first significant setback in the West for a near exact half-century, since the Knights Hospitaller had repulsed the first siege of Rhodes in 1480.

It is a testament to the respect and fear the Ottomans commanded in Europe that their defeat was celebrated throughout Christendom generally, temporarily overriding national and denominational rivalries in an outburst of collective relief and joy. In Calvinist Geneva, the redemption of Catholic Vienna was celebrated as a manifest triumph over "du plus grand tyrant et destruyseur de la chrestiente lempereur de Turquie" ("the greatest tyrant and destroyer of Christianity the Emperor of Turkey").[87] Criers in the streets of Paris reported the news of the sultan's retreat to Constantinople, with religious processions being held throughout the city to give thanks to God for the salvation of Vienna. The House of Habsburg, however, could not be ascribed too much credit in Valois France, where the outcome was recognized as "a great victory" for "Ferdinand, King of Hungary, brother of the Emperor," but one owed to the intervention of Christ, who sent a hailstorm to ravage the Ottoman troops at a critical moment.[88]

There is no doubt responsibility for the Ottoman setback can be ascribed to environmental factors beyond human agency. Contemporary observers throughout the campaign repeatedly referenced the hostile weather conditions. Ottoman historian Ismail Hakki Uzunçarsili concluded that if the weather had allowed the siege of 1529 to commence two months earlier, and the besiegers to deploy their heavy guns, "there can be no doubt that Vienna would have fallen." Had that transpired, providing for a permanent Ottoman presence at the gates of Europe, the implications for the future would have been profound, for, wrote Peter Stern, Vienna represented "a gate and key to German lands." Centuries later, Arnold Toynbee proclaimed that nothing less than "the fate of Western Christendom was at stake in the Ottoman siege of Vienna in 1529."[89] Certainly, there is no immutable law in geographic determinism that would have obliged Suleiman to abandon his prize had it been taken. As the crow flies, Vienna was only 762 miles from Constantinople – much less distance than the 1,039 miles to Tunis, 1,288 miles to Basra, or 2,911 miles to Aden, all which were to come under the authority of the Porte. In the event Suleiman had claimed the city, would Catholics and Protestants have set aside their differences and drawn closer together in a common effort against the rising Ottoman tide, empowering Habsburg authority and a more centralized Holy Roman Empire? Or would the emperor's many enemies only have been emboldened by this demonstration of Habsburg impotence, leading to the further Balkanization of Western Europe and setting the stage for further Ottoman encroachment?[90]

Such scenarios were, for now, academic, as, hunkered down behind their walls, the Habsburgs, with critical assistance from that most powerful of allies, the weather, had on this occasion proved too tough a nut to crack.[91] Charles could now arrive, unburdened, at his apotheosis. On 22 February 1530, wearing an ermine-collared mantle of purple satin inlaid with gold over a robe of white and gold brocade, the emperor knelt in the chapel of Bologna's Palazzo Pubblico to receive the crown of Lombardy from Pope Clement, designating him king of Italy, and the crown of the Holy Roman Emperor, along with a sword, orb, and scepter. Two days later – Charles's thirtieth birthday and the fifth anniversary of the Battle of Pavia – he again received the octagonal crown of the Holy Roman Emperor, this time in the Cathedral of San Petronio.

His brother, meanwhile, was proactively seeking to consolidate his authority in Hungary. In the wake of the Ottoman retreat from Vienna, a Habsburg army under von Roggendorf marched on Buda, offering 10,000 ducats for Zápolya alive, and 1,000 dead. The imperial ambassador to the Curia reported that Alvise Gritti was also trapped in the city, and in Rome, they would much prefer him being taken than his master, "for they say the former is much more dangerous, owing to his influence over Ibrahim Pasha, and if taken, ought to be drawn and quartered."[92] By mid-December the walls of the city had been reduced to rubble and the defenders reduced to eating their horses. But the Habsburg force had also been depleted by sickness and cold, and Mehmet Bey, the Ottoman *bey* of Smederevo in Serbia, was marching to Buda's succor. Playing the numbers, von Roggendorf broke the siege and withdrew. Ferdinand was successful elsewhere, capturing Esztergom and other forts along the Danube.[93]

In October 1531, Ferdinand dispatched a delegation of twenty-four ambassadors to the Ottoman capital, led by Nikola Jurišić, a Croatian nobleman and commander of the small fortress at Kőszeg on the Austrian border with Hungary. This embassy was empowered to offer Suleiman an annual subsidy if the sultan would recognize Ferdinand as king of Hungary, abandon Zápolya, and withdraw his garrison from Buda. The Porte contemptuously rejected these terms and began mobilization for a new campaign against the Habsburg heartland. Alvise Gritti wrote to Charles, warning him to beware the "huge and inestimable preparations for war that the said Turk is making both on sea and on land, such that our epoch has never seen." The only alternative to general war was for the emperor to lean on his younger brother to renounce the Habsburg claim to the throne of

Hungary.[94] There was no possibility of any such resolution to the gathering crisis. By the end of that year, Erasmus noted, it was public knowledge "the Turk will invade Germany with all his forces, in a contest for the greatest of prizes, to see whether Charles will be the monarch of the whole world or the Turk. For the world can no longer bear two suns in the sky."[95]

By April 1532, Charles had intelligence that a huge Ottoman army, led by the sultan himself, was on the march for Vienna. On this occasion, he could not simply delegate the defense of the city to his brother. As he explained to Isabella on 6 April, "in light of the duty I have to defend the faith and the Christian religion... if the Turk comes against me this year, I will go against him in person... with everything I can find to resist him."[96] Ironically, the looming Ottoman threat accomplished something no amount of negotiation had hitherto come close to achieving – bringing the empire's estranged Catholic and Lutheran factions together on common ground. In March an Imperial *Diet* had been convened in Regensburg to discuss the possibility of an interdenominational ceasefire. After negotiations moved to Nuremberg in June, a formal peace accord was reached on 23 July. For the first – and last – time, Lutherans would assemble to march alongside Catholics against a common foe under the command of Charles V. However, by this time, Suleiman was already in Belgrade.

The sultan had led his army out of Constantinople on 25 April, the invasion supported by a formidable Ottoman fleet on the Danube that shadowed the ground forces. At Osijek, the Ottoman army crossed the Drava River over twelve pontoon bridges and soon entered southern Hungary. Gábor Ágoston maintains the 1532 campaign was a skillfully choreographed imperial procession intended to broadcast Ottoman imperial grandeur, organized by Ibrahim Pasha in order to present his master as world conqueror. It was also Ibrahim's response to Charles V's coronation celebrations in Bologna in 1530. Suleiman's imperial entries into Niš and Belgrade were intended as counterpoints to Charles V's coronation cavalcade. Commissioned by Ibrahim from Venice, Suleiman's four-tier parade helmet, which he wore during these triumphal entries and during private audiences, incorporated elements from both the papal tiara and the crown that Charles V had worn during his coronation in Bologna. The message was clear: Suleiman was challenging the authority of both the pope and the emperor.[97] This point was emphasized when Ibrahim informed Habsburg envoys the sultan was in fact the divinely ordained true protector of Christendom, marching to challenge a spurious emperor who had persecuted Lutherans, destroyed Rome, and imprisoned the pope. "Spain is like a lizard," Ibrahim

Pasha sneered, "pecking here and there at a bit of weed or some grain found in the dirt, while our sultan is like a dragon which gulps down the world when it opens its mouth."[98]

Those envoys had arrived in Suleiman's camp, first at Niš and then at Belgrade, to offer a much larger annual tribute and withdraw previous Habsburg demands in relation to Buda and the recognition of Ferdinand. The sultan contemptuously dismissed them. It was too late for concessions now. "The king of Spain," he replied to Ferdinand, again refusing to recognize Charles as emperor, "has proclaimed for a long time that he wants to act against the Turks; and now, by the grace of God, I am advancing with my army against him. If he is a man who has balls and courage, let him come and draw up his army in the field ready to fight with my imperial host, and the issue will be whatever God wills."[99]

The Ottoman juggernaut continued north through western Transdanubia, taking the more direct overland route to Vienna through Székesfehérvár and Győr, slogging through the swamps south of Lake Balaton (and leaving many of their heavy siege cannons in the mire), skirting the lake itself and avoiding Buda altogether. At town after town, fortress after fortress, local commanders under the sway of Zápolya came out to greet the Ottomans and offer the keys to their garrisons. Rewards were handed out accordingly.

At Győr the sultan convened a council of war with his advisers. According to the strategic plan arrived at, the Ottoman navy would continue upriver to Bratislava, while 16,000 light-armed raiders would advance to harass the environs of Vienna and spread their habitual rapine and terror throughout the population. The main body of the army would proceed west overland to the southern edge of Lake Neusiedler. From there it would turn south towards Kőszeg, the first of the small fortified towns loyal to Ferdinand. After the army made quick work of that minor obstacle, it would move west into the grasslands and meadows of southeast Austria.

The imperial army, meanwhile, was mustering at Regensburg in southern Bavaria. As in 1529, the rains in June and July swelled the rivers, which, Charles noted, "allowed us time to repair and strengthen the fortification of Vienna."[100] And the emperor was elated at how enthusiastically his subjects had responded to his call to arms. On 9 August he wrote to his wife that all the states of the Holy Roman Empire, including the Protestants, had acted with dispatch and zeal.[101] The fact was that, when not fighting against his Valois rival in Italy, Charles could mobilize a military force comparable in size to that of Suleiman. The official estimate on 16 August placed the total combined military and auxiliary manpower available to the emperor at 222,820 men. All through spring and summer, infantry, cavalry, and artillery units derived from the financial and military support from half of Europe – Spain, Portugal, the Netherlands, the Italian states, the Holy Roman Empire, Bohemia, and Hungary – continued to muster at Vienna, where by August, Charles awaited Suleiman at the head of an army 90,000–95,000 strong.[102]

On 9 August, the advance units of the Ottoman army under Ibrahim Pasha formed up before Kőszeg.[103] Their route of march had brought the invasion force to the outskirts of Vienna almost a month earlier than had been the case in 1529, when it had only crossed the Austrian border on 19 September. As well as leaving earlier, this time the Ottomans had taken a substantially shorter route. Instead of following the Danube, taking them due north and then due west, the army proceeded along the diagonal line from Osijek directly to Kőszeg.

The defense of Kőszeg was entrusted to Nikola Jurišić, a Croatian officer in Habsburg service with impressive credentials as both a warrior and a diplomat. Ferdinand had appointed him with overall command over the forces defending the Ottoman frontier after the Battle of Mohács. Jurišić in turn had helped Ferdinand become the king of Croatia by brokering the 1527 election in Cetin. Three years later, Jurišić had been sent to Constantinople as an ambassador to negotiate with the Ottomans for peace.

Jurišić would now be put to the ultimate test. He had arrived to take command at Kőszeg only weeks before the Ottomans, who were now massing under its walls, with just ten cuirassiers and twenty-eight hussars. Even after mobilizing the able-bodied male townsfolk – far outnumbered by the several thousand women, children, and elderly now trapped within the walls – the total number of defenders amounted to no more than 700 to 800.

It should have been a walkover. Instead, the defense of Kőszeg became a legend. "I have volunteered to fight against the Turkish Emperor and his army," Jurišić wrote to Ferdinand. "I fight not because I presume to equal his force, but only so as to delay him a little while to give time for Your Royal Majesty to unite with the Christian Holy Emperor."[104] He bought much more time than anyone would have dared assume possible. Twelve days into the siege, Ottoman mines brought down a forty-foot section of the wall. But the charge of the janissaries into the breach was repulsed. When huge wooden, pyramid-shaped assault towers were rolled up to the walls, the defenders filled barrels with sulfur, tar, and tallow, set them on fire, and burned the towers to the ground.[105]

Finally, on 27 August, after another furious assault was turned back, Ibrahim Pasha offered to negotiate. These exchanges stalled, and the siege resumed. At one point eight Ottoman banners were planted on the walls, but the besiegers could not hold their ground. With no further progress, Ibrahim offered to discuss terms a second time.

The grand vizier had no idea how close he was to final victory. Jurišić himself was wounded. His store of gunpowder was virtually depleted. Half his garrison was dead, and the remaining defenders were ready to capitulate. But through adroit diplomacy, Jurišić conceded little more than the most pro forma terms of surrender. He would accept Ottoman suzerainty in principle, and, to save face, a contingent of janissaries was permitted to occupy a breach in the walls for several hours to ceremonially plant their banners in the rubble. But there would be no permanent occupation. "Even the Turks say that not once since Suleiman's accession to the throne have they been dealt such a blow by so vile and low a place as this," Jurišić, no doubt astonished he was still alive, wrote to Ferdinand.[106] The Ottomans formally broke off the siege on 29 August at 11am. To this day, the bells ring at that hour instead of at noon in Kőszeg.

The Ottomans had wasted three precious weeks on this pointless assault. Suleiman had hoped that Charles would march to relieve Kőszeg, affording him the opportunity for a decisive engagement, but throughout the siege the imperial army had remained passive as it continued to form up in Regensburg. The sultan was now forced to take stock. If his entire army could be tied down by a detachment of the enemy just a few hundred strong in a minor border post, what were his chances of reducing the imperial capital itself? Suleiman was aware that Italian, Spanish, and imperial troops, both Catholic and Lutheran, had been pouring into Vienna. The city would be far better garrisoned than it had been three years earlier, and the physical defenses had been materially modernized and expanded since the first siege.[107] Again unable to bring their heavy artillery to bear on the walls, and again operating at the limits of their supply lines at the end of the campaign season, were the Ottomans to make any attempt on Vienna now they would simply find themselves in the same tactical cul-de-sac as 1529, only facing even longer odds.

While he pondered his options, Suleiman received word the emperor's new ally, the Genoese admiral Andrea Doria, had gone on the offensive in the Adriatic and seized the fortress of Koroni in Messenia, Greece, creating a threat to his supply lines. Perhaps this was the decisive tipping point for now, instead of continuing north to Vienna, the Ottoman army turned slowly southwest towards Graz and debouched its way through the low hills and green pastures of Styria, leaving scorched earth in its wake. The focus of the campaign was now explicitly to target only civilian infrastructure in order to draw Charles out in defense of his subjects' lives and property. Wary of being drawn into another protracted siege of a military hard-point, Suleiman skirted the mountaintop bastion of Riegersburg.

By the time the Ottomans reached Graz, eleven days after leaving Kőszeg, the absence of any challenge from Charles seemed to intensify the fury of the invaders even further, and they took out their frustrations on the local populace. Again, while the Ottomans sacked the city, they did not dare assail the high walls of its imposing castle, the Schlossberg.[108] Nor were they complete masters of the open fields. Once it was confirmed the invaders would return to Constantinople via his territories, Lajos Pekry, *ban* of Croatia and Slavonia, wrote a bold letter to the Great Palatine Tamás Nádasdy, swearing "we will form up, we will rise up, and with the help of God, we will resist so that he does not cross the Mura and the Drava."[109] While this was optimistic, the Ottoman rearguard was roughly handled in an ambush at Fernitz. The outlying Ottoman detachments were subject to a much worse fate. While the advance of the main Ottoman army had been stymied at Kőszeg, Kazim Bey had been assigned a substantial body of *akinjis* with a mandate to roam on a *razzia* in as wide a radius as possible. When Kazim Bey was informed of the Ottoman retreat, he gathered his raiders at Pottenstein to link up with the main army. Of the three possible valleys he could follow, he found two had been blocked. Habsburg forces under *Landsknecht* veteran Sebastian Schertlin von Burtenbach, the Mayor of Augsburg, drove the Ottomans into the only remaining open valley, where Frederick II, count palatine of the Rhine, the Hungarian Count Bálint Török of Csesznek (who had commanded the bodyguard of King Louis at Mohács), and John Katzianer of Carniola (another veteran of Mohács, who had defected from Zápolya to Ferdinand to serve at Vienna in 1529 and been appointed commander of his Hussar bodyguard), were waiting for them with an army of *Landsknechte*, cavalry, and artillery.

The Ottoman force was completely destroyed at the ensuing Battle of Leobersdorf on 19 September, only a handful of the *akinji* limping back into Suleiman's camp. Among the dead was Kazim Bey. His magnificent helmet, studded with precious jewels and festooned with vulture feathers, had fallen into Habsburg hands. When Charles finally entered Vienna on 23 September, the helmet was presented to him as a trophy, and imperial propaganda made much of the triumph of the German eagle over the Ottoman vulture.[110] The main bulk of the Ottoman army, meanwhile, continued its withdrawal.

Suleiman arrived at Belgrade on 13 October and returned to Constantinople on 18 November.

It was an anticlimactic end to the campaign. Charles and Suleiman, the apex predators of their age, had come as close as they ever would to facing off in the kind of apocalyptic boss battle demanded by a Hollywood screenplay. The fact that didn't happen reflects the awareness on both sides that each had more to risk from defeat than they stood to gain from victory. Given the context of irresistible Ottoman momentum up to that point, the failure of Suleiman to claim Vienna in 1529 or 1532 enabled Ferdinand and Charles to emerge with enhanced reputations and a legitimate claim to have, at last, demarcated the limits of Ottoman expansion by land in Europe. In both East and West, the House of Habsburg was now recognized, the Ottoman chronicler Evliya Çelebi conceded, as "the wall around the red apple in Rome."[111]

7

SULEIMAN, PART III – KINGMAKER

The stare-down between Suleiman and Charles over Hungary had left an undefined and unstable frontier in its wake. Diplomats on both sides now rushed to fill that space. Ferdinand's ambassador, Hieronymus of Zara, arrived in Constantinople in January 1533 and negotiated the outlines of a settlement between the two rival claimants to the Crown of Hungary. Representing Charles, Cornelius Duplicius Schepper arrived in Constantinople that May, bearing the keys of the fortress of Esztergom as a symbol of Ferdinand's obeisance to the sultan. The two brothers were working at cross purposes here; Ferdinand believed that Suleiman could be persuaded to depose Zápolya in his favor, while the priority for Charles was a peace with the Ottomans that would give him a free hand in the West and the Mediterranean. Suleiman finally concluded the Treaty of Constantinople with Ferdinand on 22 June 1533.[1] Its terms confirmed the status of Zápolya as king of all Hungary while at the same time recognizing Ferdinand's possession of that part of the nation currently under his jurisdiction. Predictably, it satisfied not one of the signatories involved, but Suleiman was happy to split the difference for now for, like Charles, he had grander ambitions elsewhere and wanted the Balkan frontier kept quiet.

When the Safavid Shah Ismail had died, aged only thirty-seven, on 23 May 1524, Suleiman immediately sent a threatening letter to his successor, his ten-year-old son Tahmasp:

> I have decided to bear arms to Tabriz and Azerbaijan, and to pitch my tent in Iran and Turan, at Samarkand and in Khorasan... If you want to come and beg a crust of bread at my door for the love of God, I will be happy to oblige and you will lose nothing of your country... I will keep you in my sights and, with the grace of God, seize on you and rid the world of your poisonous existence.[2]

But there was little immediate Ottoman follow through on this belligerence. Tahmasp struggled to assert his authority, first over the factional infighting that roiled his own court, then against the rising Uzbek threat in Central Asia. With the Safavids preoccupied on his eastern flank, Suleiman was free to undertake his offensives against the Christian West. In fact, it was to his advantage to normalize trade relations with the Persians; one of his first acts as sultan was to lift the unpopular commercial blockade imposed by his father, which had the immediate effect of boosting commerce, and hence tax revenue.[3]

This reactive policy was revised after Tahmasp had the pro-Ottoman governor of Baghdad assassinated, and the sultan of the Tekkelu clan, the shah's governor in Azerbaijan, defected to the Porte. Convinced this gave him the opportunity to permanently incorporate Azerbaijan into his empire, thereby cutting the Safavids off from the Caucasus, Suleiman mobilized for his first war in the East.

On 11 June 1534, Alvise Gritti approached the Habsburg ambassador, Schepper, with an extraordinary proposal. Gritti argued Charles had been presented with a once-in-a-lifetime opportunity to destroy the Ottoman state. The sultan's fleet had left Constantinople for North Africa. The bulk of the army was in the East with Ibrahim Pasha, and Suleiman had left that very morning to follow him; hence if Charles made peace with France – by giving Milan to Francis I and making himself king of Tuscany – then his path to conquest would be clear. Ottoman Greece was populated by Christians and garrisoned with worthless troops, so the province could be conquered without drawing a sword. Charles could compel Venice, always fearful of the Turks, to join forces with him. The defenses of Constantinople were weak, hence an Imperial–Venetian fleet of some 130 galleys could take the city, especially since it would have help from within from the large Christian population at the street level and from Gritti himself within the Topkapi Palace. On the other hand, if Charles hesitated, then after the Persian campaign, Suleiman would launch an immense fleet against Italy and lead his army to Rome. Schepper should advise his emperor "that defending himself against Barbarossa will be more costly than attacking Constantinople, because there isn't a single galley left to defend the city. The Emperor's fleet will find untold riches here and will encounter no resistance. But he must hurry. If he leaves things until after the Turk returns from the East, the war will be difficult to win. One shouldn't always think of defense, but sometimes also of attack."[4] The entire concept was breathtakingly audacious, but Schepper was not impressed. He was convinced that Gritti had "given his soul to the devil to serve the sultan."[5]

Marching at the head of the vanguard, Ibrahim Pasha captured the Safavid capital, Tabriz, on 15 July 1534. Suleiman arrived in the city that September to take personal command during the War of the Two Iraqs, as it was remembered. The Ottoman offensive continued to push south, ultimately taking Baghdad in December. Tahmasp refused to give battle, relying on a scorched-earth policy coupled with a guerilla war against the Ottoman logistics chains to wear down the invasion. This was only a qualified success. While the Ottomans did not dare push onto the Iranian plateau, they now dominated the Fertile Crescent, retaining the two provinces of Iraq – *Iraq-i Ajem* (Persian Iraq) and *Iraq-i Arab* (Arab Iraq) – taken from the Safavids, and with them, the Shia holy sites of Karbala and Najaf. The port city of Basra also surrendered to the Ottomans in 1538, granting them access to the Persian Gulf. The campaign thus tightened Ottoman control over the western terminus to both the Silk Route (running from Tabriz to Erzurum and Bursa) and the Spice Route (running from Basra to Baghdad and Aleppo).[6]

Meanwhile, the artificial settlement in the Balkans was giving way. The Ottoman *sanjak-bey* of Bosnia, Gazi Husrev Bey, occupied Požega in early 1537. Ferdinand, under pressure from the local nobility, responded by launching an offensive in Slavonia. An army under Hans Katzianer, Count von Katzenstein, a veteran of the 1529 and 1532 campaigns, was committed to take Osijek. But the siege failed and the Habsburg army, trapped between the garrison of the city and an Ottoman relief force led by Semendireli Mehmed, pasha of Belgrade, was annihilated at the Battle of Gorjani on 9 October 1537. Among the fallen was another veteran of Mohács and Vienna, Pavle Bakić, the last titular despot of Serbia, whose severed head was presented to Suleiman in Constantinople.

Weary of the institutional stalemate, chafing at his subordination to the Porte, and influenced by the advice of his treasurer and chief confidante, Father George Martinuzzi, the bishop of Oradea, Zápolya came to terms with Ferdinand in the Treaty of Nagyvárad on 24 February 1538. According to their agreement, Ferdinand would recognize Zápolya as king of Hungary, but after his death, the kingdom would be transferred to Ferdinand or his heirs. If Zápolya, unmarried and already fifty years old at the time, was to father a son, Ferdinand would still succeed him, while granting Zápolya's heir the minor Habsburg principality of Szepes in lieu of the Hungarian throne.

At Székesfehérvár on 2 March 1539, Zápolya married Isabella Jagiellon, the daughter of King Sigismund I of Poland. Isabella was duly crowned queen of Hungary the same day. A year later, on 7 July 1540, the queen gave birth to a boy, John Sigismund. By the end of that same month, Zápolya was dead.

Martinuzzi then dispatched chancellor Stephen Werbőczy to Constantinople, asking Suleiman to acknowledge and protect his master's infant son. The friar also hastily convened a *diet* at Rákos, which duly elected the barely two-month-old child as King John II Sigismund of Hungary on 13 September. Suleiman was outraged that his erstwhile protégé Zápolya had struck up a secret deal with Ferdinand without so much as consulting, let alone receiving permission from, the Porte. But refusing to recognize Sigismund as the legitimate heir to the throne of Hungary in the absence of any other alternative would only enhance the claim of Ferdinand, and accordingly, the no-doubt fuming sultan had no choice but to respond positively to Martinuzzi's envoy. On 17 October, Werbőczy reported that, "with the Good Lord's help, we received from His Majesty [Suleiman] the desired response to all our proposals. His Majesty left the son of our master, born of happy memory, on his father's throne with all jurisdiction within the borders of Hungary and Transylvania."[7]

Ferdinand could have used this outcome as an opportunity to set down his own claims to the Hungarian throne and arrive at a *modus vivendi* with the new regime to ensure it served as a genuine buffer between Vienna and Constantinople. Certainly, even though he dedicated himself to securing universal recognition of his claim to be king of Hungary, he had no personal attachment to the kingdom itself. In fact, he did not set foot in its the territory on a single occasion between 1528 and 1542, his interests being represented *in absentia* through governors (Elek Thurzó, 1532–42; Pál Várdai, 1542–49). And it was not as though he was profiting from his investment. Indeed, quite the opposite. The cost of maintaining the defensive line in Hungary – which far exceeded the capacity of the Hungarians themselves to pay – had to be met by the so-called *Türkenhilfe* (Turkish tax) imposed on the Habsburg estates in Carinthia, Carniola, Styria, Lower Austria, Moravia, and throughout the Holy Roman Empire.[8] But ultimately, the obligation to maintain a forward line of defense proved decisive. As Tamás Nádasdy, the *ban* of Croatia and Slavonia put it in the summer of 1539, "If Your Holy Majesty does not support this country with your other provinces it will certainly happen that, due to the loss of this country, the other provinces of Your Holy Majesty will be lost."[9]

Accordingly, Ferdinand found himself at war with the infant Sigismund, and from October through early November 1540, Habsburg troops conquered Visegrád, Székesfehérvár, and the poorly reinforced Pest. But they failed to take the much better fortified Buda, which was vigorously defended by Martinuzzi, on the opposite bank of the Danube. Renewing the campaign in the following spring would require funds, and that meant convening the Imperial *diet*, which then inevitably picked up right where it left off by raising the religious question. When the *diet* convened in Regensburg in April, the Lutheran faction refused to commit to the war effort without guarantees that religious toleration would be respected. As usual, they got their way. On 29 July 1541, a much-amended agreement was signed in which the Lutheran princes agreed to commit 10,000 infantry and 2,000 cavalry to fight the Ottomans for three months. But this came too late to save the Habsburg cause in Hungary.

As Suleiman described it in his *fathnamas* (victory letters) to Pietro Lando, the doge of Venice, the campaign of 1541 commenced when "King Ferdinandush [Ferdinand I of Austria] the infidel, who is the king of Austria... who is cursed with unbelief... with the help of his infidel brother King of Spain Karlo [Charles V] and also with the aid of some other infidels, gathered infidel soldiers from their perverted countries" and invaded lands that belonged, by extension, to the Porte.[10] Comprised of infidels it may have been, but the Habsburg army that intervened in Hungary did not lack experience, being commanded by Wilhelm von Roggendorf and Nicholas von Salm, two veterans of the 1529 campaign in defense of Vienna.

In response, Suleiman ordered his grand vizier, the eunuch Hadım Süleyman Pasha, with the vanguard of the *kapıkulu*, and the governor of Rumelia, Ahmed Pasha, with the Rumelian field army, to advance to Buda. The sultan himself, "unfurling the flag of victory and the banner of conquest, in accordance with the happiness-marked verses written in the Qur'an, the holy honorable book," followed up with detachments from Anatolia, accompanied by his three sons, Mehmed, Selim, and Bayezid, and vizier Rüstem Pasha.[11]

The Habsburg army under von Roggendorf ("may God abandon them until the Day of Judgment") had arrived at Buda on 4 May, setting up siege guns on all sides of the city. These had opened numerous breaches in the walls by the time the Ottoman relief army arrived. The Habsburg forces pulled back, digging trenches and building field fortifications on a steep hill adjacent to Buda while scorching the earth along the shores of the Danube and fortifying some islands on the river itself.

Running battles commenced between the Ottoman vanguard and "the unblessed hell-inflicted ones" in von Roggendorf's army which played out day and night until Suleiman, advancing via a bridge over the Sava River he had ordered built at Osijek, arrived at Buda. Outmatched, von Roggendorf opted to fall back. After sunset on 21 August he began bringing up his ships to ferry the army across the Danube to Pest. Discovering this gambit, the Ottoman army launched a night assault against the Habsburg field fortifications, while Suleiman brought up his fleet, which "joined the attack on the river and broke the way of those who intended to cross over to the other side." The Habsburg staged withdrawal degenerated into a rout and the battle into a massacre; untold thousands "drowned in the water like the people of the Pharaoh."[12] Among those lost was von Roggendorf; injured in the fighting, he succumbed to his wounds two days later. Passing in triumph into Buda, Suleiman was not in the mood to indulge the taking of prisoners; "the people of hell were cleaned from the surface of the world by the swords of the valorous conquerors," he blithely informed Lando; others were "tied in chains in groups and tramped down under the horses of [the] victorious forces."[13]

On 28 August, accompanied by the leading nobility of the Hungarian estates, Martinuzzi, the queen, and the infant Sigismund arrived in the Ottoman camp to pay homage to the sultan. Suleiman welcomed the party into his tent, but when he issued the code phrase "The black soup [coffee] is still to come!" all of his guests were disarmed by the janissaries. They were ultimately allowed to depart, with one exception: Bálint Török, the *ban* of Belgrade and lord of Csesznek, whom Suleiman considered a potential threat, was taken into captivity and transferred to Yedikule Fortress, where he spent the remaining ten years of his life.

Meanwhile, Ottoman troops had been slowly infiltrating into Buda over the past week. On the orders of Hadım Süleyman Pasha, these now disarmed the garrison and seized control of the city. Thus, on 29 August, the fifteenth anniversary of the Battle of Mohács, the Ottomans formally took possession of the Hungarian capital. The royal court, the nobility, and citizens of Buda were allowed to leave the city with their possessions unharmed.

On Friday 2 September, Suleiman entered Buda. His name was celebrated during the prayer, performed in the Church of the Assumption, which the Ottomans had converted into a mosque. "My main objective was to turn the throne of Buda into a *dar al-Islam* and control the country of Hungary," Suleiman recounted. To that end, "I annexed the city of Buda and its vicinity and turned most of its churches into mosques for the people of belief."[14]

Suleiman appointed Sigismund the *sanjak-bey* of Transylvania, while the Banat was placed under the *ispán* (count) of Temes, Péter Petrović, with the rest of the trans-Tisza area being delegated to Martinuzzi. All three derived their authority exclusively from the sufferance of the sultan. Thus were the last veils stripped from the façade of Hungarian independence as the realm came to be finally and fully subsumed within the Ottoman orbit.

The result was that Hungary was subjected to a de facto tripartite division. Ferdinand occupied one slice, John II Sigismund and his tutors in Transylvania a second, and the Ottomans established direct administration in the middle territory with Buda as its center.

For obvious reasons, Isabella resented seeing her son cheated of his inheritance, and sought to repudiate the sultan's authority at the first available opportunity. She reached out to Ferdinand and at Gyalu Castle on 29 December renewed the Treaty of Nagyvárad, promising to give her son's part of the country (as well as the Holy Crown, which was in her possession) to Ferdinand, in return for the promised estates in the Szepes region.

Ferdinand stood to double his share of Hungary overnight. Once again, however, he could not seal the deal on the battlefield. In their assembly in Speyer in February 1542, the Imperial *Diet* approved the hiring of 24,000 infantrymen and 4,000 cavalry mercenaries to place at the disposal of the emperor in order to take Buda. But Charles, depressed by the destruction of his navy off the coast of Algiers in November 1541, reneged on his promise to lead the expedition personally, citing intelligence regarding an imminent French invasion. The emperor's fears were justified when Francis declared war on him in May, breaking the Truce of Nice, which had been concluded in 1538 for ten years.

Joachim II, elector of Brandenburg, proved to be a poor substitute for the emperor. Joachim had 30,000 foot soldiers and 7,000 cavalry under his command, with 15,000 local horsemen joining him in Hungary. A flotilla of 200 ships supported the expedition along its route of march down the Danube. Having reached Pest at the end of September 1542, the imperial forces commenced their investment of the city, only to lift the siege on 8 October, after just ten days in action. Decimated by typhus, the only accomplishment of the Habsburg host was to disseminate the disease throughout Europe as the army broke up and the survivors returned home. In response to this failure, led by Martinuzzi, the Transylvanian estates annulled the Gyalu arrangement in the Torda *Diet* at the end of the year and reemphasized their recognition of the elected Hungarian king, Sigismund, as their monarch.

Ferdinand could expect no assistance from Charles, who was fighting Francis on three different fronts – near Perpignan in southern France, Milan, and Antwerp. "I cannot do everything and be everywhere," the emperor wrote at the end of 1542. Therefore, "you must not count on my help, because I have enough problems – indeed, I fear, too many – of my own." Referring to Francis, he added, "I hope soon to reduce to reason our dear brother and friend, the most Christian King."[15] But the following year, the Habsburg nightmare of having to fight on two fronts was realized when Suleiman entered the war.

The sultan left Edirne on 23 April 1543. Following the Plovdiv–Sofia–Niš–Kruševac military road of his previous Hungarian campaigns, he arrived at Belgrade on 5 June. He crossed the Drava at Osijek on 22 June and arrived at Valpovo two days later. From there, Suleiman marched against Siklós, which surrendered after an eleven-day siege. Meanwhile, the *sanjak-beys* of Požega and Mohács captured Pécs, one of the largest towns in Hungary. Arriving in Buda on 23 July, the sultan and his pashas held a *divan* at which it was decided to attack Esztergom, one of Ferdinand's key fortresses, just fifty kilometers northwest of Ottoman Buda on the right bank of the Danube. Having repulsed several attacks, the castle's Spanish, Italian, and German mercenaries, some 2,200 men, surrendered on 10 August. The army then moved against Székesfehérvár, the Hungarian city of coronations and royal tombs, which surrendered on 4 September. Meanwhile, the Crimean Tatars ravaged Transdanubia.

Over the course of the campaign seasons in 1544 and 1545 the Ottomans consolidated their control by seizing Visegrád, Nógrád, and Hatvan, while in the border area of Transdanubia they occupied Simontornya, Ozora, and Tamási. With Ferdinand demonstrably unable to defend them against further Ottoman incursions, the nobles of the Trans-Tisza region opted to seek protection from Martinuzzi.

Charles and Francis, meanwhile, were busy hammering out the final details of the Treaty of Crépy, signed on 18 September 1544, by the terms of which the houses of Habsburg and Valois would resolve their differences through that age-old mechanism of dynastic politics, the marriage alliance. Francis's son Charles, Duke of Orléans, was to marry either a daughter of the emperor, whose dowry would include the Netherlands and Franche-Comté, or a daughter of Ferdinand, whose dowry would be the duchy of Milan. Francis agreed to abjure all claims to Naples and the Netherlands, to return all his conquests since the 18 June 1538 Truce of Nice, and to end the alliance with the Ottomans, instead contributing troops to a new crusade to be led by Charles. But Francis had no intention of fighting Suleiman. Neither did Charles, who had another enemy in mind. In a secret treaty that Francis signed the very next day, 19 September, the French king promised to provide the Habsburg brothers "with our full assistance and favor in the reduction and pacification of religious discord in Germany whenever it is required," to declare himself the "enemy of those who seek to prevent the said pacification," and to allow "the assistance of infantry and cavalry that we have promised against the Turks to be used if necessary against the said heretics."[16]

On 5 October 1545, the grand vizier, the sultan's son-in-law, Rüstem Pasha, finally agreed to a one-and-a-half-year truce. The Habsburgs would pay

10,000 ducats to the sultan as tribute (along with 3,000 ducats to Rüstem, and 1,000 ducats to the other viziers – the price of conducting diplomacy with the Porte). But the sudden death the very next day of Charles, Duke of Orléans, on 6 October, whose intended marriage with a Habsburg princess had been the principal rationale for French mediation of the Ottoman–Habsburg peace negotiations, reversed the French diplomatic position. The French ambassador in Constantinople would perform a complete *volte-face*, lobbying not just to dissuade Rüstem from agreeing to peace with the Habsburgs but in fact to ally with France in a joint war against them. However, Habsburg ambassador Gerard Veltwyck was able to obtain a five-year peace treaty at the end of long negotiations that played out from December 1546 to their conclusion when the terms were inked in Edirne on 19 June 1547. Over the course of these parleys, Rüstem inquired as to why the Habsburgs were so committed to pursuing their claims in Hungary when Suleiman had conquered all Hungary with his sword and was therefore sole proprietor of those lands. Veltwyck responded that the Christians regarded rule by election as superior to rule by force.[17]

Ultimately, Ferdinand agreed to pay 30,000 Hungarian gold florins annually, to be delivered to the Porte by an embassy every year in March, "in exchange for the places that are indeed part of Hungary and belong to the Christians."[18] Vienna referred to the sum as its *munus honestum et honorarium* (honest and honorable gift) to the sultan; the Ottomans considered it a *harac* (tribute), which rendered the Habsburg monarchs homage-paying vassals. Whatever its title, this donative would continue to endow the coffers in Constantinople until as late as 1606.[19]

The burden for the cost of both war and peace ultimately fell on the common people, trapped in the intractable rivalry between House Osman and House Habsburg. Sworn covenants arrived at by the magnates meant little to their subjects, for even when both sides were officially bound by treaty, not a single month passed without the forays of raiding parties, the burning down of villages, the robbing of merchants, extortion, murder, and slave-hunting *razzias*. Adding to their woes, the townsfolk along the border were liable to taxation from both sides. In the region between the Danube and Tisza rivers, more than 77 percent of the families who paid the poll tax (*cizye*) to the Ottomans in 1546 also paid the Hungarian state tax (*dica*) in 1550. There was no escape in flight, for according to the treaty of 1547, "if one of the subjects of both sides flees, all his property shall be confiscated; moreover he shall be brought back or he shall be punished in a way that it will be a warning for the others."[20]

PERSIA

Both sides wanted a free hand, the Habsburgs to put down the Protestant schismatics in Europe, the sultan to press the Porte's advantage against Persia. In 1546, the Ottoman governor of Baghdad had successfully dislodged his Safavid counterpart in Basra and established nominal control over the city. And Suleiman had a trump card to play, the arrival at his court of Alqās Mirza, the younger brother of Shah Tahmasp, exiled after a failed bid for the throne, and seeking Ottoman help for a renewed bid to secure regime change in Tabriz. Rüstem was accordingly keen to secure the Ottoman western front before turning to Persia. As he remarked to Veltwyck, "the sultan is tired of spending on the frontier 500,000 ducats every year, which is the income of Egypt, and sees also the great reputation and safety with which he can beat the enemy of the other frontier by having peace with both" Charles and Ferdinand.[21]

The defection of Alqās Mirza gave "much delight and joy" to Suleiman, who received him so well that, according to Lüfti Pasha, "Alqās could not have seen in the *vilayet* of Persia such a high and honorable position even in his dreams." This favoritism disturbed the more orthodox among the sultan's subjects. In a letter which he sent to Rüstem Pasha, Şeyh Bali Efendi, one of the leading religious scholars of the period, openly criticized Suleiman's favoritism. Asking "if on our part, we shower honors and favors on Alqās, or someone else, what will be the profit?" Şeyh Bali Efendi added that the Qizilbash "are the seeds of error and sparks... of the infernal fire... Alive or dead, in the Islamic territory they are nothing but harm, and their removal from it is very happiness."[22]

In the event, Alqās Mirza would only succeed in alienating his new compatriots as effectively as he had burned his bridges with his family, a fact reflected in his legacy to history, where he is described as *nâ-sipâs* (unfaithful) or *nâ-haqq-shinâs* (unrighteous) in Persian sources, and *khannas* (whispering Satan) in Ottoman accounts.[23] Nonetheless, this renegade's ostensible conversion having raised the possibility of a client Sunni monarch on the throne of Persia, Suleiman led the army into Anatolia on 29 March 1547. His initial strategic objective was the recapture of Van, which had been seized by Tahmasp after the Ottoman army withdrew at the conclusion of the Two Iraqs campaign in 1535. Alqās, however, urged the sultan to march directly on Tabriz, which fell without resistance, Suleiman formally entering the Safavid capital on 27 July 1547. Once again, the shah refused to meet the Ottomans in open battle. Tahmasp had instead instructed his men to lay waste to the land surrounding Tabriz, "so that no trace of grain or grass remained."[24] Accordingly, it was impossible for the Ottomans to remain in the city for more than four days, as they could find nothing edible for either man or beast, resulting in the death from hunger of several thousand horses and mules. The army took Van during its withdrawal from Tabriz.[25]

Endowing Alqās with a small force with which to penetrate into the Iranian plateau, Suleiman withdrew to Diyarbakır and then Aleppo for the winter. Alqās succeeded in looting Qom and Kashan but was repelled from Isfahan, and as his star waned and his men deserted he fell back to Fars and then Baghdad. His decision to undertake a pilgrimage to the most holy Shia sites in Najaf and Karbala proved the last straw for the Ottoman court. Summoned to account for himself, he fled, seeking sanctuary with the Kurds, who promptly handed him to Tahmasp. The shah had his brother imprisoned in the fortress of Qahqaha in Alamut, where a pair of men whose father had been murdered by Alqās took revenge by hurling him to his death from the battlements. The Ottomans made some minor gains in Georgia in 1548, but the war was clearly sputtering out; Tahmasp would not stand and give Suleiman the decisive battle he wanted, there were no more strategic objectives in Safavid territory worth taking within the orbit of Ottoman logistical capacity, and the expense of maintaining the army in the field was ruinous. Accordingly, the sultan returned to Constantinople on 21 December 1549.

The war of attrition continued to play out in the East, however, and in the absence of the sultan with the main Ottoman field army, the Safavids scored a number of local victories. In early 1550, the Safavids recaptured Shirwan. In 1551, they seized the Ottoman strongholds of Adilcevaz, Erciş, and Ahlat, while İskender Pasha, the *beylerbey* of Erzurum, was defeated by Tahmasp's second son, Ismail Mirza, who took Baku. In 1552, encouraged by the news of Ottoman intervention in Transylvania, Tahmasp drove into eastern Anatolia, taking the castles of Ahlat (slaughtering the garrison after it surrendered on terms) and Erciş. In 1553, Ismail launched another offensive into eastern Anatolia, capturing Akhlar, Arjish, and Erzurum, while in 1554, the Safavids took Tbilisi.

Clearly, the situation on the eastern frontier had deteriorated past the point where the Porte would have to directly intervene. Rüstem was appointed commander-in-chief of the Ottoman force for the projected campaign, departing Constantinople with the vanguard in mid-December 1552. The sultan followed up with the main army on 28 August 1553. But Ottoman progress would become deadlocked by internecine factional infighting with the highest possible stakes in play. The issue was the succession. The leading contender was Mustafa, the son of Suleiman's first concubine, Mahidevran. However, Suleiman's other surviving sons – Selim, Bayezid, and Cihangir – were the children of his favorite concubine,

Hürrem. Mustafa was the preferred choice of the Ottoman rank and file to succeed as sultan, having cultivated a considerable reputation as a patron of scholars and poets. Far more significantly, he commanded the loyalty of the janissaries. But the prominence of Mustafa was being undermined behind the scenes at the Topkapi Palace by the coalition of Grand Vizier Rüstem, his wife (Suleiman's only daughter) Mihrimah, and her mother, Hürrem, who worked in collaboration to facilitate the accession of Selim or Bayezid.

His mind poisoned by the influence of his most intimate advisers, who convinced the sultan his eldest son was amassing support against him in a premature bid for the throne, as Suleiman advanced into Anatolia he sent messengers ahead to Amasya summoning Mustafa to join him at Ereğli. Mustafa was trapped on the horns of an impossible dilemma. Acceding to the summons would be tantamount to throwing himself at the mercy of his enemies, but refusing to attend the sultan would simply confirm their insinuations that he was actively conspiring against his father. Though his mother pleaded with him not to go, Mustafa opted to report to Suleiman. Having surrendered his sword, upon entering the sultan's tent on 6 October he was seized and, under his father's eyes, pitilessly murdered. To deflect the outrage of the Ottoman rank and file, in particular among the janissaries, and prevent it metastasizing into insurrectionary violence, Suleiman ordered Rüstem dismissed from office, elevating Ahmed Pasha in his place.[26]

Adding to the sultan's woes, his youngest son, Cihangir, passed away from natural causes in Aleppo on 27 November. After brooding over his grief that winter, Suleiman marched out in May of the following year, advancing as far as Karabakh in the southern Caucasus, just north of the Araxes above Azerbaijan. Suleiman plundered Revan, Nakhchivan, and Karabakh, seizing much booty and many slaves, but again, the Safavids refused to meet him in open battle, once more scorching the earth as they withdrew before the sultan's advance. The Ottomans entered the completely empty and devastated cities of Erivan on 18 July and Nakhchivan four days later. After destroying a few royal buildings, they withdrew from both cities to Erzurum on 31 July under the pretext that Ramadan was approaching, but in reality because of food shortages and the spread of disease. On 28 September, the sultan departed for Amasya, where he intended to overwinter. The war was concluded the following year by the Treaty of Amasya, arrived at on 29 May 1555. This, the first formal peace treaty between the Ottoman and Safavid empires, recognized the status quo, effectively territorializing the Sunni–Shia divide within Islam. The Ottomans would retain Baghdad, Erzurum, Kars, and Van, while the Safavids maintained their hegemony over Georgia and Azerbaijan. The Safavids also agreed to stop the ritual cursing of the first three caliphs revered by Sunnis during prayers, and in exchange, the Ottomans would allow Safavid pilgrims to visit the holy cities in the Hijaz.[27] In the aftermath, Tahmasp elected to relocate the Safavid capital from Tabriz, rendered too vulnerable by its proximity to the Ottoman frontier, to Qazvin, deeper within the Iranian heartland.

Both sultan and shah were content to let sleeping dogs lie. As the Venetian *bailo* Bernardo Navagero reported to the *Serenissima*, Suleiman "has a nature inclined to quietness and, being old now, he plans to stay in peace; and he will not assemble an army other than for the purpose of defense of his lands unless he is forced by the emperor on this matter."[28]

The sultan would be denied any such opportunity to step back from his responsibilities. Simmering tension between the two rival heirs to the throne, Bayezid and Selim, erupted into outright civil war on 29 May 1559. Suleiman ordered troops led by Sokollu Mehmed Pasha to Konya to support Selim against his brother. Routed, Bayezid sought refuge at the Safavid court, proposing an alliance in order to oust his father and his brother. The proposal no doubt appealed to the shah, especially since it offered ample opportunity for Tahmasp to visit upon the Ottomans the same dynastic disruption they had imposed on him after the defection of his brother, Alqās Mirza, in 1547. But, unwilling to compromise the hard-won peace secured at Amasya, he resisted the temptation. In exchange for a substantive sum in gold, he agreed to extradite Bayezid and his four sons, who, on 25 September 1561, were all summarily garroted.[29] Peace between Constantinople and Isfahan would persist until after the death of the shah in 1576.

Could Persia have been integrated into Western schemes of an alliance against the Ottomans during this period? There were fitful attempts to do so.[30] Venice dispatched ambassadors to the Safavid court – Michele Membré in 1539, Vicenzo d'Alessandri in 1572 – to raise the possibility of joint action against the Porte. King Philip II of Spain reached out to Shah Tahmasp in the late 1550s, with the "understanding that he wants to hurt the common enemy and make war on him." Accordingly, "I very much wish to have his friendship and make arrangements with him. And this is so true that we shake hands and we help each other in any way we can to harm the Great Turk, his lands and lordships. If you fight powerfully by land, I will do the same by sea with a large number of galleys in order to damage the common enemy."[31]

Philip also urged his uncle, the Holy Roman Emperor Ferdinand, not to make peace with the Ottomans but to create an alliance with the shah via

Portugal. Tahmasp did send an envoy in 1561, and Ferdinand, intrigued by the possibilities, immediately suggested that another Persian ambassador be sent with proper credentials so that an "honorable entente and a perpetual league or at least one limited to a number of years" might be concluded.[32] That same year, Pope Pius IV sounded out Portugal's ambassador to the Holy See, Lourenço Pires de Távora, about the possibility of having the Portuguese king act as an intermediary in signing a pact with the Safavid ruler. Meanwhile, Philip II dispatched his own envoy, the English diplomat Sir Richard Shelley, who was supposed to arrive at the court of the shah via Vienna, Poland, and Russia (which had taken Kazan in 1552 and Astrakhan in 1554), then return on the sea route via Hormuz. However, this was aborted when Ferdinand and Suleiman signed an eight-year armistice in 1562.

In 1566, Philip prepared another embassy, headed by Alonso de Tovar, his ambassador in Lisbon. This mission never arrived in Iran. However, in the wake of the Battle of Lepanto, fought on 7 October 1571 (and discussed fully in Chapter 9), King Sebastian I of Portugal drafted correspondence to inform Tahmasp about the Ottoman defeat and the ensuing opportunity to forge an alliance against the Porte. But by the time the Portuguese ambassador, Miguel Abreu de Lima, presented the letters to the shah on 26 February 1575, the Holy League had dissolved. In any event, as Vincenzo d'Alessandri, a resident at the Safavid court, noted, little or nothing could be expected of Tahmasp. The shah had, he said, been immured in his palace for eleven years and cared only for women and money; he had no inclination for war; the country was in a bad state, there was much injustice and the roads were unsafe.[33] On this flat note, any prospect of a Christian–Shia coalition petered out, and the Safavids would be left on their own to fight, and lose, another war with the Ottomans between 1578 and 1590.

Predictably, in the absence of a direct Ottoman threat, the Holy Roman Empire had once more been convulsed by sectional violence. In 1534, at the head of the Schmalkaldic League's army, Landgrave Philip of Hessen forced the Habsburgs to evacuate Württemberg and restore both its former ruler and Lutheran worship. In 1542, Philip and Elector John Frederick of Saxony again deployed League forces when they declared war on Heinrich of Brunswick-Wolfenbüttel. Within the year, they invaded his territory, overthrew and imprisoned Heinrich, and oversaw the conversion of his lands, including the disputed city of Goslar. With the fall of Heinrich, the last hope of Catholicism in the North German Plain faded, as did the greatest barrier to the spread of the Protestant faith. In the years that followed, the seizure of Church possessions escalated.

Meanwhile, back in 1536 Pope Paul III had announced his intention to hold a general council of the Church in the Italian city of Mantua. This never took place, but in 1542 Paul issued a papal bull proclaiming a new general council, to be held at Trent, in order to put an end to the religious disputes between Christian princes in Europe so as to safeguard his flock "against the weapons and stratagems of the infidels," for the sultan, "our impious and merciless enemy, never rested, and took our mutual hatreds and disagreements as a profitable opportunity for himself."

On 10 June 1544, in return for a promise that religious toleration throughout the Holy Roman Empire would continue unchanged until "a general, free Christian council of the German nation" met to resolve all differences, and noting that "one must deem the king of France as much of an enemy to Christendom as the sultan, and use force against him as well as against the Turks," the *Diet* of Speyer authorized Charles to raise 24,000 infantry and 4,000 cavalry "to be employed partly against the Turk, and partly against the French king as it should seem best" to him.[34]

In reality, Charles was interested in war against neither of those external rivals, seeking peace with the Porte and partnership with Francis (through their secret annex to the 18 September 1544 Treaty of Crépy) in order to focus on the internal threat to his authority. This agenda received a further boost on 18 May 1545, when, during the *Diet* of Worms, Charles received a papal envoy, Cardinal Alessandro Farnese, Pope Paul III's secretary of state (and also his grandson), who bore a message that the Holy Father was prepared to assist the emperor with men and money if he agreed to wage war against the Lutherans. Charles had already dispatched an envoy to Constantinople with instructions to liaise with the diplomats sent by Ferdinand and by France in order to seal a deal that would prevent "those who have deviated from our Holy Faith, who call themselves Protestants, from taking advantage of the war in Hungary to reinforce their errors and make exorbitant demands," as they had done so often before. A few days later he informed Farnese that although he welcomed the pope's offer of assistance, it needed to be improved before he could commit to a campaign. A month later a new offer arrived from Rome; if the emperor declared war on the Lutherans now, the pope would contribute 200,000 ducats in cash, with another 100,000 to follow, and also pay for an expeditionary force of 12,000 foot and 500 horse. In addition, Paul III promised to authorize the sale of 500,000 ducats of monastic land in Spain to help finance the war. In Spain, Philip promised to raise a good sum of money "for resistance to the Turk, or, in case he does not come [in person], for subjugation, of those who have strayed [*desviados*]," meaning Germany's Protestants.[35]

On 2 June, Charles wrote to his sister Mary in Brussels that the Ottoman threat was less serious than had been thought, whereas the cardinal had not previously understood how unreasonable the Protestants were: they not only had no interest in sending representatives to Trent but demanded that Charles and Ferdinand give personal guarantees against any hostile action taken by the council. Mary loathed Protestants at least as much as her brother, lamenting how "the accursed sect has expanded so much that it is hard to know who the good Catholics are." However, she warned that even if it were true the Protestants could not be reduced to obedience by peaceful means, her brother ought to ask himself "whether one can reduce them to obedience by force," and "whether it were not better for the good of Christendom to leave them as they are until it pleases God to dispose otherwise."[36] She reminded Charles that a century before, another emperor, Sigismund, had "attempted to reduce the Bohemians [Hussites] by force, and sent several armies against them to that end, assisted by all the princes of Germany, but they never succeeded. In the end they had to leave them as they were."[37]

Matters escalated once it became clear the Council of Trent, which Pope Paul III convened on 13 December, ostensibly intended to serve as a forum for sectarian reconciliation, had immediately devolved into a rubber stamp for the reassertion of Catholic doctrinal absolutism and unconditional papal supremacy. The failure of the *Diet* of Regensburg in 1546 provided Charles with his *casus belli*. As he wrote to Mary on 9 June:

> The heretic Princes and Electors have decided not to attend the Diet in person; indeed they are determined to rise in revolt immediately the Diet is over, to the utter destruction of the spiritual [Catholic] lords and to the great peril of the King of the Romans [Ferdinand] and ourself. If we hesitate now we shall lose all. Thus we have determined, my brother and the Duke of Bavaria, that force alone will drive them to accept reasonable terms… unless we take immediate action all the Estates of Germany may lose their faith, and the Netherlands may follow.[38]

In March 1547, Paul III prorogued the Council of Trent and ordered that it reconvene in Bologna, in the Papal States, where no Protestant delegates could possibly be expected to come. Having mobilized papal and imperial reinforcements from Italy (in flagrant violation of his election agreement never to bring foreign troops into Germany), Charles went onto the offensive, winning a total victory over John Frederick at Mühlberg in Electoral Saxony on 23 April 1547. The elector was taken prisoner, the Schmalkaldic League's other leading figures such

Throughout the reign of Bayezid I (1389–1402) his exploits in battle expanded Ottoman frontiers both east and west, earning him the sobriquet *Yildirim* (the Thunderbolt).

Mehmed II earned his sobriquet *Fātiḥ* (the Conqueror) during his reign (1444–46, 1451–81) when he seized the prize that had eluded generations of Muslim warlords by taking Constantinople in 1453.

During the short reign (1512–20) of Selim I *Yāvuz* (the Grim) he reimposed central authority in Constantinople, demarcated the eastern frontier at Chaldiran in 1514, and overwhelmed the Mamluks in 1516–17.

Suleiman I accumulated titles including "Sultan of Sultans of East and West, world conqueror of the domains of Rum [Rome], Persia and Arabia, Hero of the Cosmos, Master of the Earth and Time" during his reign (1520–66).

Ismail I, founder of the Safavid dynasty, shah of Persia (1501–24). He reasserted Iranian national identity after centuries of foreign domination.

Tahmasp I, the second Safavid shah (1524–76), had to balance his realm's interests against those of the Ottomans to the west and the Mughals to the east.

Holy Roman Emperor Charles V dominated both Europe and the New World, but sectarian and geopolitical constraints shattered his dreams of a universal empire during his reign.

Charles V delegated to his brother, Ferdinand, archduke of Austria, the task of holding the line against the Turks in the Balkans. He succeeded as Holy Roman Emperor in 1556.

This miniature from the 16th-century Ottoman illustrated manuscript the *Hünername* depicts the Battle of Nicopolis (25 September 1396). Turkish forces, sweeping from right to left, rout the Crusader army into the Danube. The fate of the captive being led away in the lower right-hand corner was unlikely to have been a happy one; Sultan Bayezid I ordered the bulk of the prisoners taken executed.

The setting sun breaks through the clouds at the conclusion of the Battle of Varna (10 November 1444), illuminating the body of King Vladislaus I of Hungary in this 19th-century painting by Stanisław Chlebowski. The king had led an assault on Sultan Murad II's camp, only to be cut down just short of final victory. More in sorrow than in triumph, the sultan gestures to the peace treaty which was broken by the Hungarians at the behest of the papacy.

The 1453 Ottoman siege of Constantinople, depicted in this near contemporary print, is oriented with east at the top. The "city of cities" dominates the peninsula jutting into the Bosporus, with the Sea of Marmara to the right and Golden Horn to the left, cut off by the chain connecting Constantinople to Galata. Note the pontoon bridge built by the Ottomans across the Golden Horn connecting their outlying units on the north bank to their siege lines on the south; the route they took to haul their ships overland and into the Golden Horn; and the towers of the Palace of Blachernae, dominating the northwest corner of the city's defenses.

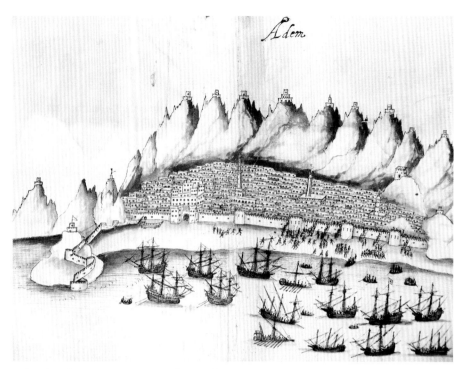

The abortive Portuguese assault on Aden (1513) is depicted in this illustration from the 16th-century *Lendas da Índia* of Gaspar Correia, who served as a scrivener to Afonso de Albuquerque, the viceroy of the *Estado da Índia*, and a possible eyewitness to this campaign. The formidable nature of the city's defenses is clear.

Mounted on a white horse, the Safavid Shah Ismail I dominates the center of this 19th-century Iranian composition of the Battle of Chaldiran (23 August 1514). The key to Ismail's first defeat is in the background: Ottoman artillery firing in a disciplined line. Through this technological edge, Sultan Selim I would emerge victorious against the Safavids and the Mamluks. It was the dawn of a new military era in the Middle East.

The Palace of the Grand Master still exudes a solemn authority in contemporary Rhodes. For over two centuries this imposing structure was the headquarters of the Knights Hospitaller. After Suleiman the Magnificent accepted the surrender of Grand Master Philippe de Villiers de L'Isle-Adam at the conclusion of the bitter siege of 1522, the sultan remarked, "It saddens me to be compelled to cast this brave old man out of his home."

This jousting sallet helmet was crafted for King Louis II of Hungary. The initials L and M, for Louis and his wife, Mary of Austria, are featured. Louis did not survive his defeat at the Battle of Mohács on 29 August 1526; fleeing the field on horseback, he was thrown into a stream and drowned under the weight of his armor.

The Ottoman victory at the Battle of Mohács (1526) was a turning point in the history of Eastern Europe. The death of King Louis II ended both the Jagiellon line and the existence of a unitary Hungarian state. From its role as the *scutum atque murus* (shield and rampart) of Christendom in the Balkans, Hungary was reduced to fragments contested between Vienna and Constantinople for the next two centuries.

These prints illuminate two key moments during the 1529–43 Ethiopian–Adal War. In the upper panel, Ethiopian churches go up in flames in the aftermath of the Battle of Wofla (28 August 1542), while Adal warlord Grañ is gunned down at the Battle of Wayna Daga (21 February 1543) in the lower panel. This conflict was of both national significance and a proxy war between Ottoman and Portuguese imperial interests.

The spire of St Stephen's Cathedral dominates the horizon in this print depicting the Ottoman siege of Vienna (1529). This campaign should have been just another high-water mark in the inexorable advance of the Turkish banner under Sultan Suleiman the Magnificent, who had already triumphed at Belgrade (1521), Rhodes (1522), and Mohács (1526).

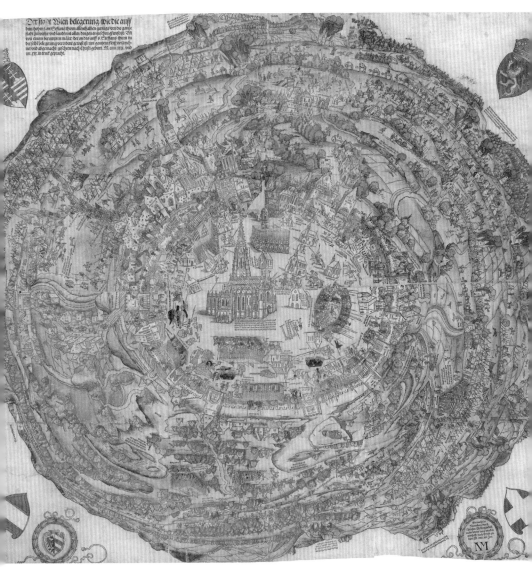

This 360-degree panorama depicting the Ottoman siege of Vienna (1529) is as close to a real-time perspective as was possible in the 16th century. Shortly after the siege was broken, a publisher from Nuremberg, Niklas Meldeman, arrived in Vienna and purchased sketches from an artist who had recorded his observations from the spire of St Stephen's Cathedral. He had this interpretation engraved, the first edition being in print by May 1530.

Suleiman the Magnificent consults with his inner circle of advisers (*divan*) at the frustrating climax to the unsuccessful Ottoman siege of Vienna (1529). Atrocious weather and the resistance of the garrison ultimately compelled the sultan to withdraw, his first setback since taking the throne nine years earlier. The official Ottoman line was that the campaign had been a success, the lands of the infidels being "wasted with fire." In fact, Vienna would define the limit of Ottoman expansion into Europe.

VII

TVNETAM CAESAR, BELLI VIRTVTE TRIVMPHANS,
INGREDITVR VICTOR, CEDENS FVGIT ILICET AFER. 1535.

For Charles V, the apotheosis of his reign was leading the successful siege of Tunis in 1535. Here, imperial troops enter the city, Charles mounted and in full armor at right. He earned the plaudits he accrued from this expedition; an amphibious operation was always a risk and he successfully coordinated the financing, recruitment, logistics, and supply chains necessary for such an offensive.

On the face of it, a partnership between the Catholic king of France and the Ottoman sultan would seem improbable, but Francis I and Suleiman I found their mutual antagonism towards the Habsburgs lent itself towards an alliance of convenience. This reached its apogee in 1543 when an Ottoman fleet under its legendary admiral Hayreddin (Barbarossa) linked up with its French counterpart to lay siege to Habsburg-aligned Nice.

This statue of Jean Parisot de Valette, the forty-ninth Grand Master of the Order of the Knights of St John, still stands today in the city that bears his name, Valletta, in recognition of his indomitable leadership in defending Malta during the Ottoman siege of 1565. Having joined the Knights Hospitaller as a young man, Valette would serve the Order with distinction, surviving the siege of Rhodes in 1522 and a year as a galley slave after defeat and capture at sea in 1541, rising to become governor of Tripoli in 1546, and succeeding as Grand Master in 1557, serving in that role until his death in 1568.

This map, one of forty panels rendered by Ignazio Danti that still decorate the Galleria delle Carte Geografiche in the Vatican, was commissioned by Pope Gregory XIII to commemorate the successful defense of Malta against the Ottoman siege of 1565. The map is oriented with west at the top; the Sciberras peninsula dominates the middle of the panel, with the fortress of St Elmo at its tip, Marsamxett Harbour to its north (left), and Grand Harbour to the south (right), punctured by the urbanized and fortified peninsulas of Birgu and Senglea.

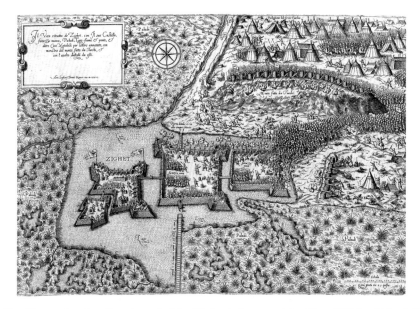

The Hungarian frontier stronghold of Szigetvár earned its title of "Island Castle" from the quasi-aquatic nature of the surrounding terrain. From the mid-16th century onwards, the name had a double meaning as the fortress stood as an island of Habsburg imperial resolve in territory increasingly absorbed into the Ottoman orbit.

This 1825 painting by Johann Peter Kraft immortalizes the last moments of Count Nicholas IV of Zrin, a Croatian aristocrat who became an icon of Hungarian national resistance for his defense of Szigetvár in 1566. Thirty-four days after the siege commenced, he led the last survivors in a final defiant sally on 7 September.

This fresco painted by Giorgio Vasari for the Vatican depicts the two fleets at the Battle of Lepanto (7 October 1571). On the left are three allegorical figures personifying the core allies of the Holy League; Spain, in full armor; the papacy, wearing the papal tiara and holding the key to the kingdom of Heaven; and Venice, accoutered as the doge. On the opposite side are three figures embodying Terror, Weakness, and Death to represent the Ottoman Empire.

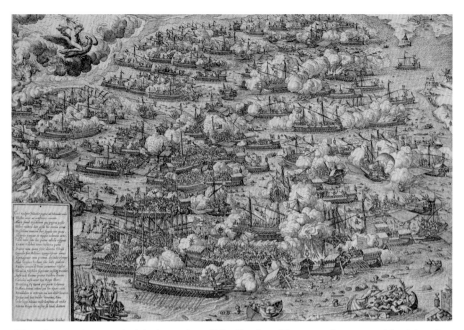

The almost claustrophobic intensity of the Battle of Lepanto is captured in this print published the following year to commemorate the triumph of the Holy League. The heavy guns mounted on board each vessel took their grim toll as the lines closed, but once they came together, desperate hand-to-hand action raged across the narrow decks for hours until one side finally broke.

Detail from the 16th-century *Suleymanname* depicting an Ottoman *akinji* light cavalry raider (right) hauling a defeated, dismounted, and lassoed Hungarian *chevalier* (left) off the battlefield. For many combatants, the primary motivation for participation in warfare during the early modern period was not national pride or religious devotion but financial gain. The taking of prisoners, destined either for ransom or the slave markets, was a regular feature of any campaign.

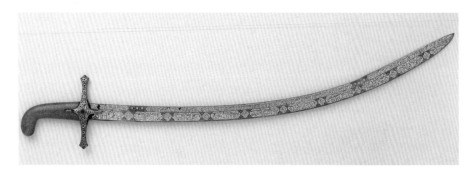

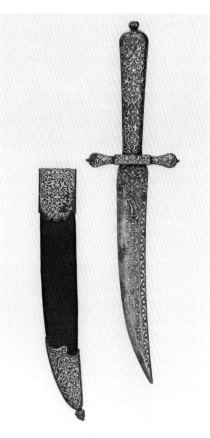

These three items reflect top of the line Ottoman military industrial production.
The saber is fitted with one of the finest and best-preserved Islamic blades of
the 16th century. Its gold inlaid decoration consists of Qur'anic inscriptions that
stress the sovereignty of God and the wisdom and power of his servant Solomon,
likely allusions to Sultan Suleiman the Magnificent. The helmet was forged from
watered steel and decorated in gold with arabesques and Qur'anic inscriptions.
The dagger has been fitted with a hilt and sheath damascened with gold
arabesques. The blade is inscribed in Persian text with a short poem celebrating
its role in the violent end to a lover's quarrel.

as Philip of Hesse soon surrendered as well, and at last a triumphant Charles seemed in a position to order the affairs of his empire as he wished.

Contributing to this newfound imperial confidence was a dramatic turnaround in Habsburg financial fortunes, which had reached a nadir in 1547 when the ever-faithful secretary of state, Francisco de los Cobos, died on 10 May while the critical cash cow of Peru was torn apart by a civil war between Crown loyalists and partisans of Gonzalo Pizarro (the half-brother of the assassinated conquistador, Francisco) that only ended with the defeat and execution of the rebel leader on 10 April 1548. By July of that year, all but 132,000 ducats in estimated Spanish revenues for 1549 had already been pre-pledged to service existing loans. A cashflow shortfall of 868,000 ducats loomed, and no investor, including Anton Fugger, was likely to accept another round of *juros* without an identifiable stream of unpledged income.

It was the Americas that came to the rescue. Two unexpected mining strikes in 1545–46 – one at Zacatecas in the northern Chichimeca territory of Mexico and a second, even larger one at Cerro de Potosi in Bolivia – changed everything. By 1548, Potosi had achieved a staggering annual output of 195 tons of silver, nine times that of Joachimstahl at its peak.[39] This not only revivified Habsburg imperial fortunes, but kickstarted European capital markets generally, enabling the West to finally and definitively shrug off the great bullion famine that had been dragging at its heels over the past two centuries.

Charles now sought to impose unity throughout his empire by instating the Augsburg Interim at the 1548 *Diet* of Augsburg. The Interim (which offered significant compromises – it recognized the existence of married clergy and allowed the laity to receive communion in both kinds) was intended to maintain order until the Council of Trent could recommence, at which point all German delegates would be persuaded to attend and contribute towards healing the religious grievances which had long troubled the Holy Roman Empire and Europe.

Meanwhile, the five-year treaty of 1547 between the Habsburgs and Porte had not even run its course when fighting broke out again in the Balkans, precipitated by the Porte's uncovering of secret negotiations between Ferdinand and the double-dealing governor of Transylvania, Martinuzzi. Despite having himself faced down two Habsburg sieges, Martinuzzi was convinced Hungary's destiny ultimately devolved upon Vienna, not Constantinople. At Nyírbátor on 8 September 1549, Martinuzzi came to an arrangement with Ferdinand's general, Nicholas Graf III von Salm, whereby Isabella and Sigismund would surrender Transylvania to Ferdinand in exchange for the Silesian duchy of Oppeln and Ratibor, plus 100,000 gold florins.

In response, Isabella sought to have John Sigismund, then not yet ten years of age, immediately crowned, and when that gambit was thwarted by Martinuzzi, convened a *diet* at Aiud on March 15 in a bid to have the regent removed from office. Though Martinuzzi had accumulated powerful enemies, including *voivodes* Elias II of Moldavia and Mircea IV of Wallachia, he still retained the upper hand politically. The *diet* dissolved, forcing Isabella and Sigismund to seek sanctuary in Alba Iulia. When word of this reached Constantinople, Suleiman was incensed; in August 1550 he tasked the Transylvanian estates with two alternatives in relation to Martinuzzi – either "cut off his head or supply him alive to the king's son [Sigismund], so that the country not be lost for the sake of such a rogue."[40]

Well aware an Ottoman military response would ensue the following campaign season, Martinuzzi appealed to Vienna for aid. On 27 April 1551, Ferdinand ordered a force under Giovanni Battista Castaldo, the margrave of Cassiano, to enter Hungary in support of the friar, whose forces laid siege to Alba Iulia from 19 May to June 10. After protracted negotiations, in which she secured the additional concession that Ferdinand would pledge his youngest daughter, Joanna (then only four years old) in marriage to Sigismund, in the Treaty of Sebeş on 19 July, Isabella agreed to abdicate in the name of her son and surrender the crown of St Stephen, this agreement being confirmed by the *Diet* of Cluj-Napoca the following month. Martinuzzi remained regent of Transylvania, and was ordained archbishop of Esztergom. On 12 October, Pope Julius III named him a cardinal, with permission to wear the habit of his order instead of a cardinal's robes.

Meanwhile, an Ottoman army under the *beylerbey* of Rumelia, Sokollu Mehmed Pasha, had departed Sofia on 10 July, seizing Bečej on 19 September. This site would subsequently be second only to Szeged as an Ottoman port and river crossing point on the lower Tisza River, especially during campaigns and raids against the castles of the Timişoara region. Sokollu also took Zrenjanin, where the garrison was commanded by friar Djordje Martinović, on 25 September, Cenad, which guarded a crossing point on the Mureş River (a tributary of the Tisza), and Lipova on 8 October, before moving south to besiege Timişoara itself. The outstanding defense of this stronghold, commanded by Stephan Lasonczy, and the approach of winter forced Sokollu to lift the siege on 16 November and pull back to Belgrade.

While the Ottoman army had been stymied at Timişoara, a Habsburg army under the joint command of Castaldo and Martinuzzi had arrived under the walls of Lipova, where the Ottoman garrison was commanded by Ulama Bey, the *sanjak-bey* of Požega, to commence its own siege on 3 November. All the while, Martinuzzi continued to communicate with Constantinople, dispatching regular tributes and assuring the Porte he was playing a long game in Ottoman interests. This double-dealing would ultimately prove his undoing. Castaldo was baffled by the intrigues of his ostensible partner; "I believe that he is more of a Turk than a Christian, and more of a Lucifer than Saint John," the general wrote to Ferdinand on 30 November; "Please God, enlighten me on what to do with this man."[41] Martinuzzi finally negotiated an end to the siege, allowing Ulama Bey and his surviving men to surrender Lipova on terms and evacuate the town during the evening of 4 December. But once the escort provided by Martinuzzi withdrew, the Ottoman column walked into an ambush set by Castaldo. Though wounded, Ulama Bey escaped, bearing word of this treachery to Constantinople. Martinuzzi, already under suspicion in his own camp, now lost all credit with the Porte. It was the Habsburgs who struck the decisive blow. On the evening of 17 December, Castaldo had Martinuzzi murdered, the sixty-nine-year-old cardinal finally succumbing to seventy-three amateurishly inflicted knife, sword, and gunshot wounds. Outraged, the pope excommunicated Ferdinand, Castaldo, and the lead assassin, Sforza Pallavicino. At the conclusion of an investigation by the Curia, during which 116 witnesses were called and a report with eighty-seven articles was compiled, Martinuzzi was found guilty of treason. On 4 February 1555, a papal bull was issued absolving Ferdinand and his associates.

Since Suleiman considered his war against the Safavids more pressing, he entrusted the reconquest of Transylvania to Sokollu Mehmed Pasha, Hadım Ali Pasha, governor-general of Buda, and Second Vizier Kara Ahmed Pasha, who was appointed commander-in-chief (*serdar*) of the campaign. The Ottoman onslaught of 1552 was irresistible. Over the course of that year, Kara Ahmed Pasha took a total of twenty-one fortresses (among them ten royal castles) from the Hungarians, keeping five of them and demolishing the rest.

Of the major urban centers, Szeged and Veszprém were taken before the Ottomans secured control of the Temes River when Timişoara fell at the end of July, its defenders massacred after surrendering on guarantees of their safety. Forewarned of their impending fate by that example, the garrison of Lipova simply fled, leaving the town to be occupied without a fight. The Ottomans then took Arad on the Maros River, opening the Maros valley towards Transylvania, and in early September, took Szolnok, and with it the only permanent bridge over the Tisza along the main military corridor leading to Buda.

Kara Ahmed Pasha conquered the entirety of the Banat region and a significant part of Slavonia, annexing vast new territories to the Ottoman Empire. He then marched on to Eger, possession of which would enable him to isolate Transylvania from Habsburg-controlled Hungary. But it was here the Ottoman juggernaut finally ground to a halt. The garrison of 1,500 professional troops and fewer than 1,000 local peoples under the command of Baron István Dobó held out against a besieging force more than twenty times their number for thirty-nine days before the Ottomans, running low on food stocks and ammunition, finally withdrew on 17 October under the shroud of an early winter.[42]

While the primary focus for 1552 was Transylvania, the Ottomans also made considerable progress in a secondary offensive into Slavonia. In addition to taking thirteen strongholds of various sizes, Mehmed Pasha, the *bey* of Sarajevo, and Ulama Bey, the *sanjak-bey* of Požega, seized Virovitica and then proceeded towards Zagreb, reaching the Čazma River and capturing the fortress of the same name, which was subsequently renamed Zacaşna and became the center of a new *sanjak*.[43] Thus, Ulama Bey secured his revenge for the treachery after the surrender of Lipova the previous year.[44]

In the summer of 1552, Hadım Ali Pasha further expanded Ottoman authority through Transdanubia by taking Veszprém and Várpalota in the vicinity of Lake Balaton. In the north, he annexed the fortresses of Drégely, Ságvár, Gyarmat, Szécsény, Hollókő, and Buják, while also bringing a large part of the area between the Drava and Sava rivers under Ottoman authority. His complete victory over a combined German and Hungarian army led by Erasmus von Teuffel in a two-day battle at Plášťovce on 9–10 August consummated these conquests.

Suleiman could be well pleased with the performance of his subordinates. The demonstrable Ottoman military hegemony enforced the Porte's political authority, as Transylvania was subsumed into a new *beylerbeyilik*, Timişoara, now recognized as the *sedd-i sugur-ı İslamiyye* (rampart of the frontiers of Islam). It was true that the new territories ran at a loss to the Ottoman treasury. However, they greatly enhanced the Porte's strategic position in relation to its Habsburg rival. And to the sultan's delight, in March 1553, Castaldo, commanding Habsburg forces in Transylvania, was forced out of the country. The Transylvanian magnates insisted that if Ferdinand was unable to protect them against the Turks, he should let them recall Isabella and Sigismund from Poland.

In 1554, Toygun Pasha of Buda occupied the fortress at Fiľakovo, establishing there the northernmost Hungarian *sanjak* administrative center in the Ottoman Empire. One of the few strongholds left in Habsburg hands was Szigetvár, which rapidly evolved into a major thorn in the Ottoman flank. In 1555, Toygun Pasha advanced into Habsburg territory, taking the castles of Kaposvár, Nagybajom, Korotna, and Babócsa, but he arrived late at Szigetvár, in mid-October, and the stout defense of the garrison, coupled with the approach of winter, compelled him to withdraw.

Ferdinand could not call upon his brother the emperor for aid because, once again, the Holy Roman Empire was being consumed with sectional strife. Charles V should have been sitting pretty in 1550. He had outlived his archrival Francis (1547), halted the territorial expansion of the Schmalkaldic League (1547), crushed the Gonzalo Pizarro rebellion in Peru (1548), and was in the midst of a five-year truce with Constantinople (1548–53). If that were not enough, his huge debt burden had been eased by the spectacular returns from Cerro de Potosi, Zacatecas, and the fledgling gold fields of upper Colombia. An annual contribution of nearly two tons of Colombian gold, nearly one-fifth of global supply, had helped to triple the value of American treasure imports to around 1 million gold pesos annually between 1541 and 1550. Additional gold strikes at Buriticá and Popayán would help to double these annual totals to nearly 2 million gold pesos in 1551–55.

But Charles was stricken with the same fatal curse that had afflicted his hapless grandfather Maximilian I – the more money he had, the more he spent. Virtually all of the emperor's American treasure shipments had already been pledged to securitize his escalating debts in Europe. The expansion of the Habsburg revenue base in the Americas merely generated fresh sources of unpledged cash flow to collateralize even more ambitious military campaigns and the assumption of even larger amounts of public debt. The cost of the emperor's triumph at Muhlberg in 1547 was nearly four times the price of his defeat at Algiers in 1541. Charles borrowed a staggering 1.2 million ducats per year between 1543 and 1551 – nearly twice the level borrowed annually in 1533–42 – obliging him to confiscate an unprecedented 2 million ducats of American treasure upon its arrival at Seville in October 1550 alone.[45]

Worst of all, this escalating death spiral of expenditure and obligation was contributing nothing towards imposing, let alone enhancing, the emperor's authority over his enemies, domestic or foreign. Cowed but unbroken by their defeat in 1547, the leading Protestant Imperial princes – Elector Maurice of Saxony, Duke John Albert I of Mecklenburg, Prince William IV of Hesse (whose father was still imprisoned by order of the emperor, alongside John Frederick), the Hohenzollern margrave Albert Alcibiades of Brandenburg-Kulmbach, and his cousin Duke Albert of Prussia – met at Lochau Castle near Torgau in May 1551 to strategize. The outcome was the Treaty of Chambord, an agreement signed on 15 January 1552 with King Henry II of France, seeking his support in a war against Charles, offering in exchange to concede the Imperial cities of Metz, Toul, Verdun, Cambrai, "and other towns of the [Holy Roman] Empire that do not speak German." Thus did the Catholic king of France add a partnership with the Protestant rebels to his alliance with the Islamic Ottoman Empire.

While the Protestant magnates luxuriated in French subsidies, Charles, his credit exhausted, was impotent to contain them: "I find neither in Augsburg nor elsewhere any man who will lend to me, howsoever large a profit be offered to him."[46] Maurice nearly captured the emperor himself at Innsbruck on the evening of 19 May, forcing Charles to flee ignominiously into the night across the mountains for the Carinthian town of Villach. Now bankrupt and isolated, Charles had no option but to appease the Lutherans. He allowed Ferdinand to negotiate the 15 August 1552 Peace of Passau, mandating no party adhering to the terms of the Confession of Augsburg "may by means of force, or in any other way, be compelled from his religion and faith to act against his own conscience and will." Charles hoped this compromise would enable him to carry on the war against France with a united empire behind him. His hopes were finally dashed by the disastrous failure of his ill-advised winter siege of Metz (23 October 1552–1 January 1553) and his defeat by the French under Duke Francis of Guise at the Battle of Renty on 13 August 1554. Having accumulated a jaw-dropping 17.6 million ducats in *juro* debt, Charles had no option other than to pre-pledge all of Spain's projected revenues (including American treasure) through 1559.[47]

The emperor had to endure one last humiliation. The terms of the Peace of Passau were reaffirmed on 25 September 1555 by the Peace of Augsburg and its declaration *Cuius regio, eius religio* (He who rules, his the religion), by which the individual princes and lords of the Holy Roman Empire were empowered to unilaterally make the decision whether their territories be Catholic or Lutheran, free from Imperial direction. Those of either denomination who now found themselves in the minority and who elected to migrate would be "hindered neither in the sale of their estates after due payment of the local taxes nor injured in their honor." Church property in Lutheran hands in 1552 was accepted as being definitively lost to the papacy. This agreement mandated official recognition of the inevitable – a religious division of Habsburg inheritance.[48] It represented the definitive failure of everything Charles had fought towards over the past thirty-five years. Instead of spiritual unity, there was now a legal framework for sectarian difference. Rather than the Holy Roman Empire becoming consolidated as a unitary state, its federalism had advanced to another level. It broke the emperor. He commenced the process of laying down his powers by abdicating as king of Spain and Sicily in favor of his son Philip on 16 January 1556. Ferdinand succeeded his brother as Holy Roman Emperor on 27 August 1556, and Charles passed into exile, finally shuffling off this mortal coil on 21 September 1558.

Whilst negotiating the unraveling of Habsburg and papal aspirations to hegemony in Christendom, Ferdinand, simultaneously under immense pressure from the unrelenting Ottoman advance in Hungary, dispatched Ferenc Zay and Antun Vrančić to Constantinople in 1553 to seek terms from the Porte. The following year, he also appointed the Flemish writer and diplomat Ogier Ghislain de Busbecq to join them. They were authorized to offer an additional annual tribute of up to 140,000 florins in exchange for Ottoman recognition of Habsburg rule in Transylvania and Hungary. The best they could do was secure a six-month truce. Having concluded the Treaty of Amasya with the Safavids to take the pressure off his eastern frontier, Suleiman now ordered mobilization for a fresh campaign in the Balkans the following year.

Seeing the writing on the wall, the Transylvanian *Diet* sent word to Ferdinand in December 1555: "We were happy to be ruled by a Christian prince and to be affiliated with the Holy Roman Emperor," but the tide had clearly turned in favor of the Porte; "Therefore, we ask Your Majesty for one of the two things: either to help us so that we can resist Süleyman, or to be so kind as to absolve us of our oath." The magnates did not wait for an answer. In January 1556, at the *Diet* of Torda, they recalled Isabella and Sigismund. In March, at the *Diet* of Sebeş, they swore allegiance to "the son of King John." Isabella and Sigismund arrived in Kolozsvár on 22 September.[49]

The following year, the new *beylerbey* of Buda, Hadım Ali Pasha, arrived under the walls of Szigetvár on 10 June. Led by Marko Horváth Stančić, the defenders withstood the ensuing forty-two-day siege. Szigetvár would have fallen, were it not for the intervention of a Habsburg force led by the Palatine Támas Nádasdy, captain general of Transdanubia, and Horváth's patron, who laid siege to the nearby Ottoman fortress of Babócsa on 18 July. Ali broke the siege of Szigetvár to relieve Babócsa but was defeated in a two-day battle on the banks of the Rinya River by Miklós Zrínyi, *ban* of Croatia and Slavonia. In August, Ferdinand's son, Archduke Ferdinand, arrived with another army and on 15 September he recaptured Korotna, massacring all the defenders in the aftermath, which induced the garrisons of the surrounding Ottoman strongholds, including Babócsa, to capitulate. Ali pulled back to Pécs, then to Buda for the winter.[50] When Horváth died in 1561, Zrínyi requested and was granted the position of chief captain at Szigetvár and administrator (*provisor*) of its estates.

In 1559, Isabella called upon a magnate ally, Menyhárt Balassa, to rid her of erstwhile supporters whom she now saw as enemies. For his reward, Balassa received the city of Satu Mare; at Sigismund's direction, he strengthened the citadel, and stocked it with artillery. Then in 1561 Balassa switched to the side of Ferdinand, giving the Habsburgs a fortified base that projected their power beyond the upper Tisza. When Balassa confiscated the income from the wine harvest in Tokaj, his action was vigorously protested by Sigismund, who dispatched forces under Stephen IX Báthory, the future *voivode* of Transylvania and king of Poland–Lithuania, supported by Mustafa Pasha, the *beylerbey* of Timişoara. But in a series of running skirmishes that lasted for much of 1562 it was Balassa, supported by Habsburg troops from Kassa (Košice), who had the better of the fighting, seizing and defending Satu Mare, Ardud, and Baia Mare.

Protracted negotiations at the Porte finally resulted in a new Habsburg–Ottoman Treaty of Constantinople in 1562, succeeding the 1547 Treaty of Edirne, in which Ferdinand renounced his claims to Transylvania and agreed to continue providing the Porte with the annual submission of 30,000 florins. The Habsburg ambassador, de Busbecq, did obtain a clause in the treaty by which Suleiman agreed that Ferdinand and his vassals – including, by name, Balassa – could freely possess what they now held outside of Transylvania proper. The treaty would be in effect for eight years.[51]

SZIGETVÁR

Inevitably, hostilities broke out again after less than a quarter of that term had expired. In 1564, Balassa started a new round of skirmishing by building a fortress on what the Transylvanians claimed was their territory. Later that year, Báthory's local partisans staged a coup, wresting Szatmár back to Sigismund's allegiance.

Most of Maximilian's advisers advocated for an immediate military response, but the cautious Archduke Ferdinand did not think Satu Mare was worth the risk of a war. Opting for a compromise, Maximilian ordered a sizable increase of the garrison of the Habsburg outpost at Kisvárda, beyond the Tisza, but north and west of Satu Mare. Meanwhile, Sigismund, supported by Mustafa Pasha, the *beylerbey* of Timişoara, and Arslan Pasha, the *beylerbey* of Buda, had already launched an offensive, and he occupied Kisvárda before the Habsburg reinforcements arrived. At Tokaj, he crossed the Tisza on a pontoon bridge (leaving his Ottoman allies behind on the left bank), and headed north towards Košice, the anchor-fortress on the Habsburg defensive line in Upper Hungary. Stalled by heavy rains, he had to pull back, leaving his artillery at Tokaj.

Ferdinand I died on 25 July, leaving the finances of his dynasty in a catastrophic condition. When Maximilian and his two brothers – Archduke Ferdinand and Archduke Charles – divided their father's debts, the total was found to exceed 12 million gulden. In Upper Hungary alone, current arrears in wages for the border garrisons amounted to 180,000 florins.[52]

Nonetheless, Maximilian decided to counterattack. To pay for a new army, he mortgaged properties, took out loans, and granted titles. To lead his forces, Maximilian obtained permission from his uncle, Philip II, to hire a veteran commander of Spanish forces in the Low Countries, Lazarus von Schwendi. To give him a co-commander who knew Upper Hungary well, Maximilian chose András Báthory, from the pro-Habsburg branch of the extended Báthory clan.

Habsburg troops departed from Košice on 1 February 1565, with an artillery train of thirty-three guns. The city of Tokaj was taken, and the besiegers were able to storm the fortress, which guarded a vital river crossing on an island in the Tisza, a few days later. The cannon were then hauled across the ice to the left bank of the Tisza. At Satu Mare, Báthory gave orders to burn the fortress; since the Szamos River was likewise frozen solid, he could not have withstood a siege. Schwendi and Báthory left a garrison in Satu Mare, and started construction of a new fortress, but the co-commanders soon quarreled, and Báthory chose to return to his estates. Schwendi's troops proceeded to capture two other strongholds, Baia Mare, near the Transylvanian border, and Ardud, south of Satu Mare. They discussed a march south to Oradea, but Maximilian rejected the idea lest it provoke a wider war.

Stephen Báthory was sent by Sigismund to offer terms. The Treaty of Szatmár (Satu Mare, 13 March 1565) stipulated that Sigismund would retain Transylvania, with Johanna of Austria, Maximilian's youngest sister, as his bride, while conceding the four counties in Upper Hungary that included Satu Mare, Mukachevo, Khust, and Tokaj, retaining only Bihor County, including Orodea.

Sigismund was only stalling for time, as he dispatched missives to his Ottoman patrons imploring them for support in upholding his claims. Seeking to avert Ottoman intervention, in a letter to Suleiman dated 9 June 1565, Maximilian offered to return Szerencs and Tokaj, but only if Sigismund agreed to pay the costs of the war – thus admitting responsibility for breaching the peace. This offer was accompanied by gifts for the sultan and his viziers, as a token of Habsburg esteem, but not the obligatory 30,000 florins in tribute for 1565.

The Porte was preoccupied with preparations for the coming invasion of Malta and did not want to be distracted by a conflict in the Balkans. However, it could not allow a key vassal to be dispossessed without a response. That summer, Ottoman forces joined Sigismund's army at Debrecen. One detachment seized Pâncota, while Hasan Pasha of Timişoara joined Sigismund in a march on Satu Mare. An attack on Schwendi's camp (on the left bank of the Szamos) was turned back, but after a seven-week siege Transylvanian and Ottoman troops forced the surrender of Ardud, where Hasan Pasha massacred the garrison, and burned the fortress. Hasan Pasha then bridged the Szamos to pursue Habsburg troops fleeing towards Kisvárda. Baia Mare also fell to the Ottomans, as the conflict continued to metastasize, spreading and drawing in more combatants; Sokollu Mustafa Bey, the *sanjak-bey* of Bosnia, was defeated in battle at Obreška, east of Zagreb, in Croatia on 10 September.

On 7 October 1565, the sultan wrote to Sigismund that he would go to war the following spring if he did not receive an ambassador from Maximilian with suitable assurances of peace. Yet the mood in Vienna was now resigned to a full-scale confrontation in the new year, and negotiations functionally ended when Maximilian refused to submit the tribute for 1565 and made no commitments concerning the return of Tokaj and other Habsburg conquests.

Domestic politics also influenced decision making in the Porte. Upon the death of Grand Vizier Semiz Ali Pasha in June 1565, Second Vizier Sokollu Mehmed was promoted to his place. By keeping Suleiman on his side during the upcoming campaign, Sokullu made sure that if the aging sultan died, he could influence the succession, ensuring Selim – Sokollu's father-in-law – succeeded to the throne.

The original start date for the campaign had been set at 5 April 1566. However, owing to the ill health of the seventy-two-year-old sultan, this was pushed back to 29 April. The specific strategic objective for the campaign – if there was one – remains unknown. Contemporaries were sure it had to be Vienna. According to Ferenc Forgách, the bishop of Oradea, Suleiman "started this last and large-scale campaign with such a huge army and with the aim of not leaving Gyula, the only significant castle held by the enemy, behind his back and capturing it, he would unite his forces, and breaking through the only gate of Hungary, he would march toward Austria."[53] If so, the campaign represented Suleiman's third – and, he must have known, last – attempt to take the city that had slipped from his grasp in 1529 and 1532. In any event, he would have been gratified to know that panic gripped the streets in the Imperial capital. The Spanish ambassador to the court of the Holy Roman Emperor, the Sieur de Chantonnay, Thomas Perrenot de Granvelle, observed that "the fear at the arrival of the Turks and the downheartedness of our men" was such that, "From Vienna and the vicinity many people are escaping, as if the siege was actually happening."[54]

After marching out from Constantinople, the Ottoman army arrived at Belgrade on 19 June. Since the Sava River was unexpectedly in flood, a pontoon bridge was constructed to enable the army's passage. Messages had been dispatched to Sigismund – now frequently referred to in official Ottoman communications as "the son of the king" (*qırāl oğlı*) – requesting him to rendezvous with the Ottoman main force at Balçık, where, after kissing the hand of the sultan, he was granted the singular honor of being recognized as "my son."[55]

Meanwhile, Second Vizier Pertev Pasha had advanced to Gyula. Commanded by László Kerecsényi, the fortress was built on an island in the Fehér-Körös River, and was defended by a garrison of some 2,000 Hungarian, Croatian, and German troops when Pertev and his 30,000-strong army commenced the siege on 2 July. Gyula was composed of three sections. The first ring, dubbed the Hussar Castle, was open from three sides and was held by the defenders for twelve days. The outer castle could only be attacked head on at a very narrow section and was held for twenty-seven days. The inner core of the fortress, including the medieval brick castle and the surrounding ramparts, held out for another nine days before finally surrendering on 2 September after a brutal, sixty-three-day fight, the longest siege in Hungary during the 16th century.[56] Advancing from Gyula, Pertev subsequently reduced the fortress of Jenő after another twenty-three days of resistance. While the ultimate success of these operations was welcome, the protracted duration of each siege was not an auspicious omen for the sultan if he intended to break through the Imperial defense line by the end of the campaign season. In addition to applying the latest scientific principles to the design of their fortifications, the Habsburgs had utilized the surrounding terrain to maximize their defensibility. Timişoara looked like an island, sited in a lake encircled by marshland. Zrenjanin stood in the Temes River on an island, surrounded by bogs. Kanjiža stood in the Tisza River, its drainage into fens and marshes making the castle inaccessible on every side for at least three kilometers.

The news only got worse when, after arriving in Belgrade on 27 June, the sultan learned of a devastating raid launched from Szigetvár against the Ottoman encampment at Siklós in which the troops of the *sanjak-bey* of Tırhala had been annihilated.

Surrounded by marshes and the thick woodlands of the Mecsek hills, Szigetvár, through controlling transportation on the Drava River and posing a constant threat to the Ottoman border castles in Slavonia, had for years impeded the Ottoman advance in South Transdanubia. The stronghold, and the troublemakers it sheltered, had long been a source of anger for Suleiman. In 1557 he complained about it in a letter to Ferdinand: "The fortress of Szigetvár belongs to the border region [next to] our well-protected domains. When the *haydud* [bandits] and robbers make trouble and commit evil acts, they take refuge in this fortress." Typically, in the spring of 1560, *hajdús* (irregular troops) from Szigetvár, Babócsa, and Csurgó drove dozens of Ottoman soldiers into the church in Mohács and set the building on fire. During the peace negotiations in 1562, this incident was still clearly on the sultan's mind: "What might make us conclude peace, if those who are in charge of [Szigetvár] will disturb it and continue the war?"[57] Setting aside any personal grudges, there were also good strategic reasons not to leave the enemy in occupation of just such a fortified stronghold astride the army's lines of communication, resupply, and retreat as it advanced. Suleiman resolved to eliminate Szigetvár before pressing on with the campaign. If his ultimate objective was Vienna, then he had not learned anything from the outcome of the last campaign against that city, more than three decades earlier, for by diverting to a minor objective instead of focusing on the grand prize, he was making the same mistake he had made in laying siege to Kőszeg in 1532.

As a diversion, part of the army was forwarded to Petrovaradin, where the Ottomans were building a bridge, suggesting the army would cross the river to Hungary there, possibly targeting Eger. The sultan also ordered the building of another bridge near Vukovar, again to confuse his enemies. Ultimately, the army crossed the Drava River into southern Transdanubia at Osijek, via a pontoon bridge the Ottomans built in seventeen days using 118 boats. The last troops crossed over on 19 July.

The Ottomans shipped their cannons and heavy military equipment on the Danube to Mohács, from whence they were transported to Szigetvár on carts. In the meantime, Arslan Pasha, the governor of Buda, had laid siege to Várpalota. Not only did he fail to take the fortress, but having received word of an approaching relief army, he retreated in such precipitous haste he left the Ottoman strongholds of Veszprém, Tata, Gesztes, and Vitány exposed. Capitalizing on his flight, Hungarian and Habsburg troops moved in and captured all of them. When Arslan hurriedly arrived at the Ottoman camp at Nagyharsány on 3 August to beg for forgiveness, Sokollu Mehmed immediately had him garroted during the noon prayer outside the sultan's tent.[58]

The sultan himself arrived at Szigetvár on 9 August, although the vanguard of his troops had arrived under the walls on 1 August and completed entrenchments encircling the fortress and the town by 5 August. The stronghold was held by a garrison of some 2,300 Croatian and Hungarian troops, led by the Croatian-born Count Nicholas IV of Zrin, the scion of a family deeply steeped in generations of armed conflict with the Ottoman antagonist. His grandfather, Count Peter II, and his uncle, Paul III, both perished in battle against the Ottomans at Krbava in 1493, while his cousin Michael was among the fallen at Mohács in 1526. His father, Count Nicholas III, and his uncle, Count John Torquatus of Krbava, *ban* of Croatia, had also found their lives subsumed into the war against the Ottomans, while Nicholas himself was a veteran of the 1529 siege of Vienna and numerous other engagements.

A Croatian–Slavonian *ban* from 1542 to 1556, in 1546 Nicholas acquired Međimurje and Čakovec in Zala County and Ozalj in Zagreb County, which became the new seats of his family. Although Nicholas had earlier possessed small estates north of the Drava River, it was at this time that he became a prominent member of the Hungarian aristocracy through a marriage alliance, endowing him with the estates of Eberau and Rotenturm in Austria and Vép in Hungary, all of which lay far enough north to be relatively safe from Ottoman attacks. This arrangement elevated him to the circle of the richest landowners, and his new residence in Eberau gave him easy access to the royal court.

Appointed royal treasurer in 1557, Nicholas served in an administrative role in Bratislava and Vienna until the post of captain general of Szigetvár became vacant in 1561 and he returned to the battlefield. In spring 1562, Nicholas personally led his soldiers across the Drava, where they crushed the troops of Arslan, *sanjak-bey* of Požega, razing the castle of Monoszló to the ground to prevent the Ottomans from fortifying it. In 1563, Nicholas was appointed captain general of Transdanubia. With this, military command of the entire area stretching from Lake Balaton to the Drava River was finally united in the hands of one man.[59]

The standard of leadership inside Szigetvár would clearly present a major obstacle to the Ottomans during the siege. So would the surrounding environment. The combination of rivers, moats, and marshes around Szigetvár (Hungarian for "Island Castle"), fed by the Almas, a tributary of the nearby Drava, made Nicholas's stronghold indeed appear to rise directly out of the water. Szigetvár was subdivided into three sections, each of which was linked to the other in sequence by bridges and causeways. The first of the three sections was the old town, with its medieval walls. The second was the so-called new town. Only then came the castle, with its state-of-the-art angle bastions, and at the very end, the citadel. In order to access this final redoubt, a besieger would have to fight their way through the other two sections first.

Ailing and gout-ridden, Suleiman set up his tent on Semlék hill, lying northeast of Szigetvár, and delegated field command to Sokollu Pasha. At dawn on 9 August the first battery of siege guns opened fire. Suffering heavy losses, that evening the defenders, after setting fire to the houses, abandoned the new town. By 19 August, after ten days of heavy bombardment, a long section of the town walls had collapsed, and with no capacity to improvise barricades, the garrison pulled out of the old town and into the castle. Six days after the capture of the old town, a stretch of the castle wall was brought down. Judging the moment had arrived, on 26 August, Sokollu Pasha ordered the first infantry assault against the castle. It was thrown back with heavy casualties.

While Nicholas and his troops put up a ferocious defense, the Imperial *Diet*, convening at Augsburg, wrangled. The primary focus for the representatives, once again, was religion, specifically whether or not to accept the outcome of the Council of Trent. As de Granvelle noted, "the main Protestant princes say that this time the emperor must clearly declare what religion he belongs to, as they wish to know whom they are dealing with. And others say that if His Majesty wishes to have help against the Turks, he must not believe that this will be provided without some concessions made to the advantage of the Protestants."[60] Direction and energy were lacking in the Imperial camp. Archduke Charles was suffering from smallpox and the aging Ferdinand, weak and thin, could hardly keep upright. By mid-August, de Granvelle concluded, one fact was now evident; should Szigetvár fall, Suleiman "could cross the entire country and rush to this place [Vienna] with no opposition."[61]

Maximilian ultimately mustered an 80,000-strong army at Győr. This was not a relief force, however. Convinced the true objective of the sultan's campaign was Vienna, the emperor ordered his troops to protect the approaches to his capital and not to intervene with the siege of Szigetvár.

On the night of 2 September, making the most of the darkness, Ottoman sappers successfully dug into the wall opposite the Hegy Bastion, the key artillery position of the castle. They spent the next three days removing the soil from the foundations, replacing it with dry wood and other flammable materials, including gunpowder. At dawn on 5 September, this mix was ignited. The fire quickly spread from the bastion to the buildings inside the castle, and proved impossible to extinguish, due to the strong wind and the heavy cannon fire targeting the bastion and its surroundings.

Nicholas managed to withstand two waves of assaults but was ultimately forced to retreat into the citadel. The struggle for Szigetvár was effectively over. The citadel was a separate headquarters, not a fortification intended to withstand a siege. On the morning of 7 September, as Ottoman artillery set the citadel ablaze, Nicholas addressed his remaining troops. "Let us go out from this burning place into the open and stand up to our enemies," he reportedly said. "Who dies – he will be with God. Who does not – his name will be honored. I will go first, and what I do, you do. And God is my witness, I will never leave you, my brothers and knights!"

As the Ottomans surged across the narrow bridge towards the citadel's gate, the defenders greeted them with a burst of grapeshot that killed hundreds. Then Nicholas, eschewing his armor, led a final counterattack, only to immediately take two musket balls to the chest and an arrow to his head. When the Ottomans finally overran the citadel, seven defenders managed to escape, and the janissaries spared a few of those captured. The rest were slain. In a final twist of fate, the toll of Ottoman casualties, already estimated in the thousands, surged even higher after the fall of Szigetvár. Those swarming through the complex in the search for plunder found only death when the slow fuse left by Nicholas in the magazine reached the powder, the resultant explosion tearing apart the citadel and anyone trapped inside.

The respect Nicholas had earned over the course of this, his last campaign, was reflected in a letter Sokollu Pasha wrote to Maximilian two months after the fall of Szigetvár: "I still regret his death, and I can prove this, because his head is not on a [spike]; I sent it up to have it cleaned; I also had his body buried, as it would have been a shame to have the body of such a brave gentleman eaten by the birds." The decapitated head was washed in vinegar and sent to the camp in Győr. From there it was taken by Nicholas's son-in-law, Boldizsár Batthyány, to Muraköz, in order that it be laid to final rest in the family monastery in Šenkovec, alongside his first wife.[62]

Was the heroic defense of Szigetvár a critical turning point in the confrontation between the Habsburg and Ottoman empires? Writing on 22 September, still unaware of the outcome of the siege, de Chantonnay mused that, in the event Suleiman did not survive the campaign, "it could be his son, seeking to counteract the poor opinion held of him, who would carry on the war, so I am not convinced that what is left of Hungary, or even of Moravia or part of Austria, would be kept." Morale in the Imperial capital was waning, and "however fortified [Vienna] may be, if the Turks should reach it, I am certain that they would conquer it in less than a month."[63] Again, there is no evidence Vienna was the end goal of the campaign, and Maximilian had succeeded in mobilizing a substantial Imperial army, in addition to which the fortifications of Vienna were vastly superior to the outdated and rundown defenses that had thwarted Suleiman's siege in 1529.

Most probably, the outcome would have been the same as in 1532; delayed by the stubborn resistance of an outlying stronghold, Suleiman would opt against risking a decisive battle so deep into enemy territory. Nonetheless, it is true that, following their pyrrhic victory at Szigetvár, the Ottomans returned to Constantinople and did not threaten the Habsburg capital again until 1683. For that reason, France's Armand Jean du Plessis, Cardinal Richelieu, retrospectively declared Szigetvár "the battle that saved civilization."[64] Géza Pálfffy also concludes that, "in early September 1566, Ottoman plans of global conquest in Europe met their end under the walls of Szigetvár."[65]

This speculation assumes Suleiman would have survived to lead his army in either direction, forward or home, for the balance of the year. He did not. At the end of his thirteenth campaign, in the forty-sixth year of his reign – the longest of any Ottoman sultan – he passed away in his tent on 6 September, the day prior to the final assault against Szigetvár.

This fact instantly became a state secret of the direst consequence. By Ottoman tradition, in the absence of a reigning sultan, the world's order (*nizam-ı alem*) was destroyed. It was vital to maintain the illusion of Suleiman's survival, for reasons both internal – keeping the army together, ensuring a smooth succession – and external – keeping the enemy guessing and at a safe distance. In this supreme challenge to his qualities of leadership, Grand Vizier Sokollu Mehmed managed to keep the sultan's death a secret for an incredible forty-eight days, buying time for the sultan's only surviving son, Selim, to receive word and return to the capital from his provincial command in Manisa on the Aegean coast of Anatolia. Sokollu managed to sustain this illusion by having doctors pretend to cure the ill sultan, by forging *fermans* (official documents) bearing Suleiman's *tuğra* (signature), by making arrangements for spending a regular winter season in Buda, and, as a last resort, by employing body doubles.

While taking all precautionary measures within the camp, Sokollu spread news and sent letters to address the rumors of the sultan's absence for the Habsburgs and Hungarians as well. To keep the enemy guessing, subsidiary Ottoman units led by the *beylerbey* of Budin and the *beylerbey* of Rumelia were assigned to seize the fortress of Babócsa, taking their own troops with them in addition to 3,000 janissaries.

In actuality, Suleiman's body had been left behind by the army when it broke camp. After receiving the customary ablutions, the sultan's corpse had been temporarily buried on the spot, in his tent under the throne. It remained there till it was exhumed, and left Szigetvár on 17 October. It was only after it arrived at Belgrade, on 24 October, that the funerary prayer (*cenaze namazı*) was celebrated in the presence of the son and heir Selim II.

Unfortunately, Selim did not have the funds available to meet the expectations of his ostensible slaves for the requisite cash bonuses that were customary during a change of regime. By the time the army reached Edirne the janissaries were in open mutiny. Admiral Piyale Pasha attempted to personally reason with the rank and file, but was knocked off his horse for his pains. Order was only restored when the financier Joseph Nasi was able to forward the new sultan the vast sums required to pacify his restless subjects. This Portuguese-born, Louvain-educated banker had moved east to Constantinople where he was free at last to discard the Christian identity he and his Jewish family had been forced to adopt in Spain, in France, in the Duchy of Burgundy, and even in Venice, in order to be able to trade and survive.

On the final stage of his last journey, Suleiman's funeral bier was officially greeted by the authorities and the people of Constantinople, and brought to the imperial mosque, where his body was finally interred.[66]

The twinned sacrifice of Count Nicholas and death of Suleiman were celebrated throughout Christendom, Catholic and Protestant.[67] It was understood to mark the end of an era, a fact reflected in the petering out of the war and the terms arrived at in its conclusion with the signing of the Treaty of Edirne on 21 February 1568. Maximilian agreed to continue submitting the annual Habsburg obligation of 30,000 florins to the Porte, and essentially conceded Ottoman hegemony over Moldavia and Wallachia. Sigismund accepted he, too, was a tributary of the Porte and renounced the title of king of Hungary, referring to himself henceforth as "Prince of Transylvania and Ruler of Parts of Hungary," specifically, of the counties east of the Tisza River.

In the short term, the treaty initiated a period of twenty-five years of relative peace between the empires, the longest era of stability the Balkans had enjoyed since the Ottomans first entered the region centuries earlier. In the longer term, the treaty formally sealed the division of the Carpathian basin into three separate parts for more than a century and a half.

8

THE MEDITERRANEAN, PART I – TUNIS, PREVEZA, AND ALGIERS

While the frontier between Habsburg and Ottoman influence in the Balkans hardened, it remained more fluid – figuratively, as well as literally – at sea in the Mediterranean. One aspect of this confrontation, however, remained consistent; as the decades progressed, the Ottoman Empire's control over coasts, ports, and sea lanes increased at the expense of all its rivals in Christendom.

Taking to the water during this period, for fisherman, merchants, and pilgrims alike, was a major gamble, for peace could prevail on land while war could continue at sea, or vice versa, and at any moment the status of the mighty and the humble could be reversed. To cite just one example, in the summer of 1540, Giannettino Doria, nephew of the famous Genoese admiral Andrea Doria, scored a major coup when he captured the notorious corsair captain Turgut Reis. His squadron of twelve galleys had been drawn up on a beach in Sardinia, where Turgut was resting the crews, drawing fresh water and repairing the hulls of his ships with molten pitch. Suddenly, the corsairs found themselves totally surrounded, with soldiers on the heights and Doria's ship-mounted cannon covering the beach. The entire squadron was taken – crew, boats, booty and all – without a shot fired. Turgut was consigned to a galley of Andrea Doria's fleet. One day, he was visited by a French Hospitaller Knight of St John named Jean Parisot de Valette. "The custom of war," Valette remarked, to which Turgut is said to have replied, "I see a change of fortunes." When last they had met, it was Turgut who commanded the corsair galley where Valette was enslaved, chained by his ankle to a bench, working at the five-man oars. Turgut endured his servitude until the spring of 1543, when the legendary corsair turned Ottoman admiral Hayreddin Reis – known and feared throughout the West as Red Beard (Barbarossa) – secured his release. Departing Toulon, where he had participated with his fleet in a joint Franco-Ottoman siege of Nice, Hayreddin, who had threatened to blockade Genoa if he didn't return to Constantinople with Turgut, met with Andrea Dora in person to arrange the 3,500 ducat ransom.[1] This was the narrative of life on and around the Mediterranean, an environment of chivalry and savagery, of fortunes made and lost, of careers rising into immortality or tumbling into degradation.

An Ottoman navy began to make its weight felt in the Mediterranean at the beginning of the 15th century. Sultan Murad II built a substantial fleet which, in 1430, helped Ottoman land forces capture Venetian-held Thessaloniki. By 1456 the Ottoman fleet of around sixty ships seized control of Genoese-ruled Enez, as well as other islands in the northern Aegean Sea.

The original headquarters for the Ottoman fleet and its *kapudan pasha* (supreme admiral) was at Gallipoli. During the 16th century, port towns such as Mytilene, Preveza, Samsun, and Vlorë would be expanded into major naval bases. Galley sailors and marines (*levents*) were recruited from Turkish, Greek, Albanian, and, at a later date, Dalmatian and North African coastal communities. Several janissary *ortas* either specialized in naval service as marines, or had historically close associations with the fleet. Thus the 88th *Orta* had an anchor for its insignia, often tattooed on the men's hands or arms, as did the 8th and 31st *Bölük* regiments. The 25th and 37th *Bölük* had a fish, while the 56th *Bölük* had a galleon. The oarsmen (*kürekçiler*) included criminals and prisoners-of-war as well as some volunteers.[2]

However, at no point during the 15th century was the Ottoman fleet a match for that of Venice, let alone Christendom collectively. During the 1463–79 war with Venice the galleys of the sultan did not win a single naval engagement. It was only during the 1499–1503 war with Venice that the Ottomans found an admiral of genius, Kemal Reis, capable of winning encounters at sea, as evidenced in his victories at Zonchio in August 1499 and Modon in August 1500.

A new generation of Ottoman mariners was rising – Piri Reis, the nephew of Kemal Reis, would serve with his uncle and, after his death in 1511, author the *Kitab-ı Bahriye* (*Book of Navigation*), a triumph in nautical cartography. Having established parity in the eastern Mediterranean, the balance in naval warfare began to tilt in favor of the Porte after the Ottomans arrived at a working relationship with the independent corsair captains operating from bases along the Maghreb coast to the west. This policy of outsourcing naval operations to the *deniz levendleri* (irregular forces of the sea) offered multiple benefits.[3] First, it enabled the Porte to maintain indirect pressure on its Western enemies, primarily Spain, Genoa, and the papacy, forcing them to divert their naval assets to the defense of their own territorial waters as opposed to contributing them to joint action against the Ottomans in the East. Second, it allowed for the Porte to identify and recruit the top tier talent in naval warfare it needed for command of the Ottoman navy. Third, the defection of these captains, with their local knowledge and connections, facilitated the incorporation of those territories, from Tunis to Algiers, into the Ottoman Empire at the expense of their native dynasties.

The corsairs in turn profited from the Ottoman connection at the beginning of the 16th century, for without the backing of a great power as a counterweight to the rising threat of Spain they were individually at risk of being forced, one by one, out of the Mediterranean altogether.

While the birth of modern Spain is closely associated with its forays west into the unexplored Atlantic, the primary focus for policy makers in the newfound kingdom was actually the defense of its own coastal waters, where the stakes were in many ways much higher. The Spanish Crown could afford to outsource its empire building in the New World to the conquistadors, who operated on their own recognizance and at their own expense. But the seesaw struggle for control of the Mediterranean demanded the personal direction of the monarch, ultimately consuming much of the wealth extracted from fabled Tenochtitlan and Cuzco.[4]

From its first phase, Spanish policy in the Mediterranean was proactive, the intent being to establish a security perimeter as far from its own shores as possible through the naval blockade of, or the outright occupation of, key ports and other strongholds along the North African coast. Queen Isabella's last will and testament explicitly stated: "I beg my daughter and her husband that they will devote themselves unremittingly to the conquest of Africa and to the war for the Faith against the Moors."[5]

Commencing with the occupation of Melilla in 1497, King Ferdinand certainly tried his best to fulfill this mandate. He took Mers El Kébir in 1505, Oran in 1509, and both Tripoli and Béjaïa in 1510, the same year the Spaniards fortified an offshore islet they dubbed the Peñon d'Alger in order to control the entrance to the port of Algiers.[6] This run of successes came to a crashing halt with the total failure of the attempt to claim Djerba in 1510, but the island was eventually taken and fortified in 1520.

Effective resistance to these Spanish incursions only developed with the arrival in the western Mediterranean of two brothers, Oruç and Hayreddin.

Oruç's first taste of life at sea was in the family business as a merchant in their native Aegean, a career path that ended when he was seized by Hospitaller privateers who killed his brother Ilyas and held him as a prisoner for nearly three years. He subsequently cut his teeth in naval combat through action against the Hospitallers while in service to the Ottoman *şehzade* Korkut. After his patron lost the struggle for power to his brother Selim, Oruç fled with him to Mamluk Egypt and eventually made his way west, where in 1504 the Hafsid sultan of Tunis, Abu Abdallah Muhammad IV al-Mutawakkil, granted him the strategically located port of Halq al-Wadi (La Goulette) as a base for his operations. Oruç and Hayreddin emerge at this point as the first of the great corsair captains of what Westerners dubbed the Barbary Coast.

Having established his reputation by seizing two papal galleys off the island of Elba and some aggressive raiding of Calabria and Apulia, by 1506 Oruç had attracted sufficient freebooters to command a fleet of eight ships. In 1510, al-Mutawakkil granted Oruç the island of Djerba, where he was appointed *caid*, a governor responsible for administration and collecting taxes.

The brothers were now in a strong enough position to break into the Spanish-held section of the Algerian coast, which would give them access to the rich shipping lanes of the West. In 1512, Oruç commanded an assault on Béjaïa. Leading from the front, Oruç had his left arm smashed by shrapnel; it had to be amputated above the elbow. He was fitted with a silver prosthetic, earning him the nickname *Gümüş Kol* (Silver Arm). In 1514, Hayreddin seized the Genoese colony of Jijil, some 150 miles east of Algiers. From this powerbase the brothers reached out to Constantinople for recognition, receiving in return a bequest of fourteen Ottoman galleys.

When Ferdinand died in 1516, the inhabitants of Algiers marked the occasion by inviting a local Berber sheikh, Selim ibn Teumi, to relieve them of their Spanish oppressors. Selim was eager to oblige, but lacked the naval force or artillery to overcome the Peñon d'Alger at the harbor entrance, and he called on the corsairs at Jijil for support. It was the chance the brothers had been waiting for; sending a force of sixteen galleots with artillery along the coast under Hayreddin, Oruç marched overland with a force of 5,000 men, mostly local Berbers bolstered by a corps of his own Turks. Before joining Selim, he invited another corsair chief called Hassan, lord of the neighboring port of Shershell, to help with the reduction of the fortress. When Hassan arrived to discuss the proposition, Oruç had him murdered, visiting the same fate on Selim – who was drowned in the local steam bath (*hammam*) while performing his customary ablutions in preparation for Friday prayers – once the Barbarossa brothers had joined forces inside Algiers. Hayreddin meanwhile eliminated any potential opposition within the city by seizing the most prominent of the independence-minded local hierarchs in the central mosque during the midday Friday prayers and subjecting them to a summary execution just outside the city gates.

Through this extremely hostile takeover, Oruç and Hayreddin were now in control of the port, and although the light guns of the galleots failed to reduce the Peñon d'Alger offshore, Oruç had himself proclaimed sultan of Algiers.

This leadership was to be tested soon enough. The regent of Spain, Cardinal-Primate Francisco Jiménez de Cisneros, appointed Diego de Vera to command an expedition of 15,000 men for the relief of the Peñon d'Alger. The operation was a fiasco; de Vera got ashore on 30 September 1516, but the Spanish were routed, losing half of the expeditionary force to a counterattack led by Oruç.

Determined to consolidate his control over the Maghreb coastline, Oruç expanded his dominions westwards in 1517, seizing the port of Ténès and the inland trading post of Tlemcen. It was near Tlemcen in 1518 that a Spanish expedition sent to retrieve their now tenuous hold on the coast caught his force in the open. Oruç died fighting side by side with his men.

Hayreddin inherited his brother's authority and his moniker in the West – Barbarossa (Red Beard). In 1519, Hayreddin reached out to Constantinople for diplomatic and military support, and was acknowledged with both. The Porte was only too happy to extend its authority into the Maghreb. Hayreddin was recognized as *beylerbey* of the province of Algeria (Cezayir-i Garb) by Sultan Selim I, who also dispatched 2,000 janissaries to his assistance. These arrived in time to reinforce the city against the threat of another Spanish invasion later that year. The viceroy of Sicily, Admiral Hugo de Moncada, had been directed by Charles V to bring together a fleet and an expeditionary force incorporating Spanish soldiers garrisoned in Naples and Sicily and contingents from Spain's Italian allies, including Genoa, the Hospitallers, the papacy, and the Gonzaga rulers of Mantua. Moncada succeeded in getting his armada into the bay of Algiers and a vanguard ashore on 17 August, but bad weather disrupted the landings and Hayreddin unleashed a counterattack on the now isolated beachhead, wiping it out. The expedition lost twenty ships, 4,000 men killed, and 3,000 taken prisoner. When Charles V offered a ransom for the captured officers, Hayreddin had all of the captives executed. When Hayreddin was offered another ransom for the return of the dead bodies, he ordered them cast into the sea.

While Hayreddin had impressed all concerned with his military prowess, politically he was still isolated, and his at least formal submission to Ottoman hegemony rankled with many local powerbrokers. In 1520, a triumvirate comprising a Hafsid prince, a sheikh of the Berber tribes of the Kabylie mountains, Ahmad ibn al-Cadi, and one of Hayreddin's own corsair captains, Kara Hasan, seized control of Algiers in 1520. Exiled from the city, Hayreddin fell back on his stronghold of Jijil and fought his way back into relevance through a string of conquests in 1521– 22, which attracted other corsairs to serve under his banner, such as Aydın Reis and Sinan Reis ("the Jew"), who joined him in 1523. Hayreddin returned to Algiers in 1525, and finally succeeded in seizing the Peñon d'Alger when, after a twenty-two-day siege, the Spanish under Governor Don Martin de Vargas surrendered on 29 May 1529. Vargas was promptly beaten to death, while the other survivors of the garrison would spend the next two years working alongside the Christian slaves of Algiers in taking apart the fortress stone by stone and using the rubble to construct a mole extending out from the harbor to link the outlying islets with the mainland, permanently denying them to the Spanish.

In 1529, while Andrea Doria and the Spanish fleet were escorting Charles to Italy for his coronation, Hayreddin dispatched Aydın Reis to ransack the Balearic Islands. In the process, Aydın encountered eight galleys under the command of Rodrigo de Portuondo, captain general of the Spanish fleet, off the island of Formentera. Outgunned but undeterred, Aydın attacked and secured a complete victory, capturing seven of the eight galleys with their crews, Portuondo being killed, shot in the chest by an Ottoman arquebusier.

The following year, Charles, now fully invested as Holy Roman Emperor, took action to bolster the defenses on the maritime frontiers of his empire. The most easterly posts that his viceroys controlled, the North African harbor-city of Tripoli in western Libya and two strategic islands due south of Sicily, Malta and Gozo, were handed over to the command of the Hospitallers, who had been homeless since being forced to evacuate Rhodes in 1522.

In 1531, while Hayreddin was besieging Cadiz, Andrea Doria descended on Cherchell, a port west of Algiers, liberating several hundred Christian slaves. Had his troops heeded Doria's orders to re-embark and depart, the expedition would have been accorded a success; instead, they dispersed in search of plunder, enabling the now-alerted Maghrebi defenses to rally. Unwilling to risk interception, Doria set sail; the men he left behind were either massacred or found themselves fated to replace the slaves they had just liberated. Hayreddin later caught up with Doria's fleet off Genoa and mauled it, burning twenty-two galleys.

TUNIS, 1535

Ottoman priorities, meanwhile, were evolving. The inconclusive campaigns of 1529 and 1532 forced the Porte to concede that the front line in the Balkans was – at least temporarily – stalemated. Meanwhile, the defection of Andrea Doria from the French to the Imperial camp in 1528 meant the Habsburgs now constituted a genuine threat at sea, a reality confirmed in 1532 when Doria seized Koroni and Patras without resistance. It was for this reason that Suleiman invited Hayreddin to Constantinople in 1533 to appoint him *kapudan pasha* of the Ottoman navy. Both men had something to gain; for the sultan, an aggressive naval commander who would take the fight to the enemy; for the corsair, the legitimacy and resources he could draw upon from the Ottoman imprimatur. Accordingly, it was at this moment that Algiers truly gravitated into the Ottoman orbit. For Hayreddin, the linchpin of the Mediterranean was Tunis. He suggested the Porte supplant the Hafsid Sultan Abu Abdallah Muhammad V al-Hasan (commonly referred to as Moulay Hasan) with his brother, Moulay Rashid. With an Ottoman vassal on the throne, the Ottoman fleet could be stationed at Tunis. "In that case, with the help of God the Sublime, it would be feasible to conquer and subdue Spain from there."[7]

In August 1533, Hayreddin set out again from Algiers with seventeen of his captains. Messina, at Sicily's northeastern tip, was sacked. Taking the island of Elba, Hayreddin seized almost the entire population under the age of twenty-five, hustling them aboard his ships, bound for the slave markets of Barbary. This did nothing to deter the French from gravitating into the Ottoman orbit. When Clement VII met with Francis at Marseilles over October–November 1533 to solemnize the marriage of his niece, Catherine de' Medici, with the king's second son, Henry, Duke of Orléans, Francis told the pope he would not only "not oppose" but would even "favor" a Turkish attack on Christendom, so as to recover from the emperor what was rightfully his: Milan.[8] This message the pope was meant to pass on, and did. Hence, Charles instructed Doria and his galleys to remain on station at Genoa to guard against action by the French in concert with Hayreddin. On the Adriatic coast of the Kingdom of Naples, a target of corsair raids since the 1480s, Viceroy Pedro de Toledo evacuated civilians from vulnerable points and strengthened garrisons and fortifications. Hayreddin apparently knew of the enemy's dispositions. Bypassing the Adriatic coast, he took his seventy galleys and thirteen *fustas* through the Straits of Messina in the summer of 1534 to strike at the undefended western coast of the kingdom. After taking the town of Reggio in the Straits of Messina and deporting its entire population as slaves to Constantinople, he sacked San Lucido and, insolently passing unopposed in sight of Naples, continued north to ravage the coastal towns of the Papal States, lying some time watering off the mouth of the Tiber. In a characteristically bold gambit, Hayreddin landed at Sperlonga and marched by night in search of Giulia Gonzaga, countess of Fondi, renowned for her beauty, who would make a prize trophy for the sultan's harem. Tipped off at the last moment, the countess fled on horseback into the darkness. Enraged, Hayreddin unleashed his men on Fondi and on a neighboring convent, whose sisters they slaughtered. For added injury, he returned to Naples to burn the six galleys Toledo had under construction there before turning east to hit Sardinia and then continuing south for his ultimate objective, Tunis.

Landing at Bizerte on 15 August with his force of 1,800 janissaries and 7,000 auxiliaries, Hayreddin advanced to La Goulette, the fort sitting astride the spit of land separating the Bay of Tunis from the sea. Hayreddin won over the garrison by bluffing that he had Moulay Rashid, Moulay Hasan's brother, on board. By the time the populace realized Rashid was actually behind bars in Constantinople, Hayreddin had already occupied the citadel and on 22 August he took control of the city, Moulay Hasan fleeing into the interior.

Suleiman was now, by extension, master of the most strategically important section of the north African coast. Tunis was now an Ottoman javelin aimed at Habsburg Sicily, barely 100 miles east-by-northeast across the water. However, while taking Tunis was easy, governing the city proved more problematic. Hayreddin was unable to pay the salaries of the janissaries in his service, who mutinied in October and again in November, obliging him to restore order by brutally suppressing the revolts in order to restore order. Moulay Hasan, meanwhile, had reached out for support from the emperor, which gave Charles the pretext for a massive amphibious operation with the ostensible goal of restoring the rightful ruler of Tunis to his throne.

Offensive operations to the far shore of the Mediterranean were inherently a gamble. That very year, the bellicose military governor of Oran, Count Alcaudete, had ordered an army inland to support another client Zayyanid prince trying to claim the throne of Tlemcen. Unlike the previous campaign against Oruç Barbarossa, when the Spaniards had enjoyed the support of many of the local tribes, on this occasion the Spanish expeditionary force was pinned down within the fortress of Tibda. Isolated from assistance, they had been overwhelmed by the Beni Rashid tribe. Only the seventy men who were taken prisoner survived.

Cardinal Tavera, president of the royal council, warned Charles against "tempting Fortune as many times as Your Majesty has done, leaving these realms [Spain] and putting yourself at risk on the sea and in lands that you do not rule" in Africa, which risked becoming "a dangerous, prolonged and uncertain business."[9] If Charles failed, Francis I would be welcomed by the Italian states as their only recourse to security against an ascendant Hayreddin.

Then there was the financial obligation. In the final analysis, total costs for the Tunis campaign would come to 1,076,652 ducats. The entire enterprise was only possible because an entirely unrelated campaign on the other side of the world had restocked the emperor's treasure chamber at La Mota.

From the very moment of its inception, the history of Spain had been intimately linked with that of the Americas. It was in the momentous year of 1492 that the Catholic monarchs Ferdinand II of Aragon and Isabella I of Castile had both conquered Granada, thereby consummating the *Reconquista*, and funded the voyage of Christopher Columbus that definitively bridged the gap between the Old World and the New. Spanish colonization and exploitation of the Americas had been institutionalized by the establishment in Seville of the Casa de la Contratación de las Indias (House of Trade) in February 1503. While the direction of Portuguese investment management had been outsourced to Florentine merchants, it was the Genoese, attracted by the opportunities emerging in the Western Hemisphere and impelled by the loss of their established eastern markets to the Ottoman Empire, who fulfilled the same role for Spain. Twenty-one of Genoa's twenty-eight noble merchant houses were represented in Seville by 1530. Great families such as Centurione, the Balbi, the Spinola, and the Sauli advanced funds in return for access to the economy of Castile and America and for *asientos* offering high rates of interest.[10] Under their auspices, Caribbean sugar, slaving, and cattle enterprises would contribute 320,000 ducats annually to Charles V's coffers by 1535.[11]

Spanish aspirations to deriving a steady flow of mineral wealth from the Caribbean would prove fleeting; an estimated fifteen tons of West Indies gold had been exported to Seville by 1520, but beyond that point the deposits were rapidly exhausted. Another huge trove of treasure was plundered from the metropolis of Tenochtitlan when the first of the great conquistadors, Hernán Cortés, conquered the heartland of Mexico, ostensibly in the name of Charles V, between 1519 and 1521. But the real prize was Peru. When Francisco Pizarro seized the Inca emperor Atahualpa at Cajamarca on 16 November 1532, he took possession of 1,356,539 pesos of gold (approximately 1,591,897 ducats), and 51,610 marks of silver.

This spectacular windfall was interpreted as a gift from God, as Gabriel de Espinosa, a companion of Pizarro, put it, "in the holy enterprise of war against the Turk, Luther, and other enemies of the faith." As treasure ships convoyed the gold and silver from Panama to Seville – the first arrived in December 1533 – Charles's royal fifth would have amounted to approximately 400,000 ducats. But for the plans Charles was forming as 1534 drew to a close, a fifth was not enough. He sequestered 60,000 ducats in treasure from private owners in December 1534, offering by way of compensation *juros* carrying an interest rate of 3 percent.[12]

On 4 March 1535 he decreed a second and much larger sequestration for 800,000 ducats, to be levied proportionally on all persons receiving shipments of more than 400 pesos (480 ducats) in gold and silver. To justify this intrusion on the rights of merchants and investors, Charles appealed to the sentiments expressed by Espinosa: "The cause of the sequestration is the dire need for fitting out armadas to resist the Grand Turk and his captains."[13]

Utilizing these funds, the emperor would be directly or indirectly responsible for about fifty of the galleys that participated in the campaign – the sixteen of Doria's that were on the Spanish's payroll, fifteen from Spain itself, commanded by Álvaro de Bazán, the Marquis of Santa Cruz, twelve from Naples, and six from Sicily. Pope Paul III paid for three papal galleys, three more outfitted at Genoa, and the five or six of Doria's that were commanded by his nephew, Antonio. The Republic of Genoa sent nine galleys, and Naples seven more. The knights of Malta sent four or five galleys, the carrack used in bombarding La Goulette, and 800 knights. Charles's brother-in-law, King John III of Portugal, had no galley fleet, but he did send 2,000 infantry and twenty-three ships of the line, including twenty caravels, two carracks, and the great galleon launched just the previous year, *São João Baptista* (popularly known as *Botafogo*, or *Spitfire*), the most powerful warship in the world, under the command of his son Luís, Duke of Beja, who joined the Imperial fleet mustering at Barcelona in April 1535. Other prominent personalities signing on for the campaign included Ferrante Gonzaga, brother of the Duke of Mantua, yearning for revenge for Barbarossa's affront to his kinswoman, the countess of Fondi, and Fernando Alvarez de Toledo, third Duke of Alba, among many other titles.

Conspicuous by his absence was the king of France. Francis I was overjoyed at the prospect of an Ottoman–Algerian victory forcing Charles to concede Milan. Paul III continued to demand that Francis I join the expedition against Tunis, alternating persuasion with threats, but all in vain. The French diplomat Guillaume du Bellay declared in 1536 that in his campaigns against the Ottomans, Charles was motivated not by a selfless devotion to his duty as the sword and shield of Christendom, but "only by a greed for glory, and by a rivalry which he and the sultan seem to have taken up, each against the other, for the monarchy of the world."[14]

After preparations that stretched through winter and into the spring, on 30 May 1535 the emperor departed from Barcelona with the fleets of Spain and Portugal to rendezvous on 11 June with the galleys of the Kingdom of Naples, the Kingdom of Sicily, the Republic of Genoa, the Papal States, and the Knights of Malta at Cagliari on the south coast of Sardinia. After taking in more recruits from Italy, Germany, and Spain, the Imperial fleet exceeded 50,000 men on 400 ships, including 26,000 infantry. The emperor also picked up intelligence on his destination, being informed by escaped slaves from Tunis that Hayreddin was fortifying La Goulette. After the emperor made landfall it would be possible to skirt the Bay of Tunis and approach the city from the west, but this was ruled inadvisable, for such an approach would leave the newly bolstered enemy fortress astride the Imperial army's lines of communication, supply, and retreat to its ships. La Goulette thus became the primary objective for the campaign, for by seizing this stronghold, Tunis itself would be neutralized.

Commanded by Doria, the combined force set sail on 15 June, arriving with favorable winds at La Goulette just twenty-four hours later. The army of the Holy Roman Emperor disembarked and encamped amid the ancient ruins of Carthage. Resistance was immediate and fierce. In the account of Seyyid Muradi, the Imperial forces were obliged to "go to ground, building tunnels like blind moles and swarming along them."[15] In reality, constructing trenches and saps were standard siege tactics. The siege was led by the young Duke of Alba, whose father had been killed during the struggle for Djerba in 1510. The German and Spanish regiments faced the north and east walls of the fort, the Italians the west, while the Knights of St John directed a coordinated naval bombardment. The earth banks that protected the strong stone vaults of the central fortress of La Goulette were pounded hour after hour, day after day, for three weeks.

Having received word of the size of the invasion fleet, Hayreddin had dispersed his own vessels throughout the ports of Algeria, and stationed his best troops, including the janissaries, in La Goulette, which had been well provisioned. The corsair Aydın Reis, called *Caccia Diavolo* (Devil Hunter) for his ferocity, and Sinan of İzmir, Barbarossa's chief lieutenant, directed the defense of the fortress. Hayreddin himself remained in the city of Tunis, directing a series of hit-and-run raids on the Imperial camp with his cavalry. But in truth he knew that only a summer storm that devastated the Imperial fleet or a plague that decimated the Imperial army could save the fortress from the vast host that besieged it.

Hayreddin soon got half his wish. As dysentery spread through the Imperial camps, the pressure increased for an assault to terminate the siege. At last, on 14 July, at the direction of two Italian military engineers, the shore-based siege guns were properly placed for a bombardment (*bateria*) from three different angles. This Imperial artillery hammered La Goulette for seven hours without interruption, supported from the sea by the two great ships built to carry heavy guns on their upper decks, the *Botafogo* and the carrack of the knights of Malta. Meanwhile, three squadrons of eight galleys each executed a naval version of firing-by-ranks, advancing and retiring by turns to fire from their prow guns the iron shot that had some chance of damaging La Goulette's curtain wall.

Finally, the galleys of the Knights of St John delivered three volleys in fast succession. It was a prearranged signal that silenced all the land batteries. Imperial troops advanced on the fort from all sides, initially under the shelter of the trenches but then in a pell-mell dash as they rushed towards the smashed walls of the bastions. The bombardment had blasted open a breach in the walls near the shore and the imperial troops poured through, encouraged by a friar bearing a crucifix. Pursued by the victorious Imperial forces, the defenders broke, falling back and into the Bay, some of them managing to escape by making their way via a causeway that led across the lake to the walls of Tunis. Most were killed or captured. The booty accumulated that day included the sixty galleys and *fustas* trapped in the harbor and hundreds of cannon, many emblazoned with the French *fleur-de-lys*, having been sold by France to her Ottoman ally.[16]

During the last days of the siege of the fort, the former Hafsid Sultan, Moulay Hasan, had ridden up from Kairouan to place some 300 tribal cavalry at the service of the emperor. After the fall of La Goulette, Moulay Hasan renewed his pleas that they should advance on Tunis, expel Barbarossa and his corsairs, and restore him to his native throne. In the ensuing council of war, some favored leaving a force to occupy La Goulette and sailing home, but the weight of opinion was for advancing to Tunis.

The lack of water and the unrelenting North African midsummer sun stretched the campaign to its breaking point. The men were forced to become their own beasts of burden as the pack animals weakened, leaving it up to the soldiers to drag the monstrous cannon through the sterile mud of the salt marshes. As Charles wrote in his own hand to his sister Mary, "We die of thirst and heat."[17] The battles fought for possession of the few good wells in the region were the fiercest, for Hayreddin knew this was the one tactical card that might reverse the imbalance of forces. He rallied the Ottoman, Arab, and Maghrebi resistance and made a stand among the stone walls and orchards surrounding Carthage. In one such engagement, Charles's horse was shot out from under him and his page-boy was gunned down at his side. In Muradi's account, "the people of Islam... cut to pieces the ill-fated treacherous ones and when the pious ones joyfully and ardently plunged their swords into the death-meriting infidels, the infidel host... turned and fled, and the Muslims repulsed three or four thousand of them and threw the King of Spain from his horse."[18] After desperate fighting, an Imperial force led by the Duke of Alba smashed through the Ottoman line. Hayreddin's men finally broke; too exhausted and dehydrated to pursue, the imperial troops dropped to their knees at the wells to drink and drink and drink.

The siege reached its climax on 21 July when the Christian slaves of Tunis, who had nothing to lose but their chains, and who had found a natural leader among their number in Paolo Simeoni, a Hospitaller knight, rose up and opened the gates to the Imperial army. With the enemy swarming inside the walls, Barbarossa fled while he still could, leading his troops in a series of quick marches into the safety of the surrounding hills. The fate of Tunis was grim. Writing in 1660, Ibn abi Dinar recounted that "a third of the inhabitants of Tunis died, another third were taken prisoner, while the final third fled. I heard it said by elders that each third represented sixty thousand souls."[19]

After three weeks of occupation the ghost city of Tunis, a wreck framed by walls, was handed back to Moulay Hasan. In exchange, by treaty signed on 6 August, the Hafsid sultan had to acknowledge that La Goulette, "occupied at great cost and with much risk, belongs now to his imperial majesty," to release any Christian slaves found in his territories, to "not make any alliances with a Muslim or Christian state that holds prejudices against his imperial majesty," and to pay an annual tribute of 2,000 ducats, six horses, and a dozen falcons.[20] Having put a bounty on Barbarossa's head – 50,000 ducats alive, 10,000 dead – Charles boarded his flagship and set sail for Sicily on 21 August.

It was the apogee of the emperor's career. A SOLIS ORTU AD OCCASUM (a phrase from Psalm 112, "From the rising to the setting of the sun") became an imperial motto. As to the escape of Hayreddin, it was considered of little consequence. "He has left in tatters, defeated," Charles commented; "he will have to look to his own defense rather than to attack and offend others."[21]

Charles had underestimated his adversary, who, far from going over onto the defensive, was already actively looking to "offend" imperial sensibilities in the most direct manner possible. Ever the calculating corsair, Hayreddin had prepared for every contingency. He had sunk fifteen galleys at the mouth of a river flowing into the sea at the port of Annaba, 200 miles up the coast from Tunis. After a forced march of five days and nights, Hayreddin reached Annaba, retrieved and refloated his boats under cover of night, and broke through the blockade of fifteen galleys under Adamo Centurione and Doria's nephew Juranetin that lay in wait for him at the entrance to the harbor. A day later, he reached sanctuary at Algiers, where he picked up eleven more galleys. Just fifteen days after that, he was back at sea, leading a fleet into the port of Mahón, the great harbor on the Balearic Island of Minorca, on 1 September. According to Spanish chronicler Francisco López de Gómara's account, he first defeated and butchered the garrison from the fortress at Ciutadella that had come out against him, then talked his way into Mahón itself under a flag of truce; once inside the walls, he had no difficulty slaughtering those who resisted, and taking away some 1,800 men, women, and children to the slave markets of Algiers.

This stinging affront to Imperial pride stripped much of its luster from the Tunis campaign, which had already been greeted with at best qualified approbation throughout Western Europe. "And when we weigh the fact of Tunis's loss, it amounts to little or nothing," an Italian chronicler concluded.

> It is more smoke than grilled meat because Barbarossa, having so many galleys, slaves, and Turks, will recover easily. In sum, the sack of Tunis is a very thin affair and of little importance... and by going to Tunis with the army His Majesty put himself in grave peril; had Barbarossa restrained himself for two or three days from fighting the army, His Majesty would certainly have been defeated, and all would have been cut down by the great and uncomfortable thirst.[22]

In distant London, Henry VIII affected disinterest, even disdain, as to the emperor's achievement; "there is no great glory in chasing a pirate," he remarked to the Imperial ambassador.[23] More concretely, on 3 October the English ambassador in France reported that the emperor's victory in Tunis mattered little to Francis I and his advisers. What would make a real difference was whether Suleiman defeated the Safavid Shah and retaliated, at which point Francis I "will little esteem the Emperor's peace, and will begin to practice for the annoyance of the Emperor, as formerly, and, as it is said, he now begins to do."[24] Henry VIII's chief minister, Thomas Cromwell, remarked that to recover Milan, Francis I would call not just on the Turk but also on the Devil.[25]

Indeed, although Francis was unable to persuade the English to join him, he renewed his efforts to obtain a formal anti-Habsburg alliance with Suleiman and Hayreddin. An interim agreement for a three-year treaty of amity was rapidly concluded with Hayreddin, and a formal embassy was dispatched to the Porte. Francis I requested financial, military, and diplomatic aid to regain what he considered his rightful possessions, including Genoa, Milan, Asti, and sovereignty over Flanders and Artois. He also wanted Ottoman aid to secure John Zápolya on the throne of Hungary and prevent Ferdinand from taking the kingdom.

A coordinated campaign was proposed, beginning with the conquest of Genoa, on the grounds that this would enable Francis to assist Hayreddin in defending Algiers, and would protect the subjects, commerce, and mutually beneficial enterprises of all three signatories. Francis offered to help his Muslim allies take Corsica, Sardinia, and Sicily. He requested the right to choose the new king of Sicily, although it was to be an Ottoman possession that would pay tribute to the sultan, and suggested the island's revenues should be used to recoup the costs of the allied campaign. The three sovereigns agreed to abide by the three-year treaty of commerce while they negotiated a full offensive-defensive treaty.[26]

French diplomat Jean de Monluc, who had acted as a personal envoy from Francis to Barbarossa in 1537, justified the Ottoman alliance on the grounds that "for the King my lord, gaining assistance from the support of the sultan is licit and allowed for any need he may have," in this case to counter "the insolence of the Imperial ministers," whose stated goal was Habsburg domination of all Europe. From this it followed that "our particular advantage was, in this case, united with the public benefit of all Christendom."[27]

PREVEZA, 1538

Meanwhile, the Venetians had been retaking their former Greek and Ionian bases, and in 1536, Andrea Doria took his fleet deep into the Aegean, seizing all the merchant ships that he came upon, before taking on and defeating a squadron of the Ottoman navy commanded by the lieutenant-governor of the Dardanelles.

In 1537, the French sent thirteen galleys to meet Hayreddin in Tunis, then accompany him to Constantinople, where the sultan had amassed an impressive fleet with the manifest goal of invading Italy. This force advanced to Vlorë in 1537 and was intended to land near Brindisi, in southern Italy while closing the Adriatic to Venetian shipping, one wing of a joint Franco-Ottoman pincer-campaign, with French armies attacking the Habsburgs' northern Italian territories.

On 23 July Ottoman troops were ferried from Vlorë to Calabria, but although thousands of *akinji* were unleashed on the peninsula, spreading terror with their raids inland, attempts to take the key port cities of Otranto and Brindisi failed, and the troops were ferried back again on 13 August. Critically, Francis had failed to keep his part of the bargain; no French troops entered Italy, leaving the Ottoman expeditionary force without support in the peninsula. The Ottoman focus transferred to the Venetian stronghold of Corfu on the opposite side of the strait linking the Adriatic to the Mediterranean. The chance to go to war with Venice, "that abject crowd of infidels ceaselessly employed in commerce, amassing wealth, and pursuing profit through cheating and treachery," was very welcome to Lüfti Pasha, who was in command of the expedition, but taking this island also made a great deal more sense from a strategic perspective than a *razzia* in Italy, for Corfu had tremendous geopolitical significance.[28] "Venice has two eyes," Piri Reis had advised Bayezid II; "Her left eye is the fortress of Modon. Her right eye is that of Corfu."[29] The Ottoman siege commenced on 25 August, this time supported by French galleys, but Suleiman was concerned over intelligence that a hastily assembled alliance between the Holy Roman Empire, Venice, and the pope had unleashed Andrea Doria at the command of a joint fleet of forty-five Spanish, eighty Venetian, and twenty-six papal galleys in pursuit of Hayreddin. Unwilling to risk his fleet being trapped between Corfu and a relief force, Suleiman ordered the siege broken, remarking "I would not exchange the life of one of my janissaries for a thousand of such fortresses."[30] The Ottomans withdrew on 6 September, Hayreddin taking a measure of revenge by ravaging the lesser Venetian bases in the Aegean, taking Syros, Aegina, Ios, Paros, Andros, Tinos, Santorini, Karpathos, Kasos, and Naxos, before returning in triumph to Constantinople with a vast sum in spoils and slaves among his prizes.

The announcement of a Holy League against the Ottomans on 8 February 1538, incorporating Venice, the Hospitallers and the papacy as well as the Habsburgs, put pressure on Francis to agree to a joint meeting at Nice (then Genoese territory) proposed by Paul III. Shuttling between Charles and Francis, who refused to share the same room together – it had been only two years since Charles had delivered a speech before the Holy Father and College of Cardinals in Rome, publicly challenging the king of France to a duel – the pope persuaded both to sign off on a ten-year truce on 18 June, leaving Milan and other issues unresolved. But Charles must have been relieved to find a face-saving formula that allowed him to back out of what had become a ruinously expensive war with relatively good grace. His abortive campaign against Provence in 1536 had obliged Cobos to lean on Adam Centurione, Ansaldo Grimaldi, and Anton Fugger for nine separate loans totaling more than 915,000 ducats between April and September of that year alone, secured mainly by the pre-pledging of future American treasure shipments. The following year, Cobos was driven to the drastic resort of a currency devaluation, the Spanish treasury being ordered to widen the official gold-to-silver ratio from 10.1:1 to 10.6:1.[31] In 1538, the treasure arriving from the New World was again sequestered, Cobos countersigning the emperor's order "To seize all the gold and silver from the Indies fleet of Blasco Nunez Vela," the first viceroy of Peru, "because there are no other means in these realms that can help and succour us."[32]

Accordingly, when Queen Eleanor of France invited her brother to meet with her husband, the emperor enthusiastically accepted. Charles greeted Francis on board his imperial galley at Aigues-Mortes on 14 July, and went on land the next day to accept the king's hospitality. Leaving subordinates to work out the details, the two sovereigns agreed in general terms to a dual marriage, with Charles's son Philip to wed one of Francis's daughters, and Francis's son Charles, the Duke of Orléans, to wed a daughter or niece of the emperor, with Milan as her dowry. Both monarchs agreed to combat the Protestant heresy in their domains, and Francis pledged to join in a grand crusade against Christendom's Muslim foes.

In addition to the forty-nine galleys from Genoa under Andrea Doria, who had overall command of the operation, the joint fleet of the Holy League was composed of eighty-one ships from Venice, personally commanded by Vincenzo Capello, the city state's *provveditore all'armata* (superintendent of the fleet); thirty-six galleys from the papacy, under another Venetian Marco Grimani; and thirty galleys from Spain, under Ferrante Gonzaga. Hayreddin did not wait for the Christian powers to mobilize their full strength. In June 1538, with ninety galleys and fifty smaller *galiots*, he sailed past the Gulf of Corinth, aiming for Corfu. Venice sent fifty-five galleys to defend the island, joined on 17 June by twenty-seven papal galleys. Neither side took decisive action, the Christians because they were outnumbered and waiting for Doria to arrive, Hayreddin because if he was caught landing the men and artillery needed for a siege of the Venetian fortress on Corfu, his galleys would be vulnerable to attack by the smaller but better-armed Christian fleet.

Hayreddin pulled his ships back into the Gulf of Arta (the bay in which the decisive Battle of Actium had been fought between Octavian and Mark Antony in 31 BC) some fifty miles south of the Venetian and Papal ships at Corfu. It was a safe anchorage with a narrow, winding entrance, shielded by islands and headlands and commanded by the guns of the Ottoman-held fortress of Preveza on the northern side of the entrance to the bay.

Doria was extraordinarily dilatory about bringing his squadron to the fleet rendezvous at Corfu. It was not until 7 September that he finally appeared with his Spanish and Genoese galleys. Then he insisted on waiting for a convoy of transports with Imperial soldiers and artillery, which did not arrive until 22 September. Finally, he was forced to wait for a favorable wind. When at last a northerly started to blow, the Holy League fleet of some 130 full-sized galleys together with at least seventy-five Venetian and Imperial transports loaded with troops and guns arrived off the entrance of the Gulf of Arta and came to anchor in the lee of Preveza Point on 25 September, with three weeks at the most before the expected break in the weather which would mark the end of the campaigning season.

The strategic situation was a stalemate. Hayreddin was effectively trapped. Sending his galleys in single file out of the Gulf of Arta into the massed firepower of the Holy League fleet would be suicide. Conversely, Doria could not force the issue. There was no way his fleet could survive crossing the bar and passing up the tortuously shoaled channel under the guns of the fortress into the semicircle of Ottoman galleys drawn up across the entrance to the bay. The key to the situation lay on land. If the Holy League could take the fort of Preveza they would be in a strong position, able to beach their galleys before the weather broke, sink blockships in the channel and trap Hayreddin inside the Gulf. If they failed to take the fort they would be forced to abandon the position for lack of safe anchorage during the winter storm season.

However, Doria overruled all proposals from his subordinates to commit to a ground assault, arguing that if the fleet were caught by one of the northwesterly gales likely at that time of year, the troops ashore would be left unsupported and at the mercy of the Ottomans. If this was his reason, it begs the question as to why he had waited so long for the troopships in the first place. An Ottoman account suggests the allied galleys did attempt to land siege forces near the fortress on 26 September and were repulsed. There was some movement of Ottoman troops along the neck of land south of the fortress on that day and a long-range, partial galley action off the Preveza narrows, but no major land engagement took place. That same night Doria decided to weigh anchor and sail south to seek shelter at the island of Levkas (just north of Ithaca, the legendary home of Odysseus) and hopefully draw Hayreddin out from his defensive position.

The Holy League fleet set sail on the following morning of 27 September, soon becoming stretched out along a line of ships extending ten miles as the galleys lost contact with the slower-moving transports. Observing an opportunity, Hayreddin signaled for his fleet to set out in pursuit and pick off any isolated stragglers. The Ottoman squadrons, commanded by a host of legendary corsair captains – among them, Hayreddin's son, Hasan; Sinan Reis; Seydi Ali Reis; Salah Reis; Turgut Reis; and Murat Reis – swiftly isolated the heavily armed and armored but lumbering great galleon of Venice, commanded by Alessandro Condalmiero, blasting away her masts to leave her dead in the water. But when the Ottomans closed in for the kill, they were exposed to her devastating firepower at point-blank range. One galley was literally blown out of the water and then immediately sank, while a half-dozen galleys more were severely disabled, some needing to be towed out of range. Even while the Ottomans set off after easier prey, Doria, ignoring appeals from Grimani and Capello, refused to come to the aid of Condalmiero. At the end of the day, Hayreddin was left in possession of the seven Christian galleys he had captured, while Condalmiero survived the attention of the Ottoman fleet and succeeded in limping back to Corfu.[33]

The Venetians never forgave Doria for his passivity, but it was ultimately rewarded when Hayreddin was caught in a storm and many of his ships were wrecked off the Dalmatian coast. Doria then turned north, to the Gulf of Valona, at the narrowest point of the Adriatic, where the guns of his fleet reduced the defenses of the Ottoman-held fort of Castelnuovo (Herceg Novi), enabling its capture. Leaving 3,500 Spanish troops under *maestre de campo* (chief of staff of the Habsburg military, second only to the *capitán general*) Luis de Sarmiento to garrison this stronghold, Doria sailed for home. Herceg Novi would have been a more strategic foothold in Ottoman Greece than Koroni was, had it been held. But the next summer, while Hayreddin blockaded the fort from the sea with the entire Ottoman fleet – 130 oared warships and 200 sail – Ulamen Bey of Bosnia encircled it from the landward side with a massive army. The ensuing siege, which played out from 18 July to 6 August, cost the Ottomans thousands of troops but ended with their taking possession of the fort and wiping out the garrison, including Sarmiento.[34]

Charles could be satisfied the Ottomans had been kept out of the western Mediterranean, but with the Holy League functionally dead, Venice was forced to sue for a humiliating, separate peace with the Porte on 2 October 1540, the price of which was a staggering 236,000 ducats a year in tribute, in addition to surrendering Monemvasia and Nafplio and ceding the Ionian and Aegean islands already claimed by Hayreddin. Venice retained from her network of strategic bases only Crete, and Cyprus further east.

Hayreddin had become such a threat to Christian interests that Charles V had spent the best part of a decade attempting through covert embassies to win him over to the Habsburg cause.[35] In April 1540, Hayreddin issued his conditions. He demanded the Spanish guarantee him possession of Algiers, Béjaïa, Annaba, Tunis, La Goulette, and Tripoli. In exchange, he would deny his corsairs the privilege of raiding imperial territory, promising that his captains would settle down as the *caids* of the cities. Free trade would be encouraged. Hayreddin pledged to supply Charles with fifty or sixty galleys to use against the Venetians, the king of France, and even against the Ottoman sultan, swearing to send his son, Hasan, to Spain as a hostage to assure the emperor of his loyalty. Charles, however, wanted to retain Béjaïa because of its long Spanish occupation and Tripoli because it belonged to the Knights of Malta. He also demanded that Hayreddin deliver him the Ottoman fleet in addition to his own.[36] These terms were too stringent, and the corsair ultimately elected to remain in the service of the Porte.

ALGIERS, 1541

The schedule for the next phase of the war was structured by the long-standing determination of the emperor to arrive at a definitive religious settlement that could provide a foundation for genuine unity of purpose under his secular authority. Negotiations between Catholic and Protestant factions had played out at Haguenau in 1540 and at Worms in January 1541, but Charles hoped for a major breakthrough at the *Diet* of Regensburg, which commenced on 5 April 1541. The terms of the 1530 Augsburg Confession were again the primary focus for debate. Though neither Martin Luther nor Pope Paul III attended, each side was represented by theologians of significant status, including Philipp Melanchthon for the Protestants and Johann Maier von Eck for the Catholics. It swiftly became apparent the two factions were by now entrenched on opposite sides of a theological divide, and the prospects for harmonizing those divisions were illusory. The final parting of the ways came when the papal legate Gasparo Contarini insisted the Catholic conferees retain the term "transubstantiation" (to which Protestants vehemently objected) as a proper way of describing how bread and wine are transformed into the body and blood of Christ in the sacrament of the Eucharist. Charles summoned the legate to his quarters on 15 May, demanding to know if peace among Christians must really be held hostage to a single word. Contarini stood firm. It had been so also in the ancient church, torn apart over the vital assertion in the Nicene Creed that God the Son is "consubstantial" with God the Father.

On 5 July, the estates on both sides rejected the emperor's efforts for church union. Although there was not to be a grand compromise, Charles stayed on in Regensburg in order to salvage something from the months of negotiation. The best he could get was an agreement on 29 July, the so-called Regensburg Interim, in which both sides agreed to refer all religious differences to the next general council, failing which a national council, or (if neither had taken place after eighteen months) another meeting of the *diet*. Until then, the religious toleration granted by the 1530 Recess of Augsburg and 1532 Peace of Nuremberg would remain in effect. This satisfied nobody, but at least gave some assurance the emperor's Catholic and Protestant subjects would not turn on each other while he was absent on his next campaign.

Accordingly, at 2pm on 29 July, before the ink had dried on the clauses committing the Lutheran magnates of the Holy Roman Empire to contribute towards Ferdinand's campaign in Hungary, Charles galloped out of Regensburg to take command of another naval operation in the Mediterranean. His original intent was to lead the fleet he had ordered to muster in the Balearic Isles in a strike directly at Constantinople itself. When she learned of this agenda, the emperor's sister, Mary, governor of the Habsburg Netherlands and widow of King Louis II of Hungary, who had fallen at Mohács, was horrified. She wrote a blistering missive to Charles warning him "you are not obliged to defend Christendom alone, or with only a little assistance, and even less to attack our common enemy, especially one as powerful as the Turks. Moreover, even if Your Majesty might want to do this you need to consider if you have the power to do it successfully," for such a venture "should not be undertaken unless it will succeed." She also reminded him of how much had gone wrong during his expedition to Tunis: "In what state would you and your army have been if Barbarossa had not come out to do battle?" Yet Tunis "is just at the doorway to your possessions." Displaying a masterful grasp of strategic realities, Mary concluded:

> Even if the campaign starts so well that Your Majesty wins some town and begins to advance, if you lack the means to press on, think what a disgrace and cause for regret it would be. And if Your Majesty wants to keep your gains, please consider what it would cost and how hard it would be to supply and defend them against such a powerful enemy, given the distances involved.[37]

Chastened, Charles scaled back his ambitious project. Algiers, closer to hand, replaced Constantinople as his intended objective. Riding non-stop through Munich and Innsbruck, then over the Brenner Pass by way of Milan and Pavia, he arrived in Genoa. His seventy-four-year-old grand admiral Andrea Doria advised against the expedition, arguing it was too late in the year for a campaign on the African shore. Charles ignored him, setting out from Genoa on 10 September to meet with Paul III at Lucca. The pope also pleaded with him not to proceed, "because the season is far advanced and these troops should be in Hungary." Charles ignored the Holy Father too, setting in motion the concentration of all Imperial assets at La Palma in Majorca. Ferrante Gonzaga, viceroy of Sicily, was ordered to mobilize at Naples the galleys of Sicily and Naples, plus troop and supply ships for men from Spanish garrisons. The Spanish galleys, commanded by

Bernardino de Mendoza, were to escort the troop and supply ships arriving at Cartagena (from northern Spain and from the Low Countries). Embarkation was complicated by a rush of gentlemen volunteers paying their own way, including Hernán Cortés, the conqueror of Mexico. Their contributions at least helped defray the immense cost of the expedition. Charles and Cobos scrambled to find the 842,000 ducats required for the 155-ship armada, 20,000 or so troops, supplies, and royal entourage for a projected five-month campaign. A Fugger commitment of around 250,000 ducats left the bulk of the campaign costs to be borne by Habsburg Naples and Sicily, who came through in July 1541 with a three-year *donativo* of 772,000 ducats. This was whittled down to around 465,000 ducats after interest and transfer charges; it is unclear how the shortfall was bridged, but as usual, Cobos somehow found a way.[38]

Charles sailed from the Genoese port of La Spezia on 27 September. Rough weather and an attack of gout meant he arrived at La Palma by way of Corsica and Sardinia on 13 October. Ferrante Gonzaga, the Duke of Alba, and the Genoese under Andrea Doria were already assembled with their contingents, but Bernardino de Mendoza was nowhere to be seen. After a few days, a galley got through with the message that Mendoza, with the combined Spanish fleet, had been at Ibiza for ten days, trying in vain to make headway for Majorca against contrary winds. Charles sent word that Mendoza should make directly for Algiers, then set sail for the city himself. On 19 October, 500 transport ships, manned by 12,000 men and carrying 24,000 soldiers, stood off the bay of Algiers. Mendóza's galleys, with another 100 troop and supply ships in their train, rendezvoused with this armada the following day.

It was late in the season, but this had its own distinct advantage as it avoided any possibility of Ottoman intervention, for Hayreddin was stationed in Constantinople and could not commit his fleet as far west as Algiers with the year already so far advanced. His deputy, the Sardinian renegade Hasan Agha who governed the Regency of Algiers in Hayreddin's stead, would have to confront the oncoming Christian armada with nothing more than the forces at his disposal, a mere 800 janissaries, and a few thousand local auxiliaries under Sheik Sidi Said Cherif.

All through Friday 21 and Saturday 22 October a heavy swell made landing impossible. But, after the emperor heard mass on Sunday morning, the weather changed, and the infantry began disembarking at a point chosen by Doria about seven miles east of Algiers. The next day, the expeditionary force commenced construction of three camps "according to nations," with the Italians closest to shore and the Spaniards occupying the lower slopes of a ridge of hills dominating the shoreline. The Spaniards then drove off detachments of Algerine skirmishers, and occupied the heights within sight of the city. With a web of trenches expanding around Algiers, all was now ready for offloading the artillery and supplies that would permit the siege to commence.

But every calculation was thrown off that evening and into the morning of 24 October, when there arose a storm of such uncommon ferocity it would be remembered by local peoples for centuries as "the wind of Charles." Hasan Agha seized the moment to launch an attack that morning, under the cover of the shrieking winds. He pushed the landing force back to the coast and seemed on the point of breaking through to Charles himself. Only the resistance of the Knights of St John gave the German troops time to come up and defend their emperor. A counterattack, led by the Knights, threw Hasan's men out of the trenches, then drove them back to the very walls of the city. However, artillery on the walls soon cleared the approaches, and as tribal warriors descended from the hills towards the embattled Christian camp, Hasan led his cavalry out of the city at a gallop in a frontal attack on the enemy lines. The emperor himself had to rally his army, and it survived until nightfall, only to be left huddling in the darkness. Having disembarked without tents or any wet-weather gear, the troops were left to be lashed unprotected by the high winds, freezing rain, and hail until the storm finally abated on 26 October.

As the skies cleared, an accounting could at last be undertaken. It made for grim reading. A staggering 140 sailing ships and fifteen galleys of the Christian armada were lost, broken to pieces as they rode in the water or dashed against the rocks, and with them much of the artillery and most of the provisions.

Doria had managed to find a safer harbor for the remainder of the fleet at Cape Matifu, five miles east of Algiers, and sent word for the emperor to join him there. Some in the emperor's council of war (among them Hernán Cortés) argued that Algiers, with its small garrison, could still be taken, but Charles this time decided discretion was the better part of valor and ordered a withdrawal. The drenched, disillusioned, and starving army (which only survived because Charles ordered the horses slaughtered and eaten) was harassed by tribesmen who now swarmed down from the mountains to join in attacking the retreating invaders, as well as by Hasan Agha, who once again led his garrison in attacking the rearguard. As a consequence of the rain, normally dry riverbeds had become all but impassible torrents, while flood plains had become marshes. When the troops reached the El Harrach River, midway to their destination, they found that flash floods had washed out the bridges. It took skilled engineers working with lumber from broken Spanish ships to rig a way across.

Upon reaching the coast on 2 November, the emperor, who wished to be one of the last to leave the African shore, waded out into the surf and was hoisted into a rowing boat. No sooner had the remnant of the fleet embarked than it was scattered by another storm. Charles was forced to seek shelter in the fortified outpost of Béjaïa until 23 November, when the weather cleared and he could set sail for Mallorca and then Cartagena, where he landed on 1 December.

With Charles chastened, the Ottomans again seized the initiative. Suleiman himself would lead the offensive by land into the Balkans against Ferdinand, delegating to Hayreddin the task of keeping Charles occupied at sea. Again, Ottoman strategic initiatives in the western Mediterranean would be staged in cooperation with the French. Suleiman departed Constantinople on 6 May 1543 at the head of his army, bound for a campaign in Hungary. Before his departure, the sultan dispatched a letter to Francis I, expressing his intentions: "I have ordered Hayreddin, my *kapudan pasha* to listen to your instructions and to form his enterprises to the ruin of your enemies."[39] The sultan's instructions to Hayreddin himself were explicit – preserve his fleet at all costs, but otherwise, use his discretion. "You are my useful and trusted servant. I rely on your piety and sound judgment in all matters. In the past you attacked those areas in the course of holy war. You know everything about the infidels and their lands. Because I rely on you completely, I placed you in command over all aspects of the imperial fleet."[40]

The Ottoman fleet, comprising 110 galleys, forty *fustes*, and three great *nefs* full of artillery and munitions, and a total of 25,000–30,000 men, sailed via the Aegean to Reggio on the Straits of Messina in Habsburg territory, which it sacked, before proceeding to Marseilles on the Mediterranean coast of France, where it arrived on 20 July to rendezvous with the French fleet under François de Bourbon, Count of Enghien. The target for the joint expedition was Nice, in territory ruled by the Duke of Savoy, the uncle of Francis I, but an ally of Charles V. When the French offered terms for the surrender of the city, the garrison prolonged the negotiations to allow reinforcements to arrive. The Ottomans deployed their artillery to breach the walls, and they captured the outer city on 22 August. The garrison sought to gain time by swearing they would surrender the citadel to the French on condition they arrange for the withdrawal of the Ottoman forces. Hayreddin suspected this was a trick, but did pull his men back to their ships. As soon as this happened, the garrison broke off negotiations and resumed fighting. The French had to not only beg Hayreddin to return to the siege, but for ammunition because their own stocks had run out.

These delays saved the day for the Imperial cause. The Duke of Savoy reached out to the Marquis del Vasto, Charles V's commander at Milan, for additional troops, which Doria transported from Genoa to Nice. A storm rolled in at the same time as the relief force. Barbarossa judged the harbor at Nice insufficiently sheltered for the Ottoman fleet and pulled his ships back to seek a haven among nearby islands. While the Ottoman ships escaped unharmed, Doria lost four of his galleys. He did, however, succeed in landing the Imperial reinforcements, obliging the French to raise the siege, burning the city as they pulled out.

This setback notwithstanding, Francis was determined to make the alliance work. On 8 September, Royal *lettres patentes* were sent to Louis Adhémar, Comte de Grignan, the governor of Provence, commanding the people of Toulon to leave the city in order to create winter accommodations for the Ottoman personnel. On 9 October, the king instructed his deputies in the field to do whatever was necessary to convince Hayreddin to remain in Provence until the following year. Hayreddin was receptive, writing to the sultan to explain that it would be risky to raise anchor for Constantinople so late in the sailing season, and in the absence of his fleet, Doria would have free rein to ravage the French coast.

Placing Toulon at Hayreddin's disposal did not solve the problem of winter quarters for the Ottoman fleet, for even at the end of the 16th century the city still had only had 637 houses within its walls. The ship's officers and crews were dispersed throughout the city, the suburbs, and in tents that sprawled over open ground. Concerned to maintain the fighting edge of these men, and meet their expectations of remuneration and reward, Hayreddin authorized small-scale raids throughout the winter against coastal towns on the Italian Riviera, including San Remo, Borghetto Santo Spirito, and Ceriale.[41]

In the spring of 1544, plans were made for a joint Ottoman–French operation against Genoa. Once again, however, negotiations dragged out, and the assembled French forces were ultimately diverted to reinforce François de Bourbon for his campaign against the Habsburgs in the Piedmont that culminated in the Battle of Cerisoles on 11 April. Hayreddin weighed anchor and departed Toulon in March, sailing for the Iles d'Hyeres, where he remained for about two months waiting to see if Francis could offer some new stratagem. But by May the Ottomans, by now convinced no campaign would be undertaken and concerned that if they remained in France any longer they would lose their window of opportunity to return home for another year, unilaterally determined the venture was over. Hayreddin sailed for Marseilles, where he freed the Muslim galley slaves, who were prisoners on French ships, then set sail for Constantinople. The expedition was not a complete loss; en route, the Ottomans sacked the island of Lipari, seizing its inhabitants and then ransoming them to the city of Messina in Sicily for 15,000 ducats and enough ship biscuit to last them the voyage home.

The fleet arrived at Constantinople on 14 October, less than a month after Francis and Charles V came to terms in the Treaty of Crépy on 18 September. The two rivals would never again clash, but after Francis died on 31 March 1547, his anti-Habsburg instincts and proclivity to an Ottoman alliance would be inherited by his son and successor, Henry II.[42]

Charles had once again achieved nothing more than maintaining the status quo, and in the process had stressed his ramshackle realm to breaking point. Like an addict, Spain could no longer function without its regular fix of bullion from the New World. The inevitable corollary of dependency on the gold and silver arriving from the Americas – inflation – was undermining the competitive basis of the Spanish economy.[43] The Habsburg state was also drowning in red ink. In the two-year 1543–44 period alone, annual short-term borrowing by the Spanish treasury averaged 1.6 million ducats – nearly four times the average level incurred between 1520 and 1542. Since the Crown was paying as much as 13 percent interest on its short-term debt, Cobos was faced with a severe cash flow problem, which could only be partially met through the increasingly regular confiscated-treasure-for-*juro* exchanges. Having exhausted both credit and good will in Spain – his presence at the *cortes* of 1542 would be his last – Charles relocated to Brussels in order to extort punitive levels of taxation from the Estates General of the Netherlands.[44]

After the death of Hayreddin on 5 July 1546, the Ottoman impetus in the Mediterranean slackened as the navy was caught up in bureaucratic infighting. The post of *kapudan pasha* was awarded to Sokollu Mehmed Pasha, who had no particular experience at sea. A veteran of the Two Iraqs campaign, he had then entered into the palace service where he held the positions of *çaşnigîrbaşı* (chief taster) and *kapıcıbaşı* (head doorkeeper). Three years later, the appointment of Sinan Pasha as *kapudan pasha* was owed to the direct influence of his brother, the Grand Vizier Rüstem Pasha, and to the indirect influence of the sultan's favorite concubine, Hürrem, whose daughter, Mihrimah, was the grand vizier's wife. Sinan's elevation was therefore an adjunct to the infighting at court where Rüstem, Hürrem, and Mihrimah schemed to prevent Mustafa, Suleiman's eldest son by an earlier concubine, from inheriting the throne.[45]

Though Turgut Reis appeared to be the best qualified candidate for the position of *kapudan pasha*, Rüstem distrusted the corsairs and blatantly favored those elevated through the palace schools of administration (*enderun*). Turgut had conquered Mahdiyya and Monastır, carving out of the dying Hafsid kingdom of Tunis a power base for himself in the Gulf of Gabes. In 1550, Charles V dispatched against Mahdiyya a combined Imperial–Hospitaller fleet under the joint command of the now eighty-four-year-old Andrea Doria, Bernardino de Mendoza, captain general of the galleys of Spain, and Claude de la Sengle, Grand Master of the Knights of Malta. After a naval bombardment breached the walls of the city it capitulated in September. Monastır was also taken, and Doria attacked Djerba the following year, almost seizing Turgut in the process.

Determined to retaliate, Suleiman ordered Sinan Pasha to lead the Ottoman navy and corsair auxiliaries under Turgut Reis and Salah Reis in a counterstrike against Tripoli. The Ottoman force staged an amphibious landing on Malta and marched against the strongholds of the Knights, but, finding these too well defended, elected to undertake a *razzia* against neighboring Gozo instead, functionally depopulating the entire island. The ensuing siege of Tripoli forced the surrender of the city on 15 August after a six-day bombardment. The garrison was constituted of only thirty knights and 630 mercenary soldiers who had been recruited from Calabria and Sicily; these latter, who hadn't been paid, mutinied and threatened to open the gates to the fort unless the leader of the Knights negotiated a surrender. Turgut had yet another ace up his sleeve – the presence in his fleet of the French ambassador, Gabriel d'Aramon, who was put in charge of negotiations with the French-speaking Knights of the Tongue of Auvergne who held Tripoli. Thanks to Turgut's lenient instructions they quickly came to terms. The knights could depart with their arms and flags flying if they left the fortifications of Tripoli unslighted.[46]

The French were, again, entirely unapologetic regarding their deepening commitment to an alliance with the Ottomans. The *Apologie pour le Roy, contre les calomnies des Imperiaulx*, published in 1551 (after d'Aramon's involvement in the fall of Tripoli) by the humanist scholar, diplomat, and royal tutor Pierre Danes dismissed the appeals to religious solidarity on the part of pro-Imperial writers as mere camouflage. Those who denounced the French monarch sought, "under the mask of religion and holiness, to confuse everything, establish a tyranny in Italy, and rob the King of his possessions."[47]

Turgut had been induced to join the expedition with the promise that he would be appointed *beylerbey* of Tripoli after the fall of the city. However, that honor was instead bestowed on Hadim Murad Agha of neighboring Tajura. Furious, Turgut retired to Edirne, where he did succeed in receiving the less prosperous *beylerbeyilik* of Tripolitania from the sultan.[48] From this powerbase, Turgut defeated Andrea Doria, who lost seven galleys, in the Battle of Ponza on 5 August 1552, and played a leading role in a combined Franco-Ottoman invasion of Corsica that wrested control of the island from Genoa the following year (and held it until it was returned in the 1559 Treaty of Cateau-Cambrésis).

These successes notwithstanding, Turgut would be disappointed once more when Rüstem Pasha dissuaded the sultan from appointing him as *kapudan pasha* to succeed Sinan Pasha when the latter died in 1554, another palace-educated official, Piyale Pasha, being appointed in his place.

Turgut, however, remained a constant threat to Christian coastal communities, most notably in the 1554 sack of Vieste in Italy, where the entire population was massacred or enslaved. Salah Reis, now *beylerbey* of Algiers, captured the Spanish *presidio* of Béjaïa in 1555; a joint French–Ottoman naval force descended on Naples that same year; Oran was taken from the Spanish in 1556, and Bizerte in 1557. The following year, an Ottoman fleet under Turgut and Piyale Pasha descended on the Balearic Isles. This vulnerable archipelago had already endured a miserable decade with isolated and exposed communities like Alcúdia (1551), Valldemossa (1552), and Andratx (1553) being selected for devastating *razzias*. Turgut's target in 1558 was Ciutadella, a port established at the western end of Minorca by the Carthaginians centuries earlier. Those townsfolk who survived the Ottoman onslaught, along with the villagers scoured from the surrounding countryside, a total of 3,452 people, would never see their homes again, a far from unusual fate for entire communities during this era. The Ottomans then set sail on the return voyage east, sacking Sorrento and depopulating Reggio en route. The arrival of the victorious Ottoman fleet in Constantinople, replete with slaves and spoils and captured ships in tow, was "a sight as joyful to the Turks as it was mournful and deplorable to us Christians," the Habsburg ambassador, Osier de Busbecq, lamented; his residence was surrounded by jeering crowds who congregated at his door "and mockingly asked my people whether they had a brother or relation or friend in the Spanish fleet; for, if so, they would have the pleasure of seeing them shortly."[49]

Another joint Franco-Ottoman campaign came to nothing when their respective fleets failed to meet at the arranged place in 1558, the Ottomans continuing on to unilaterally sack Sorrento near Naples. After they did eventually succeed in coordinating a rendezvous, the French tried to persuade Piyale Pasha to return with them to Toulon so they could combine forces and attack Bastia in Corsica, but the *kapudan pasha* declined the offer and the Ottomans returned to the Levant.

9

THE MEDITERRANEAN, PART II – MALTA, CYPRUS, AND LEPANTO

MALTA, 1565

The Treaty of Cateau-Cambrésis, signed on 3 April 1559 by Philip II of Spain and Henry II of France, finally ended the war between those two great powers and allowed for Spain to concentrate on its deteriorating strategic position in the Mediterranean. A plan proposed by Jean Parisot de Valette, Grand Master of the Knights of St John on Malta, and Juan de la Cerda, Duke of Medinaceli and viceroy of Sicily, to seize Tripoli was adopted. A Crusader fleet was mustered comprising vessels from Spanish Italy, Genoa, the Papal States, the Duchy of Savoy, the Hospitallers, and Tuscany, where Cosimo de' Medici had set up his own order of maritime knights, the Cavalieri di Santo Stefano, partly modeled on the Hospitallers, so as to play a larger role on the Mediterranean stage.[1] Overall command of the fleet was entrusted to Gian Andrea Doria, the twenty-one-year-old great-nephew of Andrea Doria.

However, delays in organization meant it was not until 1 December, long after the regular sailing season had ended, that the Crusader fleet left Syracuse, fifty-four warships and thirty-six supply ships carrying a mixed force of 12,000 men drawn from the garrisons and mercenaries in the service of the Habsburgs. The fleet only managed to get halfway across the Strait of Sicily before a storm forced it to overwinter in Malta.

In mid-February 1560, the Crusaders set out again for Tripoli. A successful landing was made, but disease, bad weather, and the lack of water forced the Crusaders to abandon the siege. To salvage something from the campaign,

Medinaceli occupied the island of Djerba on 7 March and began work on improvements to the fortress of Hamut-es-Suk on the northern shore.

Ironically, the delayed start to the Crusader offensive actually worked in its favor initially, for the Ottoman fleet had presumed that the operation had been called off and had returned to port in October 1559, leaving the sea lanes open. When word arrived that the Crusader fleet was active, Piyale Pasha immediately responded, raiding Gozo on 6 May to take prisoners for intelligence on the enemy's dispositions and intentions, and arriving off Djerba five days later. The Crusaders panicked as the eighty-six Ottoman galleys descended on the anchored invasion fleet. In the words of Busbecq, "They had neither the courage to fight nor the presence of mind to escape. A few galleys, it is true, which were cleared for action, sought safety in flight; the rest stuck fast, or broke up in the shallow water, or were surrounded by the enemy and sunk."[2]

Twenty-eight ships out of the forty-eight in the Crusader fleet were immediately sunk or taken (including the papal flagship), and 5,000 men were slain or captured. The surviving 8,000 Crusaders fled to the safety of the Hamut-es-Suk fortress. Medinaceli and Doria slipped through the Ottoman blockade on a fast cutter that night, leaving the garrison under the command of the Spaniard Álvaro de Sande, a veteran of the siege of Tunis in 1535. His position was not immediately hopeless. The fortress now boasted seventy guns, a good supply of ammunition, food enough for six months, and two large cisterns providing sufficient water for the garrison. Piyale, with only 7,000 men under his command, was actually outnumbered (though Turgut would arrive with 5,000 more men in May), and without heavy siege guns. If he could not reduce the fortress by October, he would be forced to break off and sail for home as he could not risk being at sea during the winter. Nonetheless, he imposed a tight cordon around the Hamut-es-Suk and, by redeploying the cannon from his galleys, began to compromise the defenses of the fortress, opening a breach in the outer wall and taking one of the two cisterns. No help was coming for the Crusaders. The mobilization of a relief expedition, to be recruited from all Christendom, had been announced with great fanfare, only to be quietly canceled on 15 June by Philip II, who refused to risk more money, men, or ships on a lost cause. Increasingly desperate Crusader sallies failed to break the Ottoman lines, and as summer advanced and the water supply dwindled to nothing, the situation became critical. Leading a breakout attempt, Sande himself was captured on 28 July, and the last holdouts of the garrison capitulated three days later, an ignominious end to the eighty-two-day siege.[3]

To commemorate their victory, the Ottomans built a pyramid from the skulls of those Crusaders slain on Djerba. Bleached white in the hot, dry sun, it was still visible centuries later. The holds of their ships packed with prisoners, the fleet then sailed, unhindered, for Constantinople. To drive home Ottoman supremacy, en route Piyale watered his ships at Gozo, sacked the town of Augusta on Sicily, and ravaged the coast of Abruzzo. Busbecq described how the prisoners were paraded through the streets when the Ottoman fleet arrived in Constantinople: "They were made a laughing stock, being forced to wear their armor back to front... The cries of the Turks were to be heard all around uttering insults and proclaiming themselves the masters of the whole world; for, now that the Spaniards had been vanquished, what enemy remained whom they need to fear?"[4]

The Ottomans were indeed ascendant at sea. In the summer of 1561, Turgut's command of the central Mediterranean was spectacularly confirmed when he captured the Sicilian navy's last seven galleys in an engagement fought off the corsairs' favorite anchorage, the Lipari islands. The loss of what remained of the Spanish fleet – twenty-eight galleys sunk by a storm off the coast of Málaga in 1562 – seemed to confirm the eclipse of Christian naval power. In 1563 the corsairs of Algiers felt confident enough to strike out on their own, placing Oran and its associated fortress of Mers El Kebir under siege during the summer. That year, in full view of King Philip II, a corsair vessel seized a Spanish merchant ship just three miles off Valencia, and nothing could be done about it. The raiders no longer needed the cover of night and started their landings in broad daylight. "Turgut," a French bishop wrote, "has held the kingdom of Naples in such a noose" and Christian galleys "are so harassed and confined" that Christian shipping in the Mediterranean was effectively shut down.[5]

The momentum was clearly running entirely in favor of the Ottomans, and Malta was the obvious choice as their next objective. The specific *casus belli* for the campaign was the exploits of the Hospitaller Mathurin aux Lescaut, better known as Romegas. Hailing from Provence, he was professed as a knight in 1546 and quickly established a reputation as a fearless privateer. In 1564 he served alongside García Álvarez de Toledo, 4th Marquis of Villafranca, in a Spanish campaign to reclaim the stronghold of Peñon de Velez on the North African coast (taken by Spain in 1506, it had been lost in 1522). Later that year, he led the Order's galleys in seizing the *Sultana*, a large and heavily armed Ottoman galleon under the command of Bairan Ogli Reis with 200 janissaries on board, near Kefalonia. The ship belonged to Kustir Agha, the chief eunuch of the Topkapi Palace, and bore cargo valued at 80,000 Venetian gold ducats.

Romegas also took about 300 prisoners, among them the governor of Cairo, the governor of Alexandria, and Giansevere Serchies, the former nurse of Suleiman's daughter Mihrimah, returning from a pilgrimage to Mecca. Enraged, the sultan issued orders to mobilize an expedition against Malta, giving two simple justifications: the island had become "a headquarters for infidels," and the Hospitallers "blocked the route utilized by Muslim pilgrims and merchants in the East Mediterranean, on their way to Egypt."[6] The geopolitical rationale for the campaign ran far deeper. Malta occupied a strategic position in the dead center of the Mediterranean that enabled both Christian operations against North Africa on a north–south axis, and compromised Ottoman access to the Maghreb on an east–west axis. Taking the island would reverse this paradigm; controlling Malta would empower the Ottomans with unchecked lines of communication and supply to their corsair allies, and unlimited access to the coasts of Christian Italy and Spain. In September 1563, as the Council of Trent was finally winding down, it heard a long and eloquent speech by a Hospitaller emissary, who reminded the delegates that if Malta fell, "it can scarcely be doubted that this would strike a very great wound – perhaps an incurable one – in the whole body of Christendom." The Spanish viceroy in Sicily, García Álvarez de Toledo, warned King Philip II, "If Malta is lost, not only would there be the loss of those who are therein, which would be great, but it would be simply like having the kingdoms of Sicily and Naples with a chain around their necks; and joining hands with Tripoli, [our enemies] could at any time gather together all the forces of Barbary."[7]

Philip had indulged the Grand Master with 50,000 ducats to repair the walls of Malta and another 56,000 ducats strengthening the defenses of La Goulette. However, he was not willing to intervene directly, least of all to risk his precious new fleet, which remained on station in Sicily, allowing the Ottomans complete control of the waters around Malta.

The Ottoman fleet departed from Constantinople on 29 March 1565 and set a leisurely pace as it progressed through the Aegean, rendezvousing with detachments converging from other stations. When the expedition arrived off Marsaxloxx Bay on the south coast of Malta on 18 May it comprised hundreds of ships and tens of thousands of fighting men, including janissaries and *sipahis*, plus seventy heavy siege cannon. Suleiman had assigned command of the expedition to Piyale Pasha, the hero of Djerba, who led naval operations, and the experienced fourth *vizier serdar*, Kızılahmedli Mustafa Pasha, who led the army. Both were expected to defer to the supreme authority of Turgut Reis once he joined the siege with reinforcements.

To oppose this force, a Hospitaller roll-call in early May tallied 546 knights and serving brothers. This elite was supplemented by a few thousand mercenaries and Spanish troops, and another few thousand Maltese irregulars, for a total of perhaps 6,000 men. In command was the Grand Master, Valette, whose age is variously given as sixty-seven or seventy years old at the time of the siege. A Provençal who had been professed as a knight in 1518 and survived the fall of Rhodes in 1522, he had relocated with the Order to Malta in 1530. His constant service in the struggle for control of the Mediterranean led to his being seriously wounded and his galley, the *San Giovanni*, captured by corsairs under the command of Turgut Reis in 1541. After a year at the oars as a slave (during which he learned to speak Turkish, adding that language to his fluency in French, Spanish, Greek, and Arabic) he was released in a prisoner exchange. Appointed governor of Tripoli in 1546 and captain general of the Order's fleet in 1554, he ultimately ascended to become Grand Master in 1557.

In addition to Romegas, Valette's subordinates included Sir Oliver Starkey (the last of his countrymen to represent the English langue in the wake of Henry VIII's decision to wean his country away from the Catholic Church); Luigi Broglio, commander of Fort St Elmo; Melchior d'Eguaras, captain of cavalry; Dom Mesquita of Portugal, commander of Mdina; Marshal Coppier, commander of the horse; and Vincenzo Anastagi, who would act as a conduit between Valette and García during the siege.

Aware an invasion was imminent, Valette had mobilized every asset at his disposal, recalling knights to the island, raising troops, laying in stores of food and water, and improving the fortifications, which were already formidable. Decades of labor had built out the walls and bastions on the main stronghold that dominated the Great Harbor, Fort St Angelo, at the tip of the Birgu peninsula, which extended from the south shore. This connected to the mainland via the port town of Birgu, which was walled off and defended from west to east by bastions named after the langue assigned to it – the posts of Aragon, Provence, France, Auvergne, the Genoese, and Castile. To the west of Birgu, across Kalkara Creek, defended by the posts of Germany and England, was another peninsula, Senglea. The defenses here were anchored by Fort St Michael, its wall buttressed by the posts of Carlo Ruffo (later renamed to the Post of Robles), Italy, the de Medi, and the Maltese. Finally, the Fort of St Elmo, on the tip of the Sciberras peninsula, guarded the entrance to both the Grand Harbor to its south and the Marsamxett harbor to the north.[8]

Valette had ordered the wells poisoned and the animals slaughtered, leaving nothing for the enemy, who now marched to set up camp at Marsa at the far western terminus of the Grand Harbor. It was now that the divided command structure of the Ottoman force exposed the fatal defect in its strategy. Mustafa advocated for taking the unprotected old capital, Mdina, at the island's center, then laying siege to Birgu. However, Piyale, either acting on his own initiative or determined to follow through on the predetermined orders of the Porte, insisted on anchoring his fleet at Marsamxett harbor, both to add its firepower to that of the siege guns and to shelter it from the sirocco, the hot Mediterranean winds that blow north out of the Sahara, reaching hurricane intensity during the summer season. If significant numbers of vessels were lost in a storm – still a possibility within the more open Marsaxloxx Bay – the Ottoman army would be stranded and cut off. There was also the question of logistics. Marsaxloxx was eight miles from the site of the siege, which meant moving supplies overland. That distance was not prohibitively far, but men freed from such labor could be put to better use in other ways. Additionally, men and materiel being convoyed along the land route from Marsaxloxx would be exposed to interdiction from those elements of the resistance still at large on the island, which would necessitate escorts, another drain on Ottoman manpower.[9]

Securing Marsamxett harbor as an anchorage would require first reducing Fort St Elmo at its entrance. Accordingly, the fort was invested and, commencing on 24 May, subjected to a continuous bombardment. One knight among the garrison holding St Elmo, Girolamo Pepe Napolitano, counted the shots and calculated that "a day did not pass in which six or seven hundred cannonades were not fired against it."[10] On 31 May, García urged Philip II for authority to mobilize a relief force, regardless of the risk, for "What matters is that if Malta is not helped now, I believe it will fall."[11] But the king, convinced his ships' "conservation was more important than the relief," remained unmoved.[12]

When the eighty-year-old Turgut arrived on 2 June, leading a flotilla of thirteen galleys convoying two galleots bearing 1,500 reinforcements, he reprimanded Piyale for throwing away time and resources on a secondary objective. If St Michael was taken, he explained, then St Elmo would have no value and constitute no threat, however many troops it held. However, even if St Elmo were to fall, St Michael could stand alone for years.[13]

Contemporary Christian chroniclers agreed. According to Francesco Balbi da Correggio, if Mustafa's plan to attack Mdina, Birgu, and St Michael simultaneously had been put into effect, then Malta would have fallen. "But God almighty did not wish for our defeat and through his will the two Paşas, jealous of each other, were not in agreement; the result of their errors is evident and, for us, so favorable."[14]

Although he disagreed with the rationale, now the expedition had been committed to securing St Elmo, Turgut knew the fort had to be taken. He distributed the artillery in order to bring the defense under fire from three flanks simultaneously, and pushed patrol boats into the Grand Harbor to choke off the flow of supplies and reinforcements that had been filtering into St Elmo at night. By 3 June, the Ottomans had seized the fort's ravelin and moat. However, attempts to storm St Elmo on 10, 15, and 16 June were all repulsed.

On 18 June, Turgut was mortally wounded while coordinating operations from the front-line trenches. But by 23 June, the defenses of the fort had been reduced to rubble and its garrison decimated. Aware the final assault was imminent, a pair of severely wounded knights, Juan de Guaras and Juan de Miranda, insisted on being strapped to chairs and carried to the breach in the walls; no longer able to stand, they could still wield their swords sitting down. Fighting to the last man, the defenders were overwhelmed and massacred. St Elmo was in Ottoman hands at last, and with it Marsamxett harbor, but the cost, including half the janissaries, was enormous. Frustrated, Mustafa had the bodies of slain Christians floated across the Grand Harbor on mock crucifixes. In response, Valette brought all his Ottoman prisoners to the battlements of Birgu, in plain view of the enemy, ordered them decapitated, and tossed their heads over the wall.

García had been mustering troops in Sicily, and he persuaded Philip II to authorize a *Piccolo Soccorso* (Small Relief) force of forty-two knights and some 600 men-at-arms to attempt a landing on Malta. After at least four attempts, this detachment, under the command of Melchior de Robles, a Spanish knight of the Order of St James, managed to slip through into Mdina under cover of a heavy fog on 29 June, and then into Birgu under cover of darkness on the evening of 3–4 July.

While a tremendous fillip for the garrison's morale, this feat did little to alter the strategic situation. With St Elmo reduced, the Ottoman noose began tightening around the remaining strongholds, and reinforcements continued to arrive in the Ottoman camp, including the *bey* of Algiers, Hasan Pasha (the son of Hayreddin), who pulled in at Malta with 2,500 corsairs. They would take part in Mustafa's planned concerted attack against the Senglea peninsula, which commenced on 12 July with a two-day, two-night bombardment. Shades of Constantinople in 1453, Mustafa hauled 100 small vessels across the Sciberras peninsula from the Marsamxett to the Grand Harbor, thus avoiding interdiction by the guns of Fort St Angelo, in order to launch a seaward strike led by his janissaries against the western approach to the promontory, while the corsairs attacked Fort St Michael on the landward end. When these assaults had tied down the defenders, the third prong of the offensive, an amphibious assault directly across the Grand Harbor, would go into effect.

The fighting was desperate. "I don't know if the image of hell can describe the appalling battle," chronicler Giacomo Bosio related, struggling to find the terms by which he could do justice to "the fire, the heat, the continuous flames from the flamethrowers and fire hoops; the thick smoke, the stench, the disemboweled and mutilated corpses, the clash of arms, the groans, shouts, and cries, the roar of the guns... men wounding, killing, scrabbling, throwing one another back, falling and firing."[15]

Unfortunately for the Ottomans, while the first two phases of the offensive played their parts, stretching the garrison to its limit in fighting them off, the trajectory of the naval assault force brought its boats into point-blank range of a battery of guns that had been sited by Chevalier de Guiral at the base of Fort St Angelo with the specific purpose of halting just such an amphibious attack. A single salvo sank nine out of ten vessels in the first wave, killing or drowning over 800 of the attackers, and subsequent efforts were met by equally murderous fire. The other two assaults finally petered out, the Ottomans on the western flank of the Senglea, abandoned by their boats and left trapped on the shore, being torn to shreds by a withering crossfire and then finished off by a Christian counterattack. The cost had been high – among the ranks of the garrison slain was the son of García de Toledo, the viceroy of Sicily – but Malta held.

While the Ottomans licked their wounds, Birgu and Senglea remained under what was probably the most sustained bombardment in history up to that time. Balbi claimed the enemy's guns fired 130,000 rounds over the course of the siege; by the end of July, at the height of the barrage, the thunder from the guns was so great it "could be heard distinctly in Syracuse," across the channel in Sicily; to those on the receiving end, "it seemed as if the end of the world had come."[16]

By 18 July, Ottoman engineers were all but finished with a bridge across the moat to Fort St Michael. It would have to be destroyed by hand, and Valette's nephew, Henri Parisot, volunteered to lead an attempt. After improvising a sally port by chipping away from inside the stone wall to open a gap, he led a raiding party through the breach only to be shot down before even reaching the bridge.

Even while attending to his duties coordinating the defense, Valette continued to dash off a relentless stream of correspondence to the Christian world, warning the loss of Malta would render Europe as "a fortress without a ravelin."[17] The consequences of an Ottoman victory were certainly appreciated. "We realize," Pope Pius II wrote, "in how great peril of well-being of Sicily and Italy will be put, and what great calamities threaten the Christian people, if (which God forbid!)" Malta "should come under the dominion of the impious enemy."[18]

Entirely aware of the stakes involved, García was genuinely trying to channel reinforcements to Valette. Three galleys set out in a bid to transport 600 papal troops under Pompeo Colonna and those Hospitallers who had assembled in Sicily after the siege commenced and were now desperately trying to come to the aid of their brethren. However, their attempt to run the Ottoman blockade failed.[19]

Mustafa ordered another massive double assault on 7 August, this time against Fort St Michael and Birgu itself. The Ottomans breached the town walls, and the sultan's standard was seen fluttering from the ramparts. Malta was theirs for the taking, but the Ottomans suddenly – and to the garrison inexplicably – broke off and withdrew.

Relief had come from Mdina, which captain of cavalry Vincenzo Anastagi had been using as a base for hit-and-run raids against outlying Ottoman detachments for weeks. At this critical moment, he sallied from Mdina and stormed the Ottoman camp at Marsa, massacring the sick and wounded left in the unprotected field hospital. When the Ottoman troops saw the smoke rising from their burning tents they abandoned the assault and rushed back to their camp, only to encounter the demoralizing reality of finding their comrades butchered, their possessions looted, and their shelters reduced to ash.

A war of mine and countermine commenced, with ugly skirmishes flaring up deep underground as the struggle for control of the subterranean battlefield raged with an intensity commensurate to that on the surface. On 18 August, the Ottomans finally succeeded in detonating a mine beneath the Post of Castile on the southeast corner of the Birgu wall, collapsing much of the structure. Storming parties swarmed into the breach, and again the sultan's banner was planted on what remained of the battlements. Valette led the counterattack in person and was wounded, but held the line long enough to witness the Ottoman banner being cast down and the enemy pushed back to their trenches.

The Ottomans still holding the salient of the bastion before the Post of Castile were blasted out by a countermine. The Ottomans raised a siege tower, but the garrison's engineers tunneled out through the rubble of the fort and with a point-blank salvo of chain shot destroyed the tower's legs, bringing it crashing down. Adding insult to injury, a quick-witted Christian officer had his men quickly exit from the walls and take over the wooden hulk for use as an outer bastion.

Still the Ottoman barrage continued, reducing the defenses of Malta to a shambles. "They also say," an anonymous participant commented on 2 September, "yt the battrie of ye Turkes hath so spoyled the walles of the Borgo, and saint Michaels fortresse, that cartes and chariottes may passe in at the breaches, and that it is great mervayle that euer our men could kepe them."[20] But the Ottomans were in an equally parlous condition. More and more troops were being invalided out of action with dysentery, and the freebooting corsairs were starting to slip away in search of easier prey. A report from Anastagi, the liaison with Sicily, to Ascanio della Corgna, one of the commanders of the assembling relief force, observed, "I judge and assert to you, Illustrious Excellency… that the Turks do not have more than 12 to 13,000 fighting men, of whom the only ones worth anything are the janissaries; the flower is dead, and the survivors no longer dare approach the walls, even though they are forced with cudgels by the Pashas."[21]

García had by this point mustered enough men in Sicily to be confident his intervention would be decisive. The fleet of the *Gran Soccorso* (Great Relief) set sail from Syracuse on 25 August, Gian Andrea Doria leading the way. The fleet struggled against contrary winds for days before being blown back to Sicily by a storm. García was able to regroup most of his scattered vessels at the island of Favignana, eleven miles off the westernmost tip of the island, and push forward to Linosa, but lost touch with Doria and had to lead the relief convoy in person to Gozo. Arriving at night from an unanticipated quarter, this convoy failed to rendezvous with its guides and was forced to return to Syracuse. Here, García did finally connect with Doria, and on 6 September, they set out again, and at dawn the following day, the *Gran Soccorso* finally disembarked at Mellieha Bay on the north coast of Malta. Leaving Álvaro de Sande in command – the perfect opportunity for him to avenge his honor for the debacle at Djerba – Garcia then returned to Syracuse.

Meanwhile, aware Piyale and the fleet could not remain on station off Malta indefinitely, Mustafa moved to seize Mdina in order to secure winter quarters which would enable him to maintain the Ottoman presence on the island and resume the siege when the fleet returned in the spring. When this assault broke down, he was forced to accept the siege was broken, and gave orders for the artillery to be withdrawn to the ships.

Ottoman preparations for departure were accelerated when Mustafa became aware the *Gran Soccorso* had arrived from Sicily and advanced to Mdina. On 11 September these fresh troops engaged the Ottomans at the Battle of Torre de Falca. Although exhausted after months of grueling and unrewarding service throughout the siege, the sultan's men fought desperately, and the struggle was bitter. Mustafa had his horse shot out from under him; so did Sande. Finally, the Ottomans broke, streaming back to St Paul's Bay, where Piyale was waiting offshore with the fleet. After taking on board all those who could make it to his ships, Piyale departed for Constantinople. The siege was over.

LEPANTO, 1571

Selim II ascended the Ottoman throne on 24 September 1566, following the death of his illustrious father, Suleiman the Magnificent, at Szigetvár. He was not well regarded by contemporaries; while his namesake grandfather earned the cognomen the Grim (*yavuz*), he was referred to as Selim the Drunkard (*sarı*). Ottoman historians would refer to his outstanding Grand Vizier Sokollu Mehmed Pasha as the "virtual sultan," in whose shadow Selim would become the Ottoman Empire's first sedentary ruler, fated never to leave the Topkapi Palace other than for excursions to his hunting grounds at Edirne.[22] Be that as it may, neither the change of regime in Constantinople nor the setback at Malta had any impact on the tightening Ottoman grip over the Mediterranean elsewhere. In 1566, the Ottomans seized Chios, the last island in the Aegean remaining in Christian hands, from the Genoese. Uluç Ali evicted the Hafsid Sultan, Abu al-Abbas Ahmad III (Moulay Ahmad), from Tunis in 1569. The next logical step was to detach Cyprus from the Republic of Venice. Eradicating this salient would consolidate Ottoman control over every sea lane linking the trade routes of the Levant.

On the diplomatic front, the moment was auspicious. The frontier with Persia was quiet, and in the 1568 Treaty of Edirne the Ottomans arrived at a qualified peace with Emperor Maximilian II. The Porte also had extended trade privileges to France in the capitulation of 1569, and King Charles IX did not want to risk his merchants' most favored status in the vast Ottoman domains. Another relevant consideration was the fact that in the latter part of 1569, when the decision to target Cyprus was finally taken, Spain was bogged down in two conflicts – its internal struggle to suppress the forcibly converted Moriscos in the mountains of Andalusia at home, and the revolt of its Protestant territories in the Netherlands.

When Philip II succeeded his father on the Spanish throne on 15 January 1556 – giving him sovereignty over the Netherlands in addition to Spain, Spanish America, Naples, Sicily, and Milan – he discovered that all of Spain's revenue streams had been pre-pledged through 1561 and short-term borrowing was exceeding 4 million ducats annually. Some of these loans carried interest rates as high as 49 percent. But in grand Habsburg style, the only answer to mounting debt was increasing borrowing. Anton Fugger kept the Crown afloat by advancing nearly 1.5 million ducats in loans between February 1556 and January 1557. Some 652,000 ducats (at 12 percent) in loans, guaranteed in theory by the States General of the Netherlands, and a group of wealthy state officials (as individuals), were allocated to the nearly mutinous Spanish troops fighting in the Netherlands. Another 600,000 crowns were advanced (at 23 percent) to cover unpaid salaries at the royal court in Brussels and at the front. Yet another loan of 430,000 ducats was secured against the next shipment of silver from the Americas – pre-pledged or not.

This house of cards finally collapsed in spring 1557 when Philip was forced to suspend all quarterly repayments on outstanding debt obligations in Spain. Then he shocked everyone by declaring bankruptcy that summer. Philip also confiscated the silver cargoes from the fleets that arrived on 1 July and 20 September, appropriating another 570,000 ducats that had been bound for the Fuggers' warehouse in Antwerp. The Fuggers were promised that they would be repaid (at 14 percent) by June 1559. That never happened.[23]

The Spanish state bankruptcy of June 1557 called for a massive bail-out plan. Royal creditors were forced to write down the carrying value of their outstanding claims and accept repayment in low-coupon (5 percent) *juros*, or *juros* that sold at a discount from their face value. The conversion of an avalanche of high-interest, short-term debt into long-term *juros* hit unsecured short-term debt holders especially hard. The Fuggers and a syndicate of Genoese banks had each advanced a total of 7 million ducats to the Habsburg Empire between 1521 and 1557, followed by the Welsers (4.2 million) and Schetzes (1.3 million). The financial chaos continued through the Habsburg triumph over France at the Battle of St Quentin on 10 August 1557 and the signing of the Treaty of Cateau-Cambrésis on 1 April 1559. Henry II had already declared a state bankruptcy of his own, wiping out thousands of patriotic French investors who had subscribed to the *Grand Parti*, the royal loan of 1555. Any satisfaction Philip felt at his rival's discomfort would not have survived his being forced to declare a second Spanish state bankruptcy in 1560 to work out the remaining hangover debts.

Philip could justify the fiscal emasculation of his dynasty's most loyal creditors as a matter of state security. His reigniting the smoldering divide over religion within the Habsburg realm had no rationale beyond simple dogmatic bloody-mindedness. When his reaffirmation of the anti-heresy laws in October 1565 triggered a Calvinist backlash in the Low Countries, Philip responded by appointing Fernando Alvarez de Toledo, the third Duke of Alba, as captain-general of the Netherlands. Alba arrived in Brussels on 9 August 1567 at the head of the Army of Flanders, backed by an Inquisition-style tribunal called the Council of Troubles, and authority to restore order by whatever means necessary. The subsequent campaign of repression, and the taxes imposed to enforce it, succeeded only in driving moderate Protestants, like William "the Silent" of Orange, into the rebel camp. By the end of the decade, the Netherlands were in open revolt.

Ottoman grand strategy sought to not only exploit but coordinate these twin challenges to Habsburg authority in order to prevent Spain from intervening in the eastern Mediterranean. In 1569, the Porte had been thrilled to receive word that in the Netherlands, "the Lutheran sect has brought together a large body of troops and has pillaged and plundered the provinces of the tyrannical and accursed Spanish."[24] Armed with this intelligence, the sultan authorized the establishment of a direct line of communication with the Moriscos, advising them, "The Lutheran sect does not cease its war and combat with those who are subject to the Pope and his school. You shall [therefore] secretly communicate with them, and when they set out upon war and combat with the Pope you also shall take care, jointly, to cause losses to the provinces and soldiers [of the pope] from your side."[25]

Simultaneously, Selim II dispatched an envoy to the Protestant rebels, assuring them "the announcement of our friendship, affection, compassion, and favor for you has been our imperial intention for some time," for from the moment "you have raised your sword against the papists and since you have regularly killed them, our imperial compassion and royal attention have been devoted in every way to your region." He encouraged the rebels to inform his envoy in every detail "of your conditions such that, at the time you decide upon, our victorious troops will be sent from land and sea, and, as it should be, assistance will be given." The sultan concluded by urging joint Lutheran/Morisco coordination against their collective Habsburg enemy: "You will mutually inform each other, always, and become friendly."[26]

Orders confirmed in Constantinople on 16 April 1570 for dispatch to the *beylerbey* of Algiers, Uluç Ali Pasha (who had taken Tunis in January of that year), acknowledged receiving intelligence from him that, with Ottoman support for the Moriscos, "confidence has been produced and many defeats have been given to the evil-acting Unbelievers" in Spain.[27] It is not clear whether the reinforcements from North Africa were the product of a centrally directed Ottoman strategy or the result of an initiative by Uluç Ali operating on his own recognizance.

Nonetheless, it is clear the Porte had the opportunity to proceed with, and was considering, a coordinated thrust against Habsburg interests in the western Mediterranean that involved support for the Moriscos in order to stir up resistance behind enemy lines.

However, the demands of the Cyprus campaign ultimately led to the intervention in Spain being curtailed. While "previously it had been the [sultan's] intention that the [Ottoman] fleet was to be sent to that area [the western Mediterranean] and all assistance and help were to be given to Islamic peoples," new orders mandated such endeavors would now be placed on hold, and only after Cyprus was taken would the sultan be free to concentrate his main force on coming to the relief of the Moriscos. In the meantime, they were assured of the ongoing commitment from Uluç Ali, who was ordered to be "prepared and ready to give all aid and assistance to that region, whether it be the sending of victorious troops or the giving of arms and ammunition."[28] But, in the event, organized Morisco resistance was smashed in the autumn of 1570 by a Habsburg campaign commanded by Don John.

Conversely the Ottoman position was enhanced by the outcome of the Treaty of Speyer, signed at the Imperial *Diet* in 1570, when John II Sigismund, the son of John Zápolya, renounced his crown as elected king of Hungary and assumed the title prince of Transylvania, which the emperor acknowledged. In a compromise worthy of Solomon, Sigismund also accepted Maximilian's suzerainty over Transylvania, while at the same time he himself remained an Ottoman vassal. This relative peace in the Balkans further freed up Ottoman men and materiel for a major operation in the Mediterranean.

Ottoman confidence only increased when word arrived that most of the munitions stores at the Venetian Arsenal were destroyed by fire in mid-September 1569. It was true that Venice had a peace treaty with the Porte. Selim turned to the court's *şeyhülislam* (head mufti) Ebussuud Yahya Efendi with the question of whether attacking the territory of a state with which it had a peace treaty was legally justifiable. The Ottoman supreme cleric's *fatwa* was an emphatic yes, on the grounds that Caliph Umar had conquered Cyprus in the early years of Islam, making the island an inalienable part of the *Dar al-Islam*. If retaken by the "abject Infidel," Muslims had the duty to recover it as soon as feasible. At a fundamental level, "Peace between a Muslim sovereign and the Infidels is legally permissible only as long as it is beneficial to all Muslims. Once it ceases being so, peace never is allowed."[29] Accordingly, on 28 March 1570, the Porte's emissary arrived in Venice with the sultan's ultimatum: "We demand of you Cyprus, which you shall give Us willingly or unwillingly or perforce; and do not vex our terrible sword, for We shall wage most cruel war against you everywhere; nor let you trust in your treasure, for We shall cause it suddenly to run away like a torrent; beware to defy Us."[30]

In response to the Ottoman ultimatum, a solemn vote was held in the senate; of the 220 who voted, 199 were in favor of war. On land, even prior to the formal outbreak of the conflict, the *sanjakbeyis* of the Balkan hinterland had begun sending irregular cavalry forces to raid the Venetian enclaves on the Adriatic coast. In turn, the Venetians were able to take advantage of simmering anti-Ottoman discontent around the margins of the Balkans to sponsor and partner with rebel movements in the Peloponnese and in the Himarë and Dukagjin regions of Albania. The arrival of a powerful combined arms force from Constantinople under Second Vizier Pertev Pasha and Müezzinzade (Son of the Muezzin) Ali Pasha, the admiral of the fleet, tipped the balance. Over the course of its progress from the Aegean to the Adriatic, this expedition devastated the islands of Crete, Kefalonia, and Corfu, and seized the major port cities of Ulcinj, Bar, and Budva, where Persian poet Mohammed ibn 'Abd Allah Zirek el-Hoseini, who took part in the Cyprus campaign, observed, "the soldiers, not content to seize the inhabitants' property, carried off the women, girls, boys and old men."[31]

Meanwhile, the expeditionary force for the Cyprus campaign was mustered, distributed in three successive divisions. The first and smallest (twenty-five galleys), under Murat Reis, set sail in the middle of March with orders to reach Rhodes and from there to send out scouts to observe the movements of enemy ships. The second, under the third vizier and *kapudan pasha* Piyale Pasha, consisting of sixty-five galleys and thirty other vessels, departed Constantinople on 17 April and reached Rhodes on 5 June. The third and largest squadron, under Ali Pasha and including the campaign's overall commander (*serdar*), sixth vizier Lala Mustafa Pasha, departed Constantinople on 16 May. The three divisions assembled on 10 June at Finike, a harbor on the south coast of Anatolia some 350 kilometers northwest of Cyprus. After several days attending to additional logistical details, the combined fleet set off. After a one-day stop at Limassol, on 3 July it arrived at the port of Larnaca on the southern coast of Cyprus.

The Venetians could draw some heart from their defenses on the island, which were state of the art. By the time the Ottomans attacked, eighty years of effort had gone into fortifying Famagusta. The great Land Gate with its impressive ravelin was added in 1544, and a decade later the further development of the defenses was entrusted to Count Hercules Martinengo. Under the guidance of Count Julius Savorgnano, by the end of 1565 eleven obtuse-angled artillery bastions protruded from the walls of Nicosia – by one account, "the very first European town to be surrounded by a geometrically perfect perimeter of textbook bastions."[32]

The military operations of the Ottoman conquest of Cyprus can be divided into two distinct episodes. The first was the seven-week-long Siege of Nicosia, which lasted from 22 July to 9 September 1570. This was followed by the much longer Siege of Famagusta, which held out for eleven months between 15 September 1570 and 1 August 1571. The defense of the island was entrusted to Nicolas Dandolo, a man contemporaries described as weak, stupid, and irascible. He did have two capable subordinates; the captain of Famagusta, Marco Antonio Bragadin, and Astorre Baglione.

Lala Mustafa advanced on Nicosia from the south-east, and took up positions opposite the bastions of Tripoli, D'Avila, Constanza, and Podocataro. On 30 July Mustafa began the construction of earthworks for artillery emplacements as close to the walls as he dared, simultaneously commencing sapping forward in long zigzags which went through the counterscarp and into the ditch, throwing out earth and making traverses, which were stiffened by wood fascines brought up by horses. On 9 September the forty-fifth and largest attack on the walls of Nicosia was delivered. The points of assault were the four bastions that had been battered for months. When the defenses here were overwhelmed the city fell, Dandolo being one among many thousands caught up in the subsequent massacre.

An advance guard of Ottoman cavalry arrived before Famagusta on 15 September, bearing with them a demand for the garrison to surrender, and a basket containing Dandolo's decapitated head. Bragadin ignored both the demand and the warning, which was reemphasized after the siege commenced when the severed heads of the garrison of Nicosia were paraded mounted on spears around the walls.

The Ottomans now wheeled up as many as 145 guns, including four huge cannons firing shot of up to 200 pounds in weight. These fired an estimated 120,000 iron shot and 43,000 stone rounds into the city during the course of the siege. The garrison comprised somewhere between 8,000 and 9,000 men, with ninety guns.[33]

On 16 January 1571, Marco Quirini, commanding Venetian naval assets on Crete, set sail with four transports convoying 1,700 men-at-arms, escorted by a dozen galleys. Ten days later this force brushed aside the Ottoman fleet and safely arrived with its reinforcements at Famagusta. For three weeks, Quirini rampaged off the coast of Cyprus, destroying Ottoman shore installations and interdicting Ottoman shipping. It was a vivid illustration of how exposed the Ottoman position actually was on Cyprus should the Porte lose control of the surrounding waters.

The lack of control that the Ottomans had over the approaches to Famagusta was illustrated once again when the defenders were able to construct two casemates on the inner side of the counterscarp from which flanking fire could be delivered along the line of the moat. Each casemate was connected to the walls by a ditch, and protected by a covered way. The Ottoman response was to employ their Armenian sappers and forcibly recruited local peasants to lay down an enormous system of fieldworks. The result was that for a distance of three miles south of the fortress a maze of zigzagging trenches capable of sheltering the entire Ottoman army covered the landscape, each excavated so deeply that when mounted men rode along them only the tips of their lances were visible. At the point where the saps came within artillery range of the city, forts were erected from beams and fascines packed with earth and bales of cotton.

Ten such forts were constructed, and the close-range bombardment from them started on 12 May. By 24 May the Ottomans had secured the edge of the counterscarp close to the outer ravelin by the front gate, which they then attempted to capture. The defenders replied by exploding a mine underneath the ravelin itself, so any gain was nullified.

On 3 June the Ottomans tried a new tactic, filling in the moat along a section and then cutting traverses so that they were sapping across the gap. The height of the traverses extended to the walls, so there was little that the defenders could do except throw incendiaries blindly into the passages. In this way the Ottomans gradually clawed their way towards the breaches of Famagusta, tearing down the defenders' entrenchments as they came to them and laying mines. Bragadin's men countermined as best they could, but a successful explosion under the Tower of the Arsenal on 21 June carried away all the face and the parapet of both flanks, the entire platform in front of the entrenchments and eight feet to its side. Dazed by the explosion, the company in charge of the Arsenal Tower could offer little immediate resistance to the attack which rapidly followed, but other units came to their aid and those Ottomans down in the entrenchments were deluged with incendiaries. Unfortunately, an accidental discharge of the wildfire mixture set off a load as it was being delivered to the front line, causing 500 casualties among the defenders. After five hours of bitter fighting, the Ottomans were driven off with the loss of about 600 dead.

The breach at the Arsenal was repaired during the night of 21 June. The following day another Venetian galley arrived in the harbor with assurances a relief fleet would arrive within eight days. The garrison would have to hold out until then. The explosion of a mine under the damaged ravelin of the Land Gate, which not only destroyed the ravelin but also filled the moat with its debris, heralded a fresh assault. Once again, the Ottomans drove saps closer to the breach while their guns swept the defenses so the garrison could not make repairs. The attack was eventually driven off, but not without considerable casualties among the defenders. By 28 July all the garrison's meat had been eaten, along with all the city's horses, donkeys, and cats. The following day the strongest assault yet was launched, presaged by the detonation of several mines, one of which brought down what was left of the Arsenal Tower. Such was the shortage of building materials that breaches were now being repaired using soldiers' clothing filled with earth. The following two days were defined by desperate hand-to-hand fighting over the heaps of rubble that had once been the city walls. An inventory taken on 31 July revealed that the provisions were exhausted and only seven barrels of powder remained. With no sign of the promised relief fleet, the garrison surrendered on 1 August.

The Ottomans had offered terms, including the repatriation of the garrison. These were betrayed. The rank and file were butchered as they clustered at the docks waiting for their ships home. The officers were slaughtered as they parlayed at the Pasha's tent. Only Bragadin was spared, and only in order to send a message to those still considering defiance of the Sublime Porte. After cutting off Bragadin's nose and ears, his captors humiliated and tortured him for the next two weeks. Finally, in the square adjacent to the church of St Nicholas, now converted into a mosque, he was flayed alive; starting with incisions on the soles of his feet, the skin was peeled off his body while he was still breathing. The Ottomans wrapped the skin around a life-sized straw dummy, which they dressed in Bragadin's uniform and mounted backwards on a cow. This grisly spectacle was then paraded through the streets of Famagusta before being sent on a grand tour of the Ottoman realm and ultimately presented to the sultan.

When Venice secretly dispatched an ambassador to Constantinople to open clandestine negotiations over a possible exit to the war, the Ottomans were obdurate, and unimpressed by the prospect of confronting a grand Christian coalition in the Mediterranean. Grand Vizier Sokollu Mehmed Pasha was confident the sultan "had strength enough to resist all of them, and to make war in many places at the same time; and besides, he knew perfectly well how little trust Venice could put in Christian princes."[34]

Christendom had indeed demonstrated, repeatedly, how little respect it was entitled to in terms of its capacity for collective action. And it was true, as a papal diplomat at the court of Philip II reported in April 1570, "there are few friendly feelings towards the Venetians, as they have never been willing to go to the help of others, and there is very little confidence that they will not gladly drop out of the war whenever they can, leaving the task to others and thinking only of their own interests."[35] However, after a generation spent on the back foot at sea, Western naval potential was slowly rising from its nadir during the 1550s to 1560s. The question was whether this newfound potential could be mobilized in time to make a difference.

Under Charles V, the Imperial naval presence in the Mediterranean was distributed among four fleets in being – Spain, Genoa, Naples, and Sicily – supported by the private fleets maintained by the Knights of St John of Malta, the Knights of St Stephen of Florence, and the papacy. When deemed necessary, the Imperial divisions could be united for concerted action as *La Armada de las galeras de España* under the central command of the Captain General of the Sea (*Capitán general de la Mar*).

When Philip II became king of Spain in 1556, he realized that the Spanish galley fleet was not strong enough to confront the Ottoman naval forces because the Spanish navy was mostly composed of armed merchant ships and galleys owned by the private contractors. This fact was brought home with unambiguous brutality by the decisive Ottoman victory in the naval Battle of Djerba in 1560.

In response, reform measures were introduced, which allowed for increased royal control and supervision over the fleets and a major galley construction program in Spain's Mediterranean shipyards. The papacy contributed important financial support to this program; in return, the Committee of Galleys (*Junta de Galeras*), which reported to the Council of War (*Consejo de Guerra*), was headed by the papal representative.[36]

Much of the Spanish ship-building program was funded by special ecclesiastical taxes agreed by the pope, which paid tithes and other sums to the Spanish Crown from the revenues and properties of the Church in Spain. There were some tensions between Rome and Madrid over these; the papal suspicion was that the monies were not always used for religious purposes (i.e., war against heretics and infidels). But when Pius V became pope in January 1566, he was quick to renew the largest tax, known as the *subsidio*; for Pius was obsessed with the idea of an anti-Ottoman crusade, and he knew that Spanish naval power would have to play a vital role in it.

Pius was enough of an idealist to hope that other major Catholic powers might be persuaded to join his newfound Holy League. But there was little chance of that. The Holy Roman Empire and France were too heavily invested in peace with the Porte. Poland's relations with the Ottomans – now their direct territorial neighbors – were too sensitive for any Polish ruler to contemplate going to war for the sake of a quarrel in the far-off Mediterranean. However, with undying optimism Pius did tell the papal nuncio in Poland to go to Moscow to persuade Ivan the Terrible to join the League – and, for good measure, to offer him priests to "instruct his peoples in the ceremonies of Rome." The nuncio had to explain to Pius that Ivan had just made peace with the sultan, and that there was not the slightest chance of converting him to Catholicism.[37] Ultimately, all that Pius V could muster for his grand coalition, in addition to Venice and Spain, was a handful of minor powers – his own Papal State, the Knights of Malta, and Spain's allies in Italy; Genoa, Savoy, and Tuscany.

At first, Pius grandly offered to man and equip twenty-four galleys; but the scale of the operation proved too daunting (despite his strenuous efforts to raise funds, including the appointment of sixteen new cardinals who had to pay handsomely for the privilege), so the figure was reduced to twelve.[38] On Sunday 11 June 1570, in a ceremony in the Sistine Chapel, Pius endowed Marc Antonio Colonna, Duke of Tagliacozzo and Paliano, with his commission as captain general of the papal fleet.

In early August this small body of vessels departed Ancona and sailed down the coast to Otranto, on the heel of Italy, which it reached on 6 August. Upon his arrival, Colonna was handed a letter from Philip II, notifying him the king had ordered his own naval commander, the Genoese Gian Andrea Doria, to rendezvous there with part of the Spanish fleet. Philip requested that when it came to battle, Colonna should follow Doria's lead. Philip's instructions to Doria were even more explicit; he was to proceed with caution, and to aim above all at preserving his galleys (which meant, if possible, not risking them in battle at all). Doria was happy to comply with this policy, not least because twelve of the galleys in his fleet were his own property, rented out to the king, and he would not be adequately compensated if they were lost in combat. So he sailed with deliberate slowness from Sicily to Otranto, leaving Colonna waiting for two weeks. When he finally arrived, Colonna concealed his irritation at this obvious foot-dragging and treated him with special honor. At an ensuing council of war, Doria was skeptical about undertaking any action in the eastern Mediterranean, finally conceding the combined fleet should proceed to Crete and consider its options upon arrival. On 22 August the two fleets, totaling sixty-one galleys, left Otranto, pulling in at the port of Suda on 31 August. Here they were greeted by Girolamo Zanne, the Venetian naval commander. His transit to Crete via Zadar and Corfu had been brutally impacted by typhus and dysentery. Hasty recruitment among the Cretan population could not make up for these casualties. Although the addition of other squadrons would bring the total of Venetian warships to 148, they were badly undermanned. Zanne would later put the total Venetian losses of rowers and soldiers from typhus and dysentery at over 20,000 men.

On 1 September and again on 3 September, Colonna convened a council of war. Colonna, supported by Zanne, urged that the whole fleet proceed as soon as possible to attack the Ottoman fleet at Cyprus. Doria rejected this proposal, insisting it was too late in the campaign season and that he had to start his homeward journey by the end of the month. Zanne, assuming Doria's foot-dragging was motivated by the pecuniary value of his galleys, asked Colonna, whose consummate diplomacy was the only factor holding the fleet together by this point, to inform the Genoese admiral that Venice would stand security for his galleys to the extent of 200,000 ducats and the cost of repairs. Colonna refused to deliver such an insulting message and Doria continued to veto every initiative raised. It was only after it had been agreed that his squadron need not take its turn at rearguard duty and should sail separately from the rest of the fleet that Colonna managed to move the force a few miles to Heraklion. The wrangling continued until 13 September, when Colonna finally prevailed. Doria managed to delay the expedition a little longer by demanding a formal review of the fleet. This did reveal serious weaknesses in the manning of some ships, and several galleys were set aside, with their crews and soldiers distributed among the others.

As the fleet sailed eastwards on 17 September, its combined force came to a total of 192 warships. This vast armada ground to a halt just four days later when, after pulling in to the little island of Kastellorizo, just off the Anatolian coast to the east of Rhodes, word was received of the fall of Nicosia. The fleet was now halfway from Crete to Cyprus, and Famagusta was still holding out, but only Zanne was still in favor of proceeding, and he was outvoted. Some of the captains proposed an attack on the island of Euboea (the former Venetian possession off the eastern coast of mainland Greece); Doria rejected this, as it was too close to the Ottoman heartland, suggesting some other target, such as Vlorë, Durrës, or Herceg Novi in the Adriatic. But at another meeting a few days later at Karpathos, the island between Crete and Rhodes, he bluntly announced he was immediately withdrawing with his entire contingent back to Sicily. The campaign was effectively over, and the captains returned to Crete in a mood of intense mutual hostility. Adding to their woes, a storm sank one Venetian and two papal galleys en route, then one papal and three more Venetian galleys were sunk by a storm while riding at anchor off the coast of Crete.

Colonna departed Crete with what remained of the papal fleet on 10 November, heading for Corfu. By the time he reached the island of Kefalonia, many of his soldiers and crews were dying, probably from another outbreak of typhus. Having arrived at Corfu, Colonna was pinned by contrary winds to the island for a month. Having finally set off, his flagship was struck by lightning and burned to the waterline. Colonna was forced to borrow a Venetian galley, only to be caught in another storm, driven ashore and shipwrecked a few miles from Dubrovnik. When he at last was able to return to Rome and report to Pope Pius, the Holy Father can hardly have been encouraged by his account of divided leadership and the complete lack of a strategic plan which had led to the loss of more than 20,000 men and several ships with nothing to show for it.

The alliance would have collapsed as it had in almost identical circumstances after the lost opportunity at Preveza in 1538 had it not been for the pope's fervor and diplomacy. On 20 May 1571 the official document establishing the Holy League was signed in Rome by the pope and the representatives of Venice and Spain. Its first article declared that the League would be perpetual, and that it would be offensive as well as defensive, with Algiers, Tunis, and Tripoli among its potential targets. Articles 2 and 4 stated that every spring it would assemble 200 galleys, 100 transport ships, 50,000 soldiers, and 4,500 light cavalry, and every autumn the ambassadors would meet in Rome to plan the following year's campaign. Article 7, on cost-sharing, was based on the formula used in the League of 1538: Spain would pay half, Venice one-third, and the papacy one-sixth. Two articles, 11 and 12, dealt with the thorny issue of Spain's North African concerns. If Spain were attacked by Ottoman or Barbary forces, Venice would send fifty galleys to help (and Spain, likewise, would send fifty if Venetian territory were invaded); if Spain should undertake action against Algiers, Tunis, or Tripoli in a year when there was no League campaign and no definite threat from the Ottoman fleet, Venice would contribute fifty galleys. Article 14 represented a surprising concession by Spain. It decreed that the commanders of the three contingents – Spanish, Venetian, Papal – would form a council of war, which would make decisions by majority vote. These would be binding on the captain general, even if he had been in the minority. Article 19 stipulated that Dubrovnik and its territory must not be molested in any way. Article 21 confirmed that none of the parties could act independently to negotiate peace.[39]

On the suggestion of the pope, the twenty-four-year-old Don John of Austria, the king of Spain's bastard half-brother, was appointed captain general of the Holy League fleet, with Colonna to serve as his second-in-command. Pius also had a personal stake in the campaign. Serving with the fleet were his nephew, Paolo Ghislieri (whom the pontiff had ransomed from the corsairs of Algiers), and Michele Bonelli, his twenty-year-old great-nephew, who had been appointed captain general of the papal military forces while still a teenager.

On 21 June 1571 Colonna and his men left Civitavecchia and sailed to Naples. They waited there for almost a month, partly because the Spanish galleys were not ready, and partly because of strategic uncertainties about the feasibility of the original plan, which was to rendezvous with the Venetian fleet at Corfu. News of the huge Ottoman fleet's progress northwestwards from Crete had suddenly made that very problematic.

The Ottoman fleet had mustered for the 1571 campaign season from 14 May to 10 June at Euboea under the new *kapudan pasha*, Ali Pasha, the Porte having replaced Piyale Pasha as punishment for his being outmaneuvered by Quirini off Cyprus in January. Ali Pasha commenced raiding Crete on 15 June, linking up with the Barbary corsair squadron led by Uluç Ali three days later. The combined fleet then turned west, raiding the islands of Zakynthos and Kefalonia and, on 1 July, Corfu, before undertaking a series of raids against Venetian outposts along the Adriatic coast, including Valona and, on 15 September, Parga. Ulcinj and Bar were taken. The island of Korčula, north of Dubrovnik, only held out when the women of the town donned military uniforms to deter the raiders, the Ottomans passing on to mount an assault against the island of Hvar, even further to the north.[40]

Having lost a number of men to attrition and disease, on 20 September, Ali Pasha made the decision to enter the Gulf of Patras and withdraw into the Gulf of Corinth to recruit and resupply at the port of Lepanto (modern Nafpaktos). While this allowed for a sheltered anchorage in a populated region, facilitating the drafting of crews and fighting men to compensate for the losses to his ships' complements, it left the fleet trapped in a cul-de-sac with only one exit to open water in the Ionian Sea. If the League fleet blocked that exit, Ali Pasha would have just two choices – hunker down at anchorage, or fight his way out.

The papal fleet, meanwhile, together with the three Hospitaller galleys from Malta that had joined it, finally set off from Naples for Messina, pulling in at that port on 20 July. Three days later the Corfu squadron of the Venetian fleet arrived under its new commander, Sebastiano Venier, and his deputy, Agostin Barbarigo, who had assumed command of the Venetian navy, replacing the disgraced Girolamo Zane. Venier had reluctantly abandoned Corfu to the Ottoman fleet, knowing that his own squadron (of between fifty and sixty galleys) could do nothing to protect the island without being overwhelmed. For an entire month these assembled forces were obliged to wait as the news came in of the Ottoman fleet's progress up the eastern Adriatic coast.

Don John arrived at Messina from Barcelona via Genoa and Naples on 23 August with forty-four galleys. At a council of war, Colonna and Venier favored an offensive campaign. They discussed the idea of attacking Ottoman ports in Greece and Albania, with the aim of denying the sultan's fleet any bases on the western coast of the Balkans. Colonna and Don John were privately in favor of this, but the Venetians were strongly opposed, both because their primary aim was still to save Famagusta, and because they feared the establishment of a Spanish base in Greece. Just over a week later, the remaining squadron of seventy Venetian galleys sailed into port, having made the strenuous non-stop voyage direct from Crete. At roughly the same time, Gian Andrea Doria also arrived with the Genoese galleys, and a few days later the Neapolitan squadron of thirty ships came in, under its experienced commander, Álvaro de Bazán, the Marquis of Santa Cruz. On 8 September Don John held a review of the entire fleet, which now numbered 209 galleys and six *galleasses* (heavy, three-masted galleys with decks over the rowers and built-up forecastles for artillery, ponderously slow but bristling with firepower), as well as a number of transport ships and smaller vessels. Two days later, Don John called another council of war, and the decision to mount an offensive campaign was confirmed. The fleet finally left Messina on 16 September, advancing to Crotona four days later, where it was held up by contrary winds for another week before crossing the Gulf of Taranto and arriving at Corfu on 27 September, much to the relief of its beleaguered inhabitants.

The tensions between the allied partners of the League fleet now boiled to the surface, nearly setting its constituent identities at each other's throats. When Doria announced his intention to inspect the Venetian galleys, Venier threatened to kill him, or any other Genoese, who set foot on his flagship. The task of inspecting the fleet fell to Don John, who condemned four Venetian galleys as unfit for active service, and since most of the Venetian galleys were undermanned (having struggled to compensate for the horrific losses of the previous year) they were bolstered by contingents of Habsburg men-at-arms. Friction led to a riot on board one galley, which Venier resolved by having the Spanish captain involved hanged from its yardarm. The Spanish and Venetian fleets then squared off, guns cleared for action, and it was only the diplomatic intervention of Colonna (who had already defused a similar confrontation between Spanish and Papal troops while at anchor in Naples) that prevented a bloodbath. Don John was so disgusted with Venier he refused to share the same room with him, Barbarigo being deputed to represent Venice during councils of war. The only thing holding the League fleet together at this point was word arriving about the grisly fate of Marco Antonio Bragadin. If the fleet could no longer save him, it could still avenge him.

With scouts having confirmed the Ottoman fleet was at Lepanto and giving a rough estimate of its numbers, on 3 October, the League fleet sailed south, advancing to Kefalonia on 5 October, and then pushing into the Gulf of Patras.

Aware from their own scouts that the League fleet was at Corfu, at a council of war held on 4 October, Pertau Pasha, commander of the soldiers assigned to the fleet, including the janissaries, and Mehmet Sulik Pasha (known as Sirocco), argued the Ottoman fleet should maintain a defensive position in the Gulf of Patras. They questioned the intelligence reports they had received regarding the size of the League fleet, warned that their own ships were still undermanned, and pointed out that it was late in the campaign season, which meant the League fleet would soon have to withdraw to its home ports for the winter where, after a second fruitless year and the fall of Cyprus, the centrifugal forces inherent to Christendom might tear the League apart without the Ottomans having to fire a shot in anger. However, Ali Pasha had instructions from the sultan to seek out the enemy and bring them to battle wherever possible. Though he had risen to command through his associations at court and had held administrative office as *bey* of Alexandria, he was an aggressive commander who had seen service at Djerba and Malta before taking part in the Cyprus campaign. Ali Pasha went with his instincts, siding with his more bellicose subordinates, Uluç Ali and Hayreddin's son, Hasan. He ordered the fleet to sail west for Kefalonia. If the League withdrew, he would take Corfu. If the League wanted a fight, he would give it one.

The two fleets caught sight of each other while converging some nine miles apart just before 7:30am on 7 October. The two sides were evenly matched. The League fleet, comprising 206 galleys and six *galleasses*, included 28,500 men-at-arms and 40,000 sailors and oarsmen, for a total complement of just under 70,000 men. The Ottoman fleet comprised 208 galleys, plus more than 100 additional lighter craft – fifty-six *galliots* and sixty-four *fustas*. On board were 27,000 fighting men and 50,000 sailors and oarsmen, 77,000 in total.[41] Although the League was outnumbered, it had the *galleasses* and more of its galleys were of the larger *lanterna* class. Even the *gallia sotil* (standard galley) of the League carried a much greater weight of firepower than its Ottoman counterpart. Mirroring so many previous clashes on land, this battle would be a classic confrontation between the heavier, harder-hitting Christians on one side, and the lighter, faster Muslims on the other.

On the Ottoman side, Ali Pasha, on board his flagship, the *Sultana*, held the center of the line with eighty-seven galleys. Mehmet Sulik Pasha commanded sixty galleys and two *galliots* on the right wing, hard up against the coastline, while Uluç Ali took up station with sixty-one galleys and thirty-two *galliots* on the left, where the greater speed of the lighter vessels could be put to best use in the open water of the Gulf. The reserve division of eight galleys and twenty-two *galliots* was commanded by Amurat Dragut Reis, the son of Turgut Reis. League dispositions were similar. From on board his flagship, the *Real*, Don John personally commanded the sixty-two galleys and two *galleasses* of the center division. He divided his two wings evenly, stationing Barbarigo on his left with fifty-three galleys and two *galleasses* and Doria on his right, also with fifty-three galleys and two *galleasses*. Álvaro de Bazán commanded the reserve of thirty-eight galleys.

The Ottoman right wing came into contact first, at approximately 10:30am, accelerating to outflank the League left on its shoreward side. This gambit paid immediate dividends, as Ottoman galleys swung into the flanks of their League rivals, sinking four. Barbarigo, raising his visor to make his commands heard over the din of battle, was immediately shot in the face with an arrow and mortally wounded; his nephew, Marino Contarini, moving up from the reserve squadron in his *Santa Magdelena*, was gunned down in the melee. But the left flank of the Ottoman right wing had been disrupted and delayed by the *galleasses*, commanded by the brothers Amborgio and Antonio Bragadin, kinsmen to the martyred Marc Antonio Bragadin of Famagusta, who poured fire into the approaching enemy, creating a gap between the galleys that had advanced around the League vessels at the end of the line, and those still coming up closer to the center. Observing this opportunity, Marco Quirini, the *proveditor* (quartermaster) of Venice, in command of the right flank on the League's left wing, ordered his unengaged galleys to swing around to the north and hit the Ottomans in their exposed left flank. The tables were now turned, as the Ottomans found themselves trapped between the League and the coastline. Ultimately, the ships of the Ottoman right wing were either taken, wrecked, or deliberately beached on the shore, their crews escaping on foot inland. Some were hunted down, including the mortally wounded Mehmet Sulik Pasha.

Meanwhile, the ships of the Ottoman center plowed right through the firepower of the *galleasses* in this sector at approximately 11am. The two lines collided at 11:40am, the two flagships crashing into each other, transforming a naval encounter into a savage brawl across the narrow decks. While the skilled Venetian gunners could hit a galley at up to 500 yards, most artillery fire between ships was at what the Spanish called clothes-burning range (*quemaropa*). This encounter would close up even that space. By noon, with vessels from both sides converging on their respective flagships, some thirty League and Ottoman galleys were crammed into an area measuring no more than 250 yards from north to south, and less than 200 yards from east to west. With no room to maneuver, Ali Pasha himself took up his bow and joined his archers in the bow.

A boarding party from the League flagship, the *Real*, stormed its Ottoman counterpart, the *Sultana*, across her forecastle and captured the *arrumbada*, the fighting platform constructed over her bow artillery, but were unable to push forward any further. As Ottoman reinforcements began arriving to aid the *Sultana*, driving the Christians off their flagship and taking the fight on board the *Real*, the commander of the League reserves, Bazán, committed two of his galleys, the *Faith* and *Hope* of Venice, into the fray, driving them between the *Sultana* and the Ottoman galleys moving up in her support, one of these being rammed and sunk by the *Faith* of Venice, commanded by Giovanni Battista Contarini.

Receiving reinforcements of his own from Venier in his *Capitana* of Venice, which had ranged up alongside the *Real*, Don John pushed the Ottomans off his flagship, his men in their turn surging back on board the *Sultana* in three successive assaults between 12:30pm and 1pm. Dragut Reis, commanding the Ottoman reserve, fought his way through the press of ships and succeeded in reinforcing the *Sultana*; two more League assaults on the flagship were repulsed, as were two on the adjacent galley of Pertau Pasha.

On either side of the *Real* and all down the line, the fighting was furious. Sebastiano Venier, trying to come up to the aid of the flagship in his *Capitana* of Venice, hit the *Sultana* amidships but was himself then surrounded on both sides. Only the intervention of two more Venetian galleys from the reserve saved his ship and his life, and both their captains were killed in the process. Bazán's reserve galleys were now fully committed. Marco Antonio Colonna in his Papal *Capitana* repulsed the galley of Mehmet Bey with Ali Pasha's sons on board. Don John himself fought from the prow with his two-handed sword and received a dagger thrust in the leg. The eighty-year-old Venier stood bareheaded on the deck of his galley, loosing shots from his crossbow.

The turning point came when Pertau Pasha, badly wounded, had to be evacuated, his galley then being stormed by Colonna and his flag captain, the Hospitaller knight, Romegas. The two then conferenced to strategize their next move. "The galley is ours," Romegas confirmed; "Shall we look for another, or aid the *Real*?"[42] Colonna responded by turning for the starboard side of the *Sultana*, smashing into her so hard the bows of the two ships locked together. Venier simultaneously closed in from the port side, raking the Ottoman flagship with fire; "My galley, with cannon, arquebuses, and arrows, didn't let any Turk make it from the poop to the prow of the pasha's ship," he later wrote.[43] Christian boarders swept onto the deck, fighting their way through makeshift barricades and finally reaching Ali Pasha. His head was hacked off and raised aloft, spiked on a spear tip, while the green banner entrusted to him by the sultan, heavily embroidered with texts from the Qur'an and with the name of Allah emblazoned upon it 28,900 times in golden letters, was cast down. As their flagship was triumphantly towed out of the line, those Ottoman vessels that could still do so now sought to make good their escape. But most, already committed to battle, were trapped in the chaotic maelstrom that ensued. Unable to disengage, they surrendered or were cut down, Dragut Reis among them. The battle in the center was over by 1:30pm.

While the Ottoman right flank and center had immediately closed with the enemy and engaged in furious combat, Uluç Ali on the Ottoman left flank had spent all morning not only avoiding battle but deliberately edging so far out into the open water of the gulf he had almost completely detached the Christian right from its center. Not only did he outnumber Doria by over forty vessels, many of his ships were of the lighter, faster Barbary *galliot* class. Seizing the advantage he had created, just after noon, Uluç darted right into the yawning gap and made directly for the Christian center on its exposed right flank. Seeing this, apparently without orders from Doria, Giovanni di Cardona led a group of galleys – twelve Venetian, two Sicilian-Spanish, one Savoyard, and one Papal – from the League right wing in a bid to intercept the Ottomans. Uluç immediately altered course to seize this opportunity, swarming the sixteen isolated League vessels with seventy-five of his own. The result was a massacre, with the Ottomans taking many ships, including the *Florence* and *San Giovanni*, after wiping out their entire complements. The balance only shifted when the *Resurrected Christ* of Venice, commanded by Benedetto Soranzo, surrounded and overrun, detonated her own powder magazine, nearly taking the surrounding galleys with her. Stunned by this reverse, the Ottomans were caught when Doria arrived with the rest of the League right wing, driving off the enemy and recapturing all the galleys they had taken, Doria's own *Capitana* reclaiming five vessels. Uluç left the bulk of his force to screen Doria while he led thirty of his galleys northwards to attack the League center. But by this point, the *Sultana* had been taken, and the battle was effectively over. Uluç did not want to withdraw without a prize, however; he isolated the Hospitaller galley *Capitana* under Father Giustiano, the prior of Messina, battered after participating in the brawl at the center of the line, where she had captured three Ottoman vessels. Uluç now swarmed her, wiping out her crew and towing her, stern first, out of the battle. When the League reserves began to converge on him, he cut the *Capitana* free, leaving her to drift, while summoning the Ottoman left wing to follow him out of the zone of battle and flee for the open water to the west. Some did not make it; cut off by the League rearguard, they opted to beach their ships rather than be taken. But Uluç himself did slip the closing net, flying the captured Hospitaller banner from his own masthead as a final insult while he disappeared over the horizon with about thirty vessels still under his command.

Of the Ottoman force that had entered battle that morning, roughly half of its left wing survived the clash at Lepanto. The rest of the fleet had been annihilated. When the League limped into the nearby anchorage of Porta Petala to weigh anchor for the night, it was accompanied by some 170 captured Ottoman ships.

When news arrived of the triumph at Lepanto, all Christendom erupted in celebration.[44] The seemingly inexorable Ottoman progress by land and sea over the previous decades had contributed to the cultivation of an inferiority complex in the West, where apocalypticism was rampant. Francesco Sansovino's *Lettera, o vero discorso sopra le predittioni le quali pronosticano la nostra futura felicità per la guerra del Turco l'anno 1570* and Giovanni Battista Nazari's *Discorso della future et sperata vittoria contra il Turco* had both foreseen the coming of the Antichrist in the Ottoman victory at Cyprus.[45] The total victory of the Holy League was therefore seized upon with rapturous joy as representing not merely the climax of a particular campaign but the turning point in an existential geopolitical and spiritual conflict and the lifting of a tremendous psychological burden. Miguel de Cervantes, the future author of *Don Quixote*, served in the fleet of the Holy League on board the Spanish galley *Marquesa* and was wounded three times during the battle, taking two shots from arquebus balls to the chest and being left permanently maimed in his left hand, earning him the sobriquet *El Manco de Lepanto*. For the rest of his life, he looked back with pride on his service "on the most glorious occasion that any age, past or present, ever saw, or that the future can ever hope to see."[46] In the words of his celebrated literary alter ego, it was a day "so happy to Christendom," when the nations of Europe were finally disabused "of their error in believing that the Turks were invincible by sea," for on that day "Ottoman pride and haughtiness were broken."[47]

Don John was certainly the hero of the hour. After arranging for the release of a surviving son of Ali Pasha, he even received a letter from Selim II, saluting him as "destined to be the sole cause, after a very long time, of greater harm than the sovereign and ever-felicitous House of Osman has previously received from Christians."[48] However, when viewed objectively, his victory was essentially a negative one, and ultimately quite hollow. Whatever laurels it had claimed at Lepanto, the Holy League had utterly failed to accomplish its intended goal, the relief of Cyprus, which now passed under Ottoman control for the next 300 years. Grand Vizier Sokullu Mehmet Pasha shrugged off the defeat, claiming the Holy League had "merely singed off the stubble from my master's beard, which had only grown back stronger as a result," whereas the Ottomans had succeeded in lopping off one of the arms of Christendom with the capture of Cyprus.[49] The most that can be said is that the outcome at Lepanto bought the frontier of Christendom some time. Had the Ottoman fleet prevailed, it seems likely Crete and/or Corfu would have been the next targets, the latter as a stepping-stone to a further amphibious operation directed at Apulia. Such a gambit would have played out with the at least tacit approval of the French, and the passive – or possibly, even active – support of segments of the local population. As the Huguenot diplomat Hubert Languet wrote to Augustus of Saxony in late 1572, "if the Ottomans should happen to seize some port-town of Apulia or Old Calabria and convey strong forces there, which would not be difficult, in view of the short voyage from Albania and north-western Greece, I do not doubt that many inhabitants of the Kingdom of Naples, infuriated by the Spanish tyranny, which is extremely harsh, would defect to them."[50]

While the Christian West gave itself over to emotional triumphalism, the Ottoman realm responded with cool deliberation. News of the debacle at Lepanto arrived in Constantinople less than two weeks after the battle. The *Divân-ı Hümayun* (Imperial Council) immediately made two critical decisions. The first was for the armies previously sent to Rumelia to adopt defensive measures in anticipation of a possible attack by the enemy navy, which was still active in the region, against Ottoman fortifications now left vulnerable in the Adriatic, Peloponnese, and Aegean. Such was the sense of alarm that orders were dispatched instructing local field commanders to concede outlying strongholds such as Bar and Ulcinj, demolishing their fortifications and transferring their garrisons, guns, and ammunition to other fortresses if retaining them was judged too problematic. Additionally, edicts were posted on 21 October under the imperative of *gazâ-yı ekber* (total war) for immediate initiation of a crash construction program in the empire's shipyards to make good the losses before the campaigning season of the following year, funding the program via the imposition of *avariz* (extraordinary military levy) taxes. This effort was supplemented by the expectation that the empire's most prominent statesmen would personally contribute towards the war effort (which, to their credit, they did – the vizier Lala Mustafa Pasha built three galleys in Antalya; Piyale Pasha built several galleys in Rhodes and Kocaeli; and *Reis ül-Küttab* (head of the chancery) Feridun Ahmed Bey built a *galliot* in Silivri) and through *fatwas* issued by Ebussuud Yahya Efendi, elevating those noncombatants who contributed to the defense of the realm through the provision of funds to the status of *ghazis* and *mujahids*, and confirming donations towards military expenses would qualify as *zakat*.[51]

On 28 October, Selim II appointed Uluç Ali Pasha as the new *kapudan pasha* and *beylerbey* of Algiers for his efforts in the Battle of Lepanto, upgrading his name from Uluç to Kılıç as a gesture of his enhanced prestige. In orders sent to Kılıç Ali and Pertev Pasha that same day, both were directed to bring together the ships that they still had in their possession and move to Evvoia. There, they were to recruit new oarsmen to refill the rowing desks and to secure the fortresses in the Lepanto Strait. The two men met at Evvoia on 9 November. Pertev Pasha sailed for Constantinople, and retirement, on 24 November. Kılıç Ali returned to the city, and his enhanced responsibilities, on 19 December. An edict he received from the *Divân-ı Hümayun* on 24 January 1572 charged him with evaluating the performance of his captains. Those who demonstrated merit were to be promoted in accordance with their status, a reward denied those who beached their ships; those who fled the battle were ordered to be imprisoned.[52]

Kılıç Ali was initially skeptical regarding the capacity of the Porte to meet its ambitious targets, pointing out to Grand Vizier Sokollu Mehmed Pasha that it would be relatively easy to construct the hulls of the new vessels, but manufacturing the necessary 500 or 600 anchors for 200 ships, and the matching amounts of cordage, sails, and other equipment, struck him as impossible. To this the grand vizier reportedly replied: "The might and power of this Exalted State is such that if the order were given to provide anchors of silver, cordage of silk, and sails of satin for the whole fleet, it would be possible. Whatsoever is lacking on any ship, just ask me for it." Hearing these words, Kılıç Ali kissed the grand vizier's hand, exclaiming, "For sure, I knew that you would bring the fleet to perfection!"[53]

This new fleet was mustered and passed in a grand review in its entirety at Constantinople in mid-June 1572. Giacomo Malatesta, a prisoner of war, was allowed to witness the spectacle in order that he could attest to its immensity to the pope and the Venetian Senate upon his release. In his report, Malatesta submitted that he had counted the galleys (at Sokollu's request), and that the total came to 244. Even taking into account vessels reassigned from other stations, it seems likely that at least 180 new ships had been built in eight months – a rate of production that was far beyond the capacity of any Western power, or indeed of all the Western powers put together.[54] Ottoman historian Mustafa Selâniki gloated that, "God be praised, through the excellent judgment and measures of the grand vizier a task had been accomplished that astounded the enemies of the religion… to the point of leaving them agape, their fingers in their [open] mouths."[55]

While undoubtedly impressive as a technical achievement, the wily Kılıç Ali, citing a weather-beaten infidel (*ruzgâr-dide kâfir*) who had arrived at "the essence of the problem," understood there was a critical flaw in the revivified Ottoman navy:

> Loss of ships will not bring any disaster upon the army of Islam, because they have an abundance of trees and timber in their mountains. Likewise, they will not suffer from a lack of equipment and weapons and spear-wielding soldiers. Their ocean-like supply of military manpower is well known, so that any deficiency in that respect can be ruled out. However, they have been dealt a blow in one special sense that takes time to repair… whose replacement will require many years – I mean the capture of many corsairs. The blow of the sword has descended upon able captains expert in naval matters, and at least a generation will pass before each one of them is supplanted with a man of similar caliber.[56]

Kılıç Ali would have to tread carefully and avoid any major confrontation with the League at sea before the sultan's new fleet had the experience and professionalism necessary to be competitive in such an encounter. In this, he was aided by that ancient and most decisive asset of the Porte: Christian disunity.

King Philip remained focused on the Maghreb. At the end of 1571 he allowed his representatives in Rome to sign an agreement for the following year's campaign committing the Spanish and papal fleets to muster at Messina in March and then sail east to join the Venetian navy at Corfu. But he continued to argue for a campaign in North African, not in the Balkans or Aegean. On 1 January 1572 the Venetian ambassador to Spain gave Philip a memorandum insisting the League must attack the European "center" of Ottoman power and not the African "periphery." Recognizing the need to keep the formal alliance alive, Philip responded that if European targets had to be accepted, they should be sites in the Adriatic, such as Preveza, Vlorë, and Herceg Novi, which would be useful acquisitions for his client Kingdom of Naples. However, his envoy to the *Serenissima Respublica*, Luis de Requesens, pointed out that if those places were taken, they would be claimed by Venice. A better alternative would be attacking Euboea, or islands in the Aegean, or the Peloponnese, in order to encourage a Greek rising which might interfere with the sultan's efforts to assemble a new fleet. But Philip had little real interest in any of those possible targets. He was still focused on North Africa, and on other more pressing concerns in his own domains.[57]

His opportunity came with the death of Pope Pius V on 1 May 1572. Philip immediately made preparations to withdraw from the Holy League and launch an attack on Algiers. On 20 May he sent a message to Don John, ordering him to postpone his departure for Corfu and the East and remain with his galleys in

Messina until further notice. The new pope was fully committed to carrying forward the crusade of his predecessor. After his election on 13 May, Gregory XIII summoned Marc Antonio Colonna, confirmed his appointment as commander of the papal fleet, and sent him to Naples, where the papal galleys were assembling. On 29 May, Colonna set off for Messina, arriving on 3 June. Six days later, Don John issued a grand proclamation to the people of the Peloponnese, urging them to rise up and promising help. But he was in no position to offer such aid, being under orders to remain in port. On 1 July, a frustrated Colonna issued Don John an ultimatum: if he did not allow the Spanish galleys to advance to Corfu, the League would be considered dissolved. To save the League, Don John offered a portion of his fleet – twenty-two galleys and 5,000 men-at-arms.

Colonna now had under his command 128 galleys, twenty smaller vessels, and six *galleasses*. At Corfu, he received the latest intelligence informing him Kılıç Ali had departed Constantinople on 12 June with a fleet of 130 galleys and three *galleasses*. At Igoumenitsa on the Ionian shore of Greece, Colonna received the surprising news that Philip had authorized Don John to participate in the League campaign with most, though not all, of the Spanish fleet under his command. It had apparently occurred to the king that support from the League might be decisive in his cherished plans for a North African expedition, and participation in the League now was the price he had to pay for its cooperation later. Don John sent Colonna orders to link up with him at Corfu.

Colonna, meanwhile, had sailed south on 29 July, reaching Zakynthos four days later, having been joined en route by twelve galleys from Venice's Cretan squadron. Off Monemvasia on 5 August, Colonna encountered Kılıç Ali who, unwilling to risk battle, immediately withdrew. Colonna, aware the enemy fleet comprised inexperienced personnel and was suffering from an outbreak of disease, continued to press the Ottomans for the next several days. But Kılıç Ali slipped away every time the League advanced, and on 10 August Colonna finally gave orders to withdraw for the rendezvous at Corfu. He was bitter at the lost opportunity, convinced that if Don John had joined them from the start, their combined fleet could have hunted down and destroyed Kılıç Ali, and then gained "almost all of the Peloponnese, since the Christians are standing armed and ready, awaiting the conclusion of this business."[58] For his part, Don John was enraged when he arrived at Corfu on 4 August with his fifty-three galleys only to find Colonna absent. After the two divisions did finally link up, it took another week of deliberation before the combined fleet advanced to Igoumenitsa and then set off southwards, having learned the Ottoman fleet was now at the port of Pylos on the west coast of the Peloponnese. But by the time the League galleys arrived at this point on 17 September, Kılıç Ali had withdrawn to the heavily fortified port of Methoni. Unable to accomplish anything beyond cruising impotently offshore over the next several weeks, the League fleet finally withdrew to Corfu on 19 October and then dispersed to its home ports for the winter, having accomplished nothing that year.

After another fruitless campaign, war weariness was rife in Venice. It was clear Cyprus was now irretrievably lost, and by the spring of 1573 the republic had sunk 10 million ducats into the war effort, with nothing to show for it. The senate had quietly sent an envoy to Charles IX in September to explore the possibility of using the French ambassador in Constantinople to negotiate favorable terms for peace – begging him, all the while, to keep this a secret from the other members of the League.

The French ambassador did indeed help in facilitating the two sides arriving at a treaty of peace, which was concluded on 7 March 1573, but even he was dismayed by how humiliating the terms were.[59] Venice was obliged to formally concede the loss of Cyprus and pay a lump sum indemnity of 300,000 ducats. The previously agreed annual tribute for the island of Zakynthos was now to be increased, and Venice would hand back the castle of Sopot (without which the Ottomans could not hope to control the Himarë region). Technically, each side would otherwise retain the possessions which it had held before the war. In reality, regardless of what the treaty stated, the Porte would keep Ulcinj and Bar, its gains in Albania, while Venice would surrender all of hers, retaining only a thin coastal strip of Dalmatia that included the towns of Novigrad, Nin, Zadar, Šibenik, Trogir, Split, and Kotor. And there was also an understanding that Venice would make a personal payment of 50,000 ducats to Grand Vizier Sokollu Mehmed Pasha. Such was the cost of doing business in Constantinople.[60]

Five days later, when the Venetian ambassador to Rome broke the news to Gregory XIII, the pope erupted in fury, immediately ordering him out of the room. Twice the ambassador begged leave to be heard further, and both times he was told to get out. Finally, the pope went to the window, turning his back on the unfortunate diplomat, and, "completely incandescent," ordered him once more to leave, telling him as he did so that he was excommunicated. Gregory had put much effort into continuing his predecessor's work with the League; representatives of the three powers had met in Rome over the winter, and a formal agreement to conduct another Levantine campaign had been signed by all parties (including the Venetian envoy) in February.[61] However dearly bought, Venice would remain at peace with the Ottomans for the next seventy-two years. Indeed, active Venetian collaboration with the Porte against Habsburg gambits in the Adriatic, Balkans, and Aegean would enable the Republic to retain uninterrupted access to Ottoman markets until a war between the two powers erupted over control of Crete in 1644.[62]

When Venice abandoned the League, Spain was isolated in the Mediterranean, and North Africa became the primary focus of the conflict. On 7 October 1573, the second anniversary of Lepanto, Don John led a much-depleted League fleet of no more than 107 galleys and roughly 100 transports south from Sicily. They made a good crossing, and just two days later 30,000 soldiers poured through the gates of La Goulette and advanced towards Tunis. The Ottoman *bey* and many of the inhabitants fled, and the city, which had never really recovered from its sack at the hands of Charles V in 1535, was occupied without difficulty. Abu Abdallah Muhammad VI ibn al-Hasan (Moulay Muhammad), the younger brother of the former Hafsid Sultan Moulay Ahmed, was installed as governor. Don John left a garrison under the command of Gabrio Serbelloni, a distinguished expert in fortifications and artillery, who commenced work on a new fortress linking Tunis to La Goulette, and then continued west along the Tunisian coast with his fleet, installing troops at Porto Farina and Bizerte, before setting out for home after a campaign of just one week, receiving a triumphant welcome in Palermo.

However, Serbelloni's operation was starved of resources, as Philip had to prioritize suppressing the Protestant revolt in the Netherlands, where the hard core rebels, the so-called Dutch Sea Beggars, so despised their Catholic king they openly sported crescent badges in sympathy with the Ottomans. Christian unity was also in tatters in neighboring France. The Wars of Religion between Catholics and Protestants (Huguenots) had broken out in 1562, and any hope for reconciliation evaporated when Charles IX sanctioned the St Bartholomew's Day Massacre of his Huguenot subjects on 24 August 1572.[63]

While the Christian world turned upon itself, the Ottomans spared no efforts in mobilizing a powerful expeditionary force to recover Tunis. Again, an effort was made to coordinate the war effort with pro-Ottoman partisans behind enemy lines in Spain. Selim II authorized further outreach to the Moriscos, urging them, "if in whatever year and time you will have the ability and power to move on and attack the enemies of religion" to do so, secure in the knowledge that aid "will arrive for you by sea and land," for the sultan's captains in North Africa "will render every assistance."[64] When the Ottoman navy under the command of Sinan Pasha and the *kapudan pasha* Kılıç Ali appeared off La Goulette in the second week of July 1574, it consisted of between 250 and 300 ships – larger than either fleet at Lepanto – and carried more than 40,000 soldiers. This was the largest commitment of Ottoman forces since the great land campaigns of

Suleiman the Magnificent. As soon as he knew of the approach of the Ottoman fleet, Serbelloni sent his nephew and lieutenant, Giovanni Margliani, in a light vessel to give the alarm to Don John. Since the royal half-brother had been sent to Milan to supervise overall Spanish policy in Italy, this involved an epic journey at high speed; Margliani reached Don John near Milan in less than two weeks, and then resolutely returned to what he regarded as almost certain death or captivity, taking even less time to do so.

Don John threw himself into the task of organizing a relief force, arriving at Naples with twenty-seven galleys on 17 August and summoning more. But the huge superiority of the Ottoman besieging force was already taking its toll, especially since the new Spanish fortifications were still far from complete. After five general assaults, La Goulette fell on 24 August. Tunis was finally overwhelmed on 13 September, and Serbelloni was captured; his son, Giovanpaolo, had been with him until the previous day, when he was killed by an arquebus shot to the head. There were few survivors, and most of them were wounded, including Giovanni Margliani, who had been shot in the face.[65] Moulay Muhammad, whose son, Moulay Nazar, had been killed during the siege, was shipped to Constantinople and confined in the Yedikule Fortress until his death in 1594. The Hafsid dynasty was eliminated, and Ottoman rule over Tunis confirmed. This complete victory was demonstrative proof of the Ottoman naval revival, and fully restored Ottoman military prestige. In practical terms, the Holy League had failed in all of its objectives. It failed to prevent Cyprus falling into Ottoman hands in 1571, it failed to save Venice from losing the war and signing a humiliating peace treaty in 1573, and it failed to contain Ottoman territorial aggrandizement with the occupation of Tunis in 1574. The triumph of the Holy League at Lepanto, therefore, ultimately accomplished nothing beyond indulging Western Europe with a brief spasm of psychological release from a sense of impending doom, a feat that only became more memorable with the passage of time and the emergence of a nostalgic sensibility over the end of the era of Renaissance galley warfare in the Mediterranean.[66]

10

THE EAST - FROM RED
SEA TO PERSIAN GULF TO
INDIAN OCEAN

PORTUGAL AND THE EAST

By a quirk of fate, the two powers that were ultimately responsible for containing Ottoman global hegemony – Portugal in the west of the Iberian Peninsula, Spain in the east – did so from the opposite points of the compass – Spain fighting Ottoman expansion westwards through the Mediterranean, Portugal blocking Ottoman empire-building to the east via the Indian Ocean.

"The Portuguese were the first Europeans to understand that the ocean is not a limit, but the universal waterway that unites mankind," Lord Acton concluded in a magisterial turn of phrase.[1] But there was nothing predetermined about this outcome. Prior to the 15th century, the Kingdom of Portugal was one of the poorest in Europe, so much so that it was incapable of striking its own gold coinage. It took the confluence of ruthless ambition with revolutionary advances in nautical technology to radically reverse this paradigm. Previously marginalized along the sterile western extremity of Europe, the Portuguese suddenly found themselves at the cutting edge of a new era in exploration and exploitation, as the Atlantic Ocean was transformed from a barrier to a superhighway opening up infinite vistas of opportunity. It was Portugal that drove the first wave of European empire-building, with its discovery of Madeira in 1420, the Azores in 1431, and its vessels being the first to round Cape Bojador in Africa in 1434. By 1442 at the latest, gold dust was being bartered from Saharan traders, and by the end of that decade a regular trade in gold and slaves had been opened up along the coast of Senegal. By 1457 there were sufficient stocks of gold in Lisbon for the Portuguese to at last strike their own coinage, the *cruzado* (crusade). Ever onwards the Portuguese captains roamed, reaching Sierra Leone in 1460. One of their number, Fernão Gomes, rounded Cape Palmas and arrived off Ghana in 1471. In this region, which the Portuguese came to know as the Gold Coast, Fort São Jorje da Mina, the first permanent European settlement in sub-Saharan Africa, was established in 1482. Still more horizons were destined to fall. Diogo Cão pushed south to the mouth of the Zaire River in 1483, and Bartholomew Dias rounded the Cape of Good Hope in 1488. In the grand consummation of this progress, a fleet under Vasco da Gama departed Lisbon on 8 July 1497, landed at the Cape of Good Hope on 19 November, and finally arrived in Calicut in India on 21 May 1498, after a total voyage of 316 days.[2]

From India, the voyages continued east, rushing towards the fabled spice isles of the Orient in order to claim them before they could be seized by the Spanish from the opposite direction, westwards across the Pacific. An embassy in 1518 led by Duarte Fernandes to the court of the king of Thailand was well-received by King Ramathibodi II. Attempts to arrive at a working relationship with China were less successful. In 1515, a Portuguese fleet was dispatched to Guangzhou under Fernão Peres de Andrade, bearing a diplomatic mission headed by Tomé Pires. This embassy reached the Pearl River in August 1517, but then for over two years was not permitted to proceed beyond Guangzhou. Finally achieving an audience with Ming Emperor Zhengde in 1520, Pires failed to secure diplomatic recognition or trading privileges, and was confronted with anger over the seizure of Malacca, which the Chinese regarded as a tributary state, in 1511.[3] The language barrier, cultural misunderstandings, and ongoing provocations by the Portuguese in the South China Sea led to the mission being arrested and its members incarcerated, fated to die one by one in prison. Although wildcat smuggling continued, Portugal did not secure formal trading privileges in China until the Ming court leased the "red-haired barbarians" Macao in 1557.[4] The final link in the chain of globalization was consummated in 1571 when the Portuguese formalized trade with Japan by establishing an emporium at Nagasaki, linking up with the annual Spanish silver galleons arriving in Manila from the Americas. Among the commodities traded was violence. Alongside Ronin samurai from Japan, Portuguese freelance mercenaries, men such as Diogo Veloso in Cambodia and Filipe de Brito e Nicote in Burma, were highly prized as palace guards at courts across the Asia Pacific region.[5] At the culmination of this era, the epic poem the *Lusiads* could celebrate "the famous Portuguese / To whom both Mars and Neptune bowed," eclipsing the exploits of Aeneas and Alexander:

> … those matchless heroes
> Who from Portugal's far western shores
> By oceans where none had ventured…
> Enduring hazards and assaults
> Such as drew on more than human prowess
> Among far distant peoples, to proclaim
> A New Age and win undying fame.[6]

None of this, of course, was driven by a commitment to scientific inquiry or a disinterested aspiration to discovery for its own sake. The primary motivation of the key players involved was war in the name of dynasty, kingdom, and God, expansion at sea being a logical extension of the *Reconquista*, the long-drawn-out struggle for control of the Iberian Peninsula between the slowly rising Christian states of the north and the gradually declining Muslim emirates of the south.[7] A key turning point in this process occurred on 21 August 1415, when a Portuguese fleet and army under King John I of Portugal crossed the Strait of Gibraltar to Africa and stormed the city of Ceuta. In the aftermath, one of the king's sons, Prince Henry, "gained information from Moorish prisoners and others which led him to believe that the gold-producing lands lay south of the Sahara," a contemporary chronicler, Diego Gomes, recorded, which Henry sought to reach "in order to trade with them and sustain the nobles of his household."[8]

Henry had been appointed Commander of the Order of Christ, a Portuguese crusading order created in 1319 to absorb all the knights, priories, castles, and traditions of the Templars, after their formal suppression in the rest of Europe.[9] In addition, the Order was awarded lucrative national monopolies, such as the right to trade in soap and fish, which could be profitably auctioned off to sub-licensees in a land where olive oil (the raw material of soap-making) and salted fish were the two staples of Portuguese trade. With these financial assets, between 1419 and 1434 Henry was able to commission some fifteen separate attempts to push the trade frontiers of Portugal to the south. Henry ruthlessly enforced his own hegemony over trading rights in Africa, a privilege upheld in 1456 through the papal bull *Inter Caetera* issued by Pope Nicholas V which established that the conquest, commerce, and spiritual jurisdiction of the Saracens of the West remained a monopoly of the Order of Christ. The previous year, Nicholas had issued the bull *Romanus Pontifex*, which confirmed the Portuguese Crown's right to the conquests of all coasts and territories discovered south of Cape Bojador, and forbade the subjects of all other Christian rulers from entering the region. Afonso V was bestowed with the title Lord of Guinea, affirming his right "to invade, search out, capture, vanquish, and subdue all Saracens and pagans whatsoever, and other enemies of Christ wheresoever placed, and the kingdoms, dukedoms, principalities, dominions, possessions, and all movable and immovable goods whatsoever held and possessed by them and to reduce their persons to perpetual slavery."[10] Though ostensibly united in propagating the Catholic gospel against the common Islamic foe, in reality the Iberian powers were bitter rivals, not partners.[11] The Portuguese, who had the upper hand over Castile at sea, zealously enforced their advantage in the 1479 Treaty of Alcacovas, whereby Portugal retained all rights to Africa, the Madeiras, the Azores, and the Cape Verdes in exchange for renouncing any future claims to the Canary Islands. To ensure these terms were enforced, Afonso issued orders to his captains the following year; should they encounter any Castilians "who are, or may be, on their way out to the said Guinea, or on their way back, or who are in it," the interlopers were to be seized, and, "without any further order or course of law, all may be and shall be forthwith cast into the sea, so that they may die a natural death."[12] In 1481, Portugal's claims were reconfirmed by Pope Sixtus IV in the bull *Aeterni Regis*. This was the prelude to the 1494 Treaty of Tordesillas, in which Pope Alexander VI divided the entire world between Portugal and Spain.

The modern era as we know it was thus the child of those two parents, Portugal and Spain. In 1552, Spanish chronicler Francisco López de Gómara declared the discovery of the sea routes to the East and West Indies "the greatest event since the creation of the world, apart from the incarnation and death of Him who created it." In his *An Inquiry into the Nature and Causes of the Wealth of Nations*, published in 1776 at the cusp of a new industrial era, Adam Smith rated the discovery of "a passage to the East Indies by the Cape of Good Hope" alongside the discovery of the Americas as "the two greatest and most important events recorded in the history of mankind."[13]

The transformative birth of globalization was far from bloodless. Entire ecosystems, both natural and cultural, would be swept away, unable to adapt to or compete with the sudden onslaught of biological and political competition. Even within Eurasia, long-established dynastic and economic relations would be fundamentally destabilized. Even for the protagonists, the risks involved in pioneering this new world order were considerable. Of the thirteen ships that departed Lisbon for India under Pedro Álvares Cabral on 9 March 1500, six were lost, and of those that returned the following year, two were empty when they straggled back into port. But the holds of the other five were bursting with cargo, enough to cover the costs of the expedition and return a massive profit to the Crown. The homecoming of Cabral's expedition was witnessed with deep foreboding by the Venetian ambassador to Lisbon, who reported to the senate that the ships returned laden with spices "at a price I fear to tell." The implication was clear. If the Portuguese had indeed secured a sustainable direct route to the Indies, "the King of Portugal could call himself the King of Money because all would convene to that country to obtain spices."[14]

"This is more important to the Venetian State than the Turkish War or any other war that might take place," a shocked Venetian observer, Girolamo Priuli, recorded:

> Now that this new route has been found by Portugal this King of Portugal will bring all the spices to Lisbon and there is no doubt that the Hungarians, the Germans, the Flemish and the French, and all the people from across the mountains who once came to Venice to buy spices with their money will now turn to Lisbon because it is nearer to their countries and easier to reach; also because they will be able to buy at a cheaper price, which is most important of all. This is because the spices that come to Venice pass through all of Syria and through the entire country of the sultan and everywhere they pay the most burdensome duties. Likewise, in the State of Venice they pay insupportable duties, customs, and excises. Thus with all the duties, customs, and excises... a thing that cost one ducat multiplies to sixty and perhaps to a hundred... Thus I conclude that if this voyage from Lisbon to Calicut continues as it has begun there will be a shortage of spices for the Venetian galleys and their merchants will be like a baby without its milk and nourishment. And in this I clearly see the ruin of the city of Venice, because lacking its traffic it will lack money from which has stemmed Venetian glory and fame.[15]

Venetian agent Leonardo da Ca'Masser confirmed this scenario, warning, "without doubt the king will dominate the sea completely, because it's patently obvious that the Indians can't protect the maritime trade, nor resist the shipping or artillery of this Most Serene [Portuguese] King."[16] This was not because of any deficiency in the military potential of India, where the Portuguese themselves were a microscopic minority of the population even when their empire in the East – the *Estado da Índia* – was at its height. Rather, Portuguese penetration of the subcontinent was owed to two factors; disunity, enabling the Portuguese to play the various regional dynasts off against each other, and disinterest. "Wars by sea are merchants' affairs, and of no concern to the prestige of kings," the sultan of Gujarat remarked when the Malabar coast first came under Portuguese attack. It was cost effective for local potentates to outsource their trade requirements to foreign opportunists, and if that meant tolerating the presence of such vagabond interlopers in isolated coastal enclaves, so be it.[17]

While Portugal had definitively emerged as the world's leading naval power by the beginning of the 16th century, the kingdom was still essentially a medieval society of warrior aristocrats lording over a peasant majority that lacked an entrepreneurial class (a situation only exacerbated when the Jewish population was expelled by royal decree of King Manuel I – "The Fortunate" – in 1496). In the absence of domestic capital markets, foreign financiers stepped in to offer the venture capital vital for the early expeditions to the Indies. The Florentines – always happy to take business away from the Venetians – were the first to volunteer their services, committing the front-end investment and providing the back-end distribution. It was Florentine merchant bankers like Bartholoméo Marchione, Girolano Frescobaldi, and Filippo Gualterotti who met three-quarters of the cost of the outbound Portuguese fleets, either as cash or in trade goods.

Marchione and his partners, who had outfitted one of Cabral's ships in 1500 and two of da Gama's in 1502, were responsible for four of Lopo Soares de Albergaria's in 1504, which departed Lisbon in April with the largest outbound consignment on board to date – 162 tons of Fugger copper, twenty-nine tons of lead, seventeen tons of cinnabar, and nearly two tons of silver. Having bombarded Calicut into submission, even after leaving a fleet of four ships behind to maintain Portuguese authority, Albergaria returned to Lisbon in July 1505 having bartered his trade goods for enough pepper and spices to deliver a substantive 175 percent return to his investors.[18]

By 1505, the trade in Asiatic spices accounted for 25 percent of revenues accrued by the Portuguese crown, rising to 40 percent by 1520.[19] Pepper comprised the overwhelming bulk of Portuguese-imported spices. In the fleets of 1505 and 1518, for which detailed inventories survive, 96 and 95 percent respectively of the home-bound cargoes, measured by value, consisted of this one commodity. For most of the century the Portuguese were supplying 75 percent or more of Europe's pepper imports.[20] This revenue stream fed upon itself, empowering imperial expansion and territorial aggrandizement that in turn tightened Portugal's grasp over the spice production that was becoming the life's blood of the European economy, in the process, as the Venetians had feared, reorienting the entire global system of trade and exchange away from the

Mediterranean.[21] "Born in the Indies," Spanish poet Francesco Quevedo quipped, "Sir Money is a powerful Knight."[22]

In the 15th century, German merchants wishing to buy Asian goods from Venice had to do so in Venice itself, where they were obliged to stay in the Fondaco dei Tedeschi and buy and sell under the supervision of the Venetian government. Beginning in 1501, the Portuguese began to dispose of their "Atlantic" pepper in Antwerp.[23] As the Portuguese endeavor ramped up in the Indian Ocean, its success attracted an ever-wider circle of investors, including the Affaitatis of Cremona and the two rival Augsburg-based mining concerns of Anton Welser and Jakob Fugger. The Central European mining boom had created a significant arbitrage opportunity between Europe's 10:1 to 11:1 silver-to-gold exchange ratio and the 9:1 ratio received in the Indian Ocean. Central European and Balkan silver that had been shipped east (via Venice and Cairo) for centuries was now redirected to Antwerp. The new trading pattern raised the demand (and price) for imported silver. By 1508, Antwerp was receiving 60,000 marks of Central European silver (nearly fifteen tons) annually to finance the Portuguese spice trade.

The annual volume of Malabar pepper unloaded at Antwerp more than tripled (to 8,000 quintals) between 1504 and 1511 and facilitated King Manuel's establishment of a full-scale *feitoria* (factory) at Antwerp in 1508. This allowed the Fuggers to match their copper monopoly to the growing needs of the Portuguese Crown and to enter the spice business themselves. This relationship intensified when the two partners arrived at terms for a four-year contract over 1519–23. Portugal agreed to purchase 12,000 quintals (600 tons) of Fugger copper at fourteen cruzados each in exchange for the Fuggers' right to purchase 14,000 quintals of Malabar pepper at twenty-four cruzados per quintal.

Almost everyone made money. The Portuguese Crown was happy to pay fourteen cruzados per quintal for Fugger copper because this unrefined ore could be sold at a very profitable twenty-four cruzados in Malabar. The Crown stood to realize 5.5 cruzados per quintal in profits – a 39 percent return – and profits were even higher when the copper was bartered for Malabar pepper, which could be purchased in India for as little as three cruzados per quintal and resold to European spice distributors for over twenty-four. The Fuggers would profit from both sides as well. They received a copper price that was triple their production cost (4.5 cruzados) and could mark up the retail price of their imported pepper purchases in Antwerp.[24]

This partnership pushed Venice to the brink of ruin. Prior to 1500, ten Venetian galleys had returned annually with as much as 1,750 tons of cargo from the Mamluk spice depots at Alexandria and Aleppo. With the diversion of trade to Lisbon, Venetian spice imports plummeted to around 500 tons between 1502 and 1505 – less than half of the volumes imported by Portugal during this period – and declined even further between 1508 and 1514. It was left to the Ottoman conquest of Mamluk Egypt and Syria in 1517 to bail out the reeling (but opportunistic) Venetians; the Ottomans needed Venice's European distribution network.[25]

Those seeking to make their fortunes in the East did so at considerable risk. In 1528, King John III appointed Nuno da Cunha as governor of the *Estado da Índia*, placing under his command a powerful fleet comprising eleven ships and more than 3,000 men. After setting out from Lisbon, four of those ships were lost at sea, five were forced to winter on the East Africa Coast or at Hormuz, and only two managed to reach India that year. Of the men on board, half died throughout the voyage, victims of shipwreck or disease. Shipping losses on the *carreira da Índia*, the route between Lisbon and Goa, during the 16th century were overall about 10 percent on the outbound leg, and 15 percent on the return voyage.[26] Even assuming they survived the enterprise, at roughly six months from Portugal to India, six months conducting trade, and six months making the return trip, those hoping to strike it rich in the East through commerce – the path of the *comerciante* – had to factor a year and half of their lives into the equation. Those without the capital reserves, acumen, or patience to conduct business opted to seek fame and fortune through violence – the path of the *corso* (corsair) – the code of aggressive aggrandizement later emulated by their Iberian counterparts in the Americas, the Spanish *conquistadors*.

DIU, 1509

Though profit-driven, the Portuguese enterprise in the East never lost sight of the role it played in the ancestral holy war against Islam. Outflanking the Muslim powers was a concept that had long roots in the medieval West. In 1317, a Dominican missionary named William Adam wrote a lengthy memo to a cardinal-nephew of the pope titled *De modo Sarracenos extirpandi* (*How to eradicate the Muslims*). Adam had spent nine months exploring the Indian Ocean, and he recommended enlisting the help of the Mongols to mount a naval blockade of Egypt using Genoese galleys.[27] Seven years later, Jordan of Sévérac, the Dominican friar who had taken it upon himself to establish the Catholic Church in India, wrote to his order echoing Adam's call for ships to be sent into the Indian Ocean to launch a new crusade against Egypt. "If our lord the pope would but establish a couple of galleys on this sea," he urged, "what a gain it would be! And what damage and destruction to the sultan of Alexandria!"[28]

Around the same time, a Venetian statesman named Marino Sanudo Torsello penned an elaborate manual for reviving the crusades. It came complete with detailed if inaccurate maps, and it also made the case for a naval blockade. The papacy had responded to the loss of the last Christian port in Palestine by prohibiting all trade with the Islamic world, but Rome had soon started granting exemptions to Europe's merchants, in return for a hefty consideration. Sanudo forcefully argued that Christian merchants were funding Islam's wars against Christian armies by handing over Europe's wealth in return for spices. It was abundantly clear, he pointed out, that armed expeditions alone were not going to dislodge the Muslims from the Holy Land. What was needed was a total trade embargo backed by the threat of excommunication and enforced by patrolling galleys; the blockade would fatally weaken the Egyptian sultan, since his wealth flowed from his grip over the spice trade. A crusader navy could then sail up the Nile and finish off the job. From their new base in Egypt, the knights could forge an alliance with the Mongols, attack Palestine, and retake Jerusalem. Finally, a fleet would be established in the Indian Ocean to police its peoples and trade. Sanudo pressed his plan on two successive popes and the king of France, but since it required concerted action from Europe's fractious rulers, it came to nothing.[29]

Indeed, it wasn't until the Portuguese mastered the currents and wind patterns of the Atlantic that any trans-continental agenda against Islam could be even theoretically practical. From that moment, the monarchs of Portugal were aware their potential for power projection into the Indian Ocean enabled them to serve God as well as Mammon. "We hope, with the help of God, that the great trade which now enriches the Moors of those parts, through whose hands it passes without the intervention of other persons or peoples, shall, in consequence of our regulations be diverted to the natives and ships of our own kingdom," King Manuel wrote to his Spanish counterparts, Ferdinand and Isabella, "so that henceforth Christendom shall be able to provide itself with these spices and precious stones."[30]

Thus, when Cabral set out in the quest for spices in 1500, he was also instructed to blockade the Red Sea and commence corsair operations against Islamic ports and shipping. In addition, he was ordered to establish a *feitoria* on Indian soil, which he accomplished at Calicut. However, within barely three months, an angry mob, encouraged by Middle Eastern Muslim merchants, attacked the *feitoria* and massacred its personnel. Cabral responded by first bombarding Calicut, then shifting commercial operations to Cochin and Cannanore. Calicut was again bombarded by Gama on his return in 1502, while Cochin, which welcomed the Portuguese, quickly became their principal Indian ally and the site of a new *feitoria*.

Portuguese ships continued to be dispatched to India; in 1503, three squadrons of three ships each sailed within a short time, the first under the command of Afonso de Albuquerque; then in 1504 thirteen more sailed under Lopo Soares de Albergaria and in 1505 twenty-two under Francisco de Almeida, who had been granted official authority as viceroy, the representative of the monarch with plenipotentiary powers over the emerging *Estado da Índia*. His *regimento* (instructions) from the king illustrate the extent of the geopolitical ambition now metastasizing at court:

> It seems to us that nothing would serve us better than to have a fortress at the mouth of the Red Sea or near to it – rather inside it than outside might afford the better control – because from there we could see to it that no spices might pass to the land of the sultan of Egypt, and all those in India would lose the false notion that they could trade any more, save through us.[31]

Feeding upon itself, this ambition was becoming insatiable. The following year, Almeida received additional instructions to reconnoiter and, if possible, claim Sri Lanka and Malacca for the Portuguese crown. Almeida proved more cautious, focused on consolidating Portuguese authority on the east coast of Africa and west coast of India by building fortresses at Sofala, Kilwa, Anjediva Island, Cochin, and Kannur. Though he sent his son, Lourenço de Almeida, on a diplomatic mission to the Maldives and Sri Lanka in 1507, the visit was not followed up; nor did he conduct the reconnaissance to Malacca that Manuel wanted, or seek to control the approaches to the Red Sea. As he explained to his king in 1508:

> … the more fortresses your Majesty might possess, the more your power will be divided: all your forces should be on the sea, because if there we should not be powerful (which Your Majesty forbid!), everything would be against us… In so far as you are powerful on the sea, all India will be as yours, but if you do not possess this kind of power on the sea, fortresses ashore will do you precious little good.[32]

Others among the king's subjects were more aggressive. The co-commanders of the outbound fleet in 1506, Tristão da Cunha and Afonso de Albuquerque, gave their monarch the "fortress at the mouth of the Red Sea" he wanted by seizing the fortress of Suk on Socotra Island and rechristening it São Miguel.[33] About the same time, Tristão da Cunha, commander of the Portuguese armada, landed three envoys to the Christian *negus* (emperor) of Ethiopia on the Somali coast – João Sanches, João Gomes, and the Maghrebi Sidi Mafamede – who eventually were received at the Ethiopian court around 1508.[34]

The only Portuguese setback was at the port of Hormuz in the Persian Gulf, and this was not for lack of effort. The island was a dry wasteland of volcanic rock, virtually bereft of vegetation and possessing no natural resources other than sulphur and salt. But its location astride one of the two principal routes linking the Indian Ocean to the Middle East, the Mediterranean, and Central Asia was of great strategic importance. In 1507, Albuquerque at the head of a squadron of six carracks en route to the Persian Gulf brutalized the coastal towns of Oman. The little port of Qalhat was the first to suffer his wrath. Towards the end of August, it was sacked and burned to the ground, those of its inhabitants who survived the slaughter having their ears and noses cut off by the Portuguese and dispatched to Hormuz as a sign of the approaching conqueror. Four days later, the squadron dropped anchor off Muscat. The city was stormed, plundered, and put to the torch, its population enslaved or mutilated. Sohar capitulated; Khor Fakkan was stormed and sacked.

On the evening of 26 September, Albuquerque's carracks dropped anchor in the harbor of Hormuz. So formidable were its defenses that his subordinates insisted he take stock before lunging into the fray. He freely conceded "it was a very serious undertaking, and one which required great caution," but having come this far, the expedition would benefit more from "a good, determined spirit rather than good advice."[35] The following day, battle was joined. Albuquerque was massively outnumbered, but the enemy vessels swarmed around his carracks in such numbers they only succeeded in impeding each other's progress, making themselves sitting ducks for accurate Portuguese gunfire. Having swept aside the enemy's naval assets, Albuquerque landed his men ashore. Fearing to suffer the same fate as the port towns of Oman, Hormuz surrendered.

On 10 October, after protracted negotiations, Albuquerque met with the twelve-year-old king of Hormuz, Seyf Ad-Din, and his vizier, Cogeatar, to sign the terms of capitulation. Hormuz would pay tribute to the Portuguese, who would construct a fortress on the island and be exempt from paying customs duties. Hormuz was a Safavid tributary state, but when the Portuguese were confronted by two Persian envoys who demanded the payment of the tribute,

Albuquerque presented them with guns, swords, cannonballs, and arrows, retorting that such was the "currency" struck in Portugal to pay tribute.

However, Albuquerque was not destined to consummate his subordination of Hormuz, at least, not that year. Three of his captains, unwilling to remain on station in the Gulf, sailed for India in January 1508, forcing Albuquerque to break off the occupation on 8 February. Enraged, Albuquerque vowed not to cut his beard until Hormuz was finally taken.

The Portuguese intrusion onto the trade routes of the Indian Ocean swiftly registered in Cairo, where the flow of spices, with its attendant tariffs and customs duties, suddenly dried up. This crisis made for a strange coalition of interests between the Muslim potentates of India, the Mamluks, the Ottomans, and the Venetians.[36] In 1504, the *Signoria* sent an envoy, Francesco Teldi, posing as a jewel buyer, to Cairo with instructions to arrange a secret meeting with Sultan Al-Ashraf Qansuh al-Ghawri and notify him the Portuguese had broken into the Indian Ocean, a reality that threatened to fatally undercut the established spice road into Europe via the Levant, to the detriment of both Venice and the Mamluks. The Venetian state-sponsored and defended spice trade convoys (*muda*), one to Alexandria and one to Beirut, had been halted during the Aegean war (1499–1503) with the Ottomans. Teldi was authorized to notify the sultan they would be recommended on condition the Mamluks evicted the Portuguese interlopers from the Indies and allowed the traditional rhythm of the spice network to resume. In concrete terms, Teldi urged the sultan to send envoys to the Muslim kings of Cochin and Kannur and other rulers on the west Indian coast to persuade them not to have dealings with the Portuguese, and to the kings of Calicut and Cambay to encourage them to continue their resistance against the Portuguese.[37] In return, the Mamluk sultan seconded an envoy to Venice, the Spanish-born dragoman Taghrī Birdī, who was to stay ten months in the Republic from late 1506 until mid-1507.

On two occasions, in 1507 and 1510, Kemal Reis, the first great Ottoman admiral, victor in engagements with Venice, Spain, Genoa, the papacy and the Hospitallers, who in 1501 had penetrated the Strait of Gibraltar and raided the Canary Isles in the Atlantic, commanded fleets that transported military aid to the Mamluks. In 1511, Bayezid II ordered 300 harquebuses and 2,500,000 kilograms of gunpowder, along with 30,000 arrows, be dispatched. As late as 1512, the Mamluk sultan assigned an envoy in Constantinople to request aid, including cannon, from his Ottoman counterpart. As Palmira Brummett notes, "This particular brand of gunpowder diplomacy not only protected Ottoman commercial interests in Syria and Egypt against Portuguese attacks but also provided a basis for later Ottoman expansion into Africa."[38]

Meanwhile, the imposition of Portuguese authority in India was being further tightened year by year. In 1501, Cabral established a *feitoria* in Kannur, the Portuguese presence in the city being enhanced in 1505 when the viceroy, Francisco de Almeida, constructed a fortress, the Santo Angelo, garrisoned by 150 men under the command of Lourenço de Brito. In 1506, the viceroy's son, Lourenço de Almeida, won a smashing naval victory over the Zamorin of Calicut off the harbor of Kannur. But the Portuguese overplayed their hand the following year, sinking an Indian trading vessel and killing the crew by stitching them into sails and throwing them into the sea after they failed to present a *cartaz* (license) the Portuguese obliged all merchants to purchase in order to conduct business. The Kōlattiri Raja of Kannur, supported by the Zamorin of Calicut, mobilized against the Portuguese, their combined armies investing Brito in the Santo Angelo on 27 April.

The ensuing siege set the pattern for Western imperialism during the 15th–16th centuries. While the Europeans were dominant on the oceans, they did not possess a cutting edge on land. The true secret to Western expansion was not offense, but rather, defense. European armies did not have an inherent superiority on the battlefield. What they did have was centuries of experience in building fortifications that maximized their capacity to absorb – and unleash – firepower while minimizing the number of personnel required as a garrison. Of all Europe's antagonists throughout this era, from Africa to Asia and the Americas, only the Ottomans possessed the manpower, technology, industry, and doctrine required to successfully besiege a European city or fortress, and even they were stretched to the absolute limit in every attempt, either requiring multiple efforts to take their prize (Constantinople, Belgrade, Rhodes) or being broken against the walls (Malta, Vienna). For the rest of the world, from Malacca to Cuzco, there was only frustration. This meant that Western armies penetrating the interior of any new territory could be reassured in the knowledge they had a secure base both to fall back to and project power from. Conversely, for the peoples of those territories, once the Europeans were established onshore, it would prove impossible to push them back into the sea from whence they came.

So it proved at Kannur where, despite being outnumbered by a ratio of 500:1, Brito succeeded in holding out until he was relieved by the arrival of a fleet under Tristão da Cunha on 27 August. For good measure, Cunha, accompanied by Francisco and Lourenço de Almeida, sailed on to Ponnani, a client city of Calicut, where they stormed the port on 24 November, torching every ship in the harbor.

Embassies bearing word of such atrocities were now arriving in Cairo on a regular basis. In 1506, responding to appeals for aid from Sultan Mahmud Begada of Gujarat, the Tāhirid ruler of Aden, Zāfir II, and the sharif of Mecca, Barakāt II, the Mamluk sultan established the Fifth Corps (al-tabaqa al-Khamisa), a company of arquebusiers dedicated to checking Portuguese expansion in the Red Sea, and authorized Emir Hussain Mušrif al-Kurdî to commence work on the fortification of Jeddah.

In 1507, Hussain led a joint Mamluk–Ottoman fleet to India in order to join the anti-Portuguese coalition forged by Sultan Begada of Gujarat and the Samoothiri Raja of Calicut. The arrival of Hussain's fleet at Diu in 1508 was a rather unpleasant surprise for Malik Ayaz, a former Rus slave who had risen to become ruler of the port city, a vassal of the sultan of Cambay. He agreed to having his fleet join forces with Hussain, as letters from the Mamluk sultan had requested of him, but advised Hussain against any engagement with the Portuguese until after the departure for Lisbon of the homeward bound *naus*, i.e., at the end of January or beginning of February of the following year.

After these *naus* had returned to Portugal, viceroy Almeida, convinced that no more would be coming from Portugal that year, ordered his son Lourenço to escort twenty Cochin *naus* bound for several northern ports, the last one being Chaul. The fleet that he took with him was made up of three small *naus*, a square-rigged caravel, two lateen caravels, and two galleys, manned by about 500 men. Setting out from Cochin in early January 1508, he cruised along the Malabar coast, seizing several Muslim vessels en route.

The Mamluk fleet under Hussain entered Chaul harbor on 24 March 1508, catching the Portuguese at anchor. When the two sides met in combat the following day, Lourenço made things difficult for himself by ordering his ships to fight at close quarters in unnecessarily costly boarding actions. Nonetheless, the Portuguese had the better of the fighting, capturing two Mamluk galleys and two *galliots*, while two more *galliots* cut their hawsers and fled upriver. Lourenço had the remaining Mamluk ships at his mercy when he finally opened up the distance between the fleets to use his artillery at range, only for victory to be snatched from his grasp by the arrival of the Gujarati fleet under Malik Ayaz.

That night, the now badly outnumbered Portuguese elected to break out of the harbor. At dawn, all the ships succeeded in reaching open water save the flagship, bringing up the rear of the line. Immobilized and sinking, she was stormed by waves of boarders and taken, Lourenço himself being killed.

Almeida vowed revenge – "Who ate the young rooster must now taste the old rooster," he was said to have muttered.[39] But the vengeance of the viceroy would have to wait until after the monsoon season. Further complicating matters, Afonso de Albuquerque arrived at Kannur on 5 December with orders authority over the *Estado da Índia* be handed over to him. Almeida simply ignored him, setting sail for Cochin on 12 December with a force of eighteen ships, manned by about 1,500 Portuguese and 400 auxiliaries.

After a hard fight, the Portuguese took Dabhol on 29 December and sacked it the following day. The fleet arrived off Diu on 2 February. Almeida could only risk entering the harbor with its narrow channel and shallow depth with a northeastern wind behind him and on a flood tide. When both conditions were met at 11am on 3 February, he ordered the assault. His ships immediately came under fire from both land and sea-based artillery. The *Santo Espírito* in the vanguard sank an enemy *nau* with her guns but then ran aground and was swarmed by two more *naus*, which closed in on either side. One by one, the other Portuguese ships entered the harbor and took up station against their assigned targets, subjecting them to withering fire. By 5pm the battle was over. Without losing a single ship, Almeida had sunk, captured, or scattered the entire enemy joint fleet. Hussain fled, and the following morning Malik Ayaz came to terms. Almeida, who lacked the manpower to hold, even if he could take, Diu, was content with establishing a *feitoria* in the city.

This set-piece victory, which Saturnino Monteiro describes as "one of the most important in world naval history," definitively established Portuguese authority in the Indian Ocean.[40] It broke up the emerging axis of mutual interest between the Mamluks and their potential partners in an anti-Portuguese coalition. Anthony Holland also considers the outcome at Diu "a pivotal moment in the shaping of the modern world," for had the outcome been reversed, "then the Ottomans could well have had the opportunity to take over the lucrative trade routes that were monopolized by Portugal. This raises the prospect of a much wealthier Ottoman Empire capable of financing even more ambitious military campaigns in Europe, something that could have tipped the scales" in their favor at Vienna and Malta, and then perhaps to Rome, Tangier, or further beyond.[41]

Almeida believed that control of the ocean should be maintained by naval force alone. Acquiring territory ashore and maintaining the strongholds necessary to enforce Portuguese authority on land would drain away the wealth won at sea by over-stretching Portugal's limited resources of manpower in operations which contributed nothing to generating profits. Albuquerque, on the other hand, believed that "a dominion founded on a navy alone cannot last," and advocated constructing a network of secure bases at key geopolitical chokepoints. In addition to imposing Portuguese hegemony over the local regimes, such a proactive policy would also prevent the Islamic great powers of the Levant from entering the Indian Ocean, as "the best way is to seek them there and not let them get out and set foot in India where for a certainty they would command the assistance of the Moors against us."[42]

Fortunately for Albuquerque, fifteen ships bearing 3,000 men that King Manuel had assembled for a Portuguese offensive against Calicut arrived at Cochin in November 1509. Unfortunately, they bore with them Albuquerque's cousin, the marshal of Portugal, Fernando Coutinho. He did enforce the royal writ dislodging the stubborn Almeida and confirming Albuquerque's authority as viceroy.[43] But when the expedition made landfall at Calicut on 2 January 1510, Coutinho, ignoring repeated warnings from Albuquerque, plunged deep into the city from the Portuguese beachhead and was isolated and killed in a counterattack. Albuquerque was wounded by an arrow while attempting to relieve the marshal and had to order a retreat.[44]

Albuquerque made his first decisive move in February 1510 – barely three months after assuming power as viceroy – attacking and occupying Goa, a port seized from the Delhi sultante in 1370 by the Hindu kingdom of Vijayanagara which had then been conquered by the Bahmani sultanate in 1356, recaptured by Vijayanagara in 1379, and lost to the Muslim Bijapuri sultanate in 1471. At the beginning of the 16th century the city still possessed a Hindu majority, was conveniently located between Kerala and Gujarat, offered a good defensive position with a sheltered inner harbor, and was an established port of entry for horses imported from Arabia and Iran to southern India, a trade the Portuguese wished to exploit. But before Albuquerque could consolidate his control, he was overwhelmed by a massive counterattack personally led by the Bijapuri sultan Yusuf Adil Shah, supported from within the walls by the Muslim minority, that drove him back to his ships and finally forced him to abandon Goa altogether in August. The struggle for the city had cost Albuquerque his favorite nephew and self-designated successor, Antonio de Noronha, but there was no question of this outcome being the final word on the matter. Having mustered twenty-three ships and 1,500 men at Kannur, within three months of being ousted from Goa Albuquerque returned to the city on 25 November 1510 – St Catherine's Day – and, despite being outnumbered four to one, he retook it.[45] "Our Lord has done great things for us, because he wanted us to accomplish a deed so magnificent that it surpasses even what we have prayed for," Albuquerque exulted to King Manuel. Noting that he had given explicit orders to spare the Hindu population, he continued that no such consideration had been extended to the Muslim inhabitants, who he considered a fifth column: "I have burned the town and killed everyone. For four days without any pause our men have slaughtered... wherever we have been able to get into we haven't spared the life of a single Muslim. We have herded them into the mosques and set them on fire."

Independent observers confirm the totality of the massacre. "No one escaped," wrote the Florentine merchant Piero Strozzi; "men, women, the pregnant, babes in arms." Another eyewitness, Giovanni da Empoli, a commercial agent from Tuscany, recorded that "the destruction was so great, that the river was filled with blood and dead men, so that for a week afterwards the tides deposited the corpses on the banks."[46]

The annihilation was intended to be spiritual as well as physical. "I haven't left a single gravestone or Islamic structure standing," Albuquerque continued. This tableau of violence was intended to serve a broader purpose. "The capture of Goa alone worked more to the credit of your Majesty than fifteen years' worth of armadas that were sent out to India," Albuquerque boasted to Manuel. "This use of terror will bring great things to your obedience without the need to conquer them."[47] In response to carping about the cost of maintaining Portuguese hegemony over the city, he replied that "if those of your council understood Indian affairs as I do, they would not fail to be aware that your Highness cannot rule over so extensive a territory as India by placing all your power and strength in your marine only."

Albuquerque knew that in the long run the Portuguese position rested as much on prestige as physical domination; "if once Portugal should suffer a reverse by sea, your Indian possessions have not power to hold out a day longer than the kings of the land choose to suffer it."[48]

Goa would serve as the hub of the Portuguese endeavor in Asia for the next 450 years. Its capture had significant geopolitical implications. The sultan of Gujarat authorized the Portuguese to construct a fortress in the port of Diu, Albuquerque's original choice for an Indian headquarters, while the Zamorin of Calicut also offered the right to establish a fortress in his domain. Meanwhile, after the defeat at Diu, the fall of Goa, and the collapse of the Gujarat alliance, the Mamluk sultan now lost all hope of defeating the Portuguese and stopped work on a second great fleet under construction at Suez intended for action in the Indian Ocean. In 1511, the *Signoria* dispatched another envoy, Domenico Trevisan, on a secret mission to Cairo, this time to offer the possibility of direct Venetian support for Mamluk offensive action against the Portuguese, and to urge the sultan "to get from the Turk artillery, lumber, ships and all the things necessary to pursue this [anti-Portuguese] effort."[49] But the Mamluks had lost interest in pursuing a proactive policy in the Indian Ocean, and the offer lapsed.

Having consolidated his authority over Goa, Albuquerque then set sail on 2 May 1511 for Sumatra, commanding a fleet of nineteen ships and a contingent of 1,400 soldiers, 800 Portuguese and 600 Malabar auxiliaries. On 1 July, this armada anchored off the great commercial entrepôt of Malacca. When negotiations with the sultan broke down, Albuquerque stormed and seized the city on 24 July, asserting Portuguese hegemony by erecting a fortress, a Famosa (the Renowned), for both strategic and symbolic reasons on the site of the city's principal mosque. "I hold it very certain," Albuquerque insisted, "if we take this trade of Malacca away out of their [Mamluk] hands, Cairo and Mecca will be entirely ruined, and to Venice no spices will be conveyed, except what her merchants go to buy in Portugal."[50]

When Sultan Abu Lais of Ternate permitted the Portuguese to establish a fortified warehouse on his island and agreed to maintain his traditional clove supply relationship with Malacca in 1513, Tomé Pires gloated over the geopolitical implications:

Men cannot estimate the worth of Malacca, on account of its greatness and profit. Malacca is a city that was made for merchandise, fitter than any other in the world. [T]he trade and commerce between the different nations for a thousand leagues on every hand must come to Malacca [and] while merchandise favors our faith, [the] truth is that Muhammad will be destroyed, and destroyed he cannot help but be. And true it is that this part of the world is richer and more prized than the world of the [West] Indies... Whoever is lord of Malacca has his hand on the throat of Venice. As far as from Malacca, and from Malacca to China, and from China to the Moluccas, and from the Moluccas to Java, and from Java to Malacca [and] Sumatra, [all] is in our power.[51]

Albuquerque meanwhile returned to an India roiled by dissent, motivated in part by the shifting balance of power in the Levant. While the Mamluk star was clearly waning, the rise of the Ottomans had given new heart to the anti-Portuguese resistance. Noting that conditions in the subcontinent had been completely tranquil at the time of his departure for Malacca two years previously, but upon his return he had been obliged to break another siege of Goa that had been launched against the city in his absence, Albuquerque reported to Lisbon that now, "with this news of the Ottomans, I have returned to find everywhere in rebellion. Your Highness should take note of what it will mean to have the Ottomans for neighbors, given the reputation they enjoy in these parts." Another Portuguese official, Aires da Gama, wrote to Lisbon in the following year advocating immediate military action against Gujarat, since "Diu is waiting for the Ottomans with open arms."[52]

Albuquerque set his sights on Aden. The strategic significance of this port city had placed it squarely at the center of the emerging geopolitical rivalry between the aspiring Portuguese and Ottoman hegemons. "It is by way through Aden that the Saracens of Alexandria receive all their stores of pepper and other spicery," Marco Polo had observed centuries earlier, "and there is no other route equally good and convenient by which these goods could reach that place."[53] This was no soft target. The city was situated on a rocky promontory protected on three sides by jagged and precipitous heights and walled off on the fourth, facing the sea. The assault, on Easter Sunday, 26 March 1513, was a fiasco. The preliminary barrage from the fleet made no impact on the defenses and the arquebusiers being landed from the ships' boats had to jump out and wade in the surf, rendering their gunpowder useless, when the place chosen for disembarking proved full of submerged rocks. The Portuguese who got ashore managed to storm the fort protecting the harbor and prevent its artillery from harassing the fleet at anchor. But the attempt to take the city itself by storming its wall utterly failed when the ladders brought from Cochin proved too short to reach the battlements. Those few who did reach the parapet were isolated and wiped out.

Anxious to press on into the Red Sea before the favorable easterlies failed in order to seek out the new fleet of the Mamluk sultan, Albuquerque put the debacle at Aden behind him to become the first Portuguese commander to pass through the Strait of Bab al-Mandab (the Gate of Grief) and enter the Red Sea. This feat led him to toy with concepts such as transporting workmen to Ethiopia to cut a new channel for the Nile to divert it from Egypt, and so desolate "the land of Cairo," or staging an overland expedition to sack Mecca and "carry off the body of the false Prophet."[54] None of these schemes came to fruition, but upon his return to India he addressed a letter to King Manuel in December 1513 suggesting the occupation of Massawa on the African shore and of Jeddah on the coast of Arabia. In his words, "once Jeddah was won, there will be neither a house nor an inhabitant left in Mecca, and it is granted that the *alfenados* [the henna-dyed ones, i.e., the Muslims] will abandon it since it is merely a day's journey from Jeddah. In my opinion Sir, the issue of Mecca is an easy thing; its destruction can be rapidly accomplished."[55]

Albuquerque had many enemies at court in Lisbon, and the fiasco at Aden tipped the balance against him. But he had one last campaign to fight. In 1513, Camilio Portio, on behalf of Albuquerque, had addressed an oration to Pope Leo X, stating: "There is thrown open to us by the conquest of the kingdom of Hormuz [the city-state in the Persian Gulf], the road whereby the Holy House of Jerusalem (the country in which our Savior was born) can again be recovered and rescued from the hands of those infidels who tyrannically and unrighteously possess it."[56] In March 1515, Albuquerque returned to the city with an intimidating fleet of twenty-seven vessels, 1,500 Portuguese men-at-arms, and 700 auxiliaries. Taking advantage of political infighting that had paralyzed the ruling dynasty, Albuquerque bloodlessly imposed Portuguese hegemony over Hormuz, his dominion being cemented by the construction of a fortress, Nossa Senhora da Vitoria (Our Lady of Victory). Having subdued Hormuz, Albuquerque could at last trim his beard. However, the cumulative toll of his successive campaigns and the burden of administration was severe; when he received word from Lisbon that he had been supplanted as viceroy, he died at sea en route to Goa.

Albuquerque had confidently assured the court in Lisbon that the maritime empire he had created could be maintained with "four good fortresses and a large well-armed fleet manned by three thousand Portuguese."[57] This string of fortified bases – Goa, Cochin, Hormuz, Malacca, and Mombasa – allowed the Portuguese to create a self-financing naval empire. It was predicated upon the infamous *cartaz*, a system whereby all the merchants of the Indian Ocean were required to purchase licenses in order to conduct trade. These could only be acquired at the three naval bases of Hormuz, Malacca, and Goa. Merchants not only submitted to this official protection racket, but were also simultaneously required to pay customs duties at these three ports. Thus were the Portuguese able to fund and police their vast new maritime empire.[58]

Hormuzi subordination to Portugal initially worked to its advantage. When Muqrin ibn Zamil, the king of Bahrain, a vassal of Hormuz, rebelled in 1521, the island was stormed by António Correia at the head of a combined Portuguese and Hormuzi force on 27 July, subsequently being directly administered by a Hormuzi governor. However, in mid-January 1522, Hormuz itself rose in rebellion against Portuguese authority. This was suppressed, but only after the city burned for four days and four nights. The Portuguese were rapidly learning the tough lesson that maintaining an empire was at least as problematic as winning it in the first place. The coast of Oman seethed with discontent; revolts in Sohar (1523) and Muscat (1526) had to be put down. It was a similar story in Sumatra, where the Portuguese stronghold of Malacca was under constant pressure from the surrounding Muslim sultanates of Aceh and Bintan (both in present-day Indonesia). Aceh won a victory over the Portuguese in 1522, seizing the fortress of Pacem. The following year, Bintan won a victory at the Muar River, following up by laying siege to Malacca in 1524, which was only relieved by the arrival of a fleet under Martin Afonso de Sousa at the end of July, with three *naus* and four *fustas* manned by 200 Portuguese soldiers. Having sacked the Malay port of Phang and city of Pattani, Portuguese victory was consummated when Bintan itself was seized by Pero de Mascarenhas in 1526. While the heir to the sultan of Bintan removed his court to Ugentana, authority in Malacca devolved upon two sons of Vasco da Gama, Paulo da Gama and Estêvão da Gama. After Paulo was killed in a skirmish in May 1534, Estêvão took his revenge the following year when he seized Ugentana and put it to the torch.

It could be argued the rise of anti-Portuguese militancy was derived from the perceived weakness of the *Estado da Índia* in the absence of Albuquerque. His successor, Lopo Soares de Albergaria, was charged with entering the Red Sea during 1517 in order to deliver the king's trusted aide, Duarte Galvão, as ambassador to Ethiopia. Not only did he fail to accomplish this task, he lost two priceless opportunities to enhance Portuguese authority over the region.

On 30 September 1515, a Mamluk fleet of nineteen ships under the command of Selman Reis had departed Suez in what would be the last expedition conducted by the dynasty in the Red Sea. Selman succeeded in building a fortress on the island of Kamaran off Yemen, but failed in his bid to take Aden on 17 September 1516. When Albergaria arrived at Aden the following year, he declined an invitation from the emir, who had just fought off the Mamluk expeditionary force, to establish a Portuguese presence in the city, resolving to take Jeddah instead. Although he did succeed in occupying Kamaran and destroying the fortress built by Selman Reis, his fleet was then immobilized by the monsoons, the heat and lack of drinking water costing the lives of several men, including Galvão. After being released by the elements, Albergaria was finally able to advance on Jeddah, only to be outfought by Selman Reis, who repelled his attack. Albergaria vented his frustration by sacking the Somali port of Zeila during his return journey to India. The terms of the next several viceroys were equally undistinguished. Portuguese fortresses were established at Kollam (1519) and

Chaul (1521) and in Sri Lanka at Colombo (1518). It was not until the nine-year term of Nuno da Cunha (1529–38), son of the doughty Tristão da Cunha, that the Portuguese returned to the offensive and Portuguese India arrived at its final strategic form.

The propaganda value of the defense of Jeddah by Selman Reis, who deployed artillery to repulse the Portuguese, was inestimable. As early as 1521, the Arab dynast in Basra solicited the services of Ottoman arquebusiers, "not only to fight, but also to teach how to use the firearms to the natives of the land."[59] It also enabled Selman himself to smoothly transition into the service of the Porte after the Ottoman extirpation of the Mamluk dynasty in 1517.

Selman proved adept at navigating the unsettled political environment that marked the first years of Ottoman rule. When the *beylerbey* of Egypt, Ahmed Pasha, rose up in revolt against the Porte, Selman sailed to Jeddah, where he convinced the Ottoman *bey*, Hüseyin al-Rumi, to join him in a campaign to subdue Yemen. They succeeded in dislodging the Portuguese from Kamaran and took Zabid in 1523, but a popular uprising the following year forced Selman to flee back to Suez, Hüseyin al-Rumi selling out the Ottoman state in order to take command of the insurgency and govern in his own name. Selman was soon summoned to meet Suleiman's grand vizier, Ibrahim Pasha, who had arrived in Cairo to consolidate Ottoman power and reorganize the province's administration and finances after putting down the rebellion of Ahmed Pasha.

In a report (*layiha*) written on 2 June 1525, Selman outlined to Ibrahim Pasha a bold plan to subdue Yemen as the first step in a wider campaign intended to drive the Portuguese out of the Indian Ocean: "Where our ships are ready, and, God willing, move against [the Portuguese] their total destruction will be inevitable, for one fortress is unable to support another, and they are not able to put up [a] united opposition."[60] The grand vizier amassed a substantial fleet of eighteen ships at Suez and appointed Selman admiral, but gave overall command of the expedition to Hayreddin al-Rumi. The expedition set off in late 1526, heading first for the port of Jeddah, where it intervened to subdue an armed band of Levantines who had taken control of the harbor and customs house. His appetite whetted by this minor victory, Selman was anxious to proceed with the grand geopolitical agenda he had envisioned. "With these ships and arms it is possible to capture and hold all the fortresses and ports in India which are under the rule [of] infidels," he insisted: "One cannot escape from painful feelings when one sees these ships and arms lying idly at Jeddah, while one hears about the joyful activities of the accursed Portuguese in those lands of India. If they hear those ships are not operational and lack crews they will inevitably come with a great armada for, apart from these ships, there is nothing to deter these accursed Portuguese."[61]

The Ottoman expedition duly continued on its way south, landing the bulk of its forces at the port of Mocha near the mouth of the Red Sea in January 1527. From there, the two Ottoman commanders led their army into the Yemeni interior. Hüseyin al-Rumi was dead, but the various independent warlords of the region rallied around Mustafa Bey, the ruler of Zabid since 1523. After his defeat and execution in September 1527, the Ottomans were left undisputed masters of almost all of coastal Yemen. The only major holdout was the emir of the port city of Aden, who stubbornly refused to open his gates to the Ottoman forces, although he did agree to have the sultan's name read in his congregational mosque every Friday and to strike coins in his name. Satisfied by this public (if only partial) display of submission to the Porte, Selman then headed for the island of Kamaran, just inside the Bab al-Mandab, where he set up a permanent naval base and appointed his nephew, Mustafa Bayram, as its commander. From here, Selman also established a customs house and announced that henceforth all ships traveling from India would be required to stop and pay transit fees. For the first time, the Ottomans had gained control of trade at both ends of the Red Sea. Significantly, in 1527, for the first time in more than a decade, no Portuguese fleet visited the Red Sea, Admiral Lopo Vaz de Sampaio choosing instead to stay in Goa out of fear of the Ottoman presence in Yemen.[62]

Early in 1527, the vizier of Hormuz sent Selman a letter (later intercepted by Portuguese spies) in which he asked for military assistance in liberating his island from Portuguese rule. Some months later, the Zamorin of Calicut (who had united the Muslim corsairs of the Malabar coast and forced the Portuguese to abandon a fortress there in 1524) likewise sent an embassy urging the Ottomans to send a fleet to India. Meanwhile, the corsair Mamale, who was the head of the neighboring south Indian Muslim community of Cannanore, pioneered an important new transoceanic spice route from Sumatra through the Maldives. This route allowed merchants for the first time to entirely bypass Portuguese India and sail directly to the Red Sea from the spice islands of Indonesia. As a result, by 1528 Portuguese patrols as far away as Sumatra were encountering Muslim merchant ships defended by armed escorts of Ottoman mercenaries.[63]

In 1529, a Portuguese fleet from Hormuz raided and burned several coastal settlements in the Persian Gulf in order to punish Emir Rashid, the independent ruler of Basra, for refusing to hand over an escort of fifty Ottoman mercenaries in his service. The following year, a number of armed Muslim merchant vessels from Calicut successfully evaded Portuguese patrols around Hormuz and reached Basra safely, prompting the Portuguese to retaliate by launching an attack against the island of Bahrain.[64] The tightening Portuguese control over the Persian Gulf was beginning to factor into strategic planning at the Porte. "The king of Portugal is now taken into consideration by the sultan," Daniello de Ludovisi, Venetian *bailo* in Constantinople, reported, "both because of the help that he can provide to the Safavids by means of that route, and because of the campaign which the sultan himself hopes to undertake to destroy Portuguese seapower in those parts."[65]

Meanwhile, Hayreddin al-Rumi and Selman Reis had fallen out, a dispute which ended with the murder of the latter by the former. Following Selman's assassination, the corsair's nephew, Mustafa Bayram, rallied his uncle's forces, hunted down Hayreddin al-Rumi, and ordered his execution. Declaring himself Selman's successor, Bayram briefly attempted to reestablish control over Yemen, but the political situation continued to deteriorate, and he was soon forced to abandon the mainland and fall back to Kamaran. Yemen once more descended into anarchy, gravitating out of the Ottoman orbit for the next ten years.

As news of Selman's death and his nephew's retreat spread across the sea lanes, the Ottoman strategic situation in the wider Indian Ocean region began to deteriorate as well. By the end of 1528, the Portuguese once more found the courage to dispatch a fleet to the Red Sea and captured eight large merchant vessels and forty-four small ones in the space of just a few weeks. The following year, another fleet, under Heitor da Silveira, sailed to the southern Arabian port of Shihr, whose ruler he pressured into conceding trading privileges to the Portuguese. He then attacked Mustafa Bayram and the remaining Ottoman forces in their base at Kamaran, forcing them to abandon the island and flee. Finally, Silveira headed for Aden, where the local emir (the same ruler who had refused to open his gates to Selman in 1527) now agreed to become a vassal of the king of Portugal, to pay the Portuguese a tribute of 10,000 ashrafis a year, and to prevent any ships under Aden's jurisdiction from traveling in the direction of Mecca. Adding insult to injury, upon Silveira's departure, he left behind a permanent garrison of forty Portuguese soldiers, who took possession of the citadel and insisted on participating in the emir's weekly procession to the mosque, ostentatiously brandishing their swords, muskets, and other weapons before a scandalized local population.

Having been driven out of Kamaran in 1529, Bayram fled to the port of Shihr on the south coast of Yemen, then to Diu in northwest India. He and his men could not have reached Diu at a more critical juncture, arriving just days before Nuno da Cunha, the Portuguese viceroy of the *Estado da Índia*, arrived to launch a major assault on the city by sea.

The occupation of Diu had become the singular priority for Portuguese grand strategy in the Indian Ocean. An Ottoman presence in the town would represent a permanent threat to Portuguese navigation and the strongholds on the Indian coast, all of them at leeward to that city during the Indian summer (September to April) and thus always exposed to sudden attack without warning. An attempt to storm the city by Diogo Fernandes de Beja in 1521 having been repulsed, in 1528 Nuno da Cunha left Lisbon in command of the largest fleet ever sent to India with specific instructions to construct a fortress at Diu, through diplomatic means if possible, by force if necessary. The ships and men of this armada were decimated by storms and disease, but the Portuguese retained the initiative and in February of the following year Diu's fleet was destroyed at the Battle of the Bandra River.

Although powerful reinforcements arrived under Lopo Vaz de Sampaio, Cunha continued to build out the force under his command. Throughout the monsoon (May to August) of 1530 the shipyards of Goa, Cochin, and Chaul were fully engaged in constructing new ships. When finally assembled, the fleet was the greatest that the Portuguese had ever mustered in India. It was composed of fourteen galleons, two galleasses, six *naus*, two caravels, seventeen galleys and *galliots*, 112 *bergantins, fustas*, and *catures*, and five supply ships, plus the vessels of private traders accompanying the fleet, increasing the tally to near 300 sails. The complement of fighting men comprised approximately 3,000 Portuguese and 5,000 auxiliaries, plus 1,400 Portuguese sailors, 4,000 Indian sailors and oarsmen, and 800 Malay sailors, a total of more than 14,000 men. On board the private vessels were more than 6,000 men, women, and children, some of them with the intention to settle at Diu, which was a wealthy city with a superior climate to Goa.

Under these circumstances, Diu welcomed the timely arrival of Mustafa Bayram in a fleet of twenty-six vessels, accompanied by 600 Ottoman regulars, 1,300 Arab auxiliaries, and a train of artillery, as a godsend, and the local Gujarati governor, Bahaulmulk Tughan, immediately invited Bayram to assume full responsibility for the defense of the city. Accordingly, on 15 February 1531, when the Portuguese attempted to bombard the forts protecting the entrance to Diu into submission, they were driven off by intense return fire. Bayram continued to exact heavy casualties from the besiegers with barrages from the large guns he had brought with him from Yemen, and disrupted the Portuguese siege by mining the fortifications outside the citadel with powder charges. Within just a few days, collaboration between the Ottomans and local Gujarati forces had put the Portuguese to a rout – the first "transoceanic" victory in Ottoman history, albeit one that transpired entirely without authority from Constantinople itself.[66] The victory immediately elevated Ottoman prestige throughout the region; even the recalcitrant emir of Aden, who had so scandalously agreed to become a Portuguese vassal in 1529, now declared for the Porte and ordered all forty members of the small Portuguese garrison left behind in his city arrested and put in chains.

Unable to take Diu, for the rest of the year and throughout 1532 and 1533 the frustrated Portuguese kept relentlessly attacking ships navigating the Gulf of Cambay, devastating villages along the coast both directly through raids and indirectly by cutting off trade and fishing. This accomplished little beyond further alienating regional populations and driving merchants to seek alternate paths to markets. By the mid-1530s, a new Islamic route was well established, shipping pepper directly from Aceh (whose sultan, Alaud-din Riayat Syah al-Kahar, ruled until 1571, becoming a major scourge to the Portuguese) to the Red Sea, with stops either in the Islamic Maldives or in Calicut, which though Hindu-ruled took an anti-Portuguese stance favorable to the Muslim traders. This quickly came to rival the Portuguese route in the volume of pepper shipped to Europe. It also established direct relations between Aceh and the Ottoman-ruled ports of Jeddah, Aden, and Suez.[67]

DIU, 1538

Fortunately for the Portuguese, a new power making its entrance on the scene would tip the balance back in favor of the *Estado da Índia*. Defeated by Humayun, the Mughal Emperor of Delhi, in 1534, Bahadur Shah of Gujarat retreated to Diu. Desperate for allies, he turned to the Portuguese and, on 23 December 1534, signed the Treaty of Vasai, ceding territory and the cherished right to construct a fortress at Diu. The partnership proved short lived, Bahadur Shah being killed by his erstwhile allies in February 1537 after they discovered he had been conspiring against them by reaching out to the Porte in a bid to forge a Gujarati–Ottoman alliance.

These appeals found a receptive audience. Hadım Süleyman Pasha, appointed *beylerbey* of Egypt in 1525, had been massing naval forces at Suez awaiting word to lead them against the Portuguese for over a decade; according to a 1531 report from Pero Caraldo, the Portuguese ambassador to Venice, "As soon as the fleet became ready Süleyman Pasha would set sail to look for the Armada of the King."[68] Strategic imperatives dictated otherwise until 1538, when the sultan finally ordered Süleyman Pasha to lead his fleet into the Indian Ocean.

Süleyman was a controversial choice to command the expedition. A eunuch since childhood, grotesquely overweight, and already more than eighty years old in 1538, he was loathed by his contemporaries, having cultivated a reputation for ruthlessness and cruelty bordering on the sadistic through being prepared to "spill blood on the slightest pretext."[69] Despite, or perhaps because of, these credentials, the sultan bid him to "prepare for holy war in Suez," and issued specific orders:

> Having equipped and outfitted a fleet and mustered a sufficient quantity of troops, you will cross over to India and capture and hold the ports of India; you will free that country from the harm caused by the Portuguese infidels, who have cut off the road and blocked the path to the sacred cities of Mecca and Medina (may God almighty ennoble them!), and you will put an end to their depredations at sea.[70]

While mobilizing his military assets, Süleyman Pasha also unleashed a diplomatic charm offensive, dispatching his deputy, Solak Ferhad (Ferhad the Left-Handed), on a goodwill embassy to the Muslim emirs of the region. He failed to win over the ruler of Zabid, and the emir of Aden refused to negotiate with him at all. But he received a positive response from Sultan Badr of Shihr, from Ahmed Grañ al-Mujahid, the emir of Zeila on the Horn of Africa, from Pate Marakkar, leader of the Mappilla corsairs of Calicut, and even from as far afield as Alaud-din Riayat Syah al-Kahar, the sultan of Aceh on the island of Sumatra, from where Fernão Mendes Pinto relayed a warning to Lisbon passed on to him by a local rival that Aceh intended to cultivate relations with the Porte in order to "gain naval supremacy of the Malacca strait and cut you [the Portuguese] off, as his people openly boast they will, from all your spice commerce with the Banda and Molucca islands, and block all your trade routes to China, Sunda, Borneo, Timor and Japan."[71] Thus, by 1538, Süleyman Pasha had constructed an enormous transoceanic coalition, linking Constantinople via the Red Sea to allies spanning the entire breadth of the Indian Ocean, from the Horn of Africa to Gujarat to Calicut to the Spice Islands. As Giancarlo Casale notes, this was "arguably the most geographically extensive alliance ever assembled."[72]

The Ottoman fleet departed Suez in late June. After stopping at Jeddah and the island of Kamaran for water, the fleet arrived at Aden, where Süleyman tricked the emir into boarding his ship and then executed him, along with his viziers, while Ottoman soldiers simultaneously disembarked at the harbor and took control of the citadel. As it exited the Red Sea via the Bab al-Mandab

Süleyman's armada, a powerful force estimated at about ninety ships (larger and boasting considerably more firepower than their Mediterranean counterparts) and 20,000 men (exceeding the total population of all the colonies of Portuguese Asia combined), including 7,000 janissaries, was the largest that had been seen in the Indian Ocean since the legendary fleets of the Chinese admiral Zheng He more than a century earlier.[73]

Meanwhile, in Gujarat, preparations for the siege of Diu were proceeding under the command of Khoja Zufar, the Rumi governor of Surat, whose career reflects the remarkable social mobility of the era. His family was Catholic, and he was raised in southern Italy. A merchant ship captain with his own modest fleet of three ships, he was captured during a trading mission in the Red Sea by Selman Reis. Entering the service of Mamluk Sultan Qansuh al-Ghawri in Cairo he ascended to the rank of treasurer and accompanied Hussain Mušrif al-Kurdî in the 1508 expedition to Diu. After converting to Islam, he ultimately migrated to Diu in 1531 with a substantial fortune in the train of Mustafa Bayram. Khoja Zufar subsequently emerged as a figure of considerable wealth and influence, maintaining an extensive commercial and diplomatic network that spanned the Indian Ocean, enabling him to recruit a mercenary army, ships, and crews for the siege of Diu.[74]

From his base in Surat, Khoja Zufar sent a letter to Süleyman Pasha urging him to make the fortress of Diu his primary target, and promising to provide any help necessary for the campaign. According to a Portuguese paraphrasing of his letter:

> [Khoja Zufar] asked that the fleet be sent directly to India and land at the island of Diu, where it would be very easy to capture the [Portuguese-held] fortress there since he would provide all necessary assistance. And since [Diu] is the center of all the maritime trade routes of India, from there war can be made against all the principal strongholds of the Portuguese at whatever time desired, none of which would be able to resist. The Portuguese will thus be expelled from India, trade will once again be free as it has been in times past, and the route to Muhammad's sacred residence will once again be safe from their depredations.[75]

At the end of June, the Gujarati army, totaling some 19,000 men, began to attack Diu Island. For more than a month the Portuguese, under the command of António da Silveira, managed to prevent the enemy from crossing the channel. But, on 10 August, they were forced to abandon the city and to retreat to the fortress.

Süleyman Pasha arrived at Diu on 4 September. He immediately presented the garrison with a written ultimatum. When Silveira received this missive, he remarked, "let us see what the castrated dog has to say," and read the letter in public. Asking Silveira how he would attempt to defend his pigsty with so few pigs, Süleyman promised the Portuguese free leave of people and goods so long as they returned to the coast of Malabar and handed over their weapons along with the fortress. Should they refuse this offer, Süleyman vowed to flay alive any of the garrison who fell into his possession, pointedly reminding Silveira that among the vast Ottoman host were many veterans of siege warfare who had participated in the taking of Belgrade and Rhodes.

In response, Silveira ordered paper and ink and, in the presence of all, dictated his reply:

> Most honored captain Pasha, I have carefully read your letter. If in the Island of Rhodes were the knights that are in this pigsty you could be assured that you would have not conquered it. You are to learn that here are Portuguese, used to killing many Moors and are commanded by Antonio da Silveira that has a pair of balls stronger than the balls of your canons and that all the Portuguese here have balls and do not fear those who don't have them.

After an attempt to storm the fortress failed, the allies settled down to a siege. However, the anti-Portuguese coalition was an extremely fragile one. Mahmud Shah III Gujarat – son and successor of Sultan Bahadur, whom the Portuguese had killed before the expedition – refused to cooperate with the Ottomans, fearing that if Süleyman took Diu his victory would herald the Porte establishing a permanent foothold in India. Once again, at a critical juncture an Indian potentate evaluating the implications of Portuguese vs. Ottoman hegemony in the subcontinent had determined the former was the lesser of two evils. The Ottoman underperformance in India, therefore, was the antithesis to its consistent progress in Europe. In the West, the inexorable advance of the Porte was empowered by its own absolute unity of purpose and ability to take advantage of the endemic rivalries of the European polities ostensibly ranged against it. In the East, the roles were reversed. The Portuguese, with their backs to the wall, fought with singular determination, while the Ottomans consistently failed in their efforts to build the enduring alliances with regional hegemons they needed to effectively embed their presence in the region.

Since it was not easy for the Ottoman ships to enter the channel of Diu because of the crossfire from the fortress and the sea fort, Süleyman charged

Khoja Zufar, supported by Ottoman troops and artillery, with seizing the isolated fort (garrisoned by just thirty men) the Portuguese held in the Rumi village, which would allow for an improved the liaison between the allied fleet and the army. On 10 September, after an intense artillery bombardment, the Ottomans assaulted the fort but were repulsed. Khoja Zufar then ordered a huge wooden siege tower constructed on two barges, intending to take advantage of high tide by floating the tower alongside the fort and storming the battlements. But Silveira ordered Francisco Gouveia to take two *fustas* and burn it during the night. The next day, 14 September, three *fustas* from Goa and one from Chaul arrived at Diu with reinforcements. Khoja Zufar, having received large-caliber bombards from Süleyman, subjected the Rumi village fort to a five-day bombardment that practically razed it, killing or wounding most of its occupants. But another attempt to storm the fort on 28 September again failed.

Finally, on 1 October, the surviving garrison of the village fort surrendered. Süleyman could now concentrate all his guns against the fortress, the barrage commencing on 5 October. That night, five *catures*, having slipped through the Ottoman blockade, arrived from Goa with reinforcements and gunpowder. But the bombardment continued, bringing down bastions and sections of the walls. The Portuguese frantically converted the rubble into makeshift barricades and between 10 and 26 October repulsed five concerted attempts by the Ottomans to storm the breaches.

On the night of 27 October, another relief convoy passed through the Ottoman fleet without being detected, five more *fustas* arriving from Goa with thirty soldiers and some barrels of gunpowder. The following day, the Ottomans launched simultaneous attacks, attempting to storm the fortress in its most vulnerable sector, the collapsed bastion of Gaspar de Sousa, and launching an amphibious assault against the sea fort. Both efforts were repulsed.

On 30 October, Süleyman played his last card. He embarked his men and the fleet sailed for deep water, only to return under cover of darkness that evening and landed the entire army, which attacked the fortress at dawn without a preliminary artillery barrage in order to maximize the shock value. Three times the janissaries managed to hoist their flags on the top of the ruined bastion of Gaspar de Sousa, and three times they were driven out. After four hours of fierce fighting, the Ottomans, spent, finally retreated. They were unaware the garrison had been reduced to just forty men fit to fight, and its gunpowder reserves were exhausted. To disguise the parlous condition of his command, Silveira ordered twenty men – half the total he had available – to launch a sortie, which caught the enemy troops manning the trenches off guard, returning to the fortress with an Ottoman banner.

Süleyman now commenced the evacuation of his siege lines, this time in earnest. On the night of 5–6 November, Khoja Zufar abandoned the island with his troops. On the afternoon of 6 November, a relief fleet of twenty *fustas* and four *catures* under António da Silva arrived at Diu, while Süleyman Pasha and his fleet departed. The siege was broken. According to Saturnino Monteiro:

> The siege of Diu of 1538, which broke the teeth of the Turkish Red Sea Fleet, may be looked upon, in the light of World History, as an event of no lesser importance that the seizing of Constantinople by the Turks in 1453, although in the inverse direction. If the latter opened for them the doors of the West, the former shut for them the doors of the East.[76]

DIU, 1546

The campaign against Diu was a failure, but the threat of future Ottoman intervention on a similar scale spurred diplomatic initiatives by the Portuguese. Using as his intermediary a Venetian, Duarte Catanho, King John III offered a substantive shipment of pepper in exchange for wheat, a fifteen-year truce, and guarantees of free navigation rights to Portuguese shipping in the Red Sea for commercial purposes.

While haggling over peace terms ensued, on 31 December 1540 a fleet under the command of Estêvão da Gama, a son of Vasco da Gama and the governor of the *Estado da Índia*, set sail from Goa. Although not in the same league as Süleyman Pasha's armada of 1538, this fleet was still the largest the Portuguese had ever assembled, consisting in all of more than forty vessels large and small and some 2,300 men. With this imposing force, the governor intended to penetrate deep into the Red Sea. Raiding coastal settlements along the way, his ultimate objective was to attack the main Ottoman naval base in Suez, where he hoped to burn the fleet and permanently destroy its arsenal and shipyard. Had he succeeded in doing so, it is certain that the Ottomans would have been compelled to reevaluate their newfound claims in the Indian Ocean and perhaps even reconsider the peace proposal King John had offered them two years earlier.

Almost all contemporary accounts agree, however, that the list of challenges facing the Portuguese mission was so great that its success was never a serious possibility. First of all, having never previously sailed so far into the Red Sea, the Portuguese were dangerously unfamiliar with its daunting natural impediments to navigation, which ranged from adverse winds and treacherous shoals to lack of fresh water and extreme heat. Moreover, the success of the Portuguese mission depended almost entirely on the element of surprise, a virtual impossibility given the size of their fleet and the Ottomans' intelligence network in the region. Before ever setting sail, in fact, the Portuguese learned that Khoja Zufar in Surat had been informed of their preparations and was attempting to contact the Ottomans with details about da Gama's plan of attack.

The Portuguese fleet arrived at Massawa, just inside the Bab al-Mandab, at the beginning of February 1541. Confronted by unrelenting north winds, Estêvão was forced to leave all his galleons and *naus*, with their crews, 1,000 men under the command of another kinsman, Manuel da Gama, at Massawa, and proceed into the Red Sea with only the *galliots*, *fustas*, and *catures*. Suakin was taken en route, but the winds grew steadily more obdurate until, with his men suffering severely from the heat and lack of fresh water, Estêvão could only continue with his own *galliot*, the fastest ship in India, and the fifteen *catures*, bearing a total of just 250 fighting men, the other vessels turning back for Massawa. The Portuguese finally reached the heavily guarded arsenal at Suez on 26 April, but were in no position to launch an attack, as the port was defended by a powerful battery of guns and no fewer than 2,000 Ottoman cavalry. Greeted by a heavy barrage of artillery fire and outnumbered almost ten to one, Estêvão had no choice but to call for a hasty retreat without even attempting a landing on shore.

The expedition spent another excruciating month returning to Massawa, arriving on 22 May. The port's harsh climate and almost total lack of provisions had taken a heavy toll on the Portuguese left behind, and the prospect of starvation had driven more than 100 of them to mutiny and desert, fleeing into the interior, where they were quickly surrounded and massacred by local tribesmen. Immediately upon his arrival, Estêvão ordered the retreat to Goa. But even this return passage brought little relief to the beleaguered Portuguese force, as several of the fleet's smaller vessels were caught in a storm during the passage home and lost at sea with all hands.

While the expedition had been a total failure, effectively marking an end to Portuguese adventurism in the Red Sea, it did have one very significant corollary. Before he departed Massawa for the return leg to India, Estêvão da Gama dispatched a force of 400 arquibusiers under the command of his brother, Cristóvão, charged with marching into the highlands of Ethiopia to establish contact with the legendary Prester John. Estêvão would never see his brother again, but this Portuguese intervention would have a profound impact on the future course of African history.

Peace negotiations continued to drag out, the Portuguese insisting they be able to freely trade in the Red Sea port of Jeddah while also demanding the Ottomans not build a fleet with which they could threaten Portuguese possessions in the Indian Ocean. Suleiman rejected these terms. In his counteroffer in January 1541, the sultan proposed that the parties demarcate their respective spheres of influence along the line drawn from Shihr through Aden to Zeila, and that neither empire's war fleets cross this line of demarcation. Suleiman repeated his demands in May 1542, stating that one of the conditions of the peace was that no Portuguese ship visit Shihr and Aden on the southern Yemeni coast, Zabid, Jeddah, and Suakin in the Red Sea, or any other port belonging to the Ottoman province of Habeş. In October 1544, Suleiman wrote to King John that if the Portuguese agreed to peace on the sultan's terms, "you should let us know this. If you do not agree with them, you should still let us know, so that we can take over the Indian territories accordingly."[77]

Still the war continued, playing out on many fronts. In early 1544 about 100 Portuguese freebooters sailed out from Malacca in four fustas under the command of Lançarote Guerreiro. Their intent was piracy, raiding shipping in the approaches to Tenasserim, the most important of the Thai ports. King Chairachathirat of the Ayutthaya kingdom of Siam assigned the task of hunting down and eradicating this irritant to an Ottoman mercenary captain, Heredin Mafamede. Heredin had captained one of the Ottoman galleys in Süleyman Pasha's fleet during the Diu campaign of 1538. Having become separated during the crossing of the Indian Ocean he had opted to proceed to Tenasserim, where he entered into the service of King Chairachathirat. His fleet was composed of one galley, (probably the one he had departed in from the Red Sea), four *galliots*, and five *fustas* manned by 800 fighting men, among them 300 janissaries.

Heredin caught Guerreiro while he was careening his ships in the Mergui Islands. When the Portuguese fled, Heredin made the mistake of dispersing his fleet to hunt them down, leaving his flagship isolated. In the dead of night, Guerreiro launched a desperate assault on the galley, taking it and slaughtering its complement, including Heredin. When two of the Ottoman *fustas* sailed in to report after daybreak, the Portuguese seized both of them. When two more *fustas* approached, they suffered the same fate. A storm then blew up, sinking two of the Ottoman *galliots* and the remaining *fusta*. The two surviving *galliots* were then hunted down and taken by the Portuguese.

The stakes were raised much higher on 22 April 1546, when a joint coalition between Sultan Mahmud Shah III of Gujarat, Sultan Ibrahim Adil Khan of Bijapur, and Burhan Nizam Shah I, sultan of Ahmednagar, commenced another siege of Diu. This force was once again led by Khoja Zufar, who had kept in constant contact with the Ottomans by means of his relative Mustafa al-Neshar, the governor of Zabid in Yemen and, like Khoja Zufar, another veteran of the 1538 campaign. Operations began when, at Khoja Zufar's urging, Mustafa al-Neshar agreed to send a shipment of artillery and 500 janissaries directly to Diu from the Ottoman base in Mocha. With the armies of Sultan Mahmud and Khoja Zufar already surrounding the city, this force of Ottoman auxiliaries made a dramatic entrance into Diu's harbor on 18 April 1546, "waving Turkish flags, firing a great volley of muskets, and indulging in all of the bizarre and overbearing pageantry customary of that barbarous nation," in the words of Diogo do Couto, a Portuguese historian who served with the *Estado da Índia*.[78] The siege began on the very same day, and as news of the outbreak of hostilities spread, Muslim merchants up and down the coast of India began to refuse to trade with the Portuguese in anticipation of a speedy victory for Khoja Zufar and his allies.

Having evacuated the noncombatants, the garrison, 200 Portuguese commanded by João Mascarenhas, hunkered down. Reinforcements arrived from Goa on 18 May, Governor João de Castro having dispatched 200 men under his son Fernando in a flotilla of nine light ships (*fustas* and *catures*). In prosecuting the siege, Khoja Zufar built bridges to connect the island to the mainland, then drove entrenchments and mines towards the walls, keeping the Portuguese under constant artillery fire, which was concentrated on the stretch of the ramparts between the bastions of São Tiago and São Tomé, which was the weakest section of the defenses. Whilst supervising construction of a siege tower and the filling in of the moat, Khoja Zufar ventured too close to the wall and was brought down by a bullet on 24 June. His son, Muharram, took command of the siege, and beginning on 19 July, assaults went in against the walls, reaching their climax on 27 July when a general attack was unleashed using every available fighting man against all three bastions, the São João, São Tomé, and São Tiago. To halt the tide that threatened to overwhelm the fortress the sick, the wounded, and the resident women took up arms and joined the men on the walls. In desperate fighting, the Portuguese defense prevented the enemy from entering the fortress proper, but the numbers in assault parties were so great the Portuguese were not able to expel them from those stretches of the walls they had managed to occupy.

After another general assault was repulsed, Muharram decided to resort to mining the wall while he waited for reinforcements. On 10 August the first mine was detonated, collapsing the São João bastion to the ground and killing at a single stroke the sixty-strong garrison defending it, among them Fernando de Castro. Taking advantage of the confusion within the Portuguese camp, Muharram threw his forces into a new assault, which he assumed would be the last. But the Portuguese managed to recover and once again repelled their assailants.

The end of the monsoon season was approaching and Muharram was running out of time. The bombardment intensified, and on 13 August another general assault was launched against the three bastions. Once more, the defense held, and by now, help was on the way. João de Castro had mustered thirty-seven *fustas* and 500 men under the command of another son, Álvaro. These ships were joined by other contingents from Vasai and Chaul until some sixty *fustas* and 900 men-at-arms were clustered offshore Diu, unable to break through the monsoon winds to reach the city.

At last, on 24 August, two *catures* finally managed to dock at Diu. Muharram ordered a new assault but this, too, failed. The sea began to calm and on 27 August the other reinforcements arrived, just in time to bolster the garrison, which had been reduced to less than 100 men.

João de Castro had tried – without success – to induce the Mughal emperor Selim Shah to enter the war on behalf of the beleaguered Portuguese. But the governor's personal intervention, arriving with a third relief fleet comprising sixty light ships, twelve galleons and caravels, and 1,500 men, slipping into Diu unseen over three nights, 7–10 November, turned the tide. On 11 November, having feinted a naval landing with the ships that drew the attention of the besiegers away from the city and towards an anticipated amphibious landing, de Castro and Mascarenhas burst from the gates in a powerful and totally unexpected sortie; Muharram was killed in the ensuing melee, and the besiegers routed. Among the spoils of the battle was a flag of the sultan of Cambay, which was sent to Goa. Having weathered two intensive sieges in the space of less than a decade, Diu now would remain in Portuguese hands until 19 December 1961.[79]

Although the Portuguese had defended their city, doing so had required an almost superhuman effort in which they had called upon every spare resource available in the *Estado da Índia*. And with all of their forces concentrated on Diu, they were unable to counter advances on other fronts. As a result, the Ottomans were left with a relatively free hand in what was for them an equally important theater of operations: the Persian Gulf. Here the Ottomans launched a two-pronged assault that began just as the strength of their allies in Diu was starting to falter. Hostilities commenced in August 1546, with the departure of a small squadron of four oar-powered warships from the Ottoman naval base in Aden. This squadron headed quickly up the Arabian coast, stopping first in Shihr to help the loyal Ottoman vassal Sultan Badr capture Qishn, a neighboring port city recently allied with the Portuguese. From there, the vessels proceeded next to Qalhat, which was also attacked, and then sailed as far as the Portuguese stronghold of Muscat. Taking the Portuguese garrison stationed there by surprise, the Ottomans stormed the harbor, sacked the port, and captured a merchant vessel at anchor before finally turning about and heading back towards Aden.

Meanwhile, more than 1,000 miles to the east, a much larger Ottoman force was beginning to amass around Basra, a major international center of trade occupying a commanding position at the entrance to the Persian Gulf, and a prize long coveted by the Portuguese. Until the early 1540s, Basra had been ruled by Emir Rashid, a loyal Ottoman vassal who, ever since the Ottoman conquest of Baghdad in 1534, had consistently demonstrated his allegiance to the empire by reading the Friday *huṭbe* and striking money in Suleiman's name. After Rashid's death in 1543, however, control of the city had passed to Sheyh Yahya of the Benu Aman, an ambitious tribal leader by no means favorably disposed towards the Ottomans. By using Basra as a base to gradually extend his control up the Tigris and Euphrates rivers, Sheyh Yahya had begun to restrict the free movement of merchants between Ottoman lands and the Persian Gulf and also to make friendly overtures to the Portuguese in Hormuz. With the future control of the Persian Gulf now hanging in the balance, the Ottomans therefore pounced on the opportunity to take possession of the city themselves before the Portuguese had a chance to intervene. Ayas Pasha, the governor-general of Baghdad, was the Ottoman official in charge of the campaign. He began by building a new fortress at Corna, just upriver from Basra, and then sent a letter to Sheyh Yahya demanding that the gates of the city be opened to his troops in preparation for an offensive strike against the Portuguese in Hormuz. Refusing the order, Sheyh Yahya instead forwarded this letter to Luiz Falcão, the captain of Hormuz, and offered to hand over Basra's citadel to the Portuguese in exchange for help in defending the city against the Ottomans. His tribal allies in the Shatt al-Arab sent a letter of their own to Falcão with a similar request for help, ending their plea with the following warning: "The intention of the sultan is to seize from the Portuguese the navigation of the sea... believe this and come quickly! If the Ottomans take Basra there will be nothing left to stop them from moving against you and your territories, since the route through it is much shorter than through either Suez or Jeddah."[80]

The Portuguese in Hormuz obviously agreed. One official, writing to the viceroy in India on 30 November 1546, warned:

> Sir, these are very dangerous men and very experienced in the ways and the arts of war… they have already taken control of Mecca [and the Red Sea], and if they also build a fortress in Basra they will be able to send all the ships they possess in the other sea around to this side, an eventuality which represents the greatest possible danger for all of India.[81]

A week later, the captain of Hormuz wrote to Sheyh Yahya promising help, and then sent a letter to the governor asking that a fleet be sent from Goa as quickly as possible. His plea, however, fell on deaf ears, for the Portuguese in India, thoroughly exhausted by the defense of Diu, were in no condition to provide help. With nothing more than local resistance to oppose him and with a force of more than 3,000 troops at his disposal, Ayas Pasha easily conquered Basra and put Sheyh Yahya to flight on 26 December 1546. Almost without firing a shot, the Ottomans took possession of yet another strategic outlet onto the Indian Ocean.

As Giancarlo Casale argues, the Ottoman–Portuguese war of 1538–46, where the two sides faced off through direct confrontation or via proxies in two sieges of Diu, in the Persian Gulf, and in the highlands of Ethiopia, "amounted to nothing less than the first truly global armed conflict the world had ever seen."[82] This was the first war of peripheries, the first colonial war, in which the heartlands, let alone the capitals, of the two rivals were never directly threatened. While the frontiers erupted in desperate fighting, life went on uninterrupted in both Lisbon and Constantinople.

GLOBALIZATION

The Portuguese were now clearly on the defensive. Ottoman progress only ground to a halt because of intrigue and infighting at court. Rustem Pasha, who brought down and succeeded Hadım Süleyman as grand vizier in 1544, sought to purge the clients of his rival throughout the architecture of Ottoman administration. Since Hadım Süleyman had been a proponent of an Indian Ocean strategy and his faction had driven that agenda on the Arabian and Persian frontiers, Rustem Pasha sought to reorient policy away from this periphery, going so far as to openly oppose Ayas Pasha's conquest of Basra in 1546, refusing to

supply troops for the expedition and dismissing the port as "a ruined place...
worth nothing at all."[83] A corollary was the collapse of Ottoman authority in
Zabid and Aden in 1547, the latter offering itself up to Portuguese suzerainty, an
offer seized upon with alacrity by Paio de Noronha, who arrived with two galleys
from Hormuz. In order to retrieve the situation, acting on his own recognizance,
Daud Pasha, the *beylerbey* of Egypt, mobilized a fleet comprising twenty-five
galleys and four galleons under the command of Piri Reis (then nearly ninety
years old), which retook Zabid in December 1547, while Özdemir Pasha pushed
inland, taking various settlements, including Sanaa. Piri Reis then laid siege to
Aden on 19 January 1548. Noronha was counting on the arrival of reinforcements
from Goa under Álvaro de Castro, but with no sign of the relief force he
abandoned Aden in mid-February, leaving the city to be stormed by the Ottomans
at the end of the month.

In 1550, the Arabs of Al-Qatif, which was the departure point of the caravans
transiting from the Persian Gulf to Mecca, handed over the city and its fortress
to the Ottomans. Since Al-Qatif was a vassal state of Hormuz, the king of that
city hastened to ask the Portuguese for help to retake it. The governor of the
Estado da Índia, Afonso de Noronha, sent a powerful fleet of nineteen ships and
1,000 men-at-arms under the command of his nephew, Antão de Noronha, to
the Persian Gulf, not only to recover Al-Qatif but also to help the Safavids re-
conquer Basra. After duly overwhelming the Ottoman garrison of Al-Qatif and
destroying the fortress they had constructed, Noronha proceeded to Basra, but
was wounded in taking on the fortifications guarding the approach to the city,
and fell back when warned the local tribes were massing in defense of Basra and
threatened to cut off his route back to the Persian Gulf.

By 1552, the Porte had tightened its grasp over the Persian Gulf by occupying
the entire region between Baghdad and Basra, including the marshlands at the
confluence of the Tigris and Euphrates.[84] In support of this operation, the sultan
issued orders to Piri Reis to maintain pressure on the Portuguese at sea, for "if you
leave this region, the infidel will be back and it will be certain, a threat will hover
over Basra."[85] The admiral resolved on a proactive strategy; he would take the fight
to the enemy by targeting Hormuz. Setting out from Suez in April at the head of
twenty-five galleys (*kadirga*) and four galleons (*kalyon*) with 850 soldiers on board,
he proceeded to Ras al-Hadd, a headland at the entrance to the Gulf of Oman. At
the beginning of August, an advance force commanded by his son, Mehmed Reis,
appeared under the walls of Muscat, which was taken after an eighteen-day siege,
the port being pillaged, its fortress destroyed, and 128 Portuguese, including the
local commander, João de Lisboa, being taken prisoner. Once Piri Reis arrived a

few days later, the Ottoman armada reconstituted itself as a single fighting force and continued north, reaching Hormuz the following week. By early September, large numbers of Ottoman troops had been landed on the island, and gunners had dug into positions around the city. The siege of Hormuz, perhaps the richest prize in all of Portuguese Asia, formally commenced on 19 September. The Portuguese governor, Álvaro de Noronha, conceded the town, pulling his garrison back to its citadel. Having stripped the town of its wealth, Piri Reis failed to take the citadel and, aware that the end of the monsoon season would inevitably herald the arrival of a Portuguese relief fleet, he lifted the siege on 9 October and sailed for Basra. Abandoning his fleet, Piri Reis then departed for Suez with his three fastest galleys, laden with his expedition's spoils. One of these ran aground and was lost, but the remaining two, taking advantage of a storm that scattered the Portuguese sailing to intercept them, passed unhindered into the Red Sea. However, upon his return to Cairo, Piri Reis was arrested on charges of desertion and subsequently executed on the orders of the sultan in late 1553.

Ottoman efforts in 1553 and 1554 to withdraw the ships Piri Reis had left behind from Basra to the Red Sea resulted in the same unfortunate end. In 1553, Murad Reis, the admiral of the Egyptian fleet, went overland to Basra to take personal command. Setting sail from Basra in August with fifteen galleys, one galleon, and one barco, he was intercepted by a Portuguese fleet under Diogo de Noronha, which defeated him at the Strait of Hormuz and forced him back into Basra.

The Porte next charged Seydi Ali Reis, its newly appointed admiral of the Indian Ocean fleet, with the task of retrieving the ships from Basra. Seydi Ali was a veteran of the Ottoman campaigns against Rhodes (1522), at Preveza (1538), and Tripoli (1551), and would later be author of the renowned *Mir'ātü'l-Memālik* (*Mirror of Countries*). Departing Basra on 2 July 1554, he succeeded in breaking out of the Persian Gulf, but was intercepted at Khawr Fakkan off the coast of Oman by Fernando de Menezes in command of twenty-five ships. The Ottomans succeeded in holding the Portuguese at bay in a naval engagement on 9 August, but, reinforced by an additional eleven ships, Menezes had the better of a second encounter, the Ottomans losing six ships, while two more were wrecked on the coast of Oman. Seydi Ali with his remaining nine ships made a break for Yemen, only for the prevailing westerly winds to scatter his fleet across the coast of India, he himself being cornered in the Gujarati port of Surat. Unable to run the Portuguese blockade, Seydi Ali sold the remaining ships and in late November 1554 embarked on a long and adventurous trip with some fifty companions to return to Ottoman territory overland via Ahmadabad, Lahore, Kabul, Samarkand, Bukhara, Rayy, and Qazvin, arriving in Baghdad in late February 1557. None of the ships led on campaign by Piri Reis ever returned to an Ottoman port.

Meanwhile, the Ottoman war with Iran which had commenced in 1547 had ended with the Treaty of Amasya in 1555. The following year, Álvaro de Silveira launched a campaign against Basra, only for rough weather to drive him back from the Shatt al-Arab. In 1559, the Ottoman regional *beylerbey* Mustafa Pasha made an attempt, unauthorized by the Porte, to seize Bahrain, which was held by Portuguese ally Ra'is Murad. The Ottoman supply ships were caught at anchor by a fleet under Álvaro de Silveira on 9 July, but he was then killed in battle while marching to the relief of the town. However, Mustafa Pasha would also expire from wounds suffered in this encounter, and his expedition subsequently collapsed, the last survivors abandoning the siege on terms on 6 November.

The Portuguese now restarted negotiations with the Porte, offering to concede the Red Sea to the Ottomans in exchange for recognition of their hegemony in the Persian Gulf. In 1562, Francisco Coutinho proposed the Ottomans be allowed to open factories in Cambay, Dabhol, and Calicut, and to engage in trade in India, paying tolls and taxes to the Portuguese, in exchange for which the Portuguese would be permitted to maintain factors in Basra, Alexandria, and Cairo, and to conduct commerce in the Red Sea.[86] In its counterproposal the following year, the Porte offered the Portuguese the right to establish trading houses in Basra, Cairo, and Alexandria and to trade freely in all the Ottoman-controlled ports of both the Persian Gulf and the Red Sea; in return, Ottoman merchants would be granted similar freedoms throughout the Indian Ocean, including the right to establish commercial agencies of their own "in Sind, Cambay, Dabul, Calicut, and any other ports they desired."[87]

Given the soaring costs being incurred by the *Estado da Índia*, the prospect of détente with the Ottomans was a tempting one. The Portuguese ambassador in Rome, Lourenço Pires de Távora, had urged King Sebastian I to arrive at an arrangement with the Porte, for "Your Majesty's expenses in India are very great, and will grow even greater if some solution is not found. It is precisely because of this, as no reasonable man would dispute, that an agreement with the Turk would be most profitable."[88] Ultimately, however, the offer was rejected. From a Portuguese perspective, the risks outweighed the rewards:

> The true intention of the Ottomans is not just to control the spice trade, but in the long run to become lords of all of the states of India… and incite them to rise

up against our strongholds... and in the meantime they will be left with all of the trade in spices through both the straits [of the Red Sea and Persian Gulf] that we have forbidden. Thus, the Grand Turk will become master of all without the expense of a fleet, or the need to maintain fortresses... By controlling trade, all of the Ottomans' neighbors will side with them, such that even without investing their own resources, their allies alone will be enough to push us out and make them masters of India.[89]

The Portuguese would have been wiser to strike a deal while they still had leverage, for the financial foundations of their empire were rapidly eroding. In the 1560s, Portuguese spies estimated that some 30,000–40,000 quintals of spices were passing through Alexandria alone; adding the quantities coming through the Syrian ports, it appears that the ancient spice routes had recaptured the advantage, for the annual quantities sent around the Cape to Lisbon were probably no more than 25,000–40,000 quintals. Venice, which in the early days of Portuguese disruption of all the traditional routes had sent buyers to Lisbon, was back as the major European buyer in the Levant, and was taking more than she had the previous century. By the 1580s the Portuguese share of spices had declined further, and the Levant–Venetian route dominated the trade.[90] Ironically, while the Portuguese seized control over the Indian Ocean spice trade in the middle years of the 16th century and rerouted it to their own benefit, the massive expansion in the volume of the trade that subsequently occurred under their auspices – a natural corollary of their desire to meet insatiable demand through overproduction – ultimately led to its escaping their capacity to regulate, let alone control. By the end of the century, spices were flooding into the established markets of the Levant along the age-old transit routes, and the souks and bazaars were as bustling as ever.[91]

Equally important as an explanation for the Portuguese failure to maintain their monopoly over the spice trade was the fundamental flaw of their entire business model. Unlike the Venetians, who fitted out state fleets but auctioned the ships to merchants who bought as cheaply as they could and generally acted within the disciplines of the market, the Portuguese kept spices and other important commodities as a Crown monopoly and sought to keep prices artificially high, using the profits to pay for the military force necessary to enforce the *cartaz*. Accordingly, prices at Lisbon and Antwerp – where the Portuguese established their market for northern Europe – were generally higher than prices in the Levant. More important, Portuguese colonial administrators, who were always underpaid, had no commercial incentives of their own, which only encouraged them to operate illegally by trading under the table, and it was here that the major leaks in the spice monopoly occurred.

In addition, the capacity of Portugal to enforce the *cartaz* in the first place was always compromised. Throughout the vast expanse of the *Estado da Índia*, from Mozambique to Macao, there may have been a maximum of 10,000 men available for military service at any one time. In addition to quantity, there was also the question of quality. The beggars, vagrants, convicts, and drunkards forcibly inducted into military service off the streets of Lisbon to serve in the bureaucratic inertia that defined the East at the end of the 16th century were of a very different class to the hyper-aggressive freebooters who had stamped their authority over the region at its beginning.

There were simply too few men to cover too much space, for the Portuguese empire in the East was far more widely spread than even its geographical extent implies. Because of the prevailing weather system its extremities were separated as much by the seasons as by thousands of miles of ocean. Goa, the nerve center of the entire system, could not be accessed from the African coast bases for one-third of the year because of the monsoon, while Malacca, under constant threat from local coalitions mounting vast fleets and armies, was often close to disaster before relief forces could arrive.

All of these factors contributed to Portugal accumulating a succession of budget shortfalls beginning in 1548. State revenues had collapsed to only 607,000 cruzados when the Crown finally declared bankruptcy in 1557.[92]

Barely holding their own in the field of battle and with the cherished spices literally slipping through their fingers, the Portuguese were about to come under a new form of pressure. Ottoman preparations in Basra for renewed campaigns against Bahrain in 1570 and 1575 ultimately came to nothing. However, transformative changes within the heart of the Porte itself were destined to create a significant crisis for the *Estado da Índia*, one that it would barely survive. In 1565, Semiz Ali Pasha was succeeded as grand vizier by Sokollu Mehmed Pasha, who actively sought to advance Ottoman interests through a strategic focus on the Indian Ocean. It was a propitious moment to reengage with the region, for that same year, the Deccan sultanates defeated Vijayanagara, the last great Hindu kingdom of India and a Portuguese ally, at the Battle of Talikota. The following year, Suleiman the Magnificent died. The new sultan, Selim II, who succeeded his father, was enthusiastic about proffering Ottoman aid to the distant tributaries of the Porte, who had been holding the line against Portuguese expansion at the eastern end of the Indian Ocean ever since Albuquerque's day. On 9 October 1547, Ottoman janissaries supported an Aceh assault on Malacca, burning the Portuguese ships at anchor. The Portuguese secured their revenge on 6 December, trapping and annihilating the Aceh fleet in a battle on the Perlis River. In 1551, Alauddin Riayat Shah II, the sultan of Johor, made one last effort to reclaim Malacca, the city taken by the Portuguese from his grandfather. On 12 August his forces launched their assault on the city, but it was broken.

After receiving a request for assistance from Aceh, in decrees of September 1567, Selim mustered a fleet under the command of Kurtoğlu Hizir Reis, the son of Kurtoğlu Muslihiddin Reis and *kapudan* of Suez, comprising fifteen war galleys and two transport ships loaded with "artillery pieces, muskets and other tools of war," including thirty large siege cannons. The fleet was manned by seven expert gunners, a master cannon founder from the Ottoman artillery corps, plentiful rowers, "a sufficient quantity of troops from our victorious armies," and an array of craftsmen, including sawyers, carpenters, blacksmiths, coppersmiths, caulkers, and even three goldsmiths, all of whom received a year of advanced pay before their departure.[93] The expedition bore with it an edict for Alaud-din Riayat Syah al-Kahar from Selim:

> You must persevere and exert yourself, be it by conquering the strongholds of the miserable infidels, or by freeing the people of Islam from their evil and rage. With the help of God Almighty, you must cleanse those lands of the infidel filth, so that under our Imperial rule which concludes in justice, the Muslims of that land may live in a state of tranquility and, free from anxiety, may busy themselves with earning a livelihood.[94]

This call to arms concluded with a promise of institutional support:

> If the greatest and most noble Lord in heaven so wills it, help from our courageous armies will from now on be sent to you continuously to prevent the harm caused by those enemies of the true religion and the laws of the lord of the apostles, who have overrun the lands of the Muslims.[95]

At the last minute, this grand strategic initiative, which could have had profound geopolitical implications, was aborted. An uprising in the Yemeni highlands led by the Zaydi Imam Mutahhar led to the collapse of Ottoman authority in this critical region. Sanaa and Aden fell to Mutahhar; the Ottoman squadron in Mocha fled to Jeddah; and even the loyalty of Sultan Badr in Shihr was called into question. By the end of 1567, only the tiny Ottoman garrison of Zabid still held out against the rebels, and Sokollu Mehmed Pasha was obliged to organize an emergency relief expedition. Koca Sinan Pasha, the new *bey* of Egypt, was charged with pacifying Yemen, and Kurtoğlu Hizir Reis and his fifteen galleys were reassigned for this purpose, postponing their departure for Sumatra indefinitely.[96] In the event, only the transports would arrive in Aceh. However, this contribution was sufficient to inspire a full-scale mobilization.

On 20 January 1568, while Malacca was celebrating the birthday of King Sebastian I, the governor, Leoniz Pereira, was attending a tournament when he was notified that a massive fleet had appeared offshore. He greeted the news by commenting, "How fortunate that the Acehs arrived today, allowing us to celebrate the King's birthday with a great victory!"[97] Only when the tournament had ended did he deign to observe the enemy fleet. What he saw was impressive. Sultan Alaud-din Riayat Syah al-Kahar himself had arrived in command of four galleys, three *galliots*, sixty *fustas*, more than 200 *lancharans*, about eighty *balões*, and two large *champanas* loaded with provisions and ammunition. On board were 15,000 fighting men from Aceh and 400 Ottoman soldiers, plus 200 large-caliber guns. After a protracted bombardment, Alaud-din Riayat Syah al-Kahar launched an assault in force against the city on 16 February. This was defeated with great loss, and on the evening of 25 February the demoralized sultan broke the siege, sailing for home at dawn.

A smaller Ottoman expedition did set out for Sumatra later that year; Portuguese sources reported the arrival in mid-1568 of some "500 Turks, many large bombards, abundant ammunition, many engineers and several masters of artillery" in Aceh.[98] And the Portuguese were coming under ominous pressure throughout the Indian Ocean; in the Maldives, the corsair Kutti Musa of Calicut managed to drive out the Portuguese-installed Christian king, taking control of the archipelago for himself in 1569. However, the following year, a Portuguese fleet under Luís de Melo da Silva annihilated the Aceh navy at the Simpang River in 1570, the heir to the throne of Aceh being killed in the fracas. The loss of his fleet prevented sultan Alaud-din Riayat Syah al-Kahar from laying siege to Malacca in support of his partners in the first pan-Asian alliance dedicated to collective action against the Portuguese.

The key movers in this alliance – Ali Adil Shah I, the sultan of Bijapur; Murtaza Nizam Shah, the sultan of Ahmadnagar; the Ali Raja of Kannur; and the Zamorin of Calicut – initiated the War of the League of the Indies in December 1570. The pressure on the Portuguese was immense. Chaul was subjected to a siege from 15 December 1570 to 24 July 1571, Goa from 28 December 1570 to 15 August 1571. With their backs to the wall, the

Portuguese were able to retain control over both of these key strongholds. Even minor outposts like Mangalore and Honavar also held out. The only Portuguese defeat was the surrender of Chale, which was besieged on 14 July 1571 and capitulated on 4 November, the first loss of territory conceded by the Portuguese since their arrival in India.[99] Even in Malaya, where Ali Ri'ayat Syah, who had succeeded as sultan of Aceh upon his father's death on 28 September 1571, moved against Malacca in 1573, 1575, and 1577, the Portuguese broke the siege each time.[100]

However, the survival of the *Estado da Índia* had been a near-run thing. Symbolically, its flagship, a galley of great size, was sunk during the siege of Chaul when she was struck by a large-caliber round shot which had ricocheted off a house's roof. The Portuguese had been stretched to the absolute limit. Had the Ottomans directly intervened in India during the critical years of 1570 and 1571, instead of gaining Cyprus and losing their fleet at Lepanto, they might well have broken the Portuguese dominion over the Indian Ocean Spice Route and emerged as the undisputed hegemon of a pan-Asian network of allies and client states.

This would have marked the culmination of a strategy initiated by Sokollu Mehmed Pasha who, during his long tenure as grand vizier from 1565 to 1579, undertook to expand Ottoman influence not just via the hard power of alliance building and military aggression but through the soft power of cultural exchange, centering the sultan as guarantor of the safety and security of the maritime trade and pilgrimage routes to and from Mecca and Medina.[101] This prestige was to be enhanced through the initiation of grand projects on a scale intended to eclipse the seven wonders of the ancient world.

In 1568, Sokollu ordered the governor of Egypt to commission a study by architects and engineers of the feasibility of digging a canal to link the Mediterranean with the Red Sea via Suez. One year later, troubled by the advance of Muscovite power towards the Caspian Sea, he sent an army to seize the town of Astrakhan, on the Volga Delta, and to begin excavating another canal, linking the Volga and the Don rivers.

The idea of connecting the Don and Volga was first conceived in 1563 under Suleiman the Magnificent, who hoped to check Muscovy's expansion via the lower Volga to the north Caucasus and by taking Astrakhan, captured in 1555 by Tsar Ivan IV. However, the prioritization of Ottoman interests in the Mediterranean and Balkans meant that it was only after the death of Suleiman and the accession of Selim II that Sokollu was able to revive the plan. With the canal, the grand vizier planned to transport Ottoman warships carrying siege cannons, ammunition, and provisions from the Don to the Volga. It would have enabled the Ottomans to block Russian relief forces coming downstream on the Volga, and to capture Astrakhan with the flotilla and the accompanying Ottoman and Crimean Tatar land forces.

In July 1569, the Ottoman flotilla ascended the Don from Azov and stopped south of the Ilovlya River, tributary of the Don, somewhere opposite present-day Volgograd. They attempted to dig a canal at what seemed to be the two rivers' closest point. However, the rivers were still some 50 kilometers apart and the ground was hilly. The Ottomans abandoned the plan shortly after their arrival and sent the flotilla back to Azak with most of the siege artillery. Although Ottoman and Tatar land forces reached Astrakhan by mid-September, having only light field pieces and perhaps as few as two siege cannons, they failed to capture the fort. Ending the siege after just ten days, the army reached Azak by 23 October, after a devastating one-month-long march during which hundreds died of hunger and thirst. Although Kasım Bey, the governor of Azak and the commander of the expedition, wanted to renew the operation the following spring, the attention of the Porte was now focused on the campaign against Cyprus. Thus ended the Don–Volga canal project, with which Sokollu hoped to dislodge the Russians from Astrakhan and the Lower Volga, gain direct access to the Porte's distant anti-Persian Sunni allies in Central Asia, the Uzbeks, and enable the Ottoman Black Sea fleet access to the Caspian Sea, thus to attack Safavid Persia from the north and conquer the province of Shirvan.[102]

This was empire building on a truly global scale. The twin canal projects aimed at nothing short of creating a direct maritime link between Central Asia and Mecca, allowing travelers to pass entirely by ship from Astrakhan up the Volga, then by canal to the Don, then down to the Black Sea, the Bosporus, the Dardanelles, the Aegean, and the Mediterranean, before finally crossing to Suez and into the Red Sea. Once there, such travelers would have access not only to the holy cities of Mecca and Medina but also to the far-flung communities of Muslims from the Indian Ocean who converged on the Red Sea from the opposite direction. "In short," Giancarlo Casale concludes, "Sokollu meant to make the imagined Muslim community of the 'umma a reality by creating a global transportation network, centered on the Ottoman Empire, that radiated out to the most distant corners of the Islamic world."[103]

It was not to be. At the beginning of the 1570s, the strands of Ottoman influence so patiently drawn together by Sokollu threatened to completely unravel. In distant Sumatra, the Acehnese sultan Alaud-din Riayat Syah died, ushering in an extended period of political and social turmoil that would deprive the Ottomans of their closest ally in Southeast Asia. In the highlands of Ethiopia, Christian forces handed the Ottomans a crushing and unexpected defeat at the Battle of Addi Qarro, after which they captured the strategic port of Massawa, reestablished direct contact with the Portuguese, and threatened Ottoman control of the Red Sea for the first time in more than two decades. Meanwhile, in Mughal India, the young and ambitious Emperor Akbar had begun to openly challenge the very basis of Ottoman "soft power" by advancing his own rival claim to universal sovereignty over the Islamic world.[104]

In 1573, Akbar seized the Gujarati port of Surat and thus for the first time gained control of a major outlet onto the Indian Ocean. Less than two years later, he sent several ladies of his court, including his wife and his paternal aunt, on an extended pilgrimage to Mecca, where they settled and began to distribute alms regularly in the emperor's name. Concurrently, Akbar became involved in organizing and financing the *hajj* for his Muslim subjects, setting aside funds to pay the travel expenses of all pilgrims from India wishing to make the trip, and arranging for a special royal ship to sail to Jeddah every year for their passage. At the same time, he began sending enormous quantities of gold to be distributed in alms for the poor of Mecca and Medina, along with sumptuous gifts and honorary vestments for the important dignitaries of the holy cities. In September 1579, Akbar was emboldened enough to promulgate his so-called "infallibility decree." In the months that followed, his courtiers began to experiment with an increasingly syncretic, messianic, and Akbar-centric interpretation of Islam known as the *din-i ilahi*. And Akbar himself, buttressed by this new theology of his own creation, soon began to openly mimic the Ottoman sultans' posturing as universal sovereigns by assuming titles that paralleled almost exactly the Ottomans' own dynastic claims.

In 1579, Sokollu Mehmed Pasha was unexpectedly struck down by an assassin's blade while receiving petitions at his private court in Constantinople. The following year, his successor as grand vizier, Koca Sinan Pasha, assembled a relief force in Yemen and ordered the reconquest of the stretches of Eritrean coast that had been lost to Christian Ethiopia. To ensure the area's future security, he also had money and supplies sent from Egypt for the construction of a chain of seven new fortresses along the Red Sea coast from Suakin to Massawa.

In the summer of 1581, he broadened this offensive by sending Mir Ali Bey on a raid against the strategic Portuguese fortress of Muscat. Hitting his target on 22 September, Ali Bey succeeded in seizing the town for six days before returning to the Red Sea, the holds of his three ships stuffed with plunder. Encouraged by this achievement, Ali Bey swept down the coast of East Africa in 1585, receiving a rapturous reception in Mogadishu, Malindi, and Mombasa, where the local peoples were overjoyed to see the Portuguese being swept from their shores. Having captured three fully laden Portuguese vessels, he returned safely to Mocha with some 150,000 cruzados of booty and nearly sixty Portuguese prisoners.

In the late autumn of 1588, Ali Bey again set sail from Mocha, once more bound for East Africa's Swahili Coast. His ultimate goal, according to contemporary Portuguese accounts, was an ambitious one: "to expel the Portuguese from the entire coast, even as far as Mozambique."[105] To accomplish this, however, the corsair had under his command only a small squadron of five lightly armed galleots and a contingent of no more than 300 fighting men. What he did have was a substantial battery of artillery and a positive relationship with Mombasa, where the locals welcomed his expedition. Ali Bey fortified the island in preparation for the inevitable Portuguese counterattack, and held a strong defensive position, but when the Portuguese commander, Tomé de Sousa Coutinho, arrived from Goa on 5 March 1589, he found the corsair and his men already desperately fighting off a threat from the opposite direction, a mass migration of Zimba tribesmen erupting from the interior of Africa. The Portuguese were content for the Zimba to rout the corsairs, then moved in afterwards to assign what was left of Mombasa to the control of its archrival, Malindi. Ali Bey surrendered and was taken prisoner, being brought first to Goa, then Lisbon, where he ultimately converted to Christianity.

Around the same time, Koca Sinan also dispatched a secretive embassy to India, headed by a delegation of renegade Ottoman Jews originally from Portuguese Asia. This delegation's primary mission was to open a dialogue with certain Portuguese in the *Estado da Índia* who were rumored to be disillusioned with their country's recent annexation by Spain, and who might be coaxed into an alliance with Koca Sinan as a means of maintaining their independence. Those same envoys proceeded to the Mughal court in Agra, where they privately urged Akbar to renounce his hostility towards Constantinople and join the sultan in a holy war against the Habsburgs. Akbar responded by ordering the Ottoman envoys bound in chains and banished to confinement in Lahore. According to the testimony of a Jesuit father then resident at Akbar's court, this reaction was provoked "by the arrogance both of the ambassadors themselves and of the ruler who sent them, and by the endeavor which they made to persuade him to wage war against the King of Spain and Portugal."[106]

By this point, the fire had gone out of the Ottoman rivalry with the Portuguese. The annexation of Portugal by Spain had led to a prioritization of Habsburg interests at the expense of the *Estado da Índia*. In January 1588, Philip II pointed out to his viceroy in Goa that "offensive wars have many disadvantages," and that since there were "many affairs" requiring the attention of the Habsburg monarch in Europe – not least of which was the Armada campaign against England that year – it was vital to remain on the defensive in the East. Accordingly, "it will from now on be necessary for you to preserve the gains that have already been made rather than to seek out new ventures."[107]

Both antagonists would increasingly find themselves crowded to the margins by aggressive newcomers, heralds of a new age of transnational corporate empire-building, the Dutch and English East India Companies. By 1625, conditions had already deteriorated to the point that one Ottoman author, the scholar Omer Talib, offered the following grim assessment of his empire's prospects in an era of declining global influence and authority:

> Now the Europeans have gained knowledge of the entire world, send their ships in every direction, and take possession of the most important ports... Only the things they do not consume themselves reach Istanbul and the other Muslim countries, and even then are sold at five times their original price. They derive enormous profits from this trade, and it is the main reason for the scarcity of gold and silver in the lands of the Muslims today... If nothing is done, before too long the Europeans will become lords even of the lands of Islam![108]

11

AFRICA – IN SEARCH OF PRESTER JOHN

ETHIOPIA

It was, perhaps, the most significant hoax in world history. On 18 November 1145, Bishop Hugh of Jabala in the Principality of Antioch met with Pope Eugenius III to solicit his support for the Christian realms of Outremer in the Holy Land, then under increasing pressure from the regional Islamic states after the fall of the County of Edessa the previous year. A fresh Western crusade to regain the initiative in the Levant would not occur in isolation, Hugh assured the pontiff, for one "Prester John, king and priest of a land in the extreme Orient, a Christian and a descendant of the Magi who are mentioned in the Gospel, and rules over the same people they governed... was proposing to go to Jerusalem and help the crusaders."[1]

The pope issued the bull *Quantum praedecessores* on 1 December of that year, calling for the Second Crusade. This petered out under the walls of Damascus in 1148, having accomplished nothing save destroying the marriage of King Louis VII and Queen Eleanor of France, who pointedly departed Jerusalem for home in April 1149 on separate ships. No support had been received from Prester John. His nonintervention was owed to a singular, inescapable fact. No such individual existed.

Ironically, far from invalidating the credibility of a Christian "king and priest of a land in the extreme Orient" coming to the aid of Outremer, the failure of the Second Crusade only made the Christian world cling even more desperately to the idea that such a potentate actually existed. Twenty years after the Second Crusade was summoned, a letter claiming to be from Prester John and ostensibly addressed to the Byzantine Emperor Manuel I began to circulate throughout Europe, translated from the original Latin into English, German, French, Russian, Serbian, even Hebrew. In his text, the author boasted he was "lord of lords and surpass[es], in all riches which are under the heaven, in virtue and in power, all the kings of the wide world." His realm, described as stretching "four months in one direction, indeed in the other direction no one knows how far our kingdom extends," and populated by fauns, satyrs, cyclopes, "dog-headed men, giants whose height is forty cubits," and "a bird, which is called the phoenix," strikes the modern reader as more akin to the Narnia of C.S. Lewis than anything grounded in reality. In fact, the treatise was so exaggerated in its litany of everything from sapphires to salamanders, its assertion that everyone from the Amazons to the tribes of Israel lived under the authority of Prester John, and its depiction of moral absolutes ("There is not a liar among us, nor is anyone able to lie... There is no adulterer among us... We have the most beautiful women, but they do not come to us except four times a year for the purpose of procreating children"), the mischievous, and anonymous, true author may have intended the letter to serve as parody and satire. But the popular imagination in Europe, anxious and isolated in its cul-de-sac at the western extremity of Eurasia, seized so intensely upon the legend of Prester John that his existence became taken for granted as an established reality of global geopolitics.[2]

If Prester John existed, the obvious task was to reach out and establish contact with him. The original impression created by the letter was that the realm of Prester John resided in the Far East: "Our magnificence dominates the Three Indias, and our land extends from farthest India, where the body of St Thomas the Apostle rests, to the place where the sun rises, and returns by slopes to the Babylonian Desert near the Tower of Babel." As early as 1177, Pope Alexander III dispatched the papal physician, Filippo, armed with diplomatic letters in search of Prester John. He was never heard from again, and while Marco Polo did return from his sojourn to the East in the following century, he had no luck finding the elusive Prester John either. When the Mongols erupted out of the steppes, some in Europe speculated they might be the heralds of Prester John, and indeed, some were Nestorian Christians. But the realm of the khans clearly did not conform to expectations, and as the Mongol tide receded, the search continued. Paying their respects at the court of Prester John was a specific mandate for those Portuguese captains who rounded Africa at the dawn of the 16th century. To their disappointment, he did not reside in India, and as they expanded ever further east along the trade routes to China, Japan, and the Spice Islands, it became apparent he did not call anywhere in Asia home. Slowly, the search reoriented from the east to the south, and Africa, where there was at least some parallel to the myth in fact.[3]

Alongside Armenia, Ethiopia can lay claim to be the first nation outside of the Roman Empire to convert to Christianity. Its Orthodox faith evolved in near isolation after the Arab *jihad* of the 7th century claimed the north coast of Africa and the Red Sea for Islam. But the Ethiopian nation survived and, when the Solomonic dynasty succeeded the Zagwe in 1270, began to not only assert its regional authority but actively reach out to its coreligionists in the West.

A report from 1306 identifies Ethiopian envoys in the republic of Genoa. Their *negus* (emperor), Wedem Ar'ad, had sent them to Europe to meet with Pope Clement V at Avignon and negotiate a mutual defensive pact with "the king of the Spains."[4] A delegation from *negus* Dāwit I was received in Venice in 1402. Arriving with his embassy were exotic gifts – spices, ape and zebra hides, a giant pearl, and four live leopards. The senate reciprocated with offerings of its own; accounts relate that, among other treasures, a mechanical clock, a gilded silver chalice, and a letter from the doge to the *negus* were presented to "the nuncio of Prester John."[5]

Further embassies from the *negus* arrived in Rome in 1403 and 1404, initiating a tradition whereby Ethiopian monks would undertake pilgrimage to the Eternal City, where the Santo Stefano degli Abissini complex was placed at their disposal.[6] Ethiopian observers were present at the ecclesiastical Council of Constance (1414–18), the ecumenical conclave that ended the Western Schism through the election of Pope Martin V (where, according to chronicler Ulrich von Richental, unfortunately they "knew neither Latin nor any language that one could understand").[7] In late August 1439, Pope Eugene IV dispatched the Franciscan friar Alberthus of Sarteano to summon representatives from "Prester John, the illustrious emperor of the Ethiopians" to attend the upcoming ecumenical Council in Florence.[8] In the event, Alberthus didn't get any further than the Ethiopian monastic community of Dayr al-Sultan in Jerusalem, whose abbot, Niqodemos, was careful to stress that matters of faith needed to be determined by the *negus*, and him alone. Nevertheless, in the absence of any direct instruction otherwise, he was prepared to send a delegation to attend the council in an observing capacity. Four Ethiopian monks duly presented themselves before the pope on 2 September 1441.

In 1427, Guillaume Fillastre, Cardinal of St Mark in Venice, recorded that "Christians of Prester John" had arrived in Valencia, an embassy from *negus* Yeśhāq I to King Alfonso V (*El Magnánimo*) of Aragon, seeking recognition and terms for an alliance, to be sealed through a double royal marriage binding the Solomonic Dynasty with the Crown of Aragon. Yeśhāq himself was to marry the *Infanta* Dona Juana d'Urgell, while an unnamed Ethiopian princess would wed Alfonso's considerably younger brother, the *Infante* Don Pedro.[9]

Yeśhāq also solicited the dispatch of various artisans and craftsmen to the Ethiopian court. Accordingly, when the Ethiopian ambassadors set out for home in late May 1428, they were accompanied by an Aragonese embassy, headed by Petrus of Bonia. This embassy never arrived, a fate that was only confirmed when another delegation from Ethiopia, this time dispatched by the *negus* Zar'a Yā'eqob, Yeśhāq's brother and successor, presented its credentials to Alfonso at Naples in 1450. The king wrote in reply to "our very dear friend and brother," lamenting "the loss of those thirteen men, masters in different arts, whom we dispatched a long time ago… and who, unable to pass, died on the way."[10]

Yā'eqob was a powerful warlord. It was during his reign that the Solomonic dynasty approached its apogee. In a missive to Mamluk Sultan Sayf ad-Din Jaqmaq, which reached Cairo in November 1443, the *negus* styled himself the protector of the Coptic minorities in Egypt and the Levant, concluding with a not-so-veiled threat: "And are you not aware… that the River Nile is flowing to you from our country and that we are capable of preventing the floods that irrigate your country? Nothing keeps us from so doing, only the belief in God and the care for his slaves. We have presented to you what you need to know and you should know what you have to do."[11]

Word of this exchange transferred to Europe via an embassy from Ethiopia which arrived in Jerusalem in January 1444. Accounts of its respectful reception, and the terms of the correspondence between the *negus* and the sultan, featured in a letter from the Franciscan Gandulph of Sicily to Pope Eugenius IV.

In 1445, Yā'eqob campaigned against Badlay ibn Sa'ad ad-Din, the sultan of Adal, defeating and killing him on 25 December 1445, and forcing Adal back into a tributary relationship. By 1449, Yā'eqob had pushed the frontier of Ethiopia to the shores of the long-cherished Red Sea by taking Massawa and the Dahlak Islands, reorganizing the coastal region under the administration of the *bāhr negus* (ruler of the seas), and enhancing the prospect of more direct contact between Ethiopia and the West.[12]

One Western statesman resolutely determined to take geopolitical advantage of these contacts was Alfonso V. In his letter of 1450, the Aragonese king informed Yä'eqob he was planning on sending a fleet of 150 ships to "the holy house of Jerusalem," and urged the *negus* to block the Nile and advance men to the border of Egypt.[13]

One and a half years later, no reply had arrived from Yä'eqob. In January 1452, Alfonso wrote again to the *negus*, dispatching a message with an ambassador called Michaelus to the Ethiopian court deliberately routed via Constantinople and Trabzon in order to avoid Mamluk and Ottoman territory.

After another year and a half, still no response had arrived, so in July 1453 Alfonso wrote to Yä'eqob for the third time. His letter specifies that he was sending a high-ranking member of his court – Antonius Martinez, the royal chamberlain – via yet another route. If the *negus* desired anything from the kingdom of Aragon, he should simply write back, so that Alfonso "might thereby have the capacity to act in accordance with your pleasures."[14]

What became of these embassies – and whether or not the *negus* received them, let alone considered them – must remain a mystery. But certain it is that the Mamluks and Ottomans would have had every incentive to make sure they never arrived at their intended destination.

In December 1456, Pope Calixtus III reached out to Yäeqob. Addressing himself to "the beloved son in Christ Zarajacob king of the Ethiopian realms," the pontiff preferred an offer of partnership in a crusade whereby, "between orientals and occidentals we can prepare two good armies of land and of sea," urging Yäeqob to "unite yourself to us in such a just and beautiful military enterprise, to which no other can be compared." The pope reminded the *negus* that Ethiopia controlled the sources of the Nile, "whose inundations fertilize the land where our enemies feed themselves, whom you can deprive them of it at your will."[15] Yäeqob had only to contact Ludovico, the papal legate for the naval fleet already active in the eastern Mediterranean, to do his part and join the fight.

Again, the only response was silence. In 1470, Nicola da Oliveto explained this may have been because the papacy's cherished project of starving Egypt into submission by damming the Nile was technically feasible but not possible for political reasons, owing to a medieval conception of mutually assured destruction: "They say Prester John can take away from the Moors the water of the Nile, which would not go to Cairo; but he does not want to because he fears the Moors would ruin the Temples of the Christians, which are in Jerusalem as well as in Egypt in great quantity."[16]

In 1492, an envoy from King João of Portugal, Pero da Covilhã, arrived in Ethiopia at the end of a five-year sojourn via Cairo, Goa, Calicut, Kannur, Sofala, Cairo again, Hormuz, Medina, Mecca, and Jeddah. He was received courteously, but denied permission to leave.[17] Nonetheless, once established, the Portuguese connection would rapidly become the primary conduit for Ethiopia's outreach to the West during the 16th century as ships of the *Estado da Índia* began to enter the Red Sea. The incorporation of Ethiopia as a partner in the emerging Portuguese global crusade was an integral feature of the strategic plan initiated by King Manuel I. The messianic scale of his ambition is evident in an address he made to Pope Julius II in early June 1505:

> Christians may therefore hope that shortly all the treachery and heresy of Islam will be abolished and the Holy Sepulcher of Christ… which has for a long time been trampled and ruined by these dogs… will be returned to its former liberty and in this way the Christian faith will be spread throughout the whole world. And so that this might come to pass more easily, we are already striving and hoping to ally ourselves with the most important and powerful of Christians [Prester John], sending ambassadors to him and offering the greatest help by contacting him.[18]

This ambition was mirrored in Ethiopia. In 1508, the regent Queen Eleni, governing on behalf of her just-enthroned step-great-grandson, Lebna Dengel, dispatched the first Ethiopian embassy to Portugal offering Manuel support for an anti-Islamic crusade:

> That you may cause these Moors to be wiped off the face of the earth – and we by land, brother, and you by sea, for we are powerful on the land – that they may no longer give to be eaten of dogs the offerings and gifts made at the Holy Sepulchre. And now is the time arrived of the promise made by Christ and Saint Mary His mother, Who said that in the last times the King of the parts of the Franks would rise up, and that he would put an end to the Moors.[19]

Eleni offered gold and an exchange of marriage between members of the ruling families of both states, promising "we would give you supplies as great as the mountains, and likewise we would give you men in number as the sands of the sea!" She ended by noting, "But we have no power on the sea, and you are powerful at sea. May Christ Jesus help you, for certainly the things you have done in India are marvelous!"[20]

This missive was delivered by Eleni's ambassador Mateus, who arrived in Lisbon via Goa in 1514, bearing with him a reliquary containing a fragment of the True Cross, which the king received on his knees with tears of joy.[21] In a letter to Pope Leo X that he had received an ambassador "from Prester John, most powerful lord of Christians," who had brought with him "a by no means trifling piece of the True Cross for our adoration, and a request for skillful and industrious men by whose ability and skill he believes the Nile can be… diverted from the territory and neighborhood of the sultan," Manuel confirmed he was prepared to offer "all possible aid and everything necessary for a war against the enemies of the Catholic faith, such as soldiers, arms and supplies, especially if our fleet should penetrate the Red Sea, on which his domain borders and where the forces of both can be most conveniently joined."[22] Shortly afterwards, Manuel ordered Albuquerque to send João Serrão on a scouting mission to the Red Sea, with special instructions to learn of everything he could pertaining to Ethiopia. This entirely conformed to Albuquerque's own geopolitical vision. "We have no unsettled question left in India now but that of Aden and the Red Sea," he wrote to the King from Hormuz on 22 September 1515. "May it please Our Lord, that we should fix ourselves at Massawa the port of Prester John."[23]

Portuguese chronicler João de Barros recounted how Duarte Galvão, who led the embassy that accompanied Mateus on his return journey to Ethiopia, expounded on "the destruction of the house of Mecca," and argued "there was not a more feasible way of doing this than through the strait of the Red Sea, and by joining the forces of the armadas of King D. Manuel with the people of the Abyssinian king, called Prester John." Together, "they would take the Holy House of Jerusalem from the Moors."[24]

Galvão was not destined to make this case to the *negus* in person, dying in the course of his mission. Manuel's return embassy to Ethiopia left Lisbon for Goa on 7 April 1515, taking the sea route via India that circumnavigated the African continent. It wasn't until 13 February 1520 that the Portuguese fleet finally set out on the last leg from India.

On 17 April 1520, the Portuguese diplomatic mission, now under Rodrigo de Lima, arrived in Massawa. It had taken the Portuguese nearly six years to reach Solomonic Ethiopia. More than a decade had passed since Queen Eleni had sent out her ambassadors, and the head of her mission, Mateus, would himself expire shortly after arriving home. Lima, meanwhile, met with the *bāhr negus*, explaining by way of presenting his credentials that the king of Portugal, "being aware by reports on how the Prester John was a most Christian king, in a desire for his friendship he had sent his captains over the sea to discover if there is on it some port of his, and also to make war against the Moors, the enemies of our holy faith."

In the Portuguese account, the delighted *bāhr negus* replied by confirming that "as for the clearing of the Moors out of the land, with nothing would the Prester John be better pleased, nor did he desire anything more."[25] Lima's mission finally arrived at the Solomonic court on 20 October 1521, to find the regency of Queen Eleni had ended and Lebna Dengel had assumed his full authority as *negus* with the regnal name Dāwit II. The embassy would prove a frustrating experience. The *negus* was receptive to cultural and technological exchange but sanguine about the security of his realm, which was at its ascendancy. "God has granted me repose from all my enemies," Dāwit maintained. "In all the confines of my lands, each time I march against the infidels they fly before my face."[26] The Portuguese would find themselves unable to make any progress over the next six and a half fruitless years before Dāwit would finally consent to their leaving (excepting the painter and barber, whom the *negus* expressly requested to stay behind), Lima eventually departing Ethiopia on 24 July 1527.

Dāwit, meanwhile, had dispatched his own embassy to Lisbon, led by a monk called Ṣägga Zäab at the head of a small retinue. Manuel I had died in the interim, but in 1527, Ṣägga Zäab presented King John III with a crown and letters from the *negus*, which by that point were several years out of date, but were explicit in their requests:

> I want you to send me men, artificers, to make images, and printed books, and swords, and arms for all sorts of fighting; and also masons and carpenters, and men who make medicines, and physicians, and surgeons to cure illnesses; also artificers to beat out gold, and set it, and goldsmiths and silversmiths, and men who know how to extract gold and silver and also copper from the veins, and men who can make sheet lead and earthenware; and craftsmen of any trades which are necessary in kingdoms, also gunsmiths.

Ṣägga Zäab was ultimately detained for six more years in Lisbon, which kept him from delivering his master's message to Pope Clement VII in which Dāwit "entertained hopes" to liberate the Holy Land together with the Portuguese, so that Christians from Ethiopia and Portugal might "travel to and fro without hindrance."[27]

These missed connections would represent a significant lost opportunity, for over the ensuing decade Ethiopia's regional hegemony would be completely shattered.

The Ottomans had arrived at the northern end of the Rea Sea at the same time as the Portuguese were entering from the south. Their initial impressions of Ethiopia were not favorable. A report dated 1525 and attributed to Selman Reis concluded that with just 1,000 men, "it would be easy to take the land of Ethiopia," whose warriors were dismissed as "naked infidels with wooden arrows and elephant-hide shields; apparently most of them are bare-footed, weak infidel foot-soldiers."[28] Rather than direct intervention, Ottoman involvement would be outsourced to a local confederate in the sultanate of Adal, which had been subordinated by Ethiopian kings for generations but had found new spirit under the imam Ahmed ibn Ibrahim al-Ghazi, known as Ahmed Grañ (the Left-Handed), who had seized power from sultan Abu Bakr and ruled through his brother, a puppet installed on the throne in his place.[29] Rousing the Somali tribes of the Horn of Africa with the declaration of *jihad*, Grañ won his first victory in early 1529 at the Battle of Badēqē. Dāwit extricated his army from the field, and the two sides clashed again at Shembra Kure in March. The Ethiopian right wing overwhelmed the Somalis stationed on the Adal left, but Grañ and his elite *malassy* troops – mounted and well-armed with sabers from Arabia, shields from India, and swords from North Africa – held the center. The Ethiopian line ultimately broke and Dāwit was routed.[30]

In 1531, Grañ returned to the central theater. Over the course of a grinding, day-long battle at Antukyah in February he drove the armies of two Ethiopian generals, Eslamu and Abit, off the strong defensive positions they occupied on the heights blocking his march north. Dāwit was forced to withdraw into the Ethiopian highlands and fortify the passes into Bet Amhara, leaving the territories to the east and south under the protection of his general Wasan Sagad. However, he was killed in battle near Mount Busat on 29 July and his army scattered, allowing the Adal to advance into the rugged heartland of Christian Ethiopia, despoiling Debre Birhan in April and Debre Libano in July. On 28 October, the Adal won another crushing victory at the Battle of Amba Sel, a triumph only marred by the death of Grañ's brother-in-law and right hand, Matan ibn Uthman Al Somali.

At Amba Geshen in November the Adal vanguard under Garad Ahmusa became overextended and was destroyed. But Grañ continued despoiling Ethiopia throughout 1532, unopposed, for the *negus* refused to meet him in open battle. Having established himself at Debre Birhan in Showa, by the end of the year Grañ had taken much territory and plunder from Dāwit, including Menas, his son.

Deploying cannon manned by Gujarati professionals from India, Grañ laid siege to Debre Birhan in May 1533. The Adal army broke through the first and second Ethiopian defensive lines but was unable to reach the heights of the plateau (*amba*) and had to withdraw. Despite this setback, by the end of the decade most of Ethiopia was under Adal control and much of its Christian heritage had been annihilated, including the ancient church of St Mary of Zion, which allegedly housed the Ark of the Covenant. Dāwit had been reduced to the status of a fugitive in his own country, and in 1537, another of his sons, his heir, Fiqtor, was killed.

Grañ further strengthened his hand through an open declaration of support for Hadım Süleyman Pasha as the Ottoman fleet transited the Red Sea en route to Diu in 1538. As a reward for this public display of loyalty, upon the pasha's return from India, he granted Grañ a shipment of firearms and a contingent of 200 seasoned Ottoman arquibusiers from Yemen. Their arrival endowed him with a decisive military advantage over the *negus*, enabling him to take the mountain fastness of Amba Geshen in January 1540, and with it the imperial treasury. When Dāwit died on 2 September that year, the inheritance of his son, Galawdéwos, was the shadow of an empire never reduced so low. As the Ethiopian *Chronicle of King Galawdéwos* recalled in its account of this grim era:

> Victory was taken into the hands of the Muslims… and they had dominion over the Church of Ethiopia. They won all fighting in the direction of the east and west, and in the direction of the south and north even so far that they had destroyed shrines of prayer whose walls were built with gold, silver, and precious stones from India. They killed a large number of believers by the sword. They carried off the young men, the maidens, boys and girls even to the extent that they sold them for the task of miserable enslavement.[31]

However, help was on the horizon. When Estêvão da Gama pulled in to Massawa in May 1541 at the end of his abortive raid on the Ottoman Red Sea fleet at Suez, he was greeted by the *bāhr negus*, who bore an intriguing offer. He pledged the Ethiopian Church would abandon the Coptic rite for the Catholic in exchange for Portuguese military intervention. The *bāhr negus*, who had 500 men under his command, offered to lead the Portuguese into the interior in order to link up with the main Ethiopian army under Galawdéwos. Sensing both geopolitical advantage and an opportunity to advance the cause of the one true apostolic faith, Estêvão took up this offer. When he sailed for Goa on 9 July, he left behind a force of 400 arquibusiers under the command of his twenty-five-year-old brother, Cristóvão, supported by five captains, Manuel da Cunha, João da Fonseca, Inofre de Abreu, Francisco de Abreu, and Francisco Velho.[32]

The arrival of the Portuguese could not come soon enough for the crumbling Ethiopian state, which was tottering on the edge of the abyss after Galawdéwos was defeated at the Battle of Sahart on 24 April. Cristóvão was unable to link up with the *negus*, but the ambulatory court of the queen mother, Sabla Vangel, did attach itself to his campaign.

There was no confrontation between Adal and the Portuguese after their arrival, as the newcomers were cautiously acclimatizing themselves to this new physical and political environment. It was February 1542 before the first clash occurred, the Portuguese driving an Adal screening force off a defensive position near Agame in the minor Battle of Baçente. When shortly afterwards word arrived that a Portuguese ship had arrived at Massawa from Goa, Cristóvão sent a forty-man detachment under Francisco Velho marching to the coast to rendezvous with the vessel and, if possible, escort any additional reinforcements or supplies that had been committed by his brother. Even with a reduced force, Cristóvão was now spoiling for a fight, and got one against the main Adal army on the Antalo Plain. After an exchange of insults between Grañ and Cristóvão, the Battle of Jarte was joined on 4 April.

The inequality of numbers on the respective sides was absurd. Grañ had amassed 15,000 infantry (archers and men-at-arms) and 1,500 cavalry, plus a force of 200 Ottoman arquebusiers. Ranged against this host, the roughly 350 Portuguese (the forty men under Velho had not yet returned from Massawa, and eight were dead) backed by 200 Ethiopians would inevitably have been wiped out had it not been for the ten small cannon the Portuguese had so laboriously hauled with them into the highlands. "The bombardiers acted as valiant men," Miguel de Castanhoso reported: "They shot so fast and fearlessly that the horsemen could not reach us, for the horses took fright at the fire." The Portuguese formed into a square so as to direct fire at all sides. Nonetheless, the sheer weight of Adal numbers inevitably took its toll; "the Moors did us much harm," Castanhoso admitted, "especially the Turks with arquebuses."[33] Cristóvão himself took an Ottoman bullet in one leg; dozens more men fell wounded; eleven were killed.

The turning point came when Grañ himself plunged into the thickest of the fighting to rally his army. As he did so, an arquebus shot went through his thigh, killing his horse under him. The Adal immediately retreated, bearing their wounded leader with them off the field.

Battle was rejoined on 16 April. Grañ, not yet recovered from his wound, was borne upon a litter to the field to encourage his men. Adal cavalry nearly succeeded in penetrating the Portuguese square, only to flee in disorder when a barrel of gunpowder exploded in their faces, panicking their horses. Their irrational alarm spread to the entire Adal army which routed and fled.

Two days later, Velho returned with his forty men. They had failed to find the ships at Massawa, but marched back into the line accompanied by welcome Ethiopian reinforcements, forty horsemen and 500 foot soldiers.

Both armies were forced into camp by the seasonal rains. Cristóvão sent word for Galawdéwos to join him, but while he was cut off from help arriving via the *Estado da Índia*, Grañ was in full contact with the Ottomans, appealing to Hadım Süleyman for aid. The pasha had no intention of allowing the gains of his ally to be undermined so easily, having declared in his negotiations with the Portuguese that the Horn of Africa was an area he considered to be firmly within the Ottoman sphere of influence. Hadım Süleyman dispatched a fleet of twelve Ottoman galleys from Suez, landing 900 arquibusiers and ten expert gunners at the African port of Beylul in August 1541. In return, Grañ agreed to formally recognize Ottoman suzerainty, pay 100,000 *okkas* of gold to the sultan, and send tribute worth another 2,000 *okkas* of gold annually to the Ottoman governor in Zabid, Mustafa al-Neshar.[34]

Still unable to link up with Galawdéwos, Cristóvão initiated the campaign season of 1542 by leading a raid on an outlying Ottoman garrison stationed in the Jewish hill country, securing eighty desperately needed horses, but these had not arrived in the Portuguese camp, nor had Galawdéwos marched in from Showa, when, bolstered by the reinforcements that he had had received from Hadım Süleyman, Grañ went on the offensive.[35]

Confronting his nemesis northeast of Lalibela at the Battle of Wofla on 28 August 1542, Cristóvão elected not to form a square with his force, opting instead to deploy his men in detachments on separate hills in order to pin the Adal army in a crossfire. On this occasion, however, Grañ had the advantage in firepower. Cristóvão was wounded in one leg, then the other. Francisco de Abreu was killed. Inofre de Abreu rushed forward to seize his brother's corpse only to be himself shot down. The Portuguese had the edge in hand-to-hand fighting whenever the two sides came to grips, and drove the enemy back each time, but with only eight men mounted, their counterattacks could not be sustained. "Truly, had we had the horses, which were on the way" from the Jewish hill country, Castanhoso lamented, "the victory was ours."[36] João da Fonseca and Francisco Velho were both killed, and Cristóvão again wounded, this time his arm being shattered. The Portuguese were pushed back into their camp, and then forced to flee into the surrounding heights. Cristóvão was eventually tracked down and captured. Brought before Grañ, he was tortured and finally executed. Assuming the war was effectively won, Grañ dismissed his Ottoman allies, who returned to Yemen, taking with them Cristóvão's decapitated head and the twelve Portuguese prisoners still breathing.

Roughly fifty of the Portuguese who survived the battle rallied under Manuel da Cunha and made for the coast at Massawa, hoping against hope to find a ship back to India. Another 100 survivors, scattered throughout the mountains, were brought in by the queen and mustered in the camp of the *negus* when he arrived. This combined force still had some fight left in it; at the foot of Mount Oenadias it encountered and shattered a column of reinforcements on the march to muster with Grañ.

After Manuel da Cunha and his men returned from the coast, Galawdéwos raised his camp on 6 February 1543 to confront Grañ. The two sides encountered each other near Lake Tana in the decisive Battle of Wayna Daga on 21 February. Galawdéwos formed up his army in a front line and reserve line, each of 3,500 infantry and 250 cavalry, the 150 Portuguese with him holding the center of his front line. The Adal army was mirrored but larger, constituted of a front line and reserve line, each of 7,000 infantry and 600 cavalry, Grañ's 200-strong Ottoman elite guard flanking him in the center of his front line.

The Adal had the better of the battle; Castanhoso relates that it was sixty mounted Portuguese who, "seeing that the Turks were defeating us, charged them, slaying many and driving the rest back."[37] The critical turning point came when the Portuguese cavalry vanguard encountered Grañ, fighting in the front line to rally his men, and immediately concentrated their fire against him. One of their number – accounts give the credit to João de Castilho – fired the shot that mortally wounded Grañ, who had to be led from the field, pursued by Ethiopian cavalry, one of whom later rode into the camp of the *negus* with the imam's head clenched in his teeth.

The Adal army disintegrated, with the exception of the Ottoman guard, which held its ground, their commanding officer fighting off five Ethiopian horsemen. He was charged by João Fernandes, who skewered him with his spear, only for the officer to grasp it and deliver a blow in return to Fernandes's leg above his knee that severed all the sinews. Fernandes struck the officer down with his sword, but walked with a limp for the rest of his life.

The Ottomans now broke, the vengeful Portuguese running them down and killing all but forty of them. These survivors regrouped with Grañ's widow, Bati Del Wambara, and fled with the 300 horsemen of her guard. When the victorious Ethiopians poured into the Adal camp, among the few prisoners taken that day was her son, Mohammad ibn Ahmad, who was later exchanged for Galawdéwos's brother (and ultimate successor) Menas.

In the aftermath, many Portuguese veterans of the campaign elected to remain in Ethiopia and continue to serve the *negus* as his elite troops. When the Jesuit Gonçalo met Galawdéwos in the province of Gurage in 1555 he found ninety-three Portuguese arquibusiers under the command of Captain Gaspar de Sousa serving in the royal army.[38]

Grañ's widow returned to Harar to rally his lieutenants to continue fighting the war. She agreed to marry Grañ's nephew, Nur ibn Mujahid, on condition that he would avenge her first husband's defeat. Though Galawdéwos succeeded in taking Harar and killing Sultan Barakat of Adal, the last of the Walasma line, Nur defeated the Ethiopians at the Battle of Fatagar on Good Friday, 23 March 1559.[39] Galawdéwos was killed, alongside eighteen of his Portuguese guard. This defeat reversed the Ethiopian ascendancy, and the kingdom again nearly completely unraveled. Externally, Ethiopia came under immense pressure from the animist Oromo pastoralists migrating into the highlands from the south.[40] Internally, Ethiopia was roiled by division between the Orthodox traditionalists and the converts to Catholicism.[41]

With Ethiopia divided and distracted, the Ottomans were in a position to consolidate their control over the Red Sea coast. The key figure driving this agenda was Özdemir Pasha, a former Mamluk officer now in Ottoman service. He had served in the Diu campaign of 1538, and remained in Yemen after returning from the expedition. After taking Sanaa from the Zaydi Imam Mutahhar in 1547, he was promoted *beylerbey* of Yemen in 1554.

Recalled to Constantinople, he won over the sultan for authority to lead an Ottoman campaign against Ethiopia, asserting he could do so utilizing only local resources; "neither cash nor provisions will be spent from the Imperial treasury and no requests will be made for any Janissaries to conquer more provinces for you. It is certain that – if God wills it – the entire land of the Funj [can] be conquered."[42]

On 5 July 1555, Özdemir founded the province (*eyalet*) of Habesh with its capital at Suakin. His first campaign petered out when, at the border of Upper Egypt, by the First Cataract of the Nile, his troops mutinied and he was forced to abandon the expedition, but a subsequent campaign in 1557 brought Massawa, Hergigo, and the Dahlak Islands under Ottoman suzerainty.

Pushing inland, Özdemir took the key stronghold of Debarwa in 1559. Although he died of illness while campaigning on the Ethiopian frontier in Tigre the following year, the Ottoman drive into the highlands was continued by Özdemir's son and successor as *beylerbey* of Yemen, Özdemiroglu Osman Pasha. The threat to the *Estado da Índia* implicit in the consummation of Ottoman hegemony over the interior of the Horn of Africa was recognized in the West. "If they overcome this territory they would be a great danger for India," Andre de Oviedo, archbishop of Ethiopia, warned the pope in a letter dated 15 June 1567.[43] However, with the Red Sea ports under Ottoman occupation, there was little the Portuguese could offer in support of their erstwhile ally. The Ethiopians would have to stand on their own. Under the leadership of the *negus* Sarsa Dengel, they proved capable of doing so.

At the Battle of Hadiya in 1576, Sarsa Dengel defeated Sultan Muhammad ibn Nasir of Adal, who was captured and executed, terminating the Uthman dynasty of Harar and ending the Adal threat to Ethiopia once and for all. Sarsa Dengel seized Debarwa after his victory in the Battle of Addi Qarro in 1579, in which the then *beylerbey* of Habesh, Ahmed Pasha, was killed. Debarwa was retaken by the Ottomans in 1582, but was recaptured by the Ethiopians at the end of the decade, ensuring the Ottoman military and administrative presence was restricted to the shores of the Red Sea.[44] Ultimately, an independent Christian Ethiopia would survive in the highlands of the interior but isolated from the outside world by the Muslim presence on the coast, a paradigm that continues to structure geopolitics in the region to this day.

MOROCCO

The fate of Morocco brings us back to where we started, for it was here that the rise of Portugal to world power began, and it was here that the final phase of Ottoman imperial expansion ground to a halt, just short of a breakthrough that could have fundamentally transformed the New World as well as the Old.

In some ways, neighboring Morocco was left behind by the Portuguese once they learned how the highways of the Atlantic could convey them to more lucrative – and less combative – locales in Brazil, Africa, India, and the Orient. But the crusader impulse never completely died, and in grinding, attritional warfare the Portuguese one by one stripped Morocco of its coastal port cities.

Able to descend on its targets unopposed from offshore and with a cutting edge in gunpowder technology, the Portuguese initially made steady progress.[45] The invasion of Ksar es Seghir in October 1458 was an instance of massive overkill. Gunfire from the fleet devastated the Moroccan troops who had massed amid the surf to defend their homeland. Having seized the port, its new governor, Dom Duarte de Meneses, mounted thirty-two bombards on the castle walls, cutting brutal and devastating swaths through the ranks of the Moroccan army when it attempted to recapture Ksar es Seghir in 1459.

In 1460, 1463, and again in 1464, King Afonso "the African" led or directed invasions in repeated attempts to seize the city of Tangier. These were supplemented by a series of destructive, Viking-like descents upon the coastal cities of Morocco at Larache, Tetouan, Massa, and Safi. On 24 August 1471, Afonso, at the head of a vast armada of 400 ships carrying an army of 30,000, fell upon the port city of Asilah. The storming and sack of this city so demoralized the garrison of Tangier the Portuguese were finally able to claim this prize without resistance just four days later, earning Afonso the title "King of Portugal and the two Algarves, both on this side and beyond the sea."[46]

Ottoman policy towards Morocco balanced on a very fine edge. The Porte needed the reigning Wattasid dynasty to be assertive enough to hold off the predatory Iberian powers descending on its shores, but only until the Ottomans themselves were able to arrive and stabilize the situation by absorbing Morocco into the orbit of Constantinople. For to an ambitious and far-sighted geopolitical strategist like Sultan Selim the Grim, Morocco was the grand prize. Selim recognized that his empire was boxed in to the cul-de-sac of the Mediterranean. The primary focus of his campaigns was enabling the Ottomans to break out of this geographic straitjacket. His first two campaigns were intended to impose an Ottoman presence in the Indian Ocean, enabling the Porte to contest with the Portuguese for control of its trade routes. His first campaign, the war against the Safavids, promised access to the Persian Gulf via Basra. His second campaign, the conquest of the Mamluks, allowed access to the Red Sea via Suez, Jeddah, and Aden. But it also set up his projected third campaign, intended to impose an Ottoman presence in the Atlantic Ocean, enabling the Porte to contest with the Iberian powers for control (or at least a share) of the New World. A concerted drive across the shore of North Africa from Egypt via Libya, Tunisia, and Algeria to Morocco would secure ports on the Atlantic seaboard and from these access to the Americas, which had already been marked out in the map Piri Reis shared with Selim as "Vilayet Antilia." Alan Mikhail correctly observes that Morocco:

… was much more than a frontier between empires. It stood as the fulcrum between the past and the future, between Islam and Christianity, between Eurasia and the Atlantic world. The battle for Morocco would determine whether Catholicism or its enemies prevailed, whether the Old World or the New would prove the key to global domination, whether the Ottomans or the Europeans would shape the course of world history in the early sixteenth century and beyond.[47]

By March 1519, Selim had amassed an impressive fleet in the Aegean comprising 120 heavy galleys, 150 light galleys, thirty transports, 68,000 guns, and enough cannons to outfit 112 galleys. Simultaneously, he enhanced the Ottoman sphere of influence along its line of expansion by recognizing Hayreddin Barbarossa as *beylerbey* of Algeria and dispatching 2,000 janissaries to enhance both his authority and that of the Porte. Selim held off on committing his expedition to the western Mediterranean until he was assured he could do so without stripping his defenses in the Aegean and leaving the heartland of his domain exposed to enemy action. In March 1520, he finally settled on 80,000 as the appropriate number of troops to deploy for the North Africa expedition.[48] But the grand plan was destined to die with Selim later that year. The agenda of his son and successor, Suleiman, was more narrowly focused on consolidation of territories closer to home than bold gambits venturing into the unknown.

In the absence of Ottoman intervention, Morocco would evolve on its own terms. The driving force in its revival was the Saadi family, residents of the Drâa Valley on the fringes of the Sahara, who claimed to originate in the Hijaz and be descendants of the Prophet himself. In 1510 the head of this house, Sharif Muhammad ibn Abd ar-Rahman, was publicly acknowledged by many of the tribes of southern Morocco as their judge, warlord, and mediator. He would become known by his most ardent supporters as Al-Qaim (The Awaited One). In 1513, Al-Qaim also accepted the invitation to become sheikh of the Jazuli brotherhood. The holy town of Afughal became the headquarters of this embryonic dynasty. In 1514 Sharif Al-Qaim's two sons, Sharif Ahmad al-Aruj and Sharif Muhammad esh-Sheikh, returned from their *haj* to Mecca, carrying on the *jihad* against both the Portuguese and the fading Wattasid dynasty of Morocco after their father's death in 1517.

Ahmad al-Aruj took Marrakesh from its ruling Hintata dynasty in 1524. In the 1527 Treaty of Tadla the Saadians arrived at a division of Morocco between their authority in the south and the Wattasids in the north, both sides formally agreeing to a wary partnership against the Portuguese. In 1536 the Wattasids broke the treaty, only to be defeated by the Saadian brothers at Wadi Abid. The Portuguese and the Wattasids now arrived at a three-year truce and suspended their mutual trade embargos. "Do not allow the King of Marrakesh to overcome the King of Fez," King John III of Portugal warned, "for all beside becomes secondary if this serious and disturbing business begin. The King of Marrakesh is very astute and wealthy. I am told intelligence contacts with the Turks exist."[49]

Having marginalized his brother after a power struggle between the siblings, Muhammad esh-Sheikh took Agadir from Portugal on 12 March 1541. This forced a revision of priorities in Lisbon. By this point, the cost of maintaining the string of Portuguese strongholds in Morocco exceeded the entire annual profit from the West African gold trade, consuming three-quarters of the amount that was spent upholding the entire empire in the Indian Ocean. In a brutal retrenchment, the towns of Azzemour, Mogador, and Safi, along with a number of outlying forts and local allies, were abandoned. The Portuguese presence along the coast contracted to Ceuta, Tangier, and El Jadida.[50]

Muhammad esh-Sheikh won another victory over the Wattasids at the Battle of Darna in 1545, taking the Wattasid sultan, Ahmad ibn Muhammad, prisoner. The Wattasid realm began to disintegrate, its rump state remnant in Fez falling to Muhammad esh-Sheikh in 1549. The last Wattasid sultan, Nasir al-Qasiri, still a minor, joined his father in captivity, while the regent, Ali Abu Hassun, fled, seeking asylum in Ottoman Algiers.

The rise of this energetic new regime in Morocco set alarm bells ringing on the far side of the Mediterranean. King John III of Portugal reached out to Charles V to emphasize "the great concern he ought to feel about the victorious sharif – did he expect to find a prince ruling two powerful states, so well provided with artillery, with munitions, with infantry and cavalry, with funding, and already so arrogant and self-exalted by his recent victories to be peace-loving?"[51]

Muhammad esh-Sheikh did indeed seek to build upon his bellicose reputation, but his imperial ambition was expressed along entirely unexpected lines. Instead of consummating decades of *jihad* against the Christian interlopers by eradicating the last surviving Portuguese and Spanish enclaves clustered along the coast, the sharif appointed his eldest son, Muhammad al-Harran, to lead an army into Algeria. This force seized Tlemcen, capital of the Zayyanid dynasty, in June 1551. Proclamations were issued proclaiming this was the start of a campaign of liberation that would purge the Ottoman "Sultan of Fishermen," as Suleiman was insultingly addressed, from North Africa and Egypt to make way for the authority of Muhammad esh-Sheikh, the true descendant of the family of the Prophet Muhammad. This was no empty boast, for the Islamic world was aware the Fatimid Caliphate had stormed to power during the 10th century in just such a manner, driving eastwards from out of the Maghreb to claim not just Cairo but the holy places of Jerusalem, Mecca, and Medina. The sudden, unexpected prospect of the Ottoman Empire's hard-won hegemony unraveling under pressure from the Saadian sharif of Morocco on one flank and the Shia shah of Persia on the other was a threat taken seriously in Constantinople.

Fortunately for the Porte, it had capable commanders on the ground who proved able to stabilize the Saadian situation before it could metastasize. Summoning help from the local tribes, the *beylerbey* of Algiers, Hasan Pasha, the son of Hayreddin Barbarossa, dispatched Hasan Corso, *agha* of the janissaries of Algiers, to strike back at the Saadian army, which had been left rudderless by the sudden death from disease of Crown Prince Muhammad al-Harran. The Saadian troops were surprised and defeated in January 1551 at Abu Azoun. As the Saadian army pulled back into Morocco, Corso occupied Tlemcen and established an Ottoman protectorate over the city, preparatory to the Zayyanid dynasty being extinguished and the entire territory being annexed to the Regency of Algiers.

In January 1552, Suleiman reached out to Muhammad esh-Sheikh, blaming Hasan Pasha for the conflict and offering a diplomatic resolution that would impose no obligation on the Saadians beyond accepting nominal Ottoman suzerainty. As a gesture of good faith, Hasan Pasha was recalled as *beylerbey* of Algiers, but Muhammad esh-Sheikh, no doubt stung by being addressed only as sheikh of the arabs (*shaykh al-'arab*) in this correspondence, rejected the overture. Accordingly, in 1553 Ottoman forces invaded and seized an islet offshore from Badis to utilize as a forward base. At the beginning of 1554, the Ottomans again marched into Morocco. After heavy fighting near Fez, Mohammed esh-Sheikh was defeated and forced to abandon the city, which fell on 9 January. Ali Abu Hassun was installed on the throne as a puppet ruler, and for the first time the call to prayer in the ancient mosques of Fez was called out in the name of the distant Ottoman sultan. This brief summer of Ottoman hegemony ended abruptly that same autumn. Mohammed esh-Sheikh reclaimed Fez on 13 September after he defeated and killed Ali Abu Hassun in the Battle of Tadla, bringing a definitive end to the Wattasid dynasty.

The Saadian sultan then commenced negotiations with the Count of Alcaudete, the Spanish governor of Oran, offering partnership in an anti-Ottoman alliance. The two men arrived at an agreement for a joint campaign against Algiers, Mohammed esh-Sheikh even going so far as to promise to meet the financial obligations of the Spaniards and offer one of his own sons as a hostage as proof of his intent. But the Ottomans launched a preemptive strike before this partnership could come together. The Spanish fort at Bejaia, which had resisted the siege attempts of both the Barbarossa brothers, was finally stormed in 1555 after a fourteen-day siege by Salah Reis, the new *beylerbey* of

Algiers. The following year, Salah Reis laid siege to Oran. He succeeded in destroying the forts defending the entrance to the port, but could not capture the city itself and subsequently died of the plague. Taking advantage of the Ottoman concentration of their forces against the Spanish, Mohammed esh-Sheikh was able to reoccupy Tlemcen.

In the absence of Salah Reis, and with plague raging in Algiers, Hasan Corso was advanced by the janissaries to assume authority as *beylerbey*. His rise to power reflected the meritocratic social mobility of the Ottoman state. Born Pietro Paolo Tavera, at five years old he was abducted from his native Corsica in a *razzia* and inducted into the janissary corps in Constantinople, where he was assigned the name Corso in reference to his origins. However, his fall, which would be equally dramatic, reflected the arbitrary and capricious nature of Ottoman politics. After dispatching a messenger to advise the Porte of his situation, he set out with his army against Oran, only for instructions to arrive from Constantinople expressly forbidding him to begin the siege, or, if it had commenced, ordering him immediately to raise it. When the newly appointed *beylerbey* of Algiers, Muhammad Kurdogli, arrived from Constantinople, the janissaries, offended by the imposition of an outsider at the expense of their long-serving *agha*, refused to allow him to disembark. Coming ashore only with the connivance of the corsairs, Kurdogli immediately ordered Corso be thrown from the battlements onto one of the iron hooks protruding from the walls of the city, which caught him in the ribs and held him suspended in agony for three days before he finally expired. Kurdogli was in turn assassinated the following year by Corso's friend and ally, the governor of Tlemcen, Qa'id Yusuf, himself a convert originally from Calabria in southern Italy. Yusuf died of the plague just six days later and authority devolved upon Yahyia Pasha until Hasan Pasha arrived from Constantinople in June 1557 to commence his third term as *beylerbey* and restore order in Algiers, which was threatening to devolve into anarchy.

The Ottoman line was hardening. The same mission from Constantinople conveying Hasan Pasha to Algiers also bore a message for Mohammed esh-Sheikh. The Porte now demanded, as the price of peace, the Saadian sultan order the prayer said, and coins struck, throughout his domain in the name of Suleiman.[52] When Mohammed esh-Sheikh contemptuously rejected these terms, he was assassinated in October 1557 by double agents who had been infiltrated into his entourage. The head of the Saadian sultan was severed and stuffed into a leather satchel lined with salt, which was smuggled to Algiers and then, packed in ice, on to Constantinople.

Hasan Pasha then went on to the offensive, expelling the Saadians from Tlemcen and pursuing them into Morocco. In early 1558 he encountered Abdallah al-Ghalib, who had succeeded his father, Mohammed esh-Sheikh, as the second Saadian sultan of Morocco, at Wadi al-Laban to the north of Fez. The outcome of the battle is contested, but in the aftermath, Hasan Pasha opted to retreat upon receiving intelligence of Spanish preparations for a major offensive. He embarked with his troops at the port of Qassasa in northern Morocco, just west of Melilla, and from there sailed to Algiers to prepare the defense.

The Count of Alcaudete had indeed recruited a large force in Spain that converged on Oran in two divisions, one from Cartagena under Alcaudete himself, the other from Málaga commanded by one of his sons, Don Martín de Córdoba. The target of the expedition was the port city of Mostaganem, which had been taken by the Spanish in 1506, but lost to Hayreddin Barbarossa in 1516. Spanish expeditions under Alcaudete to retake the city in 1543 and 1547 had both failed. On this occasion, the Spanish arrived at Mostaganem on 24 August and commenced siege operations, but the following day, Hasan Pasha arrived at the head of a relief army that had force-marched from Algiers, and the Spanish supply ships were seized by corsairs cruising offshore. The Spaniards attempted to slip away during the night, but the retreat swiftly degenerated into a rout. Alcaudete was killed, along with half his army, while those who survived, including his son, were destined for the slave markets of Algiers.

The political alignment of the western Mediterranean now began to stabilize. The Saadian–Ottoman spheres of influence settled along the borders of contemporary Morocco and Algeria. Neither side made any gains at the expense of the Iberian powers. The Saadians failed to take Mazagan from the Portuguese in a succession of sieges from 1561 to 1563, while the Ottoman sieges of Oran and Mers El Kébir in 1563 were both failures.

Abdallah al-Ghalib benefited from the policy of expulsion and forced conversion of the Muslim population (Moriscos) of Iberia. Between 1526 and 1570, nearly 200,000 refugees settled in Morocco; they would make up the backbone of al-Ghalib's army and the small corsair fleet he established in some of the Atlantic ports.

Abdallah al-Ghalib had commenced his reign by murdering his uncle, Ahmad al-Aruj, in order to rid himself permanently of a potential rival. Not surprisingly, three of his brothers – Ahmad al-Mansur, Abd al-Malik, and Abd al-Mu'min – fled to safety with the Ottomans in Algiers. Abdallah al-Ghalib succeeded in having Abd al-Mu'min assassinated in 1572, but Abd al-Malik survived and diligently improved his status with the Ottomans, participating in the disastrous battle at Lepanto in 1571 and the successful Ottoman siege of Tunis in 1574. Abdallah al-Ghalib died that same year, being succeeded by his son, Muhammad II al-Mutawakkil. Abd al-Malik traveled to Constantinople and obtained support from Murad III for his bid to take the Saadian throne, the sultan ordering Ramazan Pasha, the *beylerbey* of Algiers, to assist Abd al-Malik in invading Morocco. Even if the dream of an Ottoman presence in the New World had died with Selim the Grim, the acquisition of an Atlantic port would at least enable the Ottomans to outflank Spain in any future maritime conflict and would give the corsair captains of Algiers a chance to prey on the silver bullion being shipped into Seville from Peru.

On 16 March 1576 an Ottoman army, led by Abd al-Malik, was victorious at the Battle of ar-Rukn near Fez and on 14 July at the Battle of Khaynuqa'r-rayhan. In the aftermath, al-Mutawakkil fled, finding asylum in Portugal. Once on the throne, technically as an Ottoman vassal, Abd al-Malik had the Friday prayers and the *khutba* in mosques delivered in the Ottoman sultan's name, adopted Ottoman clothing, and organized his army along Ottoman lines. It was the closest the Porte had ever come to imposing its authority over the entire north coast of Africa. Nonetheless, Abd al-Malik remained wary of Ottoman intentions towards his kingdom and maintained relations with Spain as well as continuing to pursue relations with France. In order to limit Ottoman influence, Abd al-Malik sent the majority of the Ottoman troops who had been assigned to his support – including the janissaries – back to Algiers shortly after winning his throne, and was careful to entrust the highest ranks in his military to Moriscos and European mercenaries, employing them as his personal guard while on campaign.[53]

Meanwhile, his deposed nephew, al Mutawakkil, sought help from Portugal, whose king, Sebastian I, felt he had the most to lose from the increased Ottoman influence in the region. Sebastian endorsed Al-Mutawakkil's claim and in July 1578 he crossed over into northern Morocco. His army consisted of 3,000 German mercenaries, 1,000 English and Italian soldiers of fortune under the Englishman Sir Thomas Stukeley, 6,000 Portuguese peasant-soldiers under their four colonels, 2,000 Spanish infantrymen loaned by King Philip II, 2,000 Portuguese knights under the Duke D'Aveiro, and 2,500 gentleman volunteers from Portugal under Alvaro Pires de Tavora. During the campaign, the royal army was joined by a regiment of 500 Spanish soldiers led by an experienced commander, Francisco de Aldana. Finally, at Arzila, Sebastian was joined by his ally, al-Mutawakkil, who brought with him another 6,000 Berber soldiers.

However, Sebastian, who wore the helmet of King Charles V and carried the sword of Prince Henry the Navigator on this campaign, did not use the fortified Portuguese positions along the coast to his advantage, instead electing to march directly into the interior of Morocco. The Saadian army, led by Abd al-Malik, accompanied by his brother Ahmad (yet another son of Muhammad al-Sheikh), met the Portuguese at Wadi al-Makhazin near Ksar al-Kebir on 4 August.

The ensuing clash of arms, remembered as the Battle of the Three Kings, was an utter catastrophe for the Portuguese. Both Sebastian and al-Mutawakkil were killed in the battle. Sebastian's body was washed and bathed in myrrh before being delivered to King Philip, accompanied by the captive ten-year-old son of the Duke of Braganza, who was released without ransom. This gesture so impressed Philip that he sent the Moroccan court a gift by return: an emerald the size of the dead king's heart and his body weight in sapphires.[54] The corpse of al-Mutawakkil was accorded no such respect, being flayed, his carcass stuffed with straw and borne in triumph to Fez, earning him the posthumous title of al-Maslukh (the Skinned). On the Moroccan side, Abd al-Malik also died during the battle, being succeeded by his brother, Ahmad. Drawing on the prestige of the victory, he took on the regnal title al-Mansur (the Victorious), a title he would justify over the twenty-five years of his reign through his conquest of Songhai and his assertion of Morocco's autonomy and interests against both Spanish and Ottoman empires. Portugal, by contrast, was so demoralized it was annexed by King Philip II in 1580 and would remain a Spanish dependency for the next sixty years.

The last Ottoman attempt to impose the authority of the Porte over Morocco broke down because of bad blood between the commanding officer and the rank and file. In 1561, local janissaries in Algiers arrested Hasan Pasha and his allies, including Uluç Ali, and sent them in chains to Constantinople. Uluç Ali returned to the city in 1568 as *beylerbey*. This would be significant because in 1581 the janissaries, never reconciled to his administration, flatly refused his orders as *kapudan pasha* to embark on his ships for a campaign against Morocco without explicit authority from the sultan, to whom they sent envoys. Murad III ultimately aborted the entire expedition, which Uluç Ali had lobbied him for years to undertake.[55]

The anticlimactic conclusion to the 1581 campaign marked a turning point in Ottoman policy. Never again would the Porte undertake a forward naval policy in the western Mediterranean. In 1583, the proposal of Hasan Veneziano, *beylerbey* of Algiers, for a campaign against Oran was rejected, and every subsequent effort to revive the Ottoman presence in the western

Mediterranean, from the coalition of *kapudan pasha* Uluç Ali and the ambassadors of France and England lobbying to support the claim of a pretender to the throne of Portugal, to the possibility of intervention on behalf of Henri de Navarre and the Huguenots against Philip II and the Catholic League in France, came to nothing.[56]

The Catholic/Muslim dichotomy itself began to break down towards the end of the century as both sides sought to enlist the support of Protestant England. In 1586, the English ambassador to Constantinople, William Harborne, urged Sultan Murad III to enter the war against Spain:

> If... your Highness, in concert with my mistress, will wisely and bravely, without delay, send a warfleet to sea – to which course you are surely urged by God Almighty, your own pledged faith, the opportuneness of the occasion, the reputation of the glorious Ottoman race, and consideration for the safety of your Empire – then will the proud Spaniard and the false Pope, with all their followers be not only hurled down from their hope of victory, but will receive full punishment for their temerity. God only protects his own, and by your means he will so punish these idolaters that the survivors will be converted to worship the true God with us. And upon us, who fight for his glory, he will heap victory and all other good things.[57]

The Venetian ambassador to Constantinople reported that "the Turks are pleased at this English alliance as a counterpoise to Spain while they are occupied with Persian affairs." In the event, however, nothing came of this proposed partnership.[58] Undeterred, the English moved on to cultivate their relationship with Morocco.[59] The 1596 Anglo-Dutch expedition to Cadiz, which sacked and burned the city, and the Spanish fleet at anchor, played out with Moroccan support; al-Mansur's court historian al-Fishtali recorded how "the sky darkened with dissension against the tyrant on Qishtala [Philip II], and the kings of the nations of the Christians attacked him like wild dogs. The most ferocious against him, and the one most daring in attacking his kingdoms and tightening the noose around him, was Isabella [Elizabeth I] the sultana of the kingdoms of the lands of England." It was al-Mansur who "had lured her with his support and sharpened her will" against Philip; "with God helping him, he pitted her against the enemy of religion."[60]

In 1600, the Moroccan ambassador to the court of Queen Elizabeth, al-Annuri, proposed an alliance with the English "against the King of Spain, their common foe and enemy." This would not be directed solely against continental

Spain; "if the two serene majesties should forge this alliance, they could also wrest the East and West Indies from the Spanish." To this end, the sultan "would meet the needs of Her Serene Majesty's fleet in terms of wheat, munitions, gunpowder and provisions, as well as infantry and money."[61] Thus, the sultan outlined a program of action that would at least in part fulfill the Ottoman dream of an Islamic empire in the Americas.

While nothing concrete would arise from these negotiations, wittingly or no, Morocco had played a critical role in the containment of Ottoman global imperial hegemony. Just as the Safavids obstructed Ottoman expansion to the east by land, so the Saadians prevented Ottoman expansion to the west by sea. The Porte had come frustratingly close to achieving the geopolitical vision first envisioned by Selim the Grim. Egypt, Libya, Tunisia, and Algeria had all fallen under the sway of Constantinople. But Morocco, the final piece in the puzzle, lay, tantalizingly, just out of reach. "The Turkish drive toward the Atlantic was thus blocked," Abbas Hamdani concludes, "and with it all hopes of crossing the Atlantic to the New World."[62]

CONCLUSION

Much ink has been spilled over the centuries as to how and why European states were ultimately able to reshape the world in their image. Various theories on causal factors have been advanced. None individually account for the phenomenon as a whole.[1] Some perspectives, such as geographic determinism, are valid in terms of providing pieces to the puzzle. Other arguments, such as the thesis that Europe had a cutting edge on the battlefield because it underwent a revolution in military technology and strategy during the Renaissance, or that European hegemony was based on the inherent superiority of a Western way of making war, are entirely discredited.

Far from representing the vanguard of a self-confident and assured mature civilization that was initiating a preprogramed master plan of global conquest, the first Europeans to break out of their isolated and marginalized petty states penned up against the Atlantic Ocean on the periphery of Eurasia were almost frantic in their need to find some way out of the strategic dead-end in which they were trapped. At least the Portuguese captains pushing east past Africa and into the Indian Ocean were operating according to a set program with a specific end goal, securing direct access to the advanced markets of the Indies. The Spanish *Conquistadors* heading west into the *terra nullius* of the New World were desperate gamblers and freebooting cutthroats improvising as they went along, with little to no oversight, let alone strategic planning, from the distant crowned heads they ostensibly served.

There was no European-wide imperialism during the Renaissance. Only the Iberian powers built empires overseas. The English, the French, the Germans, the Italians, were all left behind. But the core motivation of the Portuguese and Spanish trailblazers was a deep-rooted, brooding conviction common throughout Christendom that Europe as a whole was under siege. This was the reality of the European worldview, shaped by millennia of experience. Using the Black Sea as a dividing line, Europe had been buffeted by wave after wave of would-be conquerors – Huns, Magyars, and Mongols from north of that line, Persians,

Arabs, and now Turks from the south. Europeans were only too aware that their little empires, kingdoms, and republics were dwarfed in size, population, wealth, and military potential by the great empires of the East – China, India, and the rising power of the Ottomans. Long after the end of the Renaissance, Christendom was still more acted upon than it was an actor. To cite just one example, up until the end of the 17th century, the number of Europeans being imported as slaves into Africa and the Middle East exceeded the number of slaves being exported out of those territories by Europeans.[2] Huge numbers of Poles, Ukrainians, and Russians, captured by Tatar marauders, were shipped across the Black Sea to Constantinople. In 1578 alone, the Ottoman treasury collected 4.5 million akçe from the slave trade in Feodosia. Since the highest tax paid for any one slave was 255 akçe, at least 17,500 slaves were sold at the chattel markets of Feodosia in that year.[3] Entire island communities of Christians in the Mediterranean were subject to depopulation by corsair slave raiders (Elba in 1544; Gozo in 1551).[4] This history accounts for why, for example, there was such a desperate, almost pathetic, need to cling to the hoax of Prester John and the conviction that, somewhere out there, poor lonely Europe had at least one friend in a wide and deeply hostile world.

The first Europeans to make their presence felt everywhere from Tenochtitlan and Cuzco to Mombasa and Goa were certainly bigoted, rapacious, and cruel, but it wasn't just a hunger for gold that drove Iberian colonization, it was a burning desire for the intangible but priceless assets of security, status, and respect. These qualities were significant by their absence throughout a Christendom watching the oncoming Ottoman leviathan with a mingled sense of awe and dread.

This attitude, a pervasive sense of impending doom, suffuses much of Western literature during this period. "They rule because God is angered," Erasmus wrote in his *Utilissima consultatio de bello Turcis inferendo* (*Very useful advice about bringing the war to the Turks*) of 1530, during the brief interregnum between the first and second Ottoman sieges of Vienna; "they fight us without God, they have Mahomet as their champion, and we have Christ – and yet it is obvious how far they have spread their tyranny, while we, stripped of so much power, ejected from much of Europe, are in danger of losing everything."[5] The strategic situation had not improved forty years later. In a sermon at St Paul's Cathedral, London, on Good Friday 1570, the firebrand preacher John Foxe would lament in sorrow and bafflement to the Lord of Hosts that "only a little angle of the West parts yet remaineth in some profession of thy name."[6]

The simple fact was that, prior to the mid-18th century at the earliest, Europeans were not militarily dominant relative to other civilizations anywhere on land in Eurasia, including in Europe. From the Renaissance until the threshold of the industrial revolution, European conquests were much less significant and extensive than those of the Ottomans, the Mughals, and the Manchus, both in terms of the economic and demographic resources captured, and the extent of the military resistance overcome. The Chinese and Ottomans had a stronger claim to pioneering key military innovations like professional standing armies equipped with gunpowder weapons supported by a complex, centralized administrative, fiscal, and logistical state apparatus than any Western power. Thus, as Jason C. Sharman concludes, "there simply was no Western military dominance for at least 250 years after the emergence of the first truly global international system."[7] The defining quality of the European confrontation with the Ottoman Empire during this period, therefore, of which Iberian imperialism was a critical component, was not the assertion of an assumed sociopolitical supremacy but rather its exact opposite, the shaking off of a deep-rooted inferiority complex.

So how did Western Europe escape the fate of Constantinople, Sofia, Belgrade, and Budapest? The Ottoman apotheosis during the long reign of Suleiman the Magnificent carried with it the seeds of future constraints on the exercise of power. So long as the Ottoman Empire continued to expand and incorporate regions rich in resources, the conquests essentially paid for themselves and contributed a net surplus to the treasury. For example, as the spoils of their wars with Safavid Persia, the Ottomans annexed the important cities of Tabriz, Ganja, Revan, Shirvan, and Tbilisi. These wealthy entrepôts of trade and commerce and their associated productive agricultural hinterlands delivered to the sultans additional tax levies amounting to 10–15 percent of total Ottoman central revenue, more than offsetting the up-front cost of the military campaigns responsible for their incorporation. The balance shifted once the tide of conquest slowed and military expenditure was of necessity increasingly devoted to defending the extended frontiers. By the end of his reign, Suleiman's imperialism had imposed severe strain on the central treasury, which had to set aside 60–70 percent of its cash revenues to meet military obligations.

While his successors spurned the options so often resorted to throughout the 16th century by their counterparts in the West – taking out loans, whether forced or otherwise, or even defaulting on sovereign debt, which Philip II was forced into on four separate occasions, in 1557, 1560, 1575, and 1596 – the Porte increasingly was forced to meet shortfalls in revenue through such expedients as debasement of the currency. Following the accession of Selim II in 1566, 450 akçes were cut from 120 dirhems of silver instead of 420, and the amount of silver in each akçe fell from 0.731 grams to 0.682. Despite this, the government continued to compel the exchange of 60 akçes for one altun gold piece. The value of silver coinage fell rapidly as the actual market price of silver collapsed to between 80 and 100 akçes per altun, and inflation inevitably ensued.

A second depreciation was undertaken in 1584–86. To meet the costs of the 1578–90 Safavid war, the Porte introduced a new standard of 800 akçe cut from 100 dirhems of silver, each akçe now weighing only 0.384 grams. So intense was the backlash the sultan was forced to order the execution of those state officials held responsible for this debasement. A new issue of coins at the end of the decade was intended to reintroduce stability, but the inflationary trends unleashed would continue to roil the economy, sparking popular unrest, particularly in Anatolia. Known as the Celali revolts, these uprisings would metastasize into open civil war against the Ottoman state, dragging out for fifteen years (approximately 1595 to 1610) in their first phase alone.[8]

Pál Fodor concludes the Ottoman Empire was extended beyond its capacities as early as 1552, when the Porte sought victory simultaneously on five different fronts – Hungary, the Mediterranean Sea, the Iranian border, Iraq, and Hormuz.[9] Even victory ultimately became self-defeating if the territories acquired ran at a net loss and represented a burden on the treasury as opposed to bringing in additional revenue.[10] By the terms of the 1555 Treaty of Amasya with the Safavid Empire, the Ottomans expanded their frontier in the Caucasus. While this looked impressive on a map and certainly contributed to the mystique of Ottoman invincibility on the battlefield, Grand Vizier Sinan Pasha was appalled at the additional fiscal strain this would impose on the Porte, which was now obliged to secure and garrison this remote borderland: "Since the fortresses were built, have we taken possession of a single village having two houses? Has a single akçe of revenue been obtained? It is beyond my comprehension what sort of a conquest this is."[11] This crisis of overextension was the destiny of every empire, before and since the rise and fall of the Ottomans. "Persia is to the sultan as is Flanders to the Spanish king or Crete to the Venetians, as the expenses are extremely high, and the income is insignificant," an Italian observer of the contemporary balance of power wrote in 1594. "There is no gain from the acquired lands."[12]

It was these realities that would constrain the strategic agenda of the Porte for, flush with success, there was no lack of vision or ambition at the courts of Suleiman's son and grandson. In his book *Tärïh-i hind-i garbï* (*History of the West Indies*), Grand Vizier Sinan Pasha revived the grand geopolitical vision of Sokollu

Mehmed Pasha, arguing the case to Sultan Murad III for the construction of a canal at Suez:

> ... even if only a drop was to be expended from the sea of power of the sultan, in the shortest time it would be possible to join the two seas [the Mediterranean and the Red]... thenceforth, from Well-Protected Constantinople, the place of prosperity and the abode of the throne of the sultans, ships and their crews would be organized and sent to the Red Sea and would have the power to protect the shores of the Holy Places. And in a short time, by an excellent plan, they would seize and subjugate most of the seaports of Sind and Hind [India] and would drive away and expel from that region the evil unbelievers, and it would be possible for the exquisite things of Sind and Hind and the rarities of Ethiopia and the Sudan, and the usual items of the Hijaz and the Yemen and the pearls of Bahrain and Aden, all to reach the capital with only a trifling effort.[13]

By September 1586, *kapudan pasha* Kılıç Ali Pasha was leaking specifics about the canal's construction to the resident French ambassador Savary de Lanscome, who duly reported to Paris that, "This grand scheme of theirs has so inflated their already habitual arrogance, and sparked their greed and ambition to such an extent, that it appears to them as if all the treasures and precious gems of India are already in their hands, and Persia ensnared in their net as well."

The Ottomans held the Portuguese presence in India "of no account whatsoever" since the *Estado da Índia* was now under Spanish authority; "And if truth be told, should their aspirations be fulfilled to build this canal, and they do send two hundred armed galleys [to India] as they say they will, then since they are already masters of Arabia they will make rapid progress with no one to stop them, and will shut the door [to India] on Lisbon and Spain."[14]

While this project would never be realized, the fact it was even raised and reported with genuine alarm to foreign capitals indicates the conventional depiction of Ottoman decay after arriving at the peak of its new world order (*nizam-i alem*) during the golden age forged by Suleiman is exaggerated. While the relentless energy that had empowered Ottoman expansion over the previous two and a half centuries did tail off, the empire remained the largest, and richest, single power in the European cockpit. It is better to appreciate Ottoman history for at least another hundred years after the death of Suleiman as representing a plateau in its potential, as opposed to any decline. Ottoman prowess in battle at every level, from tactical leadership and fighting spirit to logistics and weapons technology, was at least the equal of any rival, and certain it is that the empire was not conceding any of the ground it had accumulated. To the contrary, while territorial aggrandizement had lost the dramatic flair of previous eras, expansion continued piecemeal where appropriate. The empire held its own over the course of the first Long War with the Habsburgs (1593–1606), seizing and retaining several strategic fortresses in Hungary, including Eger (1596) and Kanizsa (1600). But this conflict lacked the edge of existential crisis that had applied in Ottoman campaigns up until the death of Suleiman, when Vienna itself was at stake, and in the final analysis, all it accomplished was to reaffirm the inherent stability of the Balkan frontier. An appreciation of this reality was coded into the Treaty of Zsitvatorok that ended the war in 1606, where the Habsburgs were recognized as sovereigns of equal rank to the Ottoman sultan, and were no longer obliged to pay the annual tribute.[15]

Subsequently, almost by mutual consent, the Christian and Islamic worlds in the eastern Mediterranean effectively turned their backs on each other, reverting from an outward-facing inter-religious war between rival faiths to a succession of inward-facing, intra-religious wars between practitioners of the same faith. After the conclusion to the Long War, the border between Habsburg and Ottoman spheres of influence would fall into stasis during the first half of the 17th century as both dynasties were drawn into protracted, enervating, and unrewarding conflicts elsewhere, Vienna into the maelstrom of the Thirty Years War (1618–48), Constantinople into a grinding series of conflicts with Safavid Persia (1603–18, 1623–39).

Meanwhile, this same process of disengagement played out in the western Mediterranean. In 1591, the Saadian Sultan Ahmad sent an army in a lightning strike south across the Sahara that defeated the ruler of Songhai, Askia Ishaq II, at the Battle of Tondibi and occupied his capital of Gao. Spain was drawn ever deeper into its self-imposed purgatory of suppressing the Protestant revolt in the Netherlands. When Philip began to confiscate American silver cargoes in Seville that had been destined for English creditors, Queen Elizabeth I increased her direct support to the rebels and unleashed her privateers against Spanish ports and shipping on both sides of the Atlantic. Philip's response, imposing a trade embargo against England, only succeeded in driving commerce from Antwerp north to Amsterdam and Hamburg. By the middle of the decade, outlays on the war represented over one-quarter of royal expenditures and over one-third of royal revenues. With deficits spiraling out of control, Philip was forced to declare another default in September 1575.[16] Negotiations with his Genoese creditors played out for months; on 4 November 1576, the soldiers of his Army of Flanders, many of whom hadn't been paid in years, took matters into their own hands, sacking Antwerp in an eleven-day rampage remembered as the Spanish Fury.[17]

France, meanwhile, consumed its own strength in a dynastic struggle that overlapped with an intractable sectional civil war between its Catholic majority and Protestant minority. Neither of these conflicts could or would be resolved on terms that accepted Catholics and Protestants could live side by side. Spain's war ended after generations of rebellion with the 1648 Peace of Münster that recognized the independence of the Netherlands; France's war ended in 1685, when King Louis XIV issued the Edict of Fontainebleau, revoking the Edict of Nantes and declaring Protestantism illegal, driving his Huguenot subjects into exile.

The long-dormant Ottoman war machine rumbled back into life under the able leadership of grand viziers Köprülü Mehmed Pasha (1656–61) and his son and successor Köprülüzade Fazil Ahmed Pasha (1661–76), who annexed slices of Hungary in 1660 and 1663, brought the protracted war with Venice (1645–69) to a successful conclusion with the conquest of Crete, and made gains at the expense of Poland–Lithuania in 1672.

But the Porte finally overreached itself when Grand Vizier Kara Mustafa Pasha (1676–83) undertook an invasion of the Habsburg heartland that culminated in his defeat during the siege of Vienna in 1683. In the Treaty of Karlowitz that concluded the ensuing second Long War (1684–99) against the anti-Ottoman coalition of the Holy League, Constantinople for the first time conceded outright territorial losses, including Budapest. The Treaty of Passarowitz (Požarevac) in 1718, which ended another Habsburg–Ottoman war, continued this trend, with Constantinople signing away Belgrade. From this point onwards, the Porte would be constantly on the defensive, the slow erosion of the Ottoman imperial perimeter earning it the sobriquet "the sick man of Europe" by the 19th century. Unable to suppress nationalist aspirations to territoriality in the Balkans, losing control of the Black Sea and Caucasus to Russia, and with its holdings in North Africa stripped away by the Western powers, by the outbreak of the First World War in 1914 the Ottoman Empire was set up for the final act; within the space of the ensuing ten years came defeat, the abolition of the caliphate, and the emergence of the modern Republic of Turkey.[18]

By first impelling and then challenging the rise of the Iberian powers, the heyday of Ottoman imperialism was integral to shaping the reality of the globalization that emerged during the 16th century.[19] Its legacy is coded into the structure of identities worldwide today. To cite just one example, it was Suleiman the Magnificent who was the godfather of Protestantism. Almost all major concessions wrested by the Lutherans from the Habsburgs were owed to the trajectory of Ottoman imperial ambition. The Recess of Speyer of 1526, the Religious Peace of Nürnberg, the Compart of Cadan, the Frankfurt Anstand, the Declaration of Regensburg, the Recess of Speyer of 1542, the Treaty of Passau, and the Religious Peace of Augsburg – all milestones in the Protestant struggle for recognition and the course of the Reformation – were deeply influenced by the ebb and flow of Ottoman aggression. As such, Stephen A. Fischer-Galati notes, "The consolidation, expansion, and legitimizing of Lutheranism in Germany by 1555 should be attributed to Ottoman imperialism more than to any other single factor."[20] Martin Luther himself would have appreciated the irony. On one occasion, he was informed by an imperial envoy to Constantinople that Suleiman had been very much interested in Luther and had inquired of his age. When informed that Luther was forty-eight years old, the sultan had remarked, "I wish he were even younger; he would find in me a gracious protector." In response, Luther made the sign of the cross and replied, "May God protect me from such a gracious protector!"[21] But, as George W. Forell notes, "instead of fearing the Turks, Luther had every reason to be grateful to them."[22]

For all its profound implications, in the final analysis, the Ottoman imperial project ultimately fell short of the truly global hegemony to which ambitious sultans and grand viziers aspired, one that would have seen the Indian Ocean crossroads of trade centered on Constantinople, and Islamic colonization of the New World directed by the Porte. In both directions, the final pieces of the geopolitical puzzle remained tantalizingly just out of reach.

As Arnold Toynbee concluded in his magisterial survey of world history, the Ottomans only just missed their opportunity to break out of the cul-de-sacs of the Mediterranean Sea to the Atlantic Ocean in one direction, and the Persian Gulf and Red Sea to the Indian Ocean in the other. To the east, the Ottoman conquest of Egypt and Iraq "came just too late to forestall the arrival of the Portuguese mariners in the Indian Ocean; and although the acquisition of seaboards on the Red Sea and on the Persian Gulf, in addition to their seaboard on the Mediterranean, gave the Osmanlis the great strategic advantage of holding the interior lines, this geographic asset did not make up for lost time."[23]

Similarly, Ottoman expansion westwards across the north coast of Africa "came just too late, and fell just too far short, to enable them to cut off, at its base, the Oceanic enterprise of the Castilians and the Portuguese," who "might have found themselves paralyzed if the Atlantic Coast of Morocco had given harbour to Ottoman fleets with the whole power of the Ottoman Empire behind them."[24]

Though in the course of their conquests the sultans were elevated to the status of caliphs, they could never quite consolidate their authority over the Muslim community as a whole, their expansion therefore being checked by the rival sect of the Safavids to the east and the rival dynasty of the Saadians to the west. Beyond these adversaries on land lay the true antagonists at sea, the Iberian powers of Portugal to the east and Spain to the west. These four states never constituted a formal alliance directed against the Porte. Their contributions to the containment of Ottoman expansionism were patchy and piecemeal, as often as not ended in defeat, and were ruinously costly.[25] But, in the final analysis, by collaborating at vital moments, by incorporating additional partners whenever possible, by committing resources to critical far-flung frontiers, and by holding on to key chokepoints, this loose coalition did just enough to win the first truly multi-continental world war.

CHRONOLOGY

1071	Battle of Manzikert (26 August) – victory of the Seljuk Turks over the Byzantine Empire opens up Anatolia to Turkish colonization.
1204	Constantinople taken by the Fourth Crusade (13 April).
1243	Battle of Köse Dağ (26 June) – defeat and subjugation of the Seljuk Turks by the Mongols.
1299	Osman I initiates the Ottoman dynasty.
1302	Battle of Bapheus (27 July) – Ottoman victory over the Byzantines.
1323	Orhan succeeds as Ottoman sultan.
1326	Bursa taken by the Ottomans (6 April) – the city serves as the first Ottoman capital.
1329	Battle of Pelekanon (10–11 June) – Ottoman victory over the Byzantines.
1331	İznik taken by the Ottomans after a three-year siege.
1337	İzmit taken by the Ottomans.
1338	Üsküdar on the Bosporus opposite Constantinople taken by the Ottomans.
1352	Çimpe taken by the Ottomans – their first possession in Europe.
1354	Gallipoli taken by the Ottomans.
1362	Murad I succeeds as Ottoman sultan.
1369	Edirne taken by the Ottomans – the city serves as the second Ottoman capital.
1371	Battle of Maritsa (26 September) – Ottoman victory over the Serbians.
1386	Niš taken by the Ottomans.
1389	First Battle of Kosovo Polje (15 June) between the Ottomans and Serbians – inconclusive outcome. Death of Murad I; Bayezid I succeeds as Ottoman sultan.

1394–1402	Ottoman siege of Constantinople.
1396	Battle of Nicopolis (25 September) – Ottoman victory over a crusader army.
1402	Battle of Ankara (20 July) – Timur defeats the Ottomans. Bayezid I taken prisoner.
1402–13	The Ottoman Interregnum, a period of dynastic civil war between the rival inheritors to Bayezid I.
1413	Battle of Çamurlu (5 July) – Mehmed defeats his final rival and reunites the Ottoman state under his reign as Sultan Mehmed I.
1421	Murad II succeeds as Ottoman sultan (26 May).
1422	Ottoman siege of Constantinople.
1430	Thessaloniki taken by the Ottomans.
1439	Srebrenica and Smederevo taken by the Ottomans.
1443–44	Crusader campaign against the Ottomans. The Crusaders take Niš but are repulsed at the Zlatitsa Pass and are forced into a fighting retreat.
1444	Battle of Varna (10 November) – decisive Ottoman victory over a crusader army. Death of King Vladislaus I of Hungary.
1448	Second Battle of Kosovo Polje (17–20 October) – Ottoman victory over the Hungarians.
1451	Mehmed II succeeds as Ottoman sultan (3 February).
1453	Constantinople taken by the Ottomans (29 May) – the city serves as the third Ottoman capital.
1456	Ottoman siege of Belgrade (4–22 July) broken.
1459	Ottomans annex Serbia.
1460	Ottomans annex the Morea.
1461	Trabzon taken by the Ottomans.
1462	Ottoman campaign in Wallachia.
1463	Ottomans annex Bosnia.
1463–79	First Ottoman–Venetian War.
1475	Battle of Vaslui (10 January) – Moldovan defeat of the Ottomans.
1475	Feodosia taken by the Ottomans; the Crimean khanate reduced to an Ottoman vassal.
1479	Albania annexed by the Ottomans.
1480	Otranto taken by the Ottomans (11 August). Ottoman siege of Rhodes (23 May–17 August) broken.
1481	Bayezid II succeeds as Ottoman sultan (3 May).

1485–91	First Ottoman–Mamluk War.
1487	Final defeat of the Karamanids confirms Ottoman hegemony in Anatolia.
1495	Manuel I succeeds as king of Portugal (25 October).
1497–99	The da Gama expedition transits from Lisbon to Calicut, opening up Africa and India to Portuguese influence.
1499–1503	Second Ottoman–Venetian War.
1509	Battle of Diu (3 February) – Portuguese victory at sea over a coalition between the Mamluks and their Indian allies.
1510	Goa taken by the Portuguese (25 November).
1511	Malacca taken by the Portuguese (15 August).
1512	Selim I succeeds as Ottoman Sultan (24 April).
1513	Portuguese attempt to storm Aden fails (26 March).
1514	Battle of Chaldiran (22 August) – Ottoman victory over the Safavids confirms Ottoman ascendancy in Transcaucasia.
1516	Battle of Marj Dabiq (24 August) – Ottoman victory over the Mamluks imposes Ottoman authority in Syria.
1517	Battle of Raydaniyya (23 January) – Ottoman victory over the Mamluks imposes Ottoman authority in Egypt.
1519	Charles V succeeds as Holy Roman Emperor (28 June).
1520	Suleiman I succeeds as Ottoman sultan (30 September).
1521	*Diet* of Worms (28 January–25 May) – Martin Luther proscribed as a heretic – the now irreparable breach with the papacy culminates in the rise of Protestantism. Hernán Cortés takes Tenochtitlan (13 August). Belgrade taken by the Ottomans (29 August). John III succeeds as king of Portugal (13 December).
1522	Rhodes taken by the Ottomans (22 December).
1526	Battle of Mohács (29 August) – Ottoman victory over the Hungarians. Death of King Louis II of Hungary. Buda (11 September) and Pest (13 September) taken by the Ottomans.
1529–43	Ethiopian–Adal War.
1529	Ottoman siege of Vienna (27 September–15 October) broken.
1532	Ottoman siege of Kőszeg (9 –29 August) ends by negotiation, stalling the Ottoman campaign against Habsburg Austria and aborting a second siege of Vienna. Pizarro seizes the Inca emperor Atahualpa at Cajamarca (16 November).

1532–36	Ottoman Campaign of the Two Iraqs – Tabriz and Baghdad taken by the Ottomans.
1534	Tunis taken by Barbarossa for the Ottomans (22 August).
1535	Tunis taken by the Habsburgs (21 July).
1537–40	Third Ottoman–Venetian War.
1538	Battle of Preveza (28 September) – Ottoman victory at sea over the Holy League. Ottoman siege of Diu (26 June–6 November) broken.
1541	Buda taken by the Ottomans (29 August) – Hungary annexed by the Ottomans. Habsburg siege of Algiers. (23 October–2 November) broken.
1542	Battle of Wofla (28 August) – Adal–Ottoman victory over the Portuguese.
1543	Battle of Wayna Daga (21 February) – Ethiopian–Portuguese alliance victory over an Adal–Ottoman alliance. Death of Adal Imam Ahmad ibn Ibrahim al-Ghazi.
1546	Gujarati siege of Diu (20 April–10 November) broken. Basra taken by the Ottomans (26 December).
1548–49	Ottoman campaigns in Transcaucasia advance the frontier at the expense of the Safavids.
1551	Tripoli taken by the Ottomans (15 August) – Ottoman hegemony in Libya asserted.
1553–55	Ottoman–Safavid War.
1556	Philip II succeeds as king of Spain (16 January). Ferdinand I succeeds as Holy Roman Emperor (27 August).
1557	Sebastian I succeeds as king of Portugal (11 June).
1560	Djerba taken by the Ottomans (31 July).
1565	Ottoman siege of Malta (18 May–8 September) broken.
1566	Ottomans take Szigetvár (8 September). Selim II succeeds as Ottoman sultan (29 September).
1570–71	The League of the Indies, a coalition of Muslim states including Bijapur, Calicut, Cannanore, and Aceh, fails to drive the Portuguese out of India.
1570–1573	Fourth Ottoman–Venetian War.
1570	Nicosia taken by the Ottomans (9 September).
1571	Famagusta taken by the Ottomans (1 August), completing the Ottoman conquest of Cyprus. Battle of Lepanto (7 October) – Holy League victory at sea over the Ottomans.

1574	Tunis taken by the Ottomans (13 September). Murad III succeeds as Ottoman sultan (27 December).
1578	Battle of Ksar al-Kebir (4 August) – Saadi Moroccan victory over the Portuguese. Death of King Sebastian I of Portugal.
1578–90	Ottoman–Safavid War concludes with Ottoman hegemony in Transcaucasia over Georgia, Azerbaijan, and Armenia.
1580	Philip II succeeds as king of Portugal (12 September).
1593–1606	Ottoman–Habsburg War.
1595	Mehmed III succeeds as Ottoman sultan (16 January).
1596	Battle of Keresztes (24–26 October) – Ottoman victory over the Habsburgs.
1598	Philip III succeeds as king of Spain (13 September).

GLOSSARY

OTTOMAN

agha	commander of the Janissaries
akinji	light cavalry
azap	conscript infantry
bashi-bazouks	irregular soldiers
bey	local governor
beylerbey	supreme governor
devshirme	military recruitment through forcible induction of non-Muslim children
divan	council
ghazi	holy warriors
janissary	member of the sultan's elite household troops
jihad	holy war
kāfirs	non-Muslims
kapikulu	sultan's household troops
kapudan pasha	grand admiral of the Ottoman navy
pasha	title
razzia	raid
reis	military rank
sanjak-bey	governor
şehzade	prince
serdar	commander-in-chief
timar	land grants
vizier	elite political advisor

WESTERN

bailo	magistrate (Venetian)
ban	governor (Bosnian)
cartaz	license required to trade in the Indian Ocean (Portuguese)
diet	legislative assembly (Latin)
feitoria	factory (Portuguese)
juros	government certificate (Spanish)
Landsknecht	mercenaries (German)
pfalzgraf	count palatine (German)

ETHIOPIAN

bāhr negus	ruler of the seas
negus	emperor

NAUTICAL

fusta	light galley
galleass	heavy, three-masted galley
galliot	small galley
naus	carrack
parandaria	heavy store ship

NOTES

PROLOGUE

1   Gerard B. Wegemer and Stephen W. Smith (eds.), *The Essential Works of Thomas More*,
    Yale University Press, New Haven, 2020, p. 1,113. For a critique of More's framing
    device, see Isabelle Bore, "Thomas More et le Grand Turc: Variations sur le theme des
    invasions Ottomanes," *Moreana*, Vol. 48, No. 185/186, December 2011, pp. 9–34.
2   Wegemer and Smith (eds.), *Thomas More*, p. 1,112.
3   Ibid., p. 1,113.
4   Ibid., p. 1,193.
5   Ibid., p. 1,195.
6   Ibid., p. 1,223.
7   Peter Ackroyd, *The Life of Thomas More*, Doubleday, New York, 1998, p. 322.
8   Wegemer and Smith (eds.), *Thomas More*, pp. 1,126–27.

CHAPTER 1: ORIGINS, TO FIRST KOSOVO AND NICOPOLIS

1   Caroline Finkel, *Osman's Dream: The History of the Ottoman Empire*, Basic Books,
    New York, 2007. Also very useful as a general introduction to Ottoman history is
    Marc David Baer, *The Ottomans: Khans, Caesars, and Caliphs*, Basic Books, New
    York, 2021. Some sources maintain the roots of Turkish ambition run much deeper.
    An account of an exchange of envoys in 568 between the khan of the Gök-Turks
    and the Byzantine Emperor Justin relates that tears filled the eyes of the Turkish
    khan on the arrival of the Byzantine envoy. When asked to explain why he wept, the
    khan answered: "We have been told by our ancestors that the time is ripe for us to
    conquer the entire world." Osman Turan, "The Ideal of World Domination among
    the Medieval Turks," *Studia Islamica*, No. 4, 1955, p. 79.
2   David Nicolle, *Cross & Crescent in the Balkans: The Ottoman Conquest of
    Southeastern Europe (14th–15th Centuries)*, Pen & Sword Books, Barnsley, 2010,
    pp. 23–24.
3   Halil Inalcik, "Osman Ghazi's Siege of Nicaea and the Battle of Bapheus," in
    Elizabeth Zachariadou (ed.), *The Ottoman Emirate (1300–1389)*, Crete University
    Press, Rethymnon, 1993, pp. 77–100. The definitive source on the protracted death

throes of the Byzantine Empire is John Julius Norwich, *Byzantium: The Decline and Fall*, Knopf, New York, 1995.

4   Georgios C. Liakopoulos, "The Ottoman Conquest of Thrace: Aspects of Historical Geography," MA Thesis, Bilkent University, 2002, p. 35.

5   Christine Isom-Verhaaren, *The Sultan's Fleet: Seafarers of the Ottoman Empire*, I.B. Tauris, London, 2022, pp. 29–57.

6   Norman Housley, "King Louis the Great of Hungary and the Crusades, 1342–82," *Slavonic and East European Review*, Vol. 62, No. 2, 1984, p. 202.

7   Thomas A. Emmert, *Serbian Golgotha: Kosovo, 1389*, Columbia University Press, New York, 1990, p. 25.

8   John V.A. Fine, *The Late Medieval Balkans: A Critical Survey from the Late Twelfth Century to the Ottoman Conquest*, University of Michigan Press, Ann Arbor, 1994, pp. 345–405.

9   The Byzantines were notorious for their capacity to provoke and exacerbate the dynastic rivalries of their foes, but the Ottomans very early proved themselves adept pupils in this art, inserting themselves into the court intrigue at Constantinople to their own great advantage. See Nevra Necipoğlu, *Byzantium between the Ottomans and the Latins: Politics and Society in the Late Empire*, Cambridge University Press, Cambridge, 2009, pp. 119–48.

10   Gábor Ágoston, *The Last Muslim Conquest*, Princeton University Press, Princeton, 2021, p. 25.

11   Necipoğlu, *Byzantium*, p. 123.

12   Anthony Luttrell, "Latin Responses to Ottoman Expansion before 1389," in Elizabeth Zachariadou (ed.), *The Ottoman Emirate (1300–1389)*, p. 126.

13   Emmert, *Serbian Golgotha*, p. 64.

14   James E. Held, "Legend of the Fall: The Battle of Kosovo, 28 June 1389," *Strategy & Tactics*, No. 262, May–June 2010, pp. 50–58.

15   Emmert, *Serbian Golgotha*, p. 45.

16   Miloš Ivanović, "Militarization of the Serbian State under Ottoman Pressure," *Hungarian Historical Review*, Vol. 8, No. 2, 2019, pp. 390–410.

17   Paul Lendvai, *The Hungarians: A Thousand Years of Victory in Defeat*, Princeton University Press, Princeton, 2004, pp. 62–74.

18   The chronology of this campaign is contested; see Radu Cârciumaru, "Historiographic Views on the so-called Battle of 'Rovine' and its Consequences," *Annales d'Université Valahia Târgoviște*, Vol. 13, No. 2, 2011, pp. 77–82.

19   It is perhaps indicative of the depressed state of mind under which Ottoman vassals labored that on the eve of the battle, according to the account of Constantine the Philosopher, Kraljević remarked to Dejanović, "I pray God to help the Christians and that I will be among the first dead in this war." John V.A. Fine, *The Late Medieval Balkans: A Critical Survey from the Late Twelfth Century to the Ottoman Conquest*, University of Michigan Press, Ann Arbor, 1994, p. 424.

20   Isom-Verhaaren, *The Sultan's Fleet*, pp. 9–28.

21   Kelly DeVries, "The Lack of a Western European Military Response to the Ottoman Invasions of Eastern Europe from Nicopolis (1396) to Mohacs (1526)," *The Journal of Military History*, Vol. 63, No. 3, July 1999, p. 545.

22   Mike Carr, "Humbert of Viennois and the Crusade of Smyrna: A Reconsideration," *Crusades*, Vol. 13, No. 1, 2014, pp. 237–51.

23   Attila Barany, "King Sigismund and the '*Passagium Generale*' (1391–96)," in Florena Ciure and Alexandru Simon (eds.), *Conferinta Internationala Sigismund de Luxemburg*, Oradea, 6–9 December 2007.

24   Nicolle, *Cross & Crescent in the Balkans*, p. 103.

25   John of Gaunt, Duke of Lancaster, a son of King Edward III of England and the father of King Henry IV, had played a crucial role in negotiating the Truce of Leulinghem in 1389, a temporary hiatus to the Hundred Years War that allowed for consideration of a crusade against the Ottomans. John intended to accompany the crusader army on its fateful journey to Nicopolis, but ill health and political responsibilities obliged him to remain at court.

26   Nicolle, *Cross & Crescent in the Balkans*, p. 112.

27   Ibid., p. 116.

28   Ibid., p. 107.

29   DeVries, "Lack of a Western European Military Response," pp. 541–42.

30   Barnaby Rogerson, *The Last Crusaders: East, West, and the Battle for the Center of the World*, Overlook Press, New York, 2010, p. 72.

31   Nicolle, *Cross & Crescent in the Balkans*, p. 121.

32   Ibid., p. 123.

33   Ibid., p. 158.

34   DeVries, "Lack of a Western European Military Response," p. 544.

35   Ibid., p. 543.

36   Nicolle, *Cross & Crescent in the Balkans*, p. 127.

37   Ibid., p. 123.

38   Mark Whelan, "Catastrophe or Consolidation? Sigismund's Response to Defeat after the Crusade of Nicopolis (1396)," in Florin Ardelean, Christopher Nicholson, and Johannes Preiser-Kapeller (eds.), *Between Worlds: The Age of the Jagiellonians*, Peter Lang, Frankfurt am Main, 2013, pp. 215–27.

39   Ágoston, *The Last Muslim Conquest*, p. 53. Ironically, it was Sigismund who presided over the Council of Constance that deposed John XXIII in 1415; by the time of his trial, Edward Gibbon wrote, "The more scandalous charges were suppressed; the vicar of Christ was accused only of piracy, rape, sodomy, murder and incest." Frank Welsh, *The Battle for Christendom: The Council of Constance, the East–West Conflict, and the Dawn of Modern Europe*, Overlook Press, Woodstock, 2008, p. 1,340.

40   Emir O. Filipović, "Colluding with the Infidel: The Alliance between Ladislaus of Naples and the Turks," *Hungarian Historical Review*, Vol. 8, No. 2, 2019, pp. 361–89.

41 From 1399 to 1402 wheat prices in Constantinople varied between 20 and 31 *hyperpyra* per *modios* (234 kilograms). By contrast, in September and October 1402, only a few months after the termination of the siege, the price of one *modios* of wheat immediately dropped down to 7 or 8 *hyperpyra*, and by 1436 further down to 4–6.25 *hyperpyra*, reaching a level comparable to recorded pre-siege prices of 5 *hyperpyra* (in 1343) and 6.75 *hyperpyra* (in 1366) per *modios*. Necipoğlup, *Byzantium*, pp. 152–53.

42 Ali Anooshahr, *The Ghazi Sultans and the Frontiers of Islam*, Routledge, New York, 2009, p. 125.

43 Ibid., p. 124.

44 Şahin Kiliç, "Byzantine-Ottoman Relations in Early 1420s," *Uludağ Üniversitesi Fen Edebiyat Fakültesi Sosyal Bilimler Dergisi*, Vol. 14, No. 25, July 2013, pp. 24–266. See also Fine, *The Late Medieval Balkans*, pp. 453–547.

45 Necipoğlu, *Byzantium*, pp. 33–34.

46 Ibid., p. 48.

47 Ibid., p. 188.

48 Barış Ünlü, "The Formation of the Ottoman Empire from a World-Centric Perspective," in Selim Karahasanoğlu and Deniz Cenk Demir (eds.), *History from Below: A Tribute in Memory of Donald Quataert*, İstanbul Bilgi Üniversitesi Yayınları, İstanbul, 2016, pp. 123–53.

49 See Jakub J. Grygiel, *Great Powers and Geopolitical Change*, Johns Hopkins University Press, Baltimore, 2006, pp. 88–122.

50 Ágoston, *The Last Muslim Conquest*, p. 40.

51 Nicolle, *Cross & Crescent in the Balkans*, p. 92.

52 Adrian Gheorghe, *The Metamorphoses of Power: Violence, Warlords, Akıncıs and the Early Ottomans (1300–1450)*, Brill, Leiden, 2023.

53 Pál Fodor, "Wolf on the Border: Yahyapaşaoğlu Bali Bey (?–1527) – Expansion and Provincial Élite in the European Confines of the Ottoman Empire in the Early Sixteenth Century," in Pál Fodor, Nándor E. Kovács, and Benedek Péri (eds.), *Studies in Honour of Prof. Géza Dávid on his Seventieth Birthday*, Research Centre for the Humanities, Hungarian Academy of Sciences, Budapest, 2019, pp. 57–87.

54 Godfrey Goodwin, *The Janissaries*, Saqi, London, 1997, p. 39. The chronicler of this tale, Konstantin Mihailović, one of the nineteen recalcitrant forced inductees, served decades in the janissary corps and survived to write a fascinating insider account of his experiences.

55 Birol Gündoğdu, "Ottoman Military Rebellions and a Delicate Relationship between the State and Janissaries in the Early Modern Era," in Birol Gündoğdu (ed.), *Reading the Ottoman Mind*, Sivas Cumhuriyet University Press, Sivas, 2023, pp. 101–29.

56 Gábor Ágoston, *Guns for the Sultan: Military Power and the Weapons Industry in the Ottoman Empire*, Cambridge University Press, Cambridge, 2005; Douglas E. Streusand, *Islamic Gunpowder Empires: Ottomans, Safavids, and Mughals*, Westview

Press, Boulder, 2011; Gábor Ágoston, "Firearms and Military Adaptation: The Ottomans and the European Military Revolution, 1450–1800," *Journal of World History*, Vol. 25, No. 1, March 2014, pp. 85–124; Kaushik Roy, *Military Transition in Early Modern Asia, 1400–1750: Cavalry, Guns, Government and Ships*, Bloomsbury, London, 2014.

57 Ebru Boyar, "Ottoman Expansion in the East," in Suraiya Faroqhi and Kate Fleet (eds.), *The Cambridge History of Turkey, Vol. 2: The Ottoman Empire as a World Power, 1453–1603*, Cambridge University Press, Cambridge, 2013, p. 84.

58 David Ayalon, *Gunpowder and Firearms in the Mamluk Kingdom: A Challenge to a Mediaeval Society*, Vallentine, Mitchell and Co., London, 1956, p. 94. See also Albrecht Fuess, "The Role of Military Technology and Firearms in the Ottoman Conquest of the Mamluk Realm 1516–1517," *The Memory of Arabs*, No. 4, 2020, pp. 9–24.

59 Abolala Soudavar, "The Early Safavids and their Cultural Interactions with Surrounding States," in Nikki R. Keddie and Rudi P. Matthee (eds.), *Iran and the Surrounding World: Interactions in Culture and Cultural Politics*, University of Washington Press, Seattle, 2002, p. 101.

60 Gábor Ágoston, "Ottoman Warfare in Europe 1453–1826," in Jeremy Black (ed.), *European Warfare 1453–1815*, Palgrave Macmillan, New York, 1999, p. 125.

61 Rhoads Murphey, *Ottoman Warfare, 1500–1700*, UCL Press, London, 1999, p. 17.

62 Noel Malcolm, *Agents of Empire*, Oxford University Press, New York, 2015, p. 329.

63 Murphey, *Ottoman Warfare*, p. 20.

64 Ágoston, *The Last Muslim Conquest*, p. 26.

65 See Helga Anetshofer, "Legends of Sarı Saltık in the Seyahatnâme and the Bektashi Oral Tradition," in Nuran Tezcan, Semih Tezcan, and Robert Dankoff (eds.), *Evilyâ Çelebi: Studies and Essays Commemorating the 400th Anniversary of his Birth*, Ministry of Culture and Tourism, Istanbul 2012, pp. 292–300; Ceren Çıkın Sungur, "A Critical Analysis of Sari Saltik as a Hero in Saltiknâme," MA Thesis, Central European University, 2020.

66 Arda Eksigil, "Ottoman Visions of the West (15th–17th Centuries)," MA Thesis, McGill University, 2014, p. 83.

67 Adrian Gheorghe, *Metamorphoses of Power*; Suraiya Faroqhi, *The Ottoman Empire and the World Around It*, I.B. Tauris, London, 2006.

68 Einar Wigen, "Ottoman Concepts of Empire," *Contributions to the History of Concepts*, Vol. 8, No. 1, Summer 2013, pp. 44–66.

69 Eksigil, "Ottoman Visions of the West," p. 18–19.

70 Robert Finlay, "Prophecy and Politics in Istanbul: Charles V, Sultan Suleyman, and the Habsburg Embassy of 1533–1534," *Journal of Early Modern History*, Vol. 2, No. 1, January 1998, p. 19.

71 See Gábor Kármán, "Sovereignty and Representation: Tributary States in the Seventeenth-century Diplomatic System of the Ottoman Empire," pp. 155–86, and Sándor Papp, "The System of Autonomous Muslim and Christian Communities,

Churches, and States in the Ottoman Empire," pp. 375–419, in Gábor Kármán and Lovro Kunčević (eds.), *The European Tributary States of the Ottoman Empire in the Sixteenth and Seventeenth Centuries*, Brill, Leiden, 2013.

72   From an Ottoman perspective, this could be a slippery definition, and the consistently worst offender was Venice. Ibrahim Peçevi, a provincial official who later became a prominent chronicler during the first half of the 16th century, warned his cohorts the "Venetians are dependent on Muslim trade. As such, they forcibly present themselves as friends of Muslims whereas in reality, they are considerably more hostile to Muslims than other infidels are." Eksigil, "Ottoman Visions of the West," p. 49.

73   Giancarlo Casale, *The Ottoman Age of Exploration*, Oxford University Press, New York, 2010, p. 138.

74   Nathan Michalewicz, "Franco-Ottoman Diplomacy during the French Wars of Religion, 1559–1610," Ph.D. Dissertation, George Mason University, 2020, p. 196.

75   Ian Almond, *Two Faiths, One Banner: When Muslims Marched with Christians Across Europe's Battlegrounds*, I.B. Tauris, London, 2009, pp. 95–137.

76   Pál Fodor, "The Ottoman Empire, Byzantium and Western Christianity: The Implications of the Siege of Belgrade, 1456," *Acta Orientalia Academiae Scientiarum Hungaricae*, Vol. 61, No. 1, 2008, p. 44.

77   Ágoston, *The Last Muslim Conquest*, p. 47.

78   Leslie Peirce, *Empress of the East: How a European Slave Girl Became Queen of the Ottoman Empire*, Basic Books, New York, 2017; Galina I. Yermolenko (ed.), *Roxolana in European Literature, History and Culture*, Ashgate, Farnham, 2010.

79   Tobias P. Graf, *The Sultan's Renegades: Christian-European Converts to Islam and the Making of the Ottoman Elite, 1575–1610*, Oxford University Press, New York, 2017; Marc David Baer, *Honored by the Glory of Islam: Conversion and Conquest in Ottoman Europe*, Oxford University Press, New York, 2008. See also "Emergence: Brokerage across Networks," pp. 28–66, and "Becoming an Empire: Imperial Institutions and Control," pp. 67–108, in Karen Barkey, *Empire of Difference: The Ottomans in Comparative Perspective*, Cambridge University Press, Cambridge, 2008.

80   Ágoston, *The Last Muslim Conquest*, p. 22.

81   Theoharis Stavrides, *The Sultan of Vezirs: The Life and Times of the Ottoman Grand Vezir Mahmud Pasha Angelović (1453–1474)*, Brill, Leiden, 2001.

82   According to one account, while cruising near the shores of Calabria Uluç anchored by Le Castella, his birthplace, where he promised to spare the fishermen if they allowed him to embrace his mother. But she refused to accept his gifts and renounced him for having turned renegade. Isom-Verhaaren, *The Sultan's Fleet*, p. 136.

83   For this remarkable story, see Emrah Safa Gürkan, "His Bailo's Kapudan: Conversion, Tangled Loyalties and Hasan Veneziano Between Istanbul and Venice (1588–1591)," *The Journal of Ottoman Studies*, Vol. XLVIII, 2016, pp. 277–319.

84 In response to the Alhambra Decree of Ferdinand and Isabella that purged their realm of Jews, Sultan Bayezid II offered asylum to tens of thousands of refugees. "You venture to call Ferdinand a wise ruler," he remarked to his courtiers, "he who has impoverished his own country and enriched mine!" Jonathan Ray, "Iberian Jewry between West and East: Jewish Settlement in the Sixteenth-Century Mediterranean," *Mediterranean Studies*, Vol. 18, 2009, pp. 44–65.

85 Noel Malcolm, *Useful Enemies: Islam and the Ottoman Empire in Western Political Thought, 1450–1750*, Oxford University Press, Oxford, 2019, p. 74.

86 Gábor Ágoston, "Ottoman and Habsburg Military Affairs in the Age of Süleyman the Magnificent," in Pál Fodor (ed.), *The Battle for Central Europe: The Siege of Szigetvár and the Death of Süleyman the Magnificent and Nicholas Zrínyi (1566)*, Brill, Leiden, 2019, p. 289. Just as the Ottoman tide was overwhelming Hungary and rising against Vienna, Ferdinand was the beneficiary of a timely infusion of bullion derived from major breakthroughs in mining technology that empowered the discovery of new sources of precious metals and the revivification of lodes assumed to be exhausted throughout the Habsburg domains. These enabled the silver and copper mines of Tyrolia, Bohemia, Saxony, Carinthia, and Thuringia to set record levels of production. Development of the massive silver strike made at Joachimstahl in Bohemia in 1516 led to it producing as much as twenty-one tons of ore annually two decades later, equivalent to 87,500 marks per year, making it the single largest silver mine in Europe. Annual copper output at Mansfeld in Thuringia reached 2,100 tons in 1526, more than double the volume produced in 1506, plus a bonus supply of separated silver. Howard J. Erlichman, *Conquest, Tribute and Trade: The Quest for Precious Metals and the Birth of Globalization*, Prometheus Books, New York, 2003, p. 127.

87 Sergio Sardone, "Forced Loans in the Spanish Empire: The First Requisition of American Treasures in 1523," *The Economic History Review*, Vol. 72, No. 1, February 2019, pp. 57–87.

88 Brian Sandberg, "Going Off to the War in Hungary: French Nobles and Crusading Culture in the Sixteenth Century," *The Hungarian Historical Review*, Vol. 4, No. 2, 2015, p. 353.

89 Malcolm, *Useful Enemies*, p. 75.

90 Nicolle, *Cross & Crescent in the Balkans*, p. 211.

91 Malcolm, *Useful Enemies*, p. 14–15. This was a common refrain in the Curia. In late August 1456, Pius's predecessor, Pope Callixtus III wrote to Juan Soler, papal ambassador to the court of King Alfonso V of Aragon, explaining that Mehmed II, "in the face of whose power even our tepid and cold Christian powers hesitated to take up the fight, unless almost all the world joined in," only "conquered so much because no Catholic resisted him." James D. Mixson, *The Crusade of 1456: Texts and Documentation in Translation*, University of Toronto Press, Toronto, 2022, p. 132.

92 See Andrew W. Devereux, *The Other Side of Empire: Just War in the Mediterranean and the Rise of Early Modern Spain*, Cornell University Press, Ithaca, 2020, pp. 43–62; Larry Silver, "Europe's Turkish Nemesis," in Barbara Fuchs and Emily Weissbourd

(eds.), *Representing Imperial Rivalry in the Early Modern Mediterranean*, University of Toronto Press, Toronto, 2015, pp. 58–79; Charlotte Colding Smith, *Images of Islam, 1453–1600: Turks in Germany and Central Europe*, Pickering & Chatto, London, 2014; Larry Silver, "East is East: Images of the Turkish Nemesis in the Habsburg World," in James G. Harper (ed.), *The Turk and Islam in the Western Eye, 1450–1750*, Taylor & Francis, New York, 2011, pp. 185–216; Mustafa Soykut, *Historical Image of the Turk in Europe, 15th Century to the Present: Political and Civilisational Aspects*, Gorgias Press, Piscataway, 2010; Paula Sutter Fichtner, *Terror and Toleration: The Habsburg Empire Confronts Islam, 1526–1850*, Reaktion Books, London, 2008.

93   Michael Angold, *The Fall of Constantinople to the Ottomans: Context and Consequences*, Routledge, New York, 2012, p. 100.

94   Mark Greengrass, *Christendom Destroyed: Europe, 1517–1648*, Penguin, New York, 2014.

95   Diarmaid MacCulloch, *The Reformation*, Penguin, New York, 2004, p. 354.

96   The best source on this subject is the magisterial John Julius Norwich, *A History of Venice*, Knopf, New York, 1982. See also Stefan Stantchevin, "Venice and the Ottoman Threat, 1381–1453," in Norman Housley (ed.), *Reconfiguring the Fifteenth-Century Crusade*, Palgrave Macmillan, New York, 2017, pp. 161–206; Robert Finlay, *Venice Besieged: Politics and Diplomacy in the Italian Wars, 1494–1534*, Ashgate, Burlington, 2008.

97   Andrew W. Deveraux, "'The ruin and slaughter of… fellow Christians': The French as a Threat to Christendom in Spanish Assertions of Sovereignty in Italy, 1479–1516," in Fuchs and Weissbourd (eds.), *Representing Imperial Rivalry*, pp. 101–25.

98   John Dotson, "Venice, Genoa and Control of the Seas in the Thirteenth and Fourteenth Centuries," in John B. Hattendorf and Richard W. Unger (eds.), *War at Sea in the Middle Ages and the Renaissance*, Boydell Press, Rochester, 2003, pp. 119–35.

99   Ágoston, *The Last Muslim Conquest*, p. 206.

100   Malcolm, *Agents of Empire*, p. 109. Of course, not everyone in France supported the pro-Ottoman agenda of their monarchs. Francois de La Noüe, a prominent Calvinist nobleman, condemned the French alliance with the Ottomans: "if we make a comparison… of the utility of all this Turkish aide with the decrease in the renown of the French among all the nations of Europe, one would have to confess that the shame [of it] has much outweighed the profit." Sandberg, "Going Off to the War in Hungary," p. 360. The French played no part in the Holy League that triumphed over the Ottoman fleet at the Battle of Lepanto in 1571, yet one contemporary account describes how "in this city of Lyon you will have heard the great bells that give full and certain testimony (with the hymns and canticles that were sung to the God of armies in great devotion and joy) for such a victory." Ibid., p. 364.

101   Bruno Simon, "Quelques Remarques sur la Relation de Marin Cavalli, Bayle a Constantinople (1560)," in J.L. Bacque-Grammont and E. van Donzel (eds.), *Proceedings: Comité international d'études pré-ottomanes et ottomanes, VIth Symposium, Cambridge, 1st-4th July 1984*, Divit Press, Istanbul, 1987, pp.147–57.

CHAPTER 2: VARNA, SECOND KOSOVO, AND CONSTANTINOPLE

1   This church conclave, intended to promote unity throughout Christendom by resolving such questions as papal supremacy and the Hussite heresy, in fact only exposed how deep-rooted those divisions were. Convened by Pope Martin V a few weeks before his death in 1431, the council was confirmed by his successor, Pope Eugenius IV, only for him to declare it adjourned shortly afterwards. The council, however, refused to be dissolved and renewed the decree *Sacrosancta* of the Council of Constance (1414–18), which declared a general council drew its powers directly from God and that even the pope was subject to its direction. Eugenius yielded in 1433 and revoked his decree of dissolution, but the council continued to advocate for measures that would restrict the authority of the papacy. After the death of Holy Roman Emperor Sigismund in 1437, the pope ordered the council transferred to Ferrara in Italy, only for a minority of the council to repudiate his decree, declare him suspended, and label him a heretic. Eugenius responded by excommunicating the dissidents, who retaliated by declaring Eugenius deposed and in 1439 electing as his successor a layman, the Duke of Savoy, Amadeus VIII, who took the papal title Pope Felix V. When Eugenius died in 1447, his successor, Nicholas V, brought about the abdication of Felix V, while that same year Sigismund's successor as Holy Roman Emperor, Frederick III, ordered the city of Basel to expel the rump council, which reconvened in Lausanne before dissolving itself in 1449.

2   John Jefferson, *The Holy Wars of King Wladislas and Sultan Murad: The Ottoman-Christian Conflict from 1438–1444*, Brill, Leiden, 2012, p. 162.

3   Ibid., p. 173.

4   Ibid., p. 257.

5   Paul Srodecki, "Władysław III and the Polish-Hungarian Bulwark *topoi* against the Background of the Ottoman Threat in the 15th Century," in Dániel Bagi, Gábor Barabás, and Zsolt Máté (eds.), *Hungaro-Polonica: Young Scholars on Medieval Polish-Hungarian Relations*, Zsolt Máté, Pécs, 2016, p. 332.

6   Jefferson, *Holy Wars*, p. 236.

7   Ibid., p. 239.

8   Joseph Held, *Hunyadi: Legend and Reality*, Columbia University Press, New York, 1985, p. 85.

9   Tamás Pálosfalvi, *From Nicopolis to Mohács: A History of Ottoman-Hungarian Warfare, 1389–1526*, Brill, Leiden, 2018, p. 98–99.

10 Accounts of the Ottoman campaign in 1442 are contradictory and my reconstruction is by no means definitive. For reference see David Weiss, "The Ottoman Campaign in Wallachia and the Battle on the River Ialomiţa (1442)," www.academia.edu/44718244/The_Ottoman_campaign_in_Wallachia_and_the_Battle_on_the_River_Ialomi%C5%A3a_1442_

11 Jefferson, *Holy Wars*, p. 335.

12 Colin Imber, *The Crusade of Varna, 1443–45*, Ashgate, Farnham, 2013, p. 56.

13 Jefferson, *Holy Wars*, p. 343.

14 After occupying Sofia, the Crusaders reconsecrated the Siyavus Pasha mosque as the Cathedral of Hagia Sophia and assembled to hear mass, presided over by the Metropolitan Bishop of Sofia. One can imagine the import such an event had for Cesarini. This ceremony, presided over by a recently liberated Orthodox bishop and attended by Latin Christians symbolized for the cardinal the entire purpose of the crusade – the expulsion of the Ottomans, the reestablishment of Christendom in the Balkans, and the strengthening of the union between the Eastern and Western Churches. The moment was not to last. Once the Crusaders withdrew, the pasha of Sofia, who had fled to nearby Radomir when the Crusaders approached, decapitated the bishop and other church officials, "gouged out the eyes of the priests, monks and infidels" he found inside the cathedral, and had the severed heads delivered to the sultan. Jefferson, *Holy Wars*, p. 339.

15 Imber, *Crusade of Varna*, p. 62.

16 Ibid., p. 120–21.

17 Ibid., p. 72.

18 Cardinal Condulmer was both a Venetian and the pope's nephew.

19 Thaddeus V. Tuleja, "Eugenius IV and the Crusade of Varna," *The Catholic Historical Review*, Vol. 35, No. 3, October 1949, pp. 257–75. Constantine Palaiologos would succeed his brother to be crowned as the last emperor of Byzantium, Constantine XI. For the place of the Morea in later Byzantine history, see Necipoğlu, *Byzantium*, pp. 235–58.

20 Jefferson, *Holy Wars*, p. 413.

21 Ibid., p. 414.

22 Pálosfalvi, *From Nicopolis to Mohács*, p. 122.

23 Imber, *Crusade of Varna*, p. 203.

24 Ibid., p. 78.

25 Ibid., p. 78–79.

26 Held, *Hunyadi*, p. 106.

27 Ivanov Ivelin, "The Crusade of Varna (1443–1445) and the Bulgarians," in Dimitar Dimitrov et al. (eds.), *Proceedings of International Conference, 2nd Southeast Europe: History, Culture, Politics, and Economy*, Filodiritto, Bologna, 2018, pp. 12–18.

28 Nevyan Mitev, "The Battle of Shumen – One of the Most Important Battles During the Crusade of Varna in the Autumn of 1444," in Zoltan Iusztin (ed.), *Politics and Society in the Central and South-Eastern Europe (13th–16th Centuries)*, Editura MEGA, Cluj-Napoca, 2019, pp. 205–14.

29 Imber, *Crusade of Varna*, p. 83.

30 For a discussion of how exactly the Ottomans were able to breach the western cordon in the straits – including the accusations made by contemporaries regarding bribery, and of whom [about whom?] – the Venetians, Genoese, or Byzantines – see Nevyan Mitev, "Notes on the Campaign of Vladislav Varnenchik in Northeastern Bulgaria in the Autumn of 1444," *Banatica*, Vol. 26, No. 2, 2016, pp. 235–56.

31 Camil Mureșanu, *John Hunyadi: Defender of Christendom*, Histria Books, Las Vegas, 2021, p. 118.

32 Imber, *Crusade of Varna*, p. 86.

33 Ibid., p. 131.

34 Ibid., p. 98.

35 Ibid., p. 98.

36 Jefferson, *Holy Wars*, p. 465.

37 Imber, *Crusade of Varna*, p. 99.

38 Jefferson, *Holy Wars*, p. 2.

39 Imber, *Crusade of Varna*, pp. 131–32.

40 Ibid., p. 132.

41 Ibid., p. 178.

42 Ibid., p. 194.

43 Ibid., p. 100.

44 Ibid., p. 132.

45 Ibid., p. 102.

46 Tasin Gemil, *Romanians and Ottomans in the XIVth–XVIth Centuries*, Editura Enciclopedică, Bucharest, 2009, p. 165.

47 The name is a portmanteau of Iskander, the Turkish for Alexander, as in "the Great," and Bey, or Beg, "lord."

48 Emanuel C. Antoche, "Hunyadi's Campaign of 1448 and the Second Battle of Kosovo Polje (October 17–20)," in Norman Housley (ed.), *Reconfiguring the Fifteenth-Century Crusade*, Palgrave Macmillan, New York, 2017, p. 250.

49 Mureșanu, *John Hunyadi*, p. 167.

50 Barnabás Bartók, "János Hunyadi: Preventing the Ottomans from Conquering Western Europe in the Fifteenth Century," Master of Military Art and Science Thesis, US Army Command and General Staff College, Fort Leavenworth, 2011, pp. 91–92.

51 Mark Whelan, "Pasquale de Sorgo and the Second Battle of Kosovo (1448): A Translation," *Slavonic and East European Review*, Vol. 94, No. 1, 2016, p. 145.

52 Mureșanu, *John Hunyadi*, p. 180.

53 Antoche, "Hunyadi's Campaign," p. 262. Saudji had fled to Hungary after his father, Savcı Bey, the youngest son of Murad I, was executed following a failed bid to usurp the throne in 1385.

54 Ibid., p. 262.

55 Hunyadi, of course, had no intention of honoring this arrangement; he appealed to Pope Nicholas V, who duly absolved him of all obligations to Branković. The feud simmered until 1451, only being resolved by the betrothal of Hunyadi's younger son, Matthias, to the despot's granddaughter, Countess Elizabeth of Cilli.

56 Pál Fodor, *The Unbearable Weight of Empire: The Ottomans in Central Europe – A Failed Attempt at Universal Monarchy (1390–1566)*, Hungarian Academy of Sciences, Budapest, 2016, p. 27.

57 Antoche, "Hunyadi's Campaign," p. 258.

58 Noel Malcolm, *Kosovo: A Short History*, New York University Press, New York, 1998, p. 90.

59 His title as metropolitan of Kiev was in fact by this point purely nominal, as he had been arrested by Grand Prince Vasili II for promulgating the Union of Latin and Orthodox Churches to the Rus and had spent two years behind bars before escaping in September 1443 and fleeing via Lithuania to Rome.

60 Fodor, *Unbearable Weight of Empire*, p. 44.

61 Nicolle, *Cross & Crescent*, p. 181.

62 Ibid., pp. 181–82.

63 Marios Philippides and Walter K. Hanak, *The Siege and the Fall of Constantinople in 1453: Historiography, Topography, and Military Studies*, Ashgate, Farnham, 2011, p. 401.

64 Philippides and Hanak, *Fall of Constantinople*, p. 384.

65 Ibid., p. 143.

66 Ibid., p. 383.

67 David Nicolle, *Constantinople, 1453: The End of Byzantium*, Osprey, Oxford, 2000; Steven Runciman, *The Fall of Constantinople, 1453*, Cambridge University Press, New York, 1965. Note that Philippides and Hanak deconstruct the account of Pseudo-Sphrantzes, exposing his substitution of Nikephoros Palaiologos in the place of Nicholas Goudeles. Philippides and Hanak, *Fall of Constantinople*, p. 152. See also Nevra Necipoglu, "Constantinopolitan Merchants and the Question of their Attitudes towards Italians and Ottomans in the late Palaiologan Period," in Cordula Scholz and Georgios Makris (eds.), *Polypleuros nous: Miscellanea für Peter Schreiner zu seinem 60*, K.G. Saur Verlag, Munich-Leipzig, 2000, pp. 251–63.

68 Philippides and Hanak, *Fall of Constantinople*, p. 500.

69 Nicolle, *Cross & Crescent*, p. 176.

70 Philippides and Hanak, *Fall of Constantinople*, p. 197.

71 Ibid., p. 486.

72 Ibid., p. 442.

73 Ibid., p. 501.

74 Ibid., p. 458.

75 Angold, *Fall of Constantinople*, p. 7.

76 Jonathan Harris, *The End of Byzantium*, Yale University Press, New Haven, 2010, p. xvii.

77 Roger Crowley, *1453: The Holy War for Constantinople and the Clash of Islam and the West*, Hyperion, New York, 2005, p. 215.

78 Donald M. Nicol, *The Immortal Emperor: The Life and Legend of Constantine Palaiologos, Last Emperor of the Romans*, Cambridge University Press, New York, 1991.

79 Philippides and Hanak, *Fall of Constantinople*, p. 461.

80   Ibid., p. 462. Hamza would later redeem himself by conducting naval operations in the Aegean after the fall of Constantinople that compelled the surrender of the remaining islands still under nominal Byzantine authority – Thasos, Limnos, and Gökçeada. In 1454, he led a naval expedition to the far side of the Black Sea that culminated in the Ottoman annexation of Abkhazia.

81   Ibid., p. 519.

82   Angold, *Fall of Constantinople*, p. 185.

83   Anastasija Ropa, "Imagining the 1456 Siege of Belgrade in '*Capystranus*,'" *The Hungarian Historical Review*, Vol. 4, No. 2, 2015, p. 271. A generation earlier, *The Chronicle of the Hungarians*, published in 1488 by royal notary John Thurocz, lamented the fall of Constantinople, "which was begging for reinforcements from Christian kings and yet was abandoned by everyone to disaster and destruction." Mixson, *The Crusade of 1456*, p. 238.

CHAPTER 3: FIRST BELGRADE, FIRST RHODES, AND OTRANTO

1   Indicating the bad blood that persisted between Hunyadi and Branković, on the night of 17 December 1455 the despot, then resident at his estate of Kupinik (Kupinovo) on the Sava just west of Belgrade, was roused by Michael Szilágyi and taken to Belgrade, where his wife Irina had to stay prisoner until he paid a ransom and surrendered two fortified places to redeem her. However, King Ladislaus invalidated the demands of Hunyadi's brother-in-law (Szilágyi was married to Hunyadi's sister, Elizabeth) in order to save Branković from further humiliation.

2   John U. Nef, "Silver Production in Central Europe, 1450–1618," *Journal of Political Economy*, Vol. 49, No. 4, August 1941, pp. 575–91.

3   John Day, "The Great Bullion Famine of the Fifteenth Century," *Past & Present*, Vol. 79, No. 1, May 1978, pp. 3–54.

4   Peter Spufford, *Money and its Use in Medieval Europe*, Cambridge University Press, Cambridge, 1988, p. 362.

5   Erlichman, *Conquest, Tribute and Trade*, p. 20.

6   Emir O. Filipović, "The Key to the Gate of Christendom? The Strategic Importance of Bosnia in the Struggle Against the Ottomans," in Norman Housley (ed.), *The Crusade in the Fifteenth Century: Converging and Competing Cultures*, Routledge, New York, 2017, pp. 155–56.

7   Mixson, *The Crusade of 1456*, pp. 41, 42.

8   Ibid., p. 47.

9   Italian humanist and poet Antonio Bonfini described the comet looking "as long as half the sky with two tails, one pointing west and the other east, colored gold and looking like an undulating flame in the distant horizon." At the other end of the world as the Ottomans knew it, the comet was also witnessed by Zara Yaqob, emperor of Ethiopia from 1434 to 1468. Believing this was a sign from God

signaling his approval for the death by stoning of a group of heretics thirty-eight days previously, the emperor ordered a church built on the site, and later constructed an extensive palace nearby, and a second church, dedicated to St Cyriacus, a complex that would evolve into Debre Birhan, the "City of Light."

10   Mixson, *The Crusade of 1456*, p. 138.

11   Ropa, "Imagining the 1456 Siege of Belgrade," p. 273.

12   Mixson, *The Crusade of 1456*, p. 118.

13   Ibid., p. 67.

14   Ibid., p. 98.

15   Ibid., p. 97.

16   Ibid., p. 161.

17   Ibid., p. 173.

18   Ibid., p. 166.

19   Ibid., p. 253.

20   Ibid., p. 87.

21   Ibid., p. 101.

22   Ibid., p. 184.

23   Ibid., p. 253.

24   Ibid., p. 92.

25   Ibid., p. 186.

26   Ibid., p. 88.

27   Ibid., p. 254.

28   Fodor, "The Ottoman Empire, Byzantium and Western Christianity," pp. 43–51.

29   Mixson, *The Crusade of 1456*, p. 143.

30   Ibid., p. 220.

31   Ibid., p. 88.

32   Ibid., p. 93.

33   Pálosfalvi, *From Nicopolis to Mohács*, p. 187.

34   Mixson, *The Crusade of 1456*, p. 106.

35   Ibid., pp. 124–25.

36   Ibid., p. 125.

37   Ibid.,, p. 141.

38   Lendvai, *The Hungarians*, pp. 75–85.

39   Nevđn Zeynep Yelçe, "The Making of Sultan Süleyman: A Study of Process/es of Image-Making and Reputation Management," Ph.D. Dissertation, Sabancı University, 2009, p. 189.

40   Anthony Bryer, "Skanderbeg, National Hero of Albania," *History Today*, Vol. 12, No. 6, June 1962, p. 434.

41   DeVries, "Lack of a Western European Military Response," p. 545.

42   Eric Brockman, *The Two Sieges of Rhodes, 1480–1522*, John Murray, London, 1969, pp. 5–6.

43 Norman Housley, *Crusading and the Ottoman Threat, 1453–1505*, Oxford University Press, Oxford, 2013, p. 99.

44 Ibid., p. 91.

45 This victory had a grim aftermath for Skanderbeg, as a number of his key lieutenants, including Moisi Golemi, pursued the defeated Ottomans too vigorously, fell into an ambush, and were returned to Constantinople, where they were publicly flayed alive, what was left of them being thrown to the dogs.

46 Bernd J. Fischer and Oliver Jens Schmitt, *A Concise History of Albania*, Cambridge University Press, Cambridge, 2022, p. 54.

47 Venice would be left suspended on the front line of Ottoman expansion and for the rest of the republic's history would be forced into the problematic position of balancing her commercial interests with her physical security. See Maria Pia Pedani, *The Ottoman-Venetian Border (15th–18th Centuries)*, Edizioni Ca' Foscari, Venice, 2017.

48 Aleksandar Krstić, "'Which Realm Will You Opt For?' – The Serbian Nobility Between the Ottomans and the Hungarians in the 15th Century," in Srđan Rudić and Selim Aslantaş (eds.), *State and Society in the Balkans Before and After Establishment of Ottoman Rule*, Institute of History, Belgrade, 2017, pp. 129–64.

49 Matei Cazacu, "The Reign of Dracula in 1448," in Kurt W. Treptow (ed.), *Dracula: Essays on the Life and Times of Vlad the Impaler*, Histria Books, Las Vegas, 2019, pp. 65–72.

50 "Letter of Vlad the Impaler to Matthias Corvinus," in Treptow (ed.), *Dracula*, p. 414.

51 Tasin Gemil, *Romanians and Ottomans in the XIVth–XVIth Centuries*, Editura Enciclopedică, Bucharest, 2009, p. 196.

52 Raymond T. McNally and Radu R. Florescu, *Dracula: Prince of Many Faces*, Hachette, New York, 2009, p. 182.

53 McNally and Florescu, *Dracula*, p. 182.

54 Kurt W. Treptow, "Aspects of the Ottoman Campaign against Vlad III Dracula in 1462," in Treptow (ed.), *Dracula*, pp. 151–67.

55 Stavrides, *The Sultan of Vezirs*, p. 142.

56 Andrei Pogăciaş, "Dracula Against the Ottomans," *Medieval Warfare*, Vol. 11, No. 4, p. 29.

57 Konstantin Mihailovic and Benjamin A. Stolz, *Memoirs of a Janissary*, Markus Wiener Publishers, Princeton, 2011, p. 67.

58 Pogăciaş, "Dracula Against the Ottomans," p. 32. Among the dead were Hamza, *bey* of Nicopolis, and Yunus, *bey* of Silistra. In deference to their rank, they had been impaled on longer stakes than those accorded the Ottoman rank and file, so that they stood out higher than the men they had commanded.

59 Kurt W. Treptow, "Ottoman Chronicles Concerning Vlad the Impaler," in Treptow (ed.), *Dracula*, p. 401.

60 Treptow (ed.), *Dracula*, p. 390.

61 Kate Fleet, "Ottoman Expansion in the Mediterranean," in Suraiya Faroqhi and Kate Fleet (eds.), *The Cambridge History of Turkey, Vol. 2*, p. 143.

62 Fleet, "Ottoman Expansion in the Mediterranean," p. 143.

63 The Ottomans placed a vassal king, Matija Šabančić, the son of Radivoj Kotromanić, uncle of Stephen Tomašević, on the throne of Bosnia in 1465. Srdjan Rudić, "Bosnian Nobility after the Fall of the Kingdom of Bosnia in 1463," in Srđan Rudić and Selim Aslantaş (eds.), *State and Society in the Balkans Before and After Establishment of Ottoman Rule*, Institute of History, Belgrade, 2017, pp. 103–28.

64 Housley, *Crusading and the Ottoman Threat*, p. 23.

65 Filipović, "Key to the Gate of Christendom," p. 156.

66 Ibid., p. 151. See also Davor Salihović, "The Process of Bordering at the Late Fifteenth-Century Hungarian-Ottoman Frontier," *History in Flux*, No. 1, 2019, pp. 93–120.

67 Boyar, "Ottoman Expansion in the East," p. 84.

68 Allouche Adel, *The Origins and Development of the Ottoman-Safavid Conflict (906–962/1500–1555)*, Verlag, Berlin, 1983, p. 13.

69 Liviu Pilat and Ovidiu Cristea, *The Ottoman Threat and Crusading on the Eastern Border of Christendom during the 15th Century*, Brill, Leiden, 2018, p. 137.

70 In an ominous gesture, Mehmed sent a victory mission to Cairo bearing the head of Zaynal Mirza, the oldest son of Uzun Hasan.

71 See Viorel Panaitein, "The Legal and Political Status of Wallachia and Moldavia in Relation to the Ottoman Porte," pp. 9–42; Radu G. Paun, "Enemies Within: Networks of Influence and the Military Revolts against the Ottoman Power (Moldavia and Wallachia, Sixteenth-Seventeenth Centuries)," pp. 209–52; and Ovidiu Cristea, "The Friend of My Friend and the Enemy of My Enemy: Romanian Participation in Ottoman Campaigns," pp. 253–74, in Gábor Kármán and Lovro Kunčević (eds.), *The European Tributary States of the Ottoman Empire in the Sixteenth and Seventeenth Centuries*, Brill, Leiden, 2013. See also Viorel Panaite, "From Allegiance to Conquest: Ottomans and Moldo-Wallachians from the Late Fourteenth to Mid Sixteenth Centuries," *Revue Études Sud-Est Europe*, Vol. XLIX, No. 1–4, 2011, pp. 197–212; Viorel Panaite, "Power Relationships in the Ottoman Empire: Sultans and the Tribute Paying Princes of Wallachia and Moldavia (16th–18th Centuries)," *Revue Études Sud-Est Europe*, Vol. XXXVII–Vol. XXXVIII, No. 51–52, 1999–2000, pp. 47–78.

72 Pilat and Cristea, *Ottoman Threat*, p. 152.

73 See Natalia Królikowska, "Sovereignty and Subordination in Crimean-Ottoman Relations (Sixteenth-Eighteenth Centuries)," pp. 43–66, and Mária Ivanics, "The Military Co-operation of the Crimean Khanate with the Ottoman Empire in the Sixteenth and Seventeenth Centuries," pp. 275–300, in Kármán and Kunčević (eds.), *European Tributary States*.

74 The two men would alternate in power during intervals that were almost as brief as they were regular. Having just begun his thirteenth year as *voivode*, Radu was first usurped by Basarab in November 1473. He regained the throne a month later, lost it again in March 1474, immediately won it back, lost it again in summer that same year, won it back in October, and was finally succeeded by Basarab when he died in January 1475.

75 Albert Weber, "Vlad's Sequel," *Medieval Warfare*, Vol. 11, No. 4, pp. 34–37.

76 McNally and Florescu, *Dracula*, p. 221.

77 Filipović, "Key to the Gate of Christendom," p. 155.

78 Ştefan Andreescu, "Military Actions of Vlad the Impaler in Southeastern Europe in 1476," in Treptow (ed.), *Dracula*, pp. 171–86.

79 David Nicolle, *Knights of Jerusalem: The Crusading Order of Hospitallers, 1100–1565*, Osprey, Oxford, 2008; Helen J. Nicholson, *The Knights Hospitaller*, Boydell Press, Woodbridge, 2003.

80 Indicative of just how parlous a state the Hospitallers had been reduced to at this point, by the time it secured control of Rhodes, the Order had mortgaged its revenues for the next twenty years to the Florentine moneylender Peruzzi.

81 Malcolm, *Agents of Empire*, p. 79.

82 The Ottoman admiral, whose cognomen Palaiologos indicated his descent from the last reigning dynasty of the Byzantine Empire, was accompanied by two other Greek renegades, Mehmed II's diplomatic councilor Demetrius, who was to meet his death during the operation, and Antonius Meligalos, who hailed from Rhodes. Presumably, this was a deliberate gambit intended to rouse the Greek Orthodox population of the island against the Catholic Hospitallers. Apparently, it failed.

83 Brockman, *Two Sieges of Rhodes*, p. 67.

84 Ibid., p. 72.

85 Theresa M. Vann and Donald J. Kagay, *Hospitaller Piety and Crusader Propaganda: Guillaume Caoursin's Description of the Ottoman Siege of Rhodes, 1480*, Taylor & Francis Group, Milton, 2015, p. 191.

86 Vann and Kagay, *Hospitaller Piety*, pp. 194–95.

87 Ibid., pp. 195–96.

88 Ibid., p. 203. Misac Pasha's decision to account for his failure in person carried with it a considerable risk, and Mehmed was indeed so enraged his initial response was to order his unfortunate subordinate executed, though the sultan ultimately relented.

89 Fleet, "Ottoman Expansion in the Mediterranean," p. 145.

90 Christine Isom-Verhaaren, *The Sultan's Fleet*, p. 83.

91 Housley, *Crusading and the Ottoman Threat*, p. 93.

92 Kenneth M. Setton, *The Papacy and the Levant*, American Philosophical Society, Philadelphia, 1976, p. 364.

93 Housley, *Crusading and the Ottoman Threat*, p. 93.

94 Daniel Baloup, "Castilian Ships to Italy's Aid. Two Letters from Diego Rodríguez de Almela about the Crusade of Otranto (1481)," *Le Moyen Age*, Vol. 2, April 2022, pp. 449–65.

95 Vann and Kagay, *Hospitaller Piety*, p. 181.

96 Yelçe, "The Making of Sultan Süleyman," pp. 186–87.

97 Fleet, "Ottoman Expansion in the Mediterranean," p. 146.

98 In 1489, d'Aubusson was awarded the title of Cardinal by Pope Innocent VIII.

99 Pedani, *Ottoman-Venetian Border*, p. 88.

100 The exemplary loyalty of Gedik Pasha gained him nothing; he was summarily arrested and executed on the orders of the very sultan he had established on the throne. Bayezid had already arranged for the liquidation of his nephew, Cem's elder son, Oguzhan. Cem's younger son, Murad, also took shelter with the Hospitallers. When Rhodes fell to Suleiman the Magnificent in 1522, the sultan had Murad and his two sons, who lived on the island as converted Christians, executed for apostasy, while Murad's wife and daughters were shipped to Constantinople as slaves.

CHAPTER 4: PERSIA, AND THE FALL OF THE MAMLUKS

1 See Borislav Grgin, "The Ottoman Influences on Croatia in the Second Half of the Fifteenth Century," *Historische Beiträge*, Vol. 21, No. 23, 2002, pp. 87–103.

2 Suzana Miljan and Hrvoje Kekez, "The Memory of the Battle of Krbava (1493) and the Collective Identity of the Croats," *The Hungarian Historical Review*, Vol. 4, No. 2, 2015, pp. 283–313. While Ivan fell in the battle, his kinsman, Bernardin Frankopan, was able to make good his escape.

3 Filipović, "Key to the Gate of Christendom," p. 164.

4 It was not until Süleyman I's campaign in 1538 that the Porte secured its rule over the region known as Budjak (southern Bessarabia between the Lower Dniester and the Lower Prut-Danube) and the coastline between the Dniester and Dnieper rivers.

5 Liviu Pilat, "The 1487 Crusade: A Turning Point in the Moldavian-Polish Relations," *Medieval and Early Modern Studies for Central and Eastern Europe*, No. II, 2010, p. 123.

6 Krzysztof Wawrzyniak, "Ottoman-Polish Diplomatic Relations in the Sixteenth Century," MA Thesis, Bilkent University, 2003, p. 28.

7 Pilat and Cristea, *Ottoman Threat*, p. 268.

8 Snezhana Rakova, "The Last Crusaders: Felix Petančić and the Unfulfilled Crusade of 1502," in Snežana Rakova and Gheorghe Lazăr (eds.), *Au Nord et au Sud du Danube: Dynamiques politiques, sociales et religieuses dans le pasée*, Editura Istros, Braila, 2019, pp. 49–73.

9 Housley, *Crusading and the Ottoman Threat*, p. 36.

10 Cihan Yüksel Muslu, *The Ottomans and the Mamluks: Imperial Diplomacy and Warfare in the Islamic World*, I.B. Tauris, London, 2014, n.p.

11 Ayfer Karakaya Stump, "Subjects of the Sultan, Disciples of the Shah: Formation and Transformation of the Kizilbash/Alevi Communities in Ottoman Anatolia," Ph.D. Dissertation, Harvard University, 2008; Andrew J. Newman, *Safavid Iran: Rebirth of a Persian Empire*, I.B. Tauris, New York, 2006.

12 Abisaab Rula Jurdi, *Converting Persia: Religion and Power in the Safavid Empire*, I.B. Tauris, London, 2004.

13 Abdurrahman Atçil, "The Safavid Threat and Juristic Authority in the Ottoman Empire during the 16th Century," *International Journal of Middle East Studies*, Vol. 49, No. 2, May 2017, pp. 295–314.

14 Zarinebaf-Shahr Fariba,: "Qızılbash 'Heresy' and Rebellion in Ottoman Anatolia During the Sixteenth Century," *Anatolia Moderna – Yeni Anadolu*, No. 7, 1997, pp. 1–15.

15 Alan Mikhail, *God's Shadow: Sultan Selim, his Ottoman Empire, and the Making of the Modern World*, W.W. Norton & Co., New York, 2020, p. 203.

16 Mikhail, *God's Shadow*, p. 194.

17 Yasin Arslantaş, "Depicting The Other: Qizilbash Image in the 16th Century Ottoman Historiography," MA Thesis, İhsan Doğramacı Bilkent University, 2013, p. 60.

18 Arslantaş, "Depicting The Other," p. 60.

19 Ibid., p. 62.

20 One of the Timurid successors, Zahir al-Din Muhammad Babur, would make his own mark on history by marching south and imposing his dynasty, the Moghuls, on India.

21 Shaybani's skull was delivered to the Mamluk sultan in Cairo with an accompanying message that it now served as nothing more than a cup for drinking the blood of the enemies of the shah. Ismail was flexing on the Mamluks, the other established Sunni regional power, during this period at least as much as he was on the Ottomans. It was also in 1511 that Ismail sent envoys through Mamluk territory bearing the *kiswa* (ritual covering) for the Kaaba in Mecca, an honor assumed by the Mamluks to be theirs by right. The following year, Ismail sent a document to the Mamluks proving he was a direct descendant of the Prophet Muhammad and therefore had an inherited right to rule the entire Islamic world. Albrecht Fuess, "Three's a Crowd: The Downfall of the Mamluks in the Near Eastern Power Struggle, 1500–1517," in Reuven Amitai and Stephan Conermann (eds.), *The Mamluk Sultanate from the Perspective of Regional and World History*, Bonn University Press, Bonn, 2019, pp. 431–52.

22 Mikhail, *God's Shadow*, p. 194.

23 Boyar, "Ottoman Expansion in the East," p. 105.

24 Arslantaş, "Depicting The Other," p. 84.

25 Ibid., p. 65.

26 The only survivors were two of Ahmed's sons, who managed to escape by fleeing to seek refuge with the Mamluks. Their reprieve was brief, however, as both died the following spring from the plague outbreak then rampant in Egypt.

27 According to the account of Muṣṭafā ʿĀlī:

> It is related that one day Pīrī Pasha expressed his fear by saying to the lands-conquering ruler [Selīm], "If you are going to kill me in the end under some pretext, it would be appropriate if you were to release me [from life] promptly." The ruler of the world laughed much and stated jokingly and with innuendo: "This is also my intention; and to render you lifeless and to raze you to the ground is what my heart and mind desire. However, there is no man who can take your place and there exists no person who can properly perform the duties of the vizier. Otherwise, to fulfill your desire is an easy task."

See H. Erdem Çýpa, *The Making of Selim: Succession, Legitimacy, and Memory in the Early Modern Ottoman World*, Indiana University Press, Bloomington, 2017.

28 Palmira J. Brummett, *Ottoman Seapower and Levantine Diplomacy in the Age of Discovery*, State University of New York Press, Albany, NY, 1994, p. 29.

29 Brummett, *Ottoman Seapower*, p. 31.

30 Ibid., p. 30.

31 Ibid., p. 36.

32 Kenneth M. Setton, "Pope Leo X and the Turkish Peril," *Proceedings of the American Philosophical Society*, Vol. 113, No. 6, December 1969, p. 371.

33 Setton, "Pope Leo X and the Turkish Peril," p. 372.

34 Rudi Matthee, "Iran's Relations with Europe in the Safavid Period: Diplomats, Missionaries, Merchants and Travel," in Rudi Matthee (ed.), *The Safavid World*, Routledge, Abingdon, 2021, p. 9.

35 Giovanni-Tommaso Minadoi, *The War Between the Turks and the Persians* (translated by Abraham Hartwell), I.B. Tauris, London, 2019, p. 2.

36 Selim also unilaterally abandoned a planned joint Venetian–Ottoman military venture against Emperor Maximilian, in which the Ottomans would have supported the Venetians against the Empire by sending 10,000 horsemen from Bosnia to Friuli and a fleet from Valona (Avlonya) to Apulia.

37 Adel, *Origins and Development of the Ottoman-Ṣafavid Conflict*, pp. 111–12.

38 Mikhail, *God's Shadow*, p. 258.

39 Spencer C. Tucker (ed.), *Middle East Conflicts from Ancient Egypt to the 21st Century, Vol. I: A–F*, ABC-Clio, Santa Barbara, 2019, p. 1,573. Zahhak "Snake Shoulder" was a demonic figure from Zoroastrian mythology who evolved into the definitive evil tyrant in the *Shāhnāmah*, the great national epic poem of Iran.

40 Finkel, *Osman's Dream*, p. 105.

41 Mikhail, *God's Shadow*, p. 257.

42 Ibid., p. 258.

43 Ibid., p. 260.

44 Boyar, "Ottoman Expansion in the East," p. 109.

45 Rogerson, *Last Crusaders*, p. 175.

46 Luís Vaz de Camões, *The Lusiads*, trans. Landweg White, Oxford University Press, Oxford, 1997, p. 217.

47 Riza Yıldırım, "Turkomans Between Two Empires: The Origins of the Qizilbash Identity in Anatolia (1447–1514)," Ph.D. Dissertation, Bilkent University, 2008, p. 582.

48 Kaveh Farrokh, *Iran at War, 1500–1988*, Osprey, Oxford, 2011, p. 24.

49 Yıldırım, "Turkomans Between Two Empires," p. 583.

50 Ibid., p. 584.

51 Portuguese intervention in the Indian Ocean only represented the final stage of a fiscal crisis that had compromised the Mamluk state over the past century; see Abdul Azim Islahi, "Economic and Financial Crises in the Fifteenth-Century Egypt: Lessons from the History," *Islamic Economic Studies*, Vol. 21, No. 2, November 2013, pp. 71–93.

52 These included the existing works at Novo Brdo, Sidrekapsi, Srebrenica, and Serez inherited from Roman times, and the previously underdeveloped deposits at Trepca and Zaplana exploited by Ottoman engineers. Just one of these sites, Sidrekapsi (east of Thessaloniki) was producing as much as ten tons of silver per year when Suleiman took the throne. A French visitor in 1554 estimated that Sidrekapsi's 600 furnaces and 6,000 miners were generating around 300,000 ducats in annual revenue. Erlichman, *Conquest, Tribute and Trade*, pp. 140–41.

53 Ágoston, *The Last Muslim Conquest*, p. 2.

54 Andrew C. Hess, "The Ottoman Conquest of Egypt (1517) and the Beginning of the Sixteenth-Century World War," *International Journal of Middle East Studies*, Vol. 4, No. 1, January 1973, p. 75.

55 Casale, *Ottoman Age of Exploration*, p. 12.

56 Setton, "Pope Leo X and the Turkish Peril," p. 411.

57 Christopher de Bellaigue, *The Lion House: The Coming of a King*, The Bodley Head, London, 2022, p. 29.

58 Setton, "Pope Leo X and the Turkish Peril," p. 411.

59 Mikhail, *God's Shadow*, pp. 332–33.

60 Jose Cutillas, "Did Shah 'Abbās I Have a Mediterranean Policy?" *Journal of Persianate Studies*, No. 8, 2015, p. 255.

61 Brummett, *Ottoman Seapower*, p. 45.

62 Farrokh, *Iran at War*, p. 16.

63 The Safavid domain's central location, along the major east–west and north–south trade routes of western Eurasia, meant that it was a crossroads for the flow of goods and precious metals in all directions. Locally produced raw silk supplied not only Iranian requirements for the weaving of brocade and taffeta, but also the needs of the flourishing silk industries of Turkey and Italy. This gave Iran a favorable balance of trade with the West that was partly drained by its deficit with India and the East Indies arising from imports of cotton textiles, indigo, sugar, and spices, despite the

lucrative export of cavalry horses, dyestuffs for the Indian cotton textile industry, and a wide variety of nuts, fruits, and other processed foods. "Persia is like a big caravanserai which has only two doors, the one on the side of Turkey by which silver from the west enters," observed a prominent European resident in Isfahan in 1660, the French cleric Raphael du Mans, exiting via the Persian Gulf for the Indies, "where all the silver of the world unloads, and from there as if fallen into an abyss, it does not re-emerge." Najaf Haider, "Global Networks of Exchange, the India Trade, and the Mercantile Economy of Safavid Iran," in Irfan Habib (ed.), *A Shared Heritage: The Growth of Civilization in India and Iran*, Tulika Books, New Delhi, 2002, p. 197.

CHAPTER 5: SULEIMAN, PART I

1 Max Kortepeter, "The Turkish Question in the Era of the Fifth Lateran Council (1512–17)," in Donald Little (ed.), *Essays on Islamic Civilization*, E.J. Brill, Leiden, 1976, pp. 162–63.

2 Ágoston, *The Last Muslim Conquest*, p. 138.

3 Nancy Bisaha, "Reactions to the Fall of Constantinople and the Concept of Human Rights," in Housley (ed.), *Reconfiguring the Fifteenth-Century Crusade*, p. 309.

4 Malcolm, *Useful Enemies*, p. 78.

5 Adam S. Francisco, *Martin Luther and Islam: A Study in Sixteenth-Century Polemics and Apologetics*, Brill, Leiden, 2007, p. 68.

6 Francisco, *Martin Luther and Islam*, p. 69.

7 Ágoston, *The Last Muslim Conquest*, p. 143.

8 James D. Tracy, *Emperor Charles V, Impresario of War: Campaign Strategy, International Finance, and Domestic Politics*, Cambridge University Press, New York, 2002, p. 53.

9 The scale of this intervention provoked a significant backlash. In his first Imperial *Diet* in 1519, convened to recognize his ascendancy as emperor, Charles was confronted with a demand to disassociate himself from his corporate sponsors: "We should consider how to limit the big trading companies which have up to now governed with their money and acted in their own interest and caused damage, disadvantages and burden to the empire, its citizens and subjects through their rise in prices." Greg Steinmetz, *The Richest Man Who Ever Lived: The Life and Times of Jacob Fugger*, Simon & Schuster, New York, 2015, pp. 163–64. When Charles imposed taxes to repay his obligations to Fugger, Spain erupted in the Revolt of the Comuneros, an insurrection that posed a potentially mortal threat to Habsburg authority. But the emperor needed Fugger more than he needed the people. After Fugger reminded Charles that without Fugger's support he would "not have acquired the Imperial Crown, as I can attest with the written statement of all the delegates of Your Imperial Majesty," and politely insisted the emperor would "graciously recognize my faithful, humble service, dedicated to the greater

well-being of Your Imperial Majesty, and order that the money which I have paid out, together with the interest upon it, shall be reckoned up and paid, without further delay," Charles not only met this obligation but ordered the *diet* to back off from its attempts to pass legislation that would break up the Fugger commercial empire: "In no way will I allow the merchants to be prosecuted." Steinmetz, *The Richest Man*, p. 190.

10   Geoffrey Parker, *Emperor: A New Life of Charles V*, Yale University Press, New Haven, 2019, p. 106. This speech was drafted for Charles by his chancellor, Mercurino de Gattinara, who hoped to unite not just Castile but all Europe behind the authority of the young new emperor: "At last to me *imperium* has been conferred by the single consent of Germany with God, as I deem, willing and commanding… For from God himself alone is empire." Patrick Wyman, *The Verge*, Grand Central Publishing, New York, 2021, p. 317.

11   Andrew W. Devereux, *The Other Side of Empire: Just War in the Mediterranean and the Rise of Early Modern Spain*, Cornell University Press, Ithaca, 2020, pp. 127–54.

12   Francisco, *Martin Luther and Islam*, p. 41.

13   Yelçe, "The Making of Sultan Süleyman," pp. 269, 270.

14   Norman Housley, "Crusading as Social Revolt: The Hungarian Peasant Uprising of 1514," *The Journal of Ecclesiastical History*, Vol. 49, No. 1, January 1998, pp. 1–28.

15   Paul H. Freedman, "Atrocities and Executions of the Peasant Rebel Leaders in Late Medieval and Early Modern Europe," in Suzana Miljan and Gerhard Jaritz (eds.), *At the Edge of the Law: Socially Unacceptable and Illegal Behaviour in the Middle Ages and the Early Modern Period*, Medium Aevum Quotidianum, Krems, 2012, pp. 73–81. See also Dénes Harai, "Couronne ardente et danse anthropophage: le décryptage de la symbolique de l'exécution de György Dózsa, chef révolté en Hongrie (1514)," *Histoire, Économie et Société*, Vol. 38, No. 1, March 2019, pp. 32–48.

16   Rogerson, *Last Crusaders*, p. 269.

17   Edgár Artner, "Magyarország és az apostoli szentszék viszonya a mohácsi vészt megelőző években, 1521–1526," in Imre Lukinich (ed.), *Mohácsi Emlékkönyv*, Királyi Magyar Egyetemi Nyomda, Budapest, 1926, p. 70.

18   Yelçe, "The Making of Sultan Süleyman," p. 255.

19   Ibid., p. 222.

20   Ibid., p. 232.

21   Ibid., p. 233.

22   Ibid., p. 266.

23   Pálosfalvi, *From Nicopolis to Mohács*, p. 390.

24   Oláh was subsequently murdered by an Ottoman rival bearing an old grudge, but that was outside of the sultan's remit.

25   Ágoston, *The Last Muslim Conquest*, p. 156.

26   Yelçe, "The Making of Sultan Süleyman," p. 271.

27 Ibid., p. 270.

28 Michael Heslop, "The Hospitallers' Dodecanese Islands Before and During the 1522 Siege of Rhodes: Help or Hindrance?" in Simon David Phillips (ed.), *The 1522 Siege of Rhodes: Causes, Course and Consequences*, Taylor & Francis Group, Milton, 2022, pp. 63–84.

29 Yelçe, "The Making of Sultan Süleyman," p. 269.

30 Brockman, *Two Sieges of Rhodes*, p. 114.

31 Ibid., p. 115.

32 Leïla Temime Blili, *The Regency of Tunis, 1535–1666: Genesis of an Ottoman Province in the Maghreb*, The American University in Cairo Press, Cairo, 2021, n.p.

33 Brockman, *Two Sieges of Rhodes*, pp. 115–16.

34 Simon David Phillips, "How Much Did the Hospitallers Know? Information, Misinformation, and Preparation," in Phillips (ed.), *The 1522 Siege of Rhodes*, pp. 40–60.

35 Yelçe, "The Making of Sultan Süleyman," p. 228.

36 Ibid., p. 273. For the agenda and influence of Gattinara, see John M. Headley, *Church, Empire and the World: The Quest for Universal Order, 1520–1640*, Ashgate, Aldershot, 1997.

37 Murphey, *Ottoman Warfare*, p. 119.

38 Kelly DeVries, "How the Sultan Won? Suleiman's Successful Siege Tactics at Rhodes," in Phillips (ed.), *The 1522 Siege of Rhodes*, p. 93.

39 DeVries, "How the Sultan Won?" p. 94.

40 Ibid., p. 95.

41 Brockman, *Two Sieges of Rhodes*, p. 135.

42 After the conquest of Rhodes, Ahmed asked for and obtained authority in Egypt, where he rebelled in 1524; when his revolt was put down he was executed, his head being borne back to Constantinople.

43 Brockman, *Two Sieges of Rhodes*, p. 148.

44 DeVries, "How the Sultan Won?" p. 98.

45 Brockman, *Two Sieges of Rhodes*, p. 149–50.

46 Richard Hakluyt, *The Principal Navigations Voyages Traffiques & Discoveries of the English Nation, Vol. V*, James MacLehose & Sons, Glasgow, 1904, p. 47.

47 Brockman, *Two Sieges of Rhodes*, p. 153.

48 Yelçe, "The Making of Sultan Süleyman," p. 191.

49 Ibid., p. 273.

50 Ibid., p. 274.

51 Ibid., p. 275.

52 Fleet, "Ottoman Expansion in the Mediterranean," p. 155.

53 Yelçe, "The Making of Sultan Süleyman," p. 310.

54 Ibid., p. 212.

55 Ibid., p. 204.

56 András Kubinyi, "The Battle of Szavaszentdemeter-Nagyolaszi (1523): Ottoman Advance and Hungarian Defence on the Eve of Mohacs," in Géza Dávid and Pál Fodor (eds.), *Ottomans, Hungarians, and Habsburgs in Central Europe: The Military Confines in the Era of Ottoman Conquest*, Brill, Leiden, 2000, pp. 71–115.

57 Adrian Magina, "As the Turks Moved on Them… New Documents on Severin and the Lower Parts of the Hungarian Kingdom Before the Battle of Mohács," in Zsuzsanna Kopeczny (ed.), *In Central and South-East Europe: Life under the Shadow of the Ottoman Empire's Expansion (15th–16th Centuries)*, Editura MEGA, Cluj-Napoca, 2021, pp. 93–100.

58 Gregory Miller, "Holy War and Holy Terror: Views of Islam in German Pamphlet Literature, 1520–1545," Ph.D. Dissertation, Boston University, 1994, p. 67.

59 Miller, "Holy War and Holy Terror," p. 70.

60 Francisco, *Martin Luther and Islam*, p. 70.

61 Malcolm, *Useful Enemies*, p. 78.

62 Parker, *Emperor*, p. 122.

63 Eric Leland Saak, *Luther and the Reformation of the Later Middle Ages*, Cambridge University Press, New York, 2017, p. 245.

64 William Bradford, *Correspondence of The Emperor Charles V*, Richard Bentley, London, 1850, p. 133.

65 James Reston, *Defenders of the Faith*, Penguin, New York, 2009, p. 168.

66 Attila Bárány, *The Jagiellonians in Europe: Dynastic Diplomacy and Foreign Relations*, Hungarian Academy of Sciences, Debrecen, 2016, p. 144.

67 Bellaigue, *The Lion House*, pp. 59–60.

68 Yelçe, "The Making of Sultan Süleyman," p. 416.

69 Parker, *Emperor*, pp. 151–52.

70 Christine Isom-Verhaaren, *Allies with the Infidel: The Ottoman and French Alliance in the Sixteenth Century*, I.B. Tauris, London, 2011.

71 Reston, *Defenders of the Faith*, pp. 171–72. In order to rationalize the Franco-Ottoman alliance from the Porte's point of view, Ibrahim Peçevi, an important Ottoman official-turned-historian, recounted the myth of a French princess, a daughter of the king of France who, during the reign of Murad II, had been seized by corsairs and brought into the Ottoman harem, where she had given birth to Murad's son, the future Mehmed II. The same story was embellished and reshaped by Evliya Çelebi, who maintained the French princess captured was in reality the mother of Prince Cem, the son of Mehmed II who had lost the succession war to his brother Bayezid and had subsequently taken refuge in Rhodes before passing into exile in Europe. According to Çelebi, Cem had faked his death and then inveigled his way into becoming king of France; it was his descendants who still governed the realm when Suleiman rose to power, explaining their receptivity to his offer of partnership. Eksigil, "Ottoman Visions of the West," pp. 35–36.

72 Fodor, *Unbearable Weight of Empire*, p. 76.

73 The League of Cognac was expanded to include England on 30 April 1527, when Henry VIII and Francis signed the Treaty of Westminster, pledging to combine their forces against Charles.

74 Parker, *Emperor*, p. 326.

75 Reston, *Defenders of the Faith*, p. 183. Reflecting the archduke's familiarity with the classics, this phrase was adapted from Horace: "*Nam tua res agitur, paries cum proximus ardet*" ("For it is your business, when your neighbor's house is ablaze").

76 Reston, *Defenders of the Faith*, p. 184.

77 Stephen A. Fischer-Galati, *Ottoman Imperialism and German Protestantism, 1521–1555*, Harvard University Press, Cambridge, 1958, p. 26.

78 Reston, *Defenders of the Faith*, p. 184.

79 Rudi Matthee and José Cutillas Ferrer (eds.), *The Spanish Monarchy and Safavid Persia in the Early Modern Period: Politics, War and Religion*, Albatros, Valencia, 2016.

80 Yelçe, "The Making of Sultan Süleyman," p. 362.

81 Ferenc Petruska, "State Organisational Prelude and Aftermath of the Battle of Mohács," in Attila Bárány (ed.), *Mercenaries and Crusaders*, Hungarian Research Network, Debrecen, 2024, pp. 425–36.

82 William H. McNeill, *Europe's Steppe Frontier, 1500–1800*, University of Chicago Press, Chicago, 1964, p. 20.

83 Pálosfalvi, *From Nicopolis to Mohács*, p. 426.

84 Yelçe, "The Making of Sultan Süleyman," p. 391.

85 Pálosfalvi, *From Nicopolis to Mohács*, p. 427.

86 Yelçe, "The Making of Sultan Süleyman," p. 375.

87 Reston, *Defenders of the Faith*, p. 189.

88 Stephen Turnbull, *The Art of Renaissance Warfare: From the Fall of Constantinople to the Thirty Years' War*, Greenhill Books, London, 2006, p. 112.

89 Láslo M. Alföldi, "The Battle of Mohacs, 1526," in János M. Bak and Béla K. Király, (eds.), *From Hunyadi to Rákóczi: War and Society in Late Medieval and Early Modern Hungary*, Columbia University Press, New York, 1982, pp. 189–202.

90 Pálosfalvi, *From Nicopolis to Mohács*, p. 440.

91 Reston, *Defenders of the Faith*, p. 192.

92 Bellaigue, *Lion House*, p. 61.

93 André Clot, *Suleiman the Magnificent*, Saqi Books, London, 2012, p. 58.

94 "May Allah be merciful to him and punish those who misled his inexperience," Suleiman noted in his diary when confirmation of the king's demise was brought to him. "It was not my wish that he should be thus cut off, while he had scarcely tasted the sweets of life and royalty." Reston, *Defenders of the Faith*, p. 194.

95 Rogerson, *Last Crusaders*, p. 247.

96 Attila Pfeiffer, "The Battle of Christians and Ottomans in the Southwest of Bačka: From the Battle of Mohács to the Peace of Zsitvatorok," *Istraživanja*, No. 28, 2017, p. 88.

97   Pfeiffer, "Battle of Christians and Ottomans," p. 88.

98   Benedek Péter Tóta, "Hungary Overrun: A Source of Fortitude and Comfort," *Moreana*, Vol. 40, No. 156, December 2003, p. 32.

99   Yelçe, "The Making of Sultan Süleyman," p. 412.

100 An exception was Venice, which, eager to ensure "the world may know of our most loving disposition" towards the sultan, dispatched Marco Minio, now Duke of Heraklion, to Constantinople in order to express its "singular pleasure" at the Ottoman triumph in Hungary. Bellaigue, *Lion House*, p. 65.

101 Yelçe, "The Making of Sultan Süleyman," p. 422.

102 Ibid., pp. 424–25.

103 Ibid., pp. 422–23.

104 Ibid., p. 496.

105 Ibid., p. 423.

106 Ibid., p. 425.

107 Hakluyt, *Principal Navigations*, pp. 61–62.

108 Ibid., pp. 61–62. p. 346.

109 Leslie S. Domonkos, "The Battle of Mohács as a Cultural Watershed," in Bak and Király (eds.), *From Hunyadi to Rákóczi*, pp. 203–24.

110 Reston, *Defenders of the Faith*, p. 200.

111 Originally a poem titled *A magyar nép zivataros századaiból* (*From the Stormy Centuries of the Hungarian nation*) written by poet Ferenc Kölcsey in 1823, the anthem was set to music composed by romantic composer Ferenc Erkel in 1844.

CHAPTER 6: SULEIMAN, PART II

1   Jourden T. Moger, "Gog at Vienna: Three Woodcut Images of the Turks as Apocalyptic Destroyers in Early Editions of the Luther Bible," *Journal of the Bible and Its Reception*, Vol. 3, No. 2, July 2016, p. 263.

2   Yelçe, "The Making of Sultan Süleyman," pp. 443–44.

3   Reston, *Defenders of the Faith*, p. 272.

4   Ágoston, *The Last Muslim Conquest*, p. 184. Remarkably, Habardanecz and Weichselberger could not communicate Suleiman's answer to their master as they were unable to read the sultan's Turkish-language letter and did not know its content. No qualified interpreter in Vienna could translate the document, and its intent was only revealed when the Ottoman army was marching against Vienna in 1529.

5   Bellaigue, *Lion House*, p. 86.

6   Reston, *Defenders of the Faith*, p. 272. Venice urged Ibrahim to send the promised Ottoman military aid to John promptly and to order the *sanjak-bey* of Bosnia to attack Ferdinand's possessions in Carniola, Carinthia, and Styria.

7   Bellaigue, *Lion House*, p. 87.

8   Ágoston, *The Last Muslim Conquest*, p. 180.

9   Karl A. Schimmer, *The Bulwark of Christendom: The Turkish Sieges of Vienna 1529 & 1683*, John Murray, London, 1847, p. 6.

10 Ágoston, *The Last Muslim Conquest*, p. 177.

11 Kenneth M. Setton, *The Papacy and the Levant, 1204–1571, Volume III: The Sixteenth Century*, The American Philosophical Society, Philadelphia, 1984, p. 327.

12 Yelçe, "The Making of Sultan Süleyman," p. 500. The *Serenissima* was, as usual, careful to play both sides. Visiting the Ottoman camp at Belgrade, Venetian secretary Maximo Leopardi assured Ibrahim the treaty was binding only on Francis, who had to sign in order to have his sons back, and that Venice had no part in it. This shameless double-dealing exasperated the Habsburg ambassador in Venice to the point he advised the emperor that, "Now is the time to root out that venomous plant [of the Republic] and strike a blow at people who have always been the promotors of discord among Christian princes and the constant abettors of the Turk." Finlay, "Prophecy and Politics in Istanbul," p. 10.

13 Reston, *Defenders of the Faith*, p. 279.

14 To this day, Vienna can be appreciated as the easternmost extension of Western Europe; the next important city downstream on the Danube – called Pressburg by the Germans, Pozsony by the Hungarians, and Bratislava by the Slovaks – is where eastern Europe begins.

15 Christian Pfister and Rudolf Brazdil, "Climatic Variability in Sixteenth-Century Europe and its Social Dimension: A Synthesis," *Climatic Change*, Vol. 43, No. 1, September 1999, p. 23.

16 Christian Pfister, et al., "Daily Weather Observations in Sixteenth-Century Europe," *Climatic Change*, Vol. 43, No. 1, September 1999, p. 130.

17 Reston, *Defenders of the Faith*, p. 280.

18 Ibid., p. 280.

19 Schimmer, *The Bulwark of Christendom*, p. 12.

20 To the Italians, these were the *guastadori* ("despoilers"); to the French, *faucheurs* ("mowers") and *ecorcheurs* ("flayers"); but the Germans labeled them simply the *sackman*, either because they filled their own sacks with plunder, or emptied those of other people.

21 Schimmer, *The Bulwark of Christendom*, p. 9.

22 Ibid., p. 13.

23 Reston, *Defenders of the Faith*, p. 276.

24 Parker, *Emperor*, pp. 189–90.

25 Stephen A. Fischer-Galati, "Ottoman Imperialism and the Lutheran Struggle for Recognition in Germany, 1520–1529," *Church History*, Vol. 23, No. 1, March 1954, pp. 46–67.

26 Francisco, *Martin Luther and Islam*, p.68.

27 George W. Forell, "Luther and the War against the Turks," *Church History*, Vol. 14, No. 4, December 1945, p. 261.

28 Forell, "Luther and the War against the Turks," pp. 267–68.

29 Ibid., p. 266.

30 Ibid., p. 264.

31 Thomas More, "A Dialogue Concerning Heresies," in Thomas M.C. Lawler, Germain Marchadour, and Richard C. Marius (eds.), *The Yale Edition of The Complete Works of St Thomas More: Volume 6*, Yale University Press, New Haven, 1981, p. 413.

32 More, "A Dialogue Concerning Heresies," p. 373.

33 Malcolm, *Useful Enemies*, p. 92.

34 Parker, *Emperor*, p. 197.

35 Beresford J. Kidd, *Documents Illustrative of the Continental Reformation*, Clarendon, Oxford, 1967, p. 301.

36 In 1539, 1545, and 1546, Protestant representatives entered negotiations with the court of Henry VIII for an alliance between England and the League.

37 Reston, *Defenders of the Faith*, p. 281.

38 Piotr Tafiłowski, "Anti-Turkish Literature in 15th–16th Century Europe," *Tarih İncelemeleri Dergisi*, Vol. 30, No. 1, 2015, pp. 231–80.

39 Miller, *Holy War*, pp. 71–72.

40 Ibid., p. 76.

41 Ibid., p. 77.

42 Francisco, *Martin Luther and Islam*, p. 73.

43 Miller, *Holy War*, pp. 73–74.

44 Ibid., p. 75. It should be borne in mind, Luther's deference to the secular power of the emperor in no way represented his desire to arrive at any kind of *modus vivendi* with the pope. To the contrary:

> The Pope, along with his following, is not content with fighting, murdering, and robbing his [armed] antagonists: he also burns, anathematizes, and persecutes the innocent [non-violent], pious, and orthodox Christians. He is the real Antichrist, for he does these things while sitting in the temple of God as head of the Church, which the Turk does not do. But if the Pope is Antichrist, the Turk is the devil incarnate. It is against both that our prayers, and those of Christendom, must be directed.

John W. Bohnstedt, "The Infidel Scourge of God: The Turkish Menace as Seen by German Pamphleteers of the Reformation Era," *Transactions of the American Philosophical Society*, Vol. 58, No. 9, 1968, p. 24.

45 Miller, *Holy War*, p. 75.

46 Ibid., p. 74.

47 Martin Luther, *Works, Vol. 46: The Christian in Society*, ed. Robert C. Schultz; trans. Charles M. Jacobs, Concordia, Saint Louis, 1967, p. 185.

48 Luther, *Works*, p. 184.

49 Ibid., p. 185. On a more practical level, Luther also advised that we should "not insufficiently arm ourselves and send our poor Germans off to be slaughtered. If we are not going to make an adequate, honest resistance that will have some reserve power, it

would be far better not to begin a war," (ibid., p. 201). For more on the pamphlet war against the Ottomans, see Bohnstedt, "The Infidel Scourge of God," pp. 1–58.

50   Forell, "Luther and the War against the Turks," p. 262. In his *Wie sich Prediger und Leien halten sollen, so der Türck das Deutsche Land überfallen wurde*, Johannes Brenz, another Lutheran reformer, made the case that "those who fight against the Turk should be confident in the knowledge that, although God sometimes gives victory to the Turk, their fighting will not be in vain, but will serve to check the Turk's advance, so that he will not become master of all the world." So far as Luther was concerned, the ultimate destiny of Christendom was out of his hands. If his exegesis could mobilize the faithful, then so much the good; if not, "then may our dear Lord Christ help and come down from Heaven with the Last Judgment and smite both Turk and Pope to the Earth, together with all tyrants and all the godless, and deliver us from all sins and from all evil." Forell, "Luther and the War against the Turks," p. 271.

51   Bohnstedt, "The Infidel Scourge of God," p. 46.

52   Ibid., p. 47.

53   Parker, *Emperor*, p. 228.

54   Fischer-Galati, *Ottoman Imperialism and German Protestantism*, p. 112.

55   Parker, *Emperor*, p. 229.

56   Roger B. Merrimen, *Suleiman the Magnificent, 1520–1566*, Harvard University Press, Cambridge, 1944, p. 106.

57   Reston, *Defenders of the Faith*, p. 281.

58   Ágoston, "Ottoman and Habsburg Military Affairs," p. 17.

59   When finally demolished at the end of the 19th century, the perimeter of the old wall would become the famous *Ringstraße*, or "Ring Street," which to this day defines the financial and cultural core of Vienna.

60   Reston, *Defenders of the Faith*, p. 282.

61   Fletcher Pratt, *The Battles that Changed History*, Hanover House, Garden City, 1956, p. 142.

62   After taking an exact account of all provisions in the city, the troops were divided into messes of four men; and to each mess a ration was allotted of eight pounds of bread and fifteen measures of wine. It was later found necessary to diminish this quantity to some of the foreign *Landsknechte*, who, unaccustomed to the potent Austrian wines, were being incapacitated for duty. Five-eighths of their wine and two pounds of their bread were struck off.

63   The Graf von Salm hailed from a small fief on the Rhine River not far from Speyer and Worms. He resided at Salm Hoff, near Marchegg in Lower Austria.

64   Schimmer, *The Bulwark of Christendom*, p. 18. Of Austria's states-deputies and councilors, the following were in the city: George von Puechhaim, governor of Lower Austria; Nicholaus Rabenhaupt, chancellor; Rudolph von Hohenfeld, Felician von Pottschach, privy councilors; John von Greissenegg, commandant of Vienna, and of the foot militia of the city; Melchior von Lamberg; Trajan von Auersberg; Bernardin Ritschen; Helfreich von Meggun; Erasmus von Obritschen;

Raimund von Dornberg; Otto von Achterdingen; John Apfalterer; Siegfried von Kollonitsch; Reinbrecht von Ebersdorf; and Hans von Eibenswald. The magistrates remaining in the city were Wolfgang Troy, burgomaster; Paul Bernfuss, judge; and the councilors Sebastian Eiseler, Sebastian Schmutz, and Wolfgang Mangold.

65 Schimmer, *The Bulwark of Christendom*, p. 19.

66 Kim Seabrook, "Siege of Vienna (1529): The Devil Let Loose," *P.O.E.*, 8 March, 2018, www.prisonersofeternity.co.uk/siege-of-vienna-1529-the-devil-let-loose/. While invaluable as an eyewitness account, von Labach's chronicle of the siege (*Warhafftige handlung Wie und welcher massen der Türck die stat Ofen und Wien belegert*, 1530) embodies the official Habsburg line, stylized as a clash of civilizations between Christianity and Islam: "In the year of our lord 1529, Sultan Suleiman, the Cruel tyrant and sworn enemy of the Christian faith, set out for Vienna with all his military equipment and forces in order to defeat Christianity and subjugate it."

67 Schimmer, *The Bulwark of Christendom*, p. 21.

68 Seabrook, "Siege of Vienna (1529)."

69 Schimmer, *The Bulwark of Christendom*, p. 24.

70 Seabrook, "Siege of Vienna (1529)."

71 Schimmer, *The Bulwark of Christendom*, p. 27.

72 The financial disadvantage of the Habsburg Crown, hamstrung as it was by being forced to appeal to the regional powerbrokers of its diverse and far-flung domains for funds, as opposed to the unitary Ottoman state, were never more evident than in this instance. At this moment of supreme trial, funding for the Habsburg river flotilla on the Danube was 40,000 florins in arrears. With great effort, a mere 800 florins had been made available. Schimmer, *The Bulwark of Christendom*, p. 37.

73 Some of the arrows, probably discharged by persons of distinction, were enhanced with costly fabric, painted, and even set with pearls, and were kept long afterwards as curiosities.

74 Seabrook, "Siege of Vienna (1529)."

75 Jan D. Lorenzen and Hannes Schuler, "1529: The Siege of Vienna," *The History Channel*, 2006, www.youtube.com/watch?v=pPXDgUrg5E8&t=2261s.

76 Lorenzen and Schuler, "1529: The Siege of Vienna." Roggendorf subsequently endowed the informant with a pension for life in return for his intelligence; this generous compensation may have expressed some consideration of the manner in which it had been extracted.

77 Schimmer, *The Bulwark of Christendom*, p. 33.

78 Ibid., p. 35.

79 Lorenzen and Schuler, "1529: The Siege of Vienna."

80 Ibid.

81 In his account, Peter Stern asserts that Suleiman made one last effort to extort at least a financial concession from Vienna, offering to break off the siege on payment to him of 200,000 florins. In their response to this ransom note, the city fathers could only lament that unfortunately, the keys to their treasury had gone missing.

82 Bellaigue, *Lion House*, p. 96.

83 Paula Sutter Fichtner, "From Rhetoric to Memory: Islam, Ottomans, and Austrian Historians in the Renaissance," *Nordic Journal of Renaissance Studies*, Vol. 16, 2019, p. 62.

84 Lorenzen and Schuler, "1529: The Siege of Vienna."

85 Nevdn Zeynep Yelçe, "Between a 'Brilliant Retreat' and a 'Tragic Defeat': Ottoman Narratives of the 1529 and 1683 Sieges of Vienna," in Seyfi Kenan and Selçuk Akşin Somel (eds.), *Dimensions of Transformation in the Ottoman Empire from the Late Medieval Age to Modernity*, Brill, Leiden, 2021, pp. 305–23.

86 Schimmer, *The Bulwark of Christendom*, pp. 44–45.

87 Sandberg, "Going Off to the War in Hungary," p. 359.

88 Ibid., p. 359.

89 Arnold J. Toynbee, "The Lost Opportunities of the Scandinavians and the Osmanlis," *A Study of History, Vol. II, Annex VII*, Oxford University Press, New York, 1934, p. 444.

90 See Theodore K. Rabb, "If Only It Had Not Been such a Wet Summer," in Robert Cowley (ed.), *What If?*, Putnam's, New York, 1999, pp. 107–120; Richard W. Bulliet, "The Other Siege of Vienna and the Ottoman Threat: An Essay in Counter-Factual History," *ReOrient*, Vol. 1, No. 1, Autumn 2015, pp. 11–22.

91 Palmira Brummett concludes: "Indeed, when one looks at the campaigns against the Habsburgs, one is tempted to say that it was not superior forces or a lack of valor that kept the Ottomans from taking Vienna but a combination of water and mud." Palmira Brummett, "The River Crossing: Breaking Points (Metaphorical and 'Real') in Ottoman Mutiny," in Jane Hathaway (ed.), *Rebellion, Repression, Reinvention: Mutiny in Comparative Perspective*, Praeger, Westport, 2001, p. 219.

92 Bellaigue, *Lion House*, p. 130.

93 Ferdinand also commenced reconstruction and modernization of the defenses of Vienna; see Ingrid Mader, "Die Wiener Befestigung vom 16. bis zum 19. Jahrhundert – Ein Überblick," *Fundort Wien*, Berichte zur Archäologie, 13/2010, pp. 27–55.

94 Bellaigue, *Lion House*, p. 132.

95 Ágoston, *The Last Muslim Conquest*, p. 200.

96 Tracy, *Emperor Charles V*, p. 138.

97 Gábor Ágoston, "Information, Ideology, and Limits of Imperial Policy: Ottoman Grand Strategy in the Context of Ottoman–Habsburg Rivalry," in Fodor (ed.), *The Battle for Central Europe*, p. 101.

98 Finlay, "Prophecy and Politics in Istanbul," p. 12.

99 Ágoston, *The Last Muslim Conquest*, p. 189.

100 Ibid., p. 189.

101 Reston, *Defenders of the Faith*, p. 331.

102 Ágoston, *The Last Muslim Conquest*, p. 189. This enormous host demanded a commensurately vast commitment from the imperial treasury. Francis also

contributed, in his own way; Charles redirected over 400,000 ducats from the French ransom negotiated at the Peace of Cambrai in order to help pay his troops.

103 Gábor Szántai, *33 Castles, Battles, Legends: Hungarian-Ottoman War Series, #1*, Gábor Szántai, Oklahoma City, 2017.

104 Bellaigue, *Lion House*, p. 148.

105 Reston, *Defenders of the Faith*, p. 333.

106 Bellaigue, *Lion House*, p. 151.

107 Heike Krause and Christoph Sonnlechner, "Landscape and Fortification of Vienna after the Ottoman Siege of 1529," *The Hungarian Historical Review*, Vol. 7, No. 3, 2018, pp. 451–76.

108 For an alternative perspective on this narrative see Zsuzsa Barbarics-Hermanik, "Die Renaissancefestung auf dem Grazer Schloßberg als strategische Antwort auf die Expansion des Osmanischen Reiches," *Historisches Jahrbuch der Stadt Graz*, Heft 49/50, 2019–2020, pp. 93–128.

109 Bariska István, "A Nádasdy család és az 1532 évi oszmán-török hadjárat," *Vasi Szemle*, Vol. 72, No. 1–6, 2018, p. 52.

110 Reston, *Defenders of the Faith*, p. 337.

111 Tasin Gemil, *Romanians and Ottomans in the XIVth–XVIth Centuries*, Editura Enciclopedică, Bucharest, 2009, p. 235

CHAPTER 7: SULEIMAN, PART III

1 The treaty was specifically between the Porte and Ferdinand, not with the Habsburgs generally; the war between Suleiman and Charles dragged on. Doria defeated the Ottoman fleet sent to evict him from Koroni in 1533, but the following year an Ottoman army laid siege to the city, which fell on 1 April 1534.

2 Clot, *Suleiman the Magnificent*, p. 55.

3 Rudi Matthee, "The Safavid-Ottoman Frontier: Iraq-I Arab as seen by the Safavids," *The International Journal of Turkish Studies*, Vol. 9, No. 1–2, Summer 2003, pp. 157–73.

4 Bellaigue, *Lion House*, p. 204.

5 Finlay, "Prophecy and Politics in Istanbul," p. 27. Gritti would be dead by the end of the year, killed alongside his two sons during the siege of Medgyes (Mediaş) in Transylvania.

6 The Ottomans formally cemented their authority at the terminus of the Persian Gulf when they marched into Basra on 26 December 1546. Jean-Louis Bacqué-Grammont, "The Eastern Policy of Süleymân the Magnificent, 1520–1533," in Halil Inalcik and Cemal Kafadar (eds.), *Süleymân the Second and His Time*, Isis Press, Istanbul, 1993, pp. 219–28.

7 Ágoston, *The Last Muslim Conquest*, p. 200.

8 James D. Tracy, "The Road to Szigetvár. Ferdinand I's Defense of His Hungarian Frontier, 1548–1564," *The Austrian History Yearbook*, No. 44, 2013, pp. 17–46.

9   Pálffy, *Hungary Between Two Empires, 1526–1711*, Indiana University Press, Bloomington, 2021, p. 31.

10 Zahit Atçıl, "The Ottoman Conquest of Buda(pest): Sultan Suleiman's Imperial Letter of Victory," in Hani Khafipour (ed.), *The Empires of the Near East and India: Source Studies of the Safavid, Ottoman, and Mughal Literate Communities*, Columbia University Press, New York, 2019, p. 283.

11 Atçıl, "The Ottoman Conquest," p. 284.

12 Ibid., p. 285.

13 Ibid., p. 285.

14 Ibid., p. 285.

15 Ágoston, *The Last Muslim Conquest*, p. 206.

16 Parker, *Emperor*, p. 306.

17 Zahit Atçıl, "State and Government in the Mid-Sixteenth Century Ottoman Empire: The Grand Vizierates of Rüstem Pasha (1544–1561)," Ph.D. Dissertation, University of Chicago, 2015, p. 75.

18 Claudia Römer and Nicolas Vatinin, "The Hungarian Frontier and Süleyman's Way to Szigetvár according to Ottoman Sources," in Fodor (ed.), *The Battle for Central Europe*, p. 344.

19 Pálffy, *Hungary Between Two Empires*, p. 18.

20 Römer and Vatinin, "The Hungarian Frontier," pp. 345–46.

21 Zahit Atçıl, "The Foundation of Peace-Oriented Foreign Policy in the Sixteenth-Century Ottoman Empire: Rüstem Pasha's Vision of Diplomacy," in Tracey A. Sowerby and Christopher Markiewicz (eds.), *Diplomatic Cultures at the Ottoman Court, c.1500–1630*, Routledge, New York, 2021, p. 140.

22 Boyar, "Ottoman Expansion in the East," p. 123.

23 Atçıl, "State and Government," p. 76.

24 Boyar, "Ottoman Expansion in the East," p. 121.

25 Interestingly, Suleiman was accompanied on this campaign by the French ambassador, Gabriel de Luetz.

26 Zahit Atçıl, "Why Did Süleyman the Magnificent Execute His Son Şehzade Mustafa in 1553?" *Osmanlı Araştırmaları*, No. 48, 2016, pp. 67–103. Rüstem did not have to wait long for his career to recover from the tactical decision – which may well have been taken on his initiative – to remove him from office. On 29 September 1555, after arriving at the Topkapi Palace for the regular *divan* meeting, Ahmed Pasha was executed by order of the sultan. That same day, Rüstem was restored to the grand vizierate.

27 Zahit Atçıl, "Warfare as a Tool of Diplomacy: Background of the First Ottoman-Safavid Treaty in 1555," *Turkish Historical Review*, Vol. 10, No. 1, June 2019, pp. 3–24.

28 Atçıl, "The Foundation of Peace-Oriented Foreign Policy," p. 141.

29 Bayezid's youngest son, not yet a year old, who had been left behind in Bursa, was subsequently executed on the orders of his grandfather, the sultan.

30 For a study of Western diplomatic approaches to Tahmasp during this period, see Kurosh Meshkat, "The Journey of Master Anthony Jenkinson to Persia, 1562–1563," *Journal of Early Modern History*, Vol. 13, No. 2, 2009, pp. 209–28.

31 Cutillas, "Did Shah 'Abbās I Have a Mediterranean Policy?" p. 263.

32 Rudi Matthee, "Distant Allies: Diplomatic Contacts Between Portugal and Iran in the Reign of Shah Tahmasb, 1524–1576," in Rudi Matthee and Jorge Flores (eds.), *Portugal, The Persian Gulf and Safavid Persia*, Peeters, Leuven, 2011, p. 235.

33 Laurence Lockhart, "European Contacts with Persia, 1350–1736," in Peter Jackson and Laurence Lockhart (eds.), *The Cambridge History of Iran VI: The Timurid and Safavid Periods*, Cambridge University Press, Cambridge, 1986, p. 384.

34 Parker, *Emperor*, p. 299–300.

35 Ibid., p. 313.

36 Mary also recoiled at the prospect of outsourcing the suppression of heresy to *Landskneche* mercenaries: "I know not whether God wishes to reduce those who have strayed [*les desvoyez*] to obedience by men whose lives are so execrable." Tracy, *Emperor Charles V*, p. 205.

37 Parker, *Emperor*, p. 315.

38 Hugh Thomas, *The Golden Empire: Spain, Charles V, and the Creation of America*, Random House, New York, 2010, pp. 374–75.

39 Erlichman, *Conquest, Tribute and Trade*, p. 214.

40 Pálffy, *Hungary Between Two Empires*, p. 48.

41 Željko Zidarić, "The Assassination of Frater Georgius Martinusius," www.academia.edu/87109015/1551_The_last_year_of_Juraj_George_Utje%C5%A1enovi%C4%87s_life, September 2022, p. 13.

42 The garrison was sustained by large quantities of the local red wine. Someone who saw the wine dripping from the whiskers of the defenders during the siege claimed they were fortified by bulls' blood, an appellation that has stuck for the local vintage to this day. Turnbull, *The Art of Renaissance Warfare*, p. 121.

43 Fodor, *Unbearable Weight*, pp. 114–15.

44 Dino Mujadžević, "Ulama-bey, Sanjakbey of Bosnia and Požega," *Prilozi Za Orijentalnu Filologiju*, No. 60, 2017, pp. 251–58.

45 Erlichman, *Conquest, Tribute and Trade*, p. 223.

46 Richard Ehrenberg, *Capital & Finance in the Age of the Renaissance: A Study of the Fuggers and their Connections*, Harcourt, Brace, New York, 1928, p. 107.

47 Erlichman, *Conquest, Tribute and Trade*, p. 229.

48 Ironically, the Lutherans hated and feared the Calvinists almost as much as they did the Catholics, so with Lutheran princes as the negotiators with the Catholics at Augsburg, the official choice of Protestantism was to be limited to Lutheranism as defined by the 1530 Augsburg Confession, with the alternative sects being denied any legal recognition. MacCulloch, *The Reformation*, p. 283.

49 Ágoston, The *Last Muslim Conquest*, p. 222.

50 Janos B. Szabó, "An Example for Some – A Lesson for Others: The First Ottoman Siege of Szigetvár and the Military Campaigns of 1555–1556," in Péter Kasza (ed.), *Remembering a Forgotten Siege: Szigetvár, 1556*, MTA Bölcsészettudományi Kutatóközpont, Budapest, 2016, pp. 121–47.

51 Atçıl, "The Foundation of Peace-Oriented Foreign Policy," p. 137.

52 James D. Tracy, "Tokaj, 1565: A Habsburg Prize of War, and an Ottoman Casus Belli," in Fodor (ed.), *The Battle for Central Europe*, p. 362.

53 Szabolcs Varga, "Miklós Zrínyi, Captain-General of Szigetvár (1561–1566) – His Organisational Activity and Death," in Fodor (ed.), *The Battle for Central Europe*, p. 390.

54 Alfredo Alvar Ezquerrain, "Intangible Cultural Exchanges: Christendom's Eastern Frontier as Seen by Philip II's Ambassador Chantonnay (1566)," in Fodor (ed.), *The Battle for Central Europe*, p. 248.

55 Kutse Altın, "The Reconstruction of the Motives and Activities of the Last Campaign of Kanuni Sultan Süleyman," in István Zimonyi (ed.), *Altaic and Chagatay Lectures: Studies in Honour of Éva Kincses-Nagy*, University of Szeged, Szeged, 2021, p. 28.

56 József Kelenik, "The Sieges of Szigetvár and Gyula, 1566," in Fodor (ed.), *The Battle for Central Europe*, p. 400.

57 Römer and Vatinin, "The Hungarian Frontier," in Fodor (ed.), *The Battle for Central Europe*, p. 349.

58 Sokollu Mehmed then had his own nephew, Szokollu Musztafa, appointed as the new pasha of Buda.

59 Damir Karbićin, "The Memory of Nicholas IV of Zrin and the Battle of Szigetvár in Croatia and the Balkans," in Fodor (ed.), *The Battle for Central Europe*, p. 510.

60 Alvar Ezquerrain, "Intangible Cultural Exchanges," in Fodor (ed.), *The Battle for Central Europe*, p. 247.

61 Ibid., p. 252.

62 Varga, "Miklós Zrínyi," p. 395.

63 Alvar Ezquerrain, "Intangible Cultural Exchanges," in Fodor (ed.), *The Battle for Central Europe*, p. 255.

64 Beginning with Brne Karnarutić's poem *Vazetje Sigeta Grada*, written within a decade of the event, and perhaps most famously represented in Miklós Zrínyi's 1651 epic poem *Szigeti Veszedelem* and Ivan Zajc's 1876 opera *Nikola Šubić Zrinjski*, the siege of Szigetvár, much like the Battle of Kosovo, would evolve into a marker for the national identity of subsequent generations.

65 Géza Pálffy, "Hungary, Vienna and the Defence System against the Ottomans in the Age of Süleyman," in Fodor (ed.), *The Battle for Central Europe*, p. 336.

66 The Ottomans also built a funerary monument at Szigetvár on the hill where the sultan's tent had been pitched and where his first burial had taken place. It was linked to a mosque, a *tekke* of dervishes who maintained it, and a barracks, until

Habsburg troops completely destroyed the entire site when they reclaimed Szigetvár in the 17th century.

67   Zsuzsa Barbarics-Hermanik, "The Entangled Memory of the Battle of Sziget (1566) in Early Modern Europe," in Fodor (ed.), *The Battle for Central Europe*, pp. 479–507. On 29 December 1566 a twenty-year-old Danish nobleman named Tycho Brahe lost a part of his nose in a duel in the Hanseatic city of Rostock located on the Baltic Sea, on the north coast of the Holy Roman Empire. The duel was the consequence of a heated dispute at a Christmas celebration in the house of one of his professors, which had taken place two days previously. It was about a mathematical formula that this young gentleman, who was a student at the University of Rostock at that time, had used to predict the death of Sultan Suleiman the Magnificent based on a lunar eclipse that he had observed over the city on 28 October. In addition to enthusiastically jumping to this conclusion, he had also composed and posted some dramatic poems in Latin hexameters at the university announcing his astrological foretelling of the death of the "Great Turk" – and in doing so, he brought this to public attention. Unfortunately, the news soon arrived that Suleiman had indeed died, but almost seven weeks before the lunar eclipse.

CHAPTER 8: THE MEDITERRANEAN, PART I

1   Rogerson, *Last Crusaders*, p. 314.

2   Nicolle, *Cross & Crescent*, p. 227.

3   Elina Gugliuzzo, "Sea Power and the Ottomans in the Early Modern Mediterranean World," in Georgios Theotokis and Aysel Yıldız (eds.), *A Military History of the Mediterranean Sea*, Brill, Leiden, 2018, pp. 79–91.

4   Andrew C. Hess, *The Forgotten Frontier: A History of the Sixteenth Century Ibero-African Frontier*, The University of Chicago Press, Chicago, 1978.

5   Rogerson, *Last Crusaders*, p. 277. See also "The African Horizon," in Andrew W. Devereux, *The Other Side of Empire: Just War in the Mediterranean and the Rise of Early Modern Spain*, Cornell University Press, Ithaca, 2020, pp. 95–126.

6   Barbara Fuchs and Yuen-Gen Liang, "A Forgotten Empire: The Spanish-North African Borderlands," *Journal of Spanish Cultural Studies*, Vol. 12, No. 3, 2011, pp. 261–73.

7   Ágoston, *The Last Muslim Conquest*, p. 194.

8   Tracy, *Emperor Charles V*, p. 145.

9   Parker, *Emperor*, p. 238.

10   Bartolomé Yun-Casalilla, *Iberian World Empires and the Globalization of Europe 1415–1668*, Palgrave Macmillan, Singapore, 2019, p. 244. See also Ruth Pike, *Enterprise and Adventure: the Genoese in Seville and the Opening of the New World*, Cornell University Press, Cornell, 1966.

11   Erlichman, *Conquest, Tribute, and Trade*, p. 86.

12 Juan M. Carretero Zamora, "Fiscalidad extraordinaria y deuda: el destino del servicio de las cortes de Castilla, 1535–1537," *Espacio, Tiempo y Forma*, Series IV, 1995, pp. 11–47.

13 Tracy, *Emperor Charles V*, p. 156.

14 Malcolm, *Useful Enemies*, p. 69.

15 Bellaigue, *Lion House*, p. 191.

16 Bruce Ware Allen, "Emperor vs. Pirate: Tunis, 1535," *Military History Quarterly*, Vol. 26, No. 2, Winter 2014, pp. 58–63.

17 Rogerson, *Last Crusaders*, p. 299.

18 Bellaigue, *Lion House*, p. 192.

19 Blili, *The Regency of Tunis*, n.p.

20 Moulay Hasan was not graced with a long term of office after regaining his throne. In 1537, a number of Tunisian cities, including Sousse and Kairouan, rebelled. Many of these were pacified by Andrea Doria during a campaign in 1539, but the following year they passed under the authority of Turgut Reis. In 1542, the sultan set sail for Italy, intending to muster support, but in his absence, his son rebelled, claiming his father intended to become a Christian in order to hand the country over to the Spanish, and seized the throne as Sultan Abu al-Abbas Ahmad III (Moulay Ahmad). Moulay Hasan returned to Tunis in the company of a mercenary, Giovanni Battista Lofredi, but he was captured and given the choice between execution or being blinded. Opting for the latter, he passed into exile and died in 1549.

21 María José Rodríguez-Salgado, "'No Great Glory in Chasing a Pirate': The Manipulation of News during the 1535 Tunis Campaign," *Mediterranea*, Vol. XVII, No. 49, August 2020, p. 440.

22 Bellaigue, *Lion House*, p. 196.

23 Rodríguez-Salgado, "'No Great Glory in Chasing a Pirate,'" p. 439.

24 Ibid., p. 440.

25 Ibid., p. 423.

26 Ibid., p. 423.

27 Malcolm, *Useful Enemies*, p. 116.

28 Fleet, "Ottoman Expansion in the Mediterranean," p. 159.

29 Svatopluk Soucek, "Naval Aspects of the Ottoman Conquests of Rhodes, Cyprus and Crete," *Studia Islamica*, No. 98/99, 2004, p. 232.

30 Soucek, "Naval Aspects," p. 230.

31 Erlichman, *Conquest, Tribute and Trade*, p. 199–200.

32 Dryden G. Liddle, "Power and Finance at the Court of Charles V: Francisco de los Cobos, Royal Secretary of Charles V," Ph.D. Dissertation, The Open University, 2010, p. 277. Charles promised not to resort to such expedients in future, "even in times of great necessity," but this pledge was hardly credible, and the arbitrary nature of his confiscations was provoking unrest at the elite level. The *Cortes* of 1538 warned Charles, "Taking the Indies money from merchants in Seville, and giving them *juros* causes much damage. There are those from whom it is taken who

can no longer do their business and, little by little, trade will decline, because they cannot make payments, and also royal revenues will decline because of the cessation of trade." Ibid., p. 278.

33 Ali Rıza İşipek, "Preveza Battle from a Naval Perspective," in Dejanirah Couto, Feza Gunergun, and Maria Pia Pedani (eds.), *Seapower, Technology and Trade: Studies in Turkish Maritime History*, Piri Reis University, Istanbul, 2014, pp. 41–47. Other Venetian territories on the Dalmatian coast were also attacked: Bar and Ulcinj were both besieged by local Ottoman forces.

34 Tracy, *Emperor Charles V*, p. 165.

35 Francesco Caprioli, "The 'Sheep' and the 'Lion': Charles V, Barbarossa, and Habsburg Diplomatic Practice in the Muslim Mediterranean (1534–1542)," *Journal of Early Modern History*, No. 25, 2021, pp. 392–421.

36 Blili, *The Regency of Tunis*, n.p.

37 Parker, *Emperor*, pp. 271–72.

38 Erlichman, *Conquest, Tribute and Trade*, p. 202.

39 Christine Isom-Verhaaren, "'Barbarossa and His Army Who Came to Succor All of Us': Ottoman and French Views of Their Joint Campaign of 1543–1544," *French Historical Studies*, Vol. 30, No. 3, Summer 2007, p. 405.

40 Christine Isom-Verhaaren, "Was there Room in Rum for Corsairs? Who Was an Ottoman in the Naval Forces of the Ottoman Empire in the 15th and 16th Centuries?" *Osmanlı Araştırmaları/The Journal of Ottoman Studies*, Vol. XLIV, 2014, p. 256.

41 Akif Tunc, "An Ottoman Winter," *History Today*, Vol. 74, No. 9, September 2024, p. 24.

42 The admiral of the French fleet, Leone Strozzi, the Knight of St John and prior of Capua, sought help from Turgut Reis in an ambitious plan to capture the future King Philip II of Spain who was sailing from Spain to Genoa in 1547.

43 Elvira Vilches, *New World Gold: Cultural Anxiety and Monetary Disorder in Early Modern Spain*, University of Chicago Press, Chicago, 2010; Mauricio Drelichman, "The Curse of Moctezuma: American Silver and the Dutch Disease," *Explorations in Economic History*, Vol. 42, No. 3, July 2005, pp. 349–80.

44 In blatant defiance of the still-binding 1312 papal decree against usury, Charles approved "lending at interest" in 1543. Erlichman, *Conquest, Tribute and Trade*, p. 208.

45 Mustafa loathed Sinan, who he described as "viciously contentious, impetuous with words, dreadful, and tyrannical!" A neutral observer, Venetian ambassador Bernardo Navagero, described him as having:

> ... little experience with maritime affairs, since he has not had any duty or practice related to the army: he is obeyed and esteemed more than any other captain on account of his brother. There is nothing he commands that is not carried out and he wants to be recognized by all as a leader. He has little courtesy and speaks with no reservation. He is irascible, or better said furious... His brother, the Pasha, loves him extremely and favours him excessively, and cannot support any talk against him. He therefore does all

that enters his head without any fear whatsoever, and everyone stays quiet even if greatly abused… There is no securer way to prevent Mustafa's succession than to prohibit with the armada his passage [to Constantinople].

Christine Isom-Verhaaren, "Was there Room in Rum for Corsairs?" pp. 256–57.

46   Rogerson, *Last Crusaders*, p. 318. For an introduction to the corsair's career, see Özlem Kumrular, "Turgut Reis (1485–1565): The Uncrowned King of the Mediterranean," in Couto, Gunergun, and Pedani (eds.), *Seapower, Technology and Trade*, pp. 48–52.

47   Malcolm, *Useful Enemies*, p. 118.

48   This kind of favoritism was endemic in the Ottoman hierarchy during this period. Rüstem Pasha also disliked Hayreddin's heir and successor in Algeria, Hasan Pasha. Recalled to Constantinople in September 1551 to explain his refusal to surrender to Rüstem the income of a *hamam* built by his father, Hasan was replaced as *beylerbey* by the grand vizier's favorite, Salah Reis. These distinctions could become a matter of life and death; the corsair Piri Reis was executed in 1553 as punishment for his failed expedition against Hormuz, whereas *enderun* graduate Hadım Süleyman Pasha, despite his similar failure before Diu in 1538, faced no penalty and later rose to become the grand vizier. Emrah Safa Gürkan, "The Centre and the Frontier: Ottoman Cooperation with the North African Corsairs in the Sixteenth Century," *Turkish Historical Review*, Vol. 1, No. 2, November 2010, p. 149.

49   Fleet, "Ottoman Expansion in the Mediterranean," pp. 162–63.

CHAPTER 9: THE MEDITERRANEAN, PART II

1   Marco Gemignani, "The Navies of the Medici: The Florentine Navy and Navy of the Sacred Military Order of St Stephen, 1547–1648," in Hattendorf and Unger (eds.), *War at Sea in the Middle Ages and the Renaissance*, pp. 169–85. Responsibility for the Tuscan fleet was entrusted to Piero Machiavelli, son of the (in)famous Florentine political philosopher Niccoló. Raymond E. Role, "Cosimo de' Medici's Holy Navy," *MHQ: The Quarterly Journal of Military History*, Vol. 15, No. 1, Autumn 2002, pp. 76–85.

2   Rogerson, *Last Crusaaders*, p. 346.

3   Bruce Ware Allen, "Disaster at Djerba," *History Today*, Vol. 67, No. 6, June 2017, pp. 24–35.

4   Rogerson, *Last Crusaders*, p. 348.

5   Roger Crowley, *Empires of the Sea: The Siege of Malta, the Battle of Lepanto, and the Contest for the Center of the World*, Random House, New York, 2008, p. 79.

6   Malcolm, *Agents of Empire*, p. 82.

7   Bruce Ware Allen, *The Great Siege of Malta: The Epic Battle between the Ottoman Empire and the Knights of St. John*, University of New England Press, Lebanon, 2015, p. 87.

8   Charles Stephenson, *The Fortifications of Malta, 1530–1945*, Osprey, Oxford, 2004.

9   Maciej Jonasz, "The Great Siege of Malta, 1565," *Strategy & Tactics*, No. 346, May–June 2024, p. 37.

10   Allen, *The Great Siege of Malta*, p. 126.

11   Ibid., p. 116.

12   Ibid., p. 170.

13   T. Mikail, P. Duggan, and Mahmut Demir, "Gelibolulu Mustafa Ali's 1591 Narrative of the Siege of Malta, and his Account of the Death of Turgut Reis related in his *Künhü'l-Ahbar*," in Maroma Camilleri (ed.), *Besieged Malta 1565, Vol. II*, Heritage Malta, Valletta, 2015, pp. 57–66.

14   Fleet, "Ottoman Expansion in the Mediterranean," p. 164.

15   Crowley, *Empires of the Sea*, p. 152.

16   Tony Rothman, "The Great Siege of Malta," *History Today*, Vol. 57, No. 1, January 2007, p. 17.

17   Crowley, *Empires of the Sea*, p. 123.

18   Ibid., p. 157.

19   No help would be coming from Venice, which had a long history of distrust and distaste towards the Hospitallers. During the siege of Rhodes in 1522, the republic had actively prevented volunteers from going to the assistance of the Order, and when the knights finally surrendered it sent a special envoy to congratulate the sultan. In 1536 and again in 1553 the republic announced a *sequestro*, a freezing of all assets and revenues of the Order in Venetian territory, as a way of strengthening its demand that the Hospitallers, dubbed the *cavalieri ladri* (thieving knights) in the republic's complaint to the pope, stop plundering Venetian and Ottoman ships. Relations deteriorated during the 1580s to the point where Venice sequestered all property of the Order in its territory, dismissed all knights who were in Venetian government service, and banned all trade and correspondence with Malta, declaring that the knights were henceforth to be treated as enemy corsairs. The Hospitallers responded by announcing they would seize any Venetian ships they encountered at sea. The imbroglio had to be defused by the intervention of the pope. Malcolm, *Agents of Empire*, p. 81 and p. 312.

20   Allen, *The Great Siege of Malta*, p. 223.

21   Rothman, "The Great Siege of Malta," p. 18.

22   Tamás Kiss, "The Selimiye Mosque, The Apocalypse and the War of Cyprus (1570–71): The Creation of Selim II's Sultanic Image," in Irina Vainovski-Mihai (ed.), *New Europe College Yearbook 2013–2014*, New Europe College, Bucharest, 2014, p. 261.

23   Confirming this was the supreme fiscal crisis of the Habsburg era, of the fifteen occasions the Indies cargoes were seized by the Habsburg monarchs during the 16th century (1523, 1535, 1538, 1545, 1553, 1555, 1556, 1557, 1558, 1566, 1577, 1583, 1587, 1590, 1596), five took place during the 1550s. Bartolomé Yun-

Casalilla, *Iberian World Empires and the Globalization of Europe 1415–1668*, Palgrave Macmillan, Singapore, 2019, p. 304.

24   Andrew C. Hess, "The Moriscos: An Ottoman Fifth Column in Sixteenth-Century Spain," *The American Historical Review*, Vol. 74, No. 1, October 1968, p. 14.

25   Hess, "The Moriscos," p. 19.

26   Ibid., p. 20.

27   Ibid., p. 14.

28   Ibid., p. 15–16.

29   Soucek, "Naval Aspects," p. 235.

30   Roger Crowley, "Bragadin's Defense," *MHQ: The Quarterly Journal of Military History*, Vol. 21, No. 3, Spring 2009, p. 66.

31   Malcolm, *Agents of Empire*, p. 165.

32   Jeremy Black, *European Warfare 1453–1815*, Macmillan, Basingstoke, 1999, p. 32.

33   Turnbull, *The Art of Renaissance Warfare*, p. 136.

34   Malcolm, *Agents of Empire*, p. 153.

35   Ibid., p. 105.

36   Hüseyin Serdar Tabakoğlu, "Commanding The Sea: The Spanish Naval High Command in the Early Modern Mediterranean," *Cihannüma*, Vol. 2, No. 1, July 2016, pp. 1–14.

37   Malcolm, *Agents of Empire*, p. 108.

38   Ibid., p. 110.

39   Ibid., pp. 153–54.

40   Ibid., p. 157.

41   Angus Konstam, *Lepanto, 1571: The Greatest Naval Battle of the Renaissance*, Osprey, Oxford, 2003, p. 20.

42   Konstam, *Lepanto*, p. 74.

43   Crowley, *Empires of the Sea*, p. 272.

44   Sectional grudges died hard. When King James VI of Scotland published an epic poem celebrating the outcome at Lepanto, he felt constrained to explain rather uncomfortably in a preface why, "contrary to my degree and religion, like a mercenary poet," a Protestant monarch had written "in praise of a foreign Papist bastard," Don John. He also tacked on to the end of his work a reminder, "God doth love his name so well, / That so he did them aid / That serv'd not right the same." MacCulloch, *The Reformation*, p. 340.

45   Kiss, "The Selimiye Mosque," p. 279. Others, such as Heinrich Müller in his *Türkische Historien* (1563) and Michel Jove in his *Vray Discours de la bataille des armes Christienne & Turquesque* (1571), anticipated the ultimate downfall of the Ottoman state, but this was more in desperate hope than expectation.

46   Miguel de Cervantes, *Adventures of Don Quixote de la Mancha*, Frederick Warne & Co., London, 1887, p. vii.

47   Ibid., p. 196.

48 Crowley, *Empires of the Sea*, p. 280.

49 Rogerson, *Last Crusaders*, p. 395.

50 Malcolm, *Agents of Empire*, p. 173. Active pro-Ottoman fifth columnists were active throughout the 16th century, such as Count Giovanni Aldobrandini of Ravenna, the philosopher (and Dominican friar) Tommaso Campanella, and the *condottiere* Ferdinando Sanseverino, Prince of Salerno.

51 İdris Bostan, "Ottoman Attitude Towards the Defeat at Lepanto (1571)," *Primavera-Verano*, Vol. 15, No. 26, 2023, pp. 191–209 (pp. 207–08).

52 Bostan, "Ottoman Attitude," p. 202.

53 Soucek, "Naval Aspects," p. 243.

54 Malcolm, *Agents of Empire*, p. 176.

55 Soucek, "Naval Aspects," p. 244.

56 Ibid., p. 246.

57 Malcolm, *Agents of Empire*, pp. 180–81.

58 Ibid., p. 184.

59 Modern commentators tend to agree. Voltaire described the peace being dictated "as if the Turks had won the battle of Lepanto."

60 Malcolm, *Agents of Empire*, p. 187. On their side, the Ottomans confirmed to the Venetians the commercial privileges previously held in the Ottoman markets, the restitution of the ships captured during the war, and, most importantly and interestingly, the protection of Venice from any punitive action by the Habsburg fleet in retaliation for Venice pulling out of the Holy League.

61 Malcolm, *Agents of Empire*, p. 188.

62 Ardian Muhaj, "The Revival of the Anti-Ottoman Projects in the Balkans after Lepanto and Venice's Struggle to Maintain Long-Lasting Peace with the Ottomans (1573–1645)," *Tarih İncelemeleri Dergisi*, Vol. 76, No. 1, 2022, pp. 203–21.

63 The Ottomans had embraced their partnership with France even more after Lepanto. Charles IX sought to take advantage of the alliance to further his coalition against Spain by placing his brother, Henri de Valois, Duke of Anjou, on the throne of Algiers. He assured Selim the Ottoman province would remain an Ottoman tributary state, and Henri would continue to pay the duties and tribute owed to the Porte by the current viceroy of Algiers. The sultan, however, refused to sanction this arrangement, explaining that, because Ottoman law and Islam were already firmly established, he could not cede Algiers to Anjou "any more than [he could] Constantinople." Nathan Michalewicz, "Franco-Ottoman Diplomacy during the French Wars of Religion, 1559–1610," Ph.D. Dissertation, George Mason University, 2020, pp. 200, 204.

64 Hess, "The Moriscos," p. 18.

65 Malcolm, *Agents of Empire*, p. 191.

66 John F. Guilmartin, Jr., *Gunpowder and Galleys: Changing Technology and Mediterranean Warfare at Sea in the Sixteenth Century*, Cambridge University Press, New York, 1974.

CHAPTER 10: THE EAST

1 John Emerich Edward Dalberg-Acton, *Lectures on Modern History, Part II: The New World*, Macmillan & Co., London, 1906, p. 52.

2 John Laband, *Bringers of War: The Portuguese in Africa during the Age of Gunpowder & Sail from the 15th to 18th Century*, Pen and Sword, Barnsley, 2013; Sanjay Subrahmanyam, *The Portuguese Empire in Asia, 1500–1700: A Political and Economic History*, John Wiley & Sons, Chichester, 2012; Malyn Newitt, *A History of Portuguese Overseas Expansion, 1400–1668*, Routledge, New York, 2005; M.N. Pearson, *Port Cities and Intruders: The Swahili Coast, India, and Portugal in the Early Modern Era*, Johns Hopkins University Press, Baltimore, 1998.

3 Cheah Boon Kheng, "Ming China's Support for Sultan Mahmud of Melaka and Its Hostility towards the Portuguese after the Fall of Melaka in 1511," *Journal of the Malaysian Branch of the Royal Asiatic Society*, Vol. 85, No. 2, December 2012, pp. 55–77.

4 Tonio Andrade, *Lost Colony: The Untold Story of China's First Victory over the West*, Princeton University Press, Princeton, 2011; Tonio Andrade, *The Gunpowder Age: China Military Innovation and the Rise of the West in World History*, Princeton University Press, Princeton, 2016; Serge Gruzinski, *The Eagle and the Dragon: Globalization and European Dreams of Conquest in China and America in the Sixteenth Century*, Polity, New York, 2014.

5 See Bailey W. Diffie and George D. Winius, *Foundations of the Portuguese Empire, 1415–1580*, University of Minnesota Press, Minneapolis, 1977, pp. 380–405. The career of de Brito was particularly incidental. After serving the king of Arakan as a mercenary in the attack on Pegu in 1599, he was subsequently placed in command of the important seaport of Syriam in the Irrawaddy Delta, where he began independently levying customs duties on coastal shipping and building up a force of Portuguese, mestizos, and Indian Muslims. To strengthen his position further he went to Goa to obtain recognition from the Viceroy, returning with reinforcements and six ships as well as the Viceroy's half-Javanese niece, Dona Luisa de Saldanha, as his bride. He overreached when he began diverting coastal shipping forcibly to Syriam, in effect monopolizing the supply of overseas imports to the interior, as well as conducting plundering forays on inland centers. In 1612, King Anaukhpetlun of Burma besieged and captured Syriam before reinforcements could arrive from Goa and Arakan. De Brito was impaled as a punishment for his sacrilege, taking three days to die, and the unfortunate Dona Luisa was sold into slavery. The surviving Portuguese and many Muslim mercenaries were settled at villages in the interior and their descendants continued to serve in Burmese armies as late as the 19th century. Ronald Findlay and Kevin H. O'Rourke, *Power and Plenty: Trade, War, and the World Economy in the Second Millennium*, Princeton University Press, Princeton, 2009, p. 196.

6 Camões, *The Lusiads*, p. 3.

7 Saul António Gomes, "The Idea of Crusade in Portugal through the Fifteenth Century," in Attila Bárány (ed.), *Mercenaries and Crusaders*, Hungarian Research Network, Debrecen, 2024, pp. 317–32.

8 Rogerson, *Last Crusaders*, p. 28.

9 Owing to the proximity of its Muslim neighbors, Portugal already possessed two indigenous crusading orders, the Knights of Avis and of Santiago.

10 Nigel Cliff, *Holy War: How Vasco da Gama's Epic Voyages Turned the Tide in a Centuries-Old Clash of Civilizations*, Harper, New York, 2011, p. 99.

11 This rivalry is the central theme of Roger Crowley, *Spice: The 16th-Century Contest that Shaped the Modern World*, Yale University Press, New Haven, 2024.

12 George Winius, "The Ocean Adventurers," in Tony Allan (ed.), *Voyages of Discovery*, Time-Life, Alexandria, 1989, p. 23.

13 Cliff, *Holy War*, p. 419.

14 Roger Crowley, *Conquerors: How Portugal Forged the First Global Empire*, Random House, New York, 2015, loc. 1719.

15 Fernand Braudel, *The Mediterranean and the Mediterranean World in the Age of Philip II, Vol. 1*, Collins, London, 1975, p. 543.

16 Crowley, *Conquerors*, loc. 2581.

17 K.S. Mathew, "Indo-Portuguese Naval Battles in the Indian Ocean during the Early Sixteenth Century," in Kaushik Roy and Peter Lorge (eds.), *Chinese and Indian Warfare – From the Classical Age to 1870*, Routledge, New York, 2015, pp. 166–80.

18 Erlichman, *Conquest, Tribute and Trade*, pp. 47–48.

19 Sanjay Subrahmanyam and Luís Filipe F. R. Thomaz, "Evolution of Empire: The Portuguese in the Indian Ocean During the Sixteenth Century," in James D. Tracy (ed.), *The Political Economy of Merchant Empires: State Power and World Trade, 1350–1750*, Cambridge University Press, Cambridge, 1991, p. 328.

20 A.R. Disney, *A History of Portugal and the Portuguese Empire: From Beginnings to 1807, Vol. 2: The Portuguese Empire*, Cambridge University Press, Cambridge, 2009, p. 150.

21 Faruk Tabak, *The Waning of the Mediterranean, 1550–1870: A Geohistorical Approach*, Johns Hopkins University Press, Baltimore, 2008.

22 Peter Padfield, *Tide of Empires: Decisive Naval Campaigns in the Rise of the West 1481–1654 (Volume I)*, Lume Books, Borough, 2021, p. 78.

23 Findlay and O'Rourke, *Power and Plenty*, p. 206.

24 Erlichman, *Conquest, Tribute and Trade*, p. 113.

25 Ibid., p. 114.

26 Disney, *A History of Portugal*, p. 158.

27 Cliff, *Holy War*, p. 115.

28 Ibid., p. 116.

29 Ibid., p. 117.

30 Luc Cuyvers, *Into the Rising Sun: Vasco da Gama and the Search for the Sea Route to the East*, TV Books, New York, 1999, p. 110.

31   Diffie and Winius, *Foundations of the Portuguese Empire*, p. 227.

32   Ibid., p. 229.

33   As a gesture of intent, the small mosque on the island was reconsecrated as a church and similarly renamed Nossa Senhora da Vitoria, "Our Lady of the Victory." However, the lack of water on the island made Portuguese occupation untenable, and Socotra was abandoned five years after it had been taken.

34   Andreu Martínez d'Alòs-Moner, "Conquistadores, Mercenaries, and Missionaries: The Failed Portuguese Dominion of the Red Sea," *Northeast African Studies*, Vol. 12, No. 1, 2012, pp. 3–4.

35   Padfield, *Tide of Empires*, p. 85.

36   See Robert Finlay, "Crisis and Crusade in the Mediterranean: Venice, Portugal and the Cape Route to India, 1498–1509," *Studi Veneziani*, Vol. 28, 1994, pp. 45–90; George Modelski, "Enduring Rivalry in the Democratic Lineage: The Venice-Portugal Case," in William R. Thompson, *Great Power Rivalries*, University of South Carolina Press, Columbia, 1999, pp. 153–71.

37   Brummett, *Ottoman Seapower*, p. 34.

38   Palmira Brummett, "Kemal Re'is and Ottoman Gunpowder Diplomacy," in Selim Deringil and Sinan Kuneralp (eds.), *Studies on Ottoman Diplomatic History, Vol. V: The Ottomans and Africa*, Isis Press, Istanbul, 1990, p. 1.

39   Diffie and Winius, *Foundations of the Portuguese Empire*, p. 237.

40   Saturnino Monteiro, *Portuguese Sea Battles, Vol. I: The First World Sea Power, 1139–1521*, Lisbon, 2014, loc. 5643.

41   Anthony Holland, *1509: The Battle of Diu*, Epic Battles of History, Anthony Holland, 2023, p. 240.

42   Padfield, *Tide of Empires*, p. 93.

43   Almeida set sail for Portugal, but was killed on the voyage home in a skirmish with native peoples in Africa near the Cape of Good Hope.

44   Diffie and Winius, *Foundations of the Portuguese Empire*, p. 247.

45   Disney, *A History of Portugal*, p. 130.

46   Crowley, *Conquerors*, loc. 4194.

47   Diffie and Winius, *Foundations of the Portuguese Empire*, p. 254.

48   Padfield, *Tide of Empires*, p. 80.

49   Brummett, *Ottoman Seapower*, p. 43.

50   Abbas Hamdani, "Ottoman Response to the Discovery of America and the New Route to India," *Journal of the American Oriental Society*, Vol. 101, No. 3, July–September 1981, p. 326.

51   Erlichman, *Conquest, Tribute and Trade*, p. 62.

52   Casale, *Ottoman Age of Exploration*, p. 28.

53   Jeffrey M. Shaw, *The Ethiopian–Adal War, 1529–1543: The Conquest of Abyssinia*, Helion & Co., Warwick, 2021, p. 33.

54   Padfield, *Tides of Empire*, p. 101.

55   D'Alòs-Moner, "Conquistadores, Mercenaries, and Missionaries," p. 5.

56 Abbas Hamdani, "Ottoman Response to the Discovery of America and the New Route to India," *Journal of the American Oriental Society*, Vol. 101, No. 3, July–September 1981, pp. 326–27.

57 Rogerson, *Last Crusaders*, p. 200.

58 Ruby Maloni, "Control of the Seas: The Historical Exegesis of the Portuguese '*Cartaz*,'" *Proceedings of the Indian History Congress*, Vol. 72, Part I, 2011, pp. 476–84.

59 Salih Özbaran, *Ottoman Expansion Towards the Indian Ocean in the 16th Century*, Bilgi University Press, Istanbul, 2009, p. 279.

60 Özbaran, *Ottoman Expansion*, p. 59.

61 Ibid., p. 72.

62 Casale, *Ottoman Age of Exploration*, p. 45.

63 Ibid., p. 45.

64 Ibid., pp. 50–51.

65 Giancarlo Casale, "Imperial Smackdown: The Portuguese Between Imamate and Caliphate in the Persian Gulf," in Rudi Mathee and Jorge Flores (eds.), *Portugal, The Persian Gulf and Safavid Persia*, Iran Heritage Foundation, Peeters, 2011, p. 186.

66 Casale, *Ottoman Age of Exploration*, p. 48. Sultan Bahadur of Gujarat rewarded Bayram and appointed him head of the arsenal at Diu, only for him to later defect to the Mughal emperor Humayun.

67 Anthony Reid, "Turkey as Aceh's Alternative Imperium," *Archipel*, Vol. 87, 2014, p. 83.

68 Özbaran, *Ottoman Expansion*, p. 79.

69 Casale, *Ottoman Age of Exploration*, p. 54.

70 Ibid., p. 82.

71 Ibid., p. 58.

72 Ibid., p. 59.

73 Giancarlo Casale, "Ottoman Warships in the Indian Ocean Armada of 1538: A Qualitative and Statistical Analysis," in Couto, Gunergun, and Pedani (eds.), *Seapower, Technology and Trade*, pp. 89–102.

74 Dejanirah Couto, "Rûmî Networks in India: A Snapshot on the Second Siege of Diu (1546)", in Couto, Gunergun, and Pedani (eds.), *Seapower, Technology and Trade*, pp. 103–14.

75 Casale, *Ottoman Age of Exploration*, p. 57.

76 Saturnino Monteiro, *Portuguese Sea Battles, Vol. II: Christianity, Commerce and Corso, 1522–1538*, Lisbon, 2014, loc. 7277.

77 Salih Özbaran, "An Imperial Letter from Süleyman the Magnificent to Dom João III Concerning Proposals for an Ottoman-Portuguese Armistice," *Portuguese Studies*, Vol. 6, 1990, pp. 24–31.

78 Casale, *Ottoman Age of Exploration*, p. 76.

79 Ricardo Bonalume Neto, "Lightning Rod of Portuguese India," *MHQ: The Quarterly Journal of Military History*, Vol. 14, No. 3, Spring 2002, pp. 68–77.

80   Casale, *Ottoman Age of Exploration*, p. 78.

81   Ibid., p. 78.

82   Ibid., p. 80.

83   Ibid., p. 88.

84   Fodor, *Unbearable Weight*, p. 122.

85   Dejanirah Couto, "Portuguese-Ottoman Rivalry in the Persian Gulf in the Mid-Sixteenth Century: The Siege of Hormuz, 1552," in Rudi Mathee and Jorge Flores (eds.), *Portugal, The Persian Gulf and Safavid Persia*, Iran Heritage Foundation, Peeters, 2011, p. 158.

86   Matthee, "Distant Allies," pp. 219–47.

87   Casale, *Ottoman Age of Exploration*, p. 115.

88   Ibid., p. 115.

89   Ibid., p. 150.

90   Padfield, *Tides of Empire*, p. 103. For all their repeated bouts of conflict in the Mediterranean, therefore, Venice ultimately owed its commerical survival to its Ottoman rival; as Findlay and O'Rourke note, "the position of Venice in the spice trade was restored by the middle of the [16th c]entury and continued to expand after that, a remarkable recovery indeed and due in large measure to the military prowess of its great Muslim ally." Findlay and O'Rourke, *Power and Plenty*, p. 205.

91   Salih Özbaran, "Ottoman Expansion in the Red Sea," in Faroqhi and Fleet (eds.), *The Ottoman Empire as a World Power, 1453–1603*, pp. 173–201. For the practical limitations of Portuguese authority in the Indian Ocean, see "A World-Economy Matures (Circa 1450–1650)" in Ravi Palat, *The Making of an Indian Ocean World-Economy, 1250–1650*, Palgrave Macmillan, New York, 2015, pp. 151–212. Ultimately, it was not the Portuguese in the 16th century but rather the Dutch and English in the 17th century who finally put paid to Venice's traditional preeminence in the spice trade. C.H.H. Wake, "The Changing Pattern of Europe's Pepper and Spice Imports, *ca.* 1400–1700," *The Journal of European Economic History*, Vol. 8, No. 2, 1979, pp. 361–403.

92   Erlichman, *Conquest, Tribute and Trade*, p. 315.

93   Casale, *Ottoman Age of Exploration*, p. 130.

94   Ibid., p. 130.

95   Ibid., p. 131.

96   These forces took Aden on 19 May 1569, preempting the arrival of a Portuguese flotilla from Hormuz that had been invited to intervene by the Zaydi commander of the garrison.

97   Saturnino Monteiro, *Portuguese Sea Battles, Vol. III: From Brazil to Japan 1539–1579*, Lisbon, 2014, loc. 5681.

98   Casale, *Ottoman Age of Exploration*, p. 133.

99   The commander of the garrison, the eighty-year-old Jorge de Castro, paid for this disgrace with his life; paroled to Goa, he was court-martialed, convicted, and executed.

100 In addition to the threat from Aceh, Malacca was also subjected to siege by the Javanese queen of Kalinyamat in 1574. This also failed.

101 This was a fundamental advantage the Ottomans maintained over their Western European rivals. As Anthony Reid notes, "The Muslim alliances spreading from the Middle East to South and Southeast Asia, unwieldy and disputatious as they always were, were better able to mobilize the 'soft power' of globalism" than their Christian antagonists, even if they had deigned attempting to do so. Reid, "Turkey as Aceh's Alternative Imperium," p. 86.

102 Gábor Ágoston, "Where Environmental and Frontier Studies Meet: Rivers, Forests, Marshes and Forts along the Ottoman–Habsburg Frontier in Hungary," in A.C.S. Peacock (ed.), *The Frontiers of the Ottoman World*, Oxford University Press, New York, 2009, pp. 60–61. The Ottomans also explored the possibility of constructing a canal that would have connected the Black Sea with the Sea of Marmara via the Sakarya River in Anatolia.

103 Casale, *Ottoman Age of Exploration*, p. 136.

104 Naimur Rahman Farooqi, "Mughal-Ottoman Relations: A Study of Political and Diplomatic Relations between Mughal India and the Ottoman Empire, 1556–1748," Ph.D. Dissertation, University of Wisconsin, 1986.

105 Giancarlo Casale, "Global Politics in the 1580s: One Canal, Twenty Thousand Cannibals, and an Ottoman Plot to Rule the World," *Journal of World History*, Vol. 18, No. 3, September 2007, p. 269.

106 Casale, *Ottoman Age of Exploration*, p. 159.

107 Ibid., p. 171.

108 Ibid., p. 200.

CHAPTER 11: AFRICA

1 Thomas Collins, "The King Who Wasn't There," *History Today*, Vol. 73, No. 5, May 2023, p. 40.

2 By the end of the century, the *Chronica* of Geoffrey of Breuil, the *Gesta Regis Henrici II et Ricardi I* of Roger of Howden, and the *De Vita Galfridi* of Gerald of Wales all referenced Prester John in their studies of history. For more on the Prester John legend, see Keagan Brewer (ed.), *Prester John: The Legend and its Sources*, Ashgate, Burlington, 2015; Christopher Taylor, "Global Circulation as Christian Enclosure: Legend, Empire, and the Nomadic Prester John," *Literature Compass*, Vol. 11, No. 7, 2014, pp. 445–59; Christopher Taylor, "Prester John, Christian Enclosure, and the Spatial Transmission of Islamic Alterity in the Twelfth-Century West," in J.C. Frakes (ed.), *Contextualizing the Muslim Other in Medieval Christian Discourse*, Palgrave Macmillan, New York, 2011, pp. 39–63; Lev N. Gumilev, *Searches for an Imaginary Kingdom: The Legend of the Kingdom of Prester John*, Cambridge University Press, Cambridge, 1987.

3   The oriental tradition took a long time to die. George Manwaring, an attendant to
    the English embassy of Anthony Sherley to Safavid Persia, recounted that upon an
    audience with Shah Abbas in 1598/99, Sherley was greeted "very royally; and the
    king gave him a crucifix of gold with diamonds, turquoises, and rubies, [and this]
    crucifix was sent [to] the king from Prester John, as the king himself did show it to
    us." Collins, "The King Who Wasn't There," p. 45.

4   Collins, "The King Who Wasn't There," p. 48.

5   Verena Krebs, *Medieval Ethiopian Kingship, Craft, and Diplomacy with Latin Europe*,
    Palgrave Macmillan, Cham, 2021, p. 21.

6   Samantha Kelly, "Ethiopians in Rome," *History Today*, Vol. 78, No. 4, September
    2024, pp. 38–53.

7   Krebs, *Medieval Ethiopian Kingship*, p. 35.

8   Ibid., p. 35.

9   Matteo Salvadore, "Faith Over Color: Ethio-European Encounters and Discourses
    in the Early Modern Era," Ph.D. Dissertation, Temple University, 2010, p. 68–69.

10 Ibid., pp. 71–72. Yeshāq's own ambassador was scarcely more fortunate. Upon
    arriving in Alexandria in 1429, the Persian merchant, Nūr al-Dīn ʿAlī al-Tabrīzī, was
    detained, tried, and convicted on charges of "importing weapons into an enemy
    country" and "playing with two religions," and publicly executed.

11 Verena Krebs, "Crusading Threats? Ethiopian-Egyptian Relations in the 1440s," in
    Benjamin Weber (ed.), *Croisades en Afrique: Les Expeditions Occidentales á
    Destination du Continent Africain, XIIIᵉ–XVIᵉ Siècles*, Presses Universitaires du Midi
    Meridiennes, Toulouse, 2019, p. 257.

12 Travis J. Owens, "Beleaguered Muslim Fortresses and Ethiopian Imperial Expansion
    from the 13th to the 16th Century," MA Thesis, Naval Postgraduate School,
    Monterey, California, 2008, p. 39. This contact always remained tenuous. Even
    after the Portuguese entered the Indian Ocean, the link to the Red Sea remained
    problematic. As João de Barros lamented, "It seems that – on account of our sins or
    as a result of some judgment of God hidden from us – at the entrance to this great
    land of Ethiopia where our ships go, he placed a menacing angel with a sword of fire
    in the form of mortal fevers which prevent us from penetrating into the interior to
    find the springs which water this earthly garden and from which flow down into the
    sea, in so many of the regions we have conquered there, rivers of gold." Cliff, *Holy
    War*, p. 402.

13 Krebs, *Medieval Ethiopian Kingship*, p. 85.

14 Ibid., p. 87.

15 Salvadore, "Faith Over Color," pp. 108–09. Callixtus was extending Yāʿeqob both
    figuratively and literally the "golden sword which Jeremiah was seen giving to the
    commander of the Maccabees." Reflecting the weight with which the papacy
    endowed the potential of an Ethiopian alliance, a whole host of precious relics was
    sent along with the pontiff's letter, including "relics from the holy Apostles Peter and
    Paul; from Saint John the Baptist; from the arm of St Andrew the Apostle; from

St James the Apostle, son of Zebedee; and from the wood of the cross on which the blessed Apostle Peter was executed." Krebs, *Medieval Ethiopian Kingship*, p. 89.

16   Salvadore, "Faith Over Color," p. 104.

17   Cates Baldridge, *Prisoners of Prester John*, McFarland & Co., Jefferson, 2012.

18   Crowley, *Conquerors*, loc. 2536.

19   Matteo Salvadore, "The Ethiopian Age of Exploration: Prester John's Discovery of Europe, 1306–1458," *Journal of World History*, Vol. 21, No. 4, December 2010, p. 622.

20   Andrew Kurt, "The Search for Prester John, a Projected Crusade and the Eroding Prestige of Ethiopian Kings, *c.*1200–*c.*1540," *Journal of Medieval History*, Vol. 39, No. 3, September 2013, p. 516.

21   Jeremy Lawrance, "The Middle Indies: Damião de Góis on Prester John and the Ethiopians," *Renaissance Studies*, Vol. 6, No. 3–4, September 1992, p. 307.

22   Krebs, *Medieval Ethiopian Kingship*, p. 147.

23   Sanceau, *Land of Prester John*, p. 44.

24   Matteo Salvadore, *The African Prester John and the Birth of Ethiopian-European Relations, 1402–1555*, Routledge, London, 2017, p. 116.

25   Salvadore, "Faith Over Color," pp. 162–63.

26   Sanceau, *Land of Prester John*, p. 105. It probably didn't help Lima's cause that almost all of the gifts with which the Portuguese mission had departed Lima – ornate, inlaid and gilded tables; velvet-covered chairs trimmed in gold; fine fabrics and finished textiles, often embroidered with religious iconography (cushions, tablecloths, cloaks, carpets, curtains, door hangings, tapestries, drapes, etc.); riding gear; fashionable golden armor trimmed in crimson satin; state-of-the-art weapons; and no less than 1,433 books – had fallen by the wayside long before the embassy arrived in the Ethiopian highlands.

27   Krebs, *Medieval Ethiopian Kingship*, p. 152.

28   A.C.S. Peacock, "The Ottomans and the Funj Sultanate in the Sixteenth and Seventeenth Centuries," *Bulletin of the School of Oriental and African Studies*, Vol. 75, No. 1, 2012, p. 91.

29   Asa J. Davis, "The Sixteenth Century Jihād in Ethiopia and the Impact on its Culture, Part One," *Journal of the Historical Society of Nigeria*, Vol. 2, No. 4, December 1963, pp. 567–92; Asa J. Davis, "The Sixteenth Century Jihād in Ethiopia and the Impact on its Culture, Part Two: Implicit Factors Behind the Movement," *Journal of the Historical Society of Nigeria*, Vol. 3, No. 1, December 1964, pp. 113–28.

30   Mohammed Hassen, "Reviewed Work(s): Ethiopia and the Red Sea: The Rise and Decline of the Solomonic Dynasty and Muslim-European Rivalry in the Region by M. Abir," *Northeast African Studies*, Vol. 6, No. 3, 1984, p. 64.

31   Shaw, *The Ethiopian–Adal War*, p. 96.

32   Ibid., p. 101.

33   Richard S. Whiteway (ed.), *The Portuguese Expedition to Abyssinia in 1541–1543*, Hakluyt Society, London, 1892, p. 46.

34 Casale, *Ottoman Age of Exploration*, p. 74.

35 C.F. Beckingham, "A Note on the Topography of Ahmad Gran's Campaigns in 1542," *Journal of Semitic Studies*, Vol. 4, No. 4, October 1959, pp. 362–73.

36 Whiteway, *The Portuguese Expedition to Abyssinia*, p. 63.

37 Ibid., p. 81.

38 Andreu Martínez d'Alòs-Moner, "Early Portuguese Emigration to the Ethiopian Highlands: Geopolitics, Missions and Métissag," in Stefan Halikowski-Smith and K.N. Chaudhuri (eds.), *Reinterpreting Indian Ocean Worlds: Essays in Honour of Kirti N. Chaudhuri*, Cambridge Scholars, Newcastle upon Tyne, 2011, pp. 2–32.

39 Paul B. Henze, *Layers of Time: A History of Ethiopia*, Palgrave Macmillan, New York, 2000, pp. 83–118.

40 Mohammed Hassen, *The Oromo and the Christian Kingdom of Ethiopia*, Boydell & Brewer, Rochester, 2015.

41 Andreu Martínez d'Alòs-Moner, *Envoys of a Human God: The Jesuit Mission to Christian Ethiopia, 1557–1632*, Brill, Leiden, 2015.

42 Peacock, "The Ottomans and the Funj Sultanate," p. 93.

43 Özbaran, *Ottoman Expansion*, p. 208.

44 Awegichew Amare Agonafir, "*Atse* Sarsa Dengel and the Rival Great Powers at His Door Steps: Vagaries of Competition and War against the Ottoman Empire, 1563-1597," *Abyssinia Journal of Business and Social Sciences*, Vol. 7, No. 2, 2022, pp. 24–32.

45 Weston F. Cook, *The Hundred Years War for Morocco: Gunpowder and the Military Revolution in the Early Modern Muslim World*, Westview, Boulder, 1994.

46 Rogerson, *Last Crusaders*, p. 49.

47 Mikhail, *God's Shadow*, p. 349.

48 Ibid., p. 351.

49 Rogerson, *Last Crusaders*, p. 219.

50 Ibid., p. 221.

51 Ibid., p. 224.

52 Jamil M. Abun-Nasr, *A History of the Maghrib in the Islamic Period*, Cambridge University Press, New York, 1987, p. 157.

53 Işıksel Güneş, "Ottoman Suzerainty Over Morocco During Abdulmelik's Reign (1576–1578): A Reassessment," in Marinos Sariyannis, et al. (eds.), *New Trends in Ottoman Studies: Papers Presented at the 20th CIEPO Symposium*, University of Crete, Rethymno, 2014, pp. 568–77.

54 Rogerson, *Last Crusaders*, p. 418.

55 Emrah Safa Gürkan, "The Centre and the Frontier: Ottoman Cooperation with the North African Corsairs in the Sixteenth Century," *Turkish Historical Review*, Vol. 1, No. 2, November 2010, p. 162.

56 Gürkan, "The Centre and the Frontier," p. 163. The Porte had already written off the Moriscos as any kind of strategic asset, for "under the Unbelievers they had become

weak, and their conditions had changed for the worse," Murad III concluded. Hess, "The Moriscos," p. 22. The Spanish resolved the possibility of any residual threat from the Morisco fifth column by expelling the entire population in 1609.

57   Isom-Verhaaren, *The Sultan's Fleet*, p. 140.

58   Ibid., p. 142.

59   See also Gerald M. MacLean and N.I. Matar, *Britain and the Islamic World, 1558–1713*, Oxford University Press, Oxford, 2011, pp. 42–78.

60   Jerry Brotton, *The Sultan and the Queen: The Untold Story of Elizabeth and Islam*, Viking, New York, 2016, p. 195.

61   Brotton, *The Sultan and the Queen*, p. 263.

62   Abbas Hamdani, "Ottoman Response to the Discovery of America and the New Route to India," *Journal of the American Oriental Society*, Vol. 101, No. 3, July–September 1981, p. 329.

CONCLUSION

1   For recent studies, see Robert B. Marks, *The Origins of the Modern World: A Global and Environmental Narrative from the Fifteenth to the Twenty-First Century*, Rowman & Littlefield, Lanham, 2019; Daniel R. Headrick, *Power over Peoples: Technology, Environments, and Western Imperialism, 1400 to the Present*, Princeton University Press, Princeton, 2012.

2   See Suraiya Faroqhi and Halil Inalcik (eds.), *Ransom Slavery along the Ottoman Borders: The Ottoman Empire and its Heritage*, Brill, Leiden, 2007.

3   Ágoston, *The Last Muslim Conquest*, p. 112.

4   See Robert C. Davis, *Christian Slaves, Muslim Masters: White Slavery in the Mediterranean, the Barbary Coast and Italy, 1500-1800*, Palgrave Macmillan, New York, 2003.

5   Desiderius Erasmus, "De Bello Turcis," in Dominic Baker-Smith (ed.), *Consultatio de bello Turcis inferendo, et obiter enarratus Psalmus*, University of Toronto Press, Toronto, 2005, p. 231.

6   MacCulloch, *The Reformation*, p. 354.

7   J.C. Sharman, *Empires of the Weak: The Real Story of European Expansion and the Creation of the New World Order*, Princeton University Press, Princeton, 2019, p. 122.

8   Omer Lutfi Barkan, "The Price Revolution of the Sixteenth Century: A Turning Point in the Economic History of the Near East, *International Journal of Middle East Studies*, Vol. 6, No. 1, January 1975, pp. 3–28. See also Erol Özvar, "Transformation of the Ottoman Empire into a Military-Fiscal State: Reconsidering the Financing of War from a Global Perspective," in Fodor (ed.), *The Battle for Central Europe*, pp. 21–63, and "Debasement and Disintegration" in Şevket Pamuk, *A Monetary History of the Ottoman Empire*, Cambridge University Press, New York, 2000, pp. 131–48.

9   Fodor, *Unbearable Weight*, p. 124. See also Subhi Labib, "The Era of Suleyman the Magnificent: Crisis of Orientation," *International Journal of Middle East Studies*, Vol. 10, 1979, pp. 435–51.

10 Feridun M. Emecen, "Ottoman Politics in the Reign of Sultan Süleyman: Government, Internal Politics and Imperial Expansion," in Fodor (ed.), *The Battle for Central Europe*, pp. 7–20.

11 Ágoston, *The Last Muslim Conquest*, p. 450.

12 Fodor, *Unbearable Weight*, p. 82.

13 Casale, "Global Politics in the 1580s," p. 286.

14 Ibid., pp. 290–91.

15 Malcolm, *Agents of Empire*, pp. 391–414.

16 A.W. Lovett, "The Castilian Bankruptcy of 1575," *The Historical Journal*, Vol. 23, No. 4, December 1980, pp. 899–911.

17 The definitive source on Habsburg finance is Mauricio Drelichman and Hans-Joachim Voth, *Lending to the Borrower from Hell: Debt, Taxes, and Default in the Age of Philip II*, Princeton University Press, Princeton, 2014.

18 Sean McMeekin, *The Ottoman Endgame: War, Revolution, and the Making of the Modern Middle East, 1908–1923*, Penguin, New York, 2015; Eugene L. Rogan, *The Fall of the Ottomans: The Great War in the Middle East*, Basic Books, New York, 2015; David Fromkin, *A Peace to End All Peace: The Fall of the Ottoman Empire and the Creation of the Modern Middle East*, Holt, New York, 2009.

19 According to Findlay and O'Rourke, "There is little doubt that had it not been for the Ottoman intervention, the Portuguese attempt at a spice monopoly would have been successful." Findlay and O'Rourke, *Power and Plenty*, p. 205.

20 Fischer-Galati, *Ottoman Imperialism and German Protestantism*, p. 117.

21 Forell, "Luther and the War against the Turks," p. 260.

22 Ibid., p. 259.

23 Toynbee, "Lost Opportunities," p. 445.

24 Ibid., pp. 444–45.

25 "Spain squandered its windfall gain" in the Americas, Dennis O. Flynn, concludes; the geopolitical ambition of the Habsburgs ultimately "dissipated its New World-based wealth on the first global war." Dennis O. Flynn, "Comparing the Tokagawa Shogunate with Hapsburg Spain: Two Silver-Based Empires in a Global Setting," in James D. Tracy (ed.), *The Political Economy of Merchant Empires*, Cambridge University Press, Cambridge, 1991, p. 348.

BIBLIOGRAPHY

Ottoman History & Heritage

Abou-El-Haj, Rifa'at Ali: *Formation of the Modern State: The Ottoman Empire, Sixteenth to Eighteenth Centuries*, Syracuse University Press, Syracuse, 2005.

Ágoston, Gábor: *Guns for the Sultan: Military Power and the Weapons Industry in the Ottoman Empire*, Cambridge University Press, Cambridge, 2005.

Akçe, Fatih: *Sultan Selim I: The Conqueror of the East*, Blue Dome Press, Clifton, 2016.

Aksan, Virginia H., and Goffman, Daniel, (eds.): *The Early Modern Ottomans: Remapping the Empire*, Cambridge University Press, Cambridge, 2009.

Amitai, Reuven, and Conermann, Stephan (eds.): *The Mamluk Sultanate from the Perspective of Regional and World History*, Bonn University Press, Bonn, 2019.

Anooshahr, Ali: *The Ghazi Sultans and the Frontiers of Islam*, Routledge, New York, 2014.

Atçıl, Zahit: "The Foundation of Peace-Oriented Foreign Policy in the Sixteenth-Century Ottoman Empire: Rüstem Pasha's Vision of Diplomacy," in Tracey A. Sowerby and Christopher Markiewicz (eds.), *Diplomatic Cultures at the Ottoman Court, c.1500–1630*, Routledge, New York, 2021, pp. 132–52.

Atçıl, Zahit: "The Ottoman Conquest of Buda(pest): Sultan Suleiman's Imperial Letter of Victory," in Hani Khafipour (ed.), *The Empires of the Near East and India: Source Studies of the Safavid, Ottoman, and Mughal Literate Communities*, Columbia University Press, New York, 2019, pp. 280–86.

Atçıl, Zahit: "Warfare as a Tool of Diplomacy: Background of the First Ottoman-Safavid Treaty in 1555," *Turkish Historical Review*, Vol. 10, No. 1, June 2019, pp. 3–24.

Atçıl, Zahit: "Why Did Süleyman the Magnificent Execute His Son Şehzade Mustafa in 1553?" *Osmanlı Araştırmaları*, No. 48, 2016, pp. 67–103.

Atçıl, Zahit: "State and Government in the Mid-Sixteenth Century Ottoman Empire: The Grand Vizierates of Rüstem Pasha (1544–1561)," Ph.D. Dissertation, University of Chicago, 2015.

Babinger, Franz: *Mehmed the Conqueror and his Time*, Princeton University Press, Princeton, 1992.

Baer, Marc D.: *Honored by the Glory of Islam: Conversion and Conquest in Ottoman Europe*, Oxford University Press, New York, 2008.

Barkey, Karen: *Empire of Difference: The Ottomans in Comparative Perspective*, Cambridge University Press, Cambridge, 2008.

Bridge, Antony: *Suleiman the Magnificent: Scourge of Heaven*, Thistle, London, 2015.

Clot, André: *Suleiman the Magnificent*, Saqi, London, 2012.

Coles, Paul: *The Ottoman Impact on Europe*, Harcourt, Brace & World, New York, 1968.

Çýpa, H. Erdem: *The Making of Selim: Succession, Legitimacy, and Memory in the Early Modern Ottoman World*, Indiana University Press, Bloomington, 2017.

Dávid, Géza, and Fodor, Pál (eds.): *Ottomans, Hungarians, and Habsburgs in Central Europe: The Military Confines in the Era of Ottoman Conquest*, Brill, Leiden, 2000.

Eksigil, Arda: "Ottoman Visions of the West (15th–17th Centuries)," MA Thesis, McGill University, 2014.

Faroqhi, Suraiya: *The Ottoman Empire and the World Around It*, I.B. Tauris, New York, 2004.

Faroqhi, Suraiya, and Fleet, Kate (eds.): *The Cambridge History of Turkey, Vol. II: The Ottoman Empire as a World Power, 1453–1603*, Cambridge University Press, Cambridge, 2012.

Finkel, Caroline: *Osman's Dream: The Story of the Ottoman Empire, 1300–1923*, Basic Books, New York, 2005.

Fodor, Pál: *In Quest of the Golden Apple: Imperial Ideology, Politics, and Military Administration in the Ottoman Empire*, Gorgias Press, Piscataway, 2010.

Fodor, Pál (ed.): *The Battle for Central Europe: The Siege of Szigetvár and the Death of Süleyman the Magnificent and Nicholas Zrínyi (1566)*, Brill, Leiden, 2019.

Gheorghe, Adrian: *The Metamorphoses of Power: Violence, Warlords, Akıncıs and the Early Ottomans (1300–1450)*, Brill, Leiden, 2023.

Goffman, Daniel: *The Ottoman Empire and Early Modern Europe*, Cambridge University Press, Cambridge, 2012.

Goodwin, Godfrey: *The Janissaries*, Saqi Essentials, London, 2006.

Goodwin, Jason: *Lords of the Horizons: A History of the Ottoman Empire*, Henry Holt, New York, 1999.

Graf, Tobias P.: *The Sultan's Renegades: Christian-European Converts to Islam and the Making of the Ottoman Elite, 1575–1610*, Oxford University Press, New York, 2017.

Gündoğdu, Birol: "Ottoman Military Rebellions and a Delicate Relationship between the State and Janissaries in the Early Modern Era," in Birol Gündoğdu (ed.), *Reading the Ottoman Mind*, Sivas Cumhuriyet University Press, Sivas, 2023, pp. 101–29.

Howard, Douglas A.: *A History of the Ottoman Empire*, Cambridge University Press, Cambridge, 2017.

Imber, Colin: *The Ottoman Empire, 1300–1650: The Structure of Power*, Palgrave Macmillan, Basingstoke, 2019.

İnalcık, Halil, and Kafadar, Cemal (eds.): *Süleymân the Second and His Time*, Isis, Istanbul, 1993.

Islahi, Abdul Azim: "Economic and Financial Crises in the Fifteenth-Century Egypt: Lessons from the History," *Islamic Economic Studies*, Vol. 21, No. 2, November 2013, pp. 71–93.

Kastritsis, Demitris J.: *The Sons of Bayezid: Empire Building and Representation in the Ottoman Civil War of 1402–1413*, Brill, Leiden, 2007.

Kunt, Metin, and Woodhead, Christine: *Süleyman the Magnificent and His Age: The Ottoman Empire in the Early Modern World*, Routledge, New York, 2013.

Mazzaoui, Michel M.: "Global Policies of Sultan Selim, 1512–1520," in Donald P. Little (ed.), *Essays on Islamic Civilization: Presented to Niyazi Berkes*, Brill, Leiden, 1976, pp. 224–43.

Mikhail, Alan: *God's Shadow: Sultan Selim, His Ottoman Empire, and the Making of the Modern World*, Liveright, New York, 2020.

Mujadžević, Dino: "Ulama-bey, Sanjakbey of Bosnia and Požega," *Prilozi Za Orijentalnu Filologiju*, No. 60, 2017, pp. 251–58.

Murphey, Rhoads: *Ottoman Warfare 1500–1700*, Rutgers University Press, Rutgers, 1999.

Muslu, Cihan Yüksel: *The Ottomans and the Mamluks: Imperial Diplomacy and Warfare in the Islamic World*, I.B. Tauris, London, 2014.

Nicolle, David: *Armies of the Ottoman Turks, 1300–1774*, Osprey, Oxford, 2007.

Nicolle, David: *The Janissaries*, Osprey, Oxford, 2008.

Özkan, Aytaç: *Great Eagle: Sultan Mehmed the Conqueror*, Blue Dome, London, 2016.

Pinto, Karen C.: *Medieval Islamic Maps: An Exploration*, The University of Chicago Press, Chicago, 2017.

Pitcher, Donald E.: *An Historical Geography of the Ottoman Empire from Earliest Times to the End of the Sixteenth Century*, Brill, Leiden, 1973.

Şahin, Kaya: *Empire and Power in the Reign of Süleyman: Narrating the Sixteenth-Century Ottoman World*, Cambridge University Press, Cambridge, 2013.

Stavrides, Theoharis: *The Sultan of Vezirs: The Life and Times of the Ottoman Grand Vezir Mahmud Pasha Angelović (1453–1474)*, Brill, Leiden, 2001.

Sugar, Peter: "A Near-Perfect Military Society: The Ottoman Empire," in L.L. Farrar, Jr. (ed.): *War: A Historical, Political and Social Study*, ABC-Clio, Santa Barbara, 1978, pp. 95–104.

Turnbull, Stephen: *The Ottoman Empire: 1326–1699*, Osprey, Oxford, 2003.

Uyar, Mesut: *A Military History of the Ottomans: From Osman to Atatürk*, Praeger, Santa Barbara, 2009.

Wittek, Paul: *Rise of the Ottoman Empire*, Routledge, New York, 2015.

Zachariadou, Elizabeth: *The Ottoman Emirate, (1300–1389)*, Crete University Press, Rethymnon, 1993.

Zarinebaf-Shahr, Fariba: "Qızılbash 'Heresy' and Rebellion in Ottoman Anatolia During the Sixteenth Century," *Anatolia Moderna – Yeni Anadolu*, No. 7, 1997, pp. 1–15.

WESTERN EUROPE IN THE OTTOMAN AGE

Blickle, Peter: *The Revolution of 1525: The German Peasants' War from a New Perspective*, Johns Hopkins University Press, Baltimore, 1981.

Brandi, Karl: *The Emperor Charles V: The Growth and Destiny of a Man and of a World-Empire* (Translated by C.V. Wedgwood), Jonathan Cape, London, 1965.

Brotton, Jerry: *This Orient Isle: Elizabethan England and the Islamic World*, Penguin, London, 2017.

Chaudhuri, K.N.: "The Containment of Islam and the Background to European Expansion," Chapter 13 in Felipe Fernández-Armesto (ed.): *An Expanding World: The European Impact on World History 1450–1800, Vol. I: The Global Opportunity*, Variorum, Aldershot, UK, 1995, pp. 299–313.

Cristini, Luca S.: *The Landsknechts*, SoldierShop, Zanica, 2016.

Drelichman, Mauricio, and Voth, Hans-Joachim: *Lending to the Borrower from Hell: Debt, Taxes, and Default in the Age of Philip II*, Princeton University Press, Princeton, 2014.

Erlichman, Howard J.: *Conquest, Tribute and Trade: The Quest for Precious Metals and the Birth of Globalization*, Prometheus Books, New York, 2003.

Fichtner, Paula S.: *Terror and Toleration: The Habsburg Empire Confronts Islam, 1526–1850*, Reaktion, London, 2008.

Fischer-Galați, Stephen A.: *Ottoman Imperialism and German Protestantism, 1521–1555*, Harvard University Press, Cambridge, 1959.

Flynn, Dennis O.: "Comparing the Tokagawa Shogunate with Hapsburg Spain: Two Silver-Based Empires in a Global Setting," in James D. Tracy (ed.), *The Political Economy of Merchant Empires*, Cambridge University Press, Cambridge, 1991, pp. 332–59.

Francisco, Adam: *Martin Luther and Islam: A Study in Sixteenth-Century Polemics and Apologetics*, Brill, Leiden, 2017.

Freedman, Paul H.: "Atrocities and Executions of the Peasant Rebel Leaders in Late Medieval and Early Modern Europe," in Suzana Miljan and Gerhard Jaritz (eds.), *At the Edge of the Law: Socially Unacceptable and Illegal Behaviour in the Middle Ages and the Early Modern Period*, Medium Aevum Quotidianum, Krems, 2012, pp. 73–81.

Harai, Dénes: "Couronne ardente et danse anthropophage: le décryptage de la symbolique de l'exécution de György Dózsa, chef révolté en Hongrie (1514)," *Histoire, Économie et Société*, Vol. 38, No. 1, March 2019, pp. 32–48.

Isom-Verhaaren, Christine: *Allies with the Infidel: The Ottoman and French Alliance in the Sixteenth Century*, I.B. Tauris, London, 2013.

Jacob, Frank, and Visoni-Alonzo, Gilmar: *The Military Revolution in Early Modern Europe: A Revision*, Palgrave Macmillan, London, 2016.

Liddle, Dryden G.: "Power and Finance at the Court of Charles V: Francisco de los Cobos, Royal Secretary of Charles V," Ph.D. Dissertation, The Open University, 2010.

Lovett, A.W.: "The Castilian Bankruptcy of 1575," *The Historical Journal*, Vol. 23, No. 4, December 1980, pp. 899–911.

MacLean, Gerald, and Matar, Nabil: *Britain and the Islamic World, 1558–1713*, Oxford University Press, Oxford, 2011.

Malcolm, Noel: *Useful Enemies: Islam and The Ottoman Empire in Western Political Thought, 1450–1750*, Oxford University Press, Oxford, 2019.

Malcolm, Noel: *Agents of Empire: Knights, Corsairs, Jesuits, and Spies in the Sixteenth-Century Mediterranean World*, Oxford University Press, Oxford, 2015.

Miller, Douglas: *The Landsknechts*, Osprey, Oxford, 1994.

Norwich, John Julius: *Four Princes: Henry VIII, Francis I, Charles V, Suleiman the Magnificent and the Obsessions that Forged Modern Europe*, Atlantic Monthly, New York, 2017.

Parker, Geoffrey: *Emperor: A New Life of Charles V*, Yale University Press, New Haven, 2019.

Pike, Ruth: *Enterprise and Adventure: The Genoese in Seville and the Opening of the New World*, Cornell University Press, Cornell, 1966.

Richards, John: *Landsknecht Soldier 1486–1560*, Osprey, Oxford, 2002.

Sardone, Sergio: "Forced Loans in the Spanish Empire: The First Requisition of American Treasures in 1523," *The Economic History Review*, Vol. 72, No. 1, February 2019, pp. 57–87.

Setton, Kenneth M.: *The Papacy and the Levant*, American Philosophical Society, Philadelphia, 1976.

Setton, Kenneth M.: "Pope Leo X and the Turkish Peril," *Proceedings of the American Philosophical Society*, Vol. 113, No. 6, December 1969, pp. 367–424.

Spufford, Peter: *Money and its Use in Medieval Europe*, Cambridge University Press, Cambridge, 1988.

Tallett, Frank: *War and Society in Early-Modern Europe, 1495–1715*, Routledge, London, 1997.

Tolan, John V., Veinstein, Gilles, Laurens, Henry, and Todd, Jane M.: *Europe and the Islamic World: A History*, Princeton University Press, Princeton, 2017.

Tracy, James D.: *Emperor Charles V, Impresario of War: Campaign Strategy, International Finance, and Domestic Politics*, Cambridge University Press, Cambridge, 2010.

Turnbull, Stephen: *The Art of Renaissance Warfare: From The Fall of Constantinople to the Thirty Years' War*, Frontline Books, Philadelphia, 2018.

Vaughan, Dorothy M.: *Europe and the Turk: A Pattern of Alliances, 1350–1700*, AMS Press, New York, 1976.

Vilches, Elvira: *New World Gold: Cultural Anxiety and Monetary Disorder in Early Modern Spain*, University of Chicago Press, Chicago, 2010.

Yun-Casalilla, Bartolomé: *Iberian World Empires and the Globalization of Europe 1415–1668*, Palgrave Macmillan, Singapore, 2019.

Zamora, Juan M. Carretero: "Fiscalidad extraordinaria y deuda: el destino del servicio de las cortes de Castilla, 1535–1537," *Espacio, Tiempo y Forma*, Series IV, 1995, pp. 11–47.

EASTERN EUROPE IN THE OTTOMAN AGE

Ágoston, Gábor: *The Last Muslim Conquest*, Princeton University Press, Princeton, 2021.

Angold, Michael: *The Fall of Constantinople to the Ottomans: Context and Consequences*, Routledge, New York, 2012.

Antov, Nikolay: *The Ottoman Wild West: The Balkan Frontier in the Fifteenth and Sixteenth Centuries*, Cambridge University Press, New York, 2017.

Bak, János M., and Király, Béla K. (eds.): *From Hunyadi to Rákóczi: War and Society in Late Medieval and Early Modern Hungary*, Columbia University Press, New York, 1982.

Bárány, Attila (ed.): *Mercenaries and Crusaders*, Hungarian Research Network, Debrecen, 2024.

Barleti, Marin: *The Siege of Shkodra: Albania's Courageous Stand against Ottoman Conquest, 1478*, Onufri, Tirana, 2012.

Bartók, Barnabás: *János Hunyadi: Preventing the Ottomans from Conquering Western Europe in the Fifteenth Century*, Master of Military Art and Science Thesis, Fort Leavenworth, Kansas, 2011.

Brackob, A.K.: *Scanderbeg: A History of George Castriota and the Albanian Resistance to Islamic Expansion in Fifteenth Century Europe*, Histria Books, Las Vegas, 2018.

Cazacu, Matei: *Dracula*, Brill, Leiden, 2017.

Dávid, Géza, and Fodor, Pál: *Ottomans, Hungarians, and Habsburgs in Central Europe: The Military Confines in the Era of Ottoman Conquest*, Brill, Leiden, 2000.

Emmert, Thomas A.: *Serbian Golgotha: Kosovo, 1389*, Columbia University Press, New York, 1990.

Engel, Pál: *The Realm of St Stephen: A History of Medieval Hungary, 895–1526*, I.B. Tauris, London, 2001.

Fine, John V.A.: *The Late Medieval Balkans; A Critical Survey from the Late Twelfth Century to the Ottoman Conquest*, The University of Michigan Press, Ann Arbor, 2009.

Fodor, Pál: *The Unbearable Weight of Empire: The Ottomans in Central Europa – A Failed Attempt at Universal Monarchy (1390–1566)*, Hungarian Academy of Sciences, Budapest Research Centre for the Humanities, 2016.

Fodor, Pál: "The Ottoman Empire, Byzantium and Western Christianity: The Implications of the Siege of Belgrade, 1456," *Acta Orientalia*, Vol. 61, No. 1–2, 2008, pp. 43–51.

Fodor, Pál (ed.): *The Battle for Central Europe: The Siege of Szigetvár and the death of Süleyman the Magnificent and Nicholas Zrínyi (1566)*, Brill, Leiden, 2019.

Hazard, Harry W. (ed.): *A History of the Crusades, Vol. 3: The Fourteenth and Fifteenth Centuries*, The University of Wisconsin Press, Madison, 2005.

Held, Joseph: *Hunyadi: Legend and Reality*, Columbia University Press, New York, 1985.

Hodgkinson, Harry: *Scanderbeg*, I.B. Tauris, London, 1999.

Housley, Norman: "Aeneas Silvius Piccolomini, Nicholas of Cusa, and the Crusade: Conciliar, Imperial, and Papal Authority," *Church History*, Vol. 86, No. 3, September 2017, pp. 643–67.

Housley, Norman: *Crusading and the Ottoman Threat, 1453–1505*, Oxford University Press, Oxford, 2013.

Housley, Norman (ed.): *Reconfiguring the Fifteenth-Century Crusade*, Palgrave Macmillan, London, 2017.

Ilich, Miljan P.: *Bosnian Phoenix: How Bosnia Saved Europe and Made Possible the Modern Age*, iUniverse, Bloomington, 2018.

Imber, Colin: *The Crusade of Varna, 1443–45 (Crusade Texts in Translation Book 14)*, Ashgate, Farnham, 2013.

Jefferson, John: *The Holy Wars of King Wladislas and Sultan Murad: The Ottoman-Christian Conflict from 1438–1444*, Brill, Boston, 2012.

Kaçar, Hilmi: "Comparison of Ottoman and Burgundian Historical Narratives on the Battle of Varna (1444)," in *Publications du Centre Européen d'Etudes Bourguignonnes*, No. 56, 2016, pp. 73–78.

Kármán, Gábor, and Kunčević, Lovro (eds.): *The European Tributary States of the Ottoman Empire in the Sixteenth and Seventeenth Centuries*, Brill, Leiden, 2013.

Miljan, Suzana, and Kekez, Hrvoje: "The Memory of the Battle of Krbava (1493) and the Collective Identity of the Croats," *The Hungarian Historical Review*, Vol. 4, No. 2, 2015, pp. 283–313.

Mitev, Nevyan: "The Battle of Shumen – One of the Most Important Battles During the Crusade of Varna in the Autumn of 1444," in Zoltan Iusztin (ed.), *Politics and Society in the Central and South-Eastern Europe (13th – 16th Centuries)*, Editura MEGA, Cluj-Napoca, 2019, pp. 205–14.

Mureşanu, Camil: *John Hunyadi: Defender of Christendom*, Histria Books, Las Vegas, 2019.

Necipoğlu, Nevra: *Byzantium between the Ottomans and the Latins: Politics and Society in the Late Empire*, Cambridge University Press, Cambridge, 2009.

Nevra Necipoglu, "Constantinopolitan Merchants and the Question of their Attitudes towards Italians and Ottomans in the late Palaiologan Period," in Cordula Scholz and Georgios Makris, (eds.), *Polypleuros nous: Miscellanea für Peter Schreiner zu seinem 60*, K.G. Saur Verlag, Munich-Leipzig, 2000, pp. 251–63.

Nicol, Donald M., *The Immortal Emperor: The Life and Legend of Constantine Palaiologos, Last Emperor of the Romans*, Cambridge University Press, New York, 1991.

Nicolle, David: *Cross and Crescent in the Balkans: The Ottoman Conquest of Southeastern Europe (14th–15th Centuries)*, Pen & Sword Military, Barnsley, 2010.

Nicolle, David: *Constantinople 1453: The End of Byzantium*, Osprey, Oxford, 2001.

Nicolle, David: *Nicopolis 1396: The Last Crusade*, Osprey, Oxford, 1999.

Nicolle, David: *Hungary and the Fall of Eastern Europe, 1000–1568*, Osprey, London, 1988.

Pálffy, Géza: *Hungary Between Two Empires, 1526–1711*, Indiana University Press, Bloomington, 2021.

Pálffy, Géza: *The Kingdom of Hungary and the Habsburg Monarchy in the Sixteenth Century*, Columbia University Press, New York, 2010.

Pálosfalvi, Tamás: *From Nicopolis to Mohács: A History of Ottoman-Hungarian Warfare, 1389–1526*, Brill, Leiden, 2018.

Perjés, Géza: *The Fall of the Medieval Kingdom of Hungary: Mohács 1526–Buda 1541*, Columbia University Press, New York, 1989.

Petrović, Sonja: "Serbian and South Slavic Folk Legends and Traditions of the Battle of Kosovo (1389): An Attempt at Systematization," *Publications of the Hellenic Folklore Research Centre: Proceedings of the 15th Congress of the International Society for Folk Narrative Research (June 21–27, 2009) Volume III*, Athens, 2014, pp. 1–12.

Pfeiffer, Attila: "The Battle of Christians and Ottomans in the Southwest of Bačka from the Battle of Mohács to the Peace of Zsitvatorok," *Istraživanja: Journal of Historical Researches*, No. 28, 2017, pp. 86–104.

Pfister, Christian, and Brazdil, Rudolf: "Climatic Variability in Sixteenth-Century Europe and its Social Dimension: A Synthesis," *Climatic Change*, Vol. 43, No. 1, September 1999, pp. 5–53.

Pfister, Christian, et al.: "Daily Weather Observations in Sixteenth-Century Europe," *Climatic Change*, Vol. 43, No. 1, September 1999, pp. 111–50.

Philippides, Marios, and Hanak, Walter K. (ed.): *The Siege and the Fall of Constantinople in 1453: Historiography, Topography, and Military Studies*, Routledge, London, 2017.

Pilat, Liviu, and Cristea, Ovidiu: *The Ottoman Threat and Crusading on the Eastern Border of Christendom During the 15th Century*, Brill, Leiden, 2018.

Pippidi, Andrei: *Visions of the Ottoman World in Renaissance Europe*, Columbia University Press, New York, 2012.

Pogăciaş, Andrei: *John Hunyadi and the Late Crusade: A Transylvanian Warlord against the Crescent*, Helion & Co., Warwick, 2021.

Popović, Marko: "Siege of Belgrade in 1521 and Restoration of Fortifications after Conquest," in Srđan Rudić, Selim Aslantaş, and Dragana Amedoski, (eds.), *Belgrade 1521–1867*, The Institute of History, Belgrade, 2018, pp. 5–27.

Reston, James: *Defenders of the Faith: Christianity and Islam Battle for the Soul of Europe, 1520–1536*, Penguin, New York, 2010.

Rogerson, Barnaby: *The Last Crusaders: East, West, and the Battle for the Center of the World*, Overlook Press, New York, 2011.

Ropa, Anastasija: "Imagining the 1456 Siege of Belgrade in *Capystranus*," *Hungarian Historical Review*, Vol. 4, No. 2, 2015, pp. 255–82.

Runciman, Steven: *The Fall of Constantinople 1453*, Cambridge University Press, Cambridge, 2015.

Sandberg, Brian: "Going Off to the War in Hungary: French Nobles and Crusading Culture in the Sixteenth Century," *The Hungarian Historical Review*, Vol. 4, No. 2, 2015, pp. 346–83.

Schimmer, Karl A., et al.: *The Bulwark of Christendom: The Turkish Sieges of Vienna 1529 & 1683*, John Murray, London, 1847.

Tóta, Benedek P.: "Hungary Overrun: A Source of Fortitude and Comfort," *Moreana*, Vol. 40, No. 156, December 2003, pp. 17–40.

Tracy, James D.: *Balkan Wars: Habsburg Croatia, Ottoman Bosnia, and Venetian Dalmatia, 1499-1617*, Rowman & Littlefield, Lanham, 2016.

Treptow, Kurt W. (ed.): *Dracula: Essays on the Life and Times of Vlad the Impaler*, Histria Books, Las Vegas, 2020.

Tuleja, Thaddeus V.: "Eugenius IV and the Crusade of Varna," *The Catholic Historical Review*, Vol. 35, No. 3, October 1949, pp. 257–75.

Vucinich, Wayne S., and Emmert, Thomas A.: *Kosovo: Legacy of a Medieval Battle*, University of Minnesota Press, Minneapolis, 1991.

Zrínyi, Miklós: *The Siege of Sziget*, Washington, DC, Catholic University of America Press, 2011.

Iran in the Ottoman Age

Allouche, Adel: *The Origins and Development of the Ottoman-Ṣafavid Conflict*, Schwarz, Berlin, 1983.

Bosworth, Clifford E.: *Iran and Islam*, Edinburgh University Press, Edinburgh, 1971.

Cutillas, Jose: "Did Shah 'Abbās I Have a Mediterranean Policy?" *Journal of Persianate Studies*, Vol. 8, No. 2, November 2015, pp. 254–75.

Farrokh, Kaveh: *Iran at War, 1500–1988*, Osprey, Oxford, 2011.

Hernán, Enrique G., Ferrer, José C., Matthee, and Rudi (eds.): *The Spanish Monarchy and Safavid Persia in the Early Modern Period: Politics, War and Religion*, Albatros, Valencia, 2016.

Matthee, Rudi: "Safavid Iran and the 'Turkish Question', or How to Avoid a War on Multiple Fronts," *Iranian Studies*, Vol. 52, No. 3–4, 2019, pp. 513–42.

Matthee, Rudi: "The Ottoman-Safavid War of 986–98/1578–90: Motives and Causes," *International Journal of Turkish Studies*, Vol. 20, No. 1–2, 2014, pp. 1–20.

Matthee, Rudi: "The Safavid-Ottoman Frontier: Iraq-i Arab as Seen by the Safavids," *International Journal of Turkish Studies*, Vol. 9, No. 1–2, 2003, pp. 157–73.

Matthee, Rudolph P., and Flores, Jorge M. (eds.): *Portugal, the Persian Gulf and Safavid Persia*, Peeters, in association with the Iran Heritage Foundation and the Freer Gallery of Art & Arthur M. Sackler Gallery, Smithsonian Institution, Leuven, 2011.

Minadoi, Giovanni-Tommaso: *The War between the Turks and the Persians: Conflict and Religion in the Safavid and Ottoman Worlds*, I.B. Tauris, London, 2019.

Newman, Andrew J.: *Safavid Iran: Rebirth of a Persian Empire*, I.B. Tauris, New York, 2006.

Yıldırım, Rıza: "Turkmens Between Two Empires: The Origins of the Qizilbash Identity in Anatolia (1447–1514)," Ph.D. Dissertation, Bilkent University, 2008.

Yıldırım, Rıza: "The Safavid-Qizilbash Ecumene and the Formation of the Qizilbash-Alevi Community in the Ottoman Empire, *c.* 1500–*c.* 1700," *Iranian Studies*, Vol. 52, No. 3–4, 2019, pp. 449–83.

The Mediterranean in the Ottoman Age

Allen, Bruce Ware: "Disaster at Djerba," *History Today*, Vol. 67, No. 6, June 2017, pp. 24–35.

Allen, Bruce Ware: *The Great Siege of Malta: The Epic Battle between the Ottoman Empire and the Knights of St John*, University Press of New England, Lebanon, 2015.

Bicheno, Hugh: *Crescent and Cross: The Battle of Lepanto 1571*, Phoenix, London, 2004.

Blili, Leïla Temime: *The Regency of Tunis, 1535–1666: Genesis of an Ottoman Province in the Maghreb*, American University of Cairo Press, Cairo, 2021.

Bostan, İdris: "Ottoman Attitude Towards the Defeat at Lepanto (1571)," *Primavera-Verano*, Vol. 15, No. 26, 2023, pp. 191–209.

Bradford, Ernle: *The Great Siege: Malta 1565*, Open Road Media, Newburyport, 2014.

Bradford, Ernle: *The Shield and the Sword: The Knights of St John*, Hodder and Stoughton, London, 1972.

Braudel, Fernand: *The Mediterranean and the Mediterranean World in the Age of Philip II*, Folio Society, London, 2000.

Brockman, Eric: *Two Sieges of Rhodes, 1480–1522*, J. Murray, London, 1969.

Capponi, Niccolo: *Victory of the West: The Great Christian-Muslim Clash at the Battle of Lepanto*, Da Capo, New York, 2008.

Caprioli, Francesco: "The 'Sheep' and the 'Lion': Charles V, Barbarossa, and Habsburg Diplomatic Practice in the Muslim Mediterranean (1534–1542), *Journal of Early Modern History*, Vol. 25, No. 5, 2021, pp. 392–421.

Cassar, George: *The Great Siege 1565 – Separating Fact from Fiction: On the Occasion of the 440th Anniversary of the Great Siege of Malta, 1565–2005*, Sacra Militia Foundation, Valletta, 2005.

Cassola, Arnold, et al.: *The 1565 Ottoman Malta Campaign Register*, Publishers Enterprise Group, Valletta, 1998.

de Correggio, Francisco Balbi: *The Siege of Malta, 1565: Translated from the Spanish Edition of 1568*, Boydell Press, Rochester, 2010.

Crowley, Roger: *Empires of the Sea: The Siege of Malta, the Battle of Lepanto, and the Contest for the Center of the World*, Random House, New York, 2009.

Devereux, Andrew W.: *The Other Side of Empire: Just War in the Mediterranean and the Rise of Early Modern Spain*, Cornell University Press, Ithaca, 2020.

Fields, Nic: *Lepanto 1571: Christian and Muslim Fleets Battle for Control of the Mediterranean*, Pen & Sword, Barnsley, 2020.

Gürkan, Emrah Safa: "The Centre and the Frontier: Ottoman Cooperation with the North African Corsairs in the Sixteenth Century," *Turkish Historical Review*, No. 1, 2010, pp. 125–63.

Heers, Jacques: *The Barbary Corsairs: Pirates, Plunder, and Warfare in the Mediterranean, 1480–1580*, Skyhorse, New York, 2018.

Hess, Andrew C.: *The Forgotten Frontier: A History of the Sixteenth Century Ibero-African Frontier*, University of Chicago Press, Chicago, 1978.

Isom-Verhaaren, Christine: *The Sultan's Fleet: Seafarers of the Ottoman Empire*, I.B. Tauris, London, 2021.

Kiss, Tamás: "Cyprus in Ottoman and Venetian Political Imagination, *c.* 1489–1582," Ph.D. Dissertation, Central European University, 2016.

Kollias, Elias: *The Knights of Rhodes – The Palace and the City*, Ekdotike Athenon, Athens, 2005.

Konstam, Angus: *Lepanto 1571: The Greatest Naval Battle of the Renaissance*, Osprey, Oxford, 2003.

Luttrell, Anthony: *The Hospitallers of Rhodes and their Mediterranean World*, Variorum, Aldershot, 1992.

Muhaj, Ardian: "The Revival of the Anti-Ottoman Projects in the Balkans after Lepanto and Venice's Struggle to Maintain Long-Lasting Peace with the Ottomans (1573–1645)," *Tarih İncelemeleri Dergisi*, Vol. 76, No. 1, 2022, pp. 203–21.

Nicholson, Helen: *The Knights Hospitaller*, Boydell Press, Woodbridge, 2013.

Nicolle, David: *Knights of Jerusalem: The Crusading Order of Hospitallers 1100–1565*, Osprey, Oxford, 2008.

Nossov, Konstantin: *The Fortress of Rhodes 1309–1522*, Osprey, Oxford, 2010.

Padfield, Peter: *Tide of Empires: Decisive Naval Campaigns in the Rise of the West, 1481–1654, (Volume I)*, Lume Books, Borough, 2021.

Phillips, Carla Rahn: "Navies and the Mediterranean in the Early Modern Period," Chapter 1 in John B. Hattendorf (ed.), *Naval Policy and Strategy in the Mediterranean*, Frank Cass, New York, 2000.

Phillips, Simon David: *The 1522 Siege of Rhodes: Causes, Course and Consequences*, Taylor & Francis Group, Milton, 2022.

Pisani, Paul George: *The Battle of Lepanto, 7 October 1571: An Unpublished Hospitaller Account*, The Salesians of Don Bosco, Silema, 2015.

Sire, H.J.A.: *The Knights of Malta*, Yale University Press, New Haven, 1996.

Smith, Douglas K., and DeVries, Kelly: *Rhodes Besieged: A New History*, History, Stroud, 2011.

Strauss, Johann: "How Cyprus came under Turkish Rule: A Conquest and the Historians," *Wiener Zeitschrift für die Kunde des Morgenlandes*, Vol. 82, 1992, pp. 325–34.

Tabak, Faruk: *The Waning of the Mediterranean, 1550–1870: A Geohistorical Approach*, Johns Hopkins University Press, Baltimore, 2008.

Tunc, Akif: "An Ottoman Winter," *History Today*, Vol. 74, No. 9, September 2024, pp. 22–24.

Williams, Phillip: *Empire and Holy War in the Mediterranean: The Galley and Maritime Conflict between the Habsburg and Ottoman Empires*, I.B. Tauris, London, 2014.

THE INDIAN OCEAN IN THE OTTOMAN AGE

Adas, Michael: *Islamic & European Expansion: The Forging of a Global Order*, Temple University Press, Philadelphia, 1993.

Alam, Muzaffar, and Subrahmanyam, Sanjay: "A View from Mecca: Notes on Gujarat, the Red Sea, and the Ottomans, 1517–39/923–946H," *Modern Asian Studies*, Vol. 51, No. 2, March 2017, pp. 268–318.

Andrade, Tonio, and Hang, Xing (eds.): *Sea Rovers, Silver, and Samurai: Maritime East Asia in Global History, 1550–1700*, University of Hawai'i Press, Honolulu, 2019.

Andrade, Tonio: *The Gunpowder Age: China, Military Innovation, and the Rise of the West in World History*, Princeton University Press, Princeton, 2017.

Basak, Sohinee: "Coastal Gujarat on the Eve of Portuguese Arrival," *Maritime Affairs: Journal of the National Maritime Foundation of India*, Vol. 10, No. 1, June 2014, pp. 95–112.

Bethencourt, Francisco, and Ramada Curto, Diogo (eds.): *Portuguese Oceanic Expansion, 1400–1800*, Cambridge University Press, Cambridge, 2011.

Boxer, Charles R.: *Portuguese Conquest and Commerce in Southern Asia, 1500–1750*, Variorum, London, 1985.

Brummett, Palmira Johnson: "The Ottomans as a World Power: What We Don't Know About Ottoman Sea-Power," *Oriente Moderno*, Nuova Serie, Anno 20 (81), No. 1, The Ottomans and the Sea (2001), pp. 1–21.

Brummett, Palmira Johnson: *Ottoman Seapower and Levantine Diplomacy in the Age of Discovery*, State University of New York Press, Albany, 1994.

Burnet, Ian: *East Indies: The 200 Year Struggle Between the Portuguese Crown, the Dutch East India Company and the English East India Company for Supremacy in the Eastern Seas*, Rosenberg, Sydney, 2013.

Carvalhal, Hélder, et al. (eds.), *The First World Empire: Portugal, War and Military Revolution* Routledge, New York, 2021.

Casale, Giancarlo: "Ottoman Warships in the Indian Ocean Armada of 1538: A Qualitative and Statistical Analysis," in Dejanirah Couto, Feza Gunergun, and Maria Pia Pedani (eds.), *Seapower, Technology and Trade: Studies in Turkish Maritime History*, Piri Reis University, Istanbul, 2014, pp. 89–102.

Casale, Giancarlo: "Imperial Smackdown: The Portuguese Between Imamate and Caliphate in the Persian Gulf," in Rudi Mathee and Jorge Flores (eds.), *Portugal, The Persian Gulf and Safavid Persia*, Iran Heritage Foundation, Peeters, 2011, pp. 177–90.

Casale, Giancarlo: *The Ottoman Age of Exploration*, Oxford University Press, Oxford, 2010.

Casale, Giancarlo: "Global Politics in the 1580s: One Canal, Twenty Thousand Cannibals, and an Ottoman Plot to Rule the World," *Journal of World History*, Vol. 18, No. 3, September 2007, pp. 267–96.

Cipolla, Carlo M.: *Guns, Sails and Empires: Technological Innovation and the Early Phases of European Expansion, 1400–1700*, Sunflower University Press, Yuma, 2002.

Cliff, Nigel: *The Last Crusade: The Epic Voyages of Vasco da Gama*, Harper, New York, 2012.

Couto, Dejanirah: "Rûmî Networks in India: A Snapshot on the Second Siege of Diu (1546)," in Dejanirah Couto, Feza Günergun, and Maria Pia Pedani Fabris (eds.): *Seapower, Technology and Trade: Studies in Turkish Maritime History*, Denizler Kitabevi, İstanbul, 2014, pp. 103–14.

Crowley, Roger: *Spice: The 16th-Century Contest that Shaped the Modern World*, Yale University Press, New Haven, 2024.

Crowley, Roger: *Conquerors: How Portugal Forged the First Global Empire*, Faber & Faber, London, 2016.

Darwin, John: *After Tamerlane: The Rise and Fall of Global Empires, 1400–2000*, Bloomsbury, New York, 2010.

de Camões, Luís Vaz: *The Lusiads*, trans. Landweg White, Oxford University Press, Oxford, 2008.

de la Garza, Andrew: *The Mughal Empire at War: Babur, Akbar and the Indian Military Revolution, 1500–1605*, Routledge, Abingdon, 2016.

Diffie, Bailey W., and Winius, George D.: *Foundations of the Portuguese Empire, 1415–1580*, University of Minnesota Press, Minneapolis, 1985.

Disney, Anthony R.: *A History of Portugal and the Portuguese Empire: From Beginnings to 1807*, Cambridge University Press, Cambridge, 2013.

Disney, Anthony R.: *The Portuguese in India and Other Studies, 1500–1700*, Ashgate, Farnham, 2009.

Gardiner, Robert: *Cogs, Caravels, and Galleons: The Sailing Ship, 1000–1650*, Naval Institute Press, Annapolis, 1994.

Glete, Jan: *Warfare at Sea, 1500–1650: Maritime Conflicts and the Transformation of Europe*, Routledge, New York, 2000.

Guilmartin, John F.: "The Revolution in Military Warfare at Sea During the Early Modern Era: Technological Origins, Operational Outcomes and Strategic Consequences," *Journal for Maritime Research*, Vol. 13, No. 2, November 2011, pp. 129–37.

Hamdani, Abbas: "Ottoman Response to the Discovery of America and the New Route to India," *Journal of the American Oriental Society*, Vol. 101, No. 3, July–September 1981, pp. 323–30.

Hess, Andrew C.: "The Ottoman Conquest of Egypt (1517) and the Beginning of the Sixteenth-Century World," *International Journal of Middle East Studies*, Vol. 4, No. 1, January 1973, pp. 55–76.

Hess, Andrew C.: "The Evolution of the Ottoman Seaborne Empire in the Age of the Oceanic Discoveries, 1453–1525," *The American Historical Review*, Vol. 75, No. 7, December 1970, pp. 1892–919.

Hoffman, Philip T.: *Why Did Europe Conquer the World?* Princeton University Press, Princeton, 2015.

Holland, Anthony: *1509: The Battle of Diu*, Epic Battles of History, Anthony Holland, 2023.

Kaushik, Roy: *Military Transition in Early Modern Asia, 1400–1750: Cavalry, Guns, Government and Ships*, Bloomsbury, London, 2015.

Kheng, Cheah Boon: "Ming China's Support for Sultan Mahmud of Melaka and Its Hostility towards the Portuguese after the Fall of Melaka in 1511," *Journal of the Malaysian Branch of the Royal Asiatic Society*, Vol. 85, No. 2, December 2012, pp. 55–77.

Laband, John: *Bringers of War: The Portuguese in Africa during the Age of Gunpowder and Sail*, Frontline Books, London, 2013.

Levenson, Jay A.: *Encompassing the Globe: Portugal and the World in the 16th and 17th Centuries*, Smithsonian Books, New York, 2007.

Marks, Robert: *The Origins of the Modern World: A Global and Environmental Narrative from the Fifteenth to the Twenty-First Century*, Rowman & Littlefield, Lanham, 2015.

Mathew, Kuzhippalli-Skaria: *Portuguese and the Sultanate of Gujarat, 1500–1573*, Mittal Publications, Delhi, 1986.

Matthews, K.S.: "Indo-Portuguese Naval Battles in the Indian Ocean during the Early Sixteenth Century," in Kaushik Roy, and Peter Lorge (eds.), *Chinese and Indian Warfare: From the Classical Age to 1870*, Routledge, Abingdon, 2015, pp. 166–80.

Monteiro, Saturnino: *Portuguese Sea Battles, Volume I: The First World Sea Power 1139–1521*, Lisbon, 2014.

Monteiro, Saturnino: *Portuguese Sea Battles, Vol. II: Christianity, Commerce and Corso, 1522–1538*, Lisbon, 2014.

Monteiro, Saturnino: *Portuguese Sea Battles, Vol. III: From Brazil to Japan, 1539–1579*, Lisbon, 2014.

Newitt, Malyn: *A History of Portuguese Overseas Expansion 1400–1668*, Routledge, London, 2004.

Özbaran, Salih: *Ottoman Expansion Towards the Indian Ocean in the 16th Century*, Bilgi University Press, Istanbul, 2009.

Parker, Charles H.: *Global Interactions in the Early Modern Age, 1400–1800*, Cambridge University Press, Cambridge, 2010.

Parker, Geoffrey: "Europe and the Wider World, 1500–1750: The Military Balance," in James D. Tracy (ed.), *The Political Economy of Merchant Empires: State Power and World Trade 1350–1750*, Cambridge University Press, Cambridge, 1990, pp. 161–95.

Pearson, Michael N.: *Port Cities and Intruders: The Swahili Coast, India and Portugal in the Early Modern Era*, Johns Hopkins University Press, Baltimore, 1998.

Pearson, Michael N.: *Merchants and Rulers in Gujarat: The Response to the Portuguese in the Sixteenth Century*, University of California Press, Berkeley, 1976.

Pissarra, José Virgilio Amaro: *Chaul e Diu, 1508 e 1509: O Domínio do Índico*, Tribuna da História, Lisbon, 2002.

Reid, Anthony: "Turkey as Aceh's Alternative Imperium," *Archipel*, Vol. 87, January 2014, pp. 81–102.

Sharman, Jason C.: *Empires of the Weak: The Real Story of European Expansion and the Creation of the New World Order*, Princeton University Press, Princeton, 2019.

Soucek, Svatopluk: "Naval Aspects of the Ottoman Conquests of Rhodes, Cyprus and Crete," *Studia Islamica*, No. 98/99, 2004, pp. 219–61.

Streusand, Douglas E.: *Islamic Gunpowder Empires: Ottomans, Safavids, and Mughals*, Westview, Boulder, 2011.

Subrahmanyam, Sanjay: *Across the Green Sea: Histories from the Western Indian Ocean, 1440–1640*, University of Texas Press, Austin, 2024.

Subrahmanyam, Sanjay: *The Portuguese Empire in Asia, 1500-1700: A Political and Economic History*, Wiley-Blackwell, Malden, 2012.

Vila-Santa, Nuno: "Noronha, the Repositioning of Diu in the Indian Ocean, and the Creation of the Northern Province (1548–1560)," *Asian Review of World Histories*, Vol. 8, No. 2, 2020, pp. 207–33.

Villiers, John, and Earle, Tom F.: *Afonso de Albuquerque, Caesar of the East*, Aris & Phillips, Warminster, 1990.

Whiteway, Richard S.: *The Rise of Portuguese Power in India 1497–1550*, Kelley, New York, 1967.

AFRICA IN THE OTTOMAN AGE

Abir, Mordechai: *Ethiopia and the Red Sea: The Rise and Decline of the Solomonic Dynasty and Muslim-European Rivalry in the Region*, Frank Cass, London, 1980.

Agonafir, Awegichew Amare: "Atse Sarsa Dengel and the Rival Great Powers at His Door Steps: Vagaries of Competition and War against the Ottoman Empire, 1563–1597," *Abyssinia Journal of Business and Social Sciences*, Vol. 7, No. 2, 2022, pp. 24–32.

al-Ḥabaša, Futūḥ: *The Conquest of Abyssinia by Shihāb al-Dīn Aḥmad ibn ʿAbd al-Qādir ʿArabfaqīh*, Tsehai Publishers and Distributors, Hollywood, 2003.

Baldridge, Cates: *Prisoners of Prester John: The Portuguese Mission to Ethiopia in search of the Mythical King, 1520–1526*, McFarland & Co., Jefferson, 2012.

Beckingham, C.F.: "A Note on the Topography of Ahmad Gran's Campaigns in 1542," *Journal of Semitic Studies*, Vol. 4, No. 4, October 1959, pp. 362–73.

Braukamper, Ulrich: "Islamic Principalities in Southeast Ethiopia between the Thirteenth and Sixteenth Centuries," *Ethiopianist Notes*, Vol. 1, No. 1, 1977, pp. 17–55, and Vol. 1, No. 2, 1977, pp. 1–42.

d'Alòs-Moner, Andreu Martínez: *Envoys of a Human God: The Jesuit Mission to Christian Ethiopia, 1557–1632*, Brill, Leiden, 2015.

d'Alòs-Moner, Andreu Martínez: "Conquistadores, Mercenaries, and Missionaries: The Failed Portuguese Dominion of the Red Sea," *Northeast African Studies*, Vol. 12, No. 1, 2012, pp. 1–28.

d'Alòs-Moner, Andreu Martínez: "Early Portuguese Emigration to the Ethiopian Highlands: Geopolitics, Missions and Métissage," Chapter 1 in Stefan Halikowski-Smith (ed.), *Reinterpreting Indian Ocean Worlds: Essays in Honour of Kirti N. Chaudhuri*, Cambridge Scholars, Newcastle upon Tyne, 2011, pp. 2–32.

d'Alòs-Moner, Andreu Martínez: "The Selling of the Negus: The Emperor of Ethiopia in Portuguese and Jesuit Imagination," *Scrinium*, Byzantinorossica, Saint Petersburg, 2005, pp. 161–73.

Davis, Asa J.: "The Sixteenth Century Jihad in Ethiopia and the Impact on its Culture (Part II): Implicit Factors behind the Movement," *Journal of the Historical Society of Nigeria*, No. 3, 1964, pp. 113–28.

Davis, Asa J.: "The Sixteenth Century Jihad in Ethiopia and the Impact on its Culture (Part I)," *Journal of the Historical Society of Nigeria*, No. 2, 1963, pp. 567–92.

Erlich, Haggai: *The Cross and the River: Ethiopia, Egypt, and the Nile*, Lynne Rienner, Boulder, 2002.

Halikowski-Smith, Stefan: "'The Friendship of Kings was in the Ambassadors': Portuguese Diplomatic Embassies in Asia and Africa during the Sixteenth and Seventeenth Centuries," *Portuguese Studies*, Vol. 22, No. 1, 2006, pp. 101–34.

Hassen, Mohammed: *The Oromo and the Christian Kingdom of Ethiopia, 1300–1700*, James Currey, Woodbridge, 2015.

Hassen, Mohammed: "Reviewed Work(s): Ethiopia and the Red Sea: The Rise and Decline of the Solomonic Dynasty and Muslim-European Rivalry in the Region by M. Abir," *Northeast African Studies*, Vol. 6, No. 3, 1984, pp. 60–65.

Headrick, Daniel R.: *Power over Peoples: Technology, Environments, and Western Imperialism, 1400 to the Present*, Princeton University Press, Princeton, 2010.

Henze, Paul B.: *Layers of Time: A History of Ethiopia*, Palgrave Macmillan, New York, 2004.

Kelly, Samantha: "Ethiopians in Rome," *History Today*, Vol. 78, No. 4, September 2024, pp. 38–53.

Kelly, Samantha (ed.): *A Companion to Medieval Ethiopia and Eritrea*, Brill, Leiden, 2020.

Krebs, Verena: *Medieval Ethiopian Kingship, Craft, and Diplomacy with Latin Europe*, Palgrave Macmillan, Cham, 2021.

Krebs, Verena: "Crusading Threats? Ethiopian-Egyptian Relations in the 1440s," in Benjamin Weber (ed.), *Croisades en Afrique: Les Expeditions Occidentales á Destination du Continent Africain, XlIIᵉ–XVIᵉ Siècles*, Presses Universitaires du Midi Meridiennes, Toulouse, 2019, pp. 245–74.

Kurt, Andrew; "The Search for Prester John: A Projected Crusade and the Eroding Prestige of Ethiopian Kings, *c.*1200–*c.*1540," *Journal of Medieval History*, Vol. 39, No. 3, September 2013, pp. 297–320.

Lawrance, Jeremy: "The Middle Indies: Damiao de Gois on Prester John and the Ethiopians," *Renaissance Studies*, Vol. 6, No. 3–4, 1992, pp. 306–24.

Maloni, Ruby: "Control of the Seas: The Historical Exegesis of the Portuguese 'Cartaz,'" *Proceedings of the Indian History Congress*, Vol. 72, No. 1, 2011, pp. 476–84.

Marcocci, Guiseppe; "Prism of Empire: The Shifting Image of Ethiopia in Renaissance Portugal (1500–1570)," in Maria Berbara and Karl A.E. Enenkel (eds.), *Portuguese Humanism and the Republic of Letters*, Brill, Leiden, 2012, pp. 447–66.

Marcus, Harold G.: *A History of Ethiopia*, University of California Press, Berkeley, 2008.

Martin, B.G.: "Mahdism, Muslim Clerics, and Holy Wars in Ethiopia, 1300–1600," in Harold G. Marcus (ed.), *Proceedings of the First United States Conference on Ethiopian Studies*, Michigan State University, East Lansing, 1975, pp. 91–100.

Owens, Travis J.: *Beleaguered Muslim Fortresses and Ethiopian Imperial Expansion from the 13th to the 16th Century*, Naval Postgraduate School, Monterey, 2008.

Özbaran, Salih: "An Imperial Letter from Süleyman the Magnificent to Dom João III Concerning Proposals for an Ottoman-Portuguese Armistice," *Portuguese Studies*, Vol. 6, 1990, pp. 24–31.

Palat, Ravi: *The Making of an Indian Ocean World-Economy, 1250–1650*, Palgrave Macmillan, New York, 2015.

Peacock, A.C.S.: "The Ottomans and the Funj Sultanate in the Sixteenth and Seventeenth Centuries," *Bulletin of the School of Oriental and African Studies*, Vol. 75, No. 1, 2012, pp. 87–111.

Salvadore, Matteo: "Muslim Partners, Catholic Foes: The Selective Isolation of Gondärine Ethiopia," *Northeast African Studies*, Vol. 12, No. 1, 2012, pp. 51–72.

Salvadore, Matteo: "The Ethiopian Age of Exploration: Prester John's Discovery of Europe, 1306–1458," *Journal of World History*, Vol. 21, No. 4, December 2010, pp. 593–627.

Salvadore, Matteo: "The Jesuit Mission to Ethiopia (1555–1634) and the Death of Prester John," Chapter 7 in Allison Kavey (ed.), *World-Building and the Early Modern Imagination*, Palgrave Macmillan, New York, 2010, pp. 141–71.

Sanceau, Elaine: *The Land of Prester John: A Chronicle of Portuguese Exploration*, Knopf, New York, 1944.

Shaw, Jeffrey M.: *The Ethiopian–Adal War, 1529–1543: The Conquest of Abyssinia*, Helion & Co., Warwick, 2021.

Tamrat, Taddesse. "The Horn of Africa: The Solomonids in Ethiopia and the States of the Horn of Africa," in D.T. Niane (ed.), *UNESCO General History of Africa, Vol. 4*, University of California Press, Berkeley, 1984, pp. 423–54.

Whiteway, Richard S. (ed.): *The Portuguese Expedition to Abyssinia in 1541–1543 by Miguel de Castanhoso*, The Hakluyt Society, London, 1892.

INDEX

517